Principles of International Investment Law

Second Edition

RUDOLF DOLZER
and
CHRISTOPH SCHREUER

OXFORD
UNIVERSITY PRESS

OXFORD

UNIVERSITY PRESS

Great Clarendon Street, Oxford, OX2 6DP,
United Kingdom

Oxford University Press is a department of the University of Oxford.
It furthers the University's objective of excellence in research, scholarship,
and education by publishing worldwide. Oxford is a registered trade mark of
Oxford University Press in the UK and in certain other countries

© Rudolf Dolzer and Christoph Schreuer, 2012

The moral rights of the authors have been asserted

First Edition published in 2008
Second Edition published in 2012

Impression: 5

British Library Cataloguing in Publication Data

Data available

ISBN 978-0-19-965179-5 (HB)
ISBN 978-0-19-965180-1 (PB)

Printed in Great Britain by
CPI Group (UK) Ltd, Croydon, CR0 4YY

Summary of Contents

Contents

Foreword to the Second Edition

Investment arbitration continues to expand and to occupy more and more arbitrators, lawyers, teachers and researchers. Looking at the state of international law in general, and of international economic law in particular, investment law has over the past decade become the most dynamic field.

With an impressive number of new awards issued since the first edition in 2008, it has become useful and necessary to prepare this new edition. We have revised all chapters. Some parts were reorganised, in particular the introductory section. Other chapters had to be entirely rewritten in the light of the fast pace of relevant jurisprudence and its new directions.

Given the favourable response of our readers to the first edition, we have continued to adhere to our style of presentation, seeking to combine the advantages of a Continental analytical study with those of a common-law case-centred approach.

In Vienna, Jane Alice Hofbauer has carefully compiled the Table of Cases for the new edition. In Bonn, Doris Gassen has, again, successfully organised the texting of the manuscript.

Rudolf Dolzer
Bonn

Christoph Schreuer
Vienna

Table of Cases

Note: **bold** page numbers refer to discussions of a case in the text, lean page references refer to cases in footnotes.

INTERNATIONAL ARBITRATIONS

WTO DISPUTE SETTLEMENT BODY

NATIONAL CASES

Table of Treaties, Conventions, Resolutions, and Rules

List of Abbreviations

AF	Additional Facility
AJIL	American Journal of International Law
ASIL Proceedings	Proceedings of the American Society of International Law
ASEAN	Association of Southeast Asian Nations
BIT	Bilateral Investment Treaty
BLEU	Belgo-Luxembourg Economic Union
BOO	Build, Operate and Own
BOT	Build, Operate and Transfer
BYIL	British Year Book of International Law
CAFTA	Central American Free Trade Agreement
CIETAC	China International Economic and Trade Arbitration Commission
DCF	Discounted Cash Flow
DR Congo	Democratic Republic of the Congo
ECHR	European Court of Human Rights
ECT	Energy Charter Treaty
EFTA	European Free Trade Association
EU	European Union
FCN	Friendship, Commerce, and Navigation
FET	Fair and Equitable Treatment
FIC	Foreign Investment Commission
FSIA	Foreign Sovereign Immunities Act
FTA	Free Trade Agreement
FTC	Free Trade Commission
GA	General Assembly
GATS	General Agreement on Trade in Services
GATT	General Agreement on Tariffs and Trade
HRLJ	Human Rights Law Journal
ICC	International Chamber of Commerce
ICJ	International Court of Justice
ICJ Rep	International Court of Justice Reports
ICLQ	International & Comparative Law Quarterly
ICSID	International Centre for Settlement of Investment Disputes

ICSID Convention	Convention on the Settlement of Investment Disputes between States and Nationals of Other States (March 1965)
ICSID Review-FILJ	ICSID Review Foreign Investment Law Journal
ILC	International Law Commission
ILM	International Legal Materials
ILR	International Law Reports
IMF	International Monetary Fund
Int. Lawyer	The International Lawyer
Iran-USCTR (or IUSCTR)	Iran-US Claims Tribunal Reports
JAA	Joint Activity Agreement
JWIT	Journal of World Investment & Trade
LCIA	London Court of International Arbitration
LIBOR	London Interbank Offered Rate
MAI	Multilateral Agreement on Investment
MFN	Most-Favoured-Nation
MIGA	Multilateral Investment Guarantee Agency
NAFTA	North American Free Trade Agreement
NGO	Non-Governmental Organization
OECD	Organization for Economic Cooperation and Development
OPIC	Overseas Private Investment Corporation
PCA	Permanent Court of Arbitration
PCIJ	Permanent Court of International Justice
PCIJ Rep	Permanent Court of International Justice Reports
Receuil	Receuil des Cours de l'Académie de droit international (Collected Courses of the Hague Academy of International Law)
RIAA	Reports of International Arbitral Awards
Stockholm Int Arb Rev	Stockholm International Arbitration Review
TDM	Transnational Dispute Management
TRIMS	Trade Related Investment Measures
UN	United Nations
UNESCO	United Nations Educational, Scientific, and Cultural Organization
UNCITRAL	United Nations Commission on International Trade Law
UNCTAD	United Nations Conference on Trade and Development
UNTS	United Nations Treaty Series
US	United States of America
VAT	Value Added Tax
VCLT	Vienna Convention on the Law of Treaties
WTO	World Trade Organization
YCA	Yearbook Commercial Arbitration

I

History, Sources, and Nature of International Investment Law

1. The history of international investment law

(a) Early developments

As early as 1796, John Adams, after having negotiated for the United States the first Treaty on Friendship, Commerce and Navigation with France, emphatically highlighted the protection of alien property by the rules of international law:

There is no principle of the law of nations more firmly established than that which entitles the property of strangers within the jurisdiction of another country in friendship with their own to the protection of its sovereign by all efforts in his power.[1]

Until the Communist Revolution in Russia in 1917 neither state practice nor the commentators of international law had reason to pay special attention to rules protecting foreign investment. Treaty practice in the nineteenth century protected alien property not on the basis of an autonomous standard, but by reference to the domestic laws of the host state. An illustration is found in Article 2(3) of the Treaty between Switzerland and the United States of 1850:

In case of...expropriation for purposes of public utility, the citizens of one of the two countries, residing or established in the other, shall be placed on an equal footing with the citizens of the country in which they reside in respect to indemnities for damages they may have sustained.[2]

The implicit assumption was that each state would in its national laws protect private property and that the extension of the domestic scheme of protection would lead to sufficient guarantees for the alien investor.

In a famous study first published in 1868, the Argentine jurist Carlos Calvo for the first time presented a new perspective of this paradigm and asserted that the international rule should in effect be understood as allowing the host state to reduce protection of alien property whilst also reducing the guarantees for property held by nationals.[3] Calvo's view would have left room for all the vagaries of domestic law,

---

[1] Cited in J B Moore, *A Digest of International Law*, vol 4 (1906) 5.
[2] Cited in R Wilson, *United States Commercial Treaties and International Law* (1960) 111.
[3] See Carlos Calvo, *Derecho Internacional Teórico y Práctico de Europa y América* (1868); Charles Calvo, *Le droit international—théorie et pratique*, vol 3 (1896) 138.

allowing both strong guarantees, but also a complete lack of protection. In addition, the Calvo doctrine is based on the view that foreigners must assert their rights before domestic courts and that they have no right of diplomatic protection by their home state or access to international tribunals. Calvo's theory was conceived against the background of gunboat diplomacy by capital-exporting countries and other practices through which these countries imposed their view of international law on foreign governments. In 1907, the Drago-Porter Convention was adopted to prevent the use of force for the collection of debt, and Calvo's radical attack on the protection of foreign citizens lost some of its justification.

On the international level, the Calvo doctrine remained at the margins of the debate, and the dominant position was that a state was bound by rules of international law, separate from national law. Elihu Root stated the prevalent position in 1910:

There is a standard of justice, very simple, very fundamental, and of such general acceptance by all civilized countries as to form a part of the international law of the world. The condition upon which any country is entitled to measure the justice due from it to an alien by the justice which it accords to its own citizens is that its system of law and administration shall conform to this general standard. If any country's system of law and administration does not conform to that standard, although the people of the country may be content or compelled to live under it, no other country can be compelled to accept it as furnishing a satisfactory measure of treatment to its citizens.[4]

Nevertheless, the conceptual reorientation proposed by Calvo was revived on a practical level in a dramatic fashion after the Russian Revolution in 1917: the Soviet Union expropriated national enterprises without compensation and justified its uncompensated expropriation of alien property by relying on the national treatment standard. The ensuing dispute led, inter alia, to the Lena Goldfields Arbitration of 1930 in which case the tribunal required the Soviet Union to pay compensation to the alien claimant, based upon the concept of unjust enrichment.[5]

In subsequent decades, a further attack upon the traditional standard of international law was mounted in 1938 by Mexico after the nationalization of US interests in the Mexican agrarian and oil business. This dispute led to a frank diplomatic exchange in which US Secretary of State Cordell Hull wrote a famous letter to his Mexican counterpart. In this letter he spelled out that the rules of international law allowed expropriation of foreign property, but required 'prompt, adequate and effective compensation'.[6] The Mexican position echoed the Calvo doctrine and also foreshadowed harsh disputes between industrialized and developing countries in later decades of post-decolonization.

---

[4] E Root, 'The Basis of Protection to Citizens Residing Abroad' (1910) 4 *AJIL* 517, 528.

[5] For an analysis of the Lena Golfields Arbitration (1930), see, inter alia, V V Veeder, 'The Lena Goldfields Arbitration: The Historical Roots of Three Ideas' (1998) 47 *ICLQ* 747; the text of the award is published as an appendix to A Nussbaum, 'The Arbitration between the Lena Goldfields, Ltd and the Soviet Government' (1950–51) 31 *ICLQ* 42.

[6] See for the correspondence G Hackworth, *Digest of International Law*, vol 3 (1942), vol 5 (1943).

(b) The emergence of an international minimum standard

The Calvo doctrine, the Russian Revolution, and the Mexican position notwithstanding, what had emerged from the various international disputes about the status of aliens in general (not just in regard to foreign investment) was a widespread sense that the alien is protected against unacceptable measures of the host state by rules of international law which are independent of those of the host state. The sum of these rules eventually came to be known as the international minimum standard.[7] The fundamental reasons that prompted the evolution and recognition of these rules are reflected in general terms in a relatively modern decision of the European Court of Human Rights:

Especially as regards a taking of property effected in the context of a social reform, there may well be good grounds for drawing a distinction between nationals and non-nationals as far as compensation is concerned. To begin with, non-nationals are more vulnerable to domestic legislation: unlike nationals, they will generally have played no part in the election or designation of its authors nor have been consulted on its adoption. Secondly, although a taking of property must always be effected in the public interest, different considerations may apply to nationals and non-nationals and there may well be legitimate reason for requiring nationals to bear a greater burden in the public interest than non-nationals.[8]

The minimum standard as it emerged historically concerned the status of the alien in general, applying to such diverse areas as procedural rights in criminal law, rights before tribunals in general, rights in matters of civil law, and rights in regard to private property held by the foreigner. An early leading case on the subject matter, *Neer v Mexico* decided in 1926, was concerned with the duty of the host state Mexico to investigate appropriately the circumstances of the unaccounted death of a US national.[9] When the claim of the widow of the US national for compensation for failure to do so was brought before a Mixed Claims Commission, the following statement was issued by the Commission in regard to the circumstances under which a host state would be liable for a violation of the minimum standard:

the treatment of an alien, in order to constitute an international delinquency, should amount to an outrage, to bad faith, to willful neglect of duty, or to an insufficiency of governmental action so far short of international standards that every reasonable and impartial man would readily recognize its insufficiency.[10]

This statement of the standard did not relate to matters of property of the alien, and was issued when matters of foreign investment and related issues such as economic growth, development, good governance, and an investment-friendly climate were

---

[7] See H Roth, *The Minimum Standard of International Law Applied to Aliens* (1949); E Borchard, *The Diplomatic Protection of Citizens Abroad* (1915).

[8] See ECtHR, *James & others v UK*, Judgment, 21 February 1986, para 63; see also *Lemire v Ukraine*, Award, 28 March 2011, para 57.

[9] *L F H Neer & Pauline Neer v United Mexican States*, IV RIAA 60 (1951).

[10] At pp 61–2.

not yet high on the international agenda. Yet this case has resurfaced in decisions of investment tribunals in the past decade.[11]

(c) Developments after the Second World War

The period between 1945 and 1990 saw major confrontations between the growing number of newly independent developing countries, on the one hand, and capital-exporting states, on the other, about the status of customary law governing foreign investment. These were often prompted by ideological positions, by an insistence on strict notions of sovereignty ('Permanent Sovereignty over Natural Resources'),[12] and by the call for economic decolonization, supported by an economic doctrine calling for independence from centres of colonialism. The new battleground chosen by developing states was now the United Nations General Assembly where they soon held and still hold the majority of votes. In 1962, half a century ago, an early confrontation ended with a compromise: GA Resolution 1803 stated that in the case of expropriation, 'appropriate compensation' would have to be paid, thus explicitly confirming neither the Hull rule nor the Calvo doctrine. Remarkably, a consensus existed then that foreign investment agreements concluded by a government must be observed in good faith.[13]

The developing states decided to take the battle further and brought it to a culmination in 1974, again in the United Nations General Assembly. Encouraged by the success of the oil-producing countries in boycotting Western states and sharp oil price increases, as well as by the then prevailing spirit of economic independence in Latin America, several resolutions were passed which called for a 'New International Economic Order'. One of its cornerstones was the apparent abolition of rules of international law governing the expropriation of alien property and their replacement by domestic rules as determined by national authorities:

Each State has the right: . . . (c) To nationalize, expropriate or transfer ownership of foreign property, in which case appropriate compensation should be paid by the State adopting such measures, taking into account its relevant laws and regulations and all circumstances that the State considers pertinent. In any case where the question of compensation gives rise to a controversy, it shall be settled under the domestic law of the nationalizing State and by its tribunals, unless it is freely and mutually agreed by all States concerned that other peaceful means be sought on the basis of the sovereign equality of States and in accordance with the principle of free choice of means.[14]

---

[11] See pp 6, 139–41.

[12] See R Dolzer, 'Permanent Sovereignty over Natural Resources and Economic Decolonization' (1986) 7 *Human Rights LJ* 217; K Gess, 'Permanent Sovereignty over Natural Resources: An Analytical Review of the United Nations Declaration and its Genesis' (1964) 13 *ICLQ* 398; S M Schwebel, 'The Story of the UN's Declaration on Permanent Sovereignty over Natural Resources' (1963) 49 *American Bar Association Journal* 463; C Brower and J Tepe, 'The Charter of Economic Rights and Duties of States: A Reflection or Rejection of International Law?' (1975) 9 *Int'l Lawyer* 295.

[13] 'Foreign investment agreements freely entered into by or between sovereign States shall be observed in good faith'; see UN GA Res 1803 (14 December 1962) para 8.

[14] UN GA Res 3281 (12 December 1974) ('Charter of Economic Rights and Duties of States').

Of course, this period of confrontation led to insecurity about the customary international rules governing foreign investment.[15] This phase lasted essentially until around 1990. At that time it became clear that, together with the end of the Soviet Union, the Socialist view of property had collapsed and that the call for economic independence had brought a major financial crisis, rather than more welfare upon the people of Latin America. From that time onwards, Latin American states started to conclude bilateral investment treaties the spirit of which was at odds with the Calvo doctrine, and the annual calls for 'permanent sovereignty' in the UN General Assembly came to an end.[16]

At the same time, international financial institutions revised their position on the role of private investment. The so-called Washington Consensus,[17] with its new emphasis on the private sector in the process of development, summarized the now dominant approach to development and its concomitant positive view of private foreign investment. In 1992, the new approach crystallized in the Preamble of the World Bank's Guidelines on the Treatment of Foreign Direct Investment. It recognizes:

that a greater flow of foreign direct investment brings substantial benefits to bear on the world economy and on the economies of developing countries in particular, in terms of improving the long term efficiency of the host country through greater competition, transfer of capital, technology and managerial skills and enhancement of market access and in terms of the expansion of international trade.[18]

Within this new climate of international economic relations, the fight of previous decades against customary rules protecting foreign investment had abruptly become anachronistic and obsolete. The tide had turned, and the new theme for capital-importing states was not to oppose classical customary law, but instead to attract additional foreign investment by granting more protection to foreign investment than required by traditional customary law, now on the basis of treaties. Five decades after it was formulated, the Hull rule became a standard element of hundreds of new bilateral investment treaties (BITs) as well as multilateral agreements, such as the Energy Charter Treaty (ECT) adopted in 1994 or the North American Free Trade Agreement (NAFTA) in which Mexico decided to join the United States and Canada, also in 1994. Developing countries started to conclude investment treaties among themselves, and the characteristics of these treaties did not significantly deviate from those concluded with developed states.[19]

---

[15] See *INA Corp v Iran*, 8 Iran–US CTR 373, 386 (1985).

[16] See T Wälde, 'A Requiem for the "New International Economic Order"'—The Rise and Fall of Paradigms in International Economic Law and a Post-Mortem with Timeless Significance' in G Hafner, G Loibl, A Rest, L Sucharipa-Behrmann, and K Zemanek (eds), *Liber Amicorum Professor Ignaz Seidl-Hohenveldern* (1998) 771.

[17] See p 87.

[18] World Bank Group, 'Guidelines on the Treatment of Foreign Direct Investment', *Legal Framework for the Treatment of Foreign Investment: Volume II: Guidelines* (1992) 35–44.

[19] See UNCTAD, *Bilateral Investment Treaties 1995–2006: Trends in Investment Rulemaking* (2007).

Ever since the early 1990s, the focus in practice has shifted to the negotiation of new treaties on foreign investment, to their understanding and interpretation. The elucidation of the state of customary law is no longer a central concern of academic commentators. However, the relevant issues have certainly not disappeared. For instance, in the context of NAFTA, the three states parties decided that the standards of 'fair and equitable treatment' and of 'full protection and security' must be understood to require host states to observe customary law and not more demanding autonomous treaty-based standards.[20] In consequence, nearly forgotten arbitral decisions—mainly the *Neer* case of 1926—were now unearthed. The importance of this award for the current state of customary law governing foreign investment has led to a debate on whether an old arbitral ruling addressing the duty to prosecute nationals suspected of a crime against a foreigner is the appropriate vantage point from which contemporary rules governing foreign investment should be developed.

(d) The evolution of investment protection treaties

The roots of modern treaty rules on foreign investment can be traced back to 1778 when the United States and France concluded their first commercial treaty, followed in the nineteenth century by treaties between the United States and their European allies and subsequently the new Latin American states.[21] These early treaties mainly addressed trade issues, but also contained rules requiring compensation in case of expropriation. After 1919, the United States negotiated a series of agreements on friendship, commerce, and navigation (FCN), followed by another series of treaties between 1945 and 1966.[22]

Rules on investment were never prominent or distinct in these FCN treaties, even though the pre-1945 treaties contained not just compensation clauses, but also provisions on the right to establish certain types of business in the partner state. After 1945, trade matters were regulated in separate treaties, and FCN treaties contained more detail on foreign investment.[23]

The era of modern investment treaties began in 1959 when Germany and Pakistan adopted a bilateral agreement which entered into force in 1962. Germany had decided to launch a programme for a series of bilateral treaties to protect its companies' foreign investments made in accordance with the laws of the host state. Soon after Germany had launched its programme and successfully negotiated its

---

[20] See pp 136 et seq.

[21] See R Wilson, *United States Commercial Treaties and International Law* (1960) 2.

[22] See K J Vandevelde, 'The Bilateral Investment Program of the United States' (1988) 21 *Cornell Int'l LJ* 201, 207–8.

[23] J W Salacuse, 'Towards a Global Treaty on Foreign Investment: The Search for a Grand Bargain' in N Horn (ed), *Arbitrating Foreign Investment Disputes* (2004) 51, 56; K J Vandevelde, 'The Bilateral Investment Program of the United States' (1988) 21 *Cornell Int'l LJ* 203.

first treaties, other European states followed suit: Switzerland concluded its first such treaty in 1961,[24] France in 1972.[25]

As to dispute settlement, the early treaties did not provide for direct investor-state dispute settlement procedures, but for the submission of disputes to the International Court of Justice or ad hoc state-to-state arbitration.[26] Starting with the treaty between Chad and Italy of 1969, BITs began offering arbitration between host states and foreign investors.

In 1977, the US State Department launched an initiative for the United States to join the European practice of the past two decades and to conclude agreements which were meant to address issues of foreign investment only, mainly to protect investments of nationals abroad.[27] Following a short period of political hesitation in view of the issue of exporting jobs by way of promoting foreign investment, and a shift of responsibility from the State Department to the United States Trade Representative during that period, the United States, between 1982 and 2011, concluded 47 bilateral treaties, mainly with developing states.[28]

A similarly significant trend was the evolution of BIT practice by Asian states. China concluded 130 treaties between 1982 and 2011.[29] India concluded its first BIT in 1994, had entered into 26 BITs by 1999, and in 2011 was a party to 83 such treaties. Japan has also decided to join the practice of other Organisation for Economic Co-operation and Development (OECD) countries and in 2011 had concluded 16 investment agreements.

At the same time, more and more developing states have negotiated BITs among themselves, altogether more than 770. In the period between 2003 and 2006, these treaties outnumbered those between developed and developing states.[30]

---

[24] Treaty between Switzerland and Tunisia of 2 December 1961; see N Huu-tru, 'Le réseau suisse d'accords bilatéraux d'encouragement et de protection des investissements' (1988) 92 *Révue Générale de Droit International Public* 577.

[25] Treaty between France and Tunisia of 30 June 1972; see P Juillard, 'Le réseau francais des conventions bilatérales d'investissement: à la recherche d'un droit perdu?' (1987) 13 *Droit et Pratique du Commerce International* 9.

[26] See eg Art 11 of the Bilateral Investment Treaty concluded between Germany and Pakistan on 25 November 1959, UNTS (1963) 24.

[27] For an historical appraisal of the US BIT Program, see K J Vandevelde, 'The BIT Program: A Fifteen-Year Appraisal', *ASIL Proceedings* (1992) 532.

[28] The authors wish to thank the Secretariat of UNCTAD for the most recent statistics for BITs.
As to BIT practice of the United States, see K J Vandevelde, *United States Investment Treaties: Policy and Practice* (1992); K J Vandevelde, 'A Brief History of International Investment Agreements' (2005) *University of California Davis J Int'l L & Pol'y* 157; S M Schwebel, 'The United States 2004 Model Bilateral Investment Treaty: An Exercise in the Regressive Development of International Law' in G Aksen, K H Böckstiegel, M J Mustill, P M Patocchi, and A M Whitesell (eds), *Liber Amicorum in Honour of Robert Briner—Global Reflections on International Law, Commerce and Dispute Resolution* (2005) 815; K Gugdeon, 'United States Bilateral Investment Treaties (1986) 4 *Int'l Tax and Business Law* 105; W Dodge, 'Investor-State Dispute Settlement Between Developed Countries: Reflections on the Australia—United States Free Trade Agreement' (2006) 39 *Vanderbilt J Int'l L* 1.

[29] On the evolution of China's attitude towards foreign investment, see D Chow, *The Legal System of the People's Republic of China in a Nutshell* (2003) 374 et seq.

[30] See UNCTAD, *Bilateral Investment Treaties 1995–2006: Trends in Investment Rulemaking* (2007) 18. Foreign investment of multinational companies based in emerging markets flowing to developed states has risen sharply in the past decade, but the volumes flowing to other developing states

One way to explain this trend is that countries with emerging markets increasingly see themselves as potential exporters of investments and wish to protect their nationals through investment agreements. While this explanation is correct, these treaties do illustrate the broader point that home states of investors are generally inclined to conclude treaties with guarantees and mechanisms going beyond the rules of customary law and that the underlying concern is not peculiar to traditional Western liberal states with outgoing foreign investment. The general point seems to be that home states of investors, whatever their historical background, consider specially negotiated rules desirable. A comparison of treaties concluded between developing countries does not reveal significant differences to agreements concluded with developed states.

(e) The quest for a multilateral framework

In 1957, Hermann Josef Abs, a prominent German banker, called for a 'Magna Charta for the Protection of Foreign Property'[31] in the form of a global treaty. Such a treaty was meant to establish not just specific standards of protection, but also a permanent arbitral tribunal charged with the application of the treaty and with the power to lay down economic sanctions against violating states, including non-signatories. When it soon became apparent that the time was not ripe for such a grand approach, Abs opted for a more modest multilateral initiative,[32] together with Sir Hartley Shawcross. These efforts finally culminated in the Abs-Shawcross Draft, which, together with other contributions such as a Swiss draft,[33] in 1962 led in turn to the first effort of the OECD, the forum of the capital-exporting countries, to prepare a multilateral treaty.[34] A second such draft was presented in 1967. However, these first efforts to create a multilateral framework remained unsuccessful, mainly due to the fact that the Convention was intended to be applicable not only to OECD member states but to all countries, and that the OECD efforts fell into a period of great divisions between capital-importing and capital-exporting countries concerning the content of recognized principles of foreign investment law.[35] Eventually, the OECD contented itself with merely recommending the draft as a model for the conclusion of bilateral investment

---

have reached a higher level; see J Santiso, 'The Emergence of Latin Multinationals', Deutsche Bank Research, 7 March 2007.

[31] Speech given at the International Industrial Development Conference (San Francisco, 15 October 1957), reprinted in *Recht der Internationalen Wirtschaft* (1957) 229.

[32] Drafts of a 'Convention on Investments Abroad', reprinted in *Recht der Internationalen Wirtschaft* (1959) 150–1.

[33] Partly reprinted in *Recht der Internationalen Wirtschaft* (1959) 151.

[34] See G A van Hecke, 'Le projet de convention de l'OCDE sur la protection des biens étrangers' (1964) 68 *Revue générale de droit international public* 641.

[35] Indeed, the Resolution of the Council of the OECD on the Draft Convention states that '[the Convention] embodies recognized principles relating to the protection of foreign property combined with rules to render more effective the application of these principles'. For the divide between developed and developing countries in the context of the discussion on a 'New International Economic Order', see p 4.

treaties by its member states.[36] This laid the groundwork for the future investment regime characterized by the lack of a universal treaty and the dominance of bilateral treaties.

In 1961, two years after the era of bilateral treaties had begun, the World Bank took the lead to address the emerging international legal framework of foreign investment, pointing to its mandate and to the link between economic development, international cooperation, and the role of private international investment. The debates then underway in the OECD, in preparation of the 1962 Draft Convention on the Protection of Foreign Property and also in the United Nations on the rules on foreign investment generally, indicated that the state of opinion regarding customary law was deeply divided and that the prospect of reaching a global consensus on the substance of investment rules was minimal.

In the World Bank, it was the then General Counsel, Aron Broches, who initiated and drove the debates on the possible scope of international consensus. Given the controversies within the United Nations, Broches properly concluded that for the time being the best contribution the Bank could make was to develop effective procedures for the impartial settlement of disputes, without attempting to seek agreement on substantive standards. This approach seemed artificial since logic would dictate that any system of dispute settlement would have to be based on a set of substantive rules which could be applied. But Broches argued that, from a pragmatic point of view, such an axiomatic approach was neither necessary nor productive.

At first sight, the Broches concept ('procedure before substance') seemed to be a limited and modest one. However, he designed what was to become, in 1965, the Convention on the Settlement of Investment Disputes between States and Nationals of Other States (ICSID Convention) establishing the International Centre for Settlement of Investment Disputes (ICSID). In retrospect, it is clear that the creation of ICSID amounted to the boldest innovative step in the modern history of international cooperation concerning the role and protection of foreign investment.

The success of this concept became apparent when the ICSID Convention quickly entered into force in 1966 and especially when in subsequent decades more and more investment treaties, bilateral and multilateral, referred to ICSID as a forum for dispute settlement. From the point of view of member states, one major advantage of the system was that investment disputes would become 'depoliticized' in the sense that they avoided confrontation between home state and host state.[37] For two decades ICSID's caseload remained quite modest. However, by the 1990s ICSID had become the main forum for the settlement of investment disputes, and Broches' vision had become a reality.

---

[36] See R Dolzer and M Stevens, *Bilateral Investment Treaties* (1995) 2.
[37] See also I Shihata, 'Towards a Greater Depoliticization of Investment Disputes: the Roles of ICSID and MIGA' in *The World Bank in a Changing World* (1991) 309.

Following its earlier efforts in the 1960s towards the creation of a multilateral investment treaty,[38] the OECD in 1995 decided to launch a new initiative in this direction. These negotiations took place from 1995 to 1998 and built, to a considerable extent, on the substance of existing bilateral treaties. The last draft for a Multilateral Agreement on Investment (MAI) dated 22 April 1998[39] indicates major areas of consensus and some points of disagreement. Although the draft shows that the negotiations had indeed progressed to a considerable extent, the discussions were halted in 1998. Several unrelated reasons had led to the break-down.[40] The United States had never stood fully behind the initiative: domestic political support necessary for ratification seemed uncertain; in addition, the level of protection for foreign investment appeared unsatisfactory due to a number of compromises. In Europe, France decided in the latter stage of the negotiations that an agreement might not be compatible with its desire to protect French culture ('*exception culturelle*'). NGOs argued that the debates within the OECD had been held without sufficient public information and input. Also, from the beginning, there was a debate as to whether the OECD, representing mainly capital-exporting countries, was the proper forum to negotiate a treaty meant to serve as a global instrument. In the end, these different aspects converged to undermine and halt support for the negotiations within the OECD.

In a partially overlapping effort, the World Trade Organization (WTO) had already placed the issue of a multilateral investment treaty on its agenda during a meeting in Singapore in 1996, in the middle of the OECD negotiations. The WTO Agreement of 1994 had embodied a first step of the trade organization into the field of foreign investment: the so-called TRIMS Agreement[41] was to regulate those aspects of foreign investment which led to direct negative consequences for a liberalized trade regime. In particular, this Agreement regulates issues of so-called performance requirements imposed by the host state upon foreign investors and aims at reducing or eliminating laws which require that local products are used in the production process by foreign investors (local content requirements). The further development of the emerging investment agenda of the WTO was addressed but not decided in 1996. In 2004, six years after the end of the OECD initiative, the efforts within the WTO to include investment issues generally into the Organization's mandate also came to a halt.[42]

---

[38] See p 8.

[39] Available at <http://www1.oecd.org/daf/mai>.

[40] See generally the different contributions to (1998) 31(3) *Cornell Int'l LJ* (symposium edition). See also Société française de droit international (ed), *Un accord multilatéral sur l'investissement: d'un forum de négociation à l'autre?* (1999); UNCTAD, *Lessons from the MAI—UNCTAD Series on Issues in International Investment Agreements* (1999); E C Nieuwenhuys and M M T A Brus (eds), *Multilateral Regulation of Investment* (2001).

[41] Agreement on Trade Related Investment Measures (TRIMS). See generally T Brewer and S Young, 'Investment Issues at the WTO: The Architecture of Rules and the Settlement of Disputes' (1998) 1 *J Int'l Economic L* 457; M Koulen, 'Foreign Investment in the WTO' in E C Nieuwenhuys and M M T A Brus (eds), *Multilateral Regulation of Investment* (2001) 181–203.

[42] See Decision of the WTO General Council of 1 August 2004 on the Doha Agenda Work Program (available at <http://www.wto.org>).

Even though developing countries had negotiated more than a thousand treaties, they were not prepared to accept a WTO-based multilateral investment treaty, arguing that such a multilateral scheme might unduly narrow their regulatory space and that the effect of such a treaty would need to be studied in greater detail. Brazil and India in particular took this position. The support of the United States for a multilateral treaty was again limited, for reasons similar to those in 1998 within the OECD.

At present, a comprehensive multilateral solution to investment issues is not in sight. It remains to be seen whether the international community will continue to develop its patchwork approach to foreign investment or whether the advantages of more global homogeneity will eventually be accepted.

(f) Recent developments

Until the early 1990s international investment law had not produced any significant case law.[43] In the meantime this situation has changed dramatically. Both in the framework of the ICSID Convention and beyond there is a veritable flood of cases that has produced and continues to produce an ever-growing case law in the field. To a large extent this dramatic increase of activity before arbitral tribunals was the direct consequence of the availability of investor-state arbitration on the basis of a rapidly growing number of BITs. Inevitably, the large number of decisions produced by differently composed tribunals has led to concerns about consistency and coherence.[44]

The success of the system of investment arbitration has also led to weariness and criticism in some quarters. Some countries have found themselves in the role of respondents more often than others and perceive the need to defend themselves repeatedly against claims by foreign investors as a serious burden. At the same time there is criticism that investment law in general and investment arbitration in particular restricts the freedom of states to take regulatory action. Therefore, enthusiasm for the current system is by no means undivided.

Under the Treaty of Lisbon, in 2009 the European Union assumed exclusive competence for foreign direct investment. This has far-reaching potential consequences for the BITs to which member states of the EU are parties. Since roughly half of all BITs worldwide have at least one EU member state as a party, the future policy of the EU on investment is likely to have global repercussions. Both BITs

---

[43] In 1970, the International Court of Justice had drawn attention to the slow evolution of investment law, discussing relevant rules on diplomatic protection:

Considering the important developments of the last half-century, the growth of foreign investments and the expansion of international activities of corporations, in particular of holding companies, which are often multinational, and considering the way in which the economic interests of states have proliferated, it may at first sight appear surprising that the evolution of the law has not gone further and that no generally accepted rules in the matter have crystallized on the international plane. (ICJ, *Case Concerning the Barcelona Traction, Light and Power Company, Ltd*, Judgment of 5 February 1970, ICJ Reports (1970) 3, 47)

[44] See R Dolzer, 'Perspectives for Investment Arbitration: Consistency as a Policy Goal?' (2012) 3 *Transnational Dispute Management*.

between EU member states (intra-EU BITs) and BITs of EU members with non-EU members (extra-EU BITs) will be affected.

With regard to intra-EU BITs, the European Commission wants all of these terminated. Some member states are strictly opposed to these plans while others have started terminating BITs with other EU members.

With regard to BITs with non-EU member states, the Commission wishes gradually to replace these by new treaties to be negotiated by the Commission on behalf of the EU. At the time of writing, negotiations are underway between the Commission and Canada, India, and Singapore.

2. The sources of international investment law

Foreign investment law consists of general international law, of standards more specific to international economic law, and of distinct rules peculiar to the protection of investment. In addition, the law of the host state plays an important role. Depending upon the circumstances of an individual case, the interplay between relevant domestic rules of the host state and applicable rules of international law may become central to the analysis of a case.[45] The domestic rules on nationality may determine jurisdiction in a particular case. Other areas of domestic law that may become relevant in a particular case include property law, commercial law, labour law, zoning law, and tax law to name just a few.

Not only is the distinction between international law and domestic law becoming blurred by the modern regime of foreign investment law,[46] but also the classical separation between public and private law, as emphasized especially in continental European legal orders, cannot be accommodated in neat categories in this field. The broader question whether international economic law allows for a useful distinction between private law and public law is particularly acute in foreign investment law. The rules governing contracts between an investor and a host state draw on both private and public law. In fact, these rules establish a link between domestic law and public international law. To a certain extent, the rules of domestic law are being confronted and superseded by rules of public international law, and in relevant international cases, the decision of arbitrators will turn on their understanding of domestic law, possibly accompanied by a process of review of domestic law under the international standards contained in treaties and in general international law.

What follows is a general survey of the most important sources of international investment law. More detailed discussion of the issues arising from these sources can be found in the relevant chapters of this book.

---

[45] For more detail see pp 288–93.
[46] See F Orrego Vicuña, 'Of Contracts and Treaties in the Global Market' (2004) 8 *Max Planck Yearbook of United Nations Law* 341.

(a) The ICSID Convention

The Convention on the Settlement of Investment Dispute between States and Nationals of other States is a multilateral treaty. It provides a procedural framework for dispute settlement between host states and foreign investors through conciliation or arbitration.[47] The Convention does not contain substantive standards of protection for investments. Also, participation in the ICSID Convention does not amount to consent to arbitration. The process whereby consent to arbitration under the ICSID Convention is given by the host state and by the investor is described at pp 254–264.

(b) Bilateral investment treaties

BITs are the most important source of contemporary international investment law. Some countries, such as Germany, Switzerland, and China, have concluded well over 100 BITs with other countries; and it is estimated that close to 3,000 BITs are in existence worldwide.

BITs provide guarantees for the investments of investors from one of the contracting states in the other contracting state. Traditionally, BITs are relatively short with no more than 12 to 14 articles. They typically consist of three parts.

The first part offers definitions, especially of the concepts of 'investment' and 'investor'.[48]

The second part consists of substantive standards for the protection of investments and investors. Typically these contain: a provision on admission of investments; a guarantee of fair and equitable treatment (FET); a guarantee of full protection and security; a guarantee against arbitrary and discriminatory treatment; a guarantee of national treatment and a guarantee of most-favoured-nation treatment (MFN clause); guarantees in case of expropriation; and guarantees concerning the free transfer of payments. These various standards and guarantees are described in some detail in Chapters V, VI, and VII. The third part deals with dispute settlement. Most BITs contain two separate provisions on dispute settlement. One provides for arbitration in the event of disputes between the host state and foreign investors (investor-state arbitration). Most BITs contain advance consent of the two states to international arbitration with investors from the other state party either before an ICSID tribunal or through some other form of arbitration. The other provision on dispute settlement in BITs provides for arbitration between the two states parties to the treaty (state-state arbitration). Whereas investor-state arbitration under BITs is very common, state-state arbitration has remained rare. The role of BITs in dispute settlement is described at pp 257–259.

The classical BIT of the past decades has addressed only issues of foreign investment. More recently there is a trend to negotiate provisions on foreign

---

[47] For details see pp 238 et seq.
[48] See p 47 et seq and pp 62 et seq.

investment in the context of wider agreements, called free trade agreements (FTAs). As the name indicates, these FTAs also address trade issues. This trend seems to have started with the agreement between Canada and the United States in 1989, which formed the basis for the NAFTA concluded in 1994 between these two states and Mexico. With the recent tendency to conclude bilateral or regional trade agreements in addition to the global rules of the WTO, states have been inclined to conclude broad agreements on economic cooperation regionally or bilaterally, instead of agreements specifically aimed at matters of trade or foreign investment. The number of these FTAs also covering rules on foreign investment has increased in recent years.[49] The European Commission is negotiating FTAs with third countries, containing provisions on trade as well as on investment.

At times, it has been argued that some BITs are negotiated in haste and without detailed consideration of their implications. Typically, capital-exporting states have formulated a model treaty for their own purpose,[50] and have presented this informal document to capital-importing states at the beginning of negotiations as a basis for the subsequent negotiations. However, developing states have gradually developed their own preferences for a certain scheme of treaties, sometimes with their own model draft. Also, treaties have been negotiated between developing countries.

As more and more treaties have been concluded, and as the international discussion on the nature and the details of these treaties has progressed, including the contours and substance of individual clauses, any argument to the effect that host states have de facto accepted investment obligations without proper knowledge of their scope and significance will become less convincing. Investment treaties are today seen as admission tickets to international investment markets.[51] Their limiting impact on the sovereignty of the host state, controversial as it may be in the individual case, is in this sense a necessary corollary to the objective of creating an investment-friendly climate.[52]

---

[49] See generally UNCTAD, *World Investment Report* (2010) 82.

[50] Most capital-exporting countries have drawn up their own model investment agreements. Also, the Asian-African Legal Consultative Committee produced a model treaty for its members in 1984, with two variants. See Asian-African Legal Consultative Committee: Models for Bilateral Agreements on Promotion and Protection of Investments, reprinted in 23 ILM 237 (1984). Meanwhile, some developing countries have adopted their own national versions. From time to time, model treaties are revised to reflect the changing circumstances and priorities. The United States, for instance, presented a new model treaty in 2012. The first US Model Treaty was adopted in 1981. See K J Vandevelde, 'The BIT Program: A Fifteen-Year Appraisal', *ASIL Proceedings* (1992) 532, 536. Obviously, model treaties have no binding force in themselves. Under certain circumstances, their content may become relevant for the interpretation of treaties. Eg, a state may be unable to rely on a certain traditional interpretation of a clause in a treaty if that clause departs from the model treaty and if the interpretation of the treaty preferred by the state is the one also offered in the model treaty. However, the point resists generalization, particularly because the negotiating history of BITs is not usually available to tribunals.

[51] See pp 20, 22.

[52] R Dolzer, 'The Impact of International Investment Treaties on Domestic Administrative Law' (2005) 37 *NYU J Int'l L & Pol* 953.

(c) Sectoral and regional treaties: the Energy Charter Treaty and NAFTA

The first multilateral treaty containing substantive rules on foreign investment is of a sectoral nature and not meant for universal membership. The ECT of 1994[53] essentially grew out of the desire of European states to cooperate closely with Russia and the new states in Eastern Europe and Central Asia in exploring and developing the energy sector, which is of crucial political, economic, and financial importance for both sides. Membership was open to all states committed to the establishment of closer cooperation and an appropriate international legal framework in the energy sector.

The scope of the ECT is not limited to investments but covers a wide range of issues such as trade, transit, energy efficiency, and dispute settlement. The chapter on investment is mostly patterned along the lines of bilateral investment treaties concluded by the member states of the European Union. Its substantive standards are similar to those contained in BITs.[54] However, the Treaty also contains some innovative features, such as special provisions concerning state entities and subnational authorities,[55] and a 'best-efforts' clause concerning non-discrimination in the pre-establishment phase,[56] coupled with an expression of intent to transform it into a legally binding obligation in the future.[57]

The Treaty entered into force in 1998. So far, 51 states and the European Union have ratified the Treaty. Russia has signed, but currently does not intend to become a party.[58] Under the Treaty, investors have the right to bring a suit before ICSID, before an arbitral tribunal established under the UNCITRAL arbitration rules, before the Arbitration Institute of the Stockholm Chamber of Commerce, or before the courts or administrative tribunals of the respondent state.[59] Thirty investment disputes were initiated between 2001 and 2011 under the framework of the ECT.

The NAFTA between Canada, Mexico, and the United States (1994)[60] addresses matters of both trade and investment. The Treaty aims at the free movement and liberalization of goods, services, people, and investment. Chapter Eleven of the NAFTA specifically addresses the treatment of investments.

---

[53] The text of the ECT can be found at 34 ILM 360 (1995). See generally C Ribeiro (ed), *Investment Arbitration and the Energy Charter Treaty* (2006); T Wälde, 'Investment Arbitration under the Energy Charter Treaty: An Overview of Selected Key Issues based on Recent Litigation Experience' in N Horn (ed), *Arbitrating Foreign Investment Disputes* (2004) 193; R Happ, 'Dispute Settlement under the Energy Charter Treaty' (2002) 45 *German Yearbook of Int'l L* 331; T Waelde, 'International Energy Law: An Introduction to Modern Concepts, Context, Policy and Players' in J P Schneider and C Theobald, *Handbuch zum Recht der Energiewirtschaft* (2003) 1129.

[54] ECT, Art 10(1) and (3).

[55] ECT, Arts 22 and 23.

[56] ECT, Art 10(2).

[57] ECT, Art 10(4).

[58] On 20 August 2009 Russia officially informed the Depository of the ECT that it did not intend to become a party.

[59] ECT, Art 26.

[60] The text of the NAFTA can be found at 32 ILM 605 (1993).

The objective enunciated in Article 102 is to increase substantially investment opportunities in the territories of the parties.[61]

The trade provisions in the NAFTA are largely built on the rules of the WTO, of which all three NAFTA countries are members. Chapter Eleven on investment amounted to a bold and innovative scheme inasmuch as it tied Mexico as a developing country to its two northern developed neighbours against a history replete with conflict, especially in investment matters.[62] In substance, Chapter Eleven builds upon the treaty practice of the United States, including the treaty with Canada concluded in 1989.

The tripartite structure of Chapter Eleven contains substantive obligations in Section A (Arts 1101 to 1114), rules on dispute settlement in Section B (Arts 1115 to 1138), and a number of definitions in Section C (Art 1139).

The substantive obligations cover traditional issues such as national treatment, MFN treatment, performance requirements, the selection of senior management and board of directors, transfers, and possible denial of benefits to investors owned or controlled by investors of non-NAFTA states. In practice, the rules on expropriation (Art 1110) and on the 'Minimum Standard of Treatment' (Art 1105) have received most attention and have led to a number of legal disputes and public controversies.

Dispute settlement is governed by Section B of Chapter Eleven. Under Article 1120 an investor may bring a suit against the host state under the ICSID Convention. But this provision is operative only if both the home state and the host state have ratified the ICSID Convention. In fact, only the United States—and not Canada or Mexico—is party to the ICSID Convention. A second choice is to submit the dispute to arbitration under the ICSID Additional Facility Rules of 1978 which do not require that both states are ICSID parties—only that one of the two states is a party. Therefore, the Additional Facility is available if the United States is either the respondent or the claimant's home state. The Additional Facility follows rules different from ICSID regarding the applicable law (no reference to the law of the host state), annulment (no annulment under ICSID rules, but review by

---

[61] See M Kinnear, A Bjorklund, and J Hannaford, *Investment Disputes under NAFTA* (2006); T Weiler (ed), *NAFTA Investment Law and Arbitration: Past Issues, Current Practice, Future Prospects* (2004); C Brower, 'NAFTA's Investment Chapter: Initial Thoughts about Second-Generation Rights' (2003) 36 *Vanderbilt J Transn'l L* 1533; C Brower, 'Structure, Legitimacy and NAFTA's Investment Chapter' (2003) 36 *Vanderbilt J Transn'l L* 37; G Aguilar Alvarez and W Park, 'The New Face of Investment Arbitration: NAFTA Chapter 11' (2003) 28 *Yale JIL* 365; B Legum, 'The Innovation of Investor-State Arbitration under NAFTA' (2002) 43 *Harvard Int'l LJ* 531; D A Gantz, 'Potential Conflicts between Investor Rights and Environmental Regulation under NAFTA's Chapter 11' (2001) 33 *George Washington International Law Review* 651; C Brower, 'Investor-State Disputes under NAFTA: The Empire Strikes Back' (2001) 40 *Columbia J Transn'l L* 43; H C Alvarez, 'Arbitration under the North American Free Trade Agreement' (2000) 16 *Arbitration International* 393; F Ortino, 'NAFTA—Fifteen Years Later' (2009) 3 *Transnational Dispute Management*. P Dumberry, *The Minimum Standard and Fair and Equitable Treatment under International Law: Examining 15 Years of NAFTA Chapter 11* (2012); A Ingelson, L Mitchell, and C Viney, 'NAFTA Takings Update' (2012) 5 *J World Energy L & Bus* 1.

[62] With regard to Mexico and NAFTA, see J Preston and S Dillon, *Opening Mexico: The Making of Democracy* (2005).

domestic courts), and enforcement (no enforcement under ICSID rules). The third possibility open to the investor is to have the arbitration governed by the UNCITRAL Arbitration Rules.

The right of the investor to file a suit against the host state under Section B is limited to breaches of the rules contained in Section A. The governing law is limited to the NAFTA itself and to applicable rules of international law (Art 1131(1)).

As regards rules in other parts of the Agreement, such as those on transparency, only the member states may bring them before an arbitral tribunal (Chapter 20, Art 2004). The member states also have the right to make a submission on a question of interpretation if they are not a party to a dispute (Art 1128).

From a broader perspective of international economic law, the most remarkable feature of the dispute resolution scheme contained in the NAFTA lies in the fact that while it addresses matters of both trade and investment, it contains separate rules on dispute resolution and, in accordance with the practice of previous decades, recognizes the right to bring a suit for an investor but not for a trader. This dualism now seems to be entrenched in state practice, some divergences and concerns notwithstanding.

(d) Customary international law

Although international investment law is dominated by treaties, customary international law still plays an important role. The treaty-based rules have to be understood and interpreted, like all treaties, in the context of the general rules of international law. Article 31(3)(c) of the Vienna Convention on the Law of Treaties provides that together with the Treaty's context 'any relevant rules of international law applicable in the relations between the parties' shall be taken into account.

Customary international law remains highly relevant for the practice of investment arbitration. Rules on attribution and other areas of state responsibility as well as rules on damages illustrate the point. Other relevant areas of customary international law are the rules on expropriation, on denial of justice, and on the nationality of investors.

In fact, the growing case law in the area of foreign investment has led to a situation in which some general rules of international law find their major practical expression in foreign investment law. The consequence is that a full contemporary understanding of these rules requires knowledge of their interpretation and application in foreign investment law cases.

A basic doctrinal issue that has arisen pertains to the impact of the large number of bilateral investment treaties on the evolution of customary law.[63] This linkage between customary law and treaty law has been at the forefront of comments which have addressed the state of customary law regarding expropriation and compensation of foreign property.[64]

---

[63] See also pp 134–9.
[64] See eg S Schwebel, 'The Reshaping of the International Law of Foreign Investment by Concordant Bilateral Investment Treaties' in S Charnovitz, D P Steger, and P van den Bossche (eds), *Law in the Service of Human Dignity—Essays in Honour of Florentino Feliciano* (2005) 241.

(e) General principles of law

General principles of law in the sense of Article 38(1)(c) of the Statute of the International Court of Justice have received increasing attention in recent practice.[65] General principles of law will acquire importance in the context of investment rules especially in the case of lacunae in the text of treaties and in the interpretation of individual terms and phrases.

Examples of general principles relied upon by tribunals include good faith,[66] *nemo auditur propriam turpitudinem allegans*,[67] estoppel,[68] *onus probandi*,[69] and the right to be heard.[70]

(f) Unilateral statements

The legal effect of unilateral statements and the conditions under which these may be considered binding have played a prominent role in some cases, especially in the context of the guarantee of fair and equitable treatment (FET). Here, the principle of good faith is closely tied to the operation of the principle of estoppel. The International Court of Justice and its predecessor have recognized that unilateral declarations will be binding if the circumstances and the wording of the statement are such that the addressees are entitled to rely on them.[71] The International Law Commission has adopted Guiding Principles applicable to unilateral declarations of states capable of creating legal obligations.[72]

This situation may also arise in the relationship between the host state and the foreign investor.[73] Arbitral tribunals have so held on the basis of the principle of good faith.[74] In *Waste Management v Mexico*, the Tribunal found that in applying the FET standard, 'it is relevant that the treatment is in breach of representations made by the host State which were reasonably relied on by the claimant'.[75]

In *Total v Argentina*[76] the Tribunal said:

---

[65] Generally see *Merrill & Ring v Canada*, Award, 31 March 2010, para 187.

[66] *Sempra v Argentina*, Award, 28 September 2007, paras 290–9 (annulled on other grounds); *Phoenix v Czech Republic*, Award, 15 April 2009, para 142; *Cementownia v Turkey*, Award, 17 September 2009, paras 138–48. See also p 156.

[67] *Rumeli v Kazakhstan*, Award, 29 July 2008, paras 310, 323.

[68] *Chevron v Ecuador*, Partial Award, 30 March 2010, paras 334 et seq; *Grynberg v Grenada*, Award, 10 December 2010, paras 7.1.1 et seq.

[69] *Alpha v Ukraine*, Award, 8 November 2010, paras 236, 237.

[70] *Fraport v Philippines*, Decision on Annulment, 23 December 2010, paras 197–208, 218–47.

[71] See *Legal Status of Eastern Greenland (Denmark v Norway)*, 5 April 1933, PCIJ, Series A/B, No 53, 22, 69; ICJ, *Nuclear Tests Cases (Australia/New Zealand v France)*, 20 December 1974, ICJ Reports (1974) 253, 268.

[72] A/CN.4/L.703.

[73] See W M Reisman and M H Arsanjani, 'The Question of Unilateral Governmental Statements as Applicable Law in Investment Disputes' (2004) 19 *ICSID Review-FILJ* 328.

[74] *Revere Copper v OPIC*, Award, 24 August 1978, 56 ILR (1980) 258, 271.

[75] *Waste Management v Mexico*, Final Award, 30 April 2004, para 98; see also *CMS v Argentina*, Decision on Jurisdiction, 17 July 2003, paras 27, 33; *LG&E v Argentina*, Award, 3 October 2006, para 133; *Mobil v Venezuela*, Decision on Jurisdiction, 10 June 2010, paras 86–141; *Cemex v Venezuela*, Decision on Jurisdiction, 30 December 2010, paras 80–139.

[76] *Total v Argentina*, Decision on Liability, 27 December 2010.

Under international law, unilateral acts, statements and conduct by States may be the source of legal obligations which the intended beneficiaries or addressees, or possibly any member of the international community, can invoke. The legal basis of that binding character appears to be only in part related to the concept of legitimate expectations—being rather akin to the principle of 'estoppel'. Both concepts may lead to the same result, namely, that of rendering the content of a unilateral declaration binding on the State that is issuing it.[77]

(g) Case law

As explained below,[78] tribunals are not bound by previous cases, but do examine and refer to them, frequently.

3. The nature of international investment law

(a) Investment law and trade law

Over time, the principles governing foreign investment have developed their own distinct features within the broader realm of international economic law. Today, it remains a matter of semantics whether it is appropriate to speak of the existence of a separate category of 'principles of foreign investment law', given their strong links to international economic law in general. But there is no doubt that the international law of foreign investment has become a specialized area of the legal profession and that special courses are offered on the subject in universities worldwide. The common usage and parlance in the terminology of international law has always been to single out and to designate distinct fields, such as the 'laws of war', or the 'law of the sea', whenever the body of rules in any one area has become extensive and dense enough to justify special attention and study.

The nature of investments makes it inevitable that the nature, structure, and purpose of foreign investment law stands out as structurally distinct in the broader realm of international law, especially in comparison to trade. In terms of legal methodology, the difference between the two fields calls for caution in assuming commonalities between foreign investment law and trade law. Whenever an analogy is proposed, or a solution is transferred from one area to the other, it must be examined in detail whether their different nature is amenable to an assumption of commonality. Often, a concept which appears to be in common turns out to have different shades and characteristics upon more detailed analysis, taking into account the peculiar business nature of long-term foreign investment projects.[79]

---

[77] At para 131. Footnote omitted.
[78] pp 33–34.   [79] See pp 204–6.

(b) Balancing duties and benefits

There have been speculations relating to the reciprocity of obligations in investment treaties, to the quid pro quo underlying these treaties, and to the mutual benefits arising from them. All these concerns relate to a common underlying theme which suggests that treaties on foreign investment in their traditional and current version place obligations solely on the host state without equal commitments on the part of the foreign investor.

Such concerns reflect the assumption that all types of treaties are necessarily based upon a similar structure and upon a pattern of reciprocity and mutuality which must be reflected in the terms of the treaty itself. However, the very nature of the law of aliens, being at the origin of foreign investment law, indicates that the *raison d'être* of this field of law does not reflect the traditional themes of reciprocity and mutuality, but instead sets accepted standards for the unilateral conduct of the host state. The context and nature of a foreign investment reveals a structural setting which does not correspond to a transaction or to an agreement in which privileges are exchanged on a mutual basis by two parties. Notions of mutuality and reciprocity are not absent from the regime of an investment treaty, but they do not operate in the same manner as in a classical agreement. Instead, they are focused on the mutual benefits of host state and investor and on the complementarity of interests flowing from the long-term commitment of resources by the foreign investor under the territorial sovereignty of the host state.

In an investment treaty, the host state deliberately renounces an element of its sovereignty in return for a new opportunity: the chance better to attract new foreign investments which it would not have acquired in the absence of a treaty. It is true that this quid pro quo underlying the choice on the part of the host state is based on a policy judgement the nature of which escapes precise evaluation. It is based upon assumptions about the effect of the treaty which are uncertain.[80] As with every treaty,[81] the acceptance of an investment treaty by a state and the determination of the desirable type and extent of obligations contained in it represent an exercise of the sovereign power to be made freely by each state in light of its circumstances and preferences.

Once the sovereign has committed itself to a treaty, the balancing of interests and aspirations is no longer subject to a unilateral decision. After the investment treaty is concluded, the investor is entitled to rely on the scheme accepted in the treaty by the host state as long as the treaty remains in force.

---

[80] See p 22.

[81] See the statement made by the Permanent Court of International Justice in the *Wimbledon* case:

> The Court declines to see in the conclusion of any Treaty by which a State undertakes to perform or refrain from performing a particular act an abandonment of its sovereignty. No doubt any convention creating an obligation of this kind places a restriction upon the exercise of the sovereign rights of the State, in the sense that it requires them to be exercised in a certain way. But the right of entering into international engagements is an attribute of State sovereignty. (*Wimbledon* (*France v Germany*), 17 August 1923, PCIJ, Series A, No 1, 25)

Investment treaties do not pit the interests and benefits of the host state against those of the investor. Instead, the motivation underlying such treaties assumes that the parties share a joint purpose. In this sense, it would be alien to the nature of an investment treaty to contrast the interests of the host state and of the foreign investor as opposed to each other. The mode and spirit of investment treaties is to understand the two interests as mutually compatible and reinforcing, held together by the joint purpose of implementing investments consistent with the business plan of the investor and the legal order of the host state.

(c) The investor's perspective: a long-term risk

Making a foreign investment is different in nature from engaging in a trade transaction. Whereas a trade deal typically consists of a one-time exchange of goods and money, the decision to invest in a foreign country initiates a long-term relationship between the investor and the host country. Often, the business plan of the investor is to sink substantial resources into the project at the outset of the investment, with the expectation of recouping this amount plus an acceptable rate of return during the subsequent period of investment, sometimes running up to 30 years or more.

A key feature in the design of such a foreign investment is to lay out in advance the risks inherent in such a long-term relationship, both from a business perspective and from the legal point of view. This involves identifying a business concept and a legal structure which is suitable to the implementation of the project in general, and minimizes risks which may arise during the period of the investment. In many cases, this task is essential for the investor as the money sunk into the project at the outset typically cannot be used subsequently at another location, because the machinery and installations of the project are specifically designed and tied to the particularities of the project and its location.

The dynamics in the relationship between the host state and the investor differ in nature before and after the investment has been made. Larger projects are typically not made under the general laws of the host country; instead, the host state and the foreign investor negotiate a deal—an investment agreement—which may adapt the general legal regime of the host country to the project-specific needs and preferences of both sides. During these negotiations, the investor will try to seek legal and other guarantees necessary in view of the nature and the length of the project. Considerations will include bilateral or multilateral treaties concluded by the host state which will provide guarantees on the level of international law. Depending on the project, the investor may be in the driver's seat during these negotiations if the host state is keen to attract the investor.

The investor will normally bear the commercial risks inherent in possible changes in the market of the project, for example new competitors, price volatilities, exchange rates, or changes affecting the financial setting. In certain transactions, provisions will be made for adaptation or renegotiation in the event of a change in the economic and financial context of the project. The political risks, that is, the risks inherent in a future intervention of the host state in the legal design of the project, will typically be addressed during these initial negotiations. Unless these risks are appropriately addressed in an applicable investment treaty, the investor may ask for protection on a number of points, such as the applicable law, the tax regime, provisions dealing with inflation, a duty of the host state to buy a certain volume of the product (especially in the field of energy production), the future pricing of the investor's product, or customs regulation for materials needed for the product, and, especially, an agreement on future dispute settlement. Such rights may be included in an investment contract between the investor and the host state.

Once these negotiations are concluded and the investor's resources are sunk into the project, the dynamics of influence and power tend to shift in favour of the host state. The central political risk which henceforth arises for the foreign investor lies in a change of position of the host government that would alter the balance of burdens, risks, and benefits which the two sides laid down when they negotiated the deal and which formed the basis of the investor's business plan and the legitimate expectations embodied in this plan. Such a change of position on the part of the host country becomes more likely with every subsequent change of government in the host state during the period of the investment.

(d) The host state's perspective: attracting foreign investment

It is reasonable to assume that the object and purpose of investment treaties is closely tied to the desirability of foreign investments, to the benefits for the host state and for the investor, to the conditions necessary for the promotion of foreign investment, and to the removal of obstacles which may stand in the way of allowing and channelling more foreign investment into the host states. Thus, the purpose of investment treaties is to address the typical risks of a long-term investment project, and thereby to provide stability and predictability in the sense of an investment-friendly climate.

Under the rules of customary international law, no state is under an obligation to admit foreign investment in its territory, generally or in any particular segment of its economy. While the right to exclude and to regulate foreign investment is an expression of state sovereignty, the power to conclude treaties with other states will also be seen as flowing from the same concept.

Once it has admitted a foreign investment, a host state is subject to a minimum standard of customary international law.[82] Modern treaties on foreign investment go beyond this minimum standard in the scope of obligations a host state owes towards a foreign investor. Whether such treaties in general, or any particular version of them, are beneficial to the host state, remains a matter for each state to decide. In particular, each state will weigh, or at least has the power to weigh, the economic and financial benefits of a treaty-based promotion of foreign investments against the consequences of being bound to the standards of protection laid down in the treaty. None of these benefits and consequences is open to a qualitatively or

---

[82] See E Root, 'The Basis of Protection to Citizens Residing Abroad' (1910) 4 *AJIL* 517, 528—see pp 134–8.

quantitatively objective assessment. Each state will exercise its sovereign prerogative in determining its preferences and priorities when it decides whether to conclude an investment treaty.

There is an ongoing debate over the impact foreign investment treaties have on the promotion of foreign investment and its geographic distribution. Empirical evidence pointing to an increase in foreign investment in a state which has been directly caused by the conclusion of new treaties remains scant, even though recent studies suggest that a positive effect will flow from such a treaty.[83] Legal security in a host country for an investment project is one of several factors that will influence an investment decision, but the driving parameters are determined not by legal but by economic considerations. Therefore, an argument that the international legal dimension will in itself prompt an increased flow of foreign investment would be unrealistic. On the other hand, globalization has led to relatively accurate real-time information about economic and legal matters around the globe, and the lack of legal stability surrounding a potential investment in a particular country may prevent a positive decision on the part of the investor. The perception of a sufficient degree of legal stability for a project, and for the investment climate in a state generally, will be one of several factors in making a decision about new foreign investment, but will not by itself serve as the decisive incentive for potential foreign investors.[84] Moreover, the perceived risk of investing in a particular country will determine the profit margin required by the investor. High-risk investments may well be undertaken but will require a higher rate of return for the investor.

Another major advantage of treaties for the protection of investments, and of investment arbitration in particular, is that investment disputes become 'depoliticized'. This means that they distance the dispute from the home state of the investor and thus avoid confrontation, at least directly, between home state and host state.[85] In other words, the dispute is removed from the political inter-state arena and moved into the judicial arena of investment arbitration. From the perspective of a host state, facing an investor before an international tribunal may

---

[83] See eg E Neumayer and L Spess, 'Do Bilateral Investment Treaties Increase Foreign Direct Investment to Developing Countries?' (2005) 33 *World Development* 1567; Z Elkins, A Guzman, and B Símmons, 'Competing for Capital: The Diffusion of Bilateral Investment Treaties, 1960–2000', Berkeley Program in Law and Economics, Annual Papers (2006); M Hallward-Driemeyer, 'Do Bilateral Investment Treaties Attract Foreign Investment?', World Bank Policy Research Working Paper No 3121; K Sauvant and L Sachs (eds), *The Effect of Treaties on Foreign Direct Investment* (2009).

[84] In 2006, the OECD adopted a Policy Framework for Investment, with a focus on ten policy areas which will determine the degree to which a country is investment friendly (investment policy, investment promotion and facilitation, trade policy, competition policy, tax policy, corporate governance, policies for promoting responsible business conduct, human resource development, infrastructure and financial services development, public governance). See OECD, Policy Framework for Investment, available at <http://www.oecd.org/dataoecd/1/31/36671400.pdf>. This Framework is also designed to promote the goals of the Millennium Declaration of the United Nations (see Preamble p 7).

[85] See C Schreuer, 'Investment Protection and International Relations' in A Reinisch and U Kriebaum (eds), *The Law of International Relations—Liber Amicorum Hanspeter Neuhold* (2007) 345.

be the lesser evil compared to being exposed to the pressure of a powerful state or the European Commission.

(e) International investment law and sovereign regulation

Conceptually, one may ask today whether the operation of the international law of foreign investment amounts to a body of international rules of administrative law governing the relationship of the foreign investor and the host state.[86] It is evident that the rules on foreign investment may reach far into segments of domestic law which would traditionally have belonged to the '*domaine reservé*' of each host country. This evolving characteristic feature of foreign investment law has led to concerns not just about the preservation of national sovereignty, but also about the democratic legitimacy of the process by which foreign investment law is developed and applied. Indeed, these concerns have not only been voiced by developing countries as recipients of foreign investments; with equal force, this linkage has been observed and criticized by segments of civil society in developed countries and in the United States after it had become a member of NAFTA and a respondent in a number of NAFTA cases.

A traditional understanding of the concept of sovereignty detached from current international economic realities may lead to the view that the international rules on foreign investment reach or even cross the lines of what is considered acceptable.[87] The rules on foreign investment touch upon domestic regulations as diverse as labour law, the organization of the judiciary, administrative principles, environmental law, health law, and, of course, rules governing property.

Rules of modern trade law also affect domestic matters, but the impact on domestic law and, thus, potential concern for national sovereignty, is more severe when rules of investment law are applied. At the same time, economic literature has emphasized that openness of an economic system to foreign competition is among the factors that contribute to economic growth and to good governance in general. Thus, investment law embodies and represents the nature and the effects of economic globalization, with the potential advantage of economic efficiency and of higher living standards coupled with a reduced legal power of the national authorities to regulate such areas which have an impact upon foreign investment.[88]

(f) International investment law and good governance

The concept of good governance has increasingly influenced the international development agenda.[89] Earlier periods of development practice after 1945 had

---

[86] See S Schill, *International Investment Law and Comparative Public Law* (2010).

[87] In response to these concerns the United States has decided to opt for a treaty that spells out definitions in great detail, so as to render arbitral decisions more predictable and to reduce the power of arbitrators.

[88] On the power of the host state to control multinational enterprises in general, see C Wallace, *The Multinational Enterprise and Legal Control—Host State Sovereignty in an Era of Economic Globalization* (2002).

[89] See generally R Dolzer, M Herdegen, and B Vogel, *Good Governance* (2007).

focused first on the significance of important individual projects and then on the role of macroeconomic policies. The new thinking, along with empirical studies, highlights the fact that all projects and policies depend in their implementation and, indeed, in their conception and formulation, on a functioning state, in particular on functioning institutions.

As a consequence, the concept of good governance has moved to the centre of international aid and poverty-reduction policies. The first coherent formulation of the concept seems to be contained in a World Bank report written on the development challenges for sub-Saharan Africa in 1989.[90] No single definition has subsequently been adopted, but the core elements have been expressed in working documents by the World Bank[91] and the International Monetary Fund.[92] In the treaty between the European Community and African, Caribbean, and Pacific States as adopted in 2000, the so-called Cotonou Agreement, the wording is as follows:

In the context of a political and institutional environment that upholds human rights, democratic principles and the rule of law, good governance is the transparent and account-able management of human, natural, economic and financial resources for the purposes of equitable and sustainable development. It entails clear decision-making procedures at the level of public authorities, transparent and accountable institutions, the primacy of law in the management and distribution of resources and capacity building for elaborating and implementing measures aiming in particular at preventing and combating corruption.[93]

The origin of the concept of good governance falls into the same period as the formulation of the Washington Consensus[94] and the beginning of the wave of investment treaties of the 1990s. The common core of the policies embodied in investment treaties, in the Washington Consensus, and in the principle of good governance lies in the recognition that institutional effectiveness, the rule of law, and an appropriate degree of stability and predictability of policies form the governmental framework for domestic economic growth and also for the willing-ness of foreign investors to enter the domestic market. Thus, investment treaties provide for external constraints and disciplines which foster and reinforce values similar to the principle of good governance with its emphasis on domestic insti-tutions and policies.

(g) Obligations for investors

BITs give guarantees to investors but do not normally address obligations of investors, although some BITs provide that investments, in order to be protected, must be in accordance with host state law.

---

[90] World Bank, *Sub-Saharan Africa: From Crisis to Sustainable Growth* (1989).
[91] See World Bank, *Governance: The World Bank's Experience* (1994) 12; compare also S Killinger, *The World Bank's Non-Political Mandate* (2003).
[92] See IMF, *Good Governance—The IMF's Role* (1997).
[93] Article 9(3); the substantive paragraph remained unchanged during the 2005 revision. See also P Hilpold, 'EU Development Cooperation at a Crossroad: The Cotonou Agreement of 23 June 2000 and the Principle of Good Governance' (2002) 7 *European Foreign Affairs Review* 53.
[94] See pp 5, 87.

On various levels, discussion has turned to the coverage by investment treaties of certain claims, including counterclaims, of the host state or obligations of the foreign investor to observe certain human rights or environmental or labour standards. Such innovations to BIT practice have indeed been proposed.[95] They would be in line with the objectives of earlier ideas pursued in the United Nations for a Code of Conduct for Transnational Corporations as well as with the more recent concepts and resolutions on corporate responsibility, as they are also in part implied in the OECD Guidelines for Multinational Enterprises adopted in 1976 and last updated in 2011, together with other efforts to promote voluntary initiatives for standards of corporate social responsibility.[96]

Within the UN these efforts to agree on non-binding rules broke down together with the failure to negotiate a multilateral treaty on foreign investment. An attempt to draw up a code of conduct on transnational corporations was made between 1977 and 1992, but was then abandoned.[97]

The OECD Guidelines, which are part of the broader OECD Declaration on International Investment and Multinational Enterprises, constitute non-binding recommendations to multinational enterprises in areas such as employment, human rights, environment, fighting bribery, science and technology, competition, taxation, information disclosure, and consumer interests. Within the administration of the adhering governments, so-called National Contact Points are charged with promotion of the Guidelines and handling inquiries about their application. All OECD member countries as well as nine non-member states have so far adhered to the OECD Guidelines.

In 2003, a group of international banks launched an initiative for a framework addressing environmental and social risks in project financing.[98] The so-called 'Equator Principles' are intended to apply to all project financings with total project capital costs over US$10 million and require, inter alia, social and environmental assessment procedures and consultation, disclosure, and monitoring mechanisms. For the applicable standards, the principles refer to various World Bank and IFC guidelines. Over 76 financial institutions have so far adopted the Equator Principles.

An effort to approach investment issues from the vantage point of human rights was made in the UN after 2000; the aim was to find a consensus on norms

---

[95] See eg H Mann, K von Moltke, A Cosbey, and L E Peterson, 'IISD Model International Agreement on Investment for Sustainable Development' (2005) available at <http://www.iisd.org>; U Kriebaum, 'Privatizing Human Rights: The Interface between International Investment Protection and Human Rights' in A Reinisch and U Kriebaum (eds), *The Law of International Relations—Liber Amicorum Hanspeter Neuhold* (2007) 165.

[96] For a survey, see UNCTAD, *World Investment Report* (2011) 111. See also A Heinemann, 'Business Enterprises in Public International Law' in U Fastenrath et al (eds), *From Bilateralism to Community Interest: Essays in Honour of Judge Bruno Simma* (2011) 718.

[97] See Draft UN Code of Conduct on Transnational Corporation, reprinted in 23 ILM 626 (1984).

[98] See S Kass and J McCarroll, 'The Revised Equator Principles' (2006) *New York LJ*, 1 September; A Hardenbrook, 'The Equator Principles: The Private Financial Sector's Attempt at Environmental Responsibility' (2007) 40 *Vanderbilt J Transn'l L* 197.

addressing responsibilities of transnational corporations,[99] and the UN named a Special Representative for human rights and transnational corporations and other business entities in 2005, tasked with 'identifying and clarifying standards of corporate responsibility and accountability with regard to human rights'. In 2011, the Special Representative prepared a Report on 'Guiding Principles on Business and Human Rights: Implementing the UN Protect, Respect and Remedy Framework'.

Whether or not the object and purpose of investment treaties—the increased flow of foreign investment—would be promoted or hindered by an extension of the subject matters of the treaties, and a corresponding new design of their nature, will have to be a necessary part of the future discussion on the usefulness of BITs in their traditional scope.

---

[99] See D Weissbrodt and M Kruger, 'Norms on the Responsibilities of Transnational Corporations and Other Business. Enterprises with Regard to Human Rights' (2003) 97 *AJIL* 901.

II

Interpretation and Application
of Investment Treaties

1. Interpreting investment treaties

As explained above (see Chapter I.2), investment law is shaped by a variety of treaties. In addition to bilateral treaties, mostly bilateral investment treaties (BITs), there are regional treaties such as the North American Free Trade Agreement (NAFTA), the Dominican Republic–Central America–United States Free Trade Agreement (CAFTA), and the Energy Charter Treaty (ECT). The Convention on the Settlement of Investment Disputes between States and Nationals of Other States (ICSID Convention), a multilateral treaty, is also frequently interpreted and applied.

The interpretation of these treaties takes place mostly by ad hoc tribunals, the composition of which varies from case to case. This makes it considerably more difficult to develop a consistent case law than in a permanent judicial institution.

(a) Methods of treaty interpretation

Most tribunals start by invoking Article 31 of the Vienna Convention on the Law of Treaties[1] (VCLT) when interpreting treaties.[2] For instance, the Tribunal in *Siemens v Argentina* stated:

---

[1] VCLT, Art 31(1) provides: 'A treaty shall be interpreted in good faith in accordance with the ordinary meaning to be given to the terms of the treaty in their context and in the light of its object and purpose.'

[2] See *AAPL v Sri Lanka*, Award, 27 June 1990, paras 38–42; *Tokios Tokelès v Ukraine*, Decision on Jurisdiction, 29 April 2004, para 27; *MTD v Chile*, Award, 25 May 2004, para 112; *Enron v Argentina*, Decision on Jurisdiction (Ancillary Claim), 2 August 2004, para 32; *Salini v Jordan*, Decision on Jurisdiction, 29 November 2004, para 75; *Plama v Bulgaria*, Decision on Jurisdiction, 8 February 2005, paras 117, 147–65; *Sempra Energy Intl v Argentina*, Decision on Jurisdiction, 11 May 2005, para 141; *Camuzzi v Argentina*, Decision on Jurisdiction, 11 May 2005, para 133; *Methanex v United States*, Award, 3 August 2005, Part II, Ch B, paras 15–23, Part IV, Ch B, para 29; *Eureko v Poland*, Partial Award, 19 August 2005, para 247; *Aguas del Tunari, SA v Bolivia*, Decision on Jurisdiction, 21 October 2005, paras 88–93, 226, 230, 239; *Saluka v Czech Republic*, Partial Award, 17 March 2006, paras 296–9; *Malaysian Historical Salvors v Malaysia*, Award, 17 May 2007, paras 65–8; *Kardassopoulos v Georgia*, Decision on Jurisdiction, 6 July 2007, paras 176–88, 206–8; *Vivendi v Argentina*, Resubmitted Case: Award, 20 August 2007, paras 7.4.2–7.4.4; *Fraport v Philippines*, Award, 16 August 2007, paras 339–42; *RSM Production v Grenada*, Award, 13 March 2009, paras 380–90; *Hrvatska Elektroprivreda v Slovenia*, Decision on Treaty Interpretation Issue, 12 June 2009, paras 151–2,

80. Both parties have based their arguments on the interpretation of the Treaty in accordance with Article 31(1) of the Vienna Convention. This Article provides that a treaty be 'interpreted in good faith in accordance with the ordinary meaning to be given to the terms of the treaty in their context and in the light of its object and purpose.' The Tribunal will adhere to these rules of interpretation in considering the disputed provisions of the Treaty. . . .[3]

At times, tribunals will also refer to the supplementary means of interpretation contained in Article 32 of the VCLT.[4] The Tribunal in *Noble Ventures v Romania*,[5] after referring to the general rule of interpretation in Article 31 of the VCLT, said:

recourse may be had to supplementary means of interpretation, including the preparatory work and the circumstances of its conclusion, only in order to confirm the meaning resulting from the application of the aforementioned methods of interpretation.[6]

A treaty's object and purpose is among the primary guides for interpretation listed in Article 31 of the VCLT. In investment treaties, the object and purpose is often sought in their preambles. These preambles highlight the positive role of foreign investment in general and the nexus between an investment-friendly climate and the flow of foreign investment in particular.[7] A typical contemporary version of a preamble reads:

The Government of X and the Government of Y; desiring to create favourable conditions for greater investment by nationals and companies of one State in the territory of the other State; recognising that the encouragement and reciprocal protection under international agreement of such investments will be conducive to the stimulation of individual business initiative and will increase prosperity in both States; have agreed as follows:[8]

Tribunals have frequently interpreted investment treaties in light of their object and purpose, often by looking at their preambles.[9] This has led to an

---

157–65, 171–94; *Romak v Uzbekistan*, Award, 26 November 2009, paras 173–97; *Millicom v Senegal*, Decision on Jurisdiction, 16 July 2010, paras 58, 70–4; *Fraport v Philippines*, Decision on Annulment, 23 December 2010, paras 73–5, 93–113; *HICEE v Slovakia*, Partial Award, 23 May 2011, paras 47–93, 110–47 (see also the Dissenting Opinion of Judge Brower).

[3] *Siemens v Argentina*, Decision on Jurisdiction, 3 August 2004, para 80.

[4] VCLT, Art 32 dealing with supplementary means of interpretation provides:

Recourse may be had to supplementary means of interpretation, including the preparatory work of the treaty and the circumstances of its conclusion, in order to confirm the meaning resulting from the application of article 31, or to determine the meaning when the interpretation according to article 31:
(a) leaves the meaning ambiguous or obscure; or
(b) leads to a result which is manifestly absurd or unreasonable.

[5] *Noble Ventures v Romania*, Award, 12 October 2005.

[6] At para 50.

[7] R Dolzer and M Stevens, *Bilateral Investment Treaties* (1995) 20–5.

[8] See preamble to the UK Model BIT.

[9] *Lauder v Czech Republic*, Award, 3 September 2001, para 292; *MTD v Chile*, Award, 25 May 2004, paras 104, 105; *Siemens v Argentina*, Decision on Jurisdiction, 3 August 2004, para 81; *CMS v Argentina*, Award, 12 May 2005, para 274; *Noble Ventures v Romania*, Award, 12 October 2005, para 52; *Aguas del Tunari, SA v Bolivia*, Decision on Jurisdiction, 21 October 2005, paras 153, 240–1, 247; *Continental Casualty Company v Argentina*, Decision on Jurisdiction, 22 February 2006, para 80; *Saluka v Czech Republic*, Partial Award, 17 March 2006, para 299; *Kardassopoulos v Georgia*, Decision on Jurisdiction, 6 July 2007, paras 178–81; *BG Group v Argentina*, Final Award, 24 December 2007,

interpretation that is favourable to the investor;[10] but this development has also attracted criticism. In particular, one tribunal warned against over-extending the method of looking at object and purpose.[11]

Closely related to object and purpose is the issue of restrictive or effective interpretation of treaties. This has arisen, in particular, in the context of interpreting treaty provisions governing the jurisdiction of tribunals. Some tribunals seem to have favoured a restrictive interpretation of treaty provisions that led to a limitation of state sovereignty.[12] Others have rejected a restrictive interpretation, at times favouring an interpretation that gives full effect to the rights of investors.[13] Most tribunals have distanced themselves from either approach and have advocated a balanced approach to interpretation.[14]

A closer look at some of these decisions would indicate that the professed preference of tribunals for one or the other method of interpretation should not necessarily be taken at face value. A tribunal's avowed predilection for a particular approach to interpretation is not always reflected in its actual decision.[15] Ultimately, what matters is what the tribunal does, not what it says it is doing.

The terms of a treaty are to be interpreted in their context. Under Article 31(2)(b) of the VCLT, context includes 'any instrument which was made by one or more parties in connexion with the conclusion of the treaty and accepted by the other parties as an instrument related to the treaty'. In *Fraport v Philippines*[16] the Tribunal interpreted the BIT between Germany and the Philippines with the help of the Philippines' Instrument of Ratification which was exchanged with Germany.[17]

---

paras 132–4; *Société Générale v Dominican Republic*, Decision on Jurisdiction, 19 September 2008, paras 21 29, 31–3, 103; *Hrvatska Elektroprivreda v Slovenia*, Decision on Treaty Interpretation Issue, 12 June 2009, paras 177–9; *Austrian Airlines v Slovakia*, Final Award, 9 October 2009, paras 101–4; *AFT v Slovakia*, Award, 5 March 2011, paras 236–7.

[10] Note that the Tribunal in *Amco v Indonesia*, in interpreting the ICSID Convention, pointed out that investment protection was also in the longer-term interest of host states: 'to protect investments is to protect the general interest of development and of developing countries' (Decision on Jurisdiction, 25 September 1983, para 23). See also Award, 20 November 1984, para 249.

[11] *Plama v Bulgaria*, Decision on Jurisdiction, 8 February 2005, para 193.

[12] *SGS v Pakistan*, Decision on Jurisdiction, 6 August 2003, para 171; *Noble Ventures v Romania*, Award, 12 October 2005, para 55.

[13] *Methanex v United States*, Preliminary Award on Jurisdiction, 7 August 2002, paras 103–5; *Aguas del Tunari, SA v Bolivia*, Decision on Jurisdiction, 21 October 2005, para 91; *SGS v Philippines*, Decision on Jurisdiction, 29 January 2004, para 116; *Eureko v Poland*, Partial Award, 19 August 2005, para 248; *Suez, Sociedad General de Aguas de Barcelona SA, and InterAguas Servicios Integrales del Agua SA v Argentina*, Decision on Jurisdiction, 16 May 2006, paras 59, 64.

[14] See pp 263–4.

[15] See eg *Noble Ventures v Romania*, Award, 12 October 2005, where the Tribunal, after subscribing to a 'restrictive interpretation' (at para 55), gives full effect to an umbrella clause (at paras 56–62). By contrast, in *El Paso Energy v Argentina*, Decision on Jurisdiction, 27 April 2006, the Tribunal expresses a preference for a 'balanced interpretation' (at para 70) but then proceeds to interpret an umbrella clause very restrictively (at paras 70–86).

[16] *Fraport v Philippines*, Award, 16 August 2007.

[17] At paras 337–43. Inexplicably, the Decision on Annulment in this case criticizes the Tribunal's use of the Instrument of Ratification. See *Fraport v Philippines*, Decision on Annulment, 23 December 2010, paras 98, 99, 107.

(b) *Travaux préparatoires*

Article 32 of the VCLT treats the *travaux préparatoires* (preparatory work) to a treaty only as a supplementary means of interpretation. In practice, resort to *travaux préparatoires* seems to be determined primarily by their availability. In the *Malaysian Historical Salvors* case the ad hoc Committee stated:

courts and tribunals interpreting treaties regularly review the *travaux préparatoires* whenever they are brought to their attention; it is mythological to pretend that they do so only when they first conclude that the term requiring interpretation is ambiguous or obscure.[18]

The drafting history of the ICSID Convention is documented in detail, readily available and easily accessible through an analytical index.[19] As a consequence, ICSID tribunals frequently have resort to its *travaux préparatoires*. By contrast, the negotiating history of BITs is typically not, or only poorly, documented. Therefore, tribunals do not usually have the possibility of relying on the *travaux préparatoires* even if they are minded to do so.[20]

The position with NAFTA occupies the middle ground. For a number of years the documents illustrating the negotiating history were not publicly available. This led to complaints about inequality of arms between a respondent state which had access to the materials and a claimant investor who did not. In July 2004 the NAFTA Free Trade Commission announced the release of the negotiating history of Chapter Eleven of the NAFTA dealing with investment.[21]

The Tribunal in *Methanex v United States*[22] stressed the limited relevance of the negotiating history of the NAFTA in light of Article 32 of the VCLT:

pursuant to Article 32, recourse may be had to supplementary means of interpretation only in the limited circumstances there specified. Other than that, the approach of the Vienna Convention is that the text of the treaty is deemed to be the authentic expression of the intentions of the parties; and its elucidation, rather than wide-ranging searches for the supposed intentions of the parties, is the proper object of interpretation.[23]

(c) Interpretative statements

Unilateral assertions of the disputing state party, on the meaning of a treaty provision, made in the process of ongoing proceedings are of limited value. Such

---

[18] *Malaysian Historical Salvors v Malaysia*, Decision on Annulment, 16 April 2009, para 57.

[19] History of the ICSID Convention: Documents Concerning the Origin and the Formulation of the Convention on the Settlement of Investment Disputes between States and Nationals of Other States, Washington, DC 1968, reprinted 2001.

[20] See *Aguas del Tunari, SA v Bolivia*, Decision on Jurisdiction, 21 October 2005, para 274, where the Tribunal deplored the lack of insight to be gained from the sparse material provided by the parties. In *Perenco v Ecuador*, Decision on Jurisdiction, 30 June 2011, paras 92–5 the Tribunal asked the parties to try to obtain the *travaux préparatoires* to the France-Ecuador BIT on a particular point.

[21] The documents are published at <http://www.naftaclaims.com/commission.htm>. It is unclear whether the available documentation covers all existing documents.

[22] *Methanex Corp v United States*, Award, 3 August 2005.

[23] At Part II, Ch B, para 22. Footnote omitted.

statements are likely to be perceived as self-serving and determined by a desire to influence the tribunal's decision in favour of the state offering the interpretation.

In one case[24] a tribunal sought information from the investor's home state on certain aspects of a BIT's interpretation; however, it did not find the information thus obtained to be of help.[25]

In another case[26] the government of the claimant's nationality (Switzerland) took the unusual step of writing to ICSID to complain about an interpretation given by an ICSID tribunal. The Swiss Government in a letter to ICSID's Deputy Secretary-General also stated that the Swiss authorities were unsure why the Tribunal had not found it necessary to inquire about their view of the meaning of the provision in the Pakistan-Switzerland BIT.[27]

Some treaties provide for a consultation mechanism concerning their interpretation or application. The BIT between the Czech Republic and the Netherlands contains such a provision, and the two states parties have issued a joint, non-binding statement which has been taken into account by tribunals.[28] The NAFTA has a mechanism whereby the Free Trade Commission (FTC)—a body composed of representatives of the three states parties—can adopt binding interpretations of the treaty.[29] The FTC made use of this method in July 2001 in interpreting the concepts of 'fair and equitable treatment' and 'full protection and security' under Article 1105 of the NAFTA.[30] NAFTA tribunals have accepted this interpretation as binding.[31]

BITs do not normally have institutional mechanisms to obtain authentic interpretations of their meaning, but the US Model BIT of 2012 provides a mechanism similar to the one in the NAFTA:

Article 30(3)

A joint decision of the Parties, each acting through its representative designated for purposes of this Article, declaring their interpretation of a provision of this Treaty shall be binding on

---

[24] *Aguas del Tunari v Bolivia*, Decision on Jurisdiction, 21 October 2005.

[25] At paras 47, 249–63.

[26] *SGS v Pakistan*, Decision on Jurisdiction, 6 August 2003, 8 ICSID Reports 406.

[27] See S A Alexandrov, 'Breaches of Contract and Breaches of Treaty' (2004) 5 *J World Investment & Trade* 555, 570–1; E Gaillard, 'Investment Treaty Arbitration and Jurisdiction Over Contract Claims—The SGS Cases Considered' in T Weiler (ed), *International Investment Law and Arbitration* (2005) 325, 341–2.

[28] *CME v Czech Republic*, Final Award, 14 March 2003, paras 87–93, 437, 504; *Eastern Sugar v Czech Republic*, Partial Award, 27 March 2007, paras 193–7.

[29] NAFTA, Art 2001(1): 'The Parties hereby establish the Free Trade Commission, comprising cabinet-level representatives of the Parties or their designees.' NAFTA, Art 1131(2): 'An interpretation by the Commission of a provision of this Agreement shall be binding on a Tribunal established under this Section.'

[30] FTC Note of Interpretation of 31 July 2001.

[31] See *Mondev v United States*, Award, 11 October 2002, paras 100 et seq; *United Parcel Service v Canada*, Award, 22 November 2002, para 97; *ADF v United States*, Award, 9 January 2003, paras 175–8; *Loewen v United States*, Award, 26 June 2003, paras 124–8; *Waste Management v Mexico*, Award, 30 April 2004, paras 90–1; *Methanex v United States*, Award, 3 August 2005, Part II, Ch H, para 23; *Grand River Enterprises v United States*, Award, 12 January 2011, paras 175–6. See also *Mexico v Metalclad*, Judgment, Supreme Court of British Columbia, 2 May 2001, 5 ICSID Reports 236, paras 61–5.

a tribunal, and any decision or award issued by a tribunal must be consistent with that joint decision.

This method may be efficient, but has a serious drawback. States may strive to issue official interpretations to influence proceedings to which they are parties. However, a mechanism whereby a party to a dispute is able to influence the outcome of judicial proceedings—by issuing an official interpretation to the detriment of the other party—is incompatible with principles of fair procedure and is hence undesirable.

(d) The authority of 'precedents'

Reliance on past decisions is a typical feature of any orderly decision process. Drawing on the experience of past decision-makers plays an important role in securing the necessary uniformity and stability of the law. A coherent case law strengthens the predictability of decisions and enhances their authority.

In investment arbitration, each tribunal is constituted ad hoc for the particular case; therefore, it is more difficult to develop a consistent case law than in an international court such as the International Court of Justice or European Court of Human Rights. Yet, tribunals do rely on previous decisions by other tribunals whenever they are able. Discussion of previous cases and of the interpretations adopted in them is a regular feature in almost every decision.[32] At the same time, it is also well established that tribunals in investment arbitration are not bound by previous decisions of other tribunals.

Despite their reliance on case law, tribunals have repeatedly pointed out that they are not bound by previous cases.[33] In *AES v Argentina*[34] the Tribunal entered into an extensive discussion of the value of previous decisions as 'precedents'. It said:

---

[32] See eg *Amco v Indonesia*, Decision on Annulment, 16 May 1986, para 44; *LETCO v Liberia*, Award, 31 March 1986, 2 ICSID Reports 346, 352; *Feldman v Mexico*, Award, 16 December 2002, para 107; *Enron v Argentina*, Decision on Jurisdiction, 14 January 2004, para 40; *Enron v Argentina*, Decision on Jurisdiction (Ancillary Claim), 2 August 2004, para 25; *AES v Argentina*, Decision on Jurisdiction, 26 April 2005, paras 17–33; *Gas Natural v Argentina*, Decision on Jurisdiction, 17 June 2005, paras 36–51; *Bayindir v Pakistan*, Decision on Jurisdiction, 14 November 2005, para 76; *Vivendi v Argentina*, Decision on Jurisdiction, 14 November 2005, para 94; *EnCana v Ecuador*, Award, 3 February 2006, para 189; *El Paso v Argentina*, Decision on Jurisdiction, 27 April 2006, para 39; *Suez v Argentina*, Decision on Jurisdiction, 16 May 2006, paras 26, 31, 60–5; *Jan de Nul v Egypt*, Decision on Jurisdiction, 16 June 2006, paras 63, 64; *Azurix v Argentina*, Award, 14 July 2006, para 391; *Pan American v Argentina*, Decision on Preliminary Objections, 27 July 2006, para 42; *ADC v Hungary*, Award, 2 October 2006, para 293; *World Duty Free v Kenya*, Award, 4 October 2006, para 16; *Saipem v Bangladesh*, Decision on Jurisdiction, 21 March 2007, para 67; *Chevron & Texaco v Ecuador*, Interim Award, 1 December 2008, paras 119–24; *Azurix v Argentina*, Decision on Annulment, 1 September 2009, paras 375–7; *Chemtura v Canada*, Award, 2 August 2010, paras 108, 109; *RosInvest v Russia*, Final Award, 12 September 2010, paras 281–6; *Grand River Enterprises v United States*, Award, 12 January 2011, paras 61, 70; *Brandes v Venezuela*, Award, 2 August 2011, para 31.

[33] *Amco v Indonesia*, Decision on Jurisdiction, 25 September 1983, 1 ICSID Reports 395; *Amco v Indonesia*, Decision on Annulment, 16 May 1986, para 44; *LETCO v Liberia*, Award, 31 March 1986, para 352; *Feldman v Mexico*, Award, 16 December 2002, para 107; *Enron v Argentina*, Decision on Jurisdiction (Ancillary Claim), 2 August 2004, para 25; *Gas Natural v Argentina*, Decision on Jurisdiction, 17 June 2005, paras 36–52; *Romak v Uzbekistan*, Award, 26 November 2009, paras 170–1.

[34] *AES Corp v Argentina*, Decision on Jurisdiction, 26 April 2005, paras 17–33.

each decision or award delivered by an ICSID Tribunal is only binding on the parties to the dispute settled by this decision or award. There is so far no rule of precedent in general international law; nor is there any within the specific ICSID system...[35]

But the Tribunal also pointed to the value of previous decisions:

Each tribunal remains sovereign and may retain, as it is confirmed by ICSID practice, a different solution for resolving the same problem; but decisions on jurisdiction dealing with the same or very similar issues may at least indicate some lines of reasoning of real interest; this Tribunal may consider them in order to compare its own position with those already adopted by its predecessors and, if it shares the views already expressed by one or more of these tribunals on a specific point of law, it is free to adopt the same solution.[36]

Having made these general points, the Tribunal proceeded to examine and rely on previous decisions by other tribunals.[37]

The Tribunal in *Saipem v Bangladesh*[38] saw it as its duty to contribute to a harmonious development of the law. It stated:

The Tribunal considers that it is not bound by previous decisions. At the same time, it is of the opinion that it must pay due consideration to earlier decisions of international tribunals. It believes that, subject to compelling contrary grounds, it has a duty to adopt solutions established in a series of consistent cases. It also believes that, subject to the specifics of a given treaty and of the circumstances of the actual case, it has a duty to seek to contribute to the harmonious development of investment law and thereby to meet the legitimate expectations of the community of States and investors towards certainty of the rule of law.[39]

In some cases tribunals have not followed earlier decisions. At times they have simply adopted a different solution without distancing themselves from the earlier decision. At other times, they have referred to an earlier decision and pointed out that they were unconvinced by the reasoning of the previous tribunal and that, therefore, their decision has departed from the one previously adopted.[40]

[35] At para 23. Footnote omitted.
[36] At para 30.
[37] At paras 51–9, 70, 73, 86, 89, 95–7. See also *Bayindir v Pakistan*, Decision on Jurisdiction, 14 November 2005, para 76: 'The Tribunal agrees that it is not bound by earlier decisions, but will certainly carefully consider such decisions whenever appropriate' (referring to *AES Corp v Argentina*); *Abaclat v Argentina*, Decision on Jurisdiction, 4 August 2011, paras 292–3.
[38] *Saipem v Bangladesh*, Decision on Jurisdiction, 21 March 2007.
[39] At para 67. Footnotes omitted. Other tribunals have adopted the same or a similar formula: *Noble Energy v Ecuador*, Decision on Jurisdiction, 5 March 2008, para 50; *Duke Energy v Ecuador*, Award, 18 August 2008, paras 116–17; *Austrian Airlines v Slovakia*, Final Award, 9 October 2009, paras 83–4; *Burlington v Ecuador*, Decision on Jurisdiction, 2 June 2010, paras 99–100; *Fakes v Turkey*, Award, 14 July 2010, para 96; *Suez v Argentina*, Decision on Liability, 30 July 2010, para 182; *Chemtura v Canada*, Award, 2 August 2010, paras 108–9.
[40] See eg *SGS v Philippines*, Decision on Jurisdiction, 29 January 2004, para 97; *Eureko v Poland*, Partial Award, 19 August 2005, paras 256–8; *El Paso Energy v Argentina*, Decision on Jurisdiction, 27 April 2006, paras 76–7; *Suez, Sociedad General de Aguas de Barcelona SA, and InterAguas Servicios Integrales del Agua SA v Argentina*, Decision on Jurisdiction, 16 May 2006, para 64; *Plama v Bulgaria*, Decision on Jurisdiction, 8 February 2005, paras 216–21; *Wintershall v Argentina*, Award, 8 December 2008, paras 178, 194; *Tza Yap Shum v Peru*, Decision on Jurisdiction, 19 June 2009, para 173; *SGS v Paraguay*, Decision on Jurisdiction, 12 February 2010, paras 41–2.

(e) Towards a greater uniformity of interpretation

The divergence of interpretations on certain issues has caused some concern and led to suggestions for improving the consistency of decisions. One perceived solution is the creation of an appeals mechanism that would open the possibility for reviewing decisions thereby increasing the chances of a consistent case law.[41] A number of US treaties foresee this possibility in the form of an appellate body or similar mechanism.[42] The US Model BIT of 2012 contains the following provision in Article 28(10):

In the event that an appellate mechanism for reviewing awards rendered by investor-State dispute settlement tribunals is developed in the future under other institutional arrangements, the Parties shall consider whether awards rendered under Article 34 should be subject to that appellate mechanism.

It is doubtful whether separate appellate bodies established under different treaties would contribute to a coherent case law. A harmonizing effect will be achieved only if the institutional mechanism applies to all, or at least many, treaties. The idea of a multilateral appeals mechanism is reflected in the Dominican Republic–CAFTA–United States Free Trade Agreement (FTA)[43] as well as in US FTAs with Singapore[44] and Chile.[45]

ICSID at one point floated a draft that foresaw the creation of an appeals facility at ICSID[46] but the idea was dropped as premature.

An appeals facility is not necessarily the best mechanism for achieving coherence and consistency in the interpretation of investment treaties. Appeal presupposes a decision being attacked for an alleged flaw in order for it to be repaired. Rather than try to fix the damage after the fact through an appeal, it is more economical and effective to address it preventively before it occurs.

A method for securing coherence and consistency that has been remarkably successful is to allow preliminary rulings while the original proceedings are still pending.[47] Under such a system, a tribunal would suspend proceedings and request a ruling on a question of law from a body established for that purpose. This

---

[41] See K P Sauvant and M Chiswick-Patterson (eds), *Appeals Mechanism in International Investment Disputes* (2008).

[42] Uruguay-US BIT, 25 October 2004, Annex E, 44 ILM 268, 296 (2005). Generally see B Legum, 'The Introduction of an Appellate Mechanism: The US Trade Act of 2002' in E Gaillard and Y Banifatemi (eds), *Annulment of ICSID Awards* (2004) 289.

[43] Dominican Republic–Central America–United States Free Trade Agreement, 5 August 2004, Art 10.20(10).

[44] Singapore-US FTA, 1 January 2004, Art 15.19(10).

[45] Chile-US FTA, 1 January 2004, Art 10.19(10).

[46] ICSID Discussion Paper, 'Possible Improvements of the Framework for ICSID Arbitration', 22 October 2004.

[47] G Kaufmann-Kohler, 'Annulment of ICSID Awards in Contract and Treaty Arbitrations: Are there Differences?' in E Gaillard and Y Banifatemi (eds), *Annulment of ICSID Awards* (2004) 289. See also G Kaufmann-Kohler, 'In Search of Transparency and Consistency: ICSID Reform Proposal' (2005) 2(5) *TDM* 8; C Schreuer, 'Preliminary Rulings in Investment Arbitration' in K P Sauvant and M Chiswick-Patterson (eds), *Appeals Mechanism in International Investment Disputes* (2008) 207.

procedure has been very successful in the framework of the European Union to secure the uniform application of EU law by domestic courts.[48]

2. Application of investment treaties in time

(a) Inter-temporal application of treaties in general

In principle, treaties apply only in relation to acts or events that occurred after their entry into force. This rule is expressed in Article 28 of the VCLT:

Article 28 Non-Retroactivity of Treaties

Unless a different intention appears from the treaty or is otherwise established, its provisions do not bind a party in relation to any act or fact which took place or any situation which ceased to exist before the date of the entry into force of the treaty with respect to that party.[49]

This means that the substantive law in force at the time an act was performed is to be applied as the standard for the act's legality. This principle is also reflected in the International Law Commission's Articles on State Responsibility:

Article 13 International Obligation in Force for a State

An act of a State does not constitute a breach of an international obligation unless the State is bound by the obligation in question at the time the act occurs.[50]

International practice has also adhered to this principle.[51] The Tribunal in *Impregilo v Pakistan*[52] said:

Impregilo complains of a number of acts for which Pakistan is said to be responsible. The legality of such acts must be determined, in each case, according to the law applicable at the time of their performance.[53]

(b) Different inter-temporal rules for jurisdiction and substance

Issues of jurisdiction and of substantive law are often subject to different inter-temporal rules. A provision on dispute settlement in a treaty that refers to any dispute arising from an investment extends to disputes relating to events that took place prior to the treaty's entry into force. This does not mean that the treaty's

---

[48] It is contained in Art 267 (ex Art 234 TEC) of the Treaty on the Functioning of the European Union.

[49] Article 2(3) of the United States Model BIT of 2012 echoes this provision.

[50] International Law Commission (ILC), Articles on State Responsibility, 2001. See J Crawford, *The International Law Commission's Articles on State Responsibility* (2002) 131.

[51] *Island of Palmas* case, II RIAA 829 at 845 (1949); *Tradex v Albania*, Decision on Jurisdiction, 24 December 1996, 5 ICSID Reports 47, 66.

[52] *Impregilo v Pakistan*, Decision on Jurisdiction, 22 April 2005.

[53] At para 311.

substantive rules are applicable to these events. Tribunals have applied different inter-temporal rules to jurisdictional clauses and to substantive provisions in treaties.[54] In *SGS v Philippines*[55] the Tribunal distinguished the application *ratione temporis* of the BIT's jurisdictional provisions from the application of the BIT's substantive standards. It said:

According to Article II of the BIT, it applies to investments 'made whether prior to or after the entry into force of the Agreement'. Article II does not, however, give the substantive provisions of the BIT any retrospective effect. The normal principle stated in Article 28 of the Vienna Convention on the Law of Treaties applies...It may be noted that in international practice a rather different approach is taken to the application of treaties to procedural or jurisdictional clauses than to substantive obligations.[56]

This means that a tribunal may have to apply different legal rules applicable at different times depending on when the acts in question occurred. These rules may be contained in customary international law[57] or in a treaty that has since been terminated.[58]

But the applicability of substantive law may have jurisdictional implications. If, under the terms of a treaty, consent to arbitration is limited to claims alleging a violation of that treaty, the date of the treaty's entry into force is also the date from which acts and events are covered by the consent.[59] Put differently, under such a consent clause the entry into force of the substantive law also determines the tribunal's jurisdiction *ratione temporis* since the tribunal may only hear claims for violation of that law. A tribunal that is competent only for alleged violations of the treaty itself will not have jurisdiction over acts that occurred before the treaty's entry into force even if those acts were illegal under customary international law.[60] For instance, under the NAFTA, the scope of consent to arbitration is limited to claims arising from alleged breaches of the NAFTA.[61]

In some cases tribunals have found that the acts in question were of a continuing character, that is, that they may have started before the treaty's entry into force but persisted thereafter.[62] The failure to pay sums due under a contract is an example of

---

[54] *Salini v Jordan*, Decision on Jurisdiction, 29 November 2004, paras 176, 177; *Impregilo v Pakistan*, Decision on Jurisdiction, 22 April 2005, para 309; *Micula v Romania*, Decision on Jurisdiction and Admissibility, 24 September 2008, paras 150–7.

[55] *SGS v Philippines*, Decision on Jurisdiction, 29 January 2004.

[56] At paras 166, 167.

[57] *Chevron v Ecuador*, Interim Award, 1 December 2008, paras 199, 201, 208–9.

[58] *Jan de Nul v Egypt*, Award, 6 November 2008, paras 132–41.

[59] *TECMED v Mexico*, Award, 29 May 2003, paras 63–8; *SGS v Philippines*, Decision on Jurisdiction, 29 January 2004, paras 166–8.

[60] In *Generation Ukraine v Ukraine*, Award, 16 September 2003, paras 11.2, 11.3, 17.1 the Tribunal found that under the terms of the applicable BIT it was competent only for disputes arising from alleged breaches of the BIT itself. Therefore, there was no jurisdiction with regard to an expropriation that had occurred before the BIT's entry into force.

[61] NAFTA, Art 1116.

[62] *Mondev v United States*, Award, 11 October 2002, paras 58, 69, 70, 73; *TECMED v Mexico*, Award, 29 May 2003, paras 63–8; *SGS v Philippines*, Decision on Jurisdiction, 29 January 2004, para 167; *Impregilo v Pakistan*, Decision on Jurisdiction, 22 April 2005, paras 312–13; *Railroad Development Corp v Guatemala*, Second Decision on Jurisdiction, 18 May 2010, paras 114–38.

a continuing breach.[63] In *Mondev v United States*[64] the dispute had already arisen before the entry into force of the NAFTA. It was beyond doubt that the NAFTA is not retrospective in effect. The Tribunal found that acts committed prior to the Treaty's entry into force might continue in effect after that date. It stated:

an act, initially committed before NAFTA entered into force, might in certain circumstances continue to be of relevance after NAFTA's entry into force, thereby becoming subject to NAFTA obligations.... Thus events or conduct prior to the entry into force of an obligation for the respondent State may be relevant in determining whether the State has subsequently committed a breach of the obligation. But it must still be possible to point to conduct of the State after that date which is itself a breach....[65]

Inter-temporal issues also arise when the alleged breach occurs not through one but through a series of acts or omissions that may be spread over time.[66] Such a composite act will be deemed to have taken place at the point of completion, that is, when the last action or omission occurred.[67] A possible example would be a continuing denial of justice.[68]

(c) The date relevant to determine jurisdiction

It is an accepted principle of international adjudication that, in the absence of treaty provisions to the contrary, the relevant date for purposes of jurisdiction is the date of the institution of proceedings.[69] The Tribunal in *Vivendi II*[70] said:

it is generally recognized that the determination of whether a party has standing in an international judicial forum, for purposes of jurisdiction to institute proceedings, is made by reference to the date on which such proceedings are deemed to have been instituted. ICSID Tribunals have consistently applied this Rule.[71]

Tribunals have applied this principle in a number of contexts. For instance, they have determined that for purposes of jurisdiction the decisive date for participation in the ICSID Convention, of the host state and of the investor's state of nationality,

---

[63] *SGS v Philippines*, Decision on Jurisdiction, 29 January 2004, para 167.

[64] *Mondev v United States*, Award, 11 October 2002.

[65] At paras 58, 70. See further *Chevron v Ecuador*, Interim Award, 1 December 2008, paras 271–84.

[66] For detailed discussion see S A Alexandrov, 'The "Baby Boom" of Treaty-Based Arbitrations and the Jurisdiction of ICSID Tribunals: Shareholders as "Investors" and Jurisdiction *Ratione Temporis*' (2005) 4 *Law and Practice of Int'l Courts and Tribunals* 19, 52–6.

[67] See ILC, Articles on State Responsibility, 2001, Art 15. See J Crawford, *The International Law Commission's Articles on State Responsibility* (2002) 141. See also Commentaries (7) and (8) at p 143.

[68] *OKO Pankki v Estonia*, Award, 19 November 2007, paras 194–6, 284; *Chevron v Ecuador*, Interim Award, 1 December 2008, paras 285–301.

[69] ICJ, *Case Concerning Questions of Interpretation and Application of the 1971 Montreal Convention Arising from the Aerial Incident at Lockerbie* (*Libyan Arab Jamahmiriya v United States of America*), Preliminary Objections, Judgment, 27 February 1998 ICJ Reports (1998) 115, para 37; *Case Concerning the Arrest Warrant of 11 April 2000* (*Democratic Republic of the Congo v Belgium*), Judgment, 14 February 2002 ICJ Reports (2002) 1, paras 26 et seq.

[70] *Vivendi v Argentina* (*Vivendi II*), Decision on Jurisdiction, 14 November 2005.

[71] At para 60.

is the date of the institution of arbitration proceedings.[72] The same principle applies to the entry into force of BITs[73] and of other treaties relevant to jurisdiction.[74] Similarly, the sale of the investment or the assignment of the claim after the institution of proceedings did not affect the claimant's standing.[75]

This principle has been mitigated by the practice of accepting jurisdiction in situations in which the requirements had not been fully satisfied at the time of instituting proceedings but had been met subsequently.[76] Where these requirements concerned specified consultation periods to reach an amicable settlement or an attempt to seek redress before the domestic courts, tribunals have found that it makes no sense to decline jurisdiction in instances where the procedural requirements have been met in the meantime and the claimant would have been able to resubmit the claim immediately.[77]

(d) Relevant dates under the ICSID Convention

The ICSID Convention entered into force on 14 October 1966, 30 days after the deposit of the twentieth ratification. It enters into force for individual states 30 days after the respective instrument of ratification has been deposited.[78] In cases where a state denounces the Convention, the denunciation takes effect six months after the receipt of a notice to that effect by the World Bank.[79]

Article 25 of the ICSID Convention relates to several dates that are critical to jurisdiction. The host state must be a party to the Convention on the date the proceedings are instituted. The same applies to the state of the investor's nationality: it must also be a party to the Convention at the time proceedings are instituted.

---

[72] See *Holiday Inns v Morocco*, P Lalive, 'The First "World Bank" Arbitration (*Holiday Inns v Morocco*)—Some Legal Problems' (1980) 51 *BYBIL* 123, 142–6; *Amco v Indonesia*, Decision on Jurisdiction, 25 September 1983, 1 ICSID Reports 403; *LETCO v Liberia*, Decision on Jurisdiction, 24 October 1984, 2 ICSID Reports 351; *Rompetrol v Romania*, Decision on Jurisdiction, 18 April 2008, para 79.

[73] *Tradex v Albania*, Decision on Jurisdiction, 24 December 1996, 5 ICSID Reports 58; *Goetz v Burundi*, Award, 10 February 1999, para 72.

[74] *Bayindir v Pakistan*, Decision on Jurisdiction, 14 November 2005, para 178.

[75] *CSOB v Slovakia*, Decision on Jurisdiction, 24 May 1999, para 31; *El Paso Energy v Argentina*, Decision on Jurisdiction, 27 April 2006, paras 117–36; *National Grid v Argentina*, Decision on Jurisdiction, 20 June 2006, paras 117–19; *Enron v Argentina*, Award, 22 May 2007, paras 196–8, 396. See also *EnCana v Ecuador*, Award, 3 February 2006, paras 123–32.

[76] For practice in the PCIJ and ICJ, see: *Mavrommatis Palestine Concessions Case*, Judgment No 2, 30 August 1924, PCIJ, Series A, No 2, 34; *Application of the Convention on the Prevention and Punishment of the Crime of Genocide* (*Bosnia and Herzegovina v Yugoslavia*), Preliminary Objections, Judgment, 11 July 1996, ICJ Reports (1996-II) 614, para 26; *Application of the Convention on the Prevention and Punishment of the Crime of Genocide* (*Croatia v Serbia*), Preliminary Objections, Judgment, 18 November 2008, ICJ Reports (2008) 441–43, paras 85, 87, 89.

[77] *SGS v Pakistan*, Decision on Jurisdiction, 6 August 2003, para 184; *Bayindir v Pakistan*, Decision on Jurisdiction, 14 November 2005, paras 88–103; *Biwater Gauff v Tanzania*, Award, 24 July 2008, para 343; *TSA Spectrum v Argentina*, Award, 19 December 2008, para 112; *AFT v Slovakia*, Award, 5 March 2011, para 204.

[78] ICSID Convention, Art 68.

[79] ICSID Convention, Art 71. Under Art 72 the denunciation does not affect the rights and obligations arising out of consent to ICSID's jurisdiction given before the notice of denunciation is received.

The temporal requirements for the investor's nationality are somewhat complex. For natural persons, under Article 25(2)(a), there are two requirements relating to two different dates: the investor must have the nationality of a state party to the Convention both on the date of consent and on the date the request for arbitration is registered. In addition, the investor must not have the host state's nationality on either date. The latter provision refers, in particular, to dual or multiple nationals. As a practical matter, the date of consent and the date of the institution of proceedings will often coincide or, at least, be very close. This is so whenever consent is based on a general offer in a treaty or in the host state's domestic legislation, which the investor simply accepts through the institution of proceedings.

For juridical persons, under Article 25(2)(b) the nationality requirement relates to only one date, the date of consent. On that date the juridical person must have the nationality of a party to the Convention other than the host state. In practical terms, the date of consent will also usually be that of the date of institution of proceedings.

As explained below in more detail,[80] under Article 25(2)(b) of the Convention, the host state and the investor may agree to treat a locally incorporated company as a foreign investor because of its foreign control. That provision refers to the date of consent as the relevant date for the nationality of the host state but is silent on the date of foreign control. Tribunals have generally also favoured the date of consent for purposes of control but have, at the same time, looked at subsequent changes up to the time of the institution of proceedings.[81] Some BITs and the ECT sensibly provide that the foreign control must exist before the dispute arises.[82]

The date of the consent to ICSID's jurisdiction is important for several reasons. Consent must exist at the time the proceedings are instituted[83] and, as explained above, the investor's nationality requirements must be met on the date of consent.

Once consent is given it becomes irrevocable, that is, it can no longer be withdrawn unilaterally.[84] Other remedies become unavailable, in principle, from the date of consent and diplomatic protection is no longer permitted.[85] In addition, the Arbitration Rules in force at the time of consent will apply unless the parties agree otherwise.[86]

The time of consent is the date by which both parties have agreed to arbitration. If the consent clause is contained in an offer by one party, its acceptance by the other party will determine the time of consent. If the host state makes a general offer to consent to arbitration in its legislation or in a treaty, the time of consent is

---

[80] Chapter III.1(d).

[81] *Amco v Indonesia*, Decision on Jurisdiction, 25 September 1983, 1 ICSID Reports 394; *Klöckner v Cameroon*, Award, 21 October 1983, 2 ICSID Reports 15; *SOABI v Senegal*, Decision on Jurisdiction, 1 August 1984, 2 ICSID Reports 183; *LETCO v Liberia*, Decision on Jurisdiction, 24 October 1984, 2 ICSID Reports 349, 351; *Vacuum Salt v Ghana*, Award, 16 February 1994, paras 35–54; *Vivendi v Argentina (Vivendi II)*, Decision on Jurisdiction, 14 November 2005, paras 21, 42–4, 65, 95–7.

[82] See ECT, Art 26(7).

[83] *Tradex v Albania*, Decision on Jurisdiction, 24 December 1996, 5 ICSID Reports 47, 57–8.

[84] Article 25(1), last sentence.   [85] Articles 26 and 27.   [86] Article 44.

determined by the investor's acceptance of the offer. This offer may be accepted simply by initiating the arbitration.

It is possible that consent to arbitration is expressed before other conditions for the jurisdiction of a tribunal are met. For instance, the parties may give their consent to ICSID arbitration before the Convention's ratification by the host state or by the investor's home state. In that case, the date of consent will be the date on which all the conditions have been met. If the host state or the investor's home state ratifies the Convention after the signature of a consent agreement, the time of consent will be the entry into force of the Convention for the respective state.[87]

The ICSID Convention provides for the withdrawal of states parties subject to a time limit. Under Article 71 of the ICSID Convention, a contracting state may denounce the Convention by written notice. Such denunciation takes effect six months after receipt of the notice. Under Article 72 of the Convention, the denunciation does not affect rights or obligations arising out of consent to ICSID's jurisdiction given before the notice of denunciation. This provision has led to a lively debate as to whether the reference to consent in Article 72 means a perfected consent agreement or a mere offer of consent.[88] So far, three states—Bolivia, Ecuador, and Venezuela—have withdrawn from the Convention.[89]

(e) Inter-temporal rules in other treaties

Treaties containing consent to arbitration often contain specific provisions determining their temporal application. Many BITs provide that they shall be applicable to all investments whether made before or after their entry into force.[90] In other words, they also protect existing investments.[91] This should not lead to the conclusion that treaties not containing a clause of this type will only apply to 'new' investments.[92] But a provision that extends the treaty's protection to existing

---

[87] See *Holiday Inns v Morocco*, Decision on Jurisdiction, 12 May 1974; Lalive, P, 'The First "World Bank" Arbitration (*Holiday Inns* v *Morocco*)—Some Legal Problems' (1980) 51 *BYBIL* 123, 142, 143, 146; *Cable TV v St Kitts and Nevis*, Award, 13 January 1997, paras 2.18, 4.09, 5.24; *Autopista v Venezuela*, Decision on Jurisdiction, 27 September 2001, paras 90, 91; *Generation Ukraine v Ukraine*, Award, 16 September 2003, paras 12.4–12.8.

[88] See C Schreuer, 'Denunciation of the ICSID Convention and Consent to Arbitration' in M Waibel, A Kaushal, Kyo-Hwa Liz Chung, and C Balchin (eds), *The Backlash against Investment Arbitration: Perceptions and Reality* (2010) 353 and the authorities cited therein.

[89] On 2 May 2007, the depositary received written notice of Bolivia's denunciation of the Convention which took effect on 3 November 2007. On 6 July 2009, the depositary received written notice of Ecuador's denunciation of the Convention which took effect on 7 January 2010. On 24 January 2012, the depositary received written notice of Venezuela's denunciation of the Convention which took effect on 25 July 2012.

[90] Argentina-Spain BIT, Art II(2); Belgium and Luxemburg-Egypt BIT, Art 12; Ukraine-US BIT, Art XII(3). See also ECT, Art 1(6).

[91] See *Genin v Estonia*, Award, 25 June 2001, para 326; *SGS v Pakistan*, Decision on Jurisdiction, 6 August 2003, para 153; *Generation Ukraine v Ukraine*, Award, 16 September 2003, para 11.1; *Pan American Energy v Argentina*, Decision on Preliminary Objections, 27 July 2006, para 211; *OKO Pankki v Estonia*, Award, 19 November 2007, paras 184–6; *Chevron & Texaco v Ecuador*, Interim Award, 1 December 2008, paras 151–89.

[92] See *Yaung Chi Oo v Myanmar*, Award, 31 March 2003, paras 69–75.

investments does not mean that acts committed before the treaty's entry into force are covered by its substantive provisions.[93]

Many BITs limit consent to arbitration to disputes arising after their entry into force.[94] For instance, the Argentina-Spain BIT, after stating that it shall also apply to investments made before its entry into force, provides:

However, this agreement shall not apply to disputes or claims originating before its entry into force.

In a number of cases tribunals have grappled with the question of the time at which the dispute had arisen.[95] In *Maffezini v Spain*[96] the respondent challenged the Tribunal's jurisdiction alleging that the dispute originated before the entry into force of the Argentina-Spain BIT. The Tribunal found that the events on which the parties disagreed began years before the BIT's entry into force; but this did not mean that a legal dispute existed at the time.[97] The Tribunal said:

there tends to be a natural sequence of events that leads to a dispute. It begins with the expression of a disagreement and the statement of a difference of views. In time these events acquire a precise legal meaning through the formulation of legal claims, their discussion and eventual rejection or lack of response by the other party. The conflict of legal views and interests will only be present in the latter stage, even though the underlying facts predate them.[98]

On that basis, the Tribunal reached the conclusion that the dispute in its technical and legal sense had begun to take shape after the BIT's entry into force. It followed that the Tribunal was competent to consider the dispute.

The time of the dispute is not identical to the time of the events leading to the dispute.[99] Normally, the allegedly illegal acts will occur some time before the dispute. Therefore, the exclusion of disputes occurring before the treaty's entry into force should not be read as excluding jurisdiction over events occurring before that date.

In *Lucchetti v Peru*[100] the BIT between Chile and Peru provided that it would not apply to disputes that arose prior to its entry into force. A series of administrative measures by local authorities had denied or withdrawn construction

---

[93] See *TECMED v Mexico*, Award, 29 May 2003, paras 53–68; *SGS v Philippines*, Decision on Jurisdiction, 29 January 2004, para 166; *Kardassopoulos v Georgia*, Decision on Jurisdiction, 6 July 2007, paras 253–5; *Bayindir v Pakistan*, Award, 27 August 2009, paras 131, 132.

[94] The Tribunal in *Salini v Jordan*, Decision on Jurisdiction, 29 November 2004, para 170 found that the phrase 'any dispute which may arise' only covered disputes that had arisen after the BIT's entry into force. See also *Impregilo v Pakistan*, Decision on Jurisdiction, 22 April 2005, paras 297–304.

[95] *Helnan v Egypt*, Decision on Jurisdiction, 17 October 2006, paras 33–57; *Toto v Lebanon*, Decision on Jurisdiction, 11 September 2009, paras 88–90; *ATA v Jordan*, Award, 18 May 2010, paras 98–109, 115–20.

[96] *Maffezini v Spain*, Decision on Jurisdiction, 25 January 2000, paras 90–8.

[97] At paras 91–8.

[98] At para 96.

[99] *Duke Energy v Peru*, Decision on Jurisdiction, 1 February 2006, paras 146–50, Decision on Annulment, 1 March 2011, paras 111–13, 170–82; *Railroad Development Corp. v Guatemala*, Second Decision on Jurisdiction, 18 May 2010, paras 126–38.

[100] *Lucchetti v Peru*, Award, 7 February 2005.

and operating licences from the investors. The investors had successfully challenged the earlier administrative acts through court proceedings that took place entirely before the BIT's entry into force. A few days after the BIT's entry into force, the municipality issued further adverse decrees. The Tribunal found that the dispute had already arisen before the BIT's entry into force and declined jurisdiction.[101]

In *Jan de Nul v Egypt*[102] the BIT between BLEU[103] and Egypt also provided that it would not apply to disputes that had arisen prior to its entry into force. A dispute already existed when, in 2002, the BIT replaced an earlier BIT of 1977. At that time the dispute was pending before the Administrative Court of Ismaïlia which eventually rendered an adverse decision in 2003, approximately one year after the new BIT's entry into force. The Tribunal accepted the claimants' contention that the dispute before it was different from the one that had been brought before the Egyptian court:

while the dispute which gave rise to the proceedings before the Egyptian courts and authorities related to questions of contract interpretation and of Egyptian law, the dispute before this ICSID Tribunal deals with alleged violations of the two BITs...[104]

This conclusion was confirmed by the fact that the court decision was a major element of the complaint. According to the Tribunal:

The intervention of a new actor, the Ismaïlia Court, appears here as a decisive factor to determine whether the dispute is a new dispute. As the Claimants' case is directly based on the alleged wrongdoing of the Ismaïlia Court, the Tribunal considers that the original dispute has (re)crystallized into a new dispute when the Ismaïlia Court rendered its decision.[105]

It followed that the Tribunal had jurisdiction over the claim.

---

[101] At paras 48–59. See also J Gaffney, 'Jurisdiction *ratione temporis* of ICSID Tribunals: *Lucchetti* and *Jan De Nul* Considered' (2006) 5 *Transnational Dispute Management*.

[102] *Jan de Nul v Egypt*, Decision on Jurisdiction, 16 June 2006.

[103] Belgo-Luxembourg Economic Union.

[104] At para 117.

[105] At para 128.

III

Investors and Investments

1. Investors

(a) Private foreign investors

International investment law is designed to promote and protect the activities of private foreign investors. This does not necessarily exclude the protection of government-controlled entities as long as they act in a commercial rather than in a governmental capacity.[1] Whether non-profit organizations may be regarded as investors is less clear and will depend on the nature of their activities.[2]

Investors are either individuals (natural persons) or companies (juridical persons). In the majority of cases the investor is a company but at times individuals also act as investors.[3] The foreignness of the investment is determined by the investor's nationality.[4] The origin of the investment, in particular of the capital, is not decisive for the question of the existence of a foreign investment.[5]

The investor's nationality determines from which treaties it may benefit.[6] If the investor wishes to rely on a bilateral investment treaty (BIT), it must show that it has the nationality of one of the two states parties. If the investor wishes to rely on a

---

[1] *CSOB v Slovakia*, Decision on Jurisdiction, 24 May 1999, paras 16–27; *Rumeli Telekom v Kazakhstan*, Award, 29 July 2008, paras 324–9. See A Broches, 'The Convention on the Settlement of Investment Disputes between States and Nationals of Other States' (1972-II) 136 Recueil des Cours 331 at 354–5.

[2] The MIGA Convention in Art 13(a)(iii) requires that an eligible investor operates on a commercial basis. The Argentina-Germany BIT includes legal persons 'whether or not organized for pecuniary gain'. Generally, see N Gallus and L E Peterson, 'International Investment Treaty protection of NGOs' (2006) 22 *Arbitration International* 527.

[3] For this reason it is most appropriate to refer to investors in general not as 'she' or 'he' but as 'it'.

[4] See A Sinclair, 'The Substance of Nationality Requirements in Investment Treaty Arbitration' (2005) 20 *ICSID Review-FILJ* 357; R Wisner and R Gallus, 'Nationality Requirements in Investor-State Arbitration' (2004) 5 *J World Investment & Trade* 927.

[5] *Tradex v Albania*, Award, 29 April 1999, paras 108–11; *Olguín v Paraguay*, Award, 26 July 2001, para 66, footnote 9; *Wena Hotels v Egypt*, Award, 8 December 2000, para 126; *Wena Hotels v Egypt*, Decision on Annulment, 5 February 2002, paras 54, 55; *Tokios Tokelès v Ukraine*, Decision on Jurisdiction, 29 April 2004, paras 74–82; *Saipem v Bangladesh*, Decision on Jurisdiction, 21 March 2007, para 106; *Lemire v Ukraine*, Decision on Jurisdiction and Liability, 14 January 2010, paras 56–9; *Mobil v Venezuela*, Decision on Jurisdiction, 10 June 2010, para 198. But see *Yaung Chi Oo v Myanmar*, Award, 31 March 2003, paras 43–5.

[6] Exceptionally, the status of foreign investor may be extended to permanent residents. See NAFTA, Art 201; ECT, Art 1(7)(a)(i). Some treaties require domicile or economic activity in the state concerned in addition to nationality.

regional treaty, such as the North American Free Trade Agreement (NAFTA) or the Energy Charter Treaty (ECT), it must show that it has the nationality of one of the states parties to the treaty. If the investor wishes to rely on the Convention on the Settlement of Investment Disputes between States and Nationals of Other States (ICSID Convention) it must show that it has the nationality of one of the states parties to the ICSID Convention.

The investor's nationality is relevant for two purposes. The substantive standards guaranteed in a treaty will only apply to the respective nationals.[7] In addition, the jurisdiction of an international tribunal is determined, inter alia, by the claimant's nationality.[8] In particular, if the host state's consent to jurisdiction is given through a treaty, it will only apply to nationals of a state that is a party to the treaty.

Traditionally, international practice on nationality issues has been shaped to a large extent by cases involving diplomatic protection of individuals and companies by their states of nationality.[9] It is sometimes questioned whether the principles developed in that context can simply be transferred to situations where the investor has direct access to international arbitration.[10] Applicable treaties as well as arbitral practice on investor protection have developed in a way that differs in several respects from the principles governing diplomatic protection.

(b) Nationality of individuals

An individual's nationality is determined primarily by the law of the country whose nationality is at issue.[11] A certificate of nationality, issued by the competent authorities of a state, is strong evidence for the existence of the nationality of that state but is not necessarily conclusive.[12]

In *Soufraki v UAE*,[13] the claimant had produced several Italian certificates of nationality. The Tribunal found that the claimant had lost that nationality as a consequence of the acquisition of Canadian nationality, a fact that was evidently unknown to the Italian authorities. As a Canadian national he was unable to rely on the BIT between Italy and the UAE. Also, ICSID jurisdiction was unavailable since Canada is not a party to the ICSID Convention. The Tribunal said:

---

[7] On the issue of rights conferred upon private investors through treaties, see O Spiermann, 'Individual Rights, State Interests and the Power to Waive ICSID Jurisdiction under Bilateral Investment Treaties' (2004) 20 *Arbitration International* 179, 183 et seq.

[8] See pp 252–3.

[9] See eg *Nottebohm Case* (*Liechtenstein v Guatemala*), ICJ Reports (1955) 4; *Case Concerning the Barcelona Traction, Light and Power Company, Limited* (*Belgium v Spain*), ICJ Reports (1970) 4. In the *Diallo* case (*Guinea v Democratic Republic of Congo*), Judgment, 24 May 2007, the ICJ confirmed, at para 61, that 'only the State of nationality may exercise diplomatic protection on behalf of the company when its rights are injured by a wrongful act of another State'.

[10] M Hirsch, *The Arbitration Mechanism of the International Centre for the Settlement of Investment Disputes* (1993) 76–7.

[11] *Pey Casado v Chile*, Award, 8 May 2008, paras 254–60.

[12] *Micula v Romania*, Decision on Jurisdiction, 24 September 2008, paras 70–106; *Tza Yap Shum v Peru*, Decision on Jurisdiction, 19 June 2009, paras 42–77.

[13] *Soufraki v United Arab Emirates*, Award, 7 July 2004.

It is accepted in international law that nationality is within the domestic jurisdiction of the State, which settles, by its own legislation, the rules relating to the acquisition (and loss) of its nationality.... But it is no less accepted that when, in international arbitral or judicial proceedings, the nationality of a person is challenged, the international tribunal is competent to pass upon that challenge.... Where, as in the instant case, the jurisdiction of an international tribunal turns on an issue of nationality, the international tribunal is empowered, indeed bound, to decide that issue.[14]

Having found that the claimant did not have Italian nationality as a matter of Italian law, the Tribunal did not find it necessary to deal with the respondent's contention that, in the absence of a genuine link, that nationality would have been ineffective.[15]

In *Olguín v Paraguay*,[16] the claimant relied on the BIT between Paraguay and Peru. The respondent objected that Olguín, in addition to his Peruvian nationality, also had US nationality and that he resided in the United States. The Tribunal found that the claimant held dual nationality and that both nationalities were effective. The fact that he had Peruvian nationality was enough, in the Tribunal's view, to afford him the protection of the BIT.[17]

Tribunals have generally been unimpressed by arguments concerning the effectiveness of a nationality. In *Micula v Romania*[18] the Tribunal said:

Nottebohm cannot be read to allow or require that a State disregard an individual's single nationality on the basis of the fact that this individual has not resided in the country of his nationality for a period of time.[19]

In *Fakes v Turkey*[20] the claimant held both Dutch and Jordanian nationalities and sought to rely on the BIT between the Netherlands and Turkey. The Tribunal rejected the respondent's argument concerning the lack of effectiveness of the Dutch nationality. The Tribunal found the rules concerning a 'genuine link' as developed in the context of diplomatic protection inapplicable. But the Tribunal left open the possibility of applying an effective nationality test in exceptional circumstances such as a nationality of convenience or a nationality passed on over several generations without any ties to the country in question.[21]

Nationals of the host state are generally excluded from international protection even if they also hold the nationality of another state. The ICSID Convention, in Article 25(2)(a), explicitly excludes dual nationals if one of their nationalities is that of the host state.

In *Champion Trading v Egypt*,[22] three of the individual claimants had dual US and Egyptian nationality. The Tribunal was unimpressed by the argument that the

---

[14] At para 55.   [15] At paras 42–6.
[16] *Olguín v Paraguay*, Award, 26 July 2001.   [17] At paras 60–2.
[18] *Micula v Romania*, Decision on Jurisdiction and Admissibility, 24 September 2008.
[19] At para 103.
[20] *Fakes v Turkey*, Award, 14 July 2010.
[21] At pp 54–81.
[22] *Champion Trading v Egypt*, Decision on Jurisdiction, 21 October 2003.

Egyptian nationality was not effective.[23] It found that the ICSID Convention had a clear and specific rule to the effect that any person who also has the nationality of the host state is excluded from bringing a claim under the Convention.[24]

On the other hand, a NAFTA tribunal found in *Feldman v Mexico*[25] that the claimant, being a citizen of the United States only, had standing despite the fact that he had his permanent residence in the host state.[26] According to the Tribunal:

under general international law, citizenship rather than residence or any other geographic affiliation is the main connecting factor between a State and an individual.[27]

In *Siag v Egypt*,[28] the claimants' Italian nationality was uncontested. The Tribunal found that they had lost their previous Egyptian nationality as a matter of Egyptian law and held that the claimants' historic and continuing residence and operation of business interests in Egypt were irrelevant. Since the claimants were not dual nationals, there was no room for a test of dominant or effective nationality.[29]

(c) Nationality of corporations

Nationality normally presupposes legal personality. Therefore, unincorporated entities and groupings will not, in general, enjoy legal protection,[30] although a treaty may provide otherwise.[31]

Corporate nationality is considerably more complex than that of individuals. Legal systems and treaties use a variety of criteria to determine whether a juridical person is a national or an investor of a particular state. Sometimes the same treaty adopts separate definitions of corporate nationality for each party.

The most commonly used criteria for corporate nationality are *incorporation* or the main *seat* of the business ('*siège social*'):

According to international law and practice, there are different possible criteria to determine a juridical person's nationality. The most widely used is the place of incorporation or registered office. Alternatively, the place of the central administration or effective seat may also be taken into consideration.[32]

---

[23] The claimants relied upon the *Nottebohm Case* (*Liechtenstein v Guatemala*), ICJ Reports (1955) 4 and upon a leading case before the Iran–US Claims Tribunal: *Decision in Case No A/18 Concerning the Question of Jurisdiction over Claims of Persons with Dual Nationality*, 5 Iran–US CTR 252 (1984 I), reprinted in 23 ILM 489 (1984).

[24] At section 3.4.1.

[25] *Feldman v Mexico*, Decision on Jurisdiction, 6 December 2000.

[26] At paras 24–37.

[27] At para 30. See also the Award in the same case, 16 December 2002, para 48.

[28] *Siag v Egypt*, Decision on Jurisdiction, 11 April 2007.

[29] At paras 195–201.

[30] *Consorzio Groupement LESI—Dipenta v Republique Algerienne*, Award, 10 January 2005, paras 37–41; *Impregilo v Pakistan*, Decision on Jurisdiction, 22 April 2005, paras 131–9.

[31] Eg the Argentina-Germany BIT in its definition of 'national' refers to 'any legal person and any commercial or other company or association with or without legal personality'.

[32] *Autopista v Venezuela*, Decision on Jurisdiction, 27 September 2001, para 107. See also *SOABI v Senegal*, Decision on Jurisdiction, 1 August 1984, para 29.

Many treaties follow one or the other of these criteria. The ECT's definition of 'investor' includes 'a company or other organization organized in accordance with the law applicable in that Contracting Party'.[33] The BIT between Poland and the United Kingdom describes corporate investors as 'any corporations, firms, organisations and associations incorporated or constituted under the law in force in that Contracting Party . . .'. The US Model BIT of 2012 describes an 'enterprise of a Party' as 'an enterprise constituted or organized under the law of a Party . . .'.

In cases in which the relevant treaties provide for incorporation as the relevant criterion, tribunals have refused to pierce the corporate veil in order to look at the nationality of the company's owners.[34] In *Tokios Tokelės v Ukraine*[35] the claimant was a business enterprise established under the laws of Lithuania; however, nationals of the Ukraine owned 99 per cent of its shares. Article 1(2)(b) of the Lithuania-Ukraine BIT defines the term 'investor', with respect to Lithuania, as 'any entity established in the territory of the Republic of Lithuania in conformity with its laws and regulations'. The respondent argued that the claimant was not a genuine entity of Lithuania because it was owned and controlled by Ukrainian nationals. Nevertheless, the majority of the Tribunal concluded that the claimant was an 'investor' of Lithuania under the BIT and a 'national of another Contracting State' under Article 25 of the ICSID Convention.[36]

In *Saluka v Czech Republic*[37] the claimant was a legal person incorporated under the laws of the Netherlands. The respondent objected that Saluka was merely a shell company controlled by its Japanese owners. In accordance with the Czech-Netherlands BIT, the definition of 'investor' in Article 1(b)(ii) includes 'legal persons constituted under the laws of [the Netherlands]'.[38] The Tribunal stated that:

[it] has some sympathy for the argument that a company which has no real connection with a State party to a BIT, and which is in reality a mere shell company controlled by another company which is not constituted under the laws of that State, should not be entitled to invoke the provisions of that treaty.[39]

Nevertheless, it found that the claimant was a Dutch company:

The Tribunal cannot in effect impose upon the parties a definition of 'investor' other than that which they themselves agreed. That agreed definition required only that the claimant-investor should be constituted under the laws of (in the present case) The Netherlands, and it is not open to the Tribunal to add other requirements which the parties could themselves have added but which they omitted to add.[40]

---

[33] ECT, Art 1(7)(a)(ii).

[34] *ADC v Hungary*, Award, 2 October 2006, paras 332–62; *Rompetrol v Romania*, Decision on Jurisdiction, 18 April 2008, paras 71, 75–110.

[35] *Tokios Tokelės v Ukraine*, Decision on Jurisdiction, 29 April 2004. See also *Wena Hotels v Egypt*, Decision on Jurisdiction, 29 June 1999, 6 ICSID Reports 74, 79–84.

[36] At paras 21–71. The decision was accompanied by a forcefully worded dissenting opinion by the Tribunal's President.

[37] *Saluka v Czech Republic*, Partial Award, 17 March 2006.

[38] At paras 1, 73, 183–6, 197.

[39] At para 240.

[40] At para 241. See also *AES Corp v Argentina*, Decision on Jurisdiction, 26 April 2005, paras 75–80.

Other treaties refer to the entity's seat or principal seat of business. For instance, the Argentina-Germany BIT refers to 'company' as a legal person 'having its seat in the territory of one of the Contracting Parties'.

Some treaties combine incorporation with seat.[41] Article I(2) of the ASEAN Agreement[42] provides:

The term 'company' of a Contracting Party shall mean a corporation, partnership or business association, incorporated or constituted under the laws in force in the territory of any Contracting party wherein the place of effective management is situated.

This provision was applied in *Yaung Chi Oo v Myanmar*,[43] in which the claimant was incorporated in Singapore, which was a party to the agreement. The Tribunal examined additionally whether it was also effectively managed from Singapore.[44]

Some treaties go beyond formal requirements such as incorporation or seat: they require a bond of economic substance between the corporate investor and the state whose nationality it claims.[45] Such an economic bond may consist of effective *control* over the corporation by nationals of the state. Alternatively, it may consist of genuine *economic activity* of the company in the state.

Under some treaties a controlling interest of nationals in a company is sufficient to establish corporate nationality.[46] In the BIT between the Netherlands and Venezuela the definition of 'nationals' in Article 1(b) covers not just legal persons incorporated in the respective state but, alternatively, legal persons not so incorporated but 'controlled, directly or indirectly' by nationals of that state. In *Mobil v Venezuela*[47] the investment had been made by the Dutch holding company through its 100 per cent-owned subsidiaries in the United States and the Bahamas. The respondent contended that the Dutch company did not, in fact, exercise genuine control over its subsidiaries. The Tribunal rejected this argument, stating:

In the present case, Venezuela Holdings (Netherlands) owns 100% of the share capital of its two American subsidiaries, which in turn own 100% of the share capital of the two Bahamas subsidiaries. Thus the share capital of Venezuela Holdings (Netherlands) in those subsidiaries makes it possible for it to exercise control on them. The Tribunal does not have to consider whether or not such control was exercised in fact.[48]

---

[41] Eg the BITs between Belgium and the Czech Republic, the BIT between Pakistan and Sweden, and the BIT between Argentina and France. See *Total v Argentina*, Decision on Jurisdiction, 25 August 2006, para 57; *Alpha v Ukraine*, Award, 8 November 2010, paras 45–55, 333–45.

[42] ASEAN Agreement for the Promotion and Protection of Investments, 15 December 1987, 27 ILM 612 (1987).

[43] *Yaung Chi Oo v Myanmar*, Award, 31 March 2003.

[44] At paras 46–52.

[45] See generally P Acconci, 'Determining the Internationally Relevant Link between a State and a Corporate Investor' (2004) 5 *J World Investment & Trade* 139.

[46] Eg the BIT between Moldova and the United States. See *Link-Trading v Moldova*, Award, 18 April 2002, para 54; See also the BIT between Ecuador and France, *Perenco v Ecuador*, Decision on Jurisdiction, 30 June 2011, para 49.

[47] *Mobil v Venezuela*, Decision on Jurisdiction, 10 June 2010.

[48] At para 160. The Tribunal relied on a protocol to the BIT which listed percentage of capital ownership as a relevant criterion for control.

Some treaties combine seat with 'a predominant interest of an investor'.[49] The BIT between Iran and Switzerland combines all the above elements and grants investor status to a legal entity if it is established under the law of the state in question and has its seat there, provided it also has real economic activities in that country. Alternatively, the same BIT grants investor status to a legal entity not incorporated in that state if it is effectively controlled by natural or juridical persons of the state.

The Multilateral Investment Guarantee Agency (MIGA) Convention requires incorporation and seat or, alternatively, control. Under Article 13(a)(ii), a juridical person will qualify as an 'eligible investor' if:

such juridical person is incorporated and has its principal place of business in a member or the majority of its capital is owned by a member or members or nationals thereof, provided that such member is not the host country in any of the above cases.

In *Champion Trading v Egypt*,[50] the Tribunal applied the BIT between Egypt and the United States. That Treaty, in its Article I(b), requires incorporation and control by nationals:

(b) 'company of a Party' means a company duly incorporated, constituted or otherwise duly organized under the applicable laws and regulations of a Party or its political subdivisions in which (i) natural persons who are nationals of such Party . . . have a substantial interest.

The corporate claimant was incorporated in the United States but was owned by five individuals most of whom were dual Egyptian and US nationals. The Tribunal found that it had jurisdiction over the corporation since the BIT did not exclude dual nationals as controlling shareholders.[51]

In *Aguas del Tunari v Bolivia*[52] the claimant was a legal person constituted under Bolivian law. It relied on the definition of 'national' in Article 1(b) of the Bolivia-Netherlands BIT which included legal persons incorporated in the host state but controlled by nationals of the other state. Aguas del Tunari argued that it was controlled by Dutch corporations. Bolivia objected, arguing that these Dutch corporations were, in turn, controlled by a US corporation. The Tribunal found that the controlling Dutch companies were more than just corporate shells set up to obtain jurisdiction over the dispute before it. Therefore, it found that the BIT's nationality requirements were fulfilled.[53]

(d) Article 25(2)(b) of the ICSID Convention: agreement to treat a local company as a foreign national because of foreign control

Host states often require that investments are made through locally incorporated companies. Normally, these local companies will not qualify as foreign investors and will hence not enjoy the ICSID Convention's protection. But the Convention

---

[49] Eg the BIT between Lithuania and Sweden.
[50] *Champion Trading v Egypt*, Decision on Jurisdiction, 21 October 2003.
[51] At section 3.4.2.
[52] *Aguas del Tunari v Bolivia*, Decision on Jurisdiction, 21 October 2005.
[53] At paras 206–323.

contains a specific provision to address the phenomenon of investments made through corporations registered in the host state. Article 25(2)(b) of the ICSID Convention deals with juridical persons incorporated in the host state but controlled by nationals of another state. These may be treated as foreign nationals on the basis of an agreement.

The relevant part of Article 25(2)(b) of the ICSID Convention provides:

'National of another Contracting State' means:... any juridical person which had the nationality of the Contracting State party to the dispute on that date and which, because of foreign control, the parties have agreed should be treated as a national of another Contracting State for the purposes of this Convention.

The application of Article 25(2)(b) requires an agreement between the host state and the investor. Such an agreement may be contained in a contract between the host state and the investor regulating the investment. Tribunals have been flexible on the form of the required agreement: the insertion of an ICSID arbitration clause in a contract was accepted as implying an agreement to treat the local company as a foreign national since, to hold otherwise, would have resulted in the ICSID clause being meaningless.[54]

Most contemporary investment arbitrations are instituted not on the basis of consent given in a contract between the host state and the investor but on the basis of an offer of consent contained in a treaty.[55] In that situation there is often no opportunity for the parties to agree to treat a particular locally incorporated company as a foreign national. Therefore, some treaties provide in general terms that companies constituted in one state but controlled by nationals of the other state shall be treated as nationals of the other state for the purposes of Article 25(2)(b).[56] The proviso in a treaty that a local company, because of foreign control, will be treated as a national of another contracting state is part of the terms of the offer of consent to jurisdiction made by the host state. When the offer to submit disputes to ICSID is accepted by the investor, that proviso becomes part of the consent agreement between the parties to the dispute.

In *Micula v Romania*[57] the relevant BIT between Romania and Sweden provided in Article 7(3):

3. For the purpose of this Article and Article 25(2)(b) of the said Washington Convention, any legal person which is constituted in accordance with the legislation of one Contracting Party and which, before a dispute arises, is controlled by an investor of the other Contracting Party, shall be treated as a legal person of the other Contracting Party.

---

[54] *Klöckner v Cameroon*, Award, 21 October 1983, 2 ICSID Reports 16; *LETCO v Liberia*, Decision on Jurisdiction, 24 October 1984, 2 ICSID Reports 349–53; *Millicom v Senegal*, Decision on Jurisdiction, 16 July 2010, paras 110–14.

[55] See Chapter X.2(f).

[56] See eg ECT, Art 26(7). See also R Dolzer and M Stevens, *Bilateral Investment Treaties* (1995) 142.

[57] *Micula v Romania*, Decision on Jurisdiction and Admissibility, 24 September 2008.

The three corporate claimants in that case were incorporated in Romania but were controlled by Swedish nationals. It followed that under Article 25(2)(b) of the ICSID Convention and Article 7(3) of the BIT the corporate claimants were to be treated as Swedish nationals.[58]

The agreement under Article 25(2)(b) must be supported by actual foreign control;[59] the agreement alone is not enough. Control would have to be exercised by a national of a state that is a party to the ICSID Convention.[60]

In *Vacuum Salt v Ghana*[61] the claimant was incorporated in Ghana. Although the agreement between the parties contained an ICSID clause and the Tribunal accepted that the ICSID clause implied an agreement to treat the claimant as a foreign national, the Tribunal found that it had to examine the existence of foreign control as a separate requirement:

the parties' agreement to treat Claimant as a foreign national 'because of foreign control' does not *ipso jure* confer jurisdiction. The reference in Article 25(2)(b) to 'foreign control' necessarily sets an objective Convention limit beyond which ICSID jurisdiction cannot exist . . .[62]

An examination of the facts revealed that there was no foreign control; therefore the Tribunal declined jurisdiction.[63]

Control over a juridical person is not a simple phenomenon. Participation in the company's capital stock or share ownership is not the only indicator of control. The existence of foreign control is a complex question requiring the examination of several factors such as equity participation, voting rights, and management.[64]

(e) Nationality planning

The foregoing sections make it clear that a prudent investor may organize its investment in a way that affords maximum protection under existing treaties. Usually this will be done through the establishment of a company in a state that has favourable treaty relations with the host state and accepts incorporation as a basis for corporate nationality. That company will then be used as a conduit for the investment. Nationality planning or 'treaty shopping' is not illegal or unethical as such, but practice demonstrates that there are limits to it. In addition, states may regard corporate structuring for the purpose of obtaining advantages from treaties as undesirable and take appropriate measures against it.

---

[58] At paras 107–16.

[59] *Klöckner v Cameroon*, Award, 21 October 1983, 2 ICSID Reports 15–16; *SOABI v Senegal*, Decision on Jurisdiction, 1 August 1984, paras 28–46; *LETCO v Liberia*, Decision on Jurisdiction, 24 October 1984, 2 ICSID Reports 352; *Autopista v Venezuela*, Decision on Jurisdiction, 27 September 2001, paras 105–34; *Millicom v Senegal*, Decision on Jurisdiction, 16 July 2010, para 109.

[60] *SOABI v Senegal*, Decision on Jurisdiction, 1 August 1984, paras 32–3.

[61] *Vacuum Salt v Ghana*, Award, 16 February 1994.

[62] At para 36.

[63] At paras 35–55.

[64] *Vacuum Salt* at paras 43–53. For a detailed discussion of control, see *Aguas del Tunari v Bolivia*, Decision on Jurisdiction, 21 October 2005, paras 225–48, 264–323.

In *Aguas del Tunari v Bolivia*[65] the Tribunal accepted the 'migration' of the controlling company from one country to another.[66] The respondent asserted that the strategic changes in the corporate structure in order to obtain the protection of a BIT amounted to fraud and abuse of corporate form. The Tribunal rejected this contention:

It is not uncommon in practice, and—absent a particular limitation—not illegal to locate one's operations in a jurisdiction perceived to provide a beneficial regulatory and legal environment in terms, for examples, of taxation or the substantive law of the jurisdiction, including the availability of a BIT.... The language of the definition of national in many BITs evidences that such national routing of investments is entirely in keeping with the purpose of the instruments and the motivations of the state parties.[67]

Not every attempt at nationality planning will succeed. In *Banro v Congo*,[68] a transfer of ownership of an investment was carried out from a company registered in a non-ICSID party, Canada, to an affiliate company in the United States, a party to the ICSID Convention. The transfer was made after the dispute had arisen and only days before instituting arbitration proceedings. This served the obvious purpose of obtaining access to ICSID and the Tribunal refused to accept jurisdiction under these circumstances.[69]

In *Phoenix v Czech Republic*[70] there was originally a dispute between the Czech state and a Czech investor. Most of the incriminated events had already occurred and the dispute was in full swing when the Czech investor tried to acquire a seemingly convenient nationality by selling the investment to an Israeli company, Phoenix, which he had established especially for that purpose. Shortly after the transfer, the company commenced ICSID arbitration, relying on the BIT between Israel and the Czech Republic. The Tribunal found that the claim constituted an abusive attempt to obtain access to the system of investment protection under the ICSID Convention. The claimant had made an investment not for the purpose of engaging in economic activity but for the sole purpose of bringing international litigation against the Czech Republic.[71]

In *Cementownia v Turkey*,[72] the claimant was a Polish company that claimed to have acquired shares in two Turkish companies. The alleged share transfers took place just 12 days before Turkey terminated concession agreements thereby, it was argued, violating its treaty obligations under the ECT. The Tribunal found that the

---

[65] *Aguas del Tunari v Bolivia*, Decision on Jurisdiction, 21 October 2005.
[66] At paras 160–80.
[67] At paras 330, 332. See also *HICEE v Slovakia*, Partial Award, 23 May 2011, para 103.
[68] *Banro v Congo*, Award, 1 September 2000, excerpts in (2002) 17 *ICSID Review-FILJ* 380.
[69] But see *Autopista v Venezuela*, Decision on Jurisdiction, 27 September 2001, paras 80–140. In that case the respondent state had consented to the transfer of the shares from Mexican to US nationals. Mexico is not a party to the ICSID Convention.
[70] *Phoenix v Czech Republic*, Award, 15 April 2009.
[71] At paras 142–5.
[72] *Cementownia v Turkey*, Award, 17 September 2009.

entire share transaction between the Turkish company and the Polish claimant was fabricated and never actually took place.[73] The Tribunal added:

Even if they did occur, the share transfers would not have been *bona fide* transactions, but rather attempts (in the face of government measures dating back some years about to culminate in the concessions' termination) to fabricate international jurisdiction where none should exist.[74]

In *Mobil v Venezuela*,[75] the investments had been made by Exxon Mobil through holding companies in Delaware and the Bahamas. After certain difficulties had arisen with the new Venezuelan Government over royalties and income tax,[76] Exxon Mobil restructured its investment by interposing a Dutch holding company. Mobil informed the Venezuelan Government of this step and the government did not raise any objection. As a consequence of the restructuring, the Delaware and Bahamian companies became 100 per cent-owned subsidiaries of the Dutch company.[77] After Mobil had completed its restructuring, Venezuela took nationalization measures. Thereupon Mobil instituted ICSID arbitration relying on the BIT between the Netherlands and Venezuela. Despite Venezuela's protestations, the Tribunal found that this form of corporate structuring was permissible. In the Tribunal's view:

204.... the aim of the restructuring of their investments in Venezuela through a Dutch holding was to protect those investments against breaches of their rights by the Venezuelan authorities by gaining access to ICSID arbitration through the BIT. The Tribunal considers that this was a perfectly legitimate goal as far as it concerned future disputes.

205. With respect to pre-existing disputes, the situation is different and the Tribunal considers that to restructure investments only in order to gain jurisdiction under a BIT for such disputes would constitute, to take the words of the Phoenix Tribunal, 'an abusive manipulation of the system of international investment protection under the ICSID Convention and the BITs'.

It appears from these cases that prospective planning within the framework of existing treaties will be accepted by tribunals.[78] 'Prospective' means that the corporate arrangements must have been in place before the facts that led to the dispute occurred[79] or, in any event, before the dispute arose. What appears to be impossible is to create a remedy for existing grievances, in particular after a dispute has arisen, by arranging for a desirable nationality.

---

[73] At para 156.
[74] At para 117.
[75] *Mobil v Venezuela*, Decision on Jurisdiction, 10 June 2010.
[76] At paras 200, 201.
[77] At paras 187–92. Under the BIT between the Netherlands and Venezuela not only companies incorporated in the Netherlands but also companies controlled by Dutch incorporated companies are deemed to be nationals of the Netherlands.
[78] See also *Millicom v Senegal*, Decision on Jurisdiction, 16 July 2010, para 84.
[79] *Société Générale v Dominican Republic*, Decision on Jurisdiction, 19 September 2008, paras 109–10.

(f) Denial of benefits

States have devised methods to counteract strategies that seek the protection of particular treaties by acquiring a favourable nationality. One such method is to require a bond of economic substance between the corporation and the state. This method has been described above.[80] Another method is the insertion of a so-called 'denial of benefits' clause into the treaty that provides consent to jurisdiction. Under such a clause, states reserve the right to deny the benefits of the treaty to a company incorporated in a state but with no economic connection to that state. The economic connection would consist in substantial business activities in the state of incorporation or ownership or control by a national of a state party to the treaty. Article 17(1) of the ECT provides:

Each Contracting Party reserves the right to deny the advantages of this Part to:
(1) a legal entity if citizens or nationals of a third state own or control such entity and if that entity has no substantial business activities in the Area of the Contracting Party in which it is organized.

Other treaties, including BITs, contain similar provisions.[81]

Tribunals have addressed this type of clause in a number of cases.[82] In *Plama v Bulgaria*,[83] the claimant was incorporated in Cyprus. After the arbitration proceedings had been instituted, Bulgaria sent a letter to ICSID purporting to exercise its right under the ECT's denial of benefits clause. Bulgaria argued that Plama had no substantial business activities in Cyprus and was controlled by nationals of states not parties to the ECT. The Tribunal found that the denial of benefits clause was drafted in permissive terms and did not operate automatically but required the actual exercise of the host state's right.[84] The exercise of that right could only be made prospectively and not retroactively after the investment had been made.[85]

In *AMTO v Ukraine*[86] the claimant was incorporated in Latvia, a party to the ECT. Ukraine objected to the Tribunal's jurisdiction based on Article 17(1) of the ECT. The Tribunal noted that the concept of a 'third state' under that provision meant a state that was not a contracting party to the ECT.[87] The burden of proof relating to the requirements of Article 17(1) of the ECT lay with the respondent invoking it. In view of the Tribunal's finding that AMTO had a substantial

---

[80] At p 49.
[81] See NAFTA, Art 1113; Argentina-United States BIT, Art I(2); US Model BIT of 2012, Art 17; Austria-Jordan BIT, Art 10.
[82] *Generation Ukraine v Ukraine*, Award, 16 September 2003, paras 15.1–15.9; *Petrobart v Kyrgyz Republic*, Award, 29 March 2005, (2005) 3 *Stockholm Int'l Arb Rev* 45, 64; *Pan American v Argentina*, Decision on Jurisdiction, 27 July 2006, paras 204, 221.
[83] *Plama v Bulgaria*, Decision on Jurisdiction, 8 February 2005. See also *Plama v Bulgaria*, Award, 27 August 2008, paras 77–95.
[84] At paras 152–8.
[85] At paras 159–65. This conclusion has been criticized: A Sinclair, 'The Substance of Nationality Requirements in Investment Treaty Arbitration' (2005) 20 *ICSID Review-FILJ* 357, 385. See also *Empresa Eléctrica del Ecuador v Ecuador*, Award, 2 June 2009, para 71.
[86] *AMTO v Ukraine*, Award, 26 March 2008.
[87] At para 62.

business activity in Latvia, there was no need to make a determination on ownership and control.[88] The Tribunal stated with respect to the requirement of
'substantial business activities' under Article 17(1) of the ECT:

the purpose of Article 17(1) is to exclude from ECT protection investors which have
adopted a nationality of convenience. Accordingly, 'substantial' in this context means 'of
substance, and not merely of form'. It does not mean 'large', and the materiality not the
magnitude of the business activity is the decisive question. In the present case, the Tribunal
is satisfied that the Claimant has substantial business activity in Latvia, on the basis of its
investment related activities conducted from premises in Latvia, and involving the employment of a small but permanent staff.[89]

(g) Shareholders as investors

Investments often take place through the acquisition of shares in a company that
has a nationality different from that of the investor. Can a shareholder pursue
claims for damage done to the company? In particular, is it possible for the
shareholder to proceed on the basis of its own nationality even if the company
does not meet the nationality requirements under the relevant treaty?[90]

In the *Barcelona Traction* case[91] the International Court of Justice (ICJ) held that
Belgium, the state of nationality of the majority shareholders of a company
incorporated in Canada, was unable to pursue claims against Spain for damage
caused to the company.[92] The ICJ acknowledged that its decision was based on
customary international law and that treaties may provide otherwise.[93] In addition,
the ICJ recognized that the exclusion of shareholders' rights against a host state
inflicting damage on a company would not necessarily apply if the company in
question was incorporated in the host state.[94]

In the *Diallo* case[95] the ICJ held that the state of nationality of the shareholder
(Guinea) was unable to exercise diplomatic protection against the state in which the
company was incorporated (Democratic Republic of Congo). The ICJ noted that
in contemporary international law the protection of shareholders is governed by

---

[88] At paras 67–70.

[89] At para 69.

[90] For detailed treatment, see S A Alexandrov, 'The "Baby Boom" of Treaty-Based Arbitrations and
the Jurisdiction of ICSID Tribunals: Shareholders as "Investors" and Jurisdiction *Ratione Temporis*'
(2005) 4 *Law and Practice of International Courts and Tribunals* 19; C Schreuer, 'Shareholder
Protection in International Investment Law' in *Festschrift für Christian Tomuschat* (2006) 601.

[91] *Barcelona Traction, Light and Power Co, Ltd (Belgium v Spain)*, Judgment, 5 February 1970, ICJ
Reports (1970) 4.

[92] See I A Laird, 'A Community of Destiny—The *Barcelona Traction* Case and the Development of
Shareholder Rights to Bring Investment Claims' in T Weiler (ed), *International Investment Law and
Arbitration: Leading Cases from the ICSID, NAFTA, Bilateral Treaties and Customary International Law*
(2005) 77–96.

[93] At paras 89–90.

[94] At para 92. See also *Pan American v Argentina*, Decision on Preliminary Objections, 27 July
2006, paras 215–16.

[95] *Diallo* case *(Guinea v Democratic Republic of Congo)*, Judgment, 24 May 2007, ICJ Reports
(2007) 582.

bilateral and multilateral treaties and by contracts between states and foreign investors. However, a 'protection by substitution', in favour of the shareholder rather than the company, is not discernible under customary international law.[96]

The issue of shareholder protection is particularly acute where, as is often the case, investments are made through companies incorporated in the host state and the local company is the immediate investor. Many states require a locally incorporated company as a precondition for the investment.

Under the conditions of Article 25(2)(b) of the ICSID Convention and provisions in some BITs, the local company might qualify as a foreign investor because of its foreign control. These provisions are discussed above.[97] A slightly different method is used by the NAFTA: an investor that owns or controls a company registered in another state party may submit a claim to arbitration on behalf of that company.[98] What these provisions have in common is that they require control over the company in question. In other words, they do not offer comfort to minority shareholders.

Most investment treaties offer a solution that gives independent standing to shareholders: the treaties include shareholding or participation in a company in their definitions of 'investment'.[99] In this way, it is not the locally incorporated company that is treated as a foreign investor; rather, the participation in the company becomes the investment. Even though the local company may be unable to pursue the claim internationally, the foreign shareholder in the company may pursue the claim in its own name. Put differently, even if the local company is not endowed with investor status, the investor's participation therein is seen as the investment. The shareholder may then pursue claims for adverse action by the host state against the company that affects its value and profitability. Arbitral practice illustrating this point is extensive.[100]

---

[96] At paras 88–90.

[97] See pp 50–2.

[98] NAFTA, Art 1117 provides in relevant part: 'An investor of a Party, on behalf of an enterprise of another Party that is a juridical person that the investor owns or controls directly or indirectly, may submit to arbitration under this Section a claim that the other Party has breached an obligation...'

[99] See R Dolzer and M Stevens, *Bilateral Investment Treaties* (1995) 27–8. See also NAFTA, Art 1139; ECT, Art 1(6)(b).

[100] See eg *Goetz v Burundi*, Decision of 2 September 1998; *Maffezini v Spain*, Decision on Jurisdiction, 25 January 2000; *Compañía de Aguas del Aconquija, & CGE v Argentina* (the *Vivendi* case), Decision on Annulment, 3 July 2002; *Azurix v Argentina*, Decision on Jurisdiction, 8 December 2003; *AMT v Zaire*, Award, 21 February 1997; *Genin v Estonia*, Award, 25 June 2001; *CME v Czech Republic*, Partial Award, 13 September 2001; *Camuzzi v Argentina*, Decision on Jurisdiction, 11 May 2005, paras 12, 78–82, 140–2; *Gas Natural v Argentina*, Decision on Jurisdiction, 17 June 2005, paras 32–5, 50–1; *AES Corp v Argentina*, Decision on Jurisdiction, 26 April 2005, paras 85–9; *Compañía de Aguas del Aconquija, PA & Vivendi Universal PA v Argentina* (*Vivendi II*), Decision on Jurisdiction, 14 November 2005, paras 88–94; *Continental Casualty v Argentina*, Decision on Jurisdiction, 22 February 2006, paras 51–4, 76–89; *Suez, Sociedad General de Aguas de Barcelona SA, and InterAguas Servicios Integrales del Agua SA v Argentina*, Decision on Jurisdiction, 16 May 2006, paras 46–51; *National Grid v Argentina*, Decision on Jurisdiction, 20 June 2006, paras 147–58, 165, Award, 3 November 2008, para 126; *Pan American v Argentina*, Decision on Preliminary Objections, 27 July 2006, paras 209–22; *Parkerings v Lithuania*, Award, 11 September 2007, paras 250–4; *Impregilo v Argentina*, Award, 21 June 2011, paras 110–40, 238–46, 271.

In *Genin v Estonia*,[101] the claimants, US nationals, were the principal shareholders of EIB, a financial institution incorporated under the law of Estonia. The BIT between Estonia and the United States in its definition of 'investment' includes 'a company or shares of stock or other interests in a company or interests in the assets thereof'. The Tribunal rejected the respondent's argument that the claim did not relate to an 'investment' as understood in the BIT:

The term 'investment' as defined in Article I(a)(ii) of the BIT clearly embraces the investment of Claimants in EIB. The transaction at issue in the present case, namely the Claimants' ownership interest in EIB, is an investment in 'shares of stock or other interests in a company' that was 'owned or controlled, directly or indirectly' by Claimants.[102]

Minority shareholders, too, have been accepted as claimants and have been granted protection under respective treaties.[103] In *CMS v Argentina*,[104] the claimant owned 29.42 per cent of TGN, a company incorporated in Argentina. The definition of 'investment' in the Argentina–US BIT includes 'a company or shares of stock or other interests in a company or interests in the assets thereof'. Argentina argued that CMS, as a minority shareholder in TGN, could not claim for any indirect damage resulting from its participation in the Argentinian company.[105] The Tribunal rejected this argument.[106] It said:

The Tribunal therefore finds no bar in current international law to the concept of allowing claims by shareholders independently from those of the corporation concerned, not even if those shareholders are minority or non-controlling shareholders.[107] ... There is indeed no requirement that an investment, in order to qualify, must necessarily be made by shareholders controlling a company or owning the majority of its shares.[108]

This practice has also been extended to indirect shareholding through an intermediate company,[109] and the same technique has been employed where the affected

---

[101] *Genin v Estonia*, Award, 25 June 2001.

[102] At para 324.

[103] See eg *AAPL v Sri Lanka*, Award, 27 June 1990; *LANCO v Argentina*, Decision on Jurisdiction, 8 December 1998; *Compañía de Aguas del Aconquija & CGE v Argentina* (the *Vivendi* case), Decision on Annulment, 3 July 2002; *CMS v Argentina*, Decision on Jurisdiction, 17 July 2003; *Champion Trading v Egypt*, Decision on Jurisdiction, 21 October 2003; *LG&E Energy v Argentina*, Decision on Jurisdiction, 30 April 2004, paras 50–63, Decision on Liability, 3 October 2006, paras 78–9; *GAMI v Mexico*, Award, 15 November 2004; *Sempra Energy v Argentina*, Decision on Jurisdiction, 11 May 2005, paras 92–4; *El Paso Energy v Argentina*, Decision on Jurisdiction, 27 April 2006, para 138; *Phoenix v Czech Republic*, Award, 15 April 2009, paras 121–3; *Hochtief v Argentina*, Decision on Jurisdiction, 24 October 2011, paras 112–19.

[104] *CMS v Argentina*, Decision on Jurisdiction, 17 July 2003.

[105] At paras 36, 37.

[106] At paras 47–65.

[107] At para 48.

[108] At para 51. To the same effect, see *Enron v Argentina*, Decision on Jurisdiction, 14 January 2004, paras 39, 44, 49, Decision on Jurisdiction (Ancillary Claim), 2 August 2004, paras 21, 22, 29, 39.

[109] See eg *Enron v Argentina*, Decision on Jurisdiction, 14 January 2004, paras 41–57, Decision on Annulment, 30 July 2010, paras 115–27; *Camuzzi v Argentina*, Decision on Jurisdiction, 11 May 2005, para 9; *Gas Natural v Argentina*, Decision on Jurisdiction, 17 June 2005, paras 9, 10, 32–5;

company was incorporated in a state other than the host state.[110] The situation is made somewhat complicated by the fact that some treaties exclude certain forms of indirect investments either explicitly or by implication.[111]

Shareholder protection is not restricted to ownership in shares; it extends to the assets of the company. Adverse action by the host state in violation of treaty guarantees affecting the company's economic position, and hence the value of shares, gives rise to rights by the shareholders.[112] In *GAMI v Mexico*,[113] the claimant, a US-registered corporation, held a 14.18 per cent equity interest in GAMI, a Mexican-registered corporation. Mexico had expropriated a number of mills belonging to GAMI. In the Tribunal's view:

> The fact that a host State does not explicitly interfere with share ownership is not decisive.... GAMI's shareholding was never expropriated as such. GAMI contends that Mexico's conduct impaired the value of its shareholding to such an extent that it must be deemed tantamount to expropriation.[114]

On the other hand, some tribunals have pointed out that the rights of foreign investors do not go beyond what could be derived from the shareholding.[115]

It follows that on the basis of treaty provisions listing participation in companies as a form of investment, shareholding in a company enjoys protection. Thus, even if the affected company does not meet the nationality requirements under the relevant treaty there will be a remedy if the shareholder does so. This is particularly relevant where, as is frequently the case, the company has the nationality of the host state and does not qualify as a foreign investor. In this situation, the company in

---

Kardassopoulos v Georgia, Decision on Jurisdiction, 6 July 2007, paras 121–4; *Noble Energy v Ecuador*, Decision on Jurisdiction, 5 March 2008, paras 70–83; *Société Générale v Dominican Republic*, Decision on Jurisdiction, 19 September 2008, paras 37, 45–52, 113–21; *Cemex v Venezuela*, Decision on Jurisdiction, 30 December 2010, paras 141–58.

[110] *Sedelmayer v Russia*, Award, 7 July 1998, Ch 2.1.1–2.1.5; *Lauder v Czech Republic*, Award, 3 September 2001; *Waste Management v Mexico*, Award, 30 April 2004; *Siemens v Argentina*, Decision on Jurisdiction, 3 August 2004, paras 122–44; *EnCana v Ecuador*, Award, 3 February 2006, paras 115–22; *Tza Yap Shum v Peru*, Decision on Jurisdiction, 19 June 2009, paras 91–111; *Mobil v Venezuela*, Decision on Jurisdiction, 10 June 2010, paras 162–6.

[111] *Berschader v Russia*, Award, 21 April 2006, paras 121–50; *HICEE v Slovakia*, Partial Award, 23 May 2011, paras 48–104, 114–15, 128–33, 146–7.

[112] *CMS v Argentina*, Decision on Jurisdiction, 17 July 2003, paras 59, 66–9, Decision on Annulment, 25 September 2007, paras 58–76; *Azurix v Argentina*, Decision on Jurisdiction, 8 December 2003, paras 69, 73, Decision on Annulment, 1 September 2009, paras 57–62, 76–80, 86–130; *Enron v Argentina*, Decision on Jurisdiction, 14 January 2004, paras 35, 43–9, 58–60, Decision on Jurisdiction (Ancillary Claim), 2 August 2004, paras 17, 34–5; *Siemens v Argentina*, Decision on Jurisdiction, 3 August 2004, paras 125, 136–50; *GAMI v Mexico*, Award, 15 November 2004, paras 26–33; *Camuzzi v Argentina*, Decision on Jurisdiction, 11 May 2005, paras 45–67; *Sempra Energy v Argentina*, Decision on Jurisdiction, 11 May 2005, paras 73–9; *Continental Casualty v Argentina*, Decision on Jurisdiction, 22 February 2006, para 79; *Bogdanov v Moldova*, Award, 22 September 2005, para 5.1; *Total v Argentina*, Decision on Jurisdiction, 25 August 2006, para 74; *RosInvest v Russia*, Final Award, 12 September 2010, paras 605–9, 625.

[113] *GAMI v Mexico*, Award, 15 November 2004.

[114] At paras 33, 35.

[115] *BG Group v Argentina*, Final Award, 24 December 2007, para 214 (this UNCITRAL Award was vacated on different grounds by the US Court of Appeals for the DC District on 17 January 2012); *El Paso v Argentina*, Award, 31 October 2011, paras 149–214.

question is not treated as the investor but as the investment. This protection extends not only to ownership in the shares but also to the assets of the company.

This generous extension of rights to shareholders can lead to some novel issues. For instance, practical problems can arise where claims are pursued in parallel, especially by different shareholders or groups of shareholders. In addition, the affected company itself may pursue certain remedies while a group of its shareholders may pursue different ones. The situation becomes even more complex where indirect shareholding through intermediaries is combined with minority shareholding. In such a case, shareholders and companies at different levels may pursue conflicting or competing litigation strategies that may be difficult to reconcile and coordinate.

2. Investments

(a) Terminology and concept

Economic science often assumes that a direct investment involves (a) the transfer of funds, (b) a longer term project, (c) the purpose of regular income, (d) the participation of the person transferring the funds, at least to some extent, in the management of the project, and (e) a business risk. These elements distinguish foreign direct investment from a portfolio investment (no element of personal management), from an ordinary transaction for purposes of sale of a good or a service (no management, no continuous flow of income), and from a short-term financial transaction.[116]

In legal terms, investment regimes need to define their scope *ratione materiae*. Contemporary treaties do not, as a rule, reflect the classical formula 'property, rights, and interests' found in traditional friendship, commerce, and navigation (FCN) treaties, in treaties to settle claims after hostilities, or in human rights documents.[117] Instead, they are built on the modern term 'investment'.[118] This usage is now fully accepted, even though the phrase 'property, rights and interests' had to a considerable extent acquired a distinct legal meaning and the term 'investment' has its origin in economic terminology and needed to be understood and defined as a legal concept when first used in investment agreements.

The reasons the drafters of investment treaties switched from 'property, rights, and interests' to 'investment' is tied to the purpose of such treaties; they were not meant to cover all types of 'property, rights, and interests'. While usage of the term 'investment' is convenient, it also presents the challenge of defining the term to

---

[116] R Dolzer, 'The Notion of Investment in Recent Practice' in S Charnovitz, D P Steger, and P van den Bosche (eds), *Law in the Service of Human Dignity: Essays in Honour of Florentino Feliciano* (2005) 261, 263; N Rubins, 'The Notion of "Investment" in International Investment Arbitration' in N Horn (ed), *Arbitrating Foreign Investment Disputes* (2004) 283.

[117] See R Dolzer, *Eigentum, Enteignung und Entschädigung im geltenden Völkerrecht* (1985) 157–63; R Lillich and B Weston, *International Claims: Their Settlement by Lump Sum Agreements* (1975) 180.

[118] In French treaties: 'investissements'; in Spanish treaties: 'inversiones'; in German treaties: 'Kapitalanlagen'; in Austrian treaties: 'Investitionen'.

make it legally manageable and operational, both for purposes of clauses which define the coverage of a BIT and also for the consent of parties to submit their disputes to arbitration.

In practice, two conceptual approaches have been developed to give legal meaning to the term. Bilateral and multilateral treaties have included specific elaborate definitions, usually at the beginning of the operative parts of the agreement. The second approach is based on the usage of the term in regular economic parlance and leaves the interpretation and application to the practice of states and tribunals.

The complexity of the current debate on the term 'investment' arises out of its simple, non-defined use in the jurisdictional clause of the ICSID Convention (Art 25). One approach to the interpretation of 'investment' in Article 25 will orient itself to the definitions in investment treaties, the other to its understanding in the economic literature. In effect, the latter approach requires two separate examinations ('a double keyhole approach'): one under the BIT, the other under Article 25.

A review of the use of the term in treaty practice and in economic discourse establishes that the two approaches may lead to different results in individual cases, but also that variants of the two versions may turn out to yield very similar or identical outcomes. The divergence in the conceptual premises has so far been resolved neither by arbitral jurisprudence nor by academic commentary. However, it appears that a synthesis of the different strands of interpretation may emerge.

(b) Investments as complex, interrelated operations

Tribunals have repeatedly emphasized that an investment typically consists of several interrelated economic activities each of which should not be viewed in isolation. The tribunal in *CSOB v Slovakia*[119] stated:

An investment is frequently a rather complex operation, composed of various interrelated transactions, each element of which, standing alone, might not in all cases qualify as an investment. Hence, a dispute that is brought before the Centre must be deemed to arise directly out of an investment even when it is based on a transaction which, standing alone, would not qualify as an investment under the Convention, provided that the particular transaction forms an integral part of an overall operation that qualifies as an investment.[120]

Whether costs arising in the course of unsuccessful negotiations for a contract amount to an investment depends upon the circumstances. In the absence of a specific applicable treaty clause, current understanding is that when the negotiations do not lead to a contract and no other type of investment is made, the

---

[119] *CSOB v Slovakia*, Decision on Jurisdiction, 24 May 1999.
[120] At para 72. See further *Enron v Argentina*, 14 January 2004, para 70; *Joy Mining v Egypt*, Award, 6 August 2004, para 54; *Mitchell v Congo*, Decision on Annulment, 1 November 2006, para 38; *Duke Energy v Peru*, Decision on Jurisdiction, 1 February 2006, para 92; *Saipem v Bangladesh*, Decision on Jurisdiction, 21 March 2007, paras 110, 114.

potential investor is not in a position to raise a claim under a BIT. The applicability of the BIT presupposes the existence of an investment. In the leading case, *Mihaly v Sri Lanka*, the majority of the Tribunal concluded: 'The Tribunal is consequently unable to accept, as a valid denomination of "investment", the unilateral or internal characterization of certain expenditures by the Claimant in preparation for a project of investment.'[121]

The *Mihaly v Sri Lanka* Tribunal even went as far as stating, in an *obiter dictum*, that the existence of a duty, on the part of the host state, to negotiate in good faith would not be covered by the notion of investment.[122]

(c) Definitions in investment protection treaties

Multilateral treaties typically define the term 'investment' and provide for ICSID jurisdiction. Examples are the NAFTA, which defines 'investment' in Article 1139[123] or the ECT with its definition in Article 1 section 6.[124] Similarly, the draft of a Multilateral Agreement on Investments[125] contained a definition along

---

[121] *Mihaly v Sri Lanka*, 15 March 2002, para 61. See further *Generation Ukraine v Ukraine*, Award, 16 September 2003, para 18.9; *PSEG v Turkey*, Decision on Jurisdiction, 4 June 2004, paras 67–105, Award, 19 January 2007, para 304.

[122] At para 51.

[123] NAFTA, Art 1139 reads: investment means:

(a) an enterprise; (b) an equity security of an enterprise; (c) a debt security of an enterprise (i) where the enterprise is an affiliate of the investor, or (ii) where the original maturity of the debt security is at least three years, but does not include a debt security, regardless of original maturity, of a state enterprise; (d) a loan to an enterprise (i) where the enterprise is an affiliate of the investor, or (ii) where the original maturity of the loan is at least three years, but does not include a loan, regardless of original maturity, to a state enterprise; (e) an interest in an enterprise that entitles the owner to share in income or profits of the enterprise; (f) an interest in an enterprise that entitles the owner to share in the assets of that enterprise on dissolution, other than a debt security or a loan excluded from subparagraph (c) or (d); (g) real estate or other property, tangible or intangible, acquired in the expectation or used for the purpose of economic benefit or other business purposes; and (h) interests arising from the commitment of capital or other resources in the territory of a Party to economic activity in such territory, such as under (i) contracts involving the presence of an investor's property in the territory of the Party, including turnkey or construction contracts, or concessions, or (ii) contracts where remuneration depends substantially on the production, revenues or profits of an enterprise;

but investment does not mean, (i) claims to money that arise solely from (i) commercial contracts for the sale of goods or services by a national or enterprise in the territory of a Party to an enterprise in the territory of another Party, or (ii) the extension of credit in connection with a commercial transaction, such as trade financing, other than a loan covered by subparagraph (d); or (j) any other claims to money, that do not involve the kinds of interests set out in subparagraphs (a) through (h).

[124] ECT, Art 1(6) reads:

'Investment' means every kind of asset, owned or controlled directly or indirectly by an Investor and includes: (a) tangible and intangible, and movable and immovable, property, and any property rights such as leases, mortgages, liens, and pledges; (b) a company or business enterprise, or shares, stock, or other forms of equity participation in a company or business enterprise, and bonds and other debt of a company or business enterprise; (c) claims to money and claims to performance pursuant to contract having an economic value and associated with an Investment; (d) Intellectual Property; (e) Returns; (f) any right conferred by law or contract or by virtue of any licences and permits granted pursuant to law to undertake any Economic Activity in the Energy Sector.

[125] See p 10.

the conventional lines of BITs together with an 'interpretative note', which would have had a limiting effect.[126]

Most bilateral treaties contain a general phrase defining investment (such as 'all assets') and several groups of illustrative categories. No special problems in interpreting such a clause will arise if the investment in question is covered by one of the illustrative categories. An example for this approach is found in the BIT between Argentina and the United States:

'investment' means every kind of investment in the territory of one Party owned or controlled directly or indirectly by nationals or companies of the other Party, such as equity, debt, and service and investment contracts; and includes without limitation: tangible and intangible property, including rights, such as mortgages, liens and pledges; a company or shares of stock or other interests in a company or interests in the assets thereof; a claim to money or a claim to performance having economic value and directly related to an investment; intellectual property which includes, inter alia, rights relating to: literary and artistic works, including sound recordings, inventions in all fields of human endeavor, industrial designs, semiconductor mask works, trade secrets, know-how, and confidential business information, and trademarks, service marks, and trade names; and any right conferred by law or contract, and any licenses and permits pursuant to law;

Other treaties are worded more in line with economic usage. For instance, the BIT between the Ukraine and Denmark (1992) focuses on the purpose of establishing lasting economic relations: 'For the purpose of this Agreement, the term "investment" shall mean every kind of asset connected with economic activities acquired for the purpose of establishing lasting economic relations...'[127]

The agreement between the United States and Chile (2003) relies—in a special, at first sight circular, way—on the term 'characteristics of an investment', referring alternatively to commitment of resources, expectation of profit, or assumption of risk:

Investment means every asset that an investor owns or controls, directly or indirectly, that has the characteristics of an investment, including such characteristics as the commitment of capital or other resources, the expectation of gain or profit, or the assumption of risk.[128]

---

[126] The draft consolidated texts provided for a broad definition of the term 'investment' ('Every kind of asset owned or controlled, directly or indirectly, by an investor'), followed by an illustrative list including claims to money, claims to performance, or intellectual property rights. However, it was foreseen that 'an interpretative note will be required to indicate that, in order to qualify as an investment under the MAI, an asset must have the characteristics of an investment, such as the commitment of capital or other resources, the expectation of gain or profit, or the assumption of risk'. See R Dolzer, 'The Notion of Investment in Recent Practice' in S Charnovitz, D P Steger, and P van den Bosche (eds), *Law in the Service of Human Dignity: Essays in Honour of Florentino Feliciano* (2005) 261, 265–6.

[127] Agreement Concerning the Promotion and Reciprocal Protection of Investments concluded between the Kingdom of Denmark and the Ukraine on 23 October 1992, Art 1(1).

[128] Free Trade Agreement between the Government of the United States of America and the Government of the Republic of Chile, Art 10.27, 6 June 2003 (available at <http://www.ustr.gov/Trade_Agreements/Bilateral/Chile_FTA/Final_Texts/Section_Index.html>).

The Free Trade Agreement between the European Free Trade Association (EFTA) and Mexico (2000) emphasizes the exercise by the investor of effective influence on management, thus implicitly distinguishing portfolio investment:

For the purpose of this Section, investment made in accordance with the laws and regulations of the Parties means direct investment, which is defined as investment for the purpose of establishing lasting economic relations with an undertaking such as, in particular, investments which give the possibility of exercising an effective influence on the management thereof.[129]

In practice, the terms 'rights conferred by contracts' or 'rights granted by the general laws' will often be part of the definition in investment agreements. The matter becomes more complicated if the definition itself contains a reference to the term 'investment' (eg 'a claim to money related to an "investment"'), as is the case in the US-Chile BIT or in a clause contained in the ECT.[130] In such circumstances, recourse to a general concept of 'investment' may be necessary.

Special issues may arise if the definition of an investment in treaties refers to rights governed by the domestic laws of the host state. This is especially so if the treaty recognizes as investments contractual rights or other rights granted under national law. In such situations, the existence of an investment will depend upon an examination of the relevant national law. For instance, an ICSID tribunal may have to rule on the validity of a contract under the national laws of the host state or may have to consider which rights are granted, or not granted, to the investor under domestic law. In the individual case, the international tribunal will take into account the understanding of the law by the organs of the host state and may defer to this understanding. But the final ruling falls to the international tribunal.

BITs frequently include the formula 'in accordance with host state law' or similar formulae in their definitions of the term 'investment'. Host states argued that this meant that the concept of 'investment', and hence the reach of protection under the treaty, had to be determined by reference to their own domestic law. Tribunals have rejected this approach. They have held that reference to a host state's domestic law concerns not the definition of the term 'investment' but solely the legality of the investment.[131] The tribunal in *Salini v Morocco*[132] stated in this respect:

[129] Free Trade Agreement between the EFTA States and the United Mexican States, Art 45, 27 November 2000 (available at <http://secretariat.efta.int>).

[130] See in this respect *Petrobart v Kyrgistan*, Award, 29 March 2005 and the discussion of the ECT, Art 1(6) ('claims to money and claims to performance pursuant to contract having an economic value and associated with an investment').

[131] *Tokios Tokelės v Ukraine*, Decision on Jurisdiction, 29 April 2004, paras 83 et seq; *PSEG v Turkey*, Decision on Jurisdiction, 4 June 2004, paras 109, 116–20; *Yaung Chi Oo v Myanmar*, Award, 31 March 2003, paras 53–62; *LESI—Dipenta v Algeria*, Award, 10 January 2005, para 24(iii); *Plama v Bulgaria*, Decision on Jurisdiction, 8 February 2005, paras 126–31; *Gas Natural v Argentina*, Decision on Jurisdiction, 17 June 2005, paras 33, 34; *Aguas del Tunari v Bolivia*, Decision on Jurisdiction, 21 October 2005, paras 139–55; *Bayindir v Pakistan*, Decision on Jurisdiction, 14 November 2005, paras 105–10; *Saluka v Czech Republic*, Partial Award, 17 March 2006, paras 183, 202–21; *Inceysa v El Salvador*, Award, 2 August 2006, paras 190–207.

[132] *Salini v Morocco*, Decision on Jurisdiction, 23 July 2003.

This provision [the required compliance with the laws and regulations of the host state] refers to the validity of the investment and not to its definition. More specifically, it seeks to prevent the Bilateral Treaty from protecting investments that should not be protected because they would be illegal.[133]

(d) 'Investment' in Article 25 of the ICSID Convention

The current wide-ranging debate on 'investment' does not arise out of the definitions in investment treaties, but out of the search for the proper understanding of the non-defined term found in the ICSID Convention. As Article 25 of the Convention serves as the jurisdictional gateway for access to ICSID, the understanding of an investment has increasingly been at the forefront of jurisdictional arguments and tribunals have had to set forth their views in decisions on jurisdiction. In disputes arising outside ICSID, the point does not normally arise in the same way.

The method of interpreting 'investment' must follow Article 31 of the Vienna Convention on the Law of Treaties. As regards the 'ordinary meaning' as the starting point, academic commentary and arbitral jurisprudence have focused in the initial phase on economic terminology, but have more recently looked to the understanding of the term in the broad treaty practice of states. The more treaties were concluded based on the same (or similar) definition by an increasing number of states, the more natural it became to rely on this contemporary legal practice, and the more artificial it appeared to turn to an amorphous understanding of the term in traditional economic literature.

This view is supported by a careful review of the *travaux préparatoires* which has established that the ICSID negotiations did not base their approach on any particular traditional (economic or legal) etymology. Indeed, the Report of the Executive Directors, which is frequently cited on this point by arbitral tribunals, summarized the negotiations by way of concluding that the negotiating parties deliberately refrained from adopting any (legal or economic) definition so as to leave room for an understanding by the parties:

No attempt was made to define the term 'investment' given the essential requirement of consent by the parties, and the mechanism through which Contracting States can make known in advance, if they so desire, the classes of disputes which they would or would not consider submitting to the Centre (Article 25(4)).[134]

As is evident from the history of the Convention, several rounds of discussions focused on efforts to delimit the term. However, the majority was not in favour of setting a minimum duration of investment, such as three or five years, or a minimum financial commitment. Also, there is no evidence in the record to the effect that parties or tribunals should turn to the term as employed in economic terminology; instead, what was to determine the content of the term 'investment'

---

[133] At para 46.   [134] 1 ICSID Reports 28, para 27.

was the manner in which the states and the parties to a dispute understood the concept.

(e) Case law

In its initial phase of the evolving case law, *Fedax v Venezuela*[135] had a major influence on the understanding of 'investment'. The Tribunal ruled that Article 25 provided a broad framework of 'investment' and also that the BIT in question (similar to other agreements) gave a very broad meaning to the term, concluding that the promissory notes held by the claimant were covered. In a separate step, the Tribunal went on to examine whether the dispute concerned an 'ordinary commercial transaction' and therefore would not be protected. In this context, relying on academic commentary, the Tribunal turned to the 'criteria approach' and listed five criteria ('the basic features of an investment') which it applied as follows to the promissory notes the claimant had acquired:

The basic features of an investment have been described as involving a certain duration, a certain regularity of profit and return, assumption of risk, a substantial commitment and a significance for the host State's development. The duration of the investment in this case meets the requirement of the Law as to contracts needing to extend beyond the fiscal year in which they are made. The regularity of profit and return is also met by the scheduling of interest payments through a period of several years. The amount of capital committed is also relatively substantial. Risk is also involved as has been explained. And most importantly, there is clearly a significant relationship between the transaction and the development of the host State, as specifically required under the Law for issuing the pertinent financial instrument. It follows that, given the particular facts of the case, the transaction meets the basic features of an investment.[136]

Among the five points in this approach, four (substantial commitment, a certain duration, assumption of risk, and a significance for the host state's development) came to be widely accepted, while regularity of profit was subsequently seldom considered relevant.

The four criteria were clearly set forth in *Salini v Morocco*[137] in 2001 and, thus, out of the legacy of the *Fedax* decision, the approach arose that would become known as the '*Salini* criteria' for investment. The four criteria were now folded into the understanding of an 'investment' within the meaning of Article 25, apparently as cumulative mandatory requirements. The criteria had their origin in the manner in which 'investment' was understood in economic terminology. Thus, economic parlance was transformed into a legal definition which relied on the existence of objective criteria inherent in a project.

An early case in which an ICSID tribunal emphasized that party autonomy finds limits in the general understanding of an 'investment' and denied its jurisdiction

---

[135] *Fedax v Venezuela*, Decision on Jurisdiction, 11 July 1997, paras 21–33.
[136] At para 43.
[137] *Salini v Morocco*, Decision on Jurisdiction, 23 July 2001, para 56.

was *Joy Mining v Egypt*.[138] In that case, the Tribunal found that the dispute essentially concerned the question whether the claimant was entitled to the release of a bank guarantee that depended upon adequate performance of equipment supplied by the claimant. The Tribunal examined whether such a bank guarantee was to be characterized as an 'investment' or as an 'ordinary feature of a sales contract'.[139] It found that 'it would really go far beyond the concept of an investment, even if broadly defined'[140] to characterize the guarantee—a contingent liability—as an investment. As for Article 25 of the ICSID Convention, the Tribunal emphasized 'that there is a limit to the freedom with which the parties may define an investment if they wish to engage the jurisdiction of ICSID tribunals'.[141] The Award notes that in 1999 ICSID refused to register a request for arbitration of a dispute arising out of a supply contract for the sale of goods.[142] The Tribunal recognized that the guarantee was given in the context of a contract with the state, which also provided for a number of services such as engineering, stocking of parts, duties of supervision, training, and technical services.[143] However, the decision does not attach significance to these elements in its analysis of an investment.

In subsequent rulings, a series of arbitral decisions cited and accepted the *Salini* approach which, for a while, appeared to be firmly accepted.[144] A degree of divergence from this line became apparent in *Malaysian Historical Salvors v Malaysia*,[145] when the Tribunal argued that the *Salini* criteria should be considered not so much for their mere existence, but for the intensity of their presence ('their quality').

The first digression from the *Salini* approach came in *Biwater Gauff v Tanzania*.[146] The case involved a water project to which the claimant had contributed more than US$ 1 million, plus personnel and know-how. The respondent's main argument to deny the existence of an investment was that the project was not reasonably profitable. The Tribunal assumed, not surprisingly, that an investment was present.

---

[138] *Joy Mining v Egypt*, Award, 6 August 2004, para 63. See also *Mitchell v Congo*, Decision on Annulment, 1 November 2006, paras 39–40, annulling the underlying Award for failure to state reasons in the context of the qualification of a legal consulting firm as an investment under the ICSID Convention.

[139] At para 44.

[140] At para 45.

[141] At para 49.

[142] At para 52.

[143] At para 55.

[144] *SGS v Pakistan*, Decision on Jurisdiction, 6 August 2003, para 133, footnote 113; *AES Corporation v Argentina*, Decision on Jurisdiction, 26 April 2005, para 88; *Bayindir v Pakistan*, Decision on Jurisdiction, 14 November 2005, paras 130–8; *Jan de Nul v Egypt*, Decision on Jurisdiction, 16 June 2006, paras 90–6; *Saipem v Bangladesh*, Decision on Jurisdiction, 21 March 2007, paras 99–106.

[145] *Malaysian Historical Salvors v Malaysia*, Award, 17 May 2007.

[146] *Biwater Gauff v Tanzania*, Award, 24 July 2008, paras 323 et seq.

The Award's reasoning amounts to a frontal attack on the *Salini* approach, even though the consequences are not drawn in an equally clear manner.[147] The *Biwater Gauff* Tribunal's criticism of the *Salini* Award rests on two points: that the text of Article 25 of the ICSID Convention contains no reference to the *Salini* criteria,[148] and that the negotiating history clearly establishes that the definition of 'investment' was intentionally left open.[149] On this basis, the Tribunal concluded that ICSID tribunals had no authority to impose their own view of appropriate fixed criteria applicable to all cases.

The *Biwater Gauff* Tribunal further elaborated that the *Salini* approach in effect may arbitrarily exclude certain types of project from protection by ICSID, that this may run counter to individual agreements among investors and host states, and that the *Salini* approach is inconsistent with the developing broad consensus reflected in bilateral investment treaties and their definitions of 'investment'. Moreover, the argument was considered untenable that only 'special and privileged arrangements' were envisaged to fall under the Convention, given that the term 'investment' was intentionally left undefined.[150]

In view of these considerations, the *Biwater Gauff* Tribunal opted for 'a more flexible and pragmatic approach', which 'takes into account the features identified in *Salini*, but along with all the circumstances of the case'.[151] It was not so much this conclusion—aiming at a compromise between party autonomy and the *Salini* approach—as the reasoning of the Tribunal which amounted to an attack on the conceptual foundations of the *Salini* approach and its progeny.

A second, harder strike against the *Salini* concept came with the Annulment Decision in *Malaysian Historical Salvors v Malaysia*.[152] This time, the critique of *Salini* was more direct and elaborate, and the *Salini*-based Award was now designated 'a gross error that gave rise to a manifest failure to exercise jurisdiction'. In an unprecedented Annulment Decision, a sizeable line of arbitral jurisprudence was to be discarded as manifestly in error.

In a first step, the Decision on Annulment concluded that, under the BIT, the claimant's contract had to be considered as an 'investment', a point left open in the Award. The Annulment Committee started its discussion of Article 25 with its view of the ordinary meaning of investment, being 'the commitment of money or other assets for the purpose of providing a return', noting that the term 'investment' is

---

[147] At para 317, the Tribunal suggests that its approach followed a series of other Awards; this reading seems to stretch earlier jurisprudence. As early as 2002, one Award had determined that 'the definition was left to be worked out in the subsequent practice of States, thereby preserving its integrity and flexibility and allowing for future progressive development of international law on the topic of investment' (*Mihaly v Sri Lanka*, Award, 15 March 2002, para 33); see also *CSOB v Slovakia*, Decision on Jurisdiction, 24 May 1999, para 90.

[148] At para 312.

[149] At para 313.

[150] At para 315.

[151] At para 316.

[152] *Malaysian Historical Salvors v Malaysia*, Decision on Annulment, 16 April 2009. The Decision came out of a divided ad hoc committee.

unqualified in Article 25.[153] Next, the Committee turned to the *travaux préparatoires* of Article 25 in considerable detail. The result was that the history nowhere points to the *Salini* criteria. The outer limits of the term 'investment' considered in the *travaux* were that simple sales and transient commercial transactions fell outside the scope of the Convention. Within these boundaries, the parties were free to submit whatever dispute they wished to be decided.[154] The *Salini* position is characterized as unduly narrowing the circumstances under which parties could have recourse to ICSID[155] and as running the 'risk of crippling the institution'.[156]

Since the decisions in *Biwater Gauff* and the *Malaysian Historical Salvors* annulment, jurisprudence has not yet settled. As shown below, some tribunals now adhere, in different versions, to the new reasoning based on party autonomy. Others continue to rely on the *Salini* approach, albeit in a modified manner, mostly without discussion of the reasons given in *Biwater Gauff* and the *Malaysia* case.

An award that clearly supports party autonomy in the definition of 'investment' was rendered in *Pantechniki v Albania*.[157] In this case, the claimant had won a bid in an international tender for works on bridges and roads. When a dispute arose concerning these works, the respondent submitted that no 'investment' within the meaning of Article 25 of the ICSID Convention had been made by the claimant.

Similar to the decision in the *Historical Salvors* annulment, the Tribunal considered that the *Salini* criteria were not found in the Convention and that they introduced elements of subjective judgement and led to unpredictability.[158] Cases which at first sight are not covered under Article 25 might nevertheless be submitted to ICSID by the parties for good reasons.[159] The Tribunal left open the circumstances under which a project might not be called an 'investment', given that it was clear that the claimant had made an investment. 'For ICSID arbitral tribunals to reject an express definition desired by two States-party to a treaty seems a step not to be taken without the certainty that the Convention compels it.'[160]

RSM v Grenada[161] considered that the *Salini* criteria ('certain objective elements') may serve only as flexible benchmarks. An agreement to express a commitment to apply for an oil and gas agreement was considered to amount to 'a readily recognizable investment', given that the claimant had agreed to supply resources for carrying out exploration. This was so even though exploration had not yet begun; the Tribunal looked to the envisaged overall project and not only to the pre-exploration phase.[162] Specifically in regard to Article 25 of the ICSID Convention, the Tribunal stated that 'certain objective elements' (which it did not specify) were required for ICSID jurisdiction, but that the parties' agreement on ICSID as the forum for dispute settlement would be viewed as a presumption in favour of the existence of an investment.

---

[153] At para 57. [154] At para 72. [155] At para 62. [156] At para 73.
[157] *Pantechniki v Albania*, Award, 30 July 2009. [158] At para 43. [159] At para 44.
[160] At para 42. [161] *RSM v Grenada*, Award, 13 March 2009. [162] At para 255.

Alpha v Ukraine[163] ruled that the definition in a BIT was entitled, in the context of Article 25, to 'great deference'[164] and should be set aside only in the presence of highly persuasive reasons. The Tribunal had earlier found that an investment is an asset 'for which "an investor of one Contracting Party" caused money or effort to be expended and from which a return or profit is expected in the territory of the other Party'.[165]

Inmaris v Ukraine[166] is based on similar reasoning. The case concerned several contracts for the financing, repair, and operation of a windjammer sail training ship.

Under the wording of the applicable BIT, these contracts fell under the definition of 'investment'. However, the respondent argued that the claimant's activity had not led to a significant contribution to Ukraine's development.

This Tribunal, too, pointed out that the ICSID Convention contains no definition along the lines of the *Salini* criteria. It was 'not persuaded to improve such a mandatory definition through case law where the Contracting States to the ICSID Convention chose not to specify one'.[167] The Tribunal underlined the role of party autonomy:

in most cases—including, in the Tribunal's view, this one—it will be appropriate to defer to the State's parties' articulation in the instrument of consent (e.g. the BIT) of what constitutes an investment. The State parties to a BIT agree to protect certain kinds of economic activity, and when they provide that disputes between investors and States relating to that activity may be resolved through, *inter alia*, ICSID arbitration, that means that they believe that that activity constitutes an 'investment' within the meaning of the ICSID Convention as well. That judgment, by States that are both Parties to the BIT and Contracting States to the ICSID Convention, should be given considerable weight and deference. A tribunal would have to have compelling reasons to disregard such a mutually agreed definition of investment.[168]

In the Tribunal's view, the *Salini* criteria may be useful to identify 'investments' in BIT or contract practice which would define the term so broadly that the provision deviated from any reasonable definition.[169] In the case presented by the claimant, no aberration of this kind was found.

With regard to other tribunals which, in principle, continue to look to the *Salini* approach in spite of the rulings in *Biwater* and *MHS*, most have modified the original concept by way of eliminating the requirement of a contribution to the host state's development. *Société Générale v Dominican Republic*[170] relied on general rules of treaty interpretation and concluded that the protections of the BIT are those listed specifically in the operative part of its text; provisions in the preamble (such as those on the transfer of capital and technology) only spell out the overall objective of the treaty, without influencing the applicable provision on 'investment'. In this view, the issue of the specific contribution of an investment does not

---

[163] *Alpha v Ukraine*, Award, 8 November 2010.   [164] At para 314.
[165] At para. 308.   [166] *Inmaris v Ukraine*, Decision on Jurisdiction, 8 March 2010.
[167] At para 129.   [168] At para 130.   [169] At para 131.
[170] *Société Générale v Dominican Republic*, Award, 19 September 2008.

arise in determining the existence of an 'investment'.[171] Therefore, the transfer of a company for a nominal price of US$2 was not excluded from the sphere of rights covered, given the relevance of other factors of the transaction, such as the market value.[172] Also, the complexity of the organizational structure on the part of a claimant has no bearing on the right to be protected under a BIT as long as no illegality is involved.[173]

According to *Fakes v Turkey*,[174] the requirement of a contribution to the economic development of the host state is not covered by the wording of Article 25. It is to be considered only as an expected consequence of an investment, uncertain at the time of the investment.[175] The Tribunal added that the ordinary meaning of 'investment' also does not pertain to matters of its legality or good faith.[176] The Tribunal ruled that the term 'investment' had an objective meaning with three criteria only (contribution, duration, risk).[177] The Award based its view of 'investment' on its understanding of the ordinary meaning, as also used in the context of the education of a child.[178]

In *Alpha v Ukraine*[179] the investor had agreed, in a number of contracts, to spend more than US$3 million on the renovation and improvement of a hotel and to assist in its promotion. In return, the investor acquired the right to a share of the regular income of the hotel.

The Tribunal considered that loans may qualify as investments,[180] as did the complex business arrangements as a whole. Also, the Award stated that the economic activities took place in the Ukraine, although the flow of the investor's money was mainly outside the Ukraine.[181] Minor errors in the documents submitted by the claimants to Ukraine would not make the investment unlawful.[182]

The conclusion was that the claimant had an investment under the applicable BIT, as the claimant had 'a claim to money' and had acquired an 'asset'. The Tribunal found that an investment is an asset 'for which an "investor of one Contracting Party" caused money or effort to be expended and from which a return or profit is expected in the territory of the other Party'.[183]

With regard to the ICSID Convention, the Tribunal emphasized that a contribution to a host state's development should not be seen as a definitional element of an investment, as its identification by the Tribunal implied second-guessing the assessments that prompted the claimant's investment.[184] More generally, as stated above, the decision of two states underlying the definition of an 'investment' in a BIT was entitled to deference and should only be set aside based on very strong grounds.[185] In addition, the claimant's project also satisfied the *Salini* criteria.[186]

---

[171] At paras 32 et seq.   [172] At para 36.   [173] At para 47.
[174] *Fakes v Turkey*, Award, 10 July, 2010.   [175] At para 111.   [176] At para 112.
[177] Following *Lesi-Dipenta v Algeria*, Award, 10 January 2005, para II.13(iv).
[178] At para 110.
[179] *Alpha v Ukraine*, Award, 8 November 2010.
[180] At para 273.   [181] At para 279.   [182] At para 297.   [183] At para 308.
[184] At para 312.   [185] At para 314.   [186] At paras 317 et seq.

The high-water mark for the autonomous approach, with a requirement of six criteria, came with *Phoenix v Czech Republic*[187] in which commitment, duration, and risk were examined. A contribution to the development of the state was not required, given that it would be impossible to ascertain;[188] instead, a contribution to the economy would suffice and such a contribution should be presumed (rebuttably) in the presence of the three first factors. However, in the Tribunal's view, for an investment to benefit from ICSID, it must also be made in accordance with the laws of the host state and, finally, the assets had to be invested bona fide.[189]

GEA v Ukraine[190] concerned a conversion contract in which the claimant agreed to provide fuel for conversion and also to assist with the delivery of logistics, pay for freight, resolve custom's matters, and supply materials. The applicable BIT implied that only such operations would be covered which by their nature had to be considered as 'investments'. The Tribunal did not elaborate on the 'nature of an investment', but was satisfied that an investment existed under the BIT in the circumstances of the case.[191] Also, immoveable property held by the investor formed an integral part of the contract and fell under the BIT.

As regards Article 25 of the ICSID Convention, the Tribunal inquired whether the claimant had made a contribution (delivery of materials), lasting a sufficient time (three years), and had undertaken a risk (market risk, credit risk, political risk). The Tribunal ruled that these three criteria were met; a link to the development of the state was not discussed. In contrast to the actual investment, the Tribunal denied that a settlement agreement, an ICC Award, or a repayment agreement pertaining to relations between an investor and a host state could be seen as an investment.[192]

The Tribunal reached its conclusions on the view that it did not have to take an independent position on the definition of an 'investment' inasmuch as it assumed that all approaches led to the same conclusion.[193]

A different line of reasoning is set forth in *Abaclat v Argentina*.[194] The Tribunal in this instance drew on the analysis in *Malicorp v Egypt*[195] and distinguished between the contribution made by an investor, reflected in Article 25 of the ICSID Convention, and the rights and values deriving from that contribution, set out in the definition of 'investment' in a BIT; values are only protected if generated by a specific contribution, contributions only if they generate a certain value.[196]

In pursuit of these premises, the *Abaclat* Tribunal concluded that an investment has to fit into the BIT definition and into the scheme of Article 25 of the ICSID Convention.[197] The Tribunal added that the silence of Article 25 on the definition of an investment was intended to leave a certain amount of room for the parties further to develop the concept of investment.[198] Article 25 was meant to encourage

---

[187] *Phoenix v Czech Republic*, Award, 15 April 2009.   [188] At para 85.
[189] At para 114.   [190] *GEA v Ukraine*, Award, 31 March 2011.
[191] At para 150.   [192] At paras 157 et seq.   [193] At para 143.
[194] *Abaclat v Argentina*, Decision on Jurisdiction, 4 August 2011.
[195] *Malicorp v Egypt*, Award, 7 April 2011, paras 109 et seq.
[196] *Abaclat* at para 350.   [197] At para 351.   [198] At para 347.

foreign investments, thereby giving the parties 'the tools to further define what kind of investment they want to promote'. The *Salini* criteria were never included in the ICSID Convention, 'while being controversial and having been applied by tribunals in varying manners and degrees . . . '.[199]

Following its distinction between rights and values, on the one hand, and contributions, on the other hand, the Tribunal considered that the purchase of security entitlements by the claimants qualified as an investment, because these entitlements were covered by BITs and amounted to a contribution.[200] As the funds were listed and protected as values under the BIT, they qualified as an 'investment' even though they were not linked to a particular enterprise or operation; the forum selection clauses had no bearing on this result. Also, the Tribunal ruled that the investments were made in Argentina where the funds were used.[201]

The borderline between an ordinary commercial transaction and an 'investment' was addressed in *Global Trading v Ukraine*.[202] The case had to address the sale of chicken by a US firm to a Ukraine state entity. The claimant pointed to the special circumstances under which the sales agreements were concluded. The Prime Minister of the Ukraine had requested the US Embassy to identify suitable US poultry exporters with the aim of reducing soaring domestic prices for poultry in the Ukraine, and the resulting poultry and purchase import programme had the purpose of promoting the economic development of the Ukraine; the state undertook to honour its contractual commitments.

The Tribunal started out from the premise that Article 25 of the ICSID Convention is of an autonomous nature, separate from the rules of a BIT. The ruling considered that the weight of authority was in favour of this view,[203] limiting the freedom of states to define the cases to be accepted by ICSID: 'Had the drafters of the Convention wished to accord an absolute freedom of that kind, they would have said so, not simply left Art. 25 without a formal definition for the term "investment".'[204] Thus, the Tribunal was not prepared to consider the argument that the lack of a definition indicated the will of the drafters to leave the matter to subsequent practice. As regards the argument by the claimants regarding the circumstances behind the sale programme, the Tribunal gave short shrift to the claimants' position; it considered that each contract was of limited duration on a commercial basis, and ruled, abruptly, that the claim was 'manifestly without merit'.[205]

The distinction between a sale and an investment was also central to the decision in *Romak v Uzbekistan*[206] which concerned deliveries of wheat over a period of five months. The Tribunal, sitting under the rules of UNCITRAL (not ICSID), considered that the word 'investment' in a BIT must have a meaning of its own. In support, the Tribunal (surprisingly) referred to the illustrative, non-exhaustive

---

[199] At para 364.   [200] At para 365.   [201] At para 374.
[202] *Global Trading v Ukraine*, Award, 1 December 2010.
[203] At para 43.
[204] At para 44.
[205] On certainty of law, see *Saba Fakes v Turkey*, Award, 10 July 2010, p 32.
[206] *Romak v Uzbekistan*, Award, 26 November 2009.

definition in the applicable BIT[207] and also to the conclusion of a trade agreement on the same day the BIT was signed.

To identify the autonomous meaning of 'investment', the Award turned to *Black's Law Dictionary*,[208] but subsequently decided to require three criteria; contribution, duration, and risk. In this context, the Tribunal assumed that the term 'investment' should be presumed to have the same meaning in the context of ICSID and outside ICSID.[209] At the same time, the Tribunal assumed that parties are free to define an 'investment' in any way they wish.[210] In the end, the Award examined the three criteria and ruled that the wheat sales satisfied none of them.

(f) Towards a new synthesis?

The evolving jurisprudence moves in meandering directions and does not follow a uniform approach. The main dividing line concerns the question whether the term 'investment' as found (but not defined) in Article 25 of the ICSID Convention must be understood on an autonomous basis ('the self-contained approach'), or whether it must be construed to refer to its understanding by the parties to the dispute in each particular case ('the party-defined approach'). Both approaches have been articulated in different variations. In particular, the *Salini* criteria were sometimes referred to as mandatory, sometimes as illustrative. The party-based approach was sometimes phrased as leaving full freedom to the parties, sometimes as restricted within reasonable boundaries.

The negotiating history of the ICSID Convention speaks in favour of a party-defined approach. From this viewpoint, there is no justification of criteria beyond the terms of the Convention or the BIT. The concrete terms by which an 'investment' is understood are those laid down by the parties, be it in a BIT or in a special agreement between the host state and the investor, and no further interpretative search for the proper meaning of the term is required. In general, the relevant segments found in the definition of BITs, being phrased in a wide manner, have so far not raised any particular problems. Exceptionally, difficulties arise when definitions of the term 'investment' use that same term.

The self-contained approach is confronted with the need to go beyond the understanding of the parties and find support for its interpretation outside the understanding of the drafters of the ICSID Convention. Beyond a non-explained, strictly intuitive conception, tribunals following this line chose to rely on their view of 'investment' either in everyday language—such as the phrase 'investment in children'—or in definitions found in dictionaries—such as *Black's Law Dictionary*.

Inasmuch as tribunals following the self-contained version aim to set out specific manageable criteria to delineate the contours of an 'investment', the task remained for these tribunals to derive, directly or indirectly, such criteria from their preferred definition.

---

[207] At para 188.
[208] '[T]he commitment of funds or other assets with the purpose to receive a profit' (at para 177).
[209] At para 194.   [210] At para 205.

Based on such definitions, or simply on intuition, these tribunals have set forth their criteria for an 'investment'. The number of criteria so established has varied in arbitral practice between three, four, and six. All these tribunals included the following three factors: a contribution by the investor, duration, and risk. Other tribunals have added to these three criteria a contribution to the development of the host state, while regularity of profit was included only occasionally. In *Phoenix v Czech Republic*, the Tribunal ruled that legality of the investment and good faith also must be present to satisfy the conditions for the existence of an investment.

The most controversial criterion has been the need for a contribution to the development of the host state, with support mainly being drawn from the reference in ICSID's preamble to 'the development of the host State'. Other tribunals have focused on such a contribution because, in their view, there is a close nexus between the presence of a contribution and development: the investor's contribution generates, according to this view, the rights and values protected in the definition of the BIT.

All variants of the autonomous understanding of investment find it difficult to support their position by reference to the negotiating history or to the text of Article 25. It has been pointed out that the examination of a contribution to the development of the host state will depend on a subjective assessment; this view is supported by the (uncontroversial) position that each state has the sovereign right to decide which foreign investments will foster the development of its economy and will accordingly admit and regulate such investments. As long as the investment is lawful, under the host state's laws, there is no room for an investment tribunal to deny protections under a BIT with the argument that the host state's development stands in the way.

The criterion of risk has also turned out to be of limited value in the characterization of an 'investment'. Practically every business deal which extends beyond the day of its conclusion will in some way involve circumstances that endanger the certainty that both sides are able and willing to comply with what was agreed. In other words, the existence of a 'duration' for an investment will, in practice, imply the existence of a risk, and the operational significance of 'risk' and 'duration' practically coincides.

Inasmuch as these considerations point to 'commitment of risk' and 'duration' as the ultimate acceptable differentiating criteria embodied in the *Salini* formula, the definition of an investment will boil down to distinguishing an 'investment' from a one-off deal in the form of a trade transaction (or sale), with no component of duration.

The remaining point is to differentiate between 'trade' and 'investment'; more precisely between an 'investment' and a one-time ordinary commercial action consisting of a one-off deal. At this point, the systematic analysis coincides with the *travaux* confirming that a one-time sale will not be considered as an 'investment', without any other definitional requirement. Moreover, the ordinary meaning of 'investment' refers to an economic transaction which is different from a trade transaction, both from the viewpoint of general usage and from the vantage point of international legal terminology. Trade and investment have for a long time been considered to be separate in international practice and in legal terminology.

Practice illustrates that issues other than the distinction of trade may arise in the definition of investment: for instance as regards a bank guarantee, articles bought by a foreign tourist, land acquired by way of inheritance, or the building of a church by a foreign organization or other matters. For such issues, the *Salini* criteria understood as benchmarks may indicate the proper solution. At the same time, the party-based approach may be limited in such cases in light of the 'nature of an investment', in line with the *travaux* of Article 25 of the ICSID Convention.[211] Tribunals may have to decide this matter without recourse to an abstract definition in light of the circumstances of each case.

Inasmuch as the will of the parties will properly be considered as the primary guidepost, deference to this will is appropriate and the 'nature of an investment' will operate as a corrective only in cases of a manifest departure from the ordinary understanding of 'investment' by the parties.

In summary, the current state of the art indicates that neither a strict insistence on objective criteria nor a strictly party-based approach may always be suitable for the general delineation of an investment. Instead, a survey of possible factual settings and existing case law appears to indicate that a combination of the flexible versions of the two approaches will best serve as the proper framework. As a result, an 'investment' within the meaning of Article 25 will exist when the parties to a BIT or an agreement between host state and investor have agreed to treat the project as an 'investment', provided that the use of that term does not stand in obvious contrast to its general understanding.

(g) Investment 'in the territory of the host state'

Some treaties refer to investments 'in the territory' of the host state.[212] At times respondents have argued that this requirement has not been met, since the would-be investor has not established a significant physical presence in the host state. The problem has arisen in cases involving financial instruments, such as loans, and in cases involving pre-shipment inspection services.[213]

In *Fedax v Venezuela* the investor had merely acquired promissory notes issued by the host country. The Tribunal rejected the respondent's argument that the claimant had not invested 'in the territory' of Venezuela:

While it is true that in some kinds of investments . . . such as the acquisition of interests in immovable property, companies and the like, a transfer of funds or value will be made into

---

[211] See *History of the Convention*, vol II, pp 952, 972, statements of A Broches.

[212] The ECT in Art 26(1) refers to investments 'in the Area' of a contracting party. NAFTA, Art 1101(1) speaks of 'investments in the territory'.

[213] In cases involving inspection services, tribunals have found that there had, in fact, been 'an injection of funds into the territory' of the host state and that 'a substantial and non-severable aspect of the overall service was provided in [the host state]' (*SGS v Pakistan*, Decision on Jurisdiction, 6 August 2003, para 136; *SGS v Philippines*, Decision on Jurisdiction, 29 January 2004, paras 99–112).

the territory of the host country, this does not necessarily happen in a number of types of investments, particularly those of a financial nature. It is a standard feature of many international financial transactions that the funds involved are not physically transferred to the territory of the beneficiary, but are put at its disposal elsewhere.[214]

Unlike cases involving the acquisition of financial instruments, tribunals have taken a restrictive approach in cases in which a physical business was in question. In *Canadian Cattlemen v United States*,[215] the Canadian claimants were engaged in the beef and cattle business and brought their claim against the United States because of alleged discrimination against them in the US market. All the investors' investments were on Canadian territory, and the dispute concerned the conditions set by the United States for cross-border trade applicable to the claimants.

The Tribunal ruled that the NAFTA protected only investments made in the territory of another state, that is, foreign investment. The Tribunal carefully reviewed the structure of the NAFTA and various relevant specific provisions; the lack of specific language in the NAFTA regarding the territory of the investment did not stand in the way of its conclusion.

In *Bayview v Mexico*,[216] the claimants, US nationals, operated a business in Texas involving farms and irrigation facilities in Texas. For this business, the claimants depended upon water carried by the Rio Bravo/Rio Grande River which originates in Mexico. When Mexico took action which affected the flow of water, the claimants submitted their case under Chapter Eleven of the NAFTA. The water rights which the claimants held in Texas were granted by the State of Texas, and Mexico was allegedly obliged to provide certain water rights to Texas following a 1969 ruling of a Texas court.

The Tribunal considered that the NAFTA only covers investments made by a national of one party in the territory of another NAFTA party, primarily regulated by the legal order of the foreign state. Here, the investment was made by US citizens on the territory of the United States,[217] and under Mexican law the claimants held no rights to water on Mexican territory.[218] The NAFTA Tribunal therefore found that it had no jurisdiction for the claim.

In *Grand River v United States*,[219] the concept of 'investment' laid down in Article 1139 of the NAFTA was at issue;[220] different from most BITs, the definition relies on the term 'enterprise' and is not worded in an open-ended manner.

The claimants' cigarette business centred on the manufacture of cigarettes in Canada and the export of the products to the United States. Similar to the decisions in *Bayview* and *Cattlemen*, the Tribunal ruled that in such a setting the claimants'

---

[214] *Fedax v Venezuela*, Decision on Jurisdiction, 11 July 1997, para 41. To the same effect: *CSOB v Slovakia*, Decision on Jurisdiction, 24 May 1999, paras 77, 78. See further *LESI & ASTALDI v Algeria*, Decision on Jurisdiction, 12 July 2006, para 73.
[215] *Canadian Cattlemen v United States*, Award on Jurisdiction, 28 January 2008.
[216] *Bayview v Mexico*, Award, 19 June 2007.
[217] At para 113.
[218] At para 116.
[219] *Grand River v United States*, Award, 11 January 2011.
[220] For the text see Appendix, p 355.

business was not considered as an 'investment' in the United States. The claimants also failed in their argument that they had established a business according to the Seneca Nation of Indians Business Code within the territory of the Seneca Nations Reservations in the State of New York, in accordance with traditional custom and practice as determined by the tribal elders.

Article 25(4) of the ICSID Convention gives contracting states the possibility of notifying the Centre of classes of disputes that they would or would not consider submitting to ICSID's jurisdiction. Such notifications are rare[221] and serve information purposes only and neither restrict nor expand ICSID's jurisdiction *ratione materiae*.

The decisive criterion for the foreignness of an investment is the nationality of the investor. An investment is foreign if it is owned or controlled by a foreign investor. There is no additional requirement of foreignness for the investment in terms of the origin of capital.[222]

---

[221] A list of notifications under Art 25(4) is available at <http://www.worldbank.org/icsid/pubs/icsid-8/icsid-8-d.htm>.

[222] *Tradex v Albania*, Award, 29 April 1999, paras 105, 108–11; *Olguín v Paraguay*, Award, 26 July 2001, para 66, footnote 9; *Tokios Tokelès v Ukraine*, Decision on Jurisdiction, 29 April 2004, para 80.

IV

Investment Contracts

1. Types of investment contracts

Large-scale investments may last for decades. They involve interests of the investor, as well as the public interests of the host state. General legislation of the host country may not sufficiently address the nature of the project and the kind of interests concerned. The legal setting of an investment may need to be adjusted to its specifics and complexities by way of an investment contract. The investment contract will also reflect the bargaining power of both sides under the circumstances of the individual project. Therefore, investors and host states often negotiate investment agreements. Not surprisingly, no general pattern applicable to all situations has emerged in practice. Even within individual sectors of the economy, typical agreements have evolved significantly over the past decades.

In practice, especially the legal regime of oil and gas projects by multinational companies has been determined in large part by investment agreements.[1] In the decades before 1945, these agreements (concessions) typically covered large areas of land, transferred title of the oil reserves to the investor, and did not contain an obligation of the investor to explore or produce oil. Under these agreements the host country would receive a bonus for the concession as such and royalties for barrels actually produced.

A second generation of agreements emerged in the 1960s and 1970s. These reflected the new power of oil-producing countries, their desire to control their resources,[2] and their aspiration to develop the necessary skills and technologies within their own borders. Often, state-owned companies were set up for the purpose of concluding and supervising agreements with foreign investors.[3] Areas with potential reserves were more restricted and closely defined, and the title to oil

---

[1] See R D Bishop, 'International Arbitration of Petroleum Disputes: The Development of a *Lex Petrolea?*' (1998) 23 *Yearbook of Commercial Arbitration* 1131; E Smith, J Dzienkowski, O Anderson, G Conine, J Lowe, and B Kramer, *International Petroleum Transactions* (2003); D Johnston, *International Petroleum Fiscal Systems and Production Sharing Contracts* (1994); A El-Kosheri and T Riad, 'The Law Governing New Generation of Petroleum Agreements: Changes in the Arbitral Process' (1986) 1 *ICSID Review-FILJ* 257; A Alkholy, 'Arbitration in Energy Disputes' (2000) 2 *J Arab Arbitration* 46; A El-Kosheri, 'Le Régime juridique créé par les accords de participation dans le domaine pétrolier' (1975) 147 *Collected Courses of the Hague Academy of International Law* 219.

[2] On the concept of 'permanent sovereignty over national resources' and UN GA Res Nos 1803 (14 December 1962) and 3281 (12 December 1974), see p 4.

[3] See pp 219 et seq.

and gas remained with the host country. The risks inherent in a failure to find suitable oil or gas were shifted to the foreign investor who was, however, allowed to recover exploration costs in cases where commercially usable reserves were found. Once oil or gas was produced, the product was divided between the two parties to the investment agreement under a negotiated formula, often subject to a gradual decrease of the rights of the investor. These arrangements were set out in so-called production-sharing or profit-sharing agreements. Increasingly, host countries tended to restrict the role of the foreign investor to the provision of technical expertise and services. Remarkably, however, exploration remained in the hands of the investor at its own risk. While this type of agreement seems preferable at first sight for the host country, especially if non-exporting, it also places the burden of financing on the host country and therefore has not been relied upon by all countries.

Beyond the area of energy exploration and production, projects creating utilities and infrastructure blossomed, especially in the early 1990s, in the era of privatization. Typical arrangements often relied on the concept of 'build, operate, and own' (BOO), placing all major benefits and risks on the investor. Sometimes, the entire project was to be transferred to the host country after a certain period (build, operate, transfer (BOT)). Joint venture arrangements with companies of the host state have their own advantages for the foreign investor, but they have sometimes also led to disappointments. Projects for construction alone usually follow a special pattern.[4]

Beyond the allocation of rights, tasks, risks, and responsibilities, investment contracts had to lay down the ground rules on which the parties agreed. These rules included, in particular, the law applicable to the project and the choice of a forum for dispute resolution. Specific provisions were often included concerning *force majeure*, good faith, and changed circumstances. From a legal perspective, the most complex and difficult questions often concerned the inclusion of clauses regulating the conduct of the parties in the event of political changes in the host country and in the event of changes in the economic equilibrium between the host state and the investor.

Occasionally, tribunals have had to define the term 'investment agreement'. In *Duke Energy v Ecuador*[5] the Tribunal very narrowly held that such an agreement must be entered into by the host state and the foreign investor, and not by a state-owned entity or a local company established by the investor.[6] In *Burlington v Ecuador*,[7] the Tribunal had to answer the question whether an agreement between the host state and a subsidiary of the claimant incorporated in a third state amounted to an 'investment agreement' between the host state and the claimant. The case concerned tax matters covered by the US-Ecuador BIT only if they arose under an 'investment agreement' between the host state and a national of the other

---

[4] See in general M Sornarajah, *The Settlement of Foreign Investment Disputes* (2000) 31–46.
[5] *Duke Energy v Ecuador*, Award, 18 August 2008.
[6] At paras 182 et seq.
[7] *Burlington v Ecuador*, Award, 2 June 2010.

party. In a split decision, following earlier jurisprudence, the Tribunal found that such an agreement was not an 'investment agreement' within the meaning of the US-Ecuador BIT.[8]

2. Applicable law

For both the state and the investor, the determination of the law applicable to the contract and the agreement on dispute resolution are often considered the most sensitive legal issues.[9] The host state will view both areas from the vantage point of protecting its national sovereignty. The investor's priority will be the choice of a legal order that provides a stable and predictable legal environment and of a forum for dispute resolution that will preclude bias or political influence against the investor.

Depending upon the bargaining power and the negotiating skill of the parties, a number of possible choices have emerged for the applicable law.[10] These range from a mere reference to the law of the host state to an exclusive choice of the rules of international law. Between these extremes, general principles of law, usage in the industry, and, more seldom, rules of natural justice or equity have been chosen. Often, a combination of national law and international rules as applicable law has been negotiated as a compromise.

The matter will also be determined by the position of international law in the domestic order of the host state. If international law is applicable, on the basis of the constitution of the host state or of legislative measures, the investor will obviously find it less difficult to accept a reference to domestic law alone. However, such rules in a constitution or legislative provisions are subject to unilateral change on the part of the host country without a right to object on the part of the investor.

Choice of law clauses may be in need of interpretation in various ways. The meaning of clauses referring to general principles of law or to the usage of trade may not be self-evident in light of the circumstances of each case. The reference to the rules or principles of international law itself may raise issues of interpretation, as will be seen in the context of the understanding of Article 42 of the Convention on the Settlement of Investment Disputes between States and Nationals of Other States (ICSID Convention).[11]

Any reference in a choice of law clause to two different legal orders or principles will, in the event of conflict or diversity between them, pose the question of the hierarchy or selection of the legal order for the individual issue concerned. A simple

---

[8] At para 234.

[9] See pp 288 et seq.

[10] The decision in *Azpetrol v Azerbaijan*, Award, 8 September 2009, paras 49–66, deals more with English contract law—being the law chosen by the parties—than with international rules. Investment tribunals do not hesitate to apply rules of a domestic legal order (of the host state or of third parties), even though they sit as international tribunals and may not have previously acquired special expertise in the domestic law to be applied.

[11] See pp 288–9.

reference to domestic law will, in itself, raise the question whether an international tribunal would, in view of its own legal basis and in light of the rules of international law applicable to aliens and foreign companies, invariably consider international rules irrelevant.[12]

The Permanent Court of International Justice, in the *Serbian Loans* case, pointed to the requirement that every contract must have a basis in a national legal order.[13] In light of that statement, tribunals have seen no reason to address the role of general rules of international law governing aliens.[14]

3. Stabilization clauses

Investment agreements are negotiated by the investor and the host state to allow for special rules between the two parties, separate from the general legislation of the host state. In principle, it will be the intention of both sides to create a legal framework that will last from the beginning to the end of their common project.

For the investor, a key concern will invariably be to safeguard the stability of the agreement. Applicable treaties between the host state and the investor's home state may provide for rules desiged to ensure or to promote stable contractual relations for their citizens—such as umbrella clauses—or a provision on fair and equitable treatment. However, such rules will not always be in place,[15] or they may not be as specific as desired by the investor. Against this background, an ongoing practice of including a stabilization clause in state-investor agreements has developed.[16] No single specific wording of such clauses has emerged and different types, with different functions and scope, have been drafted. In consequence, the significance and interpretation of each such clause will have to be assessed in light of its specific wording.

It is not surprising that investors have sought to negotiate stabilization clauses in particular with those states whose political and legal regime has in the past been subject to frequent changes or volatility. Governments of such states may have reason to agree to such clauses because they wish to attract foreign investment and because stability serves as an instrument to facilitate this goal.[17] For the host

---

[12] See p 288–93.

[13] PCIJ, Judgment No 14, Series A, No 20, 41: 'Any contract which is not a contract between States in their capacity as subjects of international law is based on the municipal law of some country.'

[14] See *Delagoa Bay Claim (UK v Portugal)*, Award, 24 July 1875, 28 RIAA 157; *Lena Goldfields v Soviet Union* (1930), (1950) 36 *Cornell LQ* 31, 42; *Aramco v Saudi Arabia* (1958) 27 ILR (1963) 117 and, on the relationship of international law with domestic law, *Ruler of Qatar v International Marine Oil Company* (1953) 20 ILR 534.

[15] For recent practice, see P Cameron, *International Energy Investment Law: The Pursuit of Stability* (2010) 233 et seq.

[16] *Amoco International Finance v Iran*, 15 Iran–US CTR 189, 239 (1987), observed that the term 'stabilization clause' normally refers to 'contract language which freezes the provisions of a national system of law chosen as the law of the contract as to the date of the contract in order to prevent the application to the contract of any future alterations of this system'.

[17] See also A Faruque, 'Validity and Efficiency of Stabilization Clauses: Legal Protection vs Fundamental Value' (2006) 23 *J Int'l Arbitration* 317, 335.

country, a stabilization clause may be more attractive than a treaty, which requires lengthy international negotiations and ratification processes. Some states have introduced specific legislation which authorizes the executive branch to conclude a special contract stabilizing the actual agreement ('Legal Stability Agreement' (LSA)).[18]

A stabilization clause in the strongest sense would require the host state not to alter its general legal regime for the area addressed in the clause. Typically, however, the investor's concern will be limited to the stability of the individual agreement it has concluded with the host state. Thus, stabilization in the form of an intangibility clause[19] will provide that changes in the law of the host state will not apply to the investment contract. It is not uncommon for the contract to limit the scope of the stabilization clause to specific areas such as tax law.[20] Another version consists of so-called freezing clauses. These will incorporate into the agreement, as the applicable law, the law of the host state as it stands at a specified time, such as the law valid when the contract enters into force.[21]

A doctrinal issue that arises for stabilization clauses in general is whether they will bind the host state or whether the sovereignty of the state will operate to allow a change of the stabilization clause itself. No international tribunal has ruled that a stabilization clause is invalid or will have no legal effect.

In *AGIP v Congo*,[22] the Tribunal had to deal with a stabilization clause that ensured that changes in domestic law by the Congo would not affect certain parts of the contract (pertaining to the nature of the protected company) with AGIP. When, later on, the Congo nationalized the company, the Tribunal examined the compatibility of the nationalization decree with the stabilization clause from the viewpoint of international law (to which the contract explicitly referred). The Tribunal ruled:

These stabilization clauses, which were freely entered into by the Government, do not affect the principle of its legislative and regulatory sovereignty since it retains both with respect to those, whether nationals of foreigners, with whom the Government has not entered into such undertakings, and that, in the present case, they are limited to rendering the modifications to the legislative regulatory provisions provided for the Agreement, unopposable to the other contracting party.

... It suffices to concentrate the examination of the compatibility of the nationalization with international law on the stabilization clauses. It is indeed in connection with these clauses that the principles of international law are used to complete the rules of Congolese law. The reference made to international law suffices to demonstrate the nationalization

---

[18] In *Duke Energy v Peru*, Award, 18 August 2008, the Tribunal had to interpret such an LSA; see also Cameron, n 15, 246 et seq on LSAs.

[19] Sometimes also called an inviolability clause; for examples see Cameron, n 15, 74.

[20] For examples, see Cameron, n 15, 70.

[21] In *Duke Energy v Peru*, Award, 18 August 2008, the Tribunal found that not only the text but also its interpretation was frozen.

[22] *AGIP v Congo*, Award, 30 November 1979.

carried out in the present case. It follows that the Government is obliged to compensate AGIP for the damage suffered by it as a result of the nationalization . . .[23]

In *LETCO v Liberia*,[24] the Tribunal explained:

This clause, commonly referred to as a 'Stabilization Clause', is commonly found in long-term development contracts and . . . is meant to avoid the arbitrary actions of the contracting government. This clause must be respected, especially in this type of agreement. Otherwise, the contracting State may easily avoid its contractual obligations by legislation.[25]

In *Aminoil v Kuwait*,[26] the Tribunal concluded that a typical stabilization clause should not be presumed to imply that a state lost the right to expropriate a contract running for a period of 60 years. The Tribunal came to the conclusion that the main effect of a stabilization clause would lie in the calculation of the amount of compensation, provoking a sharp dissent from Arbitrator Fitzmaurice.

The ruling in *Amoco International Finance v Iran*[27] follows the *Aminoil* pattern to a considerable extent, but with a different view on this point in the Concurring Opinion of Judge Brower. The majority in the *Amoco* case also took the view that a typical stabilization clause in a contract should not be understood as a renunciation on the part of the host state of its right to expropriate a concession.

None of the cases discussed here had to apply an umbrella clause in an investment treaty, which is designed to protect an investor against violation of a contractual arrangement.

The premise of this jurisprudence (mostly not articulated) is the recognition that a state has the power to bind itself, from the viewpoint of an international tribunal, and that respect for the principle *pacta sunt servanda* as well as the principle of good faith will stand in the way of an attempt to ignore the contractual bond. Tribunals have differed in their views whether a violation of the stabilization clause will require specific performance of the contract[28] or whether the aggrieved party has a right to be compensated for its loss.[29]

Special questions will arise when a stabilization clause is included in a contract between an entity created by the state, such as a national company, and a foreign investor. Here, it will be relevant whether the national company has been given the power to bind the state or whether the foreign investor may rely on such a commitment on other grounds such as good faith; tribunals have not yet clarified the point.

In the oil and gas industry, it is not infrequent that stabilization is achieved by means other than a stabilization clause in the conventional sense. One technique here is that investment agreements provide that the national oil company, being the

[23] At paras 86–8.

[24] *LETCO v Liberia*, Award, 31 March 1989.

[25] 2 ICSID Reports 368. See also *MINE v Guinea*, Decision on Annulment, 22 December 1989, paras 6.33, 6.36; *CMS v Argentina*, Award, 12 May 2005, para 151.

[26] *Aminoil v Kuwait*, Award, 24 March 1982.

[27] *Amoco International Finance v Iran*, Award, 14 July 1987.

[28] *TOPCO v Libya*, Award, 19 January 1977.

[29] *LIAMCO v Libya*, Award, 12 April 1977, with an explicit recognition of *pacta sunt servanda*.

investor's contractual partner, will pay the tax for the foreign investor and that this will also be so in the event of a future change of domestic tax law.

4. Renegotiation/adaptation

As an alternative to preserving the sanctity and stability of a contract, the more recent trend has been to agree on a renegotiation clause. Such a clause may focus on economic equilibrium rather than on legal stability.[30] The following clause was, for instance, adopted in 1994 in the Model Exploration and Production Sharing Agreement of the Sheikdom of Qatar:

Art. 34.12 Equilibrium of the Agreement

Whereas the financial position of the Contractor has been based, under the Agreement, on the laws and regulations in force at the Effective Date, it is agreed that, if any future law, decree or regulation affects Contractor's financial position, and in particular if the customs duties exceed... percent during the term of the Agreement, both parties shall enter into negotiations, in good faith, in order to reach an equitable solution that maintains the economic equilibrium of this Agreement. Failing to reach agreement on such equitable solution, the matter may be referred by either Party to arbitration pursuant to Article 31.[31]

Difficulties will arise if the circumstances triggering the right to renegotiate, usually on the part of the investor, are not described in sufficient detail in the investment contract. Beyond the triggering clause, the parties have various choices for structuring the actual process of appropriate renegotiation. Adaptation of a contract based on automatically applicable criteria is rarely foreseen. Typically, renegotiation clauses rely on criteria that leave room for negotiation. Sometimes no criteria for the process of renegotiation are included.

Obviously, renegotiation clauses provide for more flexibility than a stabilization clause, but their practicability and usefulness are questionable. The concept of an 'economic equilibrium' remains to be defined in legal terms. Moreover, a duty to

---

[30] See also R Geiger, 'Unilateral Change of Economic Developments Agreements' (1974) 23 *ICLQ* 73; M Sornarajah, 'Supremacy of the Renegotiations Clause in International Contracts' (1988) 5 *J Int'l Arb* 113; W Peter, *Arbitration and Renegotiation of International Investment Agreements* (1995) 240; A Kolo and T Wälde, 'Renegotiation and Contract Adaptation in International Investment Projects' (2000) 1 *J World Investment & Trade* 5, 7; T Waelde and G Ndi, ' "Stabilizing International Investment Commitments": International Law versus Contract Integration' (1996) 31 *Texas Int'l LJ* 228; J Salacuse, 'Renegotiating International Business Transactions: The Continuing Struggle of Life Against Form' (2001) 35 *Int'l Lawyer* 1507, 1519; J Gotanda, ' "International Commercial Arbitration: Renegotiation and Adaptation Clauses in Investment Contracts", Revisited' (2003) 36 *Vanderbilt J Transn'l L* 1461; K Berger, 'Renegotiation and Adaptation in International Investment Contracts: The Role of Contracts Drafters and Arbitrators' (2003) 36 *Vanderbilt J Transn'l L* 1347, 1361; S Kröll, 'The Renegotiation and Adaptation in Investment Contracts' in N Horn, *Arbitrating Foreign Investment Disputes* (2004).

[31] The clause is reprinted in P Bernardini, 'The Renegotiation of Investment Contracts' (1998) 13 *ICSID Review-FILJ* 411, 416; for similar clauses and their significance, see also K Berger, 'Renegotiation and Adaptation of International Investment Contracts: The Role of Contract Drafters and Arbitrators' (2003) 36 *Vanderbilt J Transn'l L* 1347.

renegotiate relies on the continued goodwill of both parties during a dispute. Therefore, the clause may not prove helpful in the context of a dispute. Thus, it is far from clear whether a duty to renegotiate will serve the practical needs of a long-term investment. If the clause should fail to produce useful results, the search for effective mechanisms for stabilization will continue.

V

Admission and Establishment

1. The move towards economic liberalism

In the late 1980s there was a growing international consensus that economic liberalism promised more growth and innovation than economic protectionism within closed national or regional borders. A now famous paper by J Williamson provided a list of conditions for successful economic growth, which eventually came to be known as the 'Washington Consensus'.[1] The 1980s were considered, from a development perspective, as the 'lost decade' in Latin America and Africa, which led to more poverty, economic stagnation, and fiscal disorder, mainly due to inward-looking, non-competitive economic policies and a lack of domestic reforms. The comparison of empirical economic data, more than ideological factors, between countries with growth (mainly in Asia) and stagnant regions pointed to economic liberalization and domestic reforms as the main driving forces of growth. The lack of support for Third World countries by the Soviet Union and its eventual collapse lent further support to this movement. Ultimately, the retreat of 'bureaucrats in business' and the move towards privatization were prompted in developing countries by the reality of insufficient services for the population, by fiscal disorder, and by the compelling need for foreign capital and technology.

The Washington Consensus has had a strong influence on international economic policies, even though it has also become clear that economic reforms need to be complemented by social and environmental policies. In current practice, the Washington Consensus is reinforced by acute competition among capital-importing states for foreign investment. Nevertheless, national policies are far from uniform in this area, and even liberal countries, such as the United States, have by no means totally opened up their economies. More recently, the global trends in national policy developments do not point in one direction. Whereas most states (mainly in Asia and Africa) have, since 2000, introduced measures with the aim of liberalizing the regime of foreign investment, others (mainly in Latin America) have adopted new regulations and restrictions.[2]

---

[1] Originally the 'Consensus' was nothing more than a research paper by John Williamson at the Washington-based Peterson Institute for International Economics; for its history, see J Williamson, 'From Reform Agenda to Damaged Brand Name—A Short History of the Washington Consensus and Suggestions for What to do Next' (2003) *Finance & Development* 10.
[2] For details, see UNCTAD, *World Investment Report* (2011) 94.

From the perspective of general international law, states are in no way compelled to admit foreign investment.[3] The economic dimension of territorial sovereignty continues to confer the right on each government to decide whether to close the national economy to foreign investors or whether to open it up, fully or with respect to certain sectors. This includes the right to determine the modalities for admission and establishment of foreign investors. Among the national considerations speaking against full liberalization are the concerns of weak domestic industries being 'crowded out', and the social effects of rapid economic change. In addition, there are moral, health, and environmental concerns and a growing agenda of national security.[4] Also, views differ as to whether it is useful to conclude treaties providing for guarantees towards liberalization or whether the flexibility inherent in domestic legislation subject to continuous review may provide more benefits for the national economy of the host state. In any event, governments negotiating investment treaties must be aware that binding commitments on admission and establishment create lasting obligations, even when economic circumstances have changed.

According to general usage, the right of 'admission' of foreign investment has been distinguished from the right of 'establishment'.[5] P Juillard uses the terms 'freedom of investment' and 'freedom of establishment'.[6] Generally speaking, the right of 'admission' concerns the right of entry of the investment in principle, whereas the right of 'establishment' pertains to the conditions under which the investor is allowed to carry out its business during the period of the investment. For an investor with a short-term business, the right of 'establishment' will be of less importance than for one who needs to rely on a longer business presence in the host state.

Typical issues of admission concern the definition of relevant economic sectors and geographic regions, the requirement of registration or of a licence, and the legal structure of an admissible investment (eg the type and seat of corporation, joint venture, restrictions of ownership). In contrast, the right of establishment is concerned with issues such as expansion of the investment, payment of taxes, or transfer of funds. An overlap may exist in important areas such as capital or performance requirements. The distinction between 'admission' and 'establishment' may be important for treaties that allow for the right of 'admission' but contain no regulation concerning 'establishment'.

2. Treaty models of admission

The policy decision of the host state whether or not to grant a right of admission is fundamental for all parties to investment treaties. On this point, there are basic

---

[3] See D Carreau and P Juillard, *Droit international économique* (2003) 361.

[4] See also GATS, Art XIV; and GATT, Art XX.

[5] I Shihata, 'Recent Trends Relating to Entry of Foreign Direct Investment' (1994) 9 *ICSID Review-FILJ* 47.

[6] P Juillard, 'Freedom of Establishment, Freedom of Capital Movements, and Freedom of Investment' (2000) 15 *ICSID Review-FILJ* 322.

differences in the regulatory approach of existing investment treaties.[7] Treaties concluded by European countries do not grant a right of admission but limit themselves to standards and guarantees for those investments which the host state has unilaterally decided to admit. A typical clause of this kind reads: 'Each Contracting State shall in its territory promote as far as possible investments by investors of the other Contracting State and admit such investments in accordance with its legislation.'[8]

An admission clause of this type means that the host state is under no obligation to revise its domestic laws of admission after ratification of the bilateral investment treaty (BIT). A possible consequence may be that nationals of the other party receive treatment less favourable under these laws than nationals of third states. Also, the host state retains the freedom to revise its laws on admission after the investment treaty has entered into force.

The United States, followed by Canada and Japan, have pursued a different admission policy than European states in negotiating investment treaties. They have negotiated treaty provisions which, to some extent, grant market access. Under these provisions, a right of admission, albeit limited in scope, is typically based on a national treatment clause. For instance, the 2004 and 2012 US Model BITs provide in their respective Articles 3 section 1: 'Each Party shall accord to investors of the other Party treatment no less favorable than that it accords, in like circumstances, to its own investors with respect to the establishment, acquisition, expansion, management, conduct, operation, and sale or other disposition of investments in its territory.'

A rule on exceptions is laid down in Article 14 section 2 of the US Model BITs: 'Articles 3 [National Treatment], 4 [Most-Favoured-Nation Treatment], 8 [Performance Requirements], and 9 [Senior Management and Boards of Directors] do not apply to any measure that a Party adopts or maintains with respect to sectors, subsectors, or activities, as set out in its Schedule to Annex II.'

But in practice no state will grant unlimited access to foreign investments. Two approaches are available in principle for treaties containing a right of admission. One approach is to identify all sectors that are open to the investors of the other party (positive list). The other is to identify all sectors that are closed (negative list). Exceptions may apply both to certain categories of investors and of investments. Some treaties provide that exceptions to be made in the future—that is, after the treaty's entry into force—must not have the effect of placing the nationals of the other state in a less favourable position. However, other treaties specifically allow the adoption of measures that are more restrictive than those existing at the time of the signature of the treaty.

The most common technique to grant a right of admission is to rely on the standard of national treatment and on a most-favoured-nation clause. The principle

---

[7] See T Pollan, *Legal Framework for the Admission of FDI* (2006).

[8] German Model Treaty of 2005, Art 2(1). On the clause 'accepted in accordance with the respective laws and regulations of either Contracting State', see *Fraport v Philippines*, Award, 16 August 2007, para 335 (subsequently annulled on different grounds).

of national treatment is simply extended to admission, combined with positive or negative lists, and with the most-favoured-nation rule.

In the context of the traditional European treaties, the application of the most-favoured-nation rule will raise the question whether its operation extends to issues of admission. This will depend primarily on the wording of the specific most-favoured-nation rule of each treaty. Some treaties specifically address the point by way of extending the most-favoured-nation rule to questions of admission.[9] Concerning the right of establishment, it would seem that the principles of national treatment and of the most-favoured-nation rules, as contained in each treaty, will apply, regardless of the existence of a right of admission, as long as the investment has been properly made.

Treaties may refer to admission under the domestic laws of the host state, which may provide requirements for admission. For treaties with no right of admission for the foreign investor, the local laws of the host state will apply, and schemes of notification, registration, and various types of approval mechanisms, including case-by-case screening, may have to be observed in accordance with the specific laws of each host state. If the treaty provides for a right of admission and the domestic rules are inconsistent with this right, an international tribunal will decide on the basis of the international obligation of the host state. Tribunals have had to address the consequences of non-compliance with admission regulations and the right of the investor to invoke a dispute settlement provision.[10]

3. Performance requirements

Obligations imposed by the host state on the investor to conduct its business in a prescribed manner ('performance requirements') have mainly been prohibited in BITs concluded by the United States and Canada. These clauses are directed against practices—such as the compulsion to use local materials, the duty to export a certain amount of products, and the obligation to hire local personnel—which may be imposed on foreign investors. These practices are deemed undesirable, since they are inconsistent with the principle of liberal markets. A typical older clause to this effect is found in the treaty between the United States and Cameroon:

Neither Party shall impose performance requirements as a condition of establishment, expansion or maintenance of investments owned by nationals or companies of the other Party, which require or enforce commitments to export goods produced, or which specify that goods or services must be purchased locally, or which impose any other similar requirements.[11]

---

[9] See Treaty between Japan and Bangladesh Concerning the Promotion and Protection of Investment concluded on 10 November 1998, Art 2(2).

[10] See pp 92–7.

[11] US-Cameroon BIT (1986), Art II section 6.

The 2004 and 2012 US Model BITs address the issue in more detail:

Neither Party may, in connection with the establishment, acquisition, expansion, management, conduct, operation, or sale or other disposition of an investment of an investor of a Party or of a non-Party in its territory, impose or enforce any requirement or enforce any commitment or undertaking: (a) to export a given level or percentage of goods or services; (b) to achieve a given level or percentage of domestic content; (c) to purchase, use, or accord a preference to goods produced in its territory, or to purchase goods from persons in its territory; (d) to relate in any way the volume or value of imports to the volume or value of exports or to the amount of foreign exchange inflows associated with such investment; (e) to restrict sales of goods or services in its territory that such investment produces or supplies by relating such sales in any way to the volume or value of its exports or foreign exchange earnings; (f) to transfer a particular technology, a production process, or other proprietary knowledge to a person in its territory; or (g) to supply exclusively from the territory of the Party the goods that such investment produces or the services that it supplies to a specific regional market or to the world market....[12]

More recently, variations of the clause have appeared and more states have included provisions on performance requirements. Also, Article 1106 of the North American Free Trade Agreement (NAFTA) contains a list of prohibited performance requirements similar to the US Model BITs.[13]

Despite the distinction between trade and investment, performance requirements were also addressed in the context of the World Trade Organization (WTO) in 1994 in the framework of the Agreement on Trade Related Investment Measures (TRIMs) which contains, in its Annex, an illustrative list of prohibited performance requirements:

1. TRIMs that are inconsistent with the obligation of national treatment... include those... which require: (a) the purchase or use by an enterprise of products of domestic

---

[12] See the 2004 and 2012 US Model BITs, Art 8.
[13] NAFTA, Art 1106 reads:

1. No Party may impose or enforce any of the following requirements, or enforce any commitment or undertaking, in connection with the establishment, acquisition, expansion, management, conduct or operation of an investment of an investor of a Party or of a non-Party in its territory: (a) to export a given level or percentage of goods or services; (b) to achieve a given level or percentage of domestic content; (c) to purchase, use or accord a preference to goods produced or services provided in its territory, or to purchase goods or services from persons in its territory; (d) to relate in any way the volume or value of imports to the volume or value of exports or to the amount of foreign exchange inflows associated with such investment; (e) to restrict sales of goods or services in its territory that such investment produces or provides by relating such sales in any way to the volume or value of its exports or foreign exchange earnings; (f) to transfer technology, a production process or other proprietary knowledge to a person in its territory, except when the requirement is imposed or the commitment or undertaking is enforced by a court, administrative tribunal or competition authority to remedy an alleged violation of competition laws or to act in a manner not inconsistent with other provisions of this Agreement; or (g) to act as the exclusive supplier of the goods it produces or services it provides to a specific region or world market....

On the understanding of these provisions, see *Merrill & Ring v Canada*, Award, 31 March 2010, paras 111 et seq (requirement of advertisement for the export of logs not a restriction on the export of logs, because of a lack of sufficient connection with export itself).

origin or from any domestic source, whether specified in terms of particular products, in terms of volume or value of products, or in terms of a proportion of volume or value of its local production; or (b) that an enterprise's purchases or use of imported products be limited to an amount related to the volume or value of local products that it exports.

2. TRIMs that are inconsistent with the obligation of general elimination of quantitative restrictions . . . include those which . . . restrict: (a) the importation by an enterprise of products used in or related to its local production, generally or to an amount related to the volume or value of local production that it exports; (b) the importation by an enterprise of products used in or related to its local production by restricting its access to foreign exchange to an amount related to the foreign exchange inflows attributable to the enterprise; or (c) the exportation or sale for export by an enterprise of products, whether specified in terms of particular products, in terms of volume or value of products, or in terms of a proportion of volume or value of its local production.

Issues of competing jurisdiction and of consistency would arise if such measures were to be challenged both before the WTO dispute settlement system and before a tribunal with its jurisdictional basis in a BIT.[14] Furthermore, the admissibility of performance requirements applying only to foreign investors remains to be clarified under the standard of national treatment.

With regard to the hiring and presence of non-local personnel to manage a foreign investment in the host country, a few treaties contain language to the effect that applications by such persons will receive 'sympathetic consideration'[15] or that quotas or numerical restrictions will not be allowed in that context.[16] As regards appointment of top personnel by the investor, some treaties recognize this freedom, subject, however, to the laws of the host state.[17]

4. Non-compliance by investor with host state law and international public policy

Many investment treaties provide that they cover investments made 'in accordance with the laws' of the host state. For example, Article 1(1) of the German-Philippines BIT reads: 'the term "investment" shall mean any kind of asset accepted in accordance with the respective laws and regulations of either Contracting State . . . '

Sometimes, the requirement of compliance of the investment with domestic laws is part of the definition of 'investment'; sometimes it is found in other parts of the treaty.[18] In *Plama v Bulgaria*, the Tribunal pointed to an obligation of the investor

---

[14] An investor would presumably have a right to invoke the TRIMs Agreement before an investment tribunal if both states parties concerned are members of the WTO. This would be beyond doubt if a BIT refers to other existing international obligations that could be invoked by the investor.

[15] See Protocol to the Treaty between Germany and Bosnia & Herzegovina concluded on 18 October 2001, para 3(c). See also on this point UNCTAD, *Bilateral Investment Treaties 1995–2005: Trends in Investment Rulemaking*, Draft (2006) 129 et seq.

[16] See Art VII(1)(b) of the Treaty between the United States and Nicaragua concerning the Encouragement and Reciprocal Protection of Investments, signed on 1 July 1995.

[17] See Treaty between Australia and Egypt on the Promotion and Protection of Investments of 3 May 2001, Art 5.

[18] See U Kriebaum, 'Illegal Investments' (2010) *Austrian Yearbook on Int'l Arbitration* 307; C Knahr, 'Investments "in accordance with host state law"' (2007) 5 *Transnational Dispute Management*.

to act in good faith, especially for the purposes of state approval of the investment.[19]

The rules on admission may create obligations for the host state. At the same time, they may limit the right of the investor to invoke the dispute settlement clause of a treaty in cases where the investor ignores the rules on admission. Whenever a clause 'in accordance with the laws of the host state' is contained in a treaty, it may be understood to imply that investments made in violation of national laws are not covered by the treaty. Therefore, the words 'in accordance with the laws' relate not just to the laws on admission and establishment but also to other rules of the domestic legal order, including those relating to corruption. As a result, investments made in violation of domestic rules may be outside the substantive guarantees contained in the relevant agreement, depending upon the nature and gravity of the violation.[20]

In *Plama v Bulgaria*,[21] the claimant had misrepresented his role as investor to the host state in a privatization agreement, leading the government to believe that the claimant had substantial assets; in reality, the claimant had very limited resources and managerial capacity.[22] The Tribunal found that the claimant's conduct amounted to deliberate concealment and to fraud. While the Energy Charter Treaty (ECT), being the applicable treaty, does not contain a clause requiring conformity with the laws of the host state, the Tribunal pointed to the rule of law as a fundamental aim of the ECT and to the principle of good faith emanating from Bulgarian law and international law. On this basis, the Tribunal denied the claimant the right to invoke the substantive rights of the ECT.[23]

Alasdair Ross Anderson v Costa Rica[24] concerned the claimants' deposits in Costa Rica in a fund run as a criminal Ponzi scheme in which incoming funds were not used as investments but as payments to other depositors and the fund manager. While the claimants themselves had not committed a crime, they had failed to exercise the kind of due diligence which a reasonable investor would have undertaken to ensure compliance with local laws.[25] As the applicable BIT required such compliance, the Tribunal declined jurisdiction.

In *Hamester v Ghana*,[26] the Tribunal stated that an investment will not be protected if it has been created in violation of the national or international principles of good faith or of the host state's law, independent of the language of the BIT.[27] This rule applies to conduct at the time of the initiation of the investment, not to subsequent performance.[28]

---

[19] *Plama v Bulgaria*, Award, 27 August 2008, para 144.
[20] According to *Rumeli v Kazakhstan*, Award, 29 July 2008, para 319, protection of a BIT will be denied only in cases of a breach of fundamental legal principles of the host country (following *LESI v Algeria*, Decision on Jurisdiction, 12 July 2006, para 73).
[21] *Plama v Bulgaria*, Award, 27 August 2008.
[22] At para 133.
[23] At para 146.
[24] *Alasdair Ross Anderson v Costa Rica*, Award, 19 May 2010.
[25] At para 58.
[26] *Hamester v Ghana*, Award, 18 June 2010.
[27] At paras 123, 124.
[28] At para 127. The Tribunal followed *Fraport v Philippines*, Award, 16 August 2007, para 344.

Beyond the substantive scope of a treaty, the issue was bound to arise whether an 'in accordance with host state law' clause will also affect the right of an investor to invoke a provision on dispute settlement. In *Salini v Morocco*,[29] Article 1(1) of the applicable BIT defined the term 'investment' as 'all categories of assets invested ... in accordance with the laws and regulations of the aforementioned party'. The Tribunal rejected the argument advanced by the respondent whereby Article 1(1) referred to the law of the host state for the definition of 'investment'. In the view of the Tribunal, the provision referred to the validity of the investment and not to its definition. It found that such a provision 'seeks to prevent the Bilateral Treaty from protecting investments that should not be protected, particularly because they would be illegal'.[30] No infringement of the laws or regulations of the host state had been established in the case.

The applicable BIT in the *Tokios Tokelės*[31] case also defined the term 'investment' as 'every kind of asset invested by an investor of one Contracting Party in the territory of the other Contracting Party in accordance with the laws and regulations of the latter'. The respondent state argued that the name under which the claimant had registered its local subsidy did not correspond to a recognized legal form under Ukrainian law and that it had identified errors in the documents provided by the investor, including the absence of necessary signatures or notarizations. For the Tribunal, these irregularities did not affect the protection of the investment under the bilateral treaty: relying on the decision in *Salini v Morocco*, the arbitrators found that the purpose of such provisions was merely 'to prevent the Bilateral Treaty from protecting investments that should not be protected, particularly because they would be illegal'.[32] Noting that the object and purpose of investment treaties is to provide broad protection for investors and their investment[33] and that the governmental authorities of the respondent had registered the claimant's subsidiary as a valid enterprise, the Tribunal concluded:

Even if we were able to confirm the Respondent's allegations, which would require a searching examination of minute details of administrative procedures in Ukrainian law, to exclude an investment on the basis of such minor errors would be inconsistent with the object and purpose of the Treaty. In our view, the Respondent's registration of each of the Claimant's investments indicates that the 'investment' in question was made in accordance with the laws and regulations of Ukraine.[34]

In *Desert Line v Yemen*,[35] the Tribunal emphasized that a host state which has for some time tolerated a legal situation is thereafter precluded from insisting later, against the investor, that the situation was unlawful from the beginning.[36]

---

[29] *Salini v Morocco*, Decision on Jurisdiction, 23 July 2001.
[30] At para 46.
[31] *Tokios Tokelės v Ukraine*, Decision on Jurisdiction, 29 April 2004.
[32] At para 84.
[33] At para 85.
[34] At para 86.
[35] *Desert Line v Yemen*, Award, 6 February 2008.
[36] At paras 97–123.

In *Railroad Development v Guatemala*,[37] arising under the rules of the Central America Free Trade Agreement (CAFTA), the claimant's investment in the railroad business was not acquired in accordance with the provisions of local law, but the government was aware of the situation and did not object for many years; as in the *Desert Line* case, the Tribunal ruled that principles of fairness precluded the respondent from raising an objection to the Tribunal's jurisdiction.[38]

In *Kardassopoulos v Georgia*,[39] the host state argued that the Joint Venture Agreement with the claimant was void *ab initio* because the state entities which had signed had acted *ultra vires*. The Tribunal found several reasons why the claim submitted was nevertheless protected under the BIT. Primarily, the Tribunal pointed to assurances given to the investor.[40]

In *Aguas del Tunari v Bolivia*,[41] the Tribunal had to interpret a BIT which provided that each party would promote cooperation through the protection of investments 'within the framework of its law and regulation' and that investments would be admitted by each party 'subject to its right to exercise powers conferred by its laws or regulations'. The respondent did not allege any fraud, but argued that these clauses subjected the dispute to the domestic tribunals. The Tribunal found that the first clause only referred to the state's duty to promote cooperation. With regard to the admission clause, the Tribunal also interpreted its scope in a limited manner and tried to explain its position in light of the object and purpose of the treaty as follows:

The Tribunal notes that the reference specifically subjects the State's duty to admit investments not to the laws and regulations of Bolivia, but rather to the 'right to exercise powers' conferred by such laws or regulations. The Tribunal finds this language significant as it implies an act at the time of admittance in accordance with the laws or regulations in force at that time.[42]

The first case in which a tribunal denied jurisdiction on the basis that a violation of the 'in accordance with the laws' clause had occurred was *Inceysa Vallisoletana v El Salvador*.[43] The Tribunal had to apply the BIT between Spain and El Salvador, which did not refer to compliance with national laws in the definition of investment but in the provisions on admission and protection.

The Tribunal found that in the bidding process that led to award of the concession, the claimant had presented false information on its financial status, about the experience and ability of its administrator, and about the identity and experience of a strategic partner supporting the claimant's bid. The Tribunal referred to the principle of good faith, to international public policy, and to the rule that no one should benefit from his own wrongdoing. The Tribunal ruled that

---

[37] *Railroad Development Corp v Guatemala*, Decision on Jurisdiction, 18 May 2010.
[38] At paras 145 et seq.
[39] *Kardassopoulos v Georgia*, Decision on Jurisdiction, 6 July 2007.
[40] At paras 171–94.
[41] *Aguas del Tunari v Bolivia*, Decision on Jurisdiction, 21 October 2005.
[42] At para 147.
[43] *Inceysa Vallisoletana v El Salvador*, Award, 2 August 2006.

El Salvador had given its consent to jurisdiction by the International Centre for Settlement of Investment Disputes (ICSID) on the condition that the claimant would act in accordance with the law:

In conclusion, the Tribunal considers that, because Inceysa's investment was made in a manner that was clearly illegal, it is not included within the scope of consent expressed by Spain and the Republic of El Salvador in the BIT and, consequently, the disputes arising from it are not subject to the jurisdiction of the Centre. Therefore, this Arbitral Tribunal declares itself incompetent to hear the dispute brought before it.[44]

The Tribunal found that these considerations applied not only to the consent given under a treaty but also to the jurisdictional rules contained in domestic legislation.

In *Fraport v Philippines*,[45] the Tribunal applied the BIT between Germany and the Philippines which defines 'investment' as assets 'accepted in accordance with the respective laws and regulations of either Contracting State'. In addition, the treaty's provision on admission refers to 'investments in accordance with its Constitution, laws and regulations'.

Legislation in the Philippines contained restrictions on shareholding and management by foreigners in public utility enterprises. The Tribunal found that Fraport had sought to circumvent this legislation by way of secret shareholder agreements. It concluded that, in view of the investor's conscious violation of the host state's law, it had no jurisdiction:

Fraport knowingly and intentionally circumvented the ADL [that is, domestic legislation] by means of secret shareholder agreements. As a consequence, it cannot claim to have made an investment 'in accordance with law'. Nor can it claim that high officials of the Respondent subsequently waived the legal requirements and validated Fraport's investment, for the Respondent's officials could not have known of the violation. Because there is no 'investment in accordance with law', the Tribunal lacks jurisdiction *ratione* materiae.[46]

The *Fraport* Award was annulled, on 23 December 2010, on the ground that the right to be heard had not been properly observed.[47]

Outside the context of a treaty, in an arbitration based exclusively on a contract between the investor and the host state, the Tribunal in *World Duty Free v Kenya*[48] had to decide whether acts of bribery during negotiation of the contract prevented the claimant from complaining about violations of the contract by the respondent state. The Tribunal emphatically found that this was the case. As bribery was contrary to the international public order of most states and to the applicable national laws and regulations, the contract was void and the investor could not complain of violations of the contract on the part of the host state:

---

[44] At para 257.
[45] *Fraport v Philippines*, Award, 16 August 2007.
[46] At para 401.
[47] *Fraport v Philippines*, Decision on Annulment, 23 December 2010, paras 218 et seq.
[48] *World Duty Free v Kenya*, Award, 4 October 2006.

In light of domestic laws and international conventions relating to corruption, and in light of the decisions taken in this matter by courts and arbitral tribunals, this Tribunal is convinced that bribery is contrary to the international public policy of most, if not all, States or, to use another formula, to transnational public policy. Thus, claims based on contracts of corruption or on contracts obtained by corruption cannot be upheld by this Arbitral Tribunal.[49]

---

[49] At para 157.

VI

Expropriation

The rules of international law governing the expropriation of alien property have long been of central concern to foreigners in general and to foreign investors in particular. Expropriation is the most severe form of interference with property. All expectations of the investor are destroyed if the investment is taken without adequate compensation.

On the level of customary international law, the minimum standard for the protection of aliens came to place limitations on the territorial sovereignty of the host state and to protect alien property. On the level of treaty law, all modern agreements on foreign investment contain specific provisions covering preconditions for and consequences of expropriation.

1. The right to expropriate

Consistent with the notion of territorial sovereignty, the classical rules of international law have accepted the host state's right to expropriate alien property in principle. Indeed, state practice has considered this right to be so fundamental that even modern investment treaties (often entitled agreements 'for the promotion and protection of foreign investment') respect this position. Treaty law typically addresses only the conditions and consequences of an expropriation, leaving the right to expropriate as such unaffected.[1]

Even clauses in agreements between the host state and the investor that freeze the applicable law for the period of the agreement ('stabilization clauses')[2] will not necessarily stand in the way of a lawful expropriation. The position is less clear if such an agreement explicitly excludes the right to expropriate. Except in extreme circumstances, an international tribunal will probably interpret such a clause in a literal manner. In practice, however, such far-reaching provisions have played no significant role.

---

[1] Some states (eg Ecuador, Peru) have in the past provided in their constitutions that their contractual agreements with foreign investors may not be changed by a unilateral act. But they have not gone as far as excluding the right to expropriate. Article 249 of the Constitution of Ecuador (1998) provided for all contracts relating to public services: 'The agreed contractual conditions cannot be modified unilaterally by law or other measures.' Article 62 of the 1993 Peruvian Constitution states: 'Through contract-laws, the State can establish guarantees and grant assurances. They may not be amended legislatively.'

[2] See pp 82 et seq.

2. The three branches of the law

Beyond the right of the host state to expropriate, international law on expropriation has developed three branches, which regulate the scope and conditions of the exercise of this power. The first one defines the interests that will be protected. This facet has not traditionally been in the forefront of academic and practical discussions but has received some prominence more recently. Most contemporary treaties, in their provisions dealing with expropriation, refer to 'investments'. Similarly, the jurisdiction of arbitral tribunals is typically restricted to disputes arising from 'investments'. Therefore, it is 'investments' as defined in these treaties that are protected.[3]

The second branch concerns the definition of an expropriation. While this matter raises no questions in cases of a formal expropriation, the issue may acquire a high degree of complexity when the host state interferes with the rights of the foreign owner without a formal taking of title. Indeed, in the practice of the past three decades, most cases relating to expropriation have turned on the controversy of whether or not a 'taking' had actually occurred. Matters of public health, the environment, or general changes in the regulatory system may prompt a state to regulate foreign investments. This has led to claims against the state on the basis that a regulatory taking or indirect expropriation has occurred. The elements of indirect expropriation are discussed below.[4]

The third branch of the law on expropriation relates to the conditions under which a state may expropriate alien property. The classical requirements for lawful expropriation are a public purpose, non-discrimination, as well as prompt, adequate, and effective compensation. In practice, the requirement of compensation has turned out to be the most controversial aspect. This issue is discussed in the next section.

3. The legality of the expropriation

It is today generally accepted that the legality of a measure of expropriation is conditioned on three (or four) requirements. These requirements are contained in most treaties. They are also seen to be part of customary international law. These requirements must be fulfilled cumulatively:

- The measure must serve a public purpose. Given the broad meaning of 'public purpose', it is not surprising that this requirement has rarely been questioned by the foreign investor. However, tribunals did address the significance of the term and its limits in some cases.[5]

---

[3] For the concept of an investment, see pp 60 et seq. See further p 248.
[4] See pp 101 et seq.
[5] See eg *ADC v Hungary*, Award, 2 October 2006, paras 429–33.

- The measure must not be arbitrary and discriminatory within the generally accepted meaning of the terms.

- Some treaties explicitly require that the procedure of expropriation must follow principles of due process.[6] Due process is an expression of the minimum standard under customary international law and of the requirement of fair and equitable treatment. Therefore, it is not clear whether such a clause, in the context of the rule on expropriation, adds an independent requirement for the legality of the expropriation.

- The expropriatory measure must be accompanied by prompt, adequate, and effective compensation. Adequate compensation is generally understood today to be equivalent to the market value of the expropriated investment.

Of these requirements for the legality of an expropriation, the measure of compensation has been by far the most controversial. In the period between roughly 1960 and 1990, the rules of customary law on compensation were at the centre of the debate on expropriation. They were discussed in the broader context of economic decolonization, the notion of 'Permanent Sovereignty over Natural Resources', and of the call for a new international economic order. Today, these fierce debates are over and nearly all expropriation cases before tribunals follow the treaty-based standard of compensation in accordance with the fair market value. In the terminology of the earlier decades this means 'full' or 'adequate' compensation. However, this does not mean that the amount of compensation is easy to determine. Especially in cases of foreign enterprises operating on the basis of complex contractual agreements, the task of valuation requires close cooperation of valuation experts and the legal profession.

Various methods may be employed to determine market value. The discounted cash flow method will often be a relevant yardstick, rather than book value or replacement value, in the case of a going concern that has already produced income. Before the point of reaching profitability, the liquidation value will be the more appropriate measure.[7]

A traditional issue that has never been entirely resolved concerns the consequences of an illegal expropriation. In the case of an indirect expropriation, illegality will be the rule, since there will be no compensation.

According to one school of thought, the measure of damages for an illegal expropriation is no different from compensation for a lawful taking. The better view is that an illegal expropriation will fall under the general rules of state responsibility, while this is not so in the case of a lawful expropriation accompanied by compensation. In the case of an illegal act the damages should, as far as possible, restore the situation that would have existed had the illegal act not been committed. By contrast, compensation for a lawful expropriation should represent the market value at the time of the taking. The result of these two methods can be markedly

---

[6] See eg the 2004 and 2012 US Model BITs, Art 6(1)(d).
[7] See pp 296–7.

different.[8] The difference will mainly concern the amount of lost profits. The issue of compensation and damages is discussed in more detail in Chapter X on the settlement of investment disputes.[9]

The requirement of 'prompt' compensation means 'without undue delay'.[10] The requirement of 'effective' compensation means that payment is to be made in a convertible currency.[11]

4. Direct and indirect expropriation

The difference between a direct or formal expropriation and an indirect expropriation turns on whether the legal title of the owner is affected by the measure in question. Today direct expropriations have become rare.[12] States are reluctant to jeopardize their investment climate by taking the drastic and conspicuous step of an open taking of foreign property. An official act that takes the title of the foreign investor's property will attract negative publicity and is likely to do lasting damage to the state's reputation as a venue for foreign investments.

As a consequence, indirect expropriations have gained in importance. An indirect expropriation leaves the investor's title untouched but deprives him of the possibility of utilizing the investment in a meaningful way. A typical feature of an indirect expropriation is that the state will deny the existence of an expropriation and will not contemplate the payment of compensation.

(a) Broad formulae: their substance and evolution

The contours of the definition of an indirect expropriation are not precisely drawn. An increasing number of arbitral cases and a growing body of literature on the subject have shed some light on the issue but the debate goes on.[13] In some recent decisions by the International Centre for Settlement of Investment Disputes (ICSID), tribunals have interpreted the concept of indirect expropriation narrowly and have preferred to find a violation of the standard of fair and equitable treatment.[14]

The concept of indirect expropriation as such was clearly recognized in the early case law of arbitral tribunals and of the Permanent Court of International Justice

[8] See eg D W Bowett, 'State Contracts with Aliens: Contemporary Developments on Compensation for Termination or Breach' (1988) 59 *BYIL* 47; *Case Concerning the Factory at Chorzów*, 1928, PCIJ, Series A, No 17, 47. For a full discussion, see I Marboe, 'Compensation and Damages in International Law, The Limits of "Fair Market Value"' (2006) 7 *J World Investment & Trade* 723.

[9] See pp 294–7.

[10] R Dolzer and M Stevens, *Bilateral Investment Treaties* (1995) 112.

[11] Dolzer and Stevens, n 11.

[12] But see *Funnekotter v Zimbabwe*, Award, 22 April 2009.

[13] See Y Fortier and S L Drymer, 'Indirect Expropriation in the Law of International Investment: I Know It When I See It, or Caveat Investor' (2004) 19 *ICSID Review-FILJ* 293.

[14] See pp 117 et seq.

(PCIJ) in the 1920s and 1930s.[15] Today it is generally accepted that certain types of measures affecting foreign property will be considered an expropriation, and require compensation, even though the owner retains the formal title. What was and remains contentious is drawing the line between non-compensable regulatory and other governmental activity and measures amounting to indirect, compensable expropriation. The issue is of equal importance to the host state, which may wish to broaden the range of non-compensable activities, and to the foreign investor, who will argue in favour of a broad understanding of the concept of indirect takings.

Bilateral and multilateral treaties and draft treaties typically contain a reference to indirect expropriation or to measures tantamount to expropriation. The Abs–Shawcross Draft Convention on Investment Abroad (1959) referred to 'measures against nationals of another Party to deprive them directly or indirectly of their property'. Essentially, the same wording appears in the 1967 Organisation for Economic Co-operation and Development (OECD) Draft Convention on the Protection of Foreign Property. The Draft United Nations Code of Conduct on Transnational Corporations referred to '[a]ny such taking of property whether direct or indirect'. The 1992 World Bank Guidelines on the Treatment of Foreign Direct Investment speaks of expropriation or 'measures which have similar effects'. Similarly, the 1998 OECD Draft for a Multilateral Agreement on Investment refers to 'measures having equivalent effect'. Another variation is contained in the North American Free Trade Agreement (NAFTA) of 1992, which speaks of 'a measure tantamount to nationalization or expropriation'. The 1994 Energy Charter Treaty similarly refers to 'a measure or measures having effect equivalent to nationalization or expropriation'.

Most current bilateral investment treaties contain similar language. The current French Model Treaty states: 'Neither Contracting Party shall take any measures of expropriation or nationalization or any other measures having the effect of dispos-session, direct or indirect, of nationals or companies of the other Contracting Party of their investments.'[16] According to the German Model Treaty '[i]nvestments by investors of either Contracting State shall not directly or indirectly be expropriated, nationalized or subjected to any other measure the effects of which would be tantamount to expropriation or nationalization'.[17] The Model Treaty used by the United Kingdom provides that '[i]nvestments of nationals or companies of either Contracting Party shall not be nationalized, expropriated or subjected to measures having effect equivalent to nationalization or expropriation'.[18]

The 2004 and 2012 US Model BITs approach the issue in greater detail. After stating in Article 6(1) that '[n]either Party may expropriate or nationalize a covered investment either directly or indirectly through measures equivalent to expropriation or nationalization',[19] a special Annex B entitled 'Expropriation' adds:

---

[15] See *Norwegian Shipowners' Claims*, I RIAA 307 (1922); *Case Concerning Certain German Interests in Polish Upper Silesia*, 1926, PCIJ, Series A, No 7, 3.

[16] French Model Treaty, Art 6(2).   [17] German Model Treaty, Art 4(2).

[18] UK Model Treaty, Art 5(1).   [19] See US Model BITs, Art 6(1).

(a) The determination of whether an action or series of actions by a Party, in a specific fact situation, constitutes an indirect expropriation, requires a case-by-case, fact-based inquiry that considers, among other factors: (i) the economic impact of the government action, although the fact that an action or series of actions by a Party has an adverse effect on the economic value of an investment, standing alone, does not establish that an indirect expropriation has occurred; (ii) the extent to which the government action interferes with distinct, reasonable investment-backed expectations; and (iii) the character of the government action.

(b) Except in rare circumstances, non-discriminatory regulatory actions by a Party that are designed and applied to protect legitimate public welfare objectives, such as public health, safety, and the environment, do not constitute indirect expropriations.[20]

Among the broader formulae proposed in general studies and drafts, some have received special attention in the decisions of arbitral tribunals and in academic writings. Harvard Professors Sohn and Baxter included in their 1961 Draft Convention on the International Responsibility of States for Injuries to Aliens, a version that is elaborate and contains specific categories of indirect takings:

A taking of property includes not only an outright taking of property but also any such unreasonable interference with the use, enjoyment, or disposal of property as to justify an inference that the owner thereof will not be able to use, enjoy, or dispose of the property within a reasonable period of time after the inception of such interference.[21]

The 1986 *Restatement (Third) of the Foreign Relations Law of the United States* (§ 712) is much shorter and in its text only speaks of a 'taking'. Comment (g) refers to actions 'that have the effect of "taking" the property, in whole or in large part, outright or in stages ("creeping expropriation")'.

A United Nations Conference on Trade and Development (UNCTAD) study, prepared in 2000, uses different language and considers that 'measures short of physical takings may amount to takings in that they result in the effective loss of management, use or control, or a significant depreciation of the value, of the assets of a foreign investor'.[22]

In an early influential article Gordon Christie reviewed the then existing case law and pointed to certain recognized groups and categories of indirect takings, without an attempt to present a general formula.[23] Judge Rosalyn Higgins, in her 1982 Hague Lectures, questioned the usefulness of a distinction between non-compensable bona fide governmental regulation and 'taking' for a public purpose:

Is this distinction intellectually viable? Is not the State in both cases (that is, either by a taking for a public purpose, or by regulating) purporting to act in the common good? And in each case has the owner of the property not suffered loss? Under international law standards,

---

[20] 2004 and 2012 US Model BITs, Annex B, para 4.

[21] L B Sohn and R R Baxter, 'Responsibility of States for Injuries to the Economic Interests of Aliens' (1961) 55 *AJIL* 545, 553 (Art 10(3)(a)).

[22] UNCTAD, *Series on Issues in International Investment Agreements: 'Taking of Property'* (2000) 4.

[23] G C Christie, 'What Constitutes a Taking of Property under International Law?' (1962) 38 *BYBIL* 307.

a regulation that amounted (by virtue of its scope and effect) to a taking, would need to be 'for a public purpose' (in the sense of a general, rather than for a private, interest). And just compensation would be due.[24]

It has been argued elsewhere that the international law of expropriation has essentially grown out of, and mirrored, parallel domestic laws.[25] As a consequence of this linkage, it appears plausible that measures that are, under the rules of key domestic laws, normally considered regulatory without requiring compensation, will not require compensation under international law either.

The importance of the effect of a measure for the question of whether an expropriation has occurred was highlighted by Reisman and Sloane:

tribunals have increasingly accepted that expropriation must be analyzed in consequential rather than in formal terms. What matters is the effect of governmental conduct—whether malfeasance, misfeasance, or nonfeasance, or some combination of the three—on foreign property rights or control over an investment, not whether the state promulgates a formal decree or otherwise expressly proclaims its intent to expropriate. For purposes of state responsibility and the obligation to make adequate reparation, international law does not distinguish indirect from direct expropriations.[26] [Footnotes omitted]

In recent jurisprudence, the formula most often found is that an expropriation will be assumed in the event of a 'substantial deprivation' of an investment.[27]

The oscillating understanding of this approach may be illustrated in light of relevant jurisprudence.

(b) Judicial and arbitral practice: some illustrative cases

Cases decided by tribunals demonstrate the variety of scenarios in which the question of indirect expropriation may arise. Tribunals have had to adapt their focus of inquiry to these different circumstances; consequently, an emphasis on different aspects of the law should not necessarily be construed as an expression of inconsistency. Often, the facts of a case simply highlight only one specific factor and neglect of other possible factors does not result from oversight but from irrelevance to the specific circumstances. A short survey of cases may serve to demonstrate the diversity of factual bases and of the reasoning of tribunals.

The *Oscar Chinn* case[28] concerned the interests of a British shipping company in the Congo. In the aftermath of the economic crisis of 1929, the Belgian Government intervened in the shipping trade on the Congo River by reducing the prices charged by Mr Chinn's only competitor, the partly state-owned company

---

[24] R Higgins, 'The Taking of Property by the State: Recent Developments in International Law' (1982-III) 176 *Recueil des Cours* 259, 331.

[25] R Dolzer, 'Indirect Expropriation of Alien Property' (1986) 1 *ICSID Review-FILJ* 41.

[26] W M Reisman and R D Sloane, 'Indirect Expropriation and its Valuation in the BIT Generation' (2003) 74 *BYBIL* 115, 121.

[27] See eg *Société Générale v Dominican Republic*, Award, 19 September 2008, para 64; *Alpha Projectholding v Ukraine*, Award, 8 November 2010, para 408.

[28] *Oscar Chinn Case (UK v Belgium)*, 12 December 1934, PCIJ, Series A/B, No 63, 4.

UNATRA. The government had also granted corresponding subsidies to UNA-TRA in order to keep the transport system on the Congo River viable. This made Oscan Chinn's business economically unsustainable. The PCIJ concluded that there was no taking. It said:

The Court... is unable to see in his [Mr Chinn's] original position—which was characterized by the possession of customers and the possibility of making a profit—anything in the nature of a genuine vested right. Favourable business conditions and good-will are transient circumstances, subject to inevitable changes;... No enterprise... can escape from the chances and hazards resulting from general economic conditions.[29]

The arbitration in *Revere Copper v OPIC*[30] concerned a dispute arising from the insurance by the US Overseas Private Investment Corporation (OPIC)[31] of an investment made by the US claimant in Jamaica. Revere Copper had made substantial investments in the Jamaican bauxite mining sector. An agreement concluded in 1967 between RJA, the investor's local subsidiary, and the Jamaican Government fixed the taxes and royalties to be paid by RJA for a period of 25 years and provided that no further taxes or financial burdens would be imposed on RJA by the Jamaican authorities. However, in 1972, the newly elected Jamaican Government announced far-reaching reform of the bauxite sector and, in 1974, increased the revenues to be paid by RJA so drastically that RJA ceased operating in 1975.

Revere Copper then sought recovery under its OPIC insurance contract, alleging that the measures adopted by the Jamaican Government amounted to an expropriation of Revere's investment. The General Terms and Conditions of the OPIC contract defined 'expropriatory action', inter alia, as: 'any action which... for a period of one year directly results in preventing... the Foreign Enterprise from exercising effective control over the use or disposition of substantial portion of its property or from constructing the project or operating the same.' Although there had been no direct interference with Revere's physical property, the majority of the Tribunal found that the repudiation of the guarantees given to Revere amounted to an action that had resulted in preventing the foreign enterprise from exercising effective control over the use or disposition of a substantial portion of its property:

OPIC argues that RJA still has all the rights and property that it had before the events of 1974: it is in possession of the plant and other facilities; it has its Mining Lease; it can operate as it did before. This may be true in a formal sense but... we do not regard RJA's 'control' of the use and operation of its properties as any longer 'effective' in view of the destruction by Government actions of its contract rights.[32]

The Arbitral Tribunal came to this conclusion by emphasizing that 'control in a large industrial enterprise... is exercised by a continuous stream of decisions'[33] and

---

[29] At 27.   [30] *Revere Copper v OPIC*, Award, 24 August 1978.
[31] On investment insurance and OPIC, see pp 228 et seq.
[32] *Revere Copper v OPIC*, 291–2.
[33] At 292.

that without the repudiated agreement between RJA and Jamaica, '[t]here is no way in which rational decisions can be made'.[34]

Sporrong & Lönnroth v Sweden[35] is the leading case for the jurisprudence of the European Court of Human Rights (ECtHR) on matters regarding the protection of private property.[36] The case was brought before the Court by two Swedish citizens whose properties had been subject to long-term expropriation permits granted by the Swedish Government to the local authorities of the city of Stockholm. The permits, issued in 1956 and 1971, only authorized the city of Stockholm to do so if it deemed it necessary for the achievement of a projected urban construction scheme. The expropriation permits lasted 23 and eight years, respectively, but the local authorities never exercised their power of formal expropriation. Certain constraints with regard to construction and renovation of the properties were imposed upon the owners. In 1979, the city of Stockholm renounced its construction plans and the expropriation permits were no longer extended.

The affected owners argued that the measures adopted by the Swedish Government constituted a violation of Article 1 of the First Additional Protocol to the European Convention for the Protection of Human Rights and Fundamental Freedoms (ECHR),[37] as they had been hindered from selling their properties at an acceptable price and from undertaking necessary renovations during the existence of the expropriation permits.

The Court ruled that the applicants had not been formally deprived of their possessions. The Court acknowledged that '[i]n the absence of formal expropriation, that is to say a transfer of ownership, the Court considers that it must look behind the appearances and investigate the realities of the situation complained of' and that 'it has to be ascertained whether that situation amounted to a de facto expropriation, as was argued by the applicants'.[38]

But the majority also found that there had been no indirect expropriation in the case before it:

although the right in question lost some of its substance, it did not disappear. The effects of the measures involved are not such that they can be assimilated to a deprivation of possessions. The Court observes in this connection that the applicants could continue to utilise their possessions and that, although it became more difficult to sell properties in

---

[34] At 292.

[35] ECtHR, *Sporrong & Lönnroth v Sweden*, 23 September 1982, Series A, 52.

[36] More generally on the practice of the ECtHR, see A Van Rijn, 'Right to the Peaceful Enjoyment of One's Possessions (Article 1 of Protocol No 1)' in P van Dijk, G J H van Hoof, A van Rijn, and L Zwaak (eds), *Theory and Practice of the European Convention on Human Rights* (2006) 863–93.

[37] Article 1 reads:

(1) Every natural or legal person is entitled to the peaceful enjoyment of his possessions. No one shall be deprived of his possessions except in the public interest and subject to the conditions provided for by law and by the general principles of international law. (2) The preceding provisions shall not, however, in any way impair the right of a State to enforce such laws as it deems necessary to control the use of property in accordance with the general interest or to secure the payment of taxes or other contributions or penalties.

[38] *Sporrong & Lönnroth v Sweden*, para 63.

Stockholm affected by expropriation permits and prohibitions on construction, the possibility of selling subsisted.[39]

The Court also held that the second paragraph of Article 1 had no relevance because the measures were designed to lead to an expropriation and not meant to limit or control the use of the properties.[40]

The Court then turned to the first sentence of the first paragraph of Article 1 and found that for the purposes of this provision 'the Court must determine whether a fair balance was struck between the demands of the general interest of the community and the requirements of the protection of the individual's fundamental rights'.[41]

While recognizing that the contracting states 'should enjoy a wide margin of appreciation in order to implement their town-planning policy',[42] the Court held that the inflexibility of the Swedish legislation, which excluded the possibility of seeking a reduction of the time limits or claiming compensation, failed to strike a fair balance between the requirements of the general interest and the protection of the right of property and therefore amounted to a violation of Article 1 of the First Additional Protocol.[43]

The reasoning of the Court demonstrates that each treaty-based provision has to be read and understood in context and that analogies to provisions in other treaties or to rules of customary law may therefore not be appropriate. The tripartite structure of Article 1 of the First Additional Protocol to the ECHR is peculiar to this particular treaty.[44]

In *Goetz v Burundi*,[45] an ICSID tribunal had to rule on the revocation, by the host state, of a free-zone status accorded to a foreign investor. Although there had been no formal taking of property, the Tribunal had no difficulty in finding that the government's actions constituted a measure having effect similar to expropriation:

> Since... the revocation of the Minister for Industry and Commerce of the free zone certificate forced them to halt all activities... which deprived their investments of all utility and deprived the claimant investors of the benefit which they could have expected from their investments, the disputed decision can be regarded as a 'measure having similar effect' to a measure depriving of or restricting property within the meaning of Article 4 of the Investment Treaty.[46]

In *Metalclad v Mexico*,[47] a US company had been granted a permit for the development and operation of a hazardous waste landfill by the Mexican Federal Government. Subsequently, the local municipal authorities refused to grant the necessary construction permit and the regional government declared the land in question a national area for the protection of cacti. The Arbitral Tribunal found a violation of Article 1110 of the NAFTA, which provides that '[n]o Party may

---

[39] At para 63.   [40] At para 64.   [41] At para 69.   [42] At para 69.   [43] At para 73.
[44] See also p 29.
[45] *Goetz v Burundi*, Award, 10 February 1999.
[46] At para 124.
[47] *Metalclad Corp v Mexico*, Award, 30 August 2000.

directly or indirectly nationalize or expropriate an investment of an investor of another Party in its territory or take a measure tantamount to nationalization or expropriation of such an investment'. An oft-repeated passage in the Tribunal's Award reads:

Thus, expropriation under NAFTA includes not only open, deliberate and acknowledged takings of property, such as outright seizure or formal or obligatory transfer of title in favour of the host State, but also covert or incidental interference with the use of property which has the effect of depriving the owner, in whole or in significant part, of the use or reasonably-to-be-expected economic benefit of property even if not necessarily to the obvious benefit of the host State.[48]

In the arbitration proceeding under the UNCITRAL Rules in *CME v Czech Republic*,[49] the Tribunal had to rule on the interference by the Czech Media Council with the contract rights of the claimant's subsidary CNTS. In particular, the Czech authorities had made it possible for the investor's local partner to cancel the contract that formed the basis for the claimant's investment in the Czech Republic. The Tribunal rejected the respondent's argument that 'the Media Council's actions did not deprive the claimant of its worth, as there has been no physical taking of the property by the State'. In the Tribunal's view, this was irrelevant:

The Media Council's actions and omissions, as described above, caused the destruction of CNTS' operations, leaving CNTS as a company with assets, but without business. . . . What was touched and indeed destroyed was the Claimant's and its predecessor's invest-ment as protected by the Treaty. What was destroyed was the commercial value of the investment . . . by reason of coercion exerted by the Media Council . . .[50]

The expropriation claim is sustained despite the fact that the Media Council did not expropriate CME by express measures of expropriation. De facto expropriations or indirect expropriations, i.e. measures that do not involve an overt taking but that effectively neutralize the benefit of the property of the foreign owner, are subject to expropriation claims. This is undisputed under international law.[51]

The ICSID Award in *Middle East Cement Shipping v Egypt*[52] concerned the revocation of a free-zone licence through the prohibition on the import of cement into Egyptian territory. The prohibition resulted in a paralysis of the investor's business, which essentially consisted of importing, storing, and dispatching cement within Egypt. The Arbitral Tribunal found that the import prohibition resulted in an indirect taking of the claimant's investment:

---

[48] At para 103; referring to *Biloune v Ghana*, Award on Damages and Costs, 30 June 1990, 95 ILR (1995) 184 at para 108.

[49] *CME v Czech Republic*, Partial Award, 13 September 2001.

[50] At para 591.

[51] At para 604. The award in the parallel case, in *Lauder v Czech Republic*, Award, 3 September 2001, assumes, without authority, that a finding of an expropriation would have to benefit the host state or any other person or entity related thereto (para 203).

[52] *Middle East Cement Shipping v Egypt*, Award, 12 April 2002.

When measures are taken by a State the effect of which is to deprive the investor of the use and benefit of his investment even though he may retain nominal ownership of the respective rights being the investment, the measures are often referred to as a 'creeping' or 'indirect' expropriation or, as in the BIT, as measures 'the effect of which is tantamount to expropriation.' As a matter of fact, the investor is deprived by such measures of parts of the value of his investment. This is the case here, and, therefore, it is the Tribunal's view that such a taking amounted to an expropriation within the meaning of Art. 4 of the BIT and that, accordingly, Respondent is liable to pay compensation therefor.[53]

An expropriation claim under Chapter Fourteen of the NAFTA, devoted to cross-border investment in financial services, was adjudged in *Fireman's Fund v Mexico*.[54] This Chapter allows an expropriation claim under Article 1110, but does not allow claims pertaining to a violation of the minimum standard or the rule on national treatment. The US claimant submitted that its investment in a Mexican financial institution was expropriated by a series of actions by the Mexican Government.[55] The bank in which the claimant had invested was in a delicate financial situation, and the claimant argued that the Mexican Government had taken steps which permanently deprived it of the value of the investment. The Tribunal briefly summarized the state of the law of expropriation,[56] but eventually considered that the actual cause of the problems faced by the investor was that its investment had been risky and that the business risks involved had materialized. The Tribunal found that Mexico had discriminated against the investor and had possibly acted in an unfair manner, but had no jurisdiction in these respects under the NAFTA's rules on financial services.

Vivendi v Argentina (resubmitted)[57] concerned a concession for a water and sewage business. The claimants alleged that Argentina had unilaterally modified tariffs, used its oversight power to pepper the claimants with unjustified accusations, used the media to generate hostility towards the claimants, incited the claimants' customers not to pay, and forced the claimants to renegotiate the concession.

The Tribunal agreed that Argentina's measures went beyond partial deprivation,[58] left the concession without value, and held that they amounted to creeping expropriation. The Tribunal rejected Argentina's defence that the claimants' control of their physical assets excluded an expropriation.[59] It pointed to the effects of Argentina's destructive acts[60] and emphasized that the pursuit of a public purpose did not immunize a governmental measure from a claim of expropriation.[61]

Biwater Gauff v Tanzania[62] concerned a claim for expropriation surrounding the peculiar circumstances of the termination of a lease in the water and sewage

---

[53] At para 107.   [54] *Fireman's Fund v Mexico*, Award, 17 July 2006.
[55] At para 185.
[56] At paras 176 et seq, cited with approval in *Corn Products v Mexico*, Award, 15 January 2008, para 87.
[57] *Vivendi v Argentina*, Award, 20 August 2007.
[58] At para 7.5.11.   [59] At para 7.5.18.   [60] At para 7.5.20.
[61] At para 7.5.21.   [62] *Biwater Gauff v Tanzania*, Award, 24 July 2008.

industry. The Tribunal confirmed that the contract was an investment,[63] that an expropriation claim must be determined in light of the effect (not necessarily of an economic nature),[64] and recognized that all relevant acts of a government affecting the property must be considered on a cumulative basis.[65]

An exercise of *puissance publique* was necessary, but not a denial of justice.[66] According to this decision, an indirect expropriation has to be assumed in cases of 'a substantial deprivation of rights for at least a meaningful period of time'.[67]

In the event, the Tribunal found that the formal termination of the lease by Tanzania was of an ordinary contractual nature and could not, therefore, amount to an expropriation. In contrast, a series of acts preceding the termination did violate the treaty rule on expropriation: an inflammatory press conference by a minister, the withdrawal of VAT exemption, the forceful occupation of the claimants' facilities, usurpation of the claimants' management rights, and deportation of senior staff amounted to an indirect expropriation. In light of the arbitral jurisprudence examined, the Tribunal found that occupation and seizure, takeover of management, and deportation of management personnel in themselves led to this conclusion.

In the end, however, the claimants received no compensation; the company had significant liabilities, its contract was about to be terminated, and a willing buyer would not have paid to acquire the company.

In *Merrill & Ring Forestry v Canada*,[68] the Tribunal ruled on the claim of a US investor which considered that the Canadian Log Export Control Regime affected its business to export timber from Canada to the United States so intensely that an indirect expropriation had to be assumed.

The Tribunal did not allow the claim.[69] It considered that the type of interest asserted by the claimant could not be considered an investment, given that the Canadian regime, while regulating the export business, did not prohibit it, and did not interfere with the contract. Also, the investor had no right to sell the product in the United States for a specific price.

Moreover, the interference with the business did not reach the level of a 'substantial deprivation' inasmuch as the claimant remained in control of its business and also continued to operate at a significant profit. The control regime in question was deemed to be in accordance with the rules of the forestry sector worldwide.

Suez v Argentina[70] concerned Argentina's treatment of the claimant's right to operate, for 30 years, a water and sewage system and to receive corresponding revenue based on a tariff regime for that period. The claimant submitted that regulatory measures by Argentina, and also its refusal to adjust the tariffs, amounted

---

[63] At para 453.　　[64] At para 455.　　[65] At para 456.
[66] At para 458.　　[67] At para 463.
[68] *Merrill & Ring Forestry v Canada*, Award, 31 March 2010.
[69] At paras 139 et seq.
[70] *Suez v Argentina*, Award, 30 July 2010.

to an expropriation. On both counts, the Tribunal rejected the claim, pointing to the claimant's ongoing control of its operations.[71]

As regards the regulatory measures in particular, the Tribunal relied on the opaque concept of an 'overt taking'[72] which, in its view, did not exist despite a series of measures affecting the right to withdraw cash from bank accounts, new taxes, currency measures resulting in depreciation of the local peso, and the abandonment of an index-based scheme of tariff adjustment.[73] In principle at least, the Tribunal recognized that an examination of a taking must be targeted at the effects, not at the intention, of a measure.[74] In general, an indirect expropriation presupposed 'a substantial, permanent deprivation of the Claimant's investments or the enjoyment of those investments' economic benefits'.

The termination of the underlying concession contract by Argentina was, under the circumstances, deemed contractual in nature and did not involve the exercise of Argentina's sovereign power; as a consequence, the measure was not expropriatory in nature.[75]

In *Alpha v Ukraine*[76] the Austrian claimant had entered into a Joint Activity Agreement (JAA) with a state enterprise in regard to a hotel in the Ukraine. The hotel was originally held by the state-owned enterprise. After the claimant had entered into the JAA, the state-owned enterprise was transformed, in 2001, into a state-owned Open Joint Stock Company not subject to privatization. The claimant's argument that it lost its rights in the process of transformation was rejected by the Tribunal.[77]

In 2004, regular payments due to the claimant under the JAA were stopped by the Stock Company, amidst political and criminal turmoil. It turned out that the state had, for non-political reasons, caused the Stock Company to halt payments to the claimant for an indefinite period;[78] here, the Tribunal questioned whether any distinction between 'sovereign' and 'commercial' actions is relevant to the question whether Ukraine's actions expropriated the claimant's investment.

As a result of non-payment after 2004, the economic value of the rights held by the claimant was largely wiped out. The Tribunal concluded that the state's actions amounted to an indirect expropriation. The decision accurately illustrates that the issue of non-payment of debt resists generalization; depending upon the circumstances, non-payment may amount to expropriation.

In order to assess the current state of the law, it is prudent not just to operate with broader formulae such as 'unreasonable interference', 'measures having the effect of an expropriation', or 'measures which substantially deprive the owner of the use of the property'. More specific topics that will help to elucidate and concretize these broad formulae are expressed in the distinction between the effect

---

[71] At paras 117 et seq.   [72] At para 125.

[73] The Tribunal explained that its position was based on the legitimate right of a state to regulate its affairs: an additional defence of Argentina invoking police powers was not recognized (para 146) inasmuch as it would be duplicative.

[74] At para 122.   [75] At para 143.

[76] *Alpha v Ukraine*, Award, 8 November 2010.

[77] At paras 101 et seq.   [78] At para 412.

and purpose of a measure, in reference to the role of the intent of a government, consideration of the issue of legitimate expectations of the investor, control over the investment, the need for regulatory measures, and the duration of a measure. These issues are discussed explicitly in some decisions, although they are not necessarily the key to a fully homogeneous theory that does justice to all existing arbitral decisions. But they will assist in a better understanding of individual decisions and general trends.

Not surprisingly, significant lacunae and open issues remain in the law governing indirect expropriation. Domestic courts have grappled with the same issues for far longer. Despite the benefit of constitutional texts and the homogeneity of their national legal systems, they have been unable to resolve all problems. Sometimes these courts have stated that broad formulae will not be helpful as guidelines for judicial reasoning.[79]

(c) Effect or intention?

The effect of the measure upon the economic benefit and value as well as upon the control over the investment is the key question when it comes to deciding whether an indirect expropriation has taken place. Whenever this effect is substantial and lasts for a significant period of time, it will be assumed prima facie that a taking of the property has occurred.[80]

Tribunals have accordingly based their decisions on economic considerations. Indirect expropriation was seen to exist if the measure constituted a deprivation of the economic use and enjoyment, 'as if the rights related thereto—such as the income or benefits . . . had ceased to exist',[81] or when 'the use or enjoyment of benefits related thereto is exacted or interfered with to a similar extent'.[82] Other formulae and phrases have also been used.[83]

---

[79] See eg *Andrus v Allard*, 444 US 51, 65; 100 S Ct 318 (1979):

> There is no abstract or fixed point at which judicial intervention under the Takings Clause becomes appropriate. Formulas and factors have been developed in a variety of settings. See *Penn Central*, above, at 123–8.
>
> Resolution of each case, however, ultimately calls as much for the exercise of judgment as for the application of logic.

[80] See eg *Norwegian Shipowners' Claims*, I RIAA 307 (1922); *Goetz v Burundi*, Award, 10 February 1999; *Middle East Cement v Egypt*, Award, 12 April 2002; *Metalclad Corp v Mexico*, Award, 30 August 2000; *CME v Czech Republic*, Partial Award, 13 September 2001.

[81] *TECMED v Mexico*, Award, 29 May 2003, para 115.

[82] At para 116.

[83] See Y Fortier and S L Drymer, 'Indirect Expropriation in the Law of International Investment: I Know It When I See It, or *Caveat Investor*' (2004) 19 *ICSID Review-FILJ* 293, 305:

> the required level of interference with such rights—has been variously described as: (1) *unreasonable*; (2) an interference that renders rights so *useless that they must be deemed to have been expropriated*; (3) an interference that deprives the investor of *fundamental rights of ownership*; (4) an interference that makes rights *practically useless*; (5) an interference *sufficiently restrictive* to warrant a conclusion that the property has been 'taken'; (6) an interference that deprives, in whole or in significant part, the *use or reasonably-to-be-expected economic benefit* of the property; (7) an interference that *radically deprives* the economical use and enjoyment of an investment, as if the rights related thereto had ceased to exist; (8) an

In *RFCC v Morocco*,[84] the Tribunal stated that an indirect expropriation exists in cases where the measures have 'substantial effects of an intensity that reduces and/or removes the legitimate benefits related with the use of the rights targeted by the measure to an extent that they render their further possession useless'.[85]

Other decisions have in various wording and degrees also emphasized the effect of the measure.[86] The Tribunal in *CMS v Argentina*[87] found that no indirect expropriation had occurred when Argentina unilaterally suspended a previously agreed tariff adjustment scheme for the gas transport sector in the context of its economic and financial crisis. The US company CMS had argued, inter alia, that the suspension of the tariff adjustment formula amounted to an indirect expropriation of its investment in the Argentine gas transport sector. The Tribunal rejected this argument even though it admitted that the measures had an important effect on the claimant's business:

The essential question is therefore to establish whether the enjoyment of the property has been effectively neutralized. The standard that a number of tribunals have applied in recent cases where indirect expropriation has been contended is that of substantial deprivation. . . . the investor is in control of the investment; the Government does not manage the day-to-day operations of the company; and the investor has full ownership and control of the investment.[88]

In *Telenor v Hungary*,[89] the investor held a telecom concession which was affected by a special levy on all telecommunications service providers. The Tribunal held that in order to constitute an expropriation, the conduct complained of must have a major adverse impact on the economic value of the investment.[90] The Tribunal said:

the interference with the investor's rights must be such as substantially to deprive the investor of the economic value, use or enjoyment of its investment.[91] . . . In considering whether measures taken by government constitute expropriation the determinative factors are the intensity and duration of the economic deprivation suffered by the investor as the result of them.[92]

interference that makes *any form of exploitation of the property disappear* . . . ; (9) an interference such that the property can no longer be put to *reasonable use*.

[84] *RFCC v Morocco*, Award, 22 December 2003.

[85] At para 69 (original in French: 'avoir des effets substantiels d'une intensité certaine qui réduisent et/ou font disparaître les bénéfices légitimement attendus de l'exploitation des droits objets de ladite mesure à un point tel qu'ils rendent la détention de ces droits inutile'). See also *LESI v Algeria*, Award, 12 November 2008, para 132; *Bayindir v Pakistan*, Award, 27 August 2009, para 459.

[86] *Tippetts, Abbett, McCarthy, Stratton v TAMS-AFFA Consulting Eng'rs of Iran*; *Biloune v Ghana*, Award on Jurisdiction, 27 October 1989; *Metalclad Corp v Mexico*, Award, 30 August 2000; *Wena v Egypt*, Award on Merits, 8 December 2000; *Santa Elena v Costa Rica*, Award, 17 February 2000; *CME v Czech Republic*, Partial Award, 13 September 2001; *Middle East Cement v Egypt*, Award, 12 April 2002; *Goetz v Burundi*, Award, 10 February 1999.

[87] *CMS v Argentina*, Award, 12 May 2005.

[88] At paras 262, 263. See also *Revere Copper v OPIC*, 56 ILR (1980) 258 and the cases discussed by G H Aldrich, 'What Constitutes a Compensable Taking of Property? The Decisions of the Iran–United States Claims Tribunal' (1994) 88 *AJIL* 585.

[89] *Telenor v Hungary*, Award, 13 September 2006.

[90] At para 64.   [91] At para 65.

[92] At para 70. Footnote omitted.

In the event, the Tribunal found that the special levy amounted to a very limited sum and fell below the threshold of the standard defining an indirect expropriation.[93]

In a number of cases tribunals have pointed out that what mattered for an indirect expropriation was only the effect of the measure and that any intention to expropriate was not decisive.[94] In *Tecmed v Mexico*,[95] the Tribunal found that there had been an indirect expropriation. After explaining the concept of indirect or de facto expropriation, the Tribunal stated: 'The government's intention is less important than the effects of the measures on the owner of the assets or on the benefits arising from such assets affected by the measures; and the form of the deprivation measure is less important than its actual effects.'[96]

In *Siemens v Argentina*,[97] the Tribunal found support in the applicable BIT for its finding that what mattered for the existence of an expropriation was the effect of the measures and not the government's intention. The Argentina-Germany BIT, like many other BITs, refers to indirect expropriation in terms of a 'measure the effects of which would be tantamount to expropriation'. The Tribunal said: 'The Treaty refers to measures that have the effect of an expropriation; it does not refer to the intent of the State to expropriate.'[98]

Authority for the 'sole effect doctrine' also comes from the practice of the Iran–US Claims Tribunal. In *Starrett Housing v Iran*,[99] the Tribunal said:

it is recognized in international law that measures taken by a State can interfere with property rights to such an extent that these rights are rendered so useless that they must be deemed to have been expropriated, even though the State does not purport to have expropriated them and the legal title to the property formally remains with the original owner.[100]

Other decisions display a more differentiated approach. They take into account the context of the measure, including the purpose pursued by the host state. *Sea-Land Service Inc v Iran*[101] seems to fall into this category. Upon review of the case law, Fortier[102] has concluded that an approach balancing different factors seems to be dominant. This is certainly true for the jurisprudence of the ECtHR.[103] Also, the 2004 and 2012 US Model BITs, in their description of indirect expropriation, refer

---

[93] At para 79.

[94] See also *Azurix v Argentina*, Award, 14 July 2006, para 309.

[95] *Tecmed v Mexico*, Award, 29 May 2003, cited in *Plama v Bulgaria*, Award, 27 August 2008, para 192.

[96] At para 116 citing the decisions of the Iran–US Claims Tribunal in *Tippetts* and *Phelps Dodge*. Footnote omitted.

[97] *Siemens v Argentina*, Award, 6 February 2007.

[98] At para 270.

[99] *Starrett Housing Corp v Iran*, Iran–US Claims Tribunal, 19 December 1983, cited in *Plama v Bulgaria*, Award, 27 August 2008, para 191.

[100] At 154. See also *Tippetts, Abbett, McCarthy, Stratton v TAMS-AFFA Consulting Engineers of Iran*, Iran–US Claims Tribunal, 22 June 1984, 225–6; *Phillips Petroleum Co v Iran*, Iran–US Claims Tribunal, 29 June 1989, para 97.

[101] *Sea-Land Service Inc v Iran*, 6 Iran–US CTR 149, 166 (1984).

[102] Y Fortier and S L Drymer, 'Indirect Expropriation in the Law of International Investment: I Know It When I See It, or *Caveat Investor*' (2004) 19 *ICSID Review-FILJ* 293.

[103] See ECtHR, *Sporrong & Lönnroth v Sweden*, 23 September 1982.

not only to the economic impact of the government action but also to the objective of protecting legitimate public welfare objectives.[104] What is uncontroversial is that the mere post-facto explanation by the host state of its intention will in itself carry no decisive weight.[105]

Indeed, a number of tribunals have pointed out that a proper analysis of an expropriation claim must go beyond the technical consideration of the formalities and 'look at the real interests involved and the purpose and effect of the government measure'.[106]

(d) Legitimate expectations

An issue that is not novel as such but has more recently received increasing attention, is the existence of legitimate expectations on the part of the investor. This theme has also found expression in various forms in domestic laws. In fact, it is arguable whether the concept of legitimate expectations is part of the general principles of law. Legitimate expectations play a key role in the interpretation of the fair and equitable treatment standard;[107] but they have also entered the law governing indirect expropriations.

The general nature of the concept of legitimate expectations makes it difficult to draw mechanical conclusions from it. But it may be employed usefully in a number of settings. Legitimate expectations may be created not only by explicit undertakings on the part of the host state in contracts but also by undertakings of a more general nature. In particular, the legal framework provided by the host state will be an important source of expectations on the part of the investor. What matters for the investor's expectations is the state of the law of the host country at the time of the investment. To the extent that the state of the law was transparent and did not violate minimum standards, an investor will hardly be able to convince a tribunal that the proper application of that law led to an expropriation. This position is consistent with the power of the host state to accept and define the rights acquired by the investor at the time of the investment.[108]

Not every change in the host state's legal system affecting foreign property will violate legitimate expectations. No such violation will occur if the change remains within the boundaries of normal adjustments customary in the host state and accepted in other states. Such changes are predictable for a prudent investor at

---

[104] US Model BITs 2004 and 2012, Annex B, para 4.

[105] See *Norwegian Shipowners' Claims*, I RIAA 307 (1922); R Dolzer, 'Indirect Expropriations: New Developments?' (2003) 11 *NYU Environmental LJ* 64, 91.

[106] *S D Myers v Canada*, First Partial Award, 13 November 2000, para 285.

[107] See pp 145 et seq.

[108] See eg *Oscar Chinn v Belgium*, 12 December 1934, PCIJ, Series A/B, No 63, 84:

Mr Chinn, a British subject, when, in 1929, he entered the river transport business, could not have been ignorant of the existence of the competition which he would encounter on the part of Unatra, which had been established since 1925, of the magnitude of the capital invested in that Company, of the connection it had with the Colonial and Belgian Governments, and of the predominant role reserved to the latter with regard to the fixing and application of transport rates.

the time of the investment. For instance, the Tribunal in *Methanex v United States*[109] found that certain new environmental regulations in California should have been foreseeable for the Canadian investor.

Tribunals have relied on the legitimate expectations of investors in a number of cases relating to indirect expropriation. In *Revere Copper v OPIC*,[110] the host state had given explicit contractual assurances not to increase taxes and royalties. The Tribunal said:

We regard these principles as particularly applicable where the question is, as here, whether actions taken by a government contrary to and damaging to the economic interests of aliens are in conflict with undertakings and assurances given in good faith to such aliens as an inducement to their making the investments affected by the action.[111]

In *Metalclad v Mexico*,[112] the investor had acted in reliance on assurances to the effect that he had all necessary permits. Nevertheless, the project was foiled by the refusal of the municipality to grant a construction permit. The Tribunal put great emphasis on the expectations created by the government's assurances:

These measures, taken together with the representations of the Mexican federal government, on which Metalclad relied, and the absence of a timely, orderly or substantive basis for the denial by the Municipality of the local construction permit, amount to an indirect expropriation.[113]

In a similar way, in *Tecmed v Mexico*[114] the Tribunal, in determining that the investment had been expropriated, found that:

upon making its investment, the Claimant had legitimate reasons to believe that the operation of the Landfill would extend over the long term.... the Claimant's expectation was that of a long-term investment relying on the recovery of its investment and the estimated return through the operation of the Landfill during its entire useful life.[115]

In *Thunderbird v Mexico*,[116] the Tribunal gave a general definition of legitimate expectations:

Having considered recent investment case law and the good faith principle of international customary law, the concept of 'legitimate expectations' relates, within the context of the NAFTA framework, to a situation where a Contracting Party's conduct creates reasonable and justifiable expectations on the part of an investor (or investment) to act in reliance on said conduct, such that a failure by the NAFTA Party to honour those expectations could cause the investor (or investment) to suffer damages.[117]

---

[109] *Methanex v United States*, Award, 3 August 2005; see also *Thunderbird v Mexico*, Award, 26 January 2006.
[110] *Revere Copper v OPIC*, Award, 24 August 1978.
[111] At 271.
[112] *Metalclad v Mexico*, Award, 30 August 2000.
[113] At para 107.
[114] *Tecmed v Mexico*, Award, 29 May 2003.
[115] At para 149.
[116] *Thunderbird v Mexico*, Award, 26 January 2006.
[117] At para 147. Footnote omitted.

On the basis of this definition, the Tribunal reached the conclusion that the investor's continued operation of gaming facilities in Mexico was not based on a legitimate expectation.[118]

In *Azurix v Argentina*,[119] the Tribunal discussed the issue of legitimate expectations at some length.[120] It held that expectations 'are not necessarily based on a contract but on assurances explicit or implicit, or on representations made by the State which the investor took into account in making the investment'.[121]

On that basis it found that Argentina had created 'reasonable expectations' that it had not lived up to.[122] Remarkably, however, the Tribunal held that no indirect expropriation had taken place, since the investor had continued to exercise control over the investment.[123]

(e) Control and expropriation

It is not unusual in situations involving allegations of indirect expropriation that the investor retains control of its enterprise but the investment loses its economic viability. The overall investment may survive, but important rights that determine its profitability may be extinguished.

A number of Awards suggest that continued control of an enterprise by the investor strongly militates against a finding that an indirect expropriation has occurred. The requirement of total or substantial deprivation[124] has led these tribunals to deny the existence of an expropriation where the investor retained control over the overall investment even though it had been deprived of specific rights.[125]

As to the relationship between expropriation and the standard of fair and equitable treatment, it was stated in *Sempra v Argentina*[126] that:

fair and equitable treatment... ensures that even where there is no clear justification for making a finding of expropriation, as in the present case, there is still a standard which serves the purpose of justice and can of itself redress damage that is unlawful and that would otherwise pass unattended. Whether this result is achieved by the application of one or several standards is a determination to be made in the light of the facts of each dispute. What counts is that in the end the stability of the law and the observance of legal obligations are

[118] At para 208.
[119] *Azurix v Argentina*, Award, 14 July 2006.
[120] At paras 316–22.
[121] At para 318.
[122] See paras 316 et seq.
[123] At para 322.
[124] *Pope & Talbot v Canada*, Award, 26 June 2000, para 102; *Metalclad v Mexico*, Award, 30 August 2000, para 103; *CMS v Argentina*, Award, 12 May 2005, para 262.
[125] *Feldman v Mexico*, Award, 16 December 2002, paras 142, 152; *Occidental v Ecuador*, Award, 1 July 2004, para 89; *CMS v Argentina*, Award, 12 May 2005, paras 263, 264; *Enron v Argentina*, Award, 22 May 2007, para 245; *PSEG v Turkey*, Award, 19 January 2007, para 278; *Sempra v Argentina*, Award, 28 September 2007, para 285; *AES v Hungary*, Award, 23 September 2010, para 14.3.2.
[126] *Sempra v Argentina*, Award, 28 September 2007, para 300.

assured, thereby safeguarding the very object and purpose of the protection sought by the treaty.

The Tribunal in *Tokios Tokelés v Ukraine*[127] explained that:

one can reasonably infer that a diminution of 5% of the investment's value will not be enough for a finding of expropriation, while a diminution of 95% would likely be sufficient.

Azurix v Argentina[128] concerned breaches of a water concession by a province of Argentina. The Tribunal, although finding other breaches of the BIT, including fair and equitable treatment, denied the existence of an indirect expropriation, since the investor had retained control over the enterprise:

the impact on the investment attributable to the Province's actions was not to the extent required to find that, in the aggregate, these actions amounted to an expropriation; Azurix did not lose the attributes of ownership, at all times continued to control ABA and its ownership of 90% of the shares was unaffected. No doubt the management of ABA was affected by the Province's actions, but not sufficiently for the Tribunal to find that Azurix's investment was expropriated.[129]

Similarly, in *LG&E v Argentina*[130] the host state had violated the terms of concessions for the distribution of gas. The Tribunal, although finding that other standards had been violated, denied the existence of an expropriation in view of the investor's continuing control:

Ownership or enjoyment can be said to be 'neutralized' where a party no longer is in control of the investment, or where it cannot direct the day-to-day operations of the investment. . . . Interference with the investment's ability to carry on its business is not satisfied where the investment continues to operate, even if profits are diminished.[131]

Control is obviously an important aspect in the analysis of a taking. However, the continued exercise of control by the investor in itself is not necessarily the sole criterion. The issue becomes obvious when a host state substantially deprives the investor of the value of the investment leaving the investor with control of an entity that amounts to not much more than a shell of the former investment.

This illustrates the significance of a test which includes criteria other than control, such as economic use and benefit. Any attempt to define an indirect expropriation on the basis of one factor alone will not lead to a satisfactory result in all cases. In particular, an approach that looks exclusively at control over the overall investment is unable to contemplate the expropriation of specific rights enjoyed by the investor.

---

[127] *Tokios Tokelés v Ukraine*, Award, 26 July 2007, para 120.
[128] *Azurix v Argentina*, Award, 14 July 2006.
[129] At para 322.
[130] *LG&E v Argentina*, Decision on Liability, 3 October 2006.
[131] At paras 188, 191. Footnotes omitted.

(f) Partial expropriation

Some tribunals have accepted the possibility of an expropriation of particular rights that formed part of an overall business operation without looking at the issue of control over the entire investment.[132] In *Middle East Cement v Egypt*,[133] the investor had, inter alia, obtained an import licence for cement and had operated a ship. Egypt subsequently took measures that prevented the investor from operating its licence and seized and auctioned the ship. The investor raised a series of claims in respect of which it alleged expropriation. These included but went beyond the import licence and ownership of the ship. The Tribunal looked at these claims separately and determined in respect of each whether an expropriation had taken place. It found that the licence qualified as an investment and that the measures that prevented the exercise of the rights under it amounted to an expropriation.[134] The Tribunal examined separately whether an expropriation of the ship had occurred and gave an affirmative answer.[135] Several other claims of expropriation in respect of other rights were also examined but denied for a variety of reasons.[136] Therefore, *Middle East Cement* demonstrates that it is possible separately to expropriate specific rights enjoyed by the investor regardless of control over the overall investment.

In *Eureko v Poland*,[137] the investor had acquired a minority share in a privatized insurance company. A related agreement granted the investor the right to acquire further shares thereby gaining majority control of the company. The right to acquire the additional shares was subsequently withdrawn by the state. The original investment remained unaffected. The Tribunal found that the right to acquire further shares constituted 'assets', which were separately capable of expropriation.[138] It follows from this decision that even where control over the basic investment remains unaffected, the taking of specific rights related to the basic investment may amount to an expropriation.[139]

In *Grand River v United States*[140] the Tribunal suggested that under the rules of the NAFTA, only an expropriation of the investment as a whole will fall under the rules of the Treaty. This view of the NAFTA (and the law of expropriation in general) is too narrow; indeed, it appears from the case law discussed in the decision[141] that the Tribunal may have failed to distinguish between the questions of the definition of a taking and the extent to which an investment may have been expropriated.

---

[132] *Waste Management v Mexico*, Award, 30 April 2004, paras 141, 147; *EnCana v Ecuador*, Award, 3 February 2006, paras 172–83. For an extensive discussion, see U Kriebaum, 'Partial Expropriation' (2007) 8 *J World Investment & Trade* 69.

[133] *Middle East Cement v Egypt*, Award, 12 April 2002.

[134] At paras 101, 105, 107, 127.

[135] At paras 138, 144.

[136] At paras 152–6, 163–5.

[137] *Eureko v Poland*, Partial Award, 19 August 2005.

[138] At paras 239–41.

[139] See U Kriebaum, 'Partial Expropriation' (2007) 8 *J World Investment & Trade* 69.

[140] *Grand River v United States*, Award, 12 January 2011, para 146.

[141] At paras 148 et seq.

(g) General regulatory measures

A question of prime importance, both for the host state and for the foreign investor, is the role of the general regulatory measures of the host country under the rules of indirect expropriation.[142] Emphasis on the host state's sovereignty supports the argument that the investor should not expect compensation for a measure of general application. Indeed, one way to identify a taking may be to clarify whether the measure in question was taken in the exercise of functions that are generally considered part of a government's powers to regulate the general welfare.[143] This approach calls for a comparison of domestic legal orders.[144]

In the United States, governmental regulatory powers are referred to as 'police power'. While it is debatable whether the term 'police power' is appropriate in the modern regulatory context, some investment tribunals have relied on this term,[145] as did the US *Restatement of Foreign Relations Law*.[146]

The Iran–US Claims Tribunal ruled in *Too v Greater Modesto Insurance Associates*:[147]

A state is not responsible for loss of property or for other economic disadvantage resulting from *bona fide* general taxation or any other action that is commonly accepted as within the police power of States, provided it is not discriminatory and is not designed to cause the alien to abandon the property to the State or to sell it at a distress price.

In *Feldman v Mexico*,[148] the Tribunal stated the position as follows:

the ways in which governmental authorities may force a company out of business, or significantly reduce the economic benefits of its business, are many. In the past, confiscatory taxation, denial of access to infrastructure or necessary raw materials, imposition of unreasonable regulatory regimes, among others, have been considered to be expropriatory actions. At the same time, governments must be free to act in the broader public interest through protection of the environment, new or modified tax regimes, the granting or withdrawal of government subsidies, reductions or increases in tariff levels, imposition of zoning restrictions and the like. Reasonable governmental regulation of this type cannot be achieved if any business that is adversely affected may seek compensation, and it is safe to say that customary international law recognizes this.[149]

---

[142] On expropriatory acts by the judiciary, see *Rumeli v Kazakhstan*, Award, 29 July 2008, para 702.
[143] This was the approach taken in *Telenor v Hungary*, Award, 13 September 2006, para 78.
[144] R Dolzer, 'Indirect Expropriation of Alien Property' (1986) 1 *ICSID Review-FILJ* 41.
[145] See eg *TECMED v Mexico*, Award, 29 May 2003, paras 115, 119.
[146] American Law Institute, *Restatement (Third) of the Foreign Relations Law of the United States*, Vol 1 (1987), § 712, Comment (g):

a state is not responsible for loss of property or for other economic disadvantage resulting from *bona fide* general taxation, regulation, forfeiture for crime, or other action of the kind that is commonly accepted as within the police power of the states, if not discriminatory.

[147] *Too v Greater Modesto Insurance Associates*, 23 Iran–US CTR 378; see also *SEDCO v NIOC*, 9 Iran–US CTR 249, 275.
[148] *Feldman v Mexico*, Award, 16 December 2002.
[149] At para 103.

Similarly, the Tribunal in *SD Myers v Canada*[150] held:

The general body of precedent usually does not treat regulatory action as amounting to expropriation. Regulatory conduct by public authorities is unlikely to be the subject of legitimate complaint under Article 1110 of the NAFTA, although the Tribunal does not rule out that possibility.[151]

In *Methanex v United States*,[152] the Arbitral Tribunal found that a Californian ban of the gasoline additive MTBE did not constitute an expropriation because the measure was adopted for a public purpose, was not discriminatory, and because no specific commitments had been given to the foreign investor:

In the Tribunal's view, Methanex is correct that an intentionally discriminatory regulation against a foreign investor fulfils a key requirement for establishing expropriation. But as a matter of general international law, a non-discriminatory regulation for a public purpose, which is enacted in accordance with due process and, which affects, inter alios, a foreign investor or investment is not deemed expropriatory and compensable unless specific commitments had been given by the regulating government to the then putative foreign investor contemplating investment that the government would refrain from such regulation.[153]

Similarly, in *Saluka v Czech Republic*,[154] the Tribunal said:

In the opinion of the Tribunal, the principle that a State does not commit an expropriation and is thus not liable to pay compensation to a dispossessed alien investor when it adopts general regulations that are 'commonly accepted as within the police power of States' forms part of customary international law today. There is ample case law in support of this proposition.[155]

The Award in *Continental Casualty v Argentina*[156] refers to:

limitations to the use of property in the public interest that fall within typical government regulations of property entailing mostly inevitable limitations imposed in order to ensure the rights of others or of the general public (being ultimately beneficial also to the property affected). These restrictions do not impede the basic, typical use of a given asset and do not impose an unreasonable burden on the owner as compared with other similar situated property owners. These restrictions are not therefore considered a form of expropriation and do not require indemnification, provided however that they do not affect property in an intolerable, discriminatory or disproportionate manner.[157] [Footnotes omitted]

The references to general regulations and to non-discrimination suggest that the tribunals were influenced by the concept of national treatment. But the rules on foreign investment are not based on the principle of national treatment. General

---

[150] *SD Myers v Canada*, First Partial Award, 13 November 2000.
[151] At para 281.
[152] *Methanex v United States*, Award, 3 August 2005.
[153] At Part IV, Ch D, p 4, para 7.
[154] *Saluka v Czech Republic*, Partial Award, 17 March 2006.
[155] At para 262, citing *Methanex v United States*.
[156] *Continental Casualty v Argentina*, Award, 5 September 2008.
[157] At para 276.

regulatory rules and the measures based on them are subject to the same standards of protection that have been developed for all other instances. In the words of the decision of *Pope & Talbot v Canada*, 'a gaping loophole' would otherwise exist in the operation of the rules protecting foreigners.[158]

In *Santa Elena v Costa Rica*,[159] the Tribunal found that the fact that measures were taken for the purpose of environmental protection did not affect their nature as an expropriation. Therefore, the obligation to pay compensation remained. The Tribunal said:

Expropriatory environmental measures—no matter how laudable and beneficial to society as a whole—are in this respect, similar to any other expropriatory measures that a state may take in order to implement its policies: where property is expropriated, even for environmental purposes, whether domestic or international, the state's obligation to pay compensation remains.[160]

In *ADC v Hungary*,[161] the claimants argued that their investment in an airport project was expropriated by measures which deprived them of their rights to operate two airport terminals and to benefit from associated future business opportunities. The Tribunal accepted the claim of indirect expropriation and rejected Hungary's argument based on its right to regulate. In the view of the Tribunal:

The Tribunal cannot accept the Respondent's position that the actions taken by it against the Claimants were merely an exercise of its rights under international law to regulate its domestic economic and legal affairs. It is the Tribunal's understanding of the basic international law principles that while a sovereign State possesses the inherent right to regulate its domestic affairs, the exercise of such right is not unlimited and must have its boundaries. As rightly pointed out by the Claimants, the rule of law, which includes treaty obligations, provides such boundaries. Therefore, when a State enters into a bilateral investment treaty like the one in this case, it becomes bound by it and the investment-protection obligations it undertook therein must be honored rather than be ignored by a later argument of the State's right to regulate.

The related point made by the Respondent that by investing in a host State, the investor assumes the 'risk' associated with the State's regulatory regime is equally unacceptable to the Tribunal. It is one thing to say that an investor shall conduct its business in compliance with the host State's domestic laws and regulations. It is quite another to imply that the investor must also be ready to accept whatever the host State decides to do to it. In the present case, had the Claimants ever envisaged the risk of any possible depriving measures, the Tribunal believes that they took that risk with the legitimate and reasonable expectation that they would receive fair treatment and just compensation and not otherwise.[162]

---

[158] *Pope & Talbot v Canada*, Interim Award, 26 June 2000, para 99; see also *ADC v Hungary*, Award, 2 October 2006, paras 423, 424.

[159] *Santa Elena v Costa Rica*, Award, 17 February 2000.

[160] At para 72. The Tribunal in *Azurix* quotes this passage at para 309: *Azurix Corp v The Argentine Republic*, Award, 14 July 2006.

[161] *ADC v Hungary*, Award, 2 October 2006.

[162] At paras 423, 424.

In addition, the Tribunal made the rare finding that the host state had failed to demonstrate that its measures were in the public interest[163] and that, moreover, the taking had not taken place under due process of law.[164]

Recent decisions have sought to find a balance between the host state's right to act in the public interest and protection of the investor's rights.[165] The Tribunal in *Azurix*[166] held that the issue was whether legitimate measures serving a public purpose should give rise to a compensation claim. It found the criterion of bona fide regulation within the accepted police powers of the state insufficient and contradictory.[167] In regard to that argument, the Tribunal said:

According to it, the BIT would require that investments not be expropriated except for a public purpose and that there be compensation if such expropriation takes place and, at the same time, regulatory measures that may be tantamount to expropriation would not give rise to a claim for compensation if taken for a public purpose.[168]

The *Azurix* Tribunal approvingly quoted the ECtHR,[169] which had found that in addition to a legitimate aim in the public interest there had to be 'a reasonable relationship of proportionality between the means employed and the aim sought to be realized'. This proportionality would be lacking if the person concerned 'bears an individual and excessive burden'.[170]

The Tribunal in *LG&E v Argentina*[171] adopted a similar balancing test:

In order to establish whether State measures constitute expropriation under Article IV(1) of the Bilateral Treaty, the Tribunal must balance two competing interests: the degree of the measure's interference with the right of ownership and the power of the State to adopt its policies.... With respect to the power of the State to adopt its policies, it can generally be said that the State has the right to adopt measures having a social or general welfare purpose. In such a case, the measure must be accepted without any imposition of liability, except in cases where the State's action is obviously disproportionate to the need being addressed. The proportionality to be used when making use of this right was recognized in *Tecmed*, which observed that 'whether such actions or measures are proportional to the public interest presumably protected thereby and the protection legally granted to investments, taking into account that the significance of such impact, has a key role upon deciding the proportionality.'[172] [Footnote omitted]

---

[163] See para 433.

[164] At paras 434 et seq.

[165] For a proposal to balance investor and host state rights that goes beyond current arbitral practice, see U Kriebaum, 'Regulatory Takings: Balancing the Interests of the Investor and the State' (2007) 8 *J World Investment & Trade* 717.

[166] *Azurix v Argentina*, Award, 14 July 2006.

[167] At paras 310, 311.

[168] At para 311.

[169] *James v United Kingdom*, Judgment of 21 February 1986, paras 50 and 63.

[170] *Azurix* at para 311.

[171] *LG&E v Argentina*, Decision on Liability, 3 October 2006.

[172] At paras 189, 195.

(h) Duration of a measure

The duration of a governmental measure affecting the interests of a foreign investor is important for the assessment of whether an expropriation has occurred.[173] The Iran–US Claims Tribunal has ruled that the appointment of a temporary manager by the host state against the will of the foreign investor will constitute a taking if the consequential deprivation is not 'merely ephemeral'.[174]

Investment tribunals have also laid emphasis on the duration of the measure in question.[175] In *SD Myers v Canada*,[176] the Tribunal said:

An expropriation usually amounts to a lasting removal of the ability of an owner to make use of its economic rights although it may be that, in some contexts and circumstances, it would be appropriate to view a deprivation as amounting to an expropriation, even if it were partial or temporary.[177]

In the event, the Tribunal found that the measure had lasted for 18 months only and that this limited effect did not amount to an expropriation.[178]

In *Wena Hotels v Egypt*,[179] the Tribunal found that the seizure of the investor's hotel lasting for nearly a year was not 'ephemeral' but amounted to an expropriation.[180] In its subsequent Decision on Interpretation[181] the *Wena* Tribunal said:

It is true that the Original Tribunal did not explicitly state that such expropriation totally and permanently deprived Wena of its fundamental rights of ownership. However, in assessing the weight of the actions described above, there was no doubt in the Tribunal's mind that the deprivation of Wena's fundamental rights of ownership was so profound that the expropriation was indeed a total and permanent one.[182]

LG&E v Argentina also ruled that the duration of the measure had to be taken into account.[183] The Tribunal found that, as a rule, only an interference that is permanent will lead to an expropriation:

Similarly, one must consider the duration of the measure as it relates to the degree of interference with the investor's ownership rights. Generally, the expropriation must be

---

[173] See G C Christie, 'What Constitutes a Taking of Property under International Law?' (1962) *BYBIL* 307; J Wagner, 'International Investment, Expropriation and Environmental Protection' (1999) 29 *Golden Gate University L Rev* 465; W M Reisman and R D Sloane, 'Indirect Expropriation and its Valuation in the BIT Generation' (2003) 74 *BYBIL* 115.

[174] See *Tippetts, Abbett, McCarthy, Stratton v TAMS-AFFA Consulting Eng'rs of Iran*, 6 Iran–US CTR 219, 225 (1984); *Phelps Dodge Corp v Iran*, 10 Iran–US CTR 121 (1986); *James M Saghi, Michael R Saghi, and Allan J Saghi v Iran*, 14 Iran–US CTR 3 (1988).

[175] *TECMED v Mexico*, Award, 29 May 2003, para 116; *Generation Ukraine v Ukraine*, Award, 16 September 2003, para 20.32; *Azurix v Argentina*, Award, 14 July 2006, para 313: 'How much time is needed must be judged by the specific circumstances of each case.'

[176] *S D Myers v Canada*, First Partial Award, 13 November 2000.

[177] At para 283.

[178] At para 287.

[179] *Wena Hotels v Egypt*, Award, 8 December 2000.

[180] At para 99.

[181] *Wena Hotels v Egypt*, Decision on Interpretation, 31 October 2005.

[182] At para 120.

[183] *LG&E v Argentina*, Decision on Liability, 3 October 2006.

permanent, that is to say, it cannot have a temporary nature, unless the investment's successful development depends on the realization of certain activities at specific moments that may not endure variations.[184]

The Tribunal concluded:

Thus, the effect of the Argentine State's actions has not been permanent on the value of the Claimants' shares, and Claimants' investment has not ceased to exist. Without a permanent, severe deprivation of LG&E's rights with regard to its investment, or almost complete deprivation of the value of LG&E's investment, the Tribunal concludes that these circumstances do not constitute expropriation.[185]

(i) Creeping expropriation

The rules on protection of foreign investments must not be circumvented by way of splitting a measure amounting to an indirect expropriation into a series of cumulative steps which, taken together, have the same effect on the foreign owner. Therefore, it has long been accepted that an expropriation may occur 'outright or in stages'.[186] Thus, the term 'creeping expropriation' describes a taking through a series of acts.[187] A study by UNCTAD referred in this context to 'a slow and incremental encroachment on one or more of the ownership rights of a foreign investor that diminishes the value of its investment'.[188]

Practice has recognized the phenomenon of creeping expropriation on a number of occasions.[189] The Tribunal in *Generation Ukraine v Ukraine*[190] explained creeping expropriation as follows:

Creeping expropriation is a form of indirect expropriation with a distinctive temporal quality in the sense that it encapsulates the situation whereby a series of acts attributable to the State *over a period of time* culminate in the expropriatory taking of such property.... A plea of creeping expropriation must proceed on the basis that the investment existed at a particular point in time and that subsequent acts attributable to the State have eroded the investor's rights to its investment to an extent that is violative of the relevant international standard of protection against expropriation.[191]

---

[184] At para 193.

[185] At para 200.

[186] See American Law Institute, *Restatement (Third) of the Foreign Relations Law of the United States*, Vol 1 (1987), § 712; G C Christie, 'What Constitutes a Taking of Property under International Law?' (1962) 38 *BYBIL* 307.

[187] The term 'creeping expropriation' has also occasionally been used interchangeably with the term 'indirect expropriation'.

[188] UNCTAD, *Series on Issues in International Investment Agreements: 'Taking of Property'* (2000) 11–12.

[189] See also *Biloune v Ghana*, 95 ILR (1994) 184, 209; *TECMED v Mexico*, Award, 29 May 2003, para 144; cf also Art 15 of the ILC Articles on State Responsibility in J Crawford, *The International Law Commission's Articles on State Responsibility* (2002) 141; *Santa Elena v Costa Rica*, Award, 17 February 2000, para 76; *Azurix v Argentina*, Award, 14 July 2006, para 313.

[190] *Generation Ukraine v Ukraine*, Award, 16 September 2003; also *Rumeli v Kazakhstan*, Award, 29 July 2008.

[191] At paras 20.22, 20.26.

The decision in *Tradex v Albania*[192] emphasized the cumulative effect of the measures in question:

While the . . . Award has come to the conclusion that none of the single decisions and events alleged by Tradex to constitute an expropriation can indeed be qualified by the Tribunal as expropriation, it might still be possible that, and the Tribunal, therefore, has to examine and evaluate hereafter whether the combination of the decisions and events can be qualified as expropriation of Tradex' foreign investment in a long, step-by-step process by Albania.[193]

In *Siemens v Argentina*,[194] the host state had taken a series of adverse measures, including postponements and suspensions of the investor's profitable activities, fruitless renegotiations, and ultimately cancellation of the project. The Tribunal found that this had amounted to an expropriation and described creeping expropriation in the following terms:

By definition, creeping expropriation refers to a process, to steps that eventually have the effect of an expropriation. If the process stops before it reaches that point, then expropriation would not occur. This does not necessarily mean that no adverse effects would have occurred. Obviously, each step must have an adverse effect but by itself may not be significant or considered an illegal act. The last step in a creeping expropriation that tilts the balance is similar to the straw that breaks the camel's back. The preceding straws may not have had a perceptible effect but are part of the process that led to the break.[195]

Professor Reisman and R D Sloane have rightly pointed out that the issue must sometimes be seen in retrospect:

Discrete acts, analyzed in isolation rather than in the context of the overall flow of events, may, whether legal or not in themselves, seem innocuous vis-à-vis a potential expropriation. Some may not be expropriatory in themselves. Only, in retrospect will it become evident that those acts comprised part of an accretion of deleterious acts and omissions, which in the aggregate expropriated the foreign investor's property rights. . . . Because of their gradual and cumulative nature, creeping expropriations also render it problematic, perhaps even arbitrary, to identify a single interference (or failure to act where a duty requires it) as the 'moment of expropriation'.[196]

5. Expropriation of contractual rights

'The taking away or destruction of rights acquired, transmitted, and defined by a contract is as much a wrong, entitling the sufferer to redress, as the taking away or destruction of tangible property.' This principle, stated in 1903 by a member of the

---

[192] *Tradex v Albania*, Award, 29 April 1999.
[193] At para 191.
[194] *Siemens v Argentina*, Award, 6 February 2007.
[195] At para 263.
[196] W M Reisman and R D Sloane, 'Indirect Expropriation and its Valuation in the BIT Generation' (2003) 74 *BYBIL* 115, 123–5.

US–Venezuela Mixed Claims Commission in the *Rudloff* case,[197] was followed in 1922 by the Permanent Court of Arbitration in the *Norwegian Shipowners* case[198] and also by the PCIJ in 1926 in the *Chorzów Factory* case.[199] Cases decided in investment arbitrations[200] and by the Iran–US Claims Tribunal[201] have confirmed this position.

In *Amoco International Finance Corp v Iran* the Iran–US Claims Tribunal held that expropriation may extend to any right that can be the object of a commercial transaction.[202] The Arbitral Tribunal in *Tokios Tokelės v Ukraine* stated that all business operations associated with the physical property of the investors are covered by the term 'investment', including contractual rights.[203]

In the modern investment context, many investment decisions are accompanied and protected by specific investment agreements with the host state, often covering matters such as taxation, customs regulations, the right and duty to sell at a certain price to the host state, or pricing issues. These agreements form the legal and financial foundations of the investment, and the business decisions based upon them may collapse in their absence. Thus, it is understandable that practically all investment treaties state that contracts are covered by the term 'investment'.[204] In turn, provisions dealing with expropriation in these treaties refer to 'investments'. It follows that contracts are protected against expropriation. The Tribunal in *Siemens v Argentina*,[205] applying the BIT between Argentina and Germany, said:

---

[197] American–Venezuelan Mixed Claims Commission, *Rudloff Case*, Decision on Merits, IX RIAA 244, 250 (1959).

[198] Permanent Court of Arbitration, *Norwegian Shipowners' Claim* (*Norway v United States*), 13 October 1922, I RIAA 307 (1948). The arbitrators held that by requisitioning ships that were to be built for Norwegian citizens, the US Government also expropriated the underlying construction contracts.

[199] *Case Concerning Certain German Interests in Polish Upper Silesia*, 1926, PCIJ, Series A, No 7, 3.

[200] See *SPP v Egypt*, Award, 20 May 1992, paras 164–7; *Wena Hotels v Egypt*, Award, 8 December 2000, para 98; *CME v Czech Republic*, Partial Award, 13 September 2001, para 591; *Impregilo v Pakistan*, Decision on Jurisdiction, 22 April 2005, para 274; *Eureko v Poland*, Partial Award, 19 August 2005, para 241; *Bayindir v Pakistan*, Decision on Jurisdiction, 14 November 2005, para 255; *Azurix v Argentina*, Award, 14 July 2006, para 314; *Inmaris v Ukraine*, Decision on Jurisdiction, 8 March 2010, para 66: contracts may lead to 'a claim of money' even if the agreement is fictious.

[201] Article IV-2 of the Treaty of Amity between Iran and the USA (1955) protects not only 'property' but also 'interests in property'. According to the tribunal in *Phillips Petroleum Company v Iran*, the term 'interest in property' was 'included at the insistence of the United States for the stated purpose of ensuring that contract rights in the petroleum industry would be protected by the treaty in the same way as would the older type of property represented by a petroleum concession' (see *Phillips Petroleum Company v Iran*, Award, 29 June 1989, para 105).

[202] *Amoco International Finance Corp v Iran*, Award, 14 July 1987, para 108.

[203] *Tokios Tokelės v Ukraine*, Decision on Jurisdiction, 29 April 2004, paras 92–3.

[204] See eg Energy Charter Treaty, Art 1(6)(f): 'any right conferred by law or contract'. See also NAFTA, Art 1139. See R Dolzer and M Stevens, *Bilateral Investment Treaties* (1994); G Sacerdoti, 'Bilateral Treaties and Multilateral Instruments on Investment Protection' (1997) 269 *Collected Courses of the Hague Academy of International Law* 251, 381; R Higgins, 'The Taking of Property by the State: Recent Developments in International Law' (1982-III) 176 *Collected Courses of the Hague Academy of International Law* 263, 271; UNCTAD, *Series on Issues in International Investment Agreements: 'Taking of Property'* (2000) 36.

[205] *Siemens v Argentina*, Award, 6 February 2007.

The Contract falls under the definition of 'investments' under the Treaty and Article 4(2) refers to expropriation or nationalization of investments. Therefore, the State parties recognized that an investment in terms of the Treaty may be expropriated. There is nothing unusual in this regard. There is a long judicial practice that recognizes that expropriation is not limited to tangible property.[206]

Not every failure by a government to perform a contract amounts to an expropriation even if the violation leads to a loss of rights under the contract. A simple breach of contract at the hands of the state is not an expropriation.[207] Tribunals have found that the determining factor is whether the state acted in an official, governmental capacity.[208]

In the *Jalapa Railroad* case before the American Mexican Claims Commission (1948),[209] the decisive issue was whether the nullification of a contractual clause by the Mexican Government was 'effected arbitrarily by means of a governmental power illegal under international law'. In *Consortium RFCC v Morocco*, the Tribunal differentiated between the mere exercise of a right and an action by the host state 'in a public capacity' and placed emphasis on whether a law or a governmental decree had been passed or a judgment executed.[210]

Other tribunals have held similarly that mere breaches of contract or defects in its performance would not amount to an expropriation. What was needed was an act of public authority.[211] In *Siemens v Argentina*,[212] the Tribunal, in the course of its discussion of expropriation, found that a state party to a contract would breach the applicable treaty only if its behaviour went beyond that which an ordinary contracting party could adopt.[213] The Tribunal said:

for the State to incur international responsibility it must act as such, it must use its public authority. The actions of the State have to be based on its 'superior governmental power'. It is not a matter of being disappointed in the performance of the State in the execution of a contract but rather of interference in the contract execution through governmental action.[214]

---

[206] At para 267. The Tribunal relied on the *Norwegian Shipowners* and *Chorzów Factory* cases.

[207] For detailed discussion, see S M Schwebel, 'On Whether the Breach by a State of a Contract with an Alien is a Breach of International Law' in *International Law at the Time of its Codification, Essays in Honour of Roberto Ago, III* (1987) 401.

[208] See also the American Law Institute, *Restatement (Third) of the Foreign Relations Law of the United States*, Vol 2 (1986), p 201: 'a state is responsible for such a repudiation or breach only ... if it is akin to an expropriation in that the contract is repudiated or breached for governmental rather than commercial reasons.'

[209] American–Mexican Claims Commission, *Jalapa Railroad and Power Co*, 8 Whiteman Digest of International Law (1976) 908–9.

[210] *RFCC v Morocco*, Award, 22 December 2003, paras 60–2, 65–9, 85–9.

[211] *Impregilo v Pakistan*, Decision on Jurisdiction, 22 April 2005, para 281; *Bayindir v Pakistan*, Decision on Jurisdiction, 14 November 2005, para 257; *Azurix v Argentina*, Award, 14 July 2006, para 315.

[212] *Siemens v Argentina*, Award, 6 February 2007.

[213] At para 248.

[214] At para 253.

In particular, tribunals have held that failure to pay a debt under a contract does not amount to an expropriation.[215] *Waste Management v Mexico*[216] concerned a concession for waste disposal. The Tribunal found that the mere non-payment by the city of Acapulco of amounts due under the concession agreement did not amount to an expropriation.[217] It found that the state's failure to pay bills, did not amount to an 'outright repudiation of the transaction' and did not purport to terminate the contact. Only a decree or executive act or an exercise of legislative public authority could amount to an expropriation:

The mere non-performance of a contractual obligation is not to be equated with a taking of property, nor (unless accompanied by other elements) is it tantamount to expropriation. Any private party can fail to perform its contracts, whereas nationalization and expropriation are inherently governmental acts.[218] ...

The Tribunal concludes that it is one thing to expropriate a right under a contract and another to fail to comply with the contract. Non-compliance by a government with contractual obligations is not the same thing as, or equivalent or tantamount to, an expropriation.[219]

While these considerations are clearly helpful, they do not exhaust the subject. Indeed, the *Waste Management* tribunal itself recognized, without elaboration, that 'one could envisage conduct tantamount to an expropriation which consisted of acts and omissions not specifically or exclusively governmental'.[220] An analysis that is consistent with the approach generally valid for all acts of expropriation would not focus exclusively on the existence of formal governmental acts or the purported intentions of the government but would also contemplate other relevant factors.[221]

---

[215] *SGS v Philippines*, Decision on Jurisdiction, 29 January 2004, para 161.
[216] *Waste Management v Mexico*, Award, 30 April 2004.
[217] At paras 159–74.
[218] At para 174.
[219] At para 175. Also *Bureau Veritas v Paraguay*, Award, 29 May 2009.
[220] At para 175.
[221] See *Alpha v Ukraine*, Award, 8 November 2010, para 412; see further p 230.

VII

Standards of Protection

1. Fair and equitable treatment[1]

Most bilateral investment treaties (BITs) and other investment treaties provide for fair and equitable treatment (FET) of foreign investments.[2] For instance, the BIT between Argentina and the United States in Article II(2) a) states: 'Investment shall at all times be accorded fair and equitable treatment...'

Today, this concept is the most frequently invoked standard in investment disputes. It is also the standard with the highest practical relevance: the majority of successful claims pursued in international arbitration are based on a violation of the FET standard. It is only since 2000 that investment tribunals have started giving content to the meaning of the standard. They have since applied it to a broad range of circumstances. The evolution of this jurisprudence is traced in some detail below.

(a) History of the concept

The concept of FET is not new and has appeared in international documents for some time. Some of these documents were non-binding, others entered into force as multilateral or bilateral treaties.[3] The origin of the clause seems to date back to the treaty practice of the United States in the period of treaties on friendship, commerce, and navigation (FCN).[4] For instance, Article I section 1 of the 1954 Treaty between Germany and the United States reads: 'Each Party shall at all times

---

[1] This section draws on the two articles by C Schreuer, 'Fair and Equitable Treatment in Arbitral Practice' (2005) 6 *J World Investment & Trade* 357–86 and R Dolzer, 'Fair and Equitable Treatment: A Key Standard in Investment Treaties' (2005) 39 *International Lawyer* 87.

[2] R Dolzer and M Stevens, *Bilateral Investment Treaties* (1995) 58; S Vasciannie, 'The Fair and Equitable Treatment Standard in International Investment Law and Practice' (1999) 70 *BYBIL* 99, 113–14; I Tudor, *The Fair and Equitable Treatment Standard in International Law of Foreign Investment* (2008); K Yannaca-Small, 'Fair and Equitable Treatment Standard' in K Yannaca-Small (ed), *Arbitration under International Investment Agreements* (2010) 385; S W Schill, 'Fair and Equitable Treatment, the Rule of Law, and Comparative Public Law' in S W Schill (ed), *International Investment Law and Comparative Public Law* (2010) 151; A Diehl, *The Core Standard of International Investment Protection: Fair and Equitable Treatment* (2012).

[3] See especially UNCTAD Series on issues in international investment agreements, 'Fair and Equitable Treatment' (1999) 3–4, 7–9, 25–8, 31–2; S Vasciannie, 'The Fair and Equitable Treatment Standard in International Investment Law and Practice' (1999) 70 *BYBIL* 99, 100–11, 107–19.

[4] See R R Wilson, *United States Commercial Treaties and International Law* (1960) 113, 120.

accord fair and equitable treatment to the nationals and companies of the other Party and to their property, enterprises and other interests.'[5]

A reference to a 'just and equitable treatment' standard appeared in Article 11(2) of the Havanna Charter for an International Trade Organization of 1948.[6] The Abs–Shawcross Draft Convention on Investment Abroad of 1959 in its Article I referred to 'fair and equitable treatment to the property of the nationals of the other Parties',[7] and the subsequent Organisation for Economic Co-operation and Development (OECD) Draft Convention on the Protection of Foreign Property of 1967 in its Article 1 contained similar language.[8]

Also, the draft for a United Nations Code of Conduct on Transnational Corporations in its 1983 version provided that transnational corporations should receive fair and equitable treatment.[9] The Guidelines on the Treatment of Foreign Direct Investment adopted by the Development Committee of the Board of Governors of the International Monetary Fund (IMF) and the World Bank in 1992 in their Section III dealing with 'Treatment' provided that '2. Each State will extend to investments established in its territory by nationals of any other State fair and equitable treatment according to the standards recommended in these Guidelines'.[10]

The OECD Draft Negotiating Text for a Multilateral Agreement on Investment (MAI) of 1998 contained the following text in its section on investment protection:

1.1. Each Contracting Party shall accord to investments in its territory of investors of another Contracting Party fair and equitable treatment and full and constant protection and security. In no case shall a Contracting Party accord treatment less favourable than that required by international law.[11]

The concept of FET has also entered into a number of multilateral treaties currently in force. For instance, the Convention Establishing the Multilateral Investment Guarantee Agency of 1985 requires the availability of fair and equitable treatment as a precondition for extending insurance cover. Article 12 dealing with 'Eligible Investments' provides in part:

(d) In guaranteeing an investment, the Agency shall satisfy itself as to: ... (iv) the investment conditions in the host country, including the availability of fair and equitable treatment and legal protection for the investment.[12]

---

[5] Treaty of Friendship, Commerce and Navigation, 29 October 1954, US-FRG, 273 UNTS 4. See also Treaty of Amity, Economic Relations, and Consular Rights, 15 August 1955, US-Iran, 284 UNTS 110, 114.

[6] UNCTAD, *International Investment Instruments: A Compendium*, vol I (1996) 4. The Havana Charter never entered into force.

[7] UNCTAD, *International Investment Instruments: A Compendium*, vol V (2001) 395. The Draft Convention represented a private initiative by H Abs and Lord Shawcross.

[8] OECD Draft Convention on the Protection of Foreign Property (1967), 7 ILM 117, 119 (1968).

[9] UNCTAD, *International Investment Instruments: A Compendium*, vol I (1996) 172.

[10] 'Guidelines on the Treatment of Foreign Direct Investment' (1992) 7 *ICSID Review-FILJ* 297, 300.

[11] UNCTAD, *International Investment Instruments: A Compendium*, vol IV (2001) 148.

[12] UNCTAD, *International Investment Instruments: A Compendium*, vol I (1996) 219.

The North American Free Trade Agreement (NAFTA) of 1992 contains the FET principle in its Article 1105, paragraph 1.[13] This provision is discussed in more detail below.

The Energy Charter Treaty (ECT) of 1994 contains elaborate language around the requirement of FET in its Article 10(1):

(1) Each Contracting Party shall, in accordance with the provisions of this Treaty, encourage and create stable, equitable, favourable and transparent conditions for Investors of other Contracting Parties to make investments in its area. Such conditions shall include a commitment to accord at all times to Investments of Investors of other Contracting Parties fair and equitable treatment.[14]

(b) Heterogeneity of treaty language

Generalizations about the standard of fair and equitable treatment should be treated with caution. As with other standard clauses in investment treaties, no single frozen version exists. Indeed, the variations in this area are quite significant.[15] Every type of clause has to be interpreted in accordance with Article 31 of the Vienna Convention on the Law of Treaties (VCLT), duly taking into account its context and, as appropriate, its history. The discussion on the different types of linkage to customary law is a good example of these variations.[16]

Some treaties refer to 'equitable and reasonable' rather than 'fair and equitable'. This variation does not appear to reflect a difference in meaning.[17]

(c) Nature and function

Essentially, the purpose of the clause as used in BIT practice is to fill gaps which may be left by the more specific standards, in order to obtain the level of investor protection intended by the treaties.[18] The operation of FET clauses in investment treaties is reminiscent of codes in civil law countries which set forth a number of specific rules and complement these with a general clause of good faith as an overarching principle which fills gaps and informs the understanding of specific clauses. Indeed, the substance of the standard of fair and equitable treatment overlaps with the meaning of good faith in its broader setting, including the related notions of *venire contra factum proprium* and estoppel. In practice the FET standard may offer redress where the facts do not support a claim for expropriation.[19]

---

[13] 32 ILM 639 (1993).

[14] 34 ILM 381, 389 (1995).

[15] See R Dolzer and M Stevens, *Bilateral Investment Treaties* (1995) 58; G Sacerdoti, 'Bilateral Treaties and Multilateral Instruments on Investment Protection' (1997) 269 *Recueil des Cours* 251, 344.

[16] See pp 134 et seq.

[17] *Parkerings v Lithuania*, Award, 11 September 2007, paras 271–8.

[18] *Sempra v Argentina*, Award, 28 September 2007, para 297.

[19] *PSEG v Turkey*, Award, 19 January 2007, para 238; *Continental Casualty v Argentina*, Award, 5 September 2008, para 254.

Does FET contain two standards, namely 'fair' and 'equitable', with independent meanings for each concept? While it would not be impossible to argue along those lines, no evidence of practice seems to point in that direction. The general assumption appears to be that 'fair and equitable' must be considered to represent a single, unified standard.

At times it has been suggested that the FET standard is merely an overarching principle that embraces the other standards of treatment typically found in investment treaties.[20] While it is undeniable that there is a certain degree of interaction and overlap with other standards, it is widely accepted that FET is an autonomous standard.[21] In the majority of cases tribunals have distinguished FET from other standards and have examined separately whether there has been a violation of the respective standards.[22] There is no doubt that the FET standard is meant as a rule of international law and is not determined by the laws of the host state. Tribunals have repeatedly emphasized the independence of the FET standard from the national treatment standard.[23] The FET standard may be violated even if the foreign investor receives the same treatment as investors of the host state's nationality. For the same reason, an investor may have been treated unfairly and inequitably even if it is unable to benefit from a most-favoured-nation (MFN) clause because it cannot show that investors of other nationalities have received better treatment.[24]

Some tribunals have pointed to the vagueness and lack of definition of the FET standard[25] and the European Parliament has deplored the use of vague language in this context.[26] In fact, the lack of precision may be a virtue rather than a shortcoming. In actual practice it is impossible to anticipate in the abstract the range of possible types of infringements upon the investor's legal position. The principle of FET allows for independent and objective third party determination of this type

[20] *Noble Ventures Inc v Romania*, Award, 12 October 2005, para 182; *Lemire v Ukraine*, Decision on Jurisdiction and Liability, 14 January 2010, paras 259, 385; *Impregilo v Argentina*, Award, 21 June 2011, paras 333–4.

[21] I Tudor, *The Fair and Equitable Treatment Standard in International Law of Foreign Investment* (2008) 182–202; C Schreuer, 'Fair and Equitable Treatment (FET): Interactions with Other Standards' in G Coop and C Ribeiro (eds), *Investment Protection and the Energy Charter Treaty* (2008) 63.

[22] *Azurix v Argentina*, Award, 14 July 2006, paras 407–8; *LG&E v Argentina*, Decision on Liability, 3 October 2006, paras 162, 163; *PSEG v Turkey*, Award, 19 January 2007, paras 258–9; *Plama v Bulgaria*, Award, 27 August 2008, paras 161–3, 183–4; *El Paso v Argentina*, Award, 31 October 2011, paras 228–31.

[23] *Genin v Estonia*, Award, 25 June 2001, para 367; *SD Myers v Canada*, First Partial Award, 13 November 2000, para 259; *CME v Czech Republic*, Partial Award, 13 September 2001, para 611; *UPS v Canada*, Decision on Jurisdiction, 22 November 2002, para 80; *El Paso v Argentina*, Award, 31 October 2011, para 337.

[24] K Yannaca-Small, 'Fair and Equitable Treatment Standard' in K Yannaca-Small (ed), *Arbitration under International Investment Agreements* (2010) 385.

[25] *CMS v Argentina*, Award, 12 May 2005, para 273; *Sempra v Argentina*, Award, 28 September 2007, para 296; *Rumeli v Kazakhstan*, Award, 29 July 2008, para 610; *Suez v Argentina*, Decision on Liability, 30 July 2010, paras 196, 202; *Total v Argentina*, Decision on Liability, 27 December 2010, paras 106–9. See also P Juillard, 'L'évolution des sources du droit des investissements' (1994) 250 *Recueil des Cours* 9, 133.

[26] European Parliament Resolution of 6 April 2011 on the Future European International Investment Policy, preamble, para G.

of behaviour on the basis of a flexible standard.[27] Therefore, it is not devoid of independent legal content. Like other broad principles of law, it is susceptible to specification through judicial practice. As Prosper Weil wrote in 2000:

The standard of 'fair and equitable treatment' is certainly no less operative than was the standard of 'due process of law', and it will be for future practice, jurisprudence and commentary to impart specific content to it.[28]

Stephan Schill has pointed out that 'fair and equitable treatment can be understood as embodying the rule of law as a standard that the legal systems of host states have to embrace in their treatment of foreign investors'.[29]

Although 'fair and equitable' may be reminiscent of the extralegal concepts of fairness and equity, it should not be confused with decisions *ex aequo et bono*.[30] The Tribunal in *ADF Group* pointed out that the requirement to accord fair and equitable treatment does not allow a tribunal to adopt its own idiosyncratic standard but 'must be disciplined by being based upon state practice and judicial or arbitral case law or other sources of customary or general international law'.[31]

(d) Fair and equitable treatment and customary international law

Considerable debate has surrounded the question of whether the FET standard merely reflects the international minimum standard, as contained in customary international law, or offers an autonomous standard that is additional to general international law. As a matter of textual interpretation it seems implausible that a treaty would refer to a well-known concept such as the 'minimum standard of treatment in customary international law' by using the expression 'fair and equitable treatment'. If the parties to a treaty want to refer to customary international law, one would assume that they would refer to it as such rather than using a different expression.[32]

A number of commentators have expressed the view that FET constitutes an independent treaty standard that goes beyond a mere restatement of customary international law.[33] Prominent among the supporters of an independent concept of

---

[27] S Vasciannie, 'The Fair and Equitable Treatment Standard in International Investment Law and Practice' (1999) 70 *BYBIL* 99, 100, 104, 145.

[28] P Weil, 'The State, the Foreign Investor, and International Law: The No Longer Stormy Relationship of a *Ménage À Trois*' (2000) 15 *ICSID Review-FILJ* 401, 415.

[29] S W Schill, 'Fair and Equitable Treatment, the Rule of Law, and Comparative Public Law' in S W Schill (ed), *International Investment Law and Comparative Public Law* (2010) 151.

[30] See C Schreuer, 'Decisions Ex Aequo et Bono under the ICSID Convention' (1996) 11 *ICSID Review-FILJ* 37.

[31] *ADF v United States*, Award, 9 January 2003, para 184. See also *Mondev v United States*, Award, 11 October 2002, para 119; *Saluka v Czech Republic*, Partial Award, 17 March 2006, paras 282–4; *Enron v Argentina*, Award, 22 May 2007, paras 256–7; *MCI v Ecuador*, Award, 31 July 2007, para 370; *Total v Argentina*, Decision on Liability, 27 December 2010, paras 108–9.

[32] *Biwater Gauff v Tanzania*, Award, 24 July 2008, para 591.

[33] R Dolzer and M Stevens, *Bilateral Investment Treaties* (1995) 60; P T Muchlinski, *Multinational Enterprises and the Law* (1999) 626; UNCTAD Series on issues in international investment agreements, 'Fair and Equitable Treatment' (1999) 13, 17, 37–40, 53, 61; S Vasciannie, 'The Fair and

fair and equitable treatment is F A Mann. Writing about British BITs in 1981 he said:

It is submitted that nothing is gained by introducing the conception of a minimum standard and, more than this, it is positively misleading to introduce it. The terms 'fair and equitable treatment' envisage conduct which goes far beyond the minimum standard and afford protection to a greater extent and according to a much more objective standard than any previously employed form of words. A tribunal would not be concerned with a minimum, maximum or average standard. It will have to decide whether in all circumstances the conduct in issue is fair and equitable or unfair and inequitable. No standard defined by other words is likely to be material. The terms are to be understood and applied independently and autonomously.[34]

On the other hand, the Notes and Comments to the OECD Draft Convention on the Protection of Foreign Property of 1967 indicate that the FET standard is set by customary international law.[35] Similarly, the European Parliament in a resolution adopted in 2011 stated that in investment agreements to be concluded by the EU, fair and equitable treatment should be 'defined on the basis of the level of treatment established by international customary law'.[36]

To a certain degree this debate depends on the exact wording of the treaty clauses providing for FET. Upon closer examination these provide in varying degrees for linkage with customary international law. Some treaties simply prescribe 'fair and equitable treatment' without reference to customary international law; German, Dutch, Swedish, and Swiss BITs generally follow this pattern.

Other clauses dealing with FET treat the standard as an element of the general rules of international law; the United States[37] and Canada have followed this approach. Also, Article 1105 of the NAFTA treats FET as part of international law.

Some treaties state that FET is to be afforded 'in accordance with international law'. The French Model Treaty provides that the states parties 'shall extend fair and equitable treatment in accordance with the principles of International Law'. Some

---

Equitable Treatment Standard in International Investment Law and Practice' (1999) 70 *BYBIL* 99, 104–5, 139–44; I Tudor, *The Fair and Equitable Treatment Standard in International Law of Foreign Investment* (2008) 54–68.

[34] F A Mann, 'British Treaties for the Promotion and Protection of Investments' (1981) 52 *BYBIL* 241, 244.

[35] 7 ILM 118, 120 (1968). See also a comment by the Swiss Foreign Office of 1979 in (1980) 36 *Annuaire suisse de droit international* 178.

[36] European Parliament Resolution of 6 April 2011 on the Future European International Investment Policy, para 19.

[37] The US State Department explained its position in 1992 in terms of the FET standard being a guide to interpretation, as embodying US policy and as replicating European practice, and in 2000 as being based on standards found in customary international law. See J J Coe, 'Fair and Equitable Treatment under NAFTA's Investment Chapter', *ASIL Proceedings* (2002), 17–19. The US Model BIT of 2012 prescribes, in Art 5, para 1, that each party 'shall accord to covered investments treatment in accordance with customary international law, including fair and equitable treatment and full protection and security', adding in para 2 that this rule 'prescribes the customary international law minimum standard of treatment of aliens as the minimum standard of treatment to be afforded to covered investments', and that the concept of fair and equitable treatment does not require additional protection and does not create additional substantive rights.

treaties state that fair and equitable treatment must in no case provide for less protection than the rules of international law. Yet another version lists fair and equitable treatment in addition to the rules of international law.

By far the most intensive discussion on the relationship of the FET standard to customary international law took place in the context of Article 1105(1) of the NAFTA.[38] That provision, including its title, reads as follows:

Article 1105: Minimum Standard of Treatment

1. Each Party shall accord to investments of investors of another Party treatment in accordance with international law, including fair and equitable treatment and full protection and security.[39]

This provision has been the subject of an official interpretation by the NAFTA Free Trade Commission (FTC), a body composed of representatives of the three states parties with the power to adopt binding interpretations.[40] The FTC interpretation states that Article 1105(1) reflects the customary international law minimum standard and does not require treatment in addition to or beyond that which is required by customary international law.[41] NAFTA tribunals have accepted the FTC interpretation.[42] In addition, subsequent BIT practice of the United States[43] and of Canada[44] has followed the FTC interpretation. The US Model BITs of

---

[38] See especially C N Brower, C H Brower, and J K Sharpe, 'The Coming Crisis in the Global Adjudication System' (2003) 19 *Arbitration International* 415, 428; P Dumberry, 'The Quest to Define "Fair and Equitable Treatment" for Investors under International Law, The Case of the NAFTA Chapter 11 Pope & Talbot Awards' (2002) 3 *J World Investment* 657; P G Foy and R J C Deane, 'Foreign Investment Protection under Investment Treaties: Recent Developments under Chapter 11 of the North American Free Trade Agreement' (2001) 16 *ICSID Review-FILJ* 299; J C Thomas, 'Reflections on Article 1105 of NAFTA: History, State Practice and the Influence of Commentators' (2002) 17 *ICSID Review-FILJ* 21; K Yannaca-Small, 'Fair and Equitable Treatment Standard' in K Yannaca-Small (ed), *Arbitration under International Investment Agreements* (2010) 387–93.

[39] North American Free Trade Agreement, 8–17 December 1992, 32 ILM 605, 639 (1993) (entered into force 1 January 1994).

[40] NAFTA, Art 1132(2).

[41] FTC Note of Interpretation of 31 July 2001:

> Minimum Standard of Treatment in Accordance with International Law: 1. Article 1105 (1) prescribes the customary international law minimum standard of treatment of aliens as the minimum standard of treatment to be afforded to investments of investors of another Party. 2. The concepts of 'fair and equitable treatment' and 'full protection and security' do not require treatment in addition to or beyond that which is required by the customary international law minimum standard of treatment of aliens. 3. A determination that there has been a breach of another provision of the NAFTA, or of a separate international agreement, does not establish that there has been a breach of Article 1105(1).

[42] *Pope & Talbot v Canada*, Award on Damages, 31 May 2002, paras 17–69; *Mondev v United States*, Award, 11 October 2002, paras 100 et seq; *UPS v Canada*, Decision on Jurisdiction, 22 November 2002, para 97; *ADF v United States*, Award, 9 January 2003, paras 175–8; *Loewen v United States*, Award, 26 June 2003, paras 124–8; *Waste Management v Mexico*, Final Award, 30 April 2004, paras 90–1; *Methanex v United States*, Award, 3 August 2005, Part IV, Ch C, paras 17–24; *Thunderbird v Mexico*, Award, 26 January 2006, paras 192, 193; *Glamis Gold v United States*, Award, 8 June 2009, para 599; *Chemtura v Canada*, Award, 2 August 2010, para 121; *Grand River Enterprises v United States*, Award, 12 January 2011, paras 173–6. See also *Metalclad Corp v Mexico*, Review by British Columbia Supreme Court, 2 May 2001, 5 ICSID Reports (2002) 238, paras 61–5.

[43] See Chile-US FTA of 2003, Art 10.4; US-Uruguay BIT of 2004, Art 5.

[44] Canada Model BIT, Art 5.

2004 and of 2012, in their respective Articles 5(2), state that FET prescribes the customary international law minimum standard of treatment and that it does not require treatment in addition to or beyond that required by that standard.

The authority of this practice, developed in the NAFTA context, is of limited relevance for the interpretation of other treaties because the NAFTA has features not shared by other treaties: Article 1105 refers to the 'Minimum Standard of Treatment' in its title. It also refers to 'international law, including fair and equitable treatment'. In addition, it was the object of a binding interpretation by an authorized treaty body for the purposes of that treaty.

In contrast to the NAFTA practice, arbitral tribunals applying other treaties not containing statements about the relationship of FET to customary international law have tended to interpret the relevant provisions autonomously on the basis of their respective wording.[45] Some of these tribunals have, however, insisted that FET is not different from the international minimum standard required by international law.[46]

In *Azurix v Argentina*,[47] the Tribunal had to interpret Article II(2) of the Argentina-US BIT guaranteeing FET and full protection and security. The provision adds that investments shall 'in no case be accorded treatment less than that required by international law'. According to the Tribunal:

The clause, as drafted, permits to interpret fair and equitable treatment and full protection and security as higher standards than required by international law. The purpose of the third sentence is to set a floor, not a ceiling, in order to avoid a possible interpretation of these standards below what is required by international law.[48]

In *Vivendi v Argentina*,[49] the applicable BIT provided for 'fair and equitable treatment according to the principles of international law'. The Tribunal found that there was no basis for the view that FET was limited to the international minimum standard and that such an interpretation would run counter to the text's ordinary meaning.[50] The Tribunal said:

Article 3 refers to fair and equitable treatment *in conformity* with the principles of international law, and not to the minimum standard of treatment.... The Tribunal sees no basis for equating principles of international law with the minimum standard of treatment. First,

[45] *Tecmed v Mexico*, Award, 29 May 2003, paras 155, 156; *MTD v Chile*, Award, 25 May 2004, paras 110–12; *Occidental v Ecuador*, Award, 1 July 2004, paras 188–90; *Saluka v Czech Republic*, Partial Award, 17 March 2006, paras 286–95; *Enron v Argentina*, Award, 22 May 2007, para 258; *Sempra v Argentina*, Award, 28 September 2007, para 302; *OKO Pankki v Estonia*, Award, 19 November 2007, paras 217–30; *Continental Casualty v Argentina*, Award, 5 September 2008, para 254; *National Grid v Argentina*, Award, 3 November 2008, paras 167–73; *Bayindir v Pakistan*, Award, 27 August 2009, para 164; *Total v Argentina*, Decision on Liability, 27 December 2010, paras 125–7.

[46] *Occidental v Ecuador*, Award, 1 July 2004, paras 189, 190; *CMS v Argentina*, Award, 12 May 2005, paras 282–4; *Rumeli v Kazakhstan*, Award, 29 July 2008, para 611; *El Paso v Argentina*, Award, 31 October 2011, paras 331–7; *Lemire v Ukraine*, Decision on Jurisdiction and Responsibility, 14 January 2010, paras 247–55.

[47] *Azurix v Argentina*, Award, 14 July 2006.

[48] At para 361.

[49] *Vivendi v Argentina*, Award, 20 August 2007.

[50] At para 745.

the reference to principles of international law supports a broader reading that invites consideration of a wider range of international law principles than the minimum standard alone. Second, the wording of Article 3 requires that the fair and equitable treatment *conform* to the principles of international law, but the requirement for conformity can just as readily set a floor as a ceiling on the Treaty's fair and equitable treatment standard.[51]

There are growing doubts about the relevance of this whole debate.[52] Tribunals have indicated that the difference between the treaty standard of FET and the customary minimum standard 'when applied to the specific facts of a case, may well be more apparent than real'.[53] The Tribunal in *El Paso*[54] pointed out that the discussion was somewhat futile since the content of the international minimum standard is 'as little defined as the BIT's FET standard'.[55]

Depending on the specific wording of a particular treaty, it may overlap with or even be identical to the minimum standard required by international law. The fact that the host state has breached a rule of international law may be evidence of a violation of the fair and equitable standard,[56] but this is not the only conceivable form of breach.

The emphasis on linkages between FET and customary international law is unlikely to restrain the evolution of the FET standard. On the contrary, this may have the effect of accelerating the development of customary law through the rapidly expanding practice on FET clauses in treaties.[57] The Tribunal in *Chemtura v Canada*[58] said in this respect:

the Tribunal notes that it is not disputed that the scope of Article 1105 of NAFTA must be determined by reference to customary international law. Such determination cannot over-look the evolution of customary international law, nor the impact of BITs on this evolution.... [I]n determining the standard of treatment set by Article 1105 of NAFTA, the Tribunal has taken into account the evolution of international customary law as a result *inter alia* of the conclusion of numerous BITs providing for fair and equitable treatment.[59]

---

[51] At paras 7.4.6, 7.4.7. Emphasis in original; footnote omitted.
[52] See S W Schill, 'Fair and Equitable Treatment, the Rule of Law, and Comparative Public Law' in S W Schill (ed), *International Investment Law and Comparative Public Law* (2010) 152–4.
[53] *Saluka v Czech Republic*, Partial Award, 17 March 2006, para 291. See also *Azurix v Argentina*, Award, 14 July 2006, para 361, 364; *Occidental v Ecuador*, Award, 1 July 2004, para 190; *CMS v Argentina*, Award, 12 May 2005, paras 282–4; *Biwater Gauff v Tanzania*, Award, 24 July 2008, para 592; *Rumeli v Kazakhstan*, Award, 29 July 2008, para 611; *Duke Energy v Ecuador*, Award, 18 August 2008, paras 332–7; *Impregilo v Argentina*, Award, 21 June 2011, paras 287–9.
[54] *El Paso v Argentina*, Award, 31 October 2011.
[55] At para 335.
[56] See *SD Myers v Canada*, First Partial Award, 13 November 2000, para 264: 'the fact that a host Party has breached a rule of international law that is specifically designed to protect investors will tend to weigh heavily in favour of finding a breach of Article 1105.'
[57] R Dolzer and A von Walter, 'Fair and Equitable Treatment and Customary Law—Lines of Jurisprudence' in F Ortino, L Liberti, A Sheppard, and H Warner (eds), *Investment Treaty Law: Current Issues* (2007) 99; I Tudor, *The Fair and Equitable Treatment Standard in International Law of Foreign Investment* (2008) 83–5.
[58] *Chemtura v Canada*, Award, 2 August 2010.
[59] At paras 121, 236.

The Tribunal in *Merrill & Ring* went one step further and stated that FET had become part of customary international law:

A requirement that aliens be treated fairly and equitably in relation to business, trade and investment is the outcome of this changing reality and as such it has become sufficiently part of widespread and consistent practice so as to demonstrate that it is reflected today in customary international law as *opinio juris*.[60]

(e) The evolution of the fair and equitable treatment standard

Obviously, the standard of FET is a broad one, and its meaning will depend on the specific circumstances of the case at issue.[61] The Tribunal in *Mondev v United States* pointed out that '[a] judgment of what is fair and equitable cannot be reached in the abstract; it must depend on the facts of the particular case'.[62] Similarly, the Tribunal in *Waste Management v Mexico* noted that 'the standard is to some extent a flexible one which must be adapted to the circumstances of each case'.[63]

NAFTA tribunals have been inclined to see the standard against a historical-evolutionary background. Other tribunals have dealt with it more directly from a contemporary perspective.[64] The historical starting point for a discussion on the standard of treatment for foreigners is often seen in the *Neer* case of 1926.[65] The case did not concern an investment but the murder of a US citizen in Mexico. The charge was that the Mexican authorities had shown a lack of diligence in investigating and prosecuting the crime. The Commission said:

the treatment of an alien, in order to constitute an international delinquency, should amount to an outrage, to bad faith, to wilful neglect of duty, or to an insufficiency of governmental action so far short of international standards that every reasonable and impartial man would readily recognize its insufficiency.[66]

The Commission found that the facts did not show such a lack of diligence as would render Mexico liable and dismissed the claim.

---

[60] *Merrill & Ring Forestry v Canada*, Award, 31 March 2010, para 210.

[61] See eg G Sacerdoti, 'Bilateral Treaties and Multilateral Instruments on Investment Protection' (1997) 269 *Recueil des Cours* 251, 346; UNCTAD Series on issues in international investment treaties, 'Fair and Equitable Treatment' (1999) 22.

[62] *Mondev v United States*, Award, 11 October 2002, para 118.

[63] *Waste Management v Mexico*, Final Award, 30 April 2004, para 99. See also *Lauder v Czech Republic*, Award, 3 September 2001, para 292; *CMS v Argentina*, Award, 12 May 2005, para 273; *Noble Ventures v Romania*, Award, 12 October 2005, para 181. See also P T Muchlinski, *Multinational Enterprises and the Law* (1999) 625.

[64] R Dolzer and A von Walter, 'Fair and Equitable Treatment and Customary Law—Lines of Jurisprudence' in F Ortino, L Liberti, A Sheppard, and H Warner (eds), *Investment Treaty Law: Current Issues* (2007) 99.

[65] *Neer v Mexico*, Opinion, US–Mexico General Claims Commission, 15 October 1926 (1927) 21 *AJIL* 555; IV RIAA 60–2. See P G Foy and R J C Deane, 'Foreign Investment Protection under Investment Treaties: Recent Developments under Chapter 11 of the North American Free Trade Agreement' (2001) 16 *ICSID Review-FILJ* 299, 314; J C Thomas, 'Reflections on Article 1105 of NAFTA: History, State Practice and the Influence of Commentators' (2002) 17 *ICSID Review-FILJ* 21, 29–32; J Paulsson and G Petrochilos, '*Neer*-ly Misled?' (2007) 22 *ICSID Review-FILJ* 242.

[66] At 556.

Another frequently cited case is *ELSI (United States v Italy)*[67] decided by a Chamber of the International Court of Justice (ICJ). While the relevant treaty in that case prohibits 'arbitrary' action, this tenet may also shed light on the FET standard. The case concerned the temporary requisitioning by the mayor of Palermo of an industrial plant belonging to an Italian company owned by US shareholders. The ICJ stated:

Arbitrariness is not so much something opposed to a rule of law, as something opposed to the rule of law. . . . It is a wilful disregard of due process of law, an act which shocks, or at least surprises, a sense of judicial propriety.[68]

The Court found that the requisition order did not violate that standard.

Subsequent tribunals have specifically distanced themselves from the very high threshold for a violation of international law formulated in *Neer*. They have repeatedly embraced the less stringent standard of the *ELSI* case and have emphasized that they were dealing with an evolving concept.[69] *ADF v United States*[70] concerned domestic contents requirements in respect of government procurement for a construction project. In interpreting Article 1105 of the NAFTA, the Tribunal agreed:

that the customary international law referred to in Article 1105(1) is not 'frozen in time' and that the minimum standard of treatment does evolve. . . . [W]hat customary international law projects is not a static photograph of the minimum standard of treatment of aliens as it stood in 1927 when the Award in the *Neer* case was rendered. For both customary international law and the minimum standard of treatment of aliens it incorporates, are constantly in a process of development.[71]

Against this background it is surprising that in 2009 a NAFTA tribunal reverted to the *Neer* standard. In *Glamis Gold*[72] the Tribunal took the *Neer* decision as 'establishing' the international minimum standard. It found that the burden of proof for any change of customary international law lay with the claimant, a burden that it had been unable to discharge. It followed that the fundamentals of the *Neer* standard still apply today.[73]

---

[67] *Elettronica Sicula SpA (ELSI) (US v Italy)*, ICJ Reports (1989) 15.

[68] At para 128. For a detailed discussion of the *ELSI* case in relation to the FET standard, see S Vasciannie, 'The Fair and Equitable Treatment Standard in International Investment Law and Practice' (1999) 70 *BYBIL* 99, 134–7.

[69] *Pope & Talbot v Canada*, Award on Merits, 10 April 2001, para 118; *Pope & Talbot v Canada*, Award on Damages, 31 May 2002, paras 63, 64; *Mondev v United States*, Award, 11 October 2002, paras 116, 123, 125, 127; *GAMI v Mexico*, Award, 15 November 2004, para 95; *Eureko v Poland*, Partial Award, 19 August 2005, para 234; *Thunderbird v Mexico*, Award, 26 January 2006, para 194; *Azurix v Argentina*, Award, 14 July 2006, paras 365–8; *LG&E v Argentina*, Decision on Liability, 3 October 2006, para 123; *Vivendi v Argentina*, Award, 20 August 2007, para 7.4.7, note 325; *Merrill & Ring Forestry v Canada*, Award, 31 March 2010, paras 195–213.

[70] *ADF Group Inc v United States*, Award, 9 January 2003.

[71] At para 179.

[72] *Glamis Gold v United States*, Award, 8 June 2009.

[73] At paras 598–627.

Mercifully the *Glamis Gold* Tribunal restricted its finding to Article 1105 of the NAFTA and noted that its view did not extend to other treaty clauses on FET.[74] The Tribunal did not explain why a terse award rendered in 1926 dealing with a murder case should establish the standard for contemporary investment law. Nor does it explain why *Neer* should be authoritative while the practice of contemporary investment tribunals is not.[75]

A subsequent NAFTA tribunal, in *Merrill & Ring*, clearly distanced itself from an undifferentiated reliance on *Neer*:

the Tribunal finds that the applicable minimum standard of treatment of investors is found in customary international law and that, except for cases of safety and due process, today's minimum standard is broader than that defined in the *Neer* case and its progeny.[76]

In recent years there are indications of an approach by tribunals that stresses the need for states to maintain a regulatory space.[77] Tribunals have stressed that 'the host State's right to regulate domestic matters in the public interest has to be taken into consideration' and that a balance between the investor's rights and the host state's public interests has to be established.[78] The Tribunal in *Lemire v Ukraine*[79] said:

The protection of the legitimate expectations must be balanced with the need to maintain a reasonable degree of regulatory flexibility on the part of the host State in order to respond to changing circumstances in the public interest.[80]

(f) Methodological issues

A central methodological issue for the resolution of these questions concerns the process of reasoning by which fact-specific conclusions are drawn from the standard in individual cases. One line of reasoning derives a definition of the essential elements of the standard on the basis of abstract reasoning. A second approach resists an attempt at a broader definition and will decide ad hoc whether certain conduct satisfies the requirements of the standard.[81] Yet a third approach attempts primarily to base its decisions on previous decisions and will build upon relevant precedents to identify typical situations in which the standard has been applied. Obviously, the latter approach was not available to the first tribunals which applied the standard. The next two sections will explore the first and the third approaches.

---

[74] At paras 606–10.
[75] For a criticism of *Glamis Gold*, see Judge S M Schwebel, 'Is *Neer* Far from Fair and Equitable?' (2011) 27 *Arbitration International* 555.
[76] *Merrill & Ring Forestry v Canada*, Award, 31 March 2010, para 213.
[77] See pp 148–9.
[78] *Total v Argentina*, Decision on Liability, 27 December 2010, paras 123–4, 162, 309, 333, 429. See also *Plama v Bulgaria*, Award, 27 August 2008, para 177; *EDF v Romania*, Award, 8 October 2009, para 299; *El Paso v Argentina*, Award, 31 October 2011, para 358.
[79] *Lemire v Ukraine*, Decision on Jurisdiction and Liability, 14 January 2010.
[80] At para 500. See also para 273.
[81] *Mondev v United States*, Award, 11 October 2002, para 118.

A rule of law approach to the concept of FET would have to concentrate on a comparative analysis of domestic legal systems and of international legal regimes.[82]

In examining the state's behaviour for compliance with the FET standard some tribunals have not only looked at individual acts but have also looked at the overall cumulative impact of the measures. The Tribunal in *El Paso* adopted the concept of a composite act from Article 15 of the International Law Commission's Articles on State Responsibility and said:

Although they may be seen in isolation as reasonable measures to cope with a difficult economic situation, the measures examined can be viewed as cumulative steps which individually do not qualify as violations of FET, as pointed out earlier by the Tribunal, but which amount to a violation if their cumulative effect is considered. . . . A *creeping violation of the FET standard* could thus be described as a process extending over time and comprising a succession or an accumulation of measures which, taken separately, would not breach that standard but, when taken together, do lead to such a result.[83]

(g) Attempts to define fair and equitable treatment

In a number of cases the tribunals have tried to give a more specific meaning to the FET standard by formulating general definitions or descriptions.[84]

Genin v Estonia[85] concerned the withdrawal of a banking licence. The Tribunal stated that acts violating the fair and equitable standard:

would include acts showing a wilful neglect of duty, an insufficiency of action falling far below international standards, or even subjective bad faith.[86]

The most comprehensive definition, most often cited, was set out in *Tecmed*,[87] which concerned the withdrawal of a licence for a landfill for hazardous waste. The Tribunal found that it had to interpret the concept of FET autonomously taking into account its text according to its ordinary meaning, international law, and the good faith principle. The intention behind the concept was to strengthen the security and trust of foreign investors thereby maximizing the use of economic resources. This goal was expressed in the preamble.[88] The Tribunal defined FET in the following terms:

---

[82] S W Schill, 'Fair and Equitable Treatment, the Rule of Law, and Comparative Public Law' in S W Schill (ed), *International Investment Law and Comparative Public Law* (2010) 154–6.

[83] *El Paso v Argentina*, Award, 31 October 2011, paras 510–19 at 515, 518. Emphasis in original. See also *Bayindir v Pakistan*, Award, 27 August 2009, paras 181, 380–1.

[84] Tribunals have made frequent use of these definitions in subsequent cases. At times they have presented surveys of such definitions: *Biwater Gauff v Tanzania*, Award, 24 July 2008, paras 596–60; *Total v Argentina*, Decision on Liability, 27 December 2010, para 110; *El Paso v Argentina*, Award, 31 October 2011, paras 341–7.

[85] *Genin v Estonia*, Award, 25 June 2001 (2002) 17 *ICSID Review-FILJ* 395.

[86] At para 367. Footnote omitted. Since there were ample grounds for the action taken by the Estonian authorities, the Tribunal did not find that a violation of the FET standard had occurred.

[87] *Tecmed v Mexico*, Award, 29 May 2003.

[88] At paras 155, 156. See also *Azurix v Argentina*, Award, 14 July 2006, para 360; *MTD v Chile*, Award, 25 May 2004, paras 112, 113.

The Arbitral Tribunal considers that this provision of the Agreement, in light of the good faith principle established by international law, requires the Contracting Parties to provide to international investments treatment that does not affect the basic expectations that were taken into account by the foreign investor to make the investment. The foreign investor expects the host State to act in a consistent manner, free from ambiguity and totally transparently in its relations with the foreign investor, so that it may know beforehand any and all rules and regulations that will govern its investments, as well as the goals of the relevant policies and administrative practices or directives, to be able to plan its investment and comply with such regulations. . . . The foreign investor also expects the host State to act consistently, i.e. without arbitrarily revoking any preexisting decisions or permits issued by the State that were relied upon by the investor to assume its commitments as well as to plan and launch its commercial and business activities. The investor also expects the State to use the legal instruments that govern the actions of the investor or the investment in conformity with the function usually assigned to such instruments, and not to deprive the investor of its investment without the required compensation.[89]

MTD v Chile[90] concerned a foreign investment contract signed on behalf of Chile for the construction of a large planned community which failed because it turned out to be inconsistent with zoning regulations. The Tribunal applied a provision in the BIT between Chile and Malaysia requiring that 'Investments of investors of either Contracting Party shall at all time be accorded fair and equitable treatment'.[91] In doing so, the Tribunal agreed with a legal opinion by Judge Schwebel that fair and equitable treatment encompassed such fundamental standards as good faith, due process, non-discrimination, and proportionality. The Tribunal relied on the standard as defined in *Tecmed*.[92] It emphasized a duty to adopt proactive behaviour in favour of the investor, and stated:

fair and equitable treatment should be understood to be treatment in an even-handed and just manner, conducive to fostering the promotion of foreign investment. Its terms are framed as a pro-active statement—'to promote', 'to create', 'to stimulate'—rather than prescriptions for a passive behavior of the State or avoidance of prejudicial conduct to the investors.[93]

On the basis of this standard, the Tribunal found that the FET standard had been violated by Chile.

The ad hoc Committee in *MTD v Chile*[94] upheld the Award but criticized its reliance on the *Tecmed* standard:

the *TECMED* Tribunal's apparent reliance on the foreign investor's expectations as the source of the host State's obligations (such as the obligation to compensate for expropriation) is questionable. The obligations of the host State towards foreign investors derive

---

[89] At para 154.
[90] *MTD v Chile*, Award, 25 May 2004; the ad hoc Committee upheld the decision, see Decision on Annulment, 21 March 2007.
[91] At para 107.
[92] At paras 114–15.
[93] At para 113.
[94] *MTD v Chile*, Decision on Annulment, 21 March 2007.

from the terms of the applicable investment treaty and not from any set of expectations investors may have or claim to have.[95]

In *Saluka v Czech Republic*[96] an ailing bank in which the claimants had invested was taken over by a competitor that had received financial assistance from the state for the purpose of the takeover. By contrast, the bank had not received similar aid when the claimants attempted to negotiate the conditions to maintain the viability of the bank. The Tribunal found that there was a violation of FET and described the requirements of the FET standard in terms of consistency, transparency, and reasonableness:

A foreign investor whose interests are protected under the Treaty is entitled to expect that the [host state] will not act in a way that is manifestly inconsistent, non-transparent, unreasonable (*i.e.* unrelated to some rational policy), or discriminatory (*i.e.* based on unjustifiable distinctions).[97]

The NAFTA case, *Waste Management v Mexico*,[98] arose from a failed concession for the disposal of waste that involved a number of grievances, including the municipality's failure to pay its bills, failure to honour exclusivity of services, difficulties with a line of credit agreement, and proceedings before the Mexican courts. The Tribunal summarized its position on the FET standard in Article 1105 of the NAFTA in the following terms:

the minimum standard of treatment of fair and equitable treatment is infringed by conduct attributable to the State and harmful to the claimant if the conduct is arbitrary, grossly unfair, unjust or idiosyncratic, is discriminatory and exposes the claimant to sectional or racial prejudice, or involves a lack of due process leading to an outcome which offends judicial propriety—as might be the case with a manifest failure of natural justice in judicial proceedings or a complete lack of transparency and candour in an administrative process. In applying this standard it is relevant that the treatment is in breach of representations made by the host State which were reasonably relied on by the claimant.[99]

Discrimination against foreigners has been regarded as an important indicator of failure to grant fair and equitable treatment.[100] Awards have also included the standard of 'improper and discreditable'[101] or 'unreasonable conduct',[102] or have referred to international or comparative standards.[103]

---

[95] At para 67.
[96] *Saluka v Czech Republic*, Partial Award, 17 March 2006.
[97] At para 309.
[98] *Waste Management v Mexico*, Final Award, 30 April 2004.
[99] At para 98. On the facts of the particular case, the Tribunal found that this standard had not been violated. At para 140.
[100] *Loewen v United States*, Award, 26 June 2003, para 135; *Waste Management v Mexico*, Final Award, 30 April 2004, para 98; *MTD v Chile*, Award, 25 May 2004, para 109. But see *Grand River v United States*, Award, 12 January 2011, para 209.
[101] *Mondev v United States*, Award, 11 October 2002, para 127; *Loewen v United States*, Award, 26 June 2003, para 133 (in reference to *Mondev*).
[102] *Saluka v Czech Republic*, Partial Award, 17 March 2006, para 309.
[103] *SD Myers v Canada*, First Partial Award, 13 November 2000, para 264.

(h) Specific applications of the fair and equitable treatment standard

Broad definitions or descriptions are not the only way to gauge the meaning of an elusive concept such as FET. Another method is to identify typical factual situations to which this principle has been applied.[104] An examination of the practice of tribunals demonstrates that several principles can be identified which are embraced by the standard of fair and equitable treatment. The cases discussed below clearly speak to the central role of stability, transparency, and the investor's legitimate expectations for the current understanding of the FET standard. Other contexts in which the standard has been applied concern compliance with contractual obligations, procedural propriety and due process, acting in good faith, and freedom from coercion and harassment.[105]

aa. Stability and the protection of the investor's legitimate expectations

The investor's legitimate expectations are based on the host state's legal framework and on any undertakings and representations made explicitly or implicitly by the host state.[106] The legal framework on which the investor is entitled to rely consists of legislation and treaties, assurances contained in decrees, licences, and similar executive statements, as well as contractual undertakings. Specific representations play a central role in the creation of legitimate expectations. Undertakings and representations made explicitly or implicitly by the host state are the strongest basis for legitimate expectations. A reversal of assurances by the host state that have led to legitimate expectations will violate the principle of fair and equitable treatment.[107]

Tribunals have emphasized that the legitimate expectations of the investor will be grounded in the legal order of the host state as it stands at the time the investor acquires the investment.[108] *GAMI v Mexico* ruled categorically: 'NAFTA arbitrations have no mandate to evaluate laws and regulations that predate the decision of

---

[104] See also K Yannaca-Small, 'Fair and Equitable Treatment Standard' in K Yannaca-Small (ed), *Arbitration under International Investment Agreements* (2010) 393–407; S W Schill, 'Fair and Equitable Treatment, the Rule of Law, and Comparative Public Law' in S W Schill (ed), *International Investment Law and Comparative Public Law* (2010) 159–70.

[105] For decisions adopting similar categories for the analysis of the FET standard, see: *Biwater Gauff v Tanzania*, Award, 24 July 2008, para 602; *Rumeli v Kazakhstan*, Award, 29 July 2008, para 609; *Siag v Egypt*, Award, 1 June 2009, para 450; *Bayindir v Pakistan*, Award, 27 August 2009, para 178; *Lemire v Ukraine*, Decision on Jurisdiction and Liability, 14 January 2010, para 284; *Paushok v Mongolia*, Award, 28 April 2011, para 253.

[106] For early discussions of the relevance of the concept of legitimate expectations in foreign investment law, see R Dolzer, 'New Foundations of the Law of Expropriation of Alien Property' (1981) 75 *AJIL* 553; G Burdeau, 'Droit international et contrats d' Etat' (1982) *Annuaire francaise de droit international* 454, 470.

[107] See also W M Reisman and M H Arsanjani, 'The Question of Unilateral Governmental Statements as Applicable Law in Investment Disputes' (2004) 19 *ICSID Review-FILJ* 328; S Vasciannie, 'The Fair and Equitable Treatment Standard in International Investment Law and Practice' (1999) 70 *BYBIL* 99, 146–7; T W Wälde, 'Energy Charter Treaty-based Investment Arbitration' (2004) 5 *J World Investment* 387.

[108] C Schreuer and U Kriebaum, 'At What Time Must Legitimate Expectations Exist?' in J Werner and A H Ali (eds), *A Liber Amicorum: Thomas Wälde. Law Beyond Conventional Thought* (2009) 265.

a foreign investor to invest.'[109] Numerous tribunals have stressed that the legal framework as it existed at the time of making the investment was decisive for any legitimate expectations.[110] In *National Grid v Argentina*[111] the Tribunal said:

this standard protects the reasonable expectations of the investor at the time it made the investment and which were based on representations, commitments or specific conditions offered by the State concerned. Thus, treatment by the State should 'not affect the basic expectations that were taken into account by the foreign investor to make the investment.'[112]

In *SD Myers v Canada*, the Tribunal made the same point when it stated that the parties acted on the basis of the law as it appeared to exist at the time of the investments.[113] Also, *Feldman v Mexico* reflects the same principle by explaining that a regulation had existed at all times relevant to the investor and that no *de jure* change had been made.[114] And in *Mondev v United States* a claim was rejected on the basis that a rule on immunity that was lawful before the NAFTA entered into force could not thereafter be considered to be arbitrary or discriminatory.[115]

These decisions are consistent with the right of the host state to determine its own legal and economic order, subject to the international minimum standard. At the same time, they recognize the investor's concern for planning and stability based on that order at the time of the investment. Whereas the prudent investor will, in light of these rulings, carefully examine the laws before investing, the host state must at all times be aware that its legal order forms the basis of legitimate expectations which must be taken into account in future reforms.

These considerations indicate that while the principle of legitimate expectations inherent in FET has an objective core, its application will depend upon the expectations nurtured and fostered by the local laws as they stand specifically at the time of the investment.

In *Occidental v Ecuador*[116] the claim was directed at the inconsistent practice of the respondent's authorities in reimbursing value added tax (VAT) paid on purchases in connection with the claimant's activities. The claimant relied on the provision in the Ecuador-US BIT guaranteeing fair and equitable treatment. The

---

[109] *GAMI v Mexico*, Award, 15 November 2004, para 93.

[110] *Azinian v Mexico*, Award, 1 November 1999, paras 95–7; *Mondev v United States*, Award, 12 October 2002, para 156; *Feldman v Mexico*, Award, 16 December 2002, para 128; *LG&E v Argentina*, Decision on Liability, 3 October 2006, para 130; *Enron v Argentina*, Award, 22 May 2007, para 262; *BG v Argentina*, Final Award, 24 December 2007, paras 297–8; *Duke Energy v Ecuador*, Award, 18 August 2008, paras 340, 365; *Jan de Nul v Egypt*, Award, 6 November 2008, para 265; *Bayindir v Pakistan*, Award, 27 August 2009, paras 190, 191; *EDF v Romania*, Award, 8 October 2009, para 219; *AES v Hungary*, Award, 23 September 2010, paras 9.3.8–9.3.18; *Frontier Petroleum v Czech Republic*, Final Award, 12 November 2010, paras 287, 468.

[111] *National Grid v Argentina*, Award, 3 November 2008.

[112] At para 173. Footnote omitted.

[113] *SD Myers v Canada*, Second Partial Award, 21 October 2002.

[114] *Feldman v Mexico*, Award, 16 December 2002, para 128.

[115] *Mondev v United States*, Award, 12 October 2002, para 156; see also *Azinian v Mexico*, Award, 1 November 1999, paras 95–7; *Oscar Chinn Case (UK v Belgium)*, 12 December 1934, PCIJ, Series A/B, No 63, para 184.

[116] *Occidental v Ecuador*, Award, 1 July 2004.

Tribunal noted that the framework under which the investor had been operating had been changed in an important manner and that the clarifications sought by the investor had evoked a wholly unsatisfactory and thoroughly vague answer. 'The tax law was changed without providing any clarity about its meaning and extent and the practice and regulations were also inconsistent with such changes.'[117]

After quoting from *Metalclad* and *Tecmed*, the Tribunal reached the conclusion that the requirements, as described in these cases, were not met in the case before it.[118] The Tribunal said:

The relevant question for international law in this discussion is not whether there is an obligation to refund VAT, which is the point on which the parties have argued most intensely, but rather whether the legal and business framework meets the requirements of stability and predictability under international law. It was earlier concluded that there is not a VAT refund obligation under international law, ... but there is certainly an obligation not to alter the legal and business environment in which the investment has been made. In this case it is the latter question that triggers a treatment that is not fair and equitable.[119]

In *CMS v Argentina*[120] the respondent had given guarantees for price adjustments for the transportation of natural gas in legislation, regulations, and under a licence. Subsequently, an emergency law and other laws and regulations first suspended and then terminated these guarantees. The Tribunal referred to the preamble of the Argentina-US BIT and said:

There can be no doubt, therefore, that a stable legal and business environment is an essential element of fair and equitable treatment. .... The measures that are complained of did in fact entirely transform and alter the legal and business environment under which the investment was made. .... It has also been established that the guarantees given in this connection under the legal framework and its various components were crucial for the investment decision. .... In addition to the specific terms of the Treaty, the significant number of treaties, both bilateral and multilateral, that have dealt with this standard also unequivocally shows that fair and equitable treatment is inseparable from stability and predictability. Many arbitral decisions and scholarly writings point in the same direction.[121]

The Tribunal found that Argentina's actions had breached the FET standard.

Eureko v Poland[122] concerned a share purchase agreement between the investor and the Polish state under which the investor acquired a minority participation in a Polish company. A related agreement guaranteed to the investor the right to acquire further shares that would have given it control over the company. Subsequently, Poland changed its privatization policy and withdrew its consent to the acquisition of further shares by the investor. The Tribunal found it abundantly clear that Eureko had been treated unfairly and inequitably by Poland. The organs of the respondent

---

[117] At para 184.   [118] At paras 185, 186.   [119] At para 191.
[120] *CMS v Argentina*, Award, 12 May 2005.
[121] At paras 274–6. Footnote omitted.
[122] *Eureko v Poland*, Partial Award, 19 August 2005.

state had consciously and overtly breached Eureko's basic expectations.[123] Therefore, the Tribunal had no hesitation in concluding that the FET standard of the Netherlands-Poland BIT had been violated by the respondent.[124]

Other tribunals have similarly found that the FET principle involved the government's obligation not to frustrate the investor's legitimate expectations by arbitrarily changing the legal framework under which the investment had been made.[125] According to one view, the investor's legitimate expectations will be seriously reduced if there is general instability in the political conditions of the country concerned.[126]

Legitimate expectations are not subjective hopes and perceptions; rather, they must be based on objectively verifiable facts. Expectations are protected only if they are legitimate and reasonable in the circumstances. The Tribunal in *Suez v Argentina*[127] said:

one must not look single-mindedly at the Claimants' subjective expectations. The Tribunal must rather examine them from an objective and reasonable point of view.[128]

More recently, tribunals have increasingly emphasized that the requirement of stability is not absolute and does not affect the state's right to exercise its sovereign power to legislate and to adapt its legal system to changing circumstances.[129] What matters is whether measures exceed normal regulatory powers and fundamentally modify the regulatory framework for the investment beyond an acceptable margin of change.[130] In other words, 'changes to general legislation, in the absence of specific stabilization promises to the foreign investor, reflect a legitimate exercise of the host state's governmental powers that are not prevented by a BIT's fair and equitable treatment standard'.[131] The Tribunal in *EDF v Romania*[132] stated in this respect:

---

[123] At paras 231, 232.

[124] At para 234.

[125] *CME v Czech Republic*, Partial Award, 13 September 2001, para 611; *Bayindir v Pakistan*, Decision on Jurisdiction, 14 November 2005, paras 231–2; *LG&E v Argentina*, Decision on Liability, 3 October 2006, para 131; *PSEG v Turkey*, Award, 19 January 2007, paras 240–56; *Enron v Argentina*, Award, 22 May 2007, paras 260–2; *Sempra v Argentina*, Award, 28 September 2007, paras 300, 303; *National Grid v Argentina*, Award, 3 November 2008, paras 178–9; *Alpha v Ukraine*, Award, 8 November 2010, para 420; *Lemire v Ukraine*, Decision on Jurisdiction and Liability, 14 January 2010, para 267; Award, 28 March 2011, paras 68–73.

[126] *Bayindir v Pakistan*, Award, 27 August 2009, paras 192–7. See also U Kriebaum, 'The Relevance of Economic and Political Conditions for the Protection under Investment Treaties' (2011) 10 *Law and Practice of International Courts and Tribunals* 383.

[127] *Suez v Argentina*, Decision on Liability, 30 July 2010.

[128] At para 209.

[129] *Parkerings v Lithuania*, Award, 11 September 2007, paras 327–38; *BG Group v Argentina*, Final Award, 24 December 2007, paras 292–310; *Plama v Bulgaria*, Award, 27 August 2008, para 219; *Continental Casualty v Argentina*, Award, 5 September 2008, paras 258–61; *AES v Hungary*, Award, 23 September 2010, paras 9.3.27–9.3.35; *Paushok v Mongolia*, Award, 28 April 2011, para 302; *Impregilo v Argentina*, Award, 21 June 2011, paras 290–1; *El Paso v Argentina*, Award, 31 October 2011, paras 344–52, 365–74.

[130] *El Paso v Argentina*, Award, 31 October 2011, para 402.

[131] *Total v Argentina*, Decision on Liability, 27 December 2010, para 164. See also paras 113–24, 309, 312, 429.

[132] *EDF v Romania*, Award, 8 October 2009.

The idea that legitimate expectations, and therefore FET, imply the stability of the legal and business framework, may not be correct if stated in an overly-broad and unqualified formulation. The FET might then mean the virtual freezing of the legal regulation of economic activities, in contrast with the State's normal regulatory power and the evolutionary character of economic life. Except where specific promises or representations are made by the State to the investor, the latter may not rely on a bilateral investment treaty as a kind of insurance policy against the risk of any changes in the host State's legal and economic framework. Such expectation would be neither legitimate nor reasonable.[133]

In deciding between the investor's right to stability and the state's right to regulate, some tribunals have weighed the investor's legitimate expectations against the state's duty to act in the public interest.[134]

Particularly important in the creation of legitimate expectations are specific assurances and representations made by the host state in order to induce investors to make investments.[135] But even here some tribunals have found that mere political statements were not capable of creating reasonable expectations.[136]

bb. Transparency

Transparency is closely related to protection of the investor's legitimate expectations. Transparency means that the legal framework for the investor's operations is readily apparent and that any decisions affecting the investor can be traced to that legal framework.[137]

There is authority to the effect that transparency and the investor's legitimate expectations are protected even without a treaty guarantee of FET. In *SPP v Egypt*[138] the respondent contended that certain acts of Egyptian officials, upon which the claimants relied, were null and void because they were in conflict with the inalienable nature of the public domain and because they were not taken pursuant to the procedures prescribed by Egyptian law. The Tribunal rejected this argument and emphasized that the investor was entitled to rely on the official representations of the government:

---

[133] At para 217.
[134] *Saluka v Czech Republic*, Partial Award, 17 March 2006, para 306; *Total v Argentina*, Decision on Liability, 27 December 2010, paras 123, 309. For an instance where a tribunal found misuse of regulatory powers, see *Vivendi v Argentina*, Award, 20 August 2007, para 7.4.24.
[135] *Kardassopoulos v Georgia*, Decision on Jurisdiction, 6 July 2007, para 191; *Parkerings v Lithuania*, Award, 11 September 2007, para 331; *Sempra v Argentina*, Award, 28 September 2007, paras 298, 299; *OKO Pankki v Estonia*, Award, 19 November 2007, paras 247–8, 263; *Duke Energy v Ecuador*, Award, 18 August 2008, paras 359–64; *Continental Casualty v Argentina*, Award, 5 September 2008, paras 258–61; *Total v Argentina*, Decision on Liability, 27 December 2010, paras 119–20, 309.
[136] *Continental Casualty v Argentina*, Award, 5 September 2008, para 261(i); *El Paso v Argentina*, Award, 31 October 2011, paras 375–9, 392–5.
[137] UNCTAD Series on issues in international investment agreements, 'Fair and Equitable Treatment' (1999) 51; S W Schill, 'Fair and Equitable Treatment, the Rule of Law, and Comparative Public Law' in S W Schill (ed), *International Investment Law and Comparative Public Law* (2010) 168–9.
[138] *SPP v Egypt*, Award, 20 May 1992.

It is possible that under Egyptian law certain acts of Egyptian officials including even Presidential Decree No. 475, may be considered legally nonexistent or null and void or susceptible to invalidation. However, these acts were cloaked with the mantle of Government authority and communicated as such to foreign investors who relied on them in making their investments. . . . Whether legal under Egyptian law or not, the acts in question were the acts of Egyptian authorities, including the highest executive authority of the Government. These acts, which are now alleged to have been in violation of the Egyptian municipal legal system, created expectations protected by established principles of international law.[139]

In *Metalclad v Mexico*[140] the issue of transparency played a central role. The Federal Government of Mexico and the state government had issued construction and operating permits for the investor's landfill project. The investor was assured that it had all the permits it needed, but the municipality refused to grant a construction permit. The claimant complained about a lack of transparency surrounding the process. In interpreting Article 1105 of the NAFTA, the Tribunal said:

Prominent in the statement of principles and rules that introduces the Agreement is the reference to 'transparency' (*NAFTA Article 102(1)*). The Tribunal understands this to include the idea that all relevant legal requirements for the purpose of initiating, completing and successfully operating investments made, or intended to be made, under the Agreement should be capable of being readily known to all affected investors of another Party. There should be no room for doubt or uncertainty on such matters. Once the authorities of the central government of any Party (whose international responsibility in such matters has been identified in the preceding section) become aware of any scope for misunderstanding or confusion in this connection, it is their duty to ensure that the correct position is promptly determined and clearly stated so that investors can proceed with all appropriate expedition in the confident belief that they are acting in accordance with all relevant laws.[141]

The Tribunal held that the investor was entitled to rely on the representations of the federal officials.[142] It concluded that the acts of the state and the municipality were in violation of the FET standard under Article 1105 of the NAFTA. In the view of the Tribunal:

Mexico failed to ensure a transparent and predictable framework for Metalclad's business planning and investment. The totality of these circumstances demonstrates a lack of orderly process and timely disposition in relation to an investor of a Party acting in the expectation that it would be treated fairly and justly in accordance with the NAFTA.[143]

---

[139] At paras 82, 83.

[140] *Metalclad v Mexico*, Award, 30 August 2000. See also T Weiler, 'Good Faith and Regulatory Transparency: The Story of Metalclad v Mexico' in T Weiler (ed), *International Investment Law and Arbitration: Leading Cases* (2005) 701.

[141] At para 76.

[142] At para 89.

[143] At para 99. The Award was set aside in part by the Supreme Court of British Columbia on grounds that are peculiar to the NAFTA: the court found that the Tribunal had improperly based its award on transparency even though that principle is not contained in Chapter Eleven but in Chapter Eighteen of the NAFTA: see *Mexico v Metalclad*, Review by British Columbia Supreme Court, 2 May 2001, 5 ICSID Reports 238, paras 57–76. The court's decision appears incorrect for two reasons: first, under Art 31 of the VCLT, a treaty term must be interpreted in its context which

In *Maffezini v Spain*[144] one of the complaints concerned a 'loan' that had been transferred by a government institution from the investor's personal account without his consent. The Tribunal found that the lack of transparency associated with the loan transaction was incompatible with fair and equitable treatment. It said:

the lack of transparency with which this loan transaction was conducted is incompatible with Spain's commitment to ensure the investor a fair and equitable treatment in accordance with Article 4(1) of the same treaty. Accordingly, the Tribunal finds that, with regard to this contention, the Claimant has substantiated his claim and is entitled to compensation . . .[145]

In *Tecmed v Mexico*,[146] the dispute concerned the replacement of an unlimited licence by a licence of limited duration for the operation of a landfill. The Tribunal applied a provision in the BIT between Mexico and Spain guaranteeing fair and equitable treatment. The Tribunal found that this provision required transparency and protection of the investor's basic expectations.[147] The Tribunal explained that:

the Claimant was entitled to expect that the government's actions would be free from any ambiguity that might affect the early assessment made by the foreign investor of its real legal situation or the situation affecting its investment and the actions the investor should take to act accordingly.[148]

In consequence, the Tribunal concluded that the investor's fair expectations were frustrated by the contradiction and uncertainty in Mexico's behaviour which was:

characterized by its ambiguity and uncertainty which are prejudicial to the investor in terms of its advance assessment of the legal situation surrounding its investment and the planning of its business activity and its adjustment to preserve its rights.[149]

In *MTD v Chile*[150] the respondent had signed an investment contract for the construction of a large planned community with the country's Foreign Investment Commission (FIC) but the project failed because it turned out to be inconsistent with zoning regulations. The Tribunal found that the guarantee of FET in the BIT between Chile and Malaysia had been violated by what it described as 'the inconsistency of action between two arms of the same Government vis-à-vis the same investor'.[151] It went on to state that while it was the investor's duty to inform itself of the country's law and policy in principle:

Chile also has an obligation to act coherently and apply its policies consistently, independently of how diligent an investor is. Under international law (the law that this Tribunal has to apply to a dispute under the BIT), the State of Chile needs to be considered by the

---

includes the treaty's entire text; secondly, Art 1131 of the NAFTA, dealing with governing law, directs that a NAFTA Chapter Eleven tribunal is to decide the dispute 'in accordance with this Agreement [ie the NAFTA—not just its Chapter Eleven] and applicable rules of international law'.

[144] *Maffezini v Spain*, Award on the Merits, 13 November 2000.
[145] At para 83.
[146] *Tecmed v Mexico*, Award, 29 May 2003.
[147] See p 143.   [148] At para 167.   [149] At para 172.
[150] *MTD v Chile*, Award, 25 May 2004.   [151] At para 163.

Tribunal as a unit.... The Tribunal is satisfied, based on the evidence presented to it, that approval of an investment by the FIC for a project that is against the urban policy of the Government is a breach of the obligation to treat an investor fairly and equitably.[152]

cc. Compliance with contractual obligations

Closely related to the issue of protection of the investor's legitimate expectations is the question to what extent this protection extends to observance of obligations arising from contracts. Contractual agreements are the classical instrument in most, if not all, legal systems for the creation of legal stability and predictability. Therefore, *pacta sunt servanda* would seem to be an obvious application of the stability requirement that is so prominent in the FET standard. The connection between this aspect of FET and the umbrella clause[153] is evident.

In a number of cases dealing with the protection of the investors' legitimate expectations, these expectations were actually based on contractual arrangements with the host state. But it does not follow that every breach of a contractual obligation by a host state or one of its entities automatically amounts to a violation of the FET standard.

Some tribunals seemed to hold the view that failure to observe contractual obligations on the part of a government would be contrary to the FET standard.[154] The Tribunal in *Mondev*[155] found it clear that the protection of Article 1105(1) of the NAFTA extended to contract claims. The Tribunal said:

a governmental prerogative to violate investment contracts would appear to be inconsistent with the principles embodied in Article 1105 and with contemporary standards of national and international law concerning governmental liability for contractual performance.[156]

Similarly, in *SGS v Paraguay*,[157] a case involving unpaid invoices for pre-shipment inspections, the Tribunal spoke of a 'baseline expectation of contractual compliance'. It noted that:

a State's non-payment under a contract is, in the view of the Tribunal, capable of giving rise to a breach of a fair and equitable treatment requirement, such as, perhaps, where the non-payment amounts to a repudiation of the contract, frustration of its economic purpose, or substantial deprivation of its value.[158]

Most tribunals have adopted a more restrictive approach. They have found that a simple breach of contract by a state would not trigger a violation of the FET

---

[152] At paras 165, 166. Chile's attempt to have the Award annulled was unsuccessful: *MTD v Chile*, Decision on Annulment, 21 March 2007.

[153] See Section 3.

[154] Tentatively: *SGS v Philippines*, Decision on Jurisdiction, 29 January 2004, para 162; *Noble Ventures v Romania*, Award, 12 October 2005, para 182; *SGS v Paraguay*, Decision on Jurisdiction, 12 February 2010, paras 144–51.

[155] *Mondev v United States*, Award, 11 October 2002.

[156] At para 134.

[157] *SGS v Paraguay*, Decision on Jurisdiction, 12 February 2010.

[158] At para 146.

standard.[159] Rather, 'a breach of FET requires conduct in the exercise of sovereign powers'.[160] However, a termination of the contract, brought about through the employment of sovereign prerogative, would lead to a violation of the FET standard.[161] The same would apply to government interference with a contract between an investor and a state entity.[162]

In *Consortium RFCC v Morocco*[163] the dispute had arisen from a contract for the construction of a motorway. The Tribunal held that only measures taken by Morocco in its sovereign capacity were capable of breaching the FET standard. A violation of contractual obligations that could have been committed by an ordinary contract partner would not rise to the level of a violation of the FET standard.[164]

A simple failure to pay sums due under a contract is not a sovereign act and may not amount to a breach of the treaty-based FET standard.[165] In *Waste Management*,[166] the Tribunal described transparency and reliance as elements of the FET standard contained in Article 1105(1) of the NAFTA. One of the claims concerned the failure of the city of Acapulco to make payments under a concession agreement.[167] The Tribunal did not find that this amounted to a violation of FET:

even the persistent non-payment of debts by a municipality is not to be equated with a violation of Article 1105, provided that it does not amount to an outright and unjustified repudiation of the transaction and provided that some remedy is open to the creditor to address the problem.[168]

Impregilo v Pakistan concerned a contract for the construction of hydroelectric power facilities. The Tribunal found that a simple breach of contract did not amount to a breach of the FET standard. Responsibility under the treaty would only be caused by a misuse of public power.[169]

In *Duke Energy v Ecuador*[170] the claimant relied on power-purchase agreements between its local subsidiary and a state entity. The Tribunal pointed out that a violation of a contract does not as such amount to a violation of the treaty standard of fair and equitable treatment:

---

[159] *Parkerings v Lithuania*, Award, 11 September 2007, paras 344–5; *EDF v Romania*, Award, 8 October 2009, paras 238–60; *Burlington v Ecuador*, Award, 2 June 2010, para 204; *Hamester v Ghana*, Award, 18 June 2010, paras 332–8.

[160] *Bayindir v Pakistan*, Award, 27 August 2009, para 377. See also para 180.

[161] *Rumeli v Kazakhstan*, Award, 29 July 2008, para 615.

[162] *Alpha v Ukraine*, Award, 8 November 2010, para 422.

[163] *RFCC v Morocco*, Award, 22 December 2003.

[164] At paras 33–4.

[165] *Biwater Gauff v Tanzania*, Award, 24 July 2008, para 636. See further p 129.

[166] *Waste Management v Mexico*, Final Award, 30 April 2004.

[167] At paras 108–17.

[168] At para 115. This part of the decision is cited with approval in *GAMI v Mexico*, Award, 15 November 2004, para 101.

[169] *Impregilo v Pakistan*, Decision on Jurisdiction, 22 April 2005, paras 266–70; Award, 21 June 2011, paras 293–310.

[170] *Duke Energy v Ecuador*, Award, 18 August 2008.

Establishing a treaty breach is a different exercise from showing a contract breach. Subject to the particular question of the umbrella clause, in order to prove a treaty breach, the Claimants must establish a violation different in nature from a contract breach, in other words a violation which the State commits in the exercise of its sovereign power.[171]

Practice demonstrates that the view that a simple breach of contract is insufficient to amount to a breach of the FET standard is clearly prevalent. But this seemingly simple test leads to further questions. The distinction between sovereign and commercial acts, which is accepted in the field of state immunity, is of unclear validity in the area of state responsibility.[172] Also, even if the underlying relationship and the breach are clearly commercial, the motives of a government for a certain act may still be governmental.

dd. Procedural propriety and due process

Fair procedure is an elementary requirement of the rule of law and a vital element of FET. It includes the traditional international law concept of denial of justice.[173] Unlike other aspects of investment protection, it is generally accepted that a claim for denial of justice is conditioned on a prior exhaustion of local remedies.[174]

The US Model BIT of 2012 specifically clarifies that the FET standard covers protection from denial of justice and guarantees due process. Article 5(2)(a) provides that:

'fair and equitable treatment' includes the obligation not to deny justice in criminal, civil, or administrative adjudicatory proceedings in accordance with the principle of due process embodied in the principal legal systems of the world . . .

Tribunals have held in a number of cases that lack of a fair procedure, or serious procedural shortcomings, were important elements in finding a violation of the FET standard. Most of these cases relate to the right to be heard in judicial or administrative proceedings.

In *Metalclad v Mexico*[175] the municipality had refused to grant a construction permit. The Tribunal found that there had been a violation of the FET guarantee in Article 1105 of the NAFTA. An element in this finding was lack of procedural propriety, specifically a failure to hear the investor:

---

[171] At para 345. See also paras 342–4, 354.

[172] *Noble Ventures v Romania*, Award, 12 October 2005, para 82.

[173] For a general description of denial of justice, see *Azinian v Mexico*, Award, 1 November 1999, paras 102, 103:

A denial of justice could be pleaded if the relevant courts refuse to entertain a suit, if they subject it to undue delay, or if they administer justice in a seriously inadequate way. . . .
There is a fourth type of denial of justice, namely the clear and malicious misapplication of the law. This type of wrong doubtless overlaps with the notion of 'pretence of form' to mask a violation of international law.

Generally on denial of justice, see J Paulsson, *Denial of Justice in International Law* (2005).

[174] *Jan de Nul v Egypt*, Award, 6 November 2008, paras 255–61; *Toto v Lebanon*, Decision on Jurisdiction, 11 September 2009, para 164.

[175] *Metalclad v Mexico*, Award, 30 August 2000.

Moreover, the permit was denied at a meeting of the Municipal Town Council of which Metalclad received no notice, to which it received no invitation, and at which it was given no opportunity to appear.[176]

In *Tecmed v Mexico*,[177] the dispute arose from revocation of a licence for the operation of a landfill and involved a provision in the BIT between Mexico and Spain guaranteeing fair and equitable treatment according to international law. The Tribunal found that this standard had been violated, inter alia, because the environmental regulatory authority had failed to notify the claimant of its intentions, thereby depriving the claimant of the opportunity to express its position.[178]

In *Middle East Cement v Egypt*[179] one of the complaints concerned the seizure and auction of the claimant's ship and the lack of proper notification of the auction to the owner. The Tribunal applied provisions promising FET and full protection and security in the BIT between Greece and Egypt. It found that a matter as important as the seizure and auctioning of a ship belonging to the claimant should have been notified by direct communication. Therefore, it found that the procedure applied did not meet the requirements of the FET and full protection and security standards.[180]

Loewen v United States[181] concerned the propriety of proceedings in the Mississippi state courts against a Canadian undertaker. The trial exhibited a gross absence of due process and of protection of the investor from prejudice on account of his nationality, and the Tribunal found that the conduct of the trial was so flawed that it constituted a miscarriage of justice.[182] With regard to Article 1105 of the NAFTA, the Tribunal also recognized the significance of due process:

Manifest injustice in the sense of a lack of due process leading to an outcome which offends a sense of judicial propriety is enough...[183]

The whole trial and its resultant verdict were clearly improper and discreditable and cannot be squared with minimum standards of international law and fair and equitable treatment.[184]

Some cases concern the frustration by a state of judgments rendered by its own domestic courts.[185] In *Siag v Egypt*[186] the claimants had obtained a series of judicial rulings in their favour by Egyptian courts but the government failed to comply with these rulings. The Tribunal found that Egypt's actions constituted a denial of justice and a violation of the FET standard.

In a number of cases the claimants had complained about the length of judicial proceedings in domestic courts which had in some cases taken many years. The tribunals, while critical of delays, did not find that these amounted to a violation of

---

[176] At para 91.
[178] At para 162.
[180] At para 143.
[182] At para 54.
[185] *Petrobart v Kyrgyz Republic*, Award, 29 March 2005, 13 ICSID Reports 464–5.
[186] *Siag v Egypt*, Award, 1 June 2009, paras 451–5.

[177] *Tecmed v Mexico*, Award, 29 May 2003.
[179] *Middle East Cement v Egypt*, Award, 12 April 2002.
[181] *Loewen v United States*, Award, 26 June 2003, 42 ILM 811 (2003).
[183] At para 132. [184] At para 137.

the FET standard.[187] They cited special circumstances relating to the complexity of the issues[188] or to the political situation in the country concerned.[189]

Denial of justice is traditionally associated with the administration of justice by domestic courts[190] but investment tribunals have accepted that the procedural guarantees inherent in the FET standard extend to the activities of the host state's administrative authorities.[191] On the other hand, the requirement to afford fair procedure on the basis of the FET standard does not extend to a state entity's management of its contractual relationship with the investor.[192]

In *Thunderbird v Mexico*[193] the Tribunal held that the standards of due process and procedural fairness applicable in administrative proceedings are lower than in a judicial process. In the particular case it found no violation of the FET standard, explaining that the claimant had been given full opportunity to be heard and to present evidence and that the proceedings were subject to judicial review by the courts.[194]

ee. Good faith

As explained above, good faith is a broad principle that is one of the foundations of international law in general and of foreign investment law in particular.[195] Arbitral tribunals have confirmed that good faith is inherent in FET.[196] It is 'the common guiding beacon' to the obligation under BITs; it is 'at the heart of the concept of FET', and 'permeates the whole approach' to investor protection.[197] The Tribunal in *Tecmed*,[198] interpreting a BIT provision on FET, said:

> The Arbitral Tribunal finds that the commitment of fair and equitable treatment... is an expression and part of the *bona fide* principle recognized in international law...[199]

The FET standard in general, and the obligation to act in good faith in particular, include the obligation not to inflict damage upon an investment purposefully.[200] The Tribunal in *Waste Management*[201] found that the obligation to act in good faith was a basic obligation under the FET standard as contained in Article 1105 of

---

[187] *Frontier Petroleum v Czech Republic*, Final Award, 12 November 2010, paras 289–96, 334.

[188] *Jan de Nul v Egypt*, Award, 6 November 2008, paras 202–4.

[189] *Toto v Lebanon*, Decision on Jurisdiction, 11 September 2009, para 165.

[190] *Grand River Enterprises v United States*, Award, 12 January 2011, paras 222–36.

[191] *Rumeli v Kazakhstan*, 29 July 2008, para 623; *Chemtura v Canada*, Award, 2 August 2010, paras 211–24; *AES v Hungary*, Award, 23 September 2010, paras 9.3.36–9.3.73.

[192] *Bayindir v Pakistan*, Award, 27 August 2009, paras 343–8.

[193] *Thunderbird v Mexico*, Award, 26 January 2006.

[194] At paras 197–201.

[195] See pp 18, 132, 142 et seq.

[196] *Genin v Estonia*, Award, 25 June 2001, para 367: 'Acts that would violate this minimum standard [of fair and equitable treatment] would include... subjective bad faith.'

[197] *Sempra v Argentina*, Award, 28 September 2007, paras 297–99.

[198] *Tecmed v Mexico*, Award, 29 May 2003.

[199] At para 153, quoting I Brownlie, *Principles of Public International Law* (1989) 19.

[200] *Vivendi v Argentina*, Award, 20 August 2007, para 7.4.39.

[201] *Waste Management v Mexico*, Final Award, 30 April 2004.

the NAFTA. In particular, a deliberate conspiracy by government authorities to defeat the investment would violate this principle:

The Tribunal has no doubt that a deliberate conspiracy—that is to say, a conscious combination of various agencies of government without justification to defeat the purposes of an investment agreement—would constitute a breach of Article 1105(1). A basic obligation of the State under Article 1105(1) is to act in good faith and form, and not deliberately to set out to destroy or frustrate the investment by improper means.[202]

In *Bayindir v Pakistan*[203] the investor claimed that its expulsion was based on local favouritism and on bad faith, since the reasons given by the government did not correspond to its actual motivation.[204] The Tribunal in its Decision on Jurisdiction found that 'the allegedly unfair motives of expulsion, if proven, are capable of founding a fair and equitable treatment claim under the BIT'.[205]

In *Saluka v Czech Republic*[206] the Tribunal also gave a central role to the requirement of good faith in its description of FET:

A foreign investor protected by the Treaty may in any case properly expect that the Czech Republic implements its policies *bona fide* by conduct that is, as far as it affects the investors' investment, reasonably justifiable by public policies and that such conduct does not manifestly violate the requirements of consistency, transparency, even-handedness and non-discrimination.[207]

In *Chemtura v Canada*[208] the claimants had complained about a special review of their product, claiming that the investigation had been in bad faith. The Tribunal, after examining the circumstances in some detail, concluded that the special review had been launched out of legitimate regulatory concerns and in accordance with Canada's international commitments.

In *Frontier Petroleum v Czech Republic*[209] the Tribunal gave the following description of violations of the good faith principle:

Bad faith action by the host state includes the use of legal instruments for purposes other than those for which they were created. It also includes a conspiracy by state organs to inflict damage upon or to defeat the investment, the termination of the investment for reasons other than the one put forth by the government, and expulsion of an investment based on local favouritism. Reliance by a government on its internal structures to excuse non-compliance with contractual obligations would also be contrary to good faith.[210]

It follows from these authorities that action in bad faith against the investor would be a violation of FET. Bad faith action by the host state includes the use of legal

---

[202] At para 138.
[203] *Bayindir v Pakistan*, Decision on Jurisdiction, 14 November 2005.
[204] At paras 242, 243.
[205] At para 250.
[206] *Saluka v Czech Republic*, Partial Award, 17 March 2006.
[207] At para 307.
[208] *Chemtura v Canada*, Award, 2 August 2010, paras 143–8, 158, 184.
[209] *Frontier Petroleum v Czech Republic*, Final Award, 12 November 2010.
[210] At para 300. Footnotes omitted.

instruments for purposes other than those for which they were created. It also includes a conspiracy by state organs to inflict damage upon or to defeat the investment.

A related but different question is whether every violation of the standard of FET requires bad faith. Put differently, is it a valid defence for the host state to argue that, although its actions may have caused harm to the investor, those actions were bona fide and hence could not have violated the FET standard? Arbitral practice clearly indicates that the FET standard may be violated, even if no *mala fides* is involved.[211] For instance, the Tribunal in *Mondev*[212] said:

To the modern eye, what is unfair or inequitable need not equate with the outrageous or the egregious. In particular, a State may treat foreign investment unfairly and inequitably without necessarily acting in bad faith.[213]

The Award in *Occidental*[214] expresses the same idea. In the context of transparency and consistency as part of the FET standard the Tribunal said:

this is an objective requirement that does not depend on whether the Respondent has proceeded in good faith or not.[215]

In *CMS v Argentina*[216] the Tribunal, after finding that FET was inseparable from stability and predictability, stated:

The Tribunal believes this is an objective requirement unrelated to whether the Respondent has had any deliberate intention or bad faith in adopting the measures in question. Of course, such intention and bad faith can aggravate the situation but are not an essential element of the standard.[217]

Similarly, the Tribunal in *El Paso v Argentina*[218] said that 'a violation can be found even if there is a mere objective disregard of the rights enjoyed by the investor under the FET standard, and that such a violation does not require subjective bad faith on the part of the State'.[219]

Other tribunals have consistently adopted the same approach.[220]

---

[211] The only contrary indication would be a dictum in *Genin v Estonia*, Award, 25 June 2001, para 371: 'any procedural irregularity that may have been present would have to amount to bad faith, a willful disregard of due process of law or an extreme insufficiency of action.' However, this passage does not relate to fair and equitable treatment but to the standard of arbitrary and discriminatory measures in Art II(3)(b) of the Estonia-US BIT.

[212] *Mondev v United States*, Award, 11 October 2002.

[213] At para 116.

[214] *Occidental v Ecuador*, Award, 1 July 2004.

[215] At para 186.

[216] *CMS v Argentina*, Award, 12 May 2005.

[217] At para 280. This passage was quoted approvingly in *Vivendi v Argentina*, Award, 20 August 2007, para 7.4.12.

[218] *El Paso v Argentina*, Award, 31 October 2011.

[219] At para 372.

[220] *Tecmed v Mexico*, Award, 29 May 2003, para 153; *Loewen v United States*, Award, 26 June 2003, para 132; *Azurix v Argentina*, Award, 14 July 2006, para 372; *LG&E v Argentina*, Decision on Liability, 3 October 2006, para 129; *PSEG v Turkey*, Award, 19 January 2007, paras 245–6; *Siemens v Argentina*, Award, 6 February 2007, para 299; *Enron v Argentina*, Award, 22 May 2007, para 263;

ff. Freedom from coercion and harassment

The FET standard also applies in situations of coercion and harassment directed at the investor. In *Pope & Talbot v Canada*[221] SLD, a government regulatory authority, had launched a 'verification review' against the investor that was confrontational and aggressive. The Tribunal held that this investigation was 'more like combat than cooperative regulation'.[222] It found that these actions by the regulatory authority were 'threats and misrepresentation', 'burdensome and confrontational', and hence a violation of the FET standard.[223]

In *Tecmed v Mexico*,[224] an unlimited licence for the operation of a landfill had been replaced by a licence of limited duration. The Tribunal applied a provision in the BIT between Mexico and Spain guaranteeing FET according to international law. The Tribunal found that the denial of the permit's renewal was designed to force the investor to relocate to another site, bearing the costs and risks of a new business. The Tribunal said:

Under such circumstances, such pressure involves forms of coercion that may be considered inconsistent with the fair and equitable treatment to be given to international investments under Article 4(1) of the Agreement and objectionable from the perspective of international law.[225]

In *Total v Argentina*[226] the investor had been forced to accept conditions much less favourable that originally agreed, including an arrangement under which it had to surrender receivables in exchange for shares. The Tribunal stated:

This scheme must be considered as a kind of forced, inequitable, debt-for-equity swap, not due to unfavourable market conditions or a company's crisis (as is usually the premise of such swaps in the private market), but due to governmental policy and conduct by Argentina. As such, in the view of the Tribunal it represents a clear breach of the fair and equitable treatment obligation of the BIT for which Argentina is liable to pay damages.[227]

Desert Line v Yemen[228] concerned contracts for the construction of asphalt roads. A dispute between the parties involved armed threats and arrest of some the investor's personnel. Local arbitration resulted in an award of certain sums to the claimant who was, however, subsequently forced to accept a much reduced amount in a settlement agreement. The Tribunal found that the settlement agreement had been imposed upon the claimant under physical and financial duress. It said:

Duke Energy v Ecuador, Award, 18 August 2008, para 341; *National Grid v Argentina*, Award, 3 November 2008, para 173; *Jan de Nul v Egypt*, Award, 6 November 2008, para 185; *Bayindir v Pakistan*, Award, 27 August 2009, para 181; *RSM v Grenada*, Award, 10 December 2010, para 7.2.24.

[221] *Pope & Talbot v Canada*, Award on Merits, 10 April 2001, paras 156–81.
[222] At para 181.
[223] *Pope & Talbot v Canada*, Award on Damages, 31 May 2002, paras 67–9.
[224] *Tecmed v Mexico*, Award, 29 May 2003.
[225] At para 163. Footnote omitted.
[226] *Total v Argentina*, Decision on Liability, 27 December 2010.
[227] At para 338.
[228] *Desert Line v Yemen*, Award, 6 February 2008, paras 151–94.

the subjection of the Claimant's employees, family members, and equipment to arrest and armed interference, as well as the subsequent peremptory 'advice' that it was 'in [his] interest' to accept that the amount awarded be amputated by half, falls well short of minimum standards of international law and cannot be the result of an authentic fair and equitable negotiation.[229]

In the resulting award, the Tribunal took the unusual step of awarding not only damages for the violation of the FET standard but additionally awarded moral damages in the amount of US$1 million.

In a number of cases tribunals have found that the investors' allegations were not proven. These include complaints of a campaign to punish the investor for publishing material critical to the regime,[230] of aggressive tax inspections,[231] and generally of coercion and harassment.[232]

(i) Conclusion

As demonstrated above, tribunals have applied the FET standard to a number of typical fact situations and have now developed considerable case law in this area. The categories outlined above by no means exhaust the possibilities of the FET standard. With the progression of arbitral practice, tribunals are likely to develop these categories further and to add new ones.

Meeting the investor's central legitimate concerns of legal consistency, stability, and predictability remains a major, but not the only, ingredient of an investment-friendly climate in which the host state in turn can reasonably expect to attract foreign investment. Thus, no inconsistency between the interests of the host state and those of the investor in regard to the creation of a stable legal framework of the host state will be diagnosed. Built upon this joint perspective of host state and investor which informs the agreement laid down in an investment treaty, the standard of fair and equitable treatment will nevertheless not be understood to amount to a stabilization clause but will leave a measure of governmental space for regulation. Presumably, the degree of freedom generally considered appropriate in domestic legal orders will not be affected. Nevertheless, it is true that in effect the standard will narrow the discretionary space available to the host state. But it is also true, in principle, that this specific sort of limitation is indeed necessary to attract foreign investment and to make it viable in practice.

2. Full protection and security

(a) Concept

At first sight, the traditional notion of 'full protection and security' is amorphous and not readily amenable to operational applicability. However, as is the case for

---

[229] At para 179.
[230] *Tokios Tokelės v Ukraine*, Award, 26 July 2007, paras 123, 137.
[231] *AMTO v Ukraine*, Award, 26 March 2008, para 96.
[232] *EDF v Romania*, Award, 8 October 2009, para 300.

other standards contained in BITs, arbitral jurisprudence has gradually refined the understanding of the term. This is true both in light of the specificity of the particular wording of various treaty clauses providing protection and in regard to the particular issues falling under this concept.

Treaty practice has relied on different formulations and patterns. Whereas the traditional version (found in a series of US FCN treaties going back to the nineteenth century)[233] relies on the classical version of a guarantee which provides for 'full protection and security', other treaties have deleted the word 'full'. Another variation ensures 'protection in accordance with fair and equitable treatment'. A simple approach is restricted to the granting of 'protection' (and not 'security'), and yet another wording relies on the promise of 'legal security'. Other phrases and combinations will also be found.

These different wordings have to be applied chiefly to three different settings. In a number of earlier cases, the acts which had harmed the foreign interest were those of insurgents or rioting groups. In a second group of cases, the governmental police authorities or military units were involved. Thirdly, more recent cases have addressed governmental regulatory acts which disturb the legal stability surrounding the investor's business.

The breadth of the clause raises issues of delimitation in relation to the scope of other treaty clauses, for instance fair and equitable treatment or the umbrella clause. Especially when it comes to protection against the application of laws affecting the security and protection of the investment, the standard may acquire special importance if the treaty does not contain other clauses with a broad scope.

Some tribunals have equated the standards of full protection and security with fair and equitable treatment.[234] Other tribunals have found that the two standards were separate.[235]

(b) Standard of liability

There is broad consensus that the standard does not provide absolute protection against physical or legal infringement. In terms of the law of state responsibility, the host state is not placed under an obligation of strict liability to prevent such violations. Rather, it is generally accepted that the host state will have to exercise 'due diligence' and will have to take such measures to protect the foreign investment as are reasonable under the circumstances.[236]

---

[233] See R Wilson, *The International Law Standard in Treaties of the United States* (1952) 92–3; K Vandevelde, 'The Bilateral Investment Treaty Programme of the United States' (1988) 21 *Cornell Int'l LJ* 203, 204.

[234] *Wena Hotels v Egypt*, Award, 8 December 2000, paras 84–95; *Occidental v Ecuador*, Award, 1 July 2004, para 187; *PSEG v Turkey*, Award, 19 January 2007, paras 257–9; *National Grid v Argentina*, Award, 3 November 2008, paras 187, 189.

[235] *National Grid v Argentina*, Award, 3 November 2008, paras 187–90; *Jan de Nul v Egypt*, Award, 6 November 2008, para 269; *Azurix v Argentina*, Award, 14 July 2006, para 407. The analysis in *Suez v Argentina*, Decision on Liability, 30 July 2010, paras 165–7 on this point is ambivalent.

[236] R Dolzer and M Stevens, *Bilateral Investment Treaties* (1995) 61; see *Elettronica Sicula SpA (ELSI) (US v Italy)*, ICJ Reports (1989) 15, para 108; *AAPL v Sri Lanka*, Award, 27 June 1990, para

At the same time, the standard would be eviscerated and downgraded to a meaningless requirement if it were assumed—as was the case in *LESI v Algeria*[237]—that it accords no more protection than clauses on national treatment or most-favoured-nation treatment. Lack of resources to take appropriate action will not serve as an excuse for the host state.[238] Whenever state organs themselves act in violation of the standard, or significantly contribute to such action, no issues of attribution or due diligence will arise because the state will then be held directly responsible.

The standard will not be violated if a state exercises its right to legislate and regulate and thereby takes reasonable measures under the circumstances.[239] Recognition of a state's police power will not in itself lead to different conclusions; the existence of this power is consumed in the sovereign right to regulate, within the boundaries of international law, and does not in itself justify more far-reaching measures affecting the rights of the investor.[240]

(c) Protection against physical violence and harassment

The duty to grant physical protection and security may operate in relation to encroachment by state organs or in relation to private acts. Violence by state organs was under review in *AAPL v Sri Lanka*,[241] a case in which security forces had destroyed the investment in the course of a counter-insurgency operation. The Tribunal reviewed all circumstances and held that these actions were unwarranted and excessive.

In *Wena Hotels v Egypt*,[242] the Tribunal found Egypt liable under the standard because employees of a state entity had seized the hotel in question and because the police authorities had been aware of the seizure and had not acted to protect the investor before or after the invasive action.

In *AMT v Zaire*,[243] the host country was held liable under a protection and security clause in the applicable BIT after incidents of looting by elements of the armed forces.

In *Eureko v Poland*,[244] there was an allegation of harassment of the investor's senior representatives. The Tribunal found that there was no violation of the standard since there was no evidence that the state had authored or instigated

---

53; *TECMED v Mexico*, Award, 29 May 2003, para 177; *Noble Ventures v Romania*, Award, 12 October 2005, para 164; *Saluka v Czech Republic*, Partial Award, 17 March 2006, para 484; *Suez v Argentina*, Decision on Liability, 30 July 2010, para 158.

[237] *LESI v Algeria*, Award, 12 November 2008, para 174; the BIT applicable to that case required '*protection et securité constantes, pleines et entieres*'.

[238] But see the differentiated analysis in *Pantechniki v Albania*, Award, 30 July 2009, paras 71–84.

[239] *AES v Hungary*, Award, 23 September 2010, para 13.3.2.

[240] See *Suez v Argentina*, Decision on Liability, 30 July 2010, paras 148–50.

[241] *AAPL v Sri Lanka*, Award, 27 June 1990, paras 45 et seq, 78 et seq.

[242] *Wena Hotels v Egypt*, Award, 8 December 2000, para 84.

[243] *AMT v Zaire*, Award, 21 February 1997, paras 6.02 et seq. See also *Saluka v Czech Republic*, Partial Award, 17 March 2006, para 483.

[244] *Eureko v Poland*, Partial Award, 19 August 2005, paras 236–7.

these acts. However, the position might have been different had such actions occurred repeatedly without protective measures on the part of the state.

Other cases have concerned private violence.[245] In the *ELSI* case,[246] a Chamber of the ICJ applied a provision in an FCN treaty that granted 'the most constant protection and security'. One charge by the claimants was that the Italian authorities had allowed workers to occupy the factory. The Court found that the response of the Italian authorities had been adequate under the circumstances.[247] The Court stated that 'The reference in Article V to the provision of "constant protection and security" cannot be construed as the giving of a warranty that property shall never in any circumstances be occupied or disturbed'.[248]

In *Tecmed v Mexico*,[249] the claimant alleged that the Mexican authorities had not acted efficiently against 'social demonstrations' and disturbances at the site of the landfill under dispute. The Tribunal applied a treaty provision guaranteeing 'full protection and security to the investments . . . in accordance with International Law'. It found that there was not sufficient evidence to prove that the Mexican authorities had encouraged, fostered, or contributed to the actions in question and that there was no evidence that the authorities had not reacted reasonably.[250]

Similarly, *Noble Ventures v Romania*[251] involved demonstrations and protests by employees. The relevant treaty provision stipulated that the 'Investment shall . . . enjoy full protection and security'. The Tribunal rejected the claim, finding that it was difficult to identify any specific failure on the part of Romania to exercise due diligence in protecting the claimant.[252]

(d) Legal protection

There is also authority to the effect that the principle of full protection and security reaches beyond physical violence and requires legal protection for the investor.[253] Some treaties explicitly provide for 'full protection and legal security'.[254] However, case law supports the view that the usual formula of 'full protection and security' also provides protection against infringements of the investor's rights.

In the *ELSI* case,[255] the guarantee of 'the most constant protection and security' was also the basis for a complaint concerning the time taken (16 months) for a decision on an appeal against an order requisitioning the factory. The ICJ's

---

[245] See also *Eastern Sugar v Czech Republic*, Partial Award, 27 March 2007, para 203.
[246] *Elettronica Sicula SpA (ELSI) (US v Italy)*, ICJ Reports (1989) 15.
[247] At paras 105–8.
[248] At para 108.
[249] *TECMED v Mexico*, Award, 29 May 2003.
[250] At paras 175–7.
[251] *Noble Ventures Inc v Romania*, Award, 12 October 2005.
[252] At paras 164–6.
[253] See *CSOB v Slovakia*, Award, 29 December 2004, para 170; *National Grid v Argentina*, Award, 3 November 2008, paras 187–90; *Frontier Petroleum v Czech Republic*, Final Award, 12 November 2010, paras 260–73; *Total v Argentina*, Decision on Liability, 27 December 2010, para 343.
[254] See eg Art 4(1) of the Germany-Argentina BIT of 9 April 1991 ('*plena protección y seguridad jurídica*').
[255] *Elettronica Sicula SpA (ELSI) (US v Italy)*, ICJ Reports (1989) 15.

Chamber examined this argument and found that the time taken, though undoubtedly long, did not violate the treaty standard in view of other procedural safeguards under Italian law.[256]

In *CME v Czech Republic*,[257] a regulatory authority had created a legal situation that enabled the investor's local partner to terminate the contract on which the investment depended. The Tribunal said that 'The host State is obligated to ensure that neither by amendment of its laws nor by actions of its administrative bodies is the agreed and approved security and protection of the foreign investor's investment withdrawn or devalued'.[258]

The tribunal in *Lauder v Czech Republic*, however, denied a violation of the standard on the basis of the same facts. It reached the result that the only duty of the host state under the 'protection and security' clause had been to grant the investor access to its judicial system.[259]

In *Azurix v Argentina*,[260] the Tribunal confirmed that 'full protection and security may be breached even if no physical violence or damage occurs':[261]

The cases referred to above show that full protection and security was understood to go beyond protection and security ensured by the police. It is not only a matter of physical security; the stability afforded by a secure investment environment is as important from an investor's point of view. The tribunal is aware that in recent free trade agreements signed by the United States, for instance, with Uruguay, full protection and security is understood to be limited to the level of police protection required under customary international law. However, when the terms 'protection and security' are qualified by 'full' and no other adjective or explanation, they extend, in their ordinary meaning, the content of this standard beyond physical security.[262]

In *Siemens v Argentina*,[263] the Tribunal derived additional authority for the proposition that 'full protection and security' goes beyond physical security and extends to legal protection from the fact that the applicable BIT's definition of investment also applied to intangible assets:

As a general matter and based on the definition of investment, which includes tangible and intangible assets, the Tribunal considers that the obligation to provide full protection and security is wider than 'physical' protection and security. It is difficult to understand how the physical security of an intangible asset would be achieved.[264]

In *Vivendi v Argentina*,[265] the Tribunal had to apply a clause requiring 'full protection and security in accordance with the principle of fair and equitable

---

[256] At para 109.
[257] *CME v Czech Republic*, Partial Award, 13 September 2001, para 613.
[258] At para 613.
[259] *Lauder v Czech Republic*, Award, 3 September 2001, para 314.
[260] *Azurix v Argentina*, Award, 14 July 2006.
[261] At para 406.
[262] At para 408.
[263] *Siemens v Argentina*, Award, 6 February 2007.
[264] At para 303.
[265] *Vivendi v Argentina*, Award, 20 August 2007.

treatment'. The Tribunal found that the scope of such a provision is not limited to safeguarding 'physical possession or the legally protected terms of the operation of the investment'.[266]

Sempra v Argentina[267] recognized that the standard has traditionally developed in the context of physical protection of the investment, but that exceptionally a broader interpretation would be possible.

The investor may also have to take active measures to protect the investment. In *GEA v Ukraine*,[268] the claimant argued that the host state should have initiated proceedings to inquire into a theft of the claimant's property. The Tribunal rejected the claim because the claimant itself had not brought a criminal complaint.

Biwater Gauff v Tanzania[269] confirmed that the guarantee of 'full security' extends to actions both of the host state and of third parties.[270] Due diligence is not observed in the case of failure 'to take reasonable, precautionary and preventive action' to protect an investment.[271] Full protection implies 'a State's guarantee to stability in a secure environment, both physical, commercial and legal'.[272]

Some tribunals have denied the applicability of this standard to legal protection. According to *Suez v Argentina*,[273] the concept of 'full protection and security' would not cover issues of legal security. The Tribunal assumed, as did *Rumeli v Kazakhstan*,[274] that the traditional interpretation given to this term stands in the way of an understanding that would extend to a broader construction; without further explanation, the *Suez* Tribunal also stated that this view is supported by a textual method of interpretation.[275]

In this context it is doubtful whether it is useful to distinguish 'full protection and security' from 'protection and security' and to assume that the absence of the word 'full' means that the standard must be given a narrower meaning which extends to physical security only.[276]

The Tribunal in *Parkerings v Lithuania*[277] ruled that 'full protection and security' not only requires the prevention of damage, but also requires the host state 'to restore the previous situation' and 'to punish the author of the injury'.

---

[266] At para 7.4.15. Cited approvingly in *AES v Hungary*, Award, 23 September 2010, para 13.3.2.
[267] *Sempra v Argentina*, Award, 28 September 2007, para 323.
[268] *GEA v Ukraine*, Award, 31 March 2011, para 247.
[269] *Biwater Gauff v Tanzania*, Award, 24 July 2008.
[270] At para 730.
[271] At para 725.
[272] At para 729.
[273] *Suez v Argentina*, Decision on Liability, 30 July 2010, paras 158–73.
[274] *Rumeli v Kazakhstan*, Award, 29 July 2008, para 668. See also *BG Group v Argentina*, Final Award, 24 December 2007, paras 323–8.
[275] At para 171.
[276] See *Parkerings v Lithuania*, Award, 11 September 2007, para 354. But see also the discussion in *Suez v Argentina*, Decision on Liability, 30 July 2010, paras 161 et seq, in particular para 169.
[277] *Parkerings v Lithuania*, Award, 11 September 2007, para 355.

(e) Relationship to customary international law

Some treaty provisions on protection and security tie the standard to general international law ('full protection and security in accordance with international law'), parallel to the practice on fair and equitable treatment. Other treaties refer to protection and security and to treatment in accordance with international law as separate standards, suggesting that the two are not identical.

The question remains whether an unqualified reference to 'full protection and security' provides an autonomous treaty standard or merely serves to incorporate customary law. To clarify the issue for purposes of the NAFTA, the three parties have stated in a Note of Interpretation that the provision on full protection and security in Article 1105(1) embodies customary law,[278] as they also did in regard to fair and equitable treatment. In other words, the NAFTA parties assume that the standard reflects those requirements embodied in the concept of the minimum standard on the level of general international law as applied to aliens.[279]

In the *ELSI* case, the ICJ suggested that the standard 'may go further' than general international law,[280] even though the clause in the relevant treaty contained a reference to international law ('full protection and security required by international law'). By contrast, some tribunals have expressed the view that this standard is no more than the traditional obligation to protect aliens under customary international law.[281]

3. The umbrella clause

(a) Meaning and origin

An umbrella clause is a provision in an investment protection treaty that guarantees the observance of obligations assumed by the host state vis-à-vis the investor. These clauses are referred to as 'umbrella clauses' because they bring contractual and other commitments under the treaty's protective umbrella. At times they are also referred to as 'observance of undertakings clauses'.[282] The most contentious issue in relation to clauses of this kind is whether, and in what circumstances, they place contracts between the host state and the investor under the treaty's protection. A typical umbrella clause in a contemporary version is Article 2(2) of the British Model Treaty: 'Each Contracting Party shall observe any obligation it may

---

[278] NAFTA Free Trade Commission, Interpretative Note of 31 July 2001, cited in *Mondev v United States*, Award, 11 October 2002, para 101.

[279] See pp 136 et seq.

[280] *Elettronica Sicula SpA (ELSI) (US v Italy)*, ICJ Reports (1989) 15, para 111.

[281] *Noble Ventures v Romania*, Award, 12 October 2005, para 164; *El Paso v Argentina*, Award, 31 October 2011, para 522.

[282] For a general overview, see K Yannaca-Small, 'What About This "Umbrella Clause"' in K Yannaca-Small (ed), *Arbitration Under International Investment Agreements* (2010) 479.

have entered into with regard to investments of nationals or companies of the other Contracting Party.'

The German Model Treaty contains a similar clause in Article 8(2). Many, but by no means all, BITs contain clauses of this type. The ECT offers such a clause in Article 10(1),[283] but the NAFTA does not contain an umbrella clause.

The wording of umbrella clauses in investment treaties is not uniform. A general discussion must allow for the variation in language of these clauses and the resulting differences in interpretation. Some treaties follow the British model quoted above, whereas other treaties use more detailed wording. The investment protection treaty concluded between France and Hong Kong in 1995 states in Article III:

Without prejudice to the provisions of this Agreement, each Contracting Party shall observe any particular obligation it may have entered into with regard to investments of investors of the other Contracting Party, including provisions more favourable than those of this Agreement.

A provision that addresses the future legal order of the host state is not an umbrella clause properly speaking:

Each contracting Party shall create and maintain in its territory a legal framework apt to guarantee to investors the continuity of legal treatment, including the compliance, in good faith, of all undertakings assumed with regard to each specific investor.[284]

Umbrella clauses are by no means of recent vintage.[285] The BIT between Germany and Pakistan of 1959—the first modern investment treaty—already contained a clause of the same kind as the current German Model Treaty. In 1959, the German Government informed the German Parliament about the effect of an umbrella clause: 'The violation of such an obligation [of an investment agreement] accordingly will also amount to a violation of the international legal obligation contained in the present Treaty.'[286]

The historical-legal context in which the origin of the clause must be assessed pertains to the post-1945 controversies about the status of investment agreements as contracts subject to the domestic laws of the host state or, alternatively, as undertakings on the level of international law.[287] In 1929, the PCIJ ruled in the *Serbian Loans* case that '[a]ny contract which is not a contract between States in

---

[283] ECT, Art 10(1), last sentence: 'Each Contracting Party shall observe any obligation it has entered into with an Investor or an Investment of an Investor of any other Contracting Party.'

[284] BIT between Italy and Jordan, Art 2(4). See *Salini v Jordan*, Decision on Jurisdiction, 29 November 2004, para 126.

[285] For discussion on the origin of the clause, see A Sinclair, '"The Origins of the Umbrella Clause": The International Law of Investment Protection' (2004) 4 *Arbitration International* 411.

[286] Translation by the authors. For the original German text, see J Alenfeld, *Die Investitionsförderungsverträge der Bundesrepublik Deutschland* (1971) 97, note 180.

[287] See eg F A Mann, 'State Contracts and State Responsibility' (1960) 54 *AJIL* 572; R Jennings, 'State Contracts in International Law' (1961) 37 *BYBIL* 156; S Schwebel, 'International Protection of Contractual Agreements' (1959) *ASIL Proceedings* 273; A Verdross, 'Protection of Private Property under Quasi-International Agreements' (1959) *Nederlands Tijdschrift voor Internationaal Recht* 355; C Hyde, 'Economic Development Agreements' (1962-I) 105 *Receuil des Cours de l'Académie de droit international* 267.

their capacity as subjects of international law is based on the municipal law of some country'.[288]

Contract claims may be put under the protection of a treaty and be referred to international adjudication. This point is made in Oppenheim's *International Law* in the following words:

It is doubtful whether a breach by a state of its contractual obligations with aliens constitutes *per se* a breach of an international obligation, unless there is some such additional element as denial of justice, or expropriation, or breach of treaty, in which case it is that additional element which will constitute the basis for the state's international responsibility. However, either by virtue of a term in the contract itself or of an agreement between the state and the alien, or by virtue of an agreement between the state allegedly in breach of its contractual obligations and the state of which the alien is a national, disputes as to compliance with the terms of contracts may be referred to an internationally composed tribunal, applying, at least in part, international law.[289]

After 1945, projects for large-scale foreign investments prompted the question whether guarantees given under the domestic law of the host state provided sufficient legal stability to justify the required expenditures for such projects. Umbrella clauses were seen as a bridge between private contractual arrangements, the domestic law of the host state, and public international law allowing for more investor security. One effect of these clauses is to blur the distinction between investment arbitration and commercial arbitration.

An umbrella clause in a treaty protects a contract that an investor has entered into with the host state and is an expression of the maxim *pacta sunt servanda*. It follows that in the presence of an umbrella clause a breach by the host country of an investment contract with the foreign investor constitutes a violation of the treaty and can be raised in international arbitration.

Until 2003, the umbrella clause received little attention in academic discussion or arbitral practice, although it was often reflected in treaties. Those few authors who drew attention to the clause essentially shared the German view of the purpose of the clause as a means to elevate violations of investment contracts to the level of international law.[290] However, this phase of unanimity came to an end with the

---

[288] Judgment, No 14, PCIJ, Series A, No 20, 41; see also *Noble Ventures v Romania*, Award, 12 October 2005, para 53: 'The Tribunal recalls the well established rule of general international law that in normal circumstances per se a breach of a contract by the State does not give rise to direct international responsibility on the part of the State.'

[289] R Jennings and A Watts, *Oppenheim's International Law*, 9th edn (1996), vol 1, 927. Footnotes omitted.

[290] See eg P Weil, 'Problèmes relatifs aux contrats passés entre un Etat et un particulier' (1969) 128 *Recueil des Cours de l'Académie de droit international* 130; F A Mann, 'British Treaties for the Promotion and Protection of Investments' (1981) *BYBIL* 241, 246; R Dolzer and M Stevens, *Bilateral Investment Treaties* (1995) 81; I Shihata, 'Applicable Law in International Arbitration: Specific Aspects in Case of the Involvement of State Parties' in I Shihata and D Wolfensohn (eds), *The World Bank in a Changing World. Selected Essays and Lectures*, vol II (1995) 601; more recently, see C Schreuer, 'Travelling the BIT-Route—Of Waiting Periods, Umbrella Clauses and Forks in the Road' (2004) 5 *J World Investment and Trade* 231, 250.

arbitral decision in *SGS v Pakistan* in 2003[291] which departed fundamentally from the conventional understanding of the clause. Ever since this ruling, the purpose, meaning, and scope of the clause have caused controversy and given rise to disturbingly divergent lines of jurisprudence.

(b) Effective application of umbrella clauses

One line of decisions gives full effect to umbrella clauses. This practice is best represented by *Noble Ventures v Romania*[292] where the Tribunal had to interpret and apply the following clause in Article II(2)(c) of the BIT between the United States and Romania: 'Each party shall observe any obligation it may have entered into with regard to investments.' The US claimant in this case argued, inter alia, that Romania had breached the umbrella clause by failing to abide by its contractual obligation to renegotiate the debts of a formerly state-owned company acquired by the investor. The Tribunal insisted on the specificity of each umbrella clause, distinguishing earlier cases on this basis. The ruling emphasized that the wording obviously referred to investment contracts.[293] Consistent with Article 31 of the VCLT, it emphasized the object and purpose of investment treaties.[294] In the view of the Tribunal:

two States may include in a bilateral investment treaty a provision to the effect that, in the interest of achieving the objects and goals of the treaty, the host State may incur international responsibility by reason of a breach of its contractual obligations towards the private investor of the other Party, the breach of contract being thus 'internationalized', i.e. assimilated to a breach of the treaty.[295]

... [I]n including Art. II(2)(c) in the BIT, the Parties had as their aim to equate contractual obligations governed by municipal law to international treaty obligations as established in the BIT.

By reason therefore of the inclusion of Art. II(2)(c) in the BIT, the Tribunal therefore considers the Claimant's claims of breach of contract on the basis that any such breach constitutes a breach of the BIT.[296]

In the event, the Tribunal found that Romania had not violated its contractual obligation, and the Tribunal left open the question whether the wide scope of an umbrella clause has to be narrowed in some way.[297]

The *Noble Ventures* Tribunal was not the first to accord a broad or full scope to the clause. In *SGS v Philippines*,[298] the Tribunal, in its Decision on Jurisdiction,

---

[291] *SGS v Pakistan*, Decision on Jurisdiction, 6 August 2003.

[292] *Noble Ventures v Romania*, Award, 12 October 2005.

[293] At para 51.

[294] At para 52.

[295] At para 64. See also at para 85: 'where the acts of a governmental agency are to be attributed to the State for the purposes of applying an umbrella clause, such as Art. II(2)(c) of the BIT, breaches of a contract into which the State has entered are capable of constituting a breach of international law *by virtue of the breach of the umbrella clause*.' Emphasis in original.

[296] At paras 61, 62.

[297] At para 61.

[298] *SGS v Philippines*, Decision on Jurisdiction, 29 January 2004.

also ruled that in the presence of an umbrella clause in the Philippines-Swiss BIT, a violation of an investment agreement will lead to a violation of the investment treaty: 'Article X(2) [the umbrella clause] means what it says.'[299] The Tribunal stated:

Article X(2) makes it a breach of the BIT for the host State to fail to observe binding commitments, including contractual commitments, which it has assumed with regard to specific investments. But it does not convert the issue of the *extent* or *content* of such obligations into an issue of international law. That issue (in the present case, the issue of how much is payable for services provided under the CISS Agreement) is still governed by the investment agreement.[300]

However, *SGS v Philippines* did not carry this approach to its logical conclusion. Instead the Tribunal assumed that, due to the existence of a forum selection clause in favour of the courts of the host state, the Philippine courts were to rule on the obligations contained in the investment contract.[301]

In *Eureko v Poland*[302] the Tribunal had to rule on the umbrella clause in Article 3.5 of the treaty between the Netherlands and Poland. The Tribunal considered the ordinary meaning, the context of the clause, and the maxim of *effet utile*. It concluded that breaches by Poland of its obligations under the contracts could be breaches of the BIT's umbrella clause, even if they did not violate the BIT's other standards.[303] The Tribunal said:

The plain meaning—the 'ordinary meaning'—of a provision prescribing that a State 'shall observe any obligation it may have entered into' with regard to certain foreign investment is not obscure. The phrase, 'shall observe' is imperative and categorical. 'Any' obligations is capacious; it means not only obligations of a certain type, but 'any'—that is to say, all—obligations entered into with regard to investments of investors of the other Contracting Party.... The context of Article 3.5 [the umbrella clause] is a Treaty whose object and purpose is 'the encouragement and reciprocal protection of investment', a treaty which contains specific provisions designed to accomplish that end, of which Article 3.5 is one. It is a cardinal rule of the interpretation of treaties that each and every operative clause of a treaty is to be interpreted as meaningful rather than meaningless.[304]

In the event, the Tribunal found that Poland had violated its obligations arising from a privatization scheme vis-à-vis the investor.

---

[299] At para 119.
[300] At para 128. Emphasis in original.
[301] At para 155:

> The Philippine courts are available to hear SGS's contract claim. Until the question of the scope or extent of the Respondent's obligation to pay is clarified—whether by agreement between the parties or by proceedings in the Philippine courts as provided for in Article 12 of the CISS Agreement—a decision by this Tribunal on SGS's claim to payment would be premature.

For a critical review, see C Schreuer, 'Calvo's Grandchildren: The Return of Local Remedies in Investment Arbitration' (2004) *Law & Practice of Int'l Courts and Tribunals* 1, 11.

[302] *Eureko v Poland*, Partial Award, 19 August 2005; for a critical review, see Z Douglas, 'Nothing if not Critical for Investment Treaty Arbitration: *Occidental, Eureko* and *Methanex*' (2006) 22 *Arbitration International* 27.

[303] At para 250.   [304] At paras 246, 248.

In *SGS v Paraguay* the claim was for unpaid bills under a contract between the investor and the state for the pre-shipment inspection of goods. The BIT between Switzerland and Paraguay provided in Article 11 that '[e]ither Contracting Party shall constantly guarantee the observance of the commitments it has entered into with respect to the investments of the investors of the other Contracting Party'. The Tribunal rejected a restrictive interpretation of this umbrella clause based either on the nature of the contract or on the nature of its breach. It said:

Article 11 does not exclude commercial contracts of the State from its scope. Likewise, Article 11 does not state that its constant guarantee of observance of such commitments may be breached only through actions that a commercial counterparty cannot take, through abuses of state power, or through exertions of undue government influence.[305]

... Article 11 requires the 'observance' of commitments. Also as a matter of the ordinary meaning of the term, a failure to meet one's obligations under a contract is clearly a failure to 'observe' one's commitments. There is nothing in Article 11 that states or implies that a government will only fail to observe its commitments if it abuses its sovereign authority.[306]

In a number of other decisions tribunals similarly gave full effect to umbrella clauses and confirmed that, by virtue of such a clause, failure by the host state to meet obligations assumed in relation to investments amounted to a breach of the treaty.[307]

(c) Restrictive application of umbrella clauses

In a series of other cases tribunals have imposed various limitations on the application of the umbrella clause.[308] In *SGS v Pakistan*[309] the Swiss claimant had concluded a contract with Pakistan on pre-shipment inspection services with a forum selection clause for Pakistani courts. When Pakistan unilaterally terminated the contract, the claimant started proceedings at the International Centre for Settlement of Investment Disputes (ICSID) under the BIT between Pakistan and Switzerland. The BIT contained the following clause: 'Either Contracting Party shall constantly guarantee the observance of the commitments it has entered into with respect to the investments of the investors of the other Contracting Party.'

The Tribunal found that the proper mode of interpretation was a restrictive one (*in dubio mitius*).[310] The Tribunal made no reference to the modes of interpretation laid down in Article 31 of the VCLT which does not in its wording embrace

---

[305] *SGS v Paraguay*, Decision on Jurisdiction, 12 February 2010, para 168.

[306] *SGS v Paraguay*, Award, 10 February 2012, para 91.

[307] *LG&E v Argentina*, Decision on Liability, 3 October 2006, paras 164–75; *Siemens v Argentina*, Award, 6 February 2007, paras 196–206; *Plama v Bulgaria*, Award, 27 August 2008, paras 185–7; *Duke Energy v Ecuador*, Award, 18 August 2008, paras 314–25; *AMTO v Ukraine*, Award, 26 March 2008, paras 109–12.

[308] For a critical evaluation, see S W Schill, 'Umbrella Clauses as Public Law Concepts in Comparative Perspective' in S W Schill (ed), *International Investment Law and Comparative Public Law* (2010) 317.

[309] *SGS v Pakistan*, Decision on Jurisdiction, 6 August 2003.

[310] At para 171.

this maxim. In light of this interpretative approach, the Tribunal concluded that any other understanding would have a far-reaching impact on the sovereignty of the host state which could not be presumed in the absence of a clear expression of a corresponding will by the parties.[311]

The Tribunal presented four arguments in support of this position. First, the conventional view would also cover non-contractual obligations arising under the laws of the host state, including the smallest types of commitment, and would lead to a flood of lawsuits before international tribunals.[312] Secondly, the conventional view would make other guarantees contained in investment treaties superfluous because even a violation of a small obligation would allow a lawsuit.[313] Thirdly, the Tribunal considered that the location of the umbrella clause not in the substantive guarantees but towards the end of the treaty spoke against a far-reaching obligation.[314] And, fourthly, it pointed out that the forum selection in investment agreements would, under the conventional view, not be binding for the investor whereas the host state would be bound to honour such clauses.[315] The Tribunal did not refer to the distinction between 'commercial acts' and 'sovereign acts'.

The Tribunal denied that its position would deprive an umbrella clause of its meaning. It pointed out that the clause would be relevant in the context of implementation of the investment treaty in the domestic legal order or if the host state failed to participate in international proceedings to which it had agreed earlier.[316]

This decision was widely criticized.[317] The sharpest criticism came from the Tribunal in *SGS v Philippines*,[318] but commentators also pointed to weaknesses of the decision.[319] The most vulnerable aspect of the decision is the lack of any attempt to ground the method of interpretation in the accepted canons embodied in Article 31 of the VCLT.

For a while it seemed as though *SGS v Pakistan* would remain an isolated decision. But the decision has also found a measure of support.[320] In 2006, two nearly identical decisions—in *El Paso v Argentina*[321] and in *Pan America v*

---

[311] At paras 167, 168.   [312] At paras 166, 168.   [313] At para 168.
[314] At para 169.   [315] At para 168.   [316] At para 172.

[317] The Government of Switzerland took the unusual step of expressing its disapproval and concern over the decision in a letter of 1 October 2003 to the Deputy Secretary-General of ICSID.

[318] *SGS v Philippines*, Decision on Jurisdiction, 29 January 2004, para 125: 'Not only are the reasons given by the Tribunal in *SGS v Pakistan* unconvincing: the Tribunal failed to give any clear meaning to the "umbrella clause".' See also *Eureko v Poland*, Partial Award, 19 August 2005, para 257.

[319] S A Alexandrov, 'Breaches of Contract and Breaches of Treaty, The Jurisdiction of Treaty-based Arbitration Tribunals to Decide Breach of Contract Claims in *SGS v Pakistan* and *SGS v Philippines*' (2004) 5 *J World Investment and Trade* 555, 569; C Schreuer 'Travelling the BIT-Route—Of Waiting Periods, Umbrella Clauses and Forks in the Road' (2004) *J World Investment and Trade* 231, 253; T Wälde, 'The "Umbrella Clause" in Investment Arbitration—A Comment on Original Intentions and Recent Cases' (2005) 6 *J World Investment and Trade* 183, 225; E Gaillard, *La jurisprudence du CIRDI* (2004) 834.

[320] See eg *Toto Costruzioni Generali v Lebanon*, Decision on Jurisdiction, 11 September 2009, paras 187–202.

[321] *El Paso Energy v Argentina*, Decision on Jurisdiction, 27 April 2006.

Argentina[322]—explicitly supported the first and second arguments set out in *SGS v Pakistan* (flood of lawsuits, overreach because of wider scope than other treaty guarantees).[323] But unlike *SGS v Pakistan*, the Tribunals then introduced the distinction between the state as a merchant and the state as a sovereign. It concluded, with a broad brush, that investment arbitration will cover only disputes concerning investment agreements or state contracts in which the state is involved 'as a sovereign' but not mere commercial contracts.[324] The Tribunal in *El Paso* sought to establish a balance between the interests of the host state and those of the investor:

This Tribunal considers that a balanced interpretation is needed, taking into account both State sovereignty and the State's responsibility to create an adapted and evolutionary framework for the development of economic activities, and the necessity to protect foreign investment and its continuing flow.[325]

Thus, the decisions in *El Paso* and in *Pan American* did not restrict the scope of the umbrella clause as drastically as *SGS v Pakistan*. They accept that obligations in investment agreements are covered by the clause to the extent that they bind the state in its sovereign capacity. Essentially, the two decisions seem to echo the French concept of *contrat administratif*.[326]

The distinction between different types of investment agreement was subsequently rejected in the Award in *Siemens v Argentina*[327] where the Tribunal stated that:

The Tribunal does not subscribe to the view of the Respondent that investment agreements should be distinguished from concession agreements of an administrative nature. Such distinction has no basis in Article 7(2) of the Treaty which refers to 'any obligations', or in the definition of 'investment' in the Treaty. Any agreement related to an investment that qualifies as such under the Treaty would be part of the obligations covered under the umbrella clause.[328]

Another approach to limiting the effect of the umbrella clause does not look at the nature of the affected contract but at the nature or magnitude of its violation. The

---

[322] *Pan America/BP v Argentina*, Decision on Preliminary Objections, 27 July 2006; two out of the three arbitrators were the same as in the *El Paso* decision.

[323] See *El Paso Energy v Argentina*, Decision on Jurisdiction, 27 April 2006, paras 72–4; *Pan America/BP v Argentina*, Decision on Preliminary Objections, 27 July 2006, paras 101–3.

[324] See *El Paso Energy v Argentina*, Decision on Jurisdiction, 27 April 2006, paras 77 et seq; *Pan America/BP v Argentina*, Decision on Preliminary Objections, 27 July 2006, para 108; in *Salini v Jordan*, Award, 31 January 2006, para 155, the Tribunal had stated, in categorical terms: 'Only the State, in the exercise of its sovereign authority, and not as a contracting party, has assumed obligations under the bilateral agreement.'

[325] *El Paso Energy v Argentina*, Decision on Jurisdiction, 27 April 2006, para 70.

[326] This position is contrary to the position taken by arbitrator René-Jean Dupuy in *Texaco v Libya*, 53 ILR (1979) 389, para 72 who had held that the theory of administrative contracts had no place in international law. See also *ARAMCO v Saudi Arabia*, 27 ILR (1963) 117, 164.

[327] *Siemens v Argentina*, Award, 6 February 2007.

[328] At para 206.

Tribunal in *CMS v Argentina* referred to the distinction between governmental and commercial actions and the significance of the interference with the contract:

the tribunal believes the Respondent is correct in arguing that not all contract breaches result in breaches of the treaty. The standard of protection of the treaty will be engaged only when there is a specific breach of treaty rights and obligations or a violation of contract rights protected under the treaty. Purely commercial aspects of a contract might not be protected by the treaty in some situations, but the protection is likely to be available when there is significant interference by governments or public agencies with the rights of the investor.[329]

Similarly, in *Sempra v Argentina*[330] the Tribunal held that ordinary commercial breaches of a contract would not violate the umbrella clause in the Argentina-US BIT. Only a breach in the exercise of a sovereign state function or power but not the conduct of an ordinary contract party could effect a breach. In the particular case, the Tribunal found that the sweeping changes that Argentina had introduced were not ordinary contractual breaches but had been brought about in exercise of the state's public function. Therefore, it concluded that breaches of the obligations in question had resulted in a breach of the umbrella clause.[331]

An examination of the current strands of jurisprudence shows clearly conflicting positions. The survey of the jurisprudence interpreting the umbrella clause indicates that the understanding of the rule remains in a state of flux. However, a terminological observation and a comment on the discussion of the substance of the clause are appropriate at this stage. The terminological point concerns the distinction between 'treaty claims' and 'contract claims', introduced by the *Vivendi* Annulment Committee and subsequently often relied upon by tribunals.[332] While the simplicity of the distinction may have seemed helpful for analytical purposes at the outset, the current position of jurisprudence on the umbrella clause suggests that the contrasting of 'treaty claims' and 'contract claims' does not facilitate an understanding of the scope of the clause. The crucial point lies in recognition that certain (or all) types of violations of contracts between the state and the investor will, in the presence of an umbrella clause, amount to a violation of the investment treaty.

States entering into an investment treaty are free to fashion the scope of the treaty and the guarantees granted therein. If the parties choose to extend the scope of the agreement beyond the confines of the classical understanding of an investment treaty and also cover, to some extent, operations previously deemed 'commercial' or 'contractual' in nature, conventional terminology cannot stand in the

---

[329] *CMS v Argentina*, Award, 12 May 2005, para 299.
[330] *Sempra v Argentina*, Award, 28 September 2007.
[331] At paras 305–14.
[332] *Vivendi v Argentina*, Decision on Annulment, 3 July 2002, paras 98, 101:

In a case where the essential basis of a claim brought before an international tribunal is a breach of contract, the tribunal will give effect to any valid choice of forum clause in the contract. . . . On the other hand, where the fundamental basis of the claim is a treaty laying down an independent standard by which the conduct of the parties is to be judged, the existence of an exclusive jurisdiction clause in a contract between the claimant and the respondent state cannot operate as a bar to the application of the treaty standard.

Generally on the distinction between treaty claims and contract claims, see pp 261, 268, 272, 275–8.

way of the parties' intentions. For this reason, any attempt to define the scope of the umbrella clause by reference to abstract concepts such as 'sovereign acts', 'commercial acts', or '*contrats administratifs*' will carry no methodological power of persuasion when it comes to interpreting and applying the clause. Ultimately, no justification exists for ignoring or revising the canons of interpretation laid down in Article 31 of the VCLT. References to conventional terminological distinctions or to categories of a specific domestic legal order have no place within this canon.

(d) Umbrella clauses and privity of contract

In principle, contracts to which an umbrella clause is to apply would be between the disputing parties, that is, a state and a foreign investor. But in some cases the disputing parties and the parties to the contract on which the investor relies for the purposes of the umbrella clause are not identical. On the host state's side, the party to the contract may be a state entity or a territorial subdivision rather than the state itself. On the investor's side, the party to the contract may not be the foreign investor itself but its subsidiary in the host state. In these situations, the question arises whether an umbrella clause will protect a contract that is not directly between the host state and the investor.[333]

Noble Ventures v Romania[334] concerned a contract between the claimant and the Romanian 'State Ownership Fund', a separate legal entity. The Tribunal reached the conclusion that the contractual conduct of the Fund had to be attributed to the Romanian Government in view of the grant of governmental power to the Fund. The Tribunal found that, for the purposes of attribution, the distinction between commercial acts and sovereign acts had no relevance.[335] It followed that the umbrella clause was applicable to the contract. The Tribunal said:

where the acts of a governmental agency are to be attributed to the State for the purposes of applying an umbrella clause, such as Art. II(2)(c) of the BIT, breaches of a contract into which the State has entered are capable of constituting a breach of international law *by virtue of the breach of the umbrella clause*.[336]

In a series of other decisions, tribunals found that the umbrella clause was inapplicable where the state had not contracted in its own name.[337] In *Impregilo v Pakistan*,[338] the contracts had been concluded not with Pakistan directly but with the Pakistan Water and Power Development Authority. The claimant wanted to benefit from an umbrella clause in a third country BIT by way of an MFN clause contained in the BIT between Italy and Pakistan. The Tribunal found that

---

[333] See N Gallus, 'An Umbrella just for Two? BIT Obligations Observance Clauses and the Parties to a Contract' (2008) 24 *Arbitration International* 157.

[334] *Noble Ventures v Romania*, Award, 12 October 2005.

[335] At para 82.

[336] At para 85. Emphasis in original.

[337] *Azurix v Argentina*, Award, 14 July 2006, paras 52, 384; *AMTO v Ukraine*, Award, 26 March 2008, paras 109–12; *EDF v Romania*, Award, 8 October 2009, paras 317, 318; *Hamester v Ghana*, Award, 18 June 2010, paras 339–50.

[338] *Impregilo v Pakistan*, Decision on Jurisdiction, 22 April 2005.

contracts concluded by a separate entity of Pakistan would not be protected by an umbrella clause.[339] A similar problem arises on the investor's side when it operates through a local company that enters into a contract. The question then arises whether the foreign investor may rely on the umbrella clause in relation to a contract to which it is not a party. The ECT in Article 10(1) gives an affirmative answer to this question by referring to 'any obligations it has entered into with an Investor *or an Investment of an Investor*'.[340]

Most BITs do not contain a clarification of this kind. The practice of tribunals is divided on whether foreign investors are entitled to protection under umbrella clauses for claims arising from the contracts of their local subsidiaries. Some tribunals have allowed claims of this nature.

In *Continental Casualty v Argentina*,[341] the investor's local subsidiary, CNA, had entered into a number of contracts with Argentina. The claimant invoked the umbrella clause in respect of these contracts[342] and the Tribunal left no doubt that the umbrella clause covered contracts concluded by the investor's subsidiary. The Tribunal stated, with respect to obligations covered by the umbrella clause in Article II(2)(c) of the Argentina-US BIT:

provided that these obligations have been entered 'with regard' to investments, they may have been entered with persons or entities other than foreign investors themselves, so that an undertaking by the host State with a subsidiary such as CNA is not in principle excluded.[343]

Other tribunals have similarly extended the effect of umbrella clauses to contracts entered into by local subsidiaries of the foreign investors.[344]

In another group of cases, tribunals have concluded that successful invocation of the umbrella clause requires that the contract is directly with the foreign investor and not with its local subsidiary.[345] In *Azurix v Argentina*,[346] a concession agreement had been concluded between a province of Argentina and the subsidiary of Azurix ABA. The Tribunal recalled that Azurix and the respondent had no contractual relationship: the obligations undertaken in the concession contract

---

[339] At para 223.
[340] Emphasis added. The Reader's Guide to the ECT offers the following explanation: 'This provision covers any contract that a host country has concluded with a subsidiary of the foreign investor in the host country, or a contract between the host country and the parent company of the subsidiary.' See also *AMTO v Ukraine*, Award, 26 March 2008, para 110.
[341] *Continental Casualty v Argentina*, Award, 5 September 2008.
[342] At para 288.
[343] At para 297. See also para 98.
[344] *CMS v Argentina*, Award, 12 May 2005, paras 296–303; *Enron v Argentina*, Award, 22 May 2007, paras 269–77. The ad hoc Committee declined to annul this part of the Award: Decision on Annulment, 30 July 2010, paras 317–46; *Sempra v Argentina*, Award, 28 September 2007, paras 308–14; *Duke Energy v Ecuador*, Award, 18 August 2008, paras 314–25.
[345] *Siemens v Argentina*, Award, 6 February 2007, paras 204–6; *BG Group v Argentina*, Final Award, 24 December 2007, paras 206–15, 361–6; *El Paso v Argentina*, Award, 31 October 2011, paras 531–8.
[346] *Azurix v Argentina*, Award, 14 July 2006.

were undertaken by the province, not Argentina, in favour of ABA, not Azurix.[347] The Tribunal said:

there is no undertaking to be honored by Argentina to Azurix other than the obligations under the BIT. Even if for argument's sake, it would be possible under Article II(2)(c) [the umbrella clause] to hold Argentina responsible for the alleged breaches of the Concession Agreement by the Province, it was ABA and not Azurix which was the party to this Agreement.[348]

In *CMS v Argentina*, the claimant was a minority shareholder in a local company TGN. The Tribunal had allowed the application of the umbrella clause with respect to a licence obtained by TGN.[349] In proceedings for the Award's annulment, the ad hoc Committee noted that under Argentinian law the obligations of Argentina under the licence were obligations to TGN, not to CMS.[350] The Committee annulled the part of the Award dealing with the umbrella clause for failure to state reasons. In the Committee's view it was 'quite unclear how the Tribunal arrived at its conclusion that CMS could enforce the obligations of Argentina to TGN'.[351]

(e) Umbrella clauses and unilateral acts

In the discussion of umbrella clauses, attention is mostly centred on contracts between the host state and the investor. However, states may assume obligations not only by way of contracts but also through unilateral declarations such as legislation and executive acts.[352] Case law indicates that umbrella clauses are not restricted to contractual obligations but are capable of protecting obligations of the host state assumed unilaterally through legislation or executive acts.[353]

Tribunals have recognized, in principle, that umbrella clauses in which states undertake to observe obligations with regard to investments cover unilateral undertakings.[354] *LG&E v Argentina*,[355] involved an umbrella clause referring to the observance of 'any obligation it may have entered into with regard to investments'.[356] The case concerned the abrogation of rights granted to investors under a Gas Law and its implementing regulations. The Tribunal found that this legislation contained 'obligations' in the sense of the umbrella clause:

---

[347] At para 52.   [348] At para 384.
[349] *CMS v Argentina*, Award, 12 May 2005, paras 296–303.
[350] *CMS v Argentina*, Decision on Annulment, 25 September 2007.
[351] At para 96.
[352] W M Reisman and M H Arsanjani, 'The Question of Unilateral Governmental Statements as Applicable Law in Investment Disputes' (2004) 19 *ICSID Review-FILJ* 328.
[353] See M C Gritón Salias, 'Do Umbrella Clauses Apply to Unilateral Undertakings?' in C Binder, U Kriebaum, A Reinisch, and S Wittich (eds), *International Investment Law for the 21st Century* (2009) 490.
[354] *Enron v Argentina*, Award, 22 May 2007, paras 269–77; see also Decision on Annulment, 30 July 2010, paras 317–46; *Noble Energy v Ecuador*, Decision on Jurisdiction, 5 March 2008, paras 154–7; *Plama v Bulgaria*, Award, 27 August 2008, paras 185–7.
[355] *LG&E v Argentina*, Decision on Liability, 3 October 2006, paras 169–75.
[356] BIT between Argentina and the United States, Art II(2)(c).

These laws and regulations became obligations within the meaning of Article II(2)(c), by virtue of targeting foreign investors and applying specifically to their investments, that gave rise to liability under the umbrella clause.[357]

Some tribunals have read limitations into the clauses on the basis of the specific wording of umbrella clauses. A reference to obligations with regard to 'specific investments' was seen to exclude general legal obligations arising from legislative measures.[358] Other tribunals have found that the words 'entered into' contained in an umbrella clause could only be read as restricting the clause to contractual undertakings.[359] In *Noble Ventures v Romania*[360] the Tribunal said:

The employment of the notion 'entered into' indicates that specific commitments are referred to and not general commitments, for example by way of legislative acts. This is also the reason why Art. II(2)(c) would be very much an empty base unless understood as referring to contracts.[361]

4. Access to justice, fair procedure, and denial of justice

The 2004 and 2012 US Model BITs in Article 5(2)(a) state that the FET standard includes the obligation 'not to deny justice in criminal, civil, or administrative adjudicatory proceedings in accordance with the principle of due process embodied in the principal legal systems of the world'. It would appear that even without such a specific reference, these principles are still covered, at least in part, by the requirement of full protection and security[362] and by the rule on fair and equitable treatment.[363] Also, it is plausible to assume that the US approach refers to the relevant rules of customary law.

The standard will cover proceedings before the courts of the host state. However, depending on the wording of the treaty, it may also find application in the conduct of a party during arbitration proceedings, in particular if a party ignores a previous agreement to arbitrate.[364] Generally, the principle of denial of justice applies to actions of all branches of a government.[365] An international tribunal will decide

---

[357] At para 175.
[358] *SGS v Philippines*, Decision on Jurisdiction, 29 January 2004, para 121.
[359] *CMS v Argentina*, Decision on Annulment, 25 September 2007, para 95(a) and (b). See also *Continental Casualty v Argentina*, Award, 5 September 2008, paras 297–303.
[360] *Noble Ventures v Romania*, Award, 12 October 2005.
[361] At para 51.
[362] See pp 160 et seq.
[363] See pp 130 et seq.
[364] In *Waste Management v Mexico*, Final Award, 30 April 2004, paras 118–40, one issue was that a Mexican city refused to advance funds to cover the cost of local arbitration and the claimant then withdrew the case. The Tribunal ruled that the refusal of payment did not amount to a wrongful act.
[365] See *Petrobart v Kyrgyz Republic*, Award, 29 March 2005, pp 75–7. This case involved the improper intervention of the government in judicial proceedings. Due process and procedural fairness are not required for strictly internal governmental matters; see *Bayindir v Pakistan*, Award, 27 August 2009, paras 338 et seq.

independently whether the principle has been respected and will in this respect not be bound by the position of a domestic court.[366]

The principles of access to justice, fair procedure, and the prohibition of denial of justice relate to three stages of the judicial process: the right to bring a claim, the right of both parties to fair treatment during the proceedings, and the right to an appropriate decision at the end of the process and its enforcement. In *Azinian v Mexico*,[367] the Tribunal summarized these criteria in the following terms:

A denial of justice could be pleaded if the relevant courts refuse to entertain a suit, if they subject it to undue delay, or if they administer justice in a seriously inadequate way.... There is a fourth type of denial of justice, namely the clear and malicious misapplication of the law.[368]

The principles of international law that apply during all phases set forth a broad framework which national rules have to respect. Essentially, these principles operate as the expression of an international standard that requires the establishment of a decent and civilized system of justice as reflected in accepted international and national practice. Thus, the concept of the minimum standard of international law[369] has a substantive and a procedural side. So far, most issues of procedural propriety have in practice been reviewed under the standard of fair and equitable treatment, as discussed above.[370]

In *Duke Energy v Ecuador*,[371] the Tribunal considered that the duty to provide effective access to justice 'seeks to implement and form part of the more general guarantee against denial of justice'.[372] The case was brought by an investor who had concluded an arbitration agreement with a local Peruvian company subject to local law. In arbitration proceedings initiated by the investor in this local setting, the local arbitral tribunal had upheld a jurisdictional objection by the state, and the claimant did not challenge this award. The Tribunal did not agree with the claimant that Peru's conduct had failed to provide effective means to assert a claim.[373]

---

[366] See *Feldman v Mexico*, Award, 16 December 2002, para 140; *Himpurna v Indonesia*, XXV ICCA YB Commercial Arbitration 109, 181. Tribunals have not yet spelled out in detail under what circumstances the misapplication of domestic law may lead to international responsibility; see *Waste Management v Mexico*, Award, 30 April 2004, paras 129 et seq. As to the decision of lower courts, it is widely assumed that their rulings will not be considered to amount to an internationally wrongful act as long as a reasonable opportunity exists for the foreigner for appropriate review; see *Ambatielos Claim*, ICJ Reports (1953) 10; *Loewen v United States*, Award, 26 June 2003, para 154.

[367] *Azinian v Mexico*, Award, 1 November 1999.

[368] At paras 102, 103. See also *Mondev v United States*, Award, 11 October 2002, paras 126–7; *Parkerings v Lithuania*, Award, 11 September 2007, para 317.

[369] See p 3.

[370] See pp 154–6.

[371] *Duke Energy v Ecuador*, Award, 18 August 2008, para 391.

[372] At para 391.

[373] At paras 390–403.

As the major studies on the subject by Freeman,[374] de Visscher,[375] and Paulsson[376] show, the application of the relevant principles is rather fact-specific, but the principles as such have been generally recognized. In the broadest terms, the concept of a procedural minimum standard was expressed in the *Ambatielos* case:

The foreigner shall enjoy full freedom to appear before the courts for the protection or defence of his rights, whether as plaintiff or defendant; to bring any action provided or authorised by law; to deliver any pleading by way of defence, set off or counterclaim; to engage Counsel; to adduce evidence, whether documentary or oral or of any other kind; to apply for bail; to lodge appeals and, in short, to use the Courts fully and to avail himself of any procedural remedies or guarantees provided by the law of the land in order that justice may be administered on a footing of equality with nationals of the country.[377]

In principle, a host state is under an obligation to establish a judicial system that allows the effective exercise of the substantive rights granted to foreign investors. This does not necessarily mean that all governmental actions must be subject to judicial review. In particular, the concept of state immunity has traditionally operated in most countries to prevent lawsuits against the government in various areas. Within NAFTA, the Tribunal in *Mondev* had to decide whether the Massachusetts Tort Claims Act violated Article 1105(1) of the NAFTA inasmuch as the Act granted immunity for intentional torts to public employers that were not organized as independent corporate entities.[378] The Canadian claimant, which had done business with a Boston public authority falling under the rule of immunity, argued before a NAFTA tribunal that the rule on full protection and security in Article 1105 of the NAFTA should be interpreted so as to render unlawful the Massachusetts rules on state immunity when applied to the Boston authority. The Tribunal disagreed, pointing out that there may be sound reasons to protect a public employer from private lawsuits.

Even on the level of human rights, the ECtHR has accepted that granting immunity to a government is permitted provided that the very essence of the right is not impaired, that the law on immunity pursues a legitimate aim, and that there is a reasonable relationship of proportionality between the means employed and the aim sought to be achieved.[379]

The situation will be different if the law on immunity or its application amounts to discrimination against the foreign investor.[380] Also, any conduct ignoring an agreement to arbitrate and any undue interference with the ordinary proceedings of

---

[374] A V Freeman, *The International Responsibility of States for Denial of Justice* (1938).

[375] Ch de Visscher, 'Le Deni de justice en droit international' (1935) 54 *Collected Courses of the Hague Academy of International Law* 370.

[376] J Paulsson, *Denial of Justice in International Law* (2005).

[377] *Ambatielos Claim*, 6 March 1956 (*Greece v UK*) 23 ILR 306, 325.

[378] *Mondev v United States*, Award, 11 November 2002, paras 139–56.

[379] *Fogarty v United Kingdom*, 21 November 2001, 34 ECHR (2002) 12. In another case decided on the same day, the Court upheld an Irish law granting immunity to foreign states: *McElhinney v Ireland*, ECHR, 21 November 2001.

[380] See Ch de Visscher, 'Le Deni de justice en droit international' (1935) 54 *Collected Courses of the Hague Academy of International Law* 370, 396; J Paulsson, *Denial of Justice in International Law* (2005) 147 et seq; *Loewen v United States*, Award, 26 June 2003, 42 ILM 811 (2003), para 135.

an arbitral tribunal will be seen as unlawful.[381] Moreover, whenever a foreign investor has been subject to a seriously unlawful act, the local authorities are required to take appropriate measures to ensure that justice is done.[382]

There is no doubt that actions of courts are attributable to the state.[383] The *Chattin* decision of the Mexican–US Claims Commission (1927) summarized the duty of courts to conduct fair proceedings as follows:

Irregularity of court proceedings is proven with reference to absence of proper investigations, insufficiency of confrontations, withholding from the accused the opportunity to know all of the charges brought against him, undue delay of the proceedings, making the hearings in open court a mere formality, and a continued absence of seriousness on the part of the Court.[384]

In *Tokios Tokelės v Ukraine*,[385] the Tribunal found that a 'failure to comply with the elementary principles of justice in the conduct of criminal proceedings, when directed towards an investor in the operation of his investment, may be a breach, or an element in a breach, of an investment treaty'.

Procedural irregularity played an important role in *Loewen v United States*.[386] The Tribunal held that the conduct of the domestic trial in the proceedings against Loewen had been disgraceful and that the judge in Mississippi had failed to protect Loewen against flagrant appeals to prejudice.[387] According to the Tribunal, the trial as a whole did not satisfy the minimum standards of international law,[388] exposing the defendant to 'manifest injustice in the sense of a lack of due process leading to an outcome which offends a sense of judicial propriety'.[389] Moreover, in the view of the Tribunal, the staggering amount of punitive damages awarded to the claimants by the Mississippi jury indicated that the jury was 'swayed by prejudice, passion or sympathy'.[390]

As to retroactive application of laws, J Paulsson has rightly pointed out that, depending on the circumstances of the case, this may be seen as unlawful.[391] In

---

[381] J Paulsson, *Denial of Justice in International Law* (2005) 149.

[382] See eg *Wena Hotels v Egypt*, Award, 8 December 2000, para 84; *Tecmed v Mexico*, Award, 29 May 2003, para 177.

[383] Article 4(1) of the ILC's Articles on State Responsibility provides:

The conduct of any State organ shall be considered an act of that State under international law, whether the organ exercises legislative, executive, judicial or any other functions, whatever position it holds in the organization of the State, and whatever its character as an organ of the central government or of a territorial unit of the State.

See J Crawford, *The International Law Commission's Articles on State Responsibility: Introduction, Text and Commentaries* (2002) 94.

[384] *BE Chattin (USA v Mexico)*, 23 July 1927, IV RIAA 282, 295 (1951).

[385] *Tokios Tokelės v Ukraine*, Award, 26 July 2007, para 133.

[386] *Loewen v United States*, Award, 26 June 2003.

[387] At para 53.

[388] At para 121.

[389] At para 132; see also *Azinian v Mexico*, Award, 1 November 1999, para 99.

[390] At para 105.

[391] J Paulsson, *Denial of Justice in International Law* (2005) 199–200: 'Surprising departures from settled patterns of reasoning or outcomes, or the sudden emergence of a full-blown rule where none had existed, must be viewed with the greatest scepticism if their effect is to disadvantage a foreigner.'

principle, the correct position seems to be that the laws of the host state, as they stood at the time of the initial investment, will serve as the proper benchmark.[392]

Concerning the outcome of a case before a local court, it is clear that an investment tribunal will not act as an appeals mechanism and will not decide whether the court was in error or whether one view of the law or the other would be preferable. Nevertheless, a line will have to be drawn between an ordinary error and a gross miscarriage of justice, which may no longer be considered as an exercise of the rule of law. This line will be crossed especially when it is impossible for a third party to recognize how an impartial judge could have reached the result in question. Proof of bad faith may be relevant, but is not required in such a case.[393]

In *Chevron v Ecuador*,[394] the claimant extensively argued, with reference to case law, that Ecuadorian courts had delayed local proceedings with the result that the case was dormant for 14 years.[395] The Tribunal examined the issue in light of the treaty-based requirement for the host to provide 'effective means of asserting claims and enforcing rights', a clause found, for example, in some US treaties and in the ECT.

The Tribunal found that this provision is to be understood as *lex specialis* vis-à-vis for the rule on denial of justice,[396] even though the close link between the two standards was recognized. Claims for undue delay, for interference by the government with the judicial process, but also for manifestly unjust decisions fall under the treaty clause,[397] and individual claims have to be examined in light of all circumstances.[398] Given the specificity of the case, the Tribunal had no difficulty in finding a violation of the clause. Moreover, the Tribunal found that the clause, being different from the rule on denial of justice, did not require exhaustion of local remedies.[399]

5. Emergency, necessity, armed conflicts, and *force majeure*

The legal rules applicable to extraordinary events and periods of economic and social disorder are of direct interest both to the host state and to the foreign investor. The host state's concern is to retain sufficient legal flexibility in dealing with extraordinary situations without incurring any liability towards the foreign investor. The investor and its home state will be aware that during a longer

---

[392] See pp 145–6.

[393] But see also Paulsson, *Denial of Justice in International Law* (2005), 202, citing D P O'Connnell, *International Law*, 2nd edn (1970) 948: 'Bad faith and not judicial error seems to be at the heart of the matter, and bad faith may be indicated by an unreasonable departure from the rules of evidence and procedure.' On denial of justice based on collusion between the local partner of a foreign investor and the local judiciary, see *France v Venezuela* (*Fabiani* case), Award of 1898, *Moore's International Arbitrations*, p 4878; collusion among branches of government with the judiciary are also considered to amount to denial of justice, see *United States v Great Britain* (*Brown* case), 23 November 1923, VI RIAA 120.

[394] *Chevron v Ecuador*, Award, 30 March 2010.

[395] At paras 171 et seq.   [396] At para 242.   [397] At para 248.

[398] At para 249.   [399] At paras 276 et seq.

investment project, extraordinary situations may arise and that one of the purposes of the legal framework created by an investment treaty will be precisely to protect the investment during such difficult periods. The relevant international rules will operate and will be applied on their own, independent of domestic provisions dealing with extraordinary periods.[400]

(a) Customary international law: civil violence, military action

Under customary international law, the theme of possible or inevitable damage to the alien during periods of serious disorder and of the possible scope of protection by the host state has long occupied arbitral tribunals. Many of these cases were decided before 1930 and concerned the consequences of unrest in Central and Latin American countries upon foreign property in line with *force majeure*. The basic result emerging from these cases is summarized in the principle of non-responsibility of the host state for extraordinary events of social strife and disorder which lead to physical action against the asset of a foreign investor.[401] However, this principle is qualified by a duty of the host state to exercise due diligence, that is, to use the police and military forces to protect the interests of the alien to the extent feasible and practicable under the circumstances, both before the event and while it unfolds.[402] It has been assumed that a claimant has the burden of showing that the host state was negligent, and also that no claim will be accepted if the host state can demonstrate that foreigners have received the same treatment as nationals of the host state.[403]

In *AAPL v Sri Lanka*,[404] Sri Lanka was found liable for an attack conducted by its military forces against the investor's staff and facilities in the context of anti-terrorist activities. In the view of the Tribunal, the governmental authorities should have undertaken precautionary measures in order to resolve the situation peacefully before launching an armed attack against the investor's facilities.[405]

(b) The ILC Articles on State Responsibility

Situations beyond the control of the host state are addressed in the ILC Articles on State Responsibility under the headings *'force majeure'* (Art 23), 'distress' (Art 24), and 'necessity' (Art 25).

---

[400] See eg *Funnekotter v Zimbabwe*, Award, 22 April 2009, para 103; *Sempra v Argentina*, Award, 28 September 2007, para 257, generally explained that the solutions for periods of crisis cannot be undertaken by unilateral measures.

[401] See eg *Spanish Zone of Morocco Claim* (1924) II RIAA 615, 642; *Pinson v United Mexican States* (1928) V RIAA 327, 419 (1952); generally I Brownlie, *Principles of Public International Law*, 7th edn (2008) 466.

[402] On the duty of the host state to take reasonable precautionary and coercive action, see eg *Ziat, Ben Kiran* (1924) II RIAA 730 (1949); *Pinson v United Mexican States* (1928) V RIAA 327 (1952); see also the *Iranian Hostage Case*, ICJ Reports (1980) 3, 29 (Iran failed to control militant groups and approved of its acts).

[403] A D McNair, *International Law Opinions*, vol II (1956) 245.

[404] *AAPL v Sri Lanka*, Award, 27 June 1990, paras 72–86.   [405] At para 85.

It is widely accepted that the ILC Articles reflect customary international law.[406] *Force majeure* covers situations and events beyond the control of a state that make it objectively impossible for that state to perform its obligations. Under Article 24 of the ILC Articles, the wrongfulness of an act 'is precluded, if the author of the act in question has no other reasonable way, in a situation of distress, of saving the author's life or the lives of other persons entrusted to the author's care'. Only in the rarest of circumstances will this rule apply in the context of an investment treaty. Necessity is not defined in Article 25, but is treated by way of identifying its limits.

The common element of these concepts is that they allow a state to act in a manner that is not in conformity with existing obligations of customary, or even treaty, law. By their very nature, they are therefore of exceptional character in the general setting of the international legal order; their application must take their derogatory effect into account and must therefore place strict limitations on their negative impact on the operation of accepted international norms. This is of special importance when an investment treaty is affected which is meant to provide for long-term legal stability.

aa. Necessity

The rule of necessity, as laid down in Article 25 of the ILC Articles, can be relevant to the subject matter of an investment treaty:

1. Necessity may not be invoked by a state as a ground for precluding the wrongfulness of an act not in conformity with an international obligation of that state unless the act:
    (a) is the only means for the state to safeguard an essential interest against a grave and imminent peril; and (b) does not seriously impair an essential interest of the state or states towards which the obligation exists, or of the international community as a whole.

2. In any case, necessity may not be invoked by a state as a ground for precluding wrongfulness if:
    (a) the international obligation in question excludes the possibility of invoking necessity; or (b) the state has contributed to the situation of necessity.

As an exception to existing international obligations, tribunals have construed the rule narrowly and have refused to rely solely on the judgement of the host country in the absence of a clause allowing for self-judgment.[407]

In *CMS v Argentina*,[408] the respondent had pleaded the defence of necessity, but the Tribunal found that the conditions for its applications were not met:

---

[406] See ICJ, *Israel Security Wall Case*, Advisory Opinion, 43 ILM 1009 (2004), para 140; *Gabčíkovo-Nagymaros Project*, ICJ Reports (1997) 7, 63, para 102; see also *Russian Indemnity Case*, II RIAA 431 (1912); *Société Commerciale de Belgique*, 1939, PCIJ, Series A/B, No 78, 160.

[407] *Gabčíkovo-Nagymaros Project*, ICJ Reports (1997) 7, 63, para 51; *CMS v Argentina*, Award, 12 May 2005, para 317; *LG&E v Argentina*, Decision on Liability, 3 October 2006, paras 207–14; *Suez v Argentina*, Decision on Liability, 30 July 2010, paras 235–43.

[408] *CMS v Argentina*, Award, 12 May 2005.

the Tribunal is persuaded that the situation was difficult enough to justify the government taking action to prevent a worsening of the situation and the danger of total economic collapse.[409] . . .

A different issue, however, is whether the measures adopted were 'the only way' for the State to safeguard the interests. This is indeed debatable. . . . The International Law Commission's comment to the effect that the plea of necessity is 'excluded if there are other (otherwise lawful) means available, even if they may be more costly or less convenient,' is persuasive in assisting this Tribunal in concluding that the measures adopted were not the only steps available.[410] . . .

The second limit is the requirement for the State not to have contributed to the situation of necessity. . . . The issue, however, is whether the contribution to the crisis by Argentina has or has not been sufficiently substantial. The Tribunal, when reviewing the circumstances of the present dispute, must conclude that this was the case. The crisis was not of the making of one particular administration and found its roots in the earlier crisis of the 1980s and evolving governmental policies of the 1990s that reached a zenith in 2002 and thereafter. Therefore, the Tribunal observes that government policies and their shortcomings significantly contributed to the crisis and the emergency and while exogenous factors did fuel additional difficulties they do not exempt the Respondent from its responsibility in the matter.[411]

Therefore, the Tribunal considered that an economic crisis may give rise to a plea of necessity in principle. But it found that two requirements for a finding of necessity were not met in the particular case: the measures taken by Argentina were not the only way to cope with the situation and Argentina itself had contributed to the situation.[412] The Tribunal also found that the 'emergency' clause in the Argentina-US Treaty was not applicable.[413] In general, such an emergency clause should not be construed in a manner that places the investor in a less favourable legal situation than that accorded under customary law.

A year after the *CMS* ruling, a different view was adopted in *LG&E v Argentina*[414] in which the Tribunal accepted the respondent's plea of necessity for a limited period. This finding was based on the emergency clause of the US-Argentina BIT supported by an analysis of Article 25 of the ILC Articles. The Tribunal said:

---

[409] At para 322.   [410] At paras 323–4.

[411] At paras 328–9; *Enron v Argentina*, Award, 22 May 2007, paras 294 et seq and *Sempra v Argentina*, Award, 28 September 2007, paras 333 et seq, essentially based their decisions on the reasoning of *CMS v Argentina*. In the context of its financial crisis, Argentina argued that its measures were necessary to protect the human rights of its citizens. However, the Tribunals saw no conflict between the rights of foreign investor and human rights of nationals; see eg *Suez v Argentina*, Decision on Liability, 30 July 2010, para 240.

[412] In the same sense: *Total v Argentina*, Decision on Liability, 27 December 2010, paras 220–4, 345, 482–4; *Impregilo v Argentina*, Award, 21 June 2011, paras 344–59.

[413] At paras 353–78.

[414] *LG&E v Argentina*, Decision on Liability, 3 October 2006. For a discussion of the differences between the *CMS* and *LG&E* rulings, see A Reinisch, 'Necessity in International Investment Arbitration—An Unnecessary Split of Opinions in Recent ICSID Cases? Comments on *CMS v. Argentina* and *LG&E v Argentina*' (2007) 8 *J World Investment & Trade* 191.

In the judgment of the Tribunal, from 1 December 2001 until 26 April 2003, Argentina was in a period of crisis during which it was necessary to enact measures to maintain public order and protect its essential security interests.[415] ...

Evidence has been put before the Tribunal that the conditions as of December 2001 constituted the highest degree of public disorder and threatened Argentina's essential security interests. This was not merely a period of 'economic problems' or 'business cycle fluctuation' as Claimants described. ... Extremely severe crises in the economic, political and social sectors reached their apex and converged in December 2001, threatening total collapse of the Government and the Argentine State.[416] ...

A State may have several responses at its disposal to maintain public order or protect its essential security interests. In this sense, it is recognized that Argentina's suspension of the calculation of tariffs in U.S. dollars and the PPI adjustment of tariffs was a legitimate way of protecting its social and economic system.[417]

Both the *CMS* and the *LG&E* decisions assumed that the situation in Argentina affected, or possibly affected, an essential interest within the meaning of Article 25 of the ILC Articles.[418] But, contrary to the *CMS* ruling, the Tribunal in *LG&E* accepted the argument advanced by the respondent that the measures adopted by Argentina had been the 'only means' available. In addition, the arbitrators in *LG&E* found that Argentina had not substantially contributed to the state of emergency.[419] Consequently, in the view of the Tribunal, Argentina was exempted from liability under the emergency clause of the applicable BIT, as well as under general international law,[420] for the period between December 2001 and April 2003.

If the conditions of necessity have been met, the further question arises whether the host state has to resume performance of its obligations as soon as the situation of emergency ceases to exist and whether it has to compensate the foreign investor for the damage that arose from the suspension of its duties. Because there is no reason for the host state to benefit from the necessity and for the investor to bear the consequences, the answer to both questions will be affirmative.[421]

Thus, in *CMS v Argentina*, the Tribunal found that '[e]ven if the plea of necessity were accepted, compliance with the obligation would reemerge as soon

---

[415] At para 226.   [416] At para 231.   [417] At para 239.

[418] See para 319 of *CMS* and paras 251–7 of *LG&E*.

[419] See *LG&E* at para 257: 'There is no serious evidence in the record that Argentina contributed to the crisis resulting in the state of necessity.'

[420] At para 258:

> While this analysis concerning Article 25 of the Draft Articles on State Responsibility alone does not establish Argentina's defense, it supports the Tribunal's analysis with regard to the meaning of Article XI's requirement that the measures implemented by Argentina had to have been necessary either for the maintenance of public order or the protection of its own essential security interests.

[421] See also J Crawford, *The International Law Commission's Articles on State Responsibility: Introduction, Text and Commentaries* (2002) 189–90. Article 27 of the ILC Articles states:

> The invocation of a circumstance precluding wrongfulness in accordance with this Chapter is without prejudice to: (a) compliance with the obligation in question, if and to the extent that the circumstances precluding wrongfulness no longer exists; (b) the question of compensation for any material loss caused by the act in question.

See also *Case Concerning the Gabčíkovo-Nagymaros Project*, ICJ Reports (1997) 7, 63, paras 48, 101.

as the circumstance precluding wrongfulness no longer existed'[422] and that it was the duty of the Tribunal to determine the compensation due.[423] In *LG&E v Argentina*, however, the Tribunal explicitly excluded the measures adopted by Argentina during the period of necessity from the calculation of damages, arguing that the damage suffered during the state of necessity should be borne by the investor. In the view of the Tribunal, Argentina could only be held liable for those measures it had adopted before and after the occurrence of the state of necessity.[424]

bb. Force majeure

Whenever a state finds itself in a situation that makes it impossible to perform an obligation, the principle of *force majeure* may apply. Article 23 of the ILC Articles on State Responsibility, expresses the rule as follows:

1. The wrongfulness of an act of a State not in conformity with an international obligation of that State is precluded if the act is due to force majeure, that is the occurrence of an irresistible force or of an unforeseen event, beyond the control of the State, making it materially impossible in the circumstances to perform the obligation.
2. Paragraph 1 does not apply if:
    (a) the situation of *force majeure* is due, either alone or in combination with other factors, to the conduct of the State invoking it; or
    (b) the State has assumed the risk of that situation occurring.

It has rightly been noted that the principle of *force majeure* may be viewed as a general principle of law.[425] However, this does not mean that only one version of the principle exists in practice. Indeed, various versions have been included in oil and gas contracts[426] and the interpretation of a contractual *force majeure* clause will primarily turn on the specific language of the clause chosen by the parties.[427]

    In state practice, the principle has been understood in a narrow sense, often in regard to movement of aircraft out of control and action taken by rebels in periods of civil strife and war.[428] It is generally accepted that for the existence of *force majeure* it is not sufficient that performance becomes more difficult.[429] Lack of funds, insolvency, or other forms of political and economic crises will not amount to *force majeure*.[430]

---

[422] *CMS v Argentina*, Award, 12 May 2005, para 328.   [423] At paras 383–94.
[424] *LG&E v Argentina*, Decision on Liability, 3 October 2006, paras 260–6.
[425] J Crawford, *The International Law Commission's Articles on State Responsibility* (2002) 173.
[426] D Bishop, J Crawford, and M Reisman, *Foreign Investment Disputes* (2004) 267 et seq.
[427] If the author of the act still has a choice, but no other reasonable way to save human life, the principle of distress will apply; see J Crawford, *The International Law Commission's Articles on State Responsibility: Introduction, Text and Commentaries* (2002) 174.
[428] See the cases cited in the *Yearbook of the ILC* (1978), vol II, Part One, paras 261 et seq.
[429] J Crawford, *The International Law Commission's Articles on State Responsibility: Introduction, Text and Commentaries* (2002) 171; see also Bin Cheng, *General Principles of Law as Applied by International Tribunals* (1987), 69; R Boed, 'State of Necessity as a Justification for Internationally Wrongful Conduct' (2006) 3 *Yale Human Rights and Development LJ* 1.
[430] Crawford, n 429, 171.

The consequences of acts by the home state of the investor, which lead directly to the difficulties, will also not fall under the principle.[431] In *National Oil Co v Libyan Sun Oil*,[432] the Tribunal ruled that the US respondent company could not invoke the clause and excuse its non-performance in Libya even though the US Government had issued an order that US passports would no longer be valid for travel to Libya. The Tribunal considered that the company should have hired non-US personnel.

(c) Treaty law

For the drafters of investment treaties, the issue was whether these principles of customary law should be accepted as such or whether they should be modified in light of the object and purpose of the treaty. In practice, the choice was essentially to accept the principles. In a number of treaties concluded by European countries, the parties decided not to include any provision on extraordinary events and periods, thus tacitly accepting the applicability of the rules of customary law. US treaty practice has been more inclined to address the issue explicitly, essentially restating existing customary law instead of revising or modifying customary rules.

A special issue to be considered in the interpretation of a treaty provision on periods of emergency concerns the general object and purpose of a BIT to provide protection for the foreign investor. It has to be assumed that any provision of a BIT, including one on emergency, does not in effect lead to a level of protection lower than the one guaranteed by the general rules of general international law, in particular customary law. Whereas it is correct that parties to a BIT may, if they wish, stipulate that they agree to a lower level, an interpretation leading to such a reduction of protection will be appropriate only in the presence of clear wording which dictates such an extraordinary intention of the parties.

What most European and US treaties have in common is to require MFN treatment and national treatment when it comes to compensation schemes adopted voluntarily by the host state to deal with the consequences of an emergency. A typical clause of this type reads:

Investors of either Contracting State whose investments suffer losses in the territory of the other Contracting State owing to war or other armed conflict, revolution, a state of national emergency, or revolt, shall be accorded treatment no less favourable by such other Contracting State than that which the latter Contracting State accords to its own investors as regards restitution, indemnification, compensation or other valuable consideration. Such payments shall be freely transferable. Investors of either Contracting State shall enjoy most-favoured-nation treatment in the territory of the other Contracting State in respect of the matters provided for in this Article.[433]

---

[431] Crawford, n 429, 173.   [432] *National Oil Co v Libyan Sun Oil*, Award, 31 May 1985.
[433] See the German Model BIT, Art 4(3) and (4). Article 5(4) of the 2004 and 2012 US Model BITs reads:

> Notwithstanding Article 14 [Non-Conforming Measures] (5)(b) [subsidies and grants], each Party shall accord to investors of the other Party, and to covered investments, non-discriminatory treatment with respect to measures it adopts or maintains relating to losses suffered by investments in its territory owing to armed conflict or civil strife.

Article XI of the BIT between Argentina and the United States provides:

This Treaty shall not preclude the application by either Party of measures necessary for the maintenance of public order, the fulfillment of its obligations with respect to the mainten-ance or restoration of international peace or security, or the Protection of its own essential security interests.

The role of customary law in the interpretation of Article XI of this BIT has been prominent in cases in the wake of Argentina's measures after its economic crisis around 2002. The wording of this provision raised the question whether Article XI incorporated the customary rule of necessity or should be considered as an autono-mous standard which, in effect, was meant to lower the standard embodied in customary law. The point was decided in different ways by different tribunals, followed by requests for annulment from both sides. Alas, the annulment commit-tees also approached the issue with different methods and results. From a systemic perspective of coherence and predictability, this jurisprudence obviously did not reach a respectable result.

Among the tribunals addressing the issues, *CMS*, *Sempra*, and *Enron* concluded that Article XI is to be interpreted in a manner which reflects the customary standard of necessity.

The *CMS* ad hoc Committee[434] assumed that Article XI is to be seen as a free-standing provision which is not the same as the necessity rule under customary international law as codified in Article 25 of the ILC Articles. Moreover, the ad hoc Committee held that Article XI is a threshold requirement: if it applies, the BIT's substantive provisions do not apply.[435] Nevertheless, the ad hoc Committee did not annul the Award on this ground.

The ruling of the Committee may be subject to criticism. In laying down the proper understanding of Article XI (instead of deciding on the Award's annul-ment), it went beyond the proper role of an annulment committee. Also, the ad hoc Committee's position is difficult to reconcile with the understanding of the United States at the time of the BIT's ratification—that the clause was meant to reflect the standard of customary law. More importantly, the Decision in effect establishes a treaty standard, by way of its interpretation, that provides less protection to the investor than customary law.

The subsequent Award in *Continental Casualty*[436] did not take a position on the relationship between Article XI and customary law, but at the same time relied on the ruling of the *CMS* Annulment Committee. The *Continental* Tribunal con-cluded that measures addressing emergency situations will be justified as long as

---

Clauses of this kind are not meant to exclude compensation, but to broaden the rights of investors during the relevant periods; see eg *National Grid v Argentina*, Award, 3 November 2008, para 253; *Impregilo v Argentina*, Award, 21 June 2011, paras 337–43. More generally, see C Schreuer, 'The Protection of Investments in Armed Conflicts' (2012) 3 *Transnational Dispute Management*.

[434] *CMS v Argentina*, Decision on Annulment, 25 September 2007.
[435] At paras 128–36.
[436] *Continental Casualty v Argentina*, Award, 5 September 2008.

they are 'appropriate', 'reasonable', and 'proportional'.[437] Obviously, these criteria significantly depart from the strict rules on necessity accepted in general international law. Similarly, the Tribunal in *El Paso v Argentina*[438] held that Article XI of the BIT is *lex specialis* in relation to Article 25 of the ILC Articles and emphasized the difference of the defences based on the two provisions.[439]

Subsequent Annulment Committees went in different directions. The decision of the *Enron* Annulment Committee[440] criticized the *CMS* Annulment reasoning for acting in the way of an appeals court,[441] but nevertheless also annulled the *Enron* Award because the latter had relied on the understanding of an economist in its application of the rule of necessity.[442] The ad hoc Committee in *Sempra v Argentina*[443] followed the *CMS* Committee in its interpretation of Article XI but, unlike the *CMS* Committee, concluded that the Tribunal's understanding of Article XI as embodying the customary principle of necessity amounted to a reason for annulment.[444]

The Annulment Committee in *Continental Casualty*[445] took a less expansive view of the role of the annulment process and considered that the taking into account of rules of the World Trade Organization (WTO) into Article XI of the BIT did not provide a reason for annulment.[446]

6. Preservation of rights

The object and purpose of investment agreements is to improve the investment climate and not to derogate from such rights of the investor that are granted in other treaties[447] or in the domestic legislation of the host country. As early as 1967, the OECD Draft Convention provided:

Where a matter is covered both by the provisions of this Convention and any other international agreement, nothing in this Convention shall prevent a national of one Party who holds property in the territory of another Party from benefiting by the provisions that are most favorable to him.[448]

A classical formulation in a BIT along these lines is found in the treaty between Germany and Poland:

---

[437] At paras 219, 227.
[438] *El Paso v Argentina*, Award, 31 October 2011.
[439] At paras 552–5.
[440] *Enron v Argentina*, Decision on Annulment, 30 July 2010.
[441] At para 405.
[442] At para 393.
[443] *Sempra v Argentina*, Decision on Annulment, 29 June 2010.
[444] See paras 186–219.
[445] *Continental Casualty v Argentina*, Decision on Annulment, 16 September 2011.
[446] At para 133.
[447] An example may be found in the TRIMs Agreement of the WTO and its rules on performance requirements.
[448] Article 8 OECD Draft Convention on the Protection of Foreign Property, 7 ILM 117 (1968).

If the statutory rules of either Contracting Party or an international undertaking which may exist, or may be established in the future between the Contracting Parties, provide for a general or special regulation by virtue of which investments by investors of the other Contracting Party would benefit of a treatment more favourable than provided for by this Treaty, said regulation shall supersede the present Treaty to the extent it is more favourable.

The clause reflects the general rule that investment treaties are meant to improve the investment climate and not to reduce rights and privileges that the investor otherwise enjoys.

7. Arbitrary or discriminatory measures

The prohibition of arbitrary treatment belongs to the classical standards contained in investment treaties.[449] By definition, every state oriented at the rule of law will outlaw arbitrary action, and foreign investors properly expect that host states will follow this standard. In treaty practice, the rule against arbitrariness is often combined with the prohibition of discrimination ('shall not impair investments by arbitrary or discriminatory measures'). The separate listing of the two standards—typically separated by the word 'or'—suggests that each must be accorded its own significance and scope.[450]

(a) Arbitrary measures

aa. The meaning of arbitrary

Some treaties do not use the term 'arbitrary' but refer to 'unjustified or discriminatory action' or to 'unreasonable or discriminatory action'. It would be difficult to identify a difference between 'arbitrary' and 'unjustified' or 'unreasonable action', and presumably the terms are interchangeable. The Tribunal in *National Grid v Argentina*,[451] said in response to an argument by the claimant that the two concepts were different:

It is the view of the Tribunal that the plain meaning of the terms 'unreasonable' and 'arbitrary' is substantially the same in the sense of something done capriciously, without reason.[452]

As to the meaning of 'arbitrary' and its application to a specific case, different approaches have been employed. One reading of the clause simply refers to the ordinary meaning and seeks to extrapolate this meaning from general legal dictionaries.

---

[449] See V Heiskanen, 'Arbitrary and Unreasonable Measures' in A Reinisch (ed), *Standards of Investment Protection* (2008) 87; C Schreuer, 'Protection against Arbitrary or Discriminatory Measures' in C A Rogers and R P Alford (eds), *The Future of Investment Arbitration* (2009) 183.

[450] In this sense: *Azurix v Argentina*, Award, 14 July 2006, para 391; *Siag v Egypt*, Award, 1 June 2009, para 457; *AES v Hungary*, Award, 23 September 2010, para 10.3.2.

[451] *National Grid v Argentina*, Award, 3 November 2008.

[452] At para 197.

For instance, the Tribunal in *Lauder v Czech Republic* and subsequent decisions have consulted *Black's Law Dictionary* according to which 'arbitrary' means 'depending on individual discretion' or refers to action 'founded on prejudice or preference rather than on reason of fact'.[453]

Another approach is to contrast the notion of an 'arbitrary action' with the concept of the rule of law. In an oft-quoted passage of the *ELSI* case, the ICJ had to apply the standard ('shall not be subjected to arbitrary or discriminatory measures') and found that 'Arbitrariness is not so much something opposed to a rule of law, as something opposed to the rule of law . . . It is a wilful disregard of due process of law, an act which shocks, or at least surprises, a sense of judicial propriety'.[454]

This formula is reminiscent of the wording used in the 1920s in the *Neer* decision describing the international minimum standard.[455] The *Genin* decision quoted the *ELSI* passages and explained the standard in similar terms in the context of an alleged procedural illegality.[456] The Tribunal in *Pope & Talbot* contrasted the *ELSI* formula with the *Neer* wording and noted in regard to the decision of the ICJ:

The formulation leaves out any requirement that every reasonable and impartial person be dissatisfied and perhaps permits a bit less injury to the psyche of the observer, who need no longer be outraged, but only surprised by what the government has done.[457]

The decision in *Noble Ventures v Romania*[458] used yet another method by establishing a comparative standard. It pointed out, in the context of a judicial reorganization of a steel mill business, that arbitrariness was excluded because proceedings of the kind in question 'are provided in all legal systems and for much the same reasons'. The specific situation of the mill 'would have justified the initiation of comparable proceedings in most other countries'. In addition, the proceedings were conducted 'in accordance with the law of Romania and not against it'.

---

[453] *Lauder v Czech Republic*, Award, 3 September 2001, para 221, cited with approval in *Occidental v Ecuador*, Award, 1 July 2004, para 162 and in *CMS v Argentina*, Award, 12 May 2005, para 291; *Azurix v Argentina*, Award, 14 July 2006, para 392. See also *Siemens v Argentina*, Award, 6 February 2007, para 318; *Plama v Bulgaria*, Award, 27 August 2008, para 184; *El Paso v Argentina*, Award, 31 October 2011, para 319.

[454] ICJ, *Case Concerning Elettronica Sicula (ELSI)*, 20 July 1989, ICJ Reports (1989) 15, 76. For a similar approach, see ICJ, *Asylum Case*, 20 November 1950, ICJ Reports (1950) 266, 284.

[455] *LFH Neer & Pauline Neer v United Mexican States*, IV RIAA 60; (1926) *AJIL* 555: '[T]he treatment of an alien, in order to constitute an international delinquency, should amount to an outrage, to bad faith, to willful neglect of duty, or to an insufficiency of governmental action so far short of international standards that every reasonable and impartial man would readily recognize its insufficiency.'

[456] *Genin v Estonia*, Award, 25 June 2001, para 371: 'Any procedural irregularity that may have been present would have to amount to bad faith, a wilful disregard of due process of law or an extreme insufficiency of action.'

[457] *Pope & Talbot v Canada*, Award on Damages, 31 May 2002, para 64. To the same effect: *Azurix v Argentina*, Award, 14 July 2006, para 392.

[458] *Noble Ventures v Romania*, Award, 12 October 2005, para 178. See for a similar view L B Sohn and R R Baxter, 'Draft Convention on the International Responsibility of States for Injuries to Aliens, Art 12(a)' (1961) 55 *AJIL* 545.

In *LG&E v Argentina*[459] the Tribunal adopted the following general description of arbitrary measures:

measures that affect the investments of nationals of the other Party without engaging in a rational decision-making process. Such process would include a consideration of the effect of a measure on foreign investments and a balance of the interests of the State with any burden imposed on such investments.[460]

Contractual breaches are not sufficient to violate the standard. The Tribunal in *Duke Energy v Ecuador* held that 'contractual breaches do not amount, in themselves, to arbitrary conduct'.[461] On the other hand, a state's use of its governmental powers to interfere with contract rights may, depending on the circumstances, be arbitrary.[462]

Some tribunals have accepted the following categories of measures as arbitrary:

(a) a measure that inflicts damage on the investor without serving any apparent legitimate purpose;

(b) a measure that is not based on legal standards but on discretion, prejudice, or personal preference;

(c) a measure taken for reasons that are different from those put forward by the decision maker;

(d) a measure taken in wilful disregard of due process and proper procedure.[463]

The Tribunal in *AES v Hungary*[464] found that reasonableness had to be analysed with the help of two elements—the existence of a rational policy and the reasonableness of the act in question:

There are two elements that require to be analyzed to determine whether a state's act was unreasonable: the existence of a rational policy; and the reasonableness of the act of the state in relation to the policy. A rational policy is taken by a state following a logical (good sense) explanation and with the aim of addressing a public interest matter. Nevertheless, a rational policy is not enough to justify all the measures taken by a state in its name. A challenged measure must also be reasonable. That is, there needs to be an appropriate correlation between the state's public policy objective and the measure adopted to achieve it. This has to do with the nature of the measure and the way it is implemented.[465]

bb. Adverse intention

The relevance of an adverse intention on the part of the host state is not entirely clear. In *CME v Czech Republic*,[466] the Tribunal found that the clause was violated in

---

[459] *LG&E v Argentina*, Decision on Liability, 3 October 2006.
[460] At para 158.
[461] *Duke Energy v Ecuador*, Award, 18 August 2008, para 381.
[462] *AES v Hungary*, Award, 23 September 2010, paras 10.3.12–10.3.13.
[463] *EDF v Romania*, Award, 8 October 2009, para 303; *Lemire v Ukraine*, Decision on Jurisdiction and Liability, 14 January 2010, para 262.
[464] *AES v Hungary*, Award, 23 September 2010.
[465] At paras 10.3.7–10.3.9.
[466] *CME v Czech Republic*, Partial Award, 13 September 2001, para 612.

light of the clear intention of the respondent to deprive CME of its contractual rights. In *Enron v Argentina*[467] the Tribunal denied the existence of arbitrariness since the measures adopted 'were what the Government believed and understood was the best response to the unfolding crisis'.[468] By contrast, in *Occidental v Ecuador*,[469] the Tribunal determined that the standard was violated 'to some extent' not because of certain impugned actions but because of the 'very confusion and lack of clarity that resulted in some form of arbitrariness, even if not intended'.[470]

cc. Relationship to fair and equitable treatment and to customary international law

Given the nature and the breadth of the concept of arbitrariness, it is not surprising that it has been said that any arbitrary action will also violate the standard of fair and equitable treatment.[471] The matter has surfaced especially under the NAFTA which contains a clause on fair and equitable treatment (Art 1105),[472] but no explicit prohibition of arbitrary treatment. Tribunals established under NAFTA have considered that arbitrary treatment also violates the requirement of fair and equitable treatment.[473] The tendency to merge the two standards can also be found in the application of bilateral treaties.[474]

Despite this tendency, there are weighty arguments in favour of treating the two standards as conceptually different. There is no good reason why treaty drafters would use two different terms when they mean one and the same thing. Equally, it is difficult to see why one standard should be part of the other when the text of the treaties lists them side by side as two standards without indicating that one is merely an emanation of the other. Of course, there may be considerable overlap and one particular set of facts may violate both the FET standard and the rule against arbitrary or discriminatory treatment.[475]

A number of tribunals have, in fact, examined compliance with the standards of fair and equitable treatment and unreasonable or discriminatory treatment

---

[467] *Enron v Argentina*, Award, 22 May 2007.
[468] At para 281. See also *Sempra v Argentina*, Award, 28 September 2007, para 318.
[469] *Occidental v Ecuador*, Award, 1 July 2004.
[470] At para 163.
[471] S Vascannie, 'The Fair and Equitable Treatment Standard in International Investment Law and Practice' (1999) 70 *BYBIL* 133.
[472] See pp 136 et seq.
[473] See eg *SD Myers v Canada*, First Partial Award, 13 November 2000, para 263; *Mondev v United States*, Award, 11 October 2002, para 127; *Waste Management v Mexico*, Final Award, 30 April 2004, para 98.
[474] See *CMS v Argentina*, Award, 12 May 2005, para 290; *Impregilo v Pakistan*, Decision on Jurisdiction, 22 April 2005, paras 264 et seq; *MTD v Chile*, Award, 25 May 2004, para 196; *Noble Ventures v Romania*, Award, 12 October 2005, para 182; *Saluka v Czech Republic*, Partial Award, 17 March 2006, para 460; *PSEG v Turkey*, Award, 19 January 2007, para 261; *MCI v Ecuador*, Award, 31 July 2007, paras 366–7, 371; *Rumeli v Kazakhstan*, Award, 29 July 2008, paras 679–81; *Lemire v Ukraine*, Decision on Liability, 14 January 2010, paras 259, 356–7, 418.
[475] *Lemire v Ukraine*, Decision on Liability, 14 January 2010, para 259.

separately.[476] Although there is often no explicit discussion of the relationship of the two concepts, their sequential and separate treatment in awards indicates that the tribunals regarded them as distinct standards.

The Tribunal in *Duke Energy v Ecuador*[477] had to interpret a provision in the Ecuador-US BIT that afforded protection against impairment by arbitrary or discriminatory measures. The respondent argued that this was part of the FET standard; however, the Tribunal disagreed and said:

In view of the structure of the provisions of the BIT, the Tribunal has difficulty following Ecuador's argument that there is only one concept of fair and equitable treatment which encompasses a non-impairment notion. The Tribunal will thus make a separate determination to decide whether the contested measures were arbitrary...[478]

As with all broad standards in BITs, the relationship of the rule to customary international law may be raised. The traditional understanding of the customary minimum standard seems to have covered actions deemed arbitrary.[479] It would follow that the treaty standard against arbitrariness is also covered by customary international law.[480]

(b) Discriminatory measures

Discrimination can take a number of forms. It can be based on race, religion, political affiliation, disability, and a number of other criteria. In the context of the treatment of foreign investment, the most frequent problem is discrimination on the basis of nationality. Consequently, most of the practice dealing with discrimination focuses on nationality. In fact, discrimination on the basis of nationality is addressed in investment treaties by way of two specific standards: national treatment and MFN treatment. These standards are dealt with in separate sections of this chapter.[481] But this does not mean that the issue of discrimination is necessarily restricted to nationality.

---

[476] See *Occidental v Ecuador*, Award, 1 July 2004, paras 159–66; *Lauder v Czech Republic*, Award, 3 September 2001, paras 214–88; *Genin v Estonia*, Award, 25 June 2001, paras 368–71; *Noble Ventures v Romania*, Award, 11 October 2005, paras 175–80; *Azurix v Argentina*, Award, 14 July 2006, paras 385–93; *LG&E v Argentina*, Decision on Liability, 3 October 2006, paras 162–3; *Siemens v Argentina*, Award, 6 February 2007, paras 310–21; *BG Group v Argentina*, Final Award, 24 December 2007, para 342; *Biwater Gauff v Tanzania*, Award, 24 July 2008, paras 586–676; *Plama v Bulgaria*, Award, 27 August 2008, para 184.

[477] *Duke Energy v Ecuador*, Award, 18 August 2008, paras 367–83.

[478] At para 377.

[479] See A Verdross, 'Les règles internationales concernant le traitement des étrangers' (1931-III) 37 *Collected Courses of the Hague Academy of International Law* 323, 358–9; *Restatement (Third) of the Foreign Relations Law of the United States*, vol 2 (1986) 196–7.

[480] As regards the understanding of the concept in the WTO, see *United States–Import Prohibition of Certain Shrimp and Shrimp Products*, Report of the Appellate Body, WT/DS58/AB/R, 12 October 1998, 38 ILM 121 (1999).

[481] See Sections 8 and 9.

Under general international law there is no general obligation to treat all aliens equally and to treat them as favourably as nationals. But such an obligation may be established by treaty.[482]

A finding of discrimination is independent of a violation of domestic law. In fact, domestic law may be the cause of a violation of the international standard. In *Lauder v Czech Republic*[483] the applicable BIT offered protection against 'arbitrary and discriminatory measures'. The Tribunal said:

For a measure to be discriminatory, it does not need to violate domestic law, since domestic law can contain a provision that is discriminatory towards foreign investment, or can lack a provision prohibiting the discrimination of foreign investment.[484]

Practice dealing with discrimination has concentrated on two key issues. One concerns the basis of comparison for the alleged discrimination; the other concerns the question whether discriminatory intent is a requirement for a finding of discrimination or whether the fact of unequal treatment is sufficient.

aa. The basis of comparison

The basis of comparison is a crucial question in applying provisions dealing with non-discrimination. If the investor is entitled to non-discrimination, what group must be looked at for comparison? Only businesses engaged in exactly the same activity? Also businesses engaged in similar activity? Or businesses engaged in any economic activity?[485]

In some cases the issue of the basis of comparison did not arise since the tribunals were able to pinpoint unjustifiable differential treatment among businesses within the same area of activity.[486] In *Occidental v Ecuador*[487] the Tribunal rejected a narrow comparison that would have looked only at the same economic sector or activity.[488] In *Enron v Argentina*[489] the Tribunal looked at the question whether there had been 'any capricious, irrational or absurd differentiation' in the treatment of different sectors of the economy.[490]

---

[482] *Genin v Estonia*, Award, 25 June 2001, para 368.

[483] *Lauder v Czech Republic*, Award, 3 September 2001.

[484] At para 220.

[485] NAFTA tribunals have dealt with a similar question in a number of cases when interpreting the provision of Art 1102 of the NAFTA on national treatment. See *SD Myers v Canada*, Award on Liability, 13 November 2000, para 250; *Pope and Talbot v Canada*, Award on the Merits, 10 April 2001, paras 45–63, 68–9, 78; *Methanex v United States*, Award, 3 August 2005, Part IV, Ch B, paras 17–19, 25–37; *Feldman v Mexico*, Award, 16 December 2002, para 171.

[486] *Nycomb v Latvia*, Award, 16 December 2003, Stockholm Int'l Arb Rev 2005:1, p 53, sec 4.3.2 at p 99; *Saluka v Czech Republic*, Partial Award, 17 March 2006, paras 313–47, 466; *Lemire v Ukraine*, Decision on Jurisdiction and Liability, 14 January 2010, paras 384–5.

[487] *Occidental v Ecuador*, Award, 1 July 2004.

[488] At paras 167–76. The Tribunal added that it found the practice concerning 'like products' developed within GATT/WTO not specifically pertinent, paras 174–6.

[489] *Enron v Argentina*, Award, 22 May 2007.

[490] At para 282. See also *Sempra v Argentina*, Award, 28 September 2007, para 319.

In a number of cases tribunals found that it was not possible to compare different sectors of the economy and to establish discrimination on that basis.[491] The Tribunal in *BG Group v Argentina* found that gas distributors and other public service providers, such as electricity distributors, were not in like circumstances.[492] In *El Paso v Argentina*[493] the claimant had complained about differences in treatment between the hydrocarbons sector and the banking sector. The Tribunal stated:

It is this Tribunal's view that a differential treatment based on the existence of a different factual and legal situation does not breach the BIT's standard. Here the Tribunal is in line with the approach of other tribunals already cited and finds itself in agreement with the tribunal in *Enron*, which found no discrimination between the different sectors of the economy, although they were indeed treated differently, as there was no 'capricious, irrational or absurd differentiation in the treatment accorded to the Claimant as compared to other entities or sectors.'[494]

bb. Discriminatory intent

Tribunals generally favour an objective approach that looks at the consequences of a particular measure and not at discriminatory intent.[495] The Tribunal in *Siemens v Argentina*[496] said:

The Tribunal concurs that intent is not decisive or essential for a finding of discrimination, and that the impact of the measure on the investment would be the determining factor to ascertain whether it had resulted in non-discriminatory treatment.[497]

However, there are cases that indicate that discriminatory intent is not irrelevant. In some cases the tribunals also looked at the question whether measures had been taken in view of the investors' foreign nationality.[498] In *LG&E v Argentina*[499] the Tribunal held that either discriminatory intent or discriminatory effect would suffice. In the end it relied on the effect of the acts in question. The Tribunal said:

In the context of investment treaties, and the obligation thereunder not to discriminate against foreign investors, a measure is considered discriminatory if the intent of the measure is to discriminate or if the measure has a discriminatory effect.[500]

---

[491] *CMS v Argentina*, Award, 12 May 2005, para 293; *Metalpar v Argentina*, Award, 6 June 2008, paras 161–4; *National Grid v Argentina*, Award, 3 November 2008, paras 201–2; *El Paso v Argentina*, Award, 31 October 2011, paras 309–15.

[492] *BG Group v Argentina*, Final Award, 24 December 2007, para 357.

[493] *El Paso v Argentina*, Award, 31 October 2011, paras 305–16.

[494] At para 315. Footnote omitted.

[495] *Myers v Canada*, Award on Liability, 13 November 2000, paras 252–4; *Feldman v Mexico*, Award, 16 December 2002, para 184; *Occidental v Ecuador*, Award, 1 July 2004, para 177; *Eastern Sugar v Czech Republic*, Partial Award, 27 March 2007, para 338.

[496] *Siemens v Argentina*, Award, 6 February 2007.

[497] At para 321.

[498] *Lauder v Czech Republic*, Award, 3 September 2001, para 231. In *Methanex v United States*, Award, 3 August 2005, the Tribunal's position on this point is unclear. See Part IV, Ch B, paras 1 and 12.

[499] *LG&E v Argentina*, Decision on Liability, 3 October 2006.

[500] At para 146. Footnote omitted.

8. National treatment

(a) General meaning

Clauses on national treatment belong to the core and the standard repertoire of BITs. They are meant to provide a level playing field between the foreign investor and the local competitor. In their typical version in European BITs, the clauses state that the foreign investor and its investments are 'accorded treatment no less favourable than that which the host state accords to its own investors'.[501] Hence, the purpose of the clause is to oblige a host state to make no negative differentiation between foreign and national investors when enacting and applying its rules and regulations and thus to promote the position of the foreign investor to the level accorded to nationals. The application of the clause presupposes some type of 'treatment' by the host state; the relevant determination will look at the substance of the issue and not to the formal side.[502]

This purpose differs fundamentally from the concept of 'national treatment' as it became known a few decades ago, especially as part of the proposed 'New International Economic Order'.[503] That concept was intended to limit, as far as possible, any rights a foreign investor could derive from international law. The possibility that national law could actually be less protective for the foreign investor than the general rules of international law is anticipated in the current BITs by the words 'no less favourable', thus recognizing that other rules may be more favourable. Hence, a positive differentiation remains possible and will even be obligatory where the general standards of international law are higher than the ones applying to nationals.[504]

In BITs concluded by European states, the wording of the clause has essentially remained the same in past decades. US treaties traditionally specify that the clause will apply when 'like situations'[505] exist. In recent years there was a change in US practice from the term 'in like situations' to 'in like circumstances'.[506] This may indicate that for the US Government there are nuances between these two versions that deserve attention.[507]

---

[501] For a review of different national treatment clauses in BITs, see R Dolzer and M Stevens, *Bilateral Investment Treaties* (1995) 63–5.

[502] A broad understanding of 'treatment' is also found in *Merrill & Ring v Canada*, Award, 31 March 2010 and in *SD Myers v Canada*, Award, 13 November 2000, para 254.

[503] See p 4.

[504] See R E Vinuesa, 'National Treatment, Principle' in R Wolfrum (ed), *Encyclopedia of Public International Law*, vol VII (2012) 486.

[505] See the 1994 US Model Treaty, Art II.1 reprinted in UNCTAD (ed), *International Investment Instruments: A Compendium*, vol III (1996) 195.

[506] See the 2004 and 2012 US Model BITs, Art 3.

[507] NAFTA, Art 1102 also refers to 'like circumstances'. Article 1102(1) reads:

Each Party shall accord to investors of another Party treatment no less favourable than that it accords, in like circumstances, to its own investors with respect to the establishment, acquisition, expansion, management, conduct, operation, and sale or other disposition of investments.

All national treatment clauses apply once a business is established (post-entry national treatment). This covers both regulatory and contractual matters.[508] Some investment treaties, especially those concluded by the United States and Canada, also include provisions concerning a right of access to a national market on the basis of national treatment (pre-entry national treatment).[509]

The relative homogeneity of the clauses in BIT practice may explain why it has been said that the standard may be easier to apply than other standards. That assumption, however, seems misleading. As a matter of legal drafting technique, while the basic clause is generally the same, the practical implications differ due to more or less wide-ranging exemptions of certain business sectors. More importantly, even the basic guarantees contained in the standard itself have not yet been clarified.

It is generally agreed that the application of the clause is fact-specific.[510] As in the context of fair and equitable treatment,[511] such a statement cautions that the standard resists abstract definitions and that no hard-and-fast approach to interpreting the clause will be found. The reason will be seen immediately when the major components of the rule are considered.

(b) Application

Three steps of analysis will be necessary to determine whether the standard has been respected. First, it has to be determined whether the foreign investor and the domestic investor are placed in a comparable setting or, in US terminology, in 'a like situation' or in 'like circumstances'. Secondly, it has to be determined whether the treatment accorded to the foreign investor is at least as favourable as the treatment accorded to domestic investors.[512] Thirdly, in the case of treatment that is less favourable, it must be determined whether the differentiation was justified. Behind these seemingly simple parameters of the clause, lie complex issues that are not answered completely by existing case law. At all levels, the full factual and legal context of the relevant issues will have to be taken into account.

aa. The basis of comparison: 'like'

The first step in an application of the rule to a case concerns the comparison of the foreign investor with the domestic investor. Is it necessary to identify a domestic investor who is in exactly the same business, or is it sufficient to point to an investor

---

[508] *Bayindir v Pakistan*, Award, 27 August 2009, para 388.

[509] See p 89.

[510] The Appellate Body of the WTO has observed that the 'concept of "likeness" is a relative one that evokes the image of an accordion': *Japan—Taxes on Alcoholic Beverages II*, WT/DS8, -10, -11/AB/R (4 October 1996) H.1.(a).

[511] See pp 133–4, 139.

[512] *UPS v Canada*, Award, 24 May 2007, para 83 distinguishes three distinct elements of a review of a national treatment claim under Art 1102 of the NAFTA: (a) treatment in the areas listed in Art 1102, (b) like circumstances with local investors and investments, and (c) less favourable treatment.

who is not in the same line of business but in the same economic sector? How do we define 'business' and 'sector' in this context?

The measuring stick with which to compare the activities of national investors to those of a foreign claimant remains controversial. In *Feldman v Mexico*, 'in like circumstances' was interpreted to refer to the same business, that is, the exporting of cigarettes.[513] By contrast, the Tribunal in *Occidental v Ecuador* referred to local producers in general, 'and this cannot be done by addressing exclusively the sector in which that particular activity is undertaken'.[514]

Generally, tribunals have been cautious not to construe the basis of comparison for the applicability of the national treatment standard too narrowly. Consistent with the purpose of the rule, conditions such as 'like situations' or 'like circumstances' should be interpreted broadly in order to open the way for a full review of the measure under the national treatment clause. In general, there seems to be agreement that the overall legal context in which a measure is placed will also have to be considered when 'like circumstances' are identified and when the identity or difference of treatment is examined. In the context of the NAFTA, the *SD Myers* decision[515] ruled that the legal context of Chapter Eleven requires considering the NAFTA framework as a whole. The Tribunal said:

The Tribunal considers that the interpretation of the phrase 'like circumstances' in Article 1102 must take into account the general principles that emerge from the legal context of the NAFTA, including both its concern with the environment and the need to avoid trade distortions that are not justified by environmental concerns. The assessment of 'like circumstances' must also take into account circumstances that would justify governmental regulations that treat them differently in order to protect the public interest. The concept of 'like circumstances' invites an examination of whether a non-national investor complaining of less favourable treatment is in the same 'sector' as the national investor. The Tribunal takes the view that the word 'sector' has a wide connotation that includes the concepts of 'economic sector' and 'business sector'.[516]

Whether a violation of this standard has in fact occurred will be decided by answering the ensuing questions, namely whether a differentiation has taken place and, if so, whether this was done without justification. Tribunals have also examined whether 'like circumstances' existed in light of the question whether the compared entities were subject to 'like legal requirements' in their regulatory treatment.[517]

bb. The existence of a differentiation

With regard to the existence of a differentiation, several questions arise. Does a violation of the standard only occur on the basis of nationality-based

---

[513] *Feldman v Mexico*, Award, 16 December 2002, para 171.

[514] *Occidental v Ecuador*, Award, 1 July 2004, para 173.

[515] *SD Myers v Canada*, First Partial Award, 13 November 2000.

[516] At para 250. The Tribunal also looked at the OECD principles on foreign investment as reflected in the OECD Declaration on International and Multinational Enterprises of 1976 to define 'a like situation'. The 1993 review of that Declaration pointed to the 'same sector', at para 248.

[517] See *Grand River Enterprises v United States*, Award, 12 January 2011, para 166.

differentiations? What is the significance of a differentiation that is not nationality-based but is still not justifiable on rational grounds? Is it necessary in this context to distinguish between *de jure* and de facto discrimination? The relevance of targeting foreign nationals (as opposed to nationals) was highlighted in *Corn Products v Mexico*:[518]

While the existence of an intention to discriminate is not a requirement for a breach of Article 1102 (and both parties seemed to accept that it was not a requirement), where such an intention is shown, that is sufficient to satisfy the third requirement [treatment less favourable, see para 117]. But the Tribunal would add that, even if an intention to discriminate had not been shown, the fact that the adverse effects of the tax were felt exclusively by the HFCS producers and suppliers, all of them foreign-owned, to the benefit of the sugar producers, the majority of which were Mexican-owned, would be sufficient to establish that the third requirement of 'less favourable treatment' was satisfied.[519]

Also, the social policy behind a governmental measure will have no bearing on the question:

The problem with this argument is that it confuses the nature of the measure taken with the motive for which it was taken. The Tribunal does not doubt either that there was a crisis in the Mexican sugar industry, or that the motive for imposing the HFCS tax was to address that crisis. That does not alter the fact that the nature of the measure which Mexico took was one which treated producers of HFCS in a markedly less favourable way than Mexican producers of sugar. Discrimination does not cease to be discrimination, nor to attract the international liability stemming therefrom, because it is undertaken to achieve a laudable goal or because the achievement of that goal can be described as necessary.[520]

According to *Lauder v Czech Republic*, a discriminatory measure is simply one that fails to provide national treatment.[521] The Tribunal, however, simply states this position without considering an alternative view.[522] The *Thunderbird* Award correctly states that a violation of the national treatment standard under the NAFTA does not require the claimant to show separately that the less favourable treatment was motivated by nationality. The fact of less favourable treatment will be sufficient.[523]

Concerning the distinction between de jure and de facto differentiations, the tribunal in *ADF v United States* seemingly would have accepted the latter as well, had respective evidence been shown by the claimant.[524] A purely incidental differentiation resulting from misguided policy decisions does not suffice to show differential treatment.[525]

---

[518] *Corn Products v Mexico*, Decision on Responsibility, 15 January 2008.
[519] At para 138.
[520] At para 142.
[521] *Lauder v Czech Republic*, Award, 3 September 2001, para 220.
[522] See eg GATT 1994, Art III, which distinguishes between national treatment and discrimination.
[523] *Thunderbird v Mexico*, Award, 26 January 2006, para 177.
[524] *ADF Group Inc. v United States*, Award, 9 January 2003, para 157. Also *Corn Products v Mexico*, Award, 15 January 2008, para 115.
[525] *GAMI v Mexico*, Award, 15 November 2004, para 114.

cc. Is there a justification for the differentiation?

The third component of the clause pertains to the justification of a differentiating measure. Although most investment treaties do not explicitly say so, it is widely accepted that differentiations are justifiable if rational grounds are shown.[526] However, a precise definition of these grounds has remained elusive.

In regard to the circumstances under which different treatment is allowed under the NAFTA, *SD Myers v Canada* stated that the 'assessment of "like circumstances" must also take into account circumstances that would justify governmental regulations that treat them differently in order to protect the public interest'.[527] In *GAMI v Mexico*, the Tribunal found the solvency of an important local industry, in this case sugar, to be a legitimate policy goal and underlined that the relevant measures were not geared towards the foreign investor.[528] In *ADF v United States*, a NAFTA tribunal found no violation of the national treatment standard, as a US requirement to use locally produced steel for government projects applied equally to both national and foreign contractors.[529]

The issue may arise whether, and under what circumstances, labour laws may play a role in establishing the case for a violation of national treatment. Additionally, the issue of special treatment of domestic entities based on cultural policies may arise,[530] for instance by way of subsidies for audio-visual culture. Since the entry into force of the UNESCO Convention on the Protection and Promotion of the Diversity of Cultural Expressions, one question is whether such a differentiation is allowed or should even be promoted.[531]

In *SD Myers v Canada*, the Tribunal seems to have assumed that subsidies are allowed to promote national policies.[532] The *Oscar Chinn* case, decided by the PCIJ almost 80 years ago, also dealt with measures by a host state to support its transport industry. In a majority decision, the Court upheld the legality of the

---

[526] See R Dolzer, 'Generalklauseln in Investitionsschutzverträgen' in *Negotiating for Peace, Liber Amicorum Tono Eitel* (2003) 291, 296–305.

[527] *SD Myers v Canada*, First Partial Award, 13 November 2000, para 250.

[528] *GAMI v Mexico*, Award, 15 November 2004, paras 114–15.

[529] *ADF Group Inc. v United States*, Award, 9 January 2003, paras 156–8.

[530] See *UPS v Canada*, Award, 24 May 2007, para 156.

[531] The Convention was adopted on 20 October 2005 and entered into force on 18 March 2007. While it is widely seen to contain provisions for 'cultural exceptions' to existing international rules, especially in the field of trade, it is unclear whether Art 20 of the Convention will be able to resolve all existing doubts. Article 20 of the UNESCO Convention reads:

> (1) Parties recognize that they shall perform in good faith their obligations under this Convention and all other treaties to which they are parties. Accordingly, without subordinating this Convention to any other treaty, (a) they shall foster mutual supportiveness between this Convention and the other treaties to which they are parties; and (b) when interpreting and applying the other treaties to which they are parties or when entering into other international obligations, Parties shall take into account the relevant provisions of this Convention. (2) Nothing in this Convention shall be interpreted as modifying rights and obligations of the Parties under any other treaties to which they are parties.

[532] *SD Myers v Canada*, First Partial Award, 13 November 2000, para 255: 'CANADA's right to source all government requirements and to grant subsidies to the Canadian industry are but two examples of legitimate alternative measures.'

Belgian measures despite a treaty that provided for 'competitive equality'.[533] Today, the special legal context of a BIT and the relevant treaty in the *Oscar Chinn* case may have to be examined in a contemporary context in order to determine the persuasive power of that precedent.[534]

In *Thunderbird v Mexico*, the Tribunal held in an *obiter dictum* that no claim to national treatment could be made when the conduct of the investor was illegal according to national law, in this case gambling, even if that national law was not uniformly enforced.[535] Hence, no 'equality in injustice' can be claimed by a foreign investor under this standard.

National policies in favour of the domestic public interest can, under certain circumstances, constitute a rational ground for according less than national treatment. However, which specific grounds may be argued in this regard is unclear. One factor in deciding this question might be whether the policy in the specific case is lawful under other relevant rules of international law.

dd. The relevance of discriminatory intent

Concerning a requirement of intent on the part of the host government to favour the national, the Tribunal in *SD Myers v Canada* seems to focus on the practical impact rather than on intent.[536] In the context of the impact, the decision asks whether the host state could have achieved its goal using alternative measures that would have had a less restrictive impact on the foreign investor.[537]

The Tribunal in *Siemens v Argentina*[538] was even more explicit:

The Tribunal concurs that intent is not decisive or essential for a finding of discrimination, and that the impact of the measure on the investment would be the determining factor to ascertain whether it had resulted in non-discriminatory treatment.[539]

The Tribunals in *Feldman v Mexico*,[540] *Bayindir v Pakistan*,[541] and *Corn Products v Mexico*[542] accepted the same position.

---

[533] The *Oscar Chinn Case (UK v Belgium)*, 12 December 1934, PCIJ, Series A/B, No 63.

[534] See, for one position, T Weiler, 'Saving Oscar Chinn: Non-Discrimination in International Investment Law' in N Horn (ed), *Arbitrating Foreign Investment Disputes: Procedural and Substantive Legal Aspects* (2004) 159–92.

[535] *Thunderbird v Mexico*, Award, 26 January 2006, para 183.

[536] *SD Myers v Canada*, First Partial Award, 13 November 2000, para 254:

Intent is important, but protectionist intent is not necessarily decisive on its own. The existence of an intent to favour nationals over non-nationals would not give rise to a breach of [Article] 1102 of the NAFTA if the measure in question were to produce no adverse effect on the non-national complainant. The word 'treatment' suggests that practical impact is required to produce a breach of Article 1102, not merely a motive or intent that is in violation of Chapter 11.

[537] At para 255.

[538] *Siemens v Argentina*, Award, 6 February 2007.

[539] At para 321.

[540] *Feldman v Mexico*, Award, 16 December 2002, para 181.

[541] *Bayindir v Pakistan*, Award, 27 August 2009, para 309.

[542] See p 201.

On the other hand, the Tribunal in *Genin* seemed to require discriminatory intent as a necessary prerequisite for a finding of discrimination.[543] The *Methanex* decision also includes language that may be understood to require evidence of intent to discriminate.[544]

As regards the need to establish nationality-based discrimination, the *Feldman* ruling suggests that in view of the practical difficulty of producing evidence of this kind it is sufficient to produce proof of discrimination and not necessary to show discrimination based on nationality.[545] The burden of proof to show any discrimination at all, however, remains with the claimant.[546]

(c) The relevance of WTO case law

The significance of WTO law and its jurisprudence for the interpretation of BITs has been the subject of some debate.[547] Earlier NAFTA decisions in *SD Myers*,[548] *Pope & Talbot*,[549] and *Feldman*[550] seemed to assume that the relevant WTO jurisprudence was indeed suitable to guide NAFTA tribunals. Meanwhile, the tide seems to have turned against considering WTO jurisprudence in the interpretation and application of a BIT. This is important because the jurisprudence of the WTO requires the government making a differentiation to bear the burden of proof for the

---

[543] *Genin v Estonia*, Award, 25 June 2001, para 369.

[544] *Methanex v United States*, Final Award, 3 August 2005, Part IV, Ch B, para 12:

> In order to sustain its claim under Article 1102(3), Methanex must demonstrate, cumulatively, that California intended to favour domestic investors by discriminating against foreign investors and that Methanex and the domestic investor supposedly being favored by California are in like circumstances.

But in para 1 of the same chapter the Tribunal says: 'an affirmative finding under NAFTA Article 1102 ... does not require the demonstration of the malign intent alleged by Methanex ...'

[545] *Feldman v Mexico*, Award, 16 December 2002, para 181:

> It is clear that the concept of national treatment as embodied in NAFTA and similar agreements is designed to prevent discrimination on the basis of nationality, or 'by reason of nationality'. (US Statement of Administrative Action, Article 1102.) However, it is not self-evident, as the Respondent argues, that any departure from national treatment must be explicitly shown to be a result of the investor's nationality. There is no such language in Article 1102. Rather, Article 1102 by its terms suggests that it is sufficient to show less favorable treatment for the foreign investor than for domestic investors in like circumstances. ... For practical as well as legal reasons, the Tribunal is prepared to assume that the differential treatment is a result of the Claimant's nationality, at least in the absence of any evidence to the contrary.

See also *Occidental v Ecuador*, Award, 1 July 2004, para 177 (focusing on the 'result of the policy enacted').

[546] *ADF Group Inc. v United States*, Award, 9 January 2003, paras 156–7.

[547] For the concept of 'like products' in WTO law, see J B Goco, 'Non-Discrimination, "Likeness", and Market Definition in World Trade Organization Jurisprudence' (2006) 40(2) *J World Trade* 315. Generally, on possible linkages between investment law and WTO law, see also G Verhoosel, 'The Use of Investor–State Arbitration under Bilateral Investment Treaties to Seek Relief for Breaches of WTO Law' (2003) 6 *J Int'l Economic L* 493.

[548] *SD Myers v Canada*, First Partial Award, 13 November 2000, paras 244–7.

[549] *Pope & Talbot v Canada*, Award on Merits, 10 April 2001, paras 45–63, 68–9.

[550] *Feldman v Mexico*, Award, 16 December 2002, para 165.

legitimacy of the policy.[551] It is at least open to question whether such an approach is appropriate in the context of BITs.

An initial blow to the original approach came in 2004 when the Tribunal in *Occidental v Ecuador* rejected the argument that WTO jurisprudence should be applied to a BIT between Ecuador and the United States.[552] The Tribunal observed that while the WTO is concerned with 'like products', the BIT addressed 'like situations' and added that WTO policies concerning competitive and substitutable goods could not be treated in the same way as the BIT policies concerning 'like situations'.[553]

The second strike, even more severe than the first, came in August 2005 with the *Methanex* ruling and its detailed clause-by-clause analysis of the various parts of the NAFTA as compared to the language used in WTO law.[554] The Tribunal pointed out that the NAFTA rules use different language in different parts. In part, the language is the same as that used in the WTO, but not so in Chapter Eleven. The conclusion in *Methanex* was that the NAFTA parties were aware of the difference in language, and that in Chapter Eleven of the NAFTA, concerning foreign investment, the parties deliberately referred to 'like circumstances' as opposed to 'like goods'. Thus, the *Methanex* Tribunal ruled that 'like circumstances' in the context of a foreign investment cannot be considered to be identical with the concept of 'like goods' and that, therefore, the NAFTA investment provisions had to be interpreted autonomously, independent from trade law considerations.[555] Nevertheless, *Corn Products v Mexico*[556] suggests that the determination of a 'like product' under the rules of the General Agreement on Tariffs and Trade (GATT) and the investment provision of Article 1102 of the NAFTA are closely linked.

The *Thunderbird* Award of January 2006 states that the burden of proof to show less favourable treatment—at least prima facie—remains with the claimant.[557] This position is directly opposed to the above-mentioned development in WTO law, which calls for a shift of the burden of proof to the government in cases of

---

[551] Cf D Regan, 'Further Thoughts on the Role of Regulatory Purpose under Article III of the General Agreement on Tariffs and Trade' (2003) 37(4) *J World Trade* 737, 752; for a critical appraisal of this approach, see J Pauwelyn, 'Evidence, Proof and Persuasion in WTO Dispute Settlement—Who Bears the Burden?' (1998) 1 *J Int'l Economic L* 227.

[552] *Occidental v Ecuador*, Award, 1 July 2004.

[553] At para 176. In the particular case, the Tribunal found that the purpose of national treatment was rather the opposite of that under GATT/WTO:

> it [the national treatment] is to avoid exporters being placed at a disadvantage in foreign markets because of the indirect taxes paid in the country of origin, while in GATT/WTO the purpose is to avoid imported products being affected by a distortion of competition with similar domestic products because of taxes and other regulations in the country of destination.

[554] *Methanex v United States*, Award, 3 August 2005, Part IV, Ch B, paras 30–5.

[555] At paras 35, 37.

[556] *Corn Products v Mexico*, Award, 15 January 2008, para 122.

[557] *Thunderbird v Mexico*, Award, 26 January 2006, paras 176–8. But see also the Separate Opinion by Arbitrator Wälde (para 2).

differentiation. The divergence in the objectives and the normative structures of trade law and investment law was also highlighted in *Bayindir v Pakistan*.[558]

If this trend of divergence between trade and investment law continues, the discussion will sharpen whether this dual approach to national treatment in international economic law needs to be revisited and whether, one way or another, the concepts should be merged. From the point of view of legal clarity and predictability, such a revision would be helpful. However, given the current divergent wordings of WTO law and investment law,[559] it cannot be assumed that investment tribunals or the WTO dispute settlement bodies will change direction so as to allow for a homogeneous jurisprudence. Thus, the more practical question is whether governments will wish to revisit the two legal regimes and decide whether the different wordings reflect different underlying policies that deserve to be protected separately. If governments consider that it would be preferable to establish a single regime, a mechanism would also have to be created that would ensure consistency of jurisprudence in trade and in investment cases. For the time being, investors, traders, and governments will have to live with the dual system.

9. Most-favoured-nation treatment

(a) Introduction

MFN clauses have formed part of international economic treaties for centuries.[560] MFN treatment is not required under customary law. The simple goal of MFN clauses in treaties is to ensure that the relevant parties treat each other in a manner at least as favourable as they treat third parties. The normal effect of an MFN clause in a BIT is to widen the rights of the investor.[561] As a relative standard, an MFN clause depends for its reach and scope on the conduct of the particular state. The clause may not have any practical significance if the state concerned fails to grant any relevant benefit to a third party. However, as soon as the state does confer a relevant benefit, it is automatically extended to the beneficiary of the MFN clause. The clause will operate, in principle, in relation to all matters that fall within the scope of the treaty containing the MFN rule. Put differently, *ratione materiae*, it operates according to the requirement of sameness, the *ejusdem generis* principle, and the precise benefit granted will depend upon the right granted to the third state. Thus, considerations similar to those relevant to determine 'like circumstances' for

---

[558] *Bayindir v Pakistan*, Award, 27 August 2009, para 389.

[559] See also *UPS v Canada*, Award, 24 May 2007, para 61, dealing with the difference between the rules on state organs and state enterprises in the NAFTA and in the WTO.

[560] G Schwarzenberger, *International Law as Applied by International Courts and Tribunals*, 3rd edn (1957) 243; OECD, *International Investment Law: A Changing Landscape* (2005) 129. On the difference between MFN treatment and the general rule on non-discrimination in public international law, see UNCTAD, *Most-Favored-Nation Treatment* (2010) 23.

[561] *Tza Yap Shum v Peru*, Decision on Jurisdiction, 19 June 2009, para 196.

the purposes of national treatment will come into play.[562] In addition, issues of justification for differential treatment may arise.[563]

The traditional significance of the MFN rule in economic treaties has led to its inclusion in most investment treaties. In the realm of international trade law, the clause, as laid down in Article I of the GATT, is considered one of the cornerstones of the entire regime.[564] In trade law, the clause grants benefits wherever the parties have not previously agreed to liberalize their relations in the same way as that in a treaty with a third state.

In the context of modern investment treaties, the almost mechanical application of the MFN principle, accepted in trade law, does not operate in a similarly straightforward manner. The reason is that investment treaties contain the results of negotiations covering distinct substantive areas. When the MFN rule is applied in such a context in a mechanical manner, the effect may be to replace the negotiated substance of the treaty rather than to add an element of cooperation. Under such circumstances, the question arises whether and to what extent the MFN rule is meant to alter arrangements specifically made by the parties to the treaty. A literal application of an MFN clause may indeed have the effect of transferring a regime into the treaty in an area that the parties specifically negotiated and that they regulated in the treaty in a manner distinct from the substance of the referenced treaty. It remains an open issue whether the MFN rule should be understood in such a manner or whether the intention of the parties as laid down in the text on the substantive guarantees in the treaty will place limits on the operation of an MFN rule.

So far, most cases involving the MFN rule have concerned situations in which benefits granted in treaties with third states were invoked. The situation is less complex, and more comparable to the issues in the trade area, when parties to an investment treaty do not refer to a treaty with a third party but simply argue that nationals of third parties are treated de facto in a more favourable manner.

(b) Variations of MFN clauses

As with other standards in investment treaties, different types and versions have been adopted in treaty practice and each clause must be interpreted and applied on its own terms.[565] A classical approach can be found in Article 3 of the German

---

[562] On 'like circumstances' in the context of contractual matters, see *Bayindir v Pakistan*, Award, 27 August 2009, para 388; on procurement issues, see *Parkerings v Lithuania*, Award, 11 September 2007, paras 377–430; on 'like circumstances' in the NAFTA, see *Archer Daniels v Mexico*, Award, 21 November 2007, paras 197–204; *Corn Products v Mexico*, Decision on Responsibility, 15 January 2008, paras 120 et seq; on the difference in the operation of an MFN clause in an investment treaty and in trade law, see UNCTAD, *Most-Favored-Nation Treatment* (2010) 29 et seq.

[563] See *Parkerings v Lithuania*, Award, 11 September 2007, paras 368 et seq.

[564] See J Jackson, W Davies, and A Sykes, *Legal Problems of International Economic Relations*, 5th edn (2008).

[565] 'Each MFN clause is a world in itself, which demands an individualised interpretation to determine its scope of application': *Tza Yap Shum v Peru*, Decision on Jurisdiction, 19 June 2009,

Model Treaty, which combines the MFN standard with the national treatment standard:

(1) Neither Contracting State shall subject investments in its territory owned or controlled by investors of the other Contracting State to treatment less favourable than it accords to investments of its own investors or to investments of investors of any third State.

(2) Neither Contracting State shall subject investors of the other Contracting State, as regards their activity in connection with investments in its territory, to treatment less favourable than it accords to its own investors or to investors of any third State.

Other versions do not refer to the same 'treatment', but to 'all matters subject to this agreement': 'In all matters subject to this Agreement, this treatment shall be no less favourable than that extended by each Party to the investments made in its territory by investors of a third country.'[566]

Against the background of evolving jurisprudence, some more recent treaties explicitly refer in their MFN clauses to specific articles in the treaty in order clearly to designate the areas to which the clause is meant to apply. The United Kingdom, for instance, has in some treaties referred to subject areas such as 'management, maintenance, use, enjoyment or disposal' to which the MFN clause applies.[567] Other parties have attempted to interpret the clause restrictively in a retrospective manner: Argentina and Panama have exchanged diplomatic notes in which they state that the MFN clause in their existing BIT does not extend to dispute resolution clauses, and that 'this has always been their intention'.[568] The United Kingdom has in some of its recent treaties spelled out the scope of the MFN clause 'for the avoidance of doubt'.[569] It will depend on the circumstances of the case whether the existence of such clarifying notes or phrases may contribute to elucidating the meaning of a BIT.

(c) Method of interpretation

The rules of interpretation laid down in the VCLT will also apply to an MFN clause.[570] Thus, the primary task is to identify the ordinary meaning of the clause in its context and in light of the object and purpose of the treaty. As to supplementary means of interpretation (Art 32 VCLT), it is rare that a tribunal has before it relevant parts of the *travaux préparatoires*. However, the Tribunal in *Plama v Bulgaria* ruled that direct negotiations between the two parties to the relevant

---

para 198; in the event, the Tribunal pointed to the dispute settlement clause which allowed to expand jurisdiction beyond matters of expropriation only 'if the parties so agree'.

[566] See eg Art IV(2) of the Spain-Argentina BIT of 3 October 1991.
[567] See Art 3(2) of the BIT between the UK and Argentina of 11 December 1990.
[568] See *National Grid v Argentina*, Decision on Jurisdiction, 20 June 2006, para 85.
[569] See also Art 3(3) of the UK Model BIT.
[570] See eg *National Grid v Argentina*, Decision on Jurisdiction, 20 June 2006, para 80.

BIT, subsequent to its entry into force, with a view to concluding a new BIT were suitable indirectly to clarify the meaning of the original BIT.[571]

A particular issue of interpretation has arisen in an effort to focus on the intention of the parties. One approach would focus on identifying this intention by way of pointing to the substantive matter (as opposed to the MFN rule) negotiated by the parties as reflected in the text, based on the argument that consideration of this text will establish the real and specific will of the parties.

Attractive as this reasoning may appear at first sight, it will ultimately not be convincing. This is so because a focus on the parties' intention[572] cannot ignore the indisputable fact that the parties have included in the treaty both the negotiated substantive matter and also the MFN rule; there is no justification for deriving the parties' intention from one of these two elements alone.

Different conclusions have been drawn from provisions that exclude the applicability of MFN clauses from certain areas (customs unions, free trade areas, economic communities). Under the principle *expressio unius est exclusio alterius*, this could mean that the MFN clause is meant to operate in all other areas, including jurisdictional matters. This was the position adopted in *National Grid v Argentina*.[573] On the other hand, the *Plama* Tribunal pointed to language in a different paragraph, also addressing the MFN rule, in which the word 'privileges' appears. The *Plama* Tribunal assumed that the term 'privilege' only covered substantive protection and cannot be understood to extend to the jurisdictional rights of an investor.[574]

(d) Invoking substantive rights

For the scope *ratione materiae* of the rule, it is useful to distinguish between its applicability to substantive treaty guarantees and to matters of dispute settlement; but the normative value of this distinction is controversial.[575] The following observations cover substantive rights, whereas dispute settlement is discussed below.[576]

In *Pope & Talbot v Canada*,[577] the Tribunal relied on the MFN clause contained in Article 1103 of the NAFTA in order to underpin its argument that the FET

---

[571] *Plama v Bulgaria*, Decision on Jurisdiction, 8 February 2005, para 195.

[572] Notably, Arts 31 and 32 of the VCLT do not contain a reference to the intention of the parties to the treaty.

[573] *National Grid v Argentina*, Decision on Jurisdiction, 20 June 2006, para 82.

[574] *Plama v Bulgaria*, Decision on Jurisdiction, 8 February 2005, para 191.

[575] See *RosInvest v Russia*, Award on Jurisdiction, October 2007, paras 131–2; *Renta 4 v Russia*, Award on Preliminary Objections, 20 March 2009, paras 99–100.

[576] See pp 270–5. On measures which may trigger MFN, see UNCTAD, *Most-Favored-Nation Treatment* (2010) 28.

[577] *Pope & Talbot v Canada*, Award on Merits, 10 April 2001, para 117. The award was issued before the authoritative interpretation of NAFTA, Art 1105 by the NAFTA FTC; see p 136. Cf also the discussions in *ADF Group Inc v United States*, Award, 9 January 2003, paras 193–8; *UPS v Canada*, Award, 24 May 2007, paras 182–4; *Chemtura v Canada*, Award, 2 August 2010, paras 231–7.

standard of Article 1105 of the NAFTA could not be considered as providing less protection than other free-standing FET clauses:

This state of affairs would surely run afoul of Articles 1102 and 1103, which gave every NAFTA investor and investment the right to national and most-favored nation treatment. NAFTA investors and investments that would be denied access to the fairness elements untrammeled by the 'egregious' conduct threshold that Canada would graft onto Article 1105 would simply turn to Articles 1102 and 1103 for relief.

In *MTD v Chile*,[578] the MFN clause was combined with the obligation to accord fair and equitable treatment in the same provision of the applicable BIT between Chile and Malaysia.[579] In the Tribunal's view, this clause allowed for the invocation of other substantive obligations contained in other BITs concluded by Chile with Denmark and Croatia, namely the obligation to award permits subsequent to approval of an investment and to fulfilment of contractual obligations:

The question for the Tribunal is whether the provisions of the Croatia BIT and the Denmark BIT which deal with the obligation to award permits subsequent to approval of an investment and to fulfillment of contractual obligations, respectively, can be considered to be part of fair and equitable treatment. . . . The Tribunal has concluded that, under the BIT, the fair and equitable standard of treatment has to be interpreted in the manner most conducive to fulfill the objective of the BIT to protect investments and create conditions favorable to investments. The Tribunal considers that to include as part of the protections of the BIT those included in Article 3(1) of the Denmark BIT and Article 3(3) and (4) of the Croatia BIT is in consonance with this purpose. The Tribunal is further convinced of this conclusion by the fact that the exclusions in the MFN clause relate to tax treatment and regional cooperation, matters alien to the BIT but that, because of the general nature of the MFN clause, the Contracting Parties considered it prudent to exclude. *A contrario sensu*, other matters that can be construed to be part of the fair and equitable treatment of investors would be covered by the clause.[580]

In *Bayindir v Pakistan*,[581] the Arbitral Tribunal found that an MFN clause would permit the invocation of an FET clause contained in another BIT:

Neither in its Reply nor at the jurisdictional hearing, did Pakistan dispute Bayindir's assertion that the investment treaties which Pakistan has concluded with France, the Netherlands, China, the United Kingdom, Australia, and Switzerland contains an explicit fair and equitable treatment clause . . . Under these circumstances and for the purposes of

---

[578] *MTD v Chile*, Award, 25 May 2004, paras 103–4.

[579] 'Investments made by investors of either Contracting Party in the territory of the other Contracting Party shall receive treatment which is fair and equitable, and not less favourable than that accorded to investments made by investors of any third State.'

[580] At paras 103–4. In *Impregilo v Pakistan*, Decision on Jurisdiction, 22 April 2005, 12 ICSID Reports 245, para 223, the claimant attempted to invoke an umbrella clause contained in another BIT concluded by the respondent by relying on the MFN clause of the applicable BIT. However, the Tribunal did not find it necessary to rule on the issue because the contracts relied upon by the claimant had not been directly concluded by the respondent state.

[581] *Bayindir v Pakistan*, Decision on Jurisdiction, 14 November 2005.

assessing jurisdiction, the Tribunal considers, prima facie, that Pakistan is bound to treat investments of Turkish nationals 'fairly and equitably.'[582]

MFN clauses have also been invoked in the context of defining the standard of compensation in expropriation cases. In *CME v Czech Republic*,[583] the applicable BIT provided for 'just compensation' representing the 'genuine value of the investment affected'. In its award, the Tribunal also relied on the MFN clauses in order to rule that the compensation should represent the 'fair market value' of the investment:

The determination of compensation under the Treaty between the Netherlands and the Czech Republic on basis of the 'fair market value' finds support in the 'most favored nation' provision of Art. 3(5) of the Treaty.... The bilateral investment treaties between the United States of America and the Czech Republic provides that compensation shall be equivalent to the fair market value of the expropriated investment immediately before the expropriatory action was taken ... The Czech Republic therefore is obligated to provide no less than 'fair market value' to Claimant in respect of its investment, should (in contrast to this Tribunal's opinion) 'just compensation' representing the 'genuine value' be interpreted to be less than 'fair market value.'[584]

(e) Current state of the law

While it is important to consider the reasoning of the tribunals and their methodological approach, it is equally or more significant to focus on the holdings of the decisions.[585] The weight of authority clearly supports the view that an MFN rule grants a claimant the right to benefit from substantive guarantees contained in third treaties. The cases so far decided do not address in detail the question whether and to what extent any limits exist for the application of the rule to such substantive guarantees.

The larger group of cases deals with the applicability of MFN clauses not to substantive guarantees but to dispute settlement. That issue is discussed in Chapter X on dispute settlement.[586] As can be seen there, practice in that field is less straightforward and to some extent divided.

On this basis, it is too early to conclude in broader terms in which direction the jurisprudence may evolve in regard to the effect of an MFN clause for the invocation of another treaty. One view would be that so far no tribunal has permitted the invocation of the clause in a manner that would have led to 'regime change' in regard to the basic treaty containing the clause. This would mean that an MFN clause will operate only to the extent that the provision in the other treaty is compatible in principle with the scheme negotiated by the parties in the basic treaty

---

[582] At paras 231–2. See also *Bayindir v Pakistan*, Award, 27 August 2009, paras 163–7.
[583] *CME v Czech Republic*, Final Award, 14 March 2003.
[584] At para 500.
[585] In *Bayindir v Pakistan*, Decision on Jurisdiction, 14 November 2005, paras 201 et seq, the Tribunal discussed de facto discrimination, but, in spite of the decision's wording, focused on the requirement of national treatment rather than the MFN rule.
[586] See pp 270–5.

and departs from it only in a detail consistent with that broader scheme. This view would have to explain under what circumstances the two treaties are seen to be 'compatible in principle'. A different view would adopt a literal interpretation that would extend the operation of the MFN clause to all areas of other treaties, regardless of any comparison or judgement on compatibility. Even under this view, the *ejusdem generis* rule would apply.

In *Hochtief v Argentina*,[587] the Tribunal addressed attempts to distinguish procedural and substantive rights and found that there was no basis for such a distinction in the context of the MFN rule in investment treaties:

This is clear if one considers the case of a claim to money or to performance having an economic value, both of which are stipulated by Article 1(c) of the Argentina-Germany BIT to be within the definition of an investment, or of intellectual property rights, addressed in Article 1(d). The argument that although a State could not cancel such claims or intellectual property rights without violating the BIT, it could cancel the right to pursue the claims or enforce the intellectual property rights through litigation or arbitration without violating the BIT is nonsensical. It is nonsensical because the right to enforcement is an essential component of the property rights themselves, and not a wholly distinct right.[588]

As to the limits of the MFN rule, the Tribunal assumed that the rule is not intended to 'create wholly new rights where none otherwise existed' in the BIT; the reason given is that the MFN rule refers to a standard and not to the extent of rights of third parties.[589] The Tribunal did not elaborate or explain how this position is anchored in an MFN rule that is not in any way qualified.

10. Transfer of funds

Conditions for the transfer of funds by investors into the host state and out of the host state are of key concern for both the investor and the host state. The investor will typically need to import funds into the host state to start a production facility or to expand its business. Repatriation of capital, including profits, into the home country or a third country will often be the major business purpose of the investment. In the words of *Continental Casualty v Argentina*,[590] the right of transfer 'is fundamental to the freedom to make a foreign investment and an essential element of the promotional role of BITs'.

The host state will want to administer its currency and its foreign reserves. Large currency transfers into and out of the country need to be monitored and controlled in order to protect national policies. Experience has shown that sudden short-term capital inflows, and especially capital flight, may lead to instability in the domestic financial markets.

---

[587] *Hochtief v Argentina*, Decision on Jurisdiction, 24 October 2011.
[588] At para 67.
[589] At para 81.
[590] *Continental Casualty v Argentina*, Award, 5 September 2008, para 239.

Thus, the interests of the foreign investor and those of the host state in the admissibility of foreign transfers will often diverge. Therefore, investment treaties invariably cover this subject. Separate types of restrictions are found in the IMF's Articles of Agreement, in rules adopted in the OECD, and in the GATT regime.[591]

The modalities of regulation in treaties vary considerably, and no single pattern is dominant. Monetary and financial policies, the volume of the domestic capital market, historical experience, and the simple bargaining power of the parties will influence the outcome of treaty negotiations. The types of transfer covered by the transfer clause in the Argentina-US BIT of 1991 were under consideration in *Continental Casualty v Argentina*.[592] The Tribunal ruled that only 'transfers... essential for, or typical to the making, controlling, maintenance, disposition of investments' are covered, in contrast to a mere 'change of type, location and currency of part of an investor's existing investment, namely a part of the freely disposable funds, held short term at its banks'.[593]

All treaty schemes are negotiated against the background of the host state's 'monetary sovereignty'. This means that the host state has 'the exclusive right to determine its own monetary unit, to give the unit legal meaning, to fix the exchange rate and to regulate, restrict or prohibit the conversion and transfer of foreign exchange'.[594] The rules of the IMF, which have been accepted in principle by 184 states, do not allow restrictions by the member states of so-called 'current transactions'.[595] This leaves them the power to regulate the inflow and outflow of 'capital transactions' as opposed to 'current transactions'.[596]

---

[591] On the overlap with BITs and the legal consequences, see R Dolzer, 'Transfer of Funds: Investment Rules and their Relationship to other International Agreements' in *International Monetary and Financial Law* (2010) 533.

[592] *Continental Casualty v Argentina*, Award, 5 September 2008, paras 241 et seq.

[593] At paras 240, 241.

[594] R Dolzer and M Stevens, *Bilateral Investment Treaties* (1995) 85.

[595] Article VIII of the IMF's Articles of Agreement states:

> ... Section 2. Avoidance of restrictions on current payments: (a) Subject to the provisions of Article VII, Section 3(b) and Article XIV, Section 2, no member shall, without the approval of the Fund, impose restrictions on the making of payments and transfers for current international transactions. (b) Exchange contracts which involve the currency of any member and which are contrary to the exchange control regulations of that member maintained or imposed consistently with this Agreement shall be unenforceable in the territories of any member. In addition, members may, by mutual accord, cooperate in measures for the purpose of making the exchange control regulations of either member more effective, provided that such measures and regulations are consistent with this Agreement.

[596] Article XXX(d) of the IMF's Articles of Agreement defines payments for current transactions in the following terms:

> Payments for current transactions means payments which are not for the purpose of transferring capital, and include, without limitation: (1) all payments due in connection with foreign trade, other current business, including services, and normal short-term banking and credit facilities; (2) payments due as interests on loans and as net income from other investments; (3) payments of moderate amount for amortization of loans or for depreciation of direct investments; and (4) moderate remittances for family living expenses. The Fund may, after consultation with the members concerned, determine whether certain specific transactions are to be considered current transactions or capital transactions.

Rules on transfer deal with the investor's right to make transfers, the types of payment covered by this right, with convertibility and exchange rates, and with limitations on the freedom of transfer.[597] In relation to the applicable IMF Rules, the Tribunal in *Continental Casualty v Argentina*[598] properly considered that the BIT provisions on transfer are more liberal and will have to be considered as *lex specialis*.

A major point of divergence between treaties relates to the question whether the right to transfer funds concerns only the transfer out of the host country or whether it covers inward transfers as well.[599] Most treaties cover both directions, but some treaties only address the duty of the host state to guarantee the right to transfer investments and returns abroad, thus referring only to outward payments. If transfers are allowed in general terms, such as 'in relation to investments', both directions of transfer are covered.

Practically no treaty grants an absolute right to make transfers to investors. Some treaties state that the rights guaranteed to the investor exist only 'subject to the laws' of the host state. For the investor, such a restriction substantially reduces the value of the right to transfer, especially since the national laws of the host state may be revised in the future as the host state deems appropriate.

The right to transfer is sometimes limited to certain types of transfer. Often, the principal rules guarantee the right of free transfer 'of payments resulting from investment activities', or they permit all transfers 'related to an investment' or 'in connection with an investment'.[600] In other treaties, the right to make transfers is not generalized. Types of payment covered by the transfer clause are often indicated in specific categories; sometimes in an exhaustive manner, sometimes in an illustrative manner. Such categories may refer to profits, interest, dividends, other current income, funds necessary to finance an investment, proceeds of liquidation, payments under a contract, management fees, royalties, or other items. Often, returns, loan payments, liquidation proceeds, or payments from licences and royalties are guaranteed free transfer, whereas qualifications of this right may be found for the transfer of salaries.

Most treaties state that the investor has the right to carry out the transfer in a freely convertible currency, that the transfer takes place at the official rate of exchange of the host state on the date of the transfer, and that the transfer will be authorized 'without delay', 'without undue delay', or that the procedures are carried out 'expeditiously'.[601] It remains the investor's responsibility to comply with the established procedure to obtain the necessary authorizations.[602]

---

[597] Measures by the host state which affect the opportunity to earn profits will not be deemed to violate the provision on the right of transfer. See *Biwater Gauff v Tanzania*, Award, 24 July 2008, para 735.

[598] At paras 243–4.

[599] UNCTAD, *Bilateral Investment Treaties 1995–2006: Trends in Investment Rulemaking* (2007) 57 et seq.

[600] R Dolzer and M Stevens, *Bilateral Investment Treaties* (1995) 87–8.

[601] Sometimes a specific time limit is mentioned, such as one month, three months, or four months.

[602] *Metalpar v Argentina*, Award, 6 June 2008, paras 176–9.

Today a liberalization of financial markets is considered advantageous for the investor and for the host state. But the experience of host states, during periods of financial disorder, indicates that in those times the government may need the power to place restrictions on the right to transfer.

Three approaches can be found in recent treaty practice to allow such restrictions.[603] Some treaties are based on the view that the short-term withdrawal of funds by the investor is undesirable under all circumstances and therefore only allow transfer out of the host country one year after the capital has entered the territory. A second approach is to place restrictions on the right to transfer during periods of severe balance-of-payments crises, external financial difficulties, or other exceptional circumstances affecting monetary policies or the exchange rate. A third approach, more recently favoured by Canada, the United States, and Japan, specifically concerns the right to restrict the freedom to provide financial services during extraordinary periods, preserving the right of the host and the home state to maintain 'the safety, soundness, integrity or financial responsibility of financial institutions'.[604] Clauses of this kind will be especially important in the context of treaties that cover the right to provide financial services. However, this approach may in the future also receive more attention in all treaties covering the right to transfer funds.

---

[603] UNCTAD, *Bilateral Investment Treaties 1995–2006: Trends in Investment Rulemaking* (2007) 62 et seq.

[604] See Art 20 (Financial Services) of the 2004 and 2012 US Model BITs:

1. Notwithstanding any other provision of this Treaty, a Party shall not be prevented from adopting or maintaining measures relating to financial services for prudential reasons, including for the protection of investors, depositors, policy holders, or persons to whom a fiduciary duty is owed by a financial services supplier, or to ensure the integrity and stability of the financial system. It is understood that the term 'prudential reasons' includes the maintenance of the safety, soundness, integrity, or financial responsibility of individual financial institutions....

On the NAFTA Rules, see *Fireman's Fund v Mexico*, Award, 17 July 2006, paras 156 et seq.

VIII

State Responsibility and Attribution

1. Organs, provinces, and municipalities

Under customary international law, a state is responsible for all its organs. Similarly, the state is responsible for its territorial units such as provinces and municipalities. This principle of attribution follows from the concept of the unity of the state and applies to organs at all levels and regardless of the position of the organ in the state's administrative organization. Therefore, lower level officials may incur the state's responsibility in the same way as the highest representatives of the state. The state's responsibility extends to all branches of the government, that is, to the executive, the legislature, and to the judiciary.

This principle of attribution is set out in the International Law Commission's (ILC's) Articles on State Responsibility[1] in the following terms:

Article 4 Conduct of organs of a State

1. The conduct of any State organ shall be considered an act of that State under international law, whether the organ exercises legislative, executive, judicial or any other functions, whatever position it holds in the organization of the State, and whatever its character as an organ of the central government or of a territorial unit of the State.
2. An organ includes any person or entity which has that status in accordance with the internal law of the State.[2]

The Commentary to the ILC's Articles adds the following explanation:

(6) Thus the reference to a State organ in article 4 is intended in the most general sense. It is not limited to the organs of the central government, to officials at a high level or to persons with responsibility for the external relations of the State. It extends to organs of government of whatever kind or classification, exercising whatever functions, and at whatever level in the hierarchy, including those at provincial or even local level. No distinction is made for this purpose between legislative, executive or judicial organs.[3]

---

[1] Articles on Responsibility of States for Internationally Wrongful Acts adopted by the International Law Commission at its 53rd session in 2001.
[2] J Crawford, *The International Law Commission's Articles on State Responsibility* (2002) 94.
[3] Crawford, n 2, p 95.

(a) State organs

The practice of investment tribunals has followed the principle of responsibility for all state organs and has applied it to the relationship of states with foreign investors. The tribunal in *CMS v Argentina*[4] said:

In so far as the international liability of Argentina under the Treaty is concerned, it also does not matter whether some actions were taken by the judiciary and others by an administrative agency, the executive or the legislative branch of the State. Article 4 of the Articles on State Responsibility adopted by the International Law Commission is abundantly clear on this point.[5]

More specifically, tribunals have held that actions by a variety of state organs were attributable to the state. These included action by a government minister,[6] the armed forces and police,[7] the state treasury,[8] the legislature,[9] and the courts.[10] In *MCI Power v Ecuador*,[11] the Tribunal looked to a combination of the institutional structure, the composition, and the functions when determining that a public-sector agency (Instituto Ecuatoriana de Electrificación) was a state organ. On the other hand, tribunals have refused to find that actions by private persons were attributable to the state.[12]

Acts of a state's organs will be attributed to that state even if they are contrary to law and even if they are in violation of instructions. Put differently, a state cannot plead that the actions of its organs were *ultra vires*. The ILC Articles on State Responsibility say in this respect:

Article 7 Excess of authority or contravention of instructions

The conduct of an organ of a State or of a person or entity empowered to exercise elements of the governmental authority shall be considered an act of the State under international law if the organ, person or entity acts in that capacity, even if it exceeds its authority or contravenes instructions.

---

[4] *CMS v Argentina*, Decision on Jurisdiction, 17 July 2003.

[5] At para 108. See also *Loewen v United States*, Decision on Jurisdiction, 9 January 2001, para 70; *Alpha v Ukraine*, Award, 8 November 2010, paras 399–403.

[6] *Texaco v Libya*, Preliminary Award, 27 November 1975, para 23.

[7] See *Amco v Indonesia*, Award, 20 November 1984, paras 155, 170–2; *AAPL v Sri Lanka*, Award, 27 June 1990.

[8] *Eureko v Poland*, Partial Award, 19 August 2005, paras 115–34.

[9] *Nycomb v Latvia*, Award, 16 December 2003, Stockholm Int'l Arb Rev 2005:1, sec 4.2 at p 93.

[10] *Amco v Indonesia*, Award, 20 November 1984, para 150; *Azinian v Mexico*, Award, 1 November 1999, paras 97–103; *Loewen v United States*, Decision on Jurisdiction, 9 January 2001, paras 47–60; *Saipem v Bangladesh*, Award, 30 June 2009, paras 188–90; *RosInvest v Russia*, Final Award, 12 September 2010, paras 602–3.

[11] *MCI Power v Ecuador*, Award, 31 July 2007, para 225.

[12] *Tradex v Albania*, Award, 29 April 1999, paras 136, 147, 165, 169, 175, 198. The Tribunal found that the occupation of a farm, which was part of a foreign investment, by villagers could not be attributed to Albania. In *Bayindir v Pakistan*, Award, 27 August 2009, para 119 the Tribunal decided that the relevant entity was not a state organ because it had separate personality and the acts in question were those of a party to a contract.

This principle has been accepted in arbitral practice. In *SPP v Egypt*,[13] the respondent contended that certain acts of Egyptian officials, upon which the claimants relied, were null and void because they were in conflict with the inalienable nature of the public domain and because they were not taken pursuant to the procedures prescribed by Egyptian law. The Tribunal rejected this argument and emphasized that the investor was entitled to rely on the official representations of the government:

Whether legal under Egyptian law or not, the acts in question were the acts of Egyptian authorities, including the highest executive authority of the Government. These acts, which are now alleged to have been in violation of the Egyptian municipal legal system, created expectations protected by established principles of international law.[14]

In *Kardassopoulos v Georgia*,[15] the claimant had received several representations from the host state to the effect that a concession was valid and that its investment was in accordance with local law. Before the Tribunal, Georgia argued that the concessions had been awarded in breach of Georgian law and were void *ab initio*. The Tribunal, relying on Article 7 of the ILC Articles and on *SPP v Egypt*, ruled that the representations were attributable to Georgia and that the claimant had a corresponding legitimate expectation and the host was estopped from arguing before a tribunal that the concession was void *ab initio*.

(b) Provinces and municipalities

The same principles of attribution apply to the acts of territorial units of states, such as provinces and municipalities. Some treaties for the protection of investments specifically state that they apply to the political subdivisions of the parties.[16] The Energy Charter Treaty (ECT) in Article 23(1) contains a provision on the observance of the treaty by sub-national authorities:

Each Contracting Party is fully responsible under this Treaty for the observance of all provisions of the Treaty, and shall take such reasonable measures as may be available to it to ensure such observance by regional and local governments and authorities within its Area.

This provision restates rather than amends the traditional rule of attribution.

Investment tribunals have consistently applied the rule that the central government is responsible for the acts of its territorial units. The Tribunal in *Vivendi I*[17] said in this respect:

it is well established that actions of a political subdivision of federal state, such as the Province of Tucumán in the federal state of the Argentine Republic, are attributable to the

---

[13] *SPP v Egypt*, Award, 20 May 1992.
[14] At para 83.
[15] *Kardassopoulos v Georgia*, Decision on Jurisdiction, 6 July 2007, paras 185–94. See also *OKO Pankki v Estonia*, Award, 19 November 2007, para 274.
[16] The Argentina-US BIT, Art XIII provides: 'This Treaty shall apply to the political subdivisions of the Parties.'
[17] *Vivendi v Argentina*, Award, 21 November 2000.

central government. It is equally clear that the internal constitutional structure of a country cannot alter these obligations.[18]

Tribunals have applied this rule to provinces,[19] constituent states,[20] and municipalities.[21]

2. State entities

(a) The role of state entities

In a number of countries, policy issues and operational matters concerning foreign investments are not handled by the central government. Instead, state entities have been created for the purpose of dealing with foreign investors (or with all investors). The position within the hierarchy of the government and the degree of legal independence of these entities vary. The reasons for the establishment of these separate entities are primarily specialization and efficiency.[22]

The existence of these separate national entities in the field of foreign investment must be reconciled with the international principle of the unity of the state. This has raised issues of attribution of acts of these entities to the state, which are not restricted to the field of foreign investment. Domestic classifications will not be decisive in this context. These issues form part of general international law, and they play a significant role in matters of state responsibility. In the field of foreign investment, matters of attribution have most often come up on the side of the respondent when a state argues that acts by state entities cannot be attributed to the state. However, the issue may also be relevant for a claimant whom a respondent considers as a state entity rather than a national of another state.[23]

In principle, state entities are separate and their acts will not be attributed to the state. However, several exceptions qualify this principle: the separation will not be respected if the corporate veil has been created as a means for fraud and evasion.[24] Also, conduct will be attributed to the state in cases where the corporation exercises

---

[18] At para 49. Footnotes omitted. In the same sense: *ADF v United States*, Award, 9 January 2003, para 166.

[19] *Enron v Argentina*, Decision on Jurisdiction, 14 January 2004, para 32. See also the case of *Heirs of the Duc de Guise*, 15 September 1951, XIII RIAA 150, 161, in which the Franco-Italian Conciliation Commission held that the Italian state was responsible for the conduct of Sicily even though Sicily enjoyed a status of autonomy in Italian law.

[20] *Mondev v United States*, Award, 11 October 2002, para 67.

[21] *Metalclad v Mexico*, Award, 30 August 2000, para 73; *Tokios Tokelės v Ukraine*, Decision on Jurisdiction, 29 April 2004, para 102.

[22] See, generally, L Schicho, *State Entities in International Investment Law* (2012); Organisation for Economic Co-operation and Development (OECD), *Public Sector Modernisation: Changing Organisational Structures*, OECD Policy Brief (2004).

[23] In *CSOB v Slovak Republic*, Decision on Jurisdiction, 24 May 1999, paras 15 et seq, the legal status of the claimant as a foreign private party (as opposed to a state agency) was in dispute. See at pp 250–1.

[24] See International Court of Justice, *Barcelona Traction Case*, Judgment, 5 February 1970, ICJ Reports (1970) 3, 39, paras 56–8.

public power.[25] Another exception concerns a situation of ownership by the state where control is exercised in order 'to achieve a particular result'.[26]

In general, matters of state responsibility, including attribution, are regulated in customary international law. Exceptionally, there are provisions in treaties that provide for the responsibility of states for action of their entities.[27] In *Genin v Estonia*,[28] this principle was reflected in a specific provision of the bilateral investment treaty (BIT). The Tribunal said:

> The Bank of Estonia is an agency of a Contracting State. The Estonian central bank is a 'state agency', as defined by the BIT, which stipulates in Article II 2(b) that 'Each Party shall ensure that any state enterprise that it maintains or establishes acts in a manner that is not inconsistent with the Party's obligations under this Treaty wherever such enterprise exercises any regulatory, administrative or other governmental authority that the Party has delegated to it, such as the power to expropriate, grant licenses....' The Republic of Estonia is therefore the appropriate Respondent to a complaint relating to the conduct of the Bank of Estonia.[29]

Matters of attribution governed by general international law include the question whether contracts or other acts undertaken by state entities are binding for the state that created those entities.[30] Questions have also arisen as to whether commitments undertaken by state entities can be considered to amount to jurisdictional consent

---

[25] See eg *Phillips Petroleum v Iran*, 21 Iran–US CTR 79 (1989).

[26] See J Crawford, *The International Law Commission's Articles on State Responsibility* (2002) 113, para 6; also *Foremost Teheran v Iran*, 10 Iran–US CTR 288 (1986); *American Bell v Iran*, 12 Iran–US CTR 170 (1986).

[27] ECT, Art 22 provides for special legal obligations of each state in regard to activities on the part of state enterprises:

> (1) Each Contracting Party shall ensure that any state enterprise which it maintains or establishes shall conduct its activities in relation to the sale or provision of goods and services in its Area in a manner consistent with the Contracting Party's obligations under Part III of this Treaty. (2) No Contracting Party shall encourage or require such a state enterprise to conduct its activities in its Area in a manner inconsistent with the Contracting Party's obligations under other provisions of this Treaty. (3) Each Contracting Party shall ensure that if it establishes or maintains an entity and entrusts the entity with regulatory, administrative or other governmental authority, such entity shall exercise that authority in a manner consistent with the Contracting Party's obligations under this Treaty. (4) No Contracting Party shall encourage or require any entity to which it grants exclusive or special privileges to conduct its activities in its Area in a manner inconsistent with the Contracting Party's obligations under this Treaty.

It is reasonable to assume that under certain circumstances these obligations of the host state go beyond the requirements under customary law.

[28] *Genin v Estonia*, Award, 25 June 2001.

[29] At para 327.

[30] This area of the law is closely connected with the view that a state cannot invoke provisions of domestic law as a defence against the violation of an international obligation (see Vienna Convention on the Law of Treaties, Art 27). See also in this respect, the decision of the ad hoc Committee in *Vivendi v Argentina*, Decision on Annulment, 3 July 2002, at para 101–7 (emphasizing the distinction between issues of attribution and responsibility in view of the unclear reasoning of the first *Vivendi* decision). In *Perenco v Ecuador*, Decision on Jurisdiction, 30 June 2011, paras 182–219 a contractual clause was to be applied which defined the parties to the contract as 'the Ecuadoran State, through Petroecuador, and the Contractor'. The Tribunal concluded that Petroecuador had a separate legal personality, but this did not mean that Petroecuador became a party to that contract.

on the part of the state itself, and also whether actions taken by those entities must be attributed to the state when it comes to liability for violation of treaty rights and relevant rights of the investor under general international law. Considerations of state unity also arise when the state entity is the respondent and measures by the state affect the relationship between the foreign investor and the state entity.

(b) Structure, function, and control

The relevant rules of attribution,[31] as found in general international law, are reflected in the ILC's Articles on State Responsibility.[32] The Articles differentiate between conduct by organs of the state (see Art 4, quoted above) and other entities, which are empowered to exercise elements of governmental authority, in Article 5. That Article provides:

Article 5 Conduct of persons or entities exercising elements of governmental authority

The conduct of a person or entity which is not an organ of the State under Article 4 but which is empowered by the law of that State to exercise elements of the governmental authority shall be considered an act of the State under international law, provided the person or entity is acting in that capacity in the particular instance.

Whereas Article 4 refers to attribution on the basis of structure, Article 5 refers to attribution on the basis of function. Recent jurisprudence of the International Centre for Settlement of Investment Disputes (ICSID) reflects this terminology referring to a 'structural test' (corresponding to the rule in Art 4) and a 'functional test' (along the lines of Art 5).[33]

Article 5 of the ILC's Articles covers the exercise of governmental authority by entities that do not fall into the category of 'organs of state'. The key term is 'governmental authority', and relevant cases will often turn on the meaning of this concept. The Commentary to the ILC's Articles adds the following explanation:

If it is to be regarded as an act of the State for purposes of international responsibility, the conduct of an entity must accordingly concern governmental activity and not other private or commercial activity in which the entity may engage. Thus, for example, the conduct of a railway company to which certain police powers have been granted will be regarded as an act of the State under international law if it concerns the exercise of those powers, but not if it concerns other activities (e.g. the sale of tickets or the purchase of rolling-stock).[34]

---

[31] On the development of the law, see K H Böckstiegel, 'Arbitration and State Enterprises' (1985) 1 *Arbitration International* 195.

[32] See eg *Noble Ventures v Romania*, Award, 12 October 2005, para 69.

[33] For a different understanding of these terms, see *LESI v Algeria*, Award, 12 November 2008, paras 106 et seq.

[34] J Crawford, *The International Law Commission's Articles on State Responsibility* (2002) 101. In *LESI v Algeria*, Award, 12 November 2008, the Tribunal examined, in paras 102 et seq, not just whether the entity in question exercised governmental functions and whether the act in question was of a governmental nature, but also whether the act was to be attributed in view of the specific complaint under the relevant standard of protection. On the need to consider (a) not only the powers of the entity in general, but (b) also the specific act in question, see *Jan de Nul v Egypt*, Award, 6 November 2008, paras 163–71 and *Hamester v Ghana*, Award, 18 June 2010, paras 202 et seq.

For the purpose of determining what is 'governmental', the ILC Commentary proposes to rely on the particular society and its traditions.[35] An alternative approach would be to focus on a comparative standard and to consider, from an objective point of view, what is normally regarded as 'governmental authority' in a contemporary setting. The formal designation in the particular domestic legal system should not be decisive. However, the manner in which the entity is empowered by the state, the content of the powers conferred, and the links between the entity and the state organs must be considered in the context of each case.

In addition to structure and function, the ILC Articles also use the criterion of state control over the entity. Article 8 of the Articles provides:

Article 8 Conduct directed or controlled by a State

The conduct of a person or group of persons shall be considered an act of a State under international law if the person or group of persons is in fact acting on the instructions of, or under the direction and control of, that State in carrying out the conduct.

The Commentary to the ILC Articles explains that 'where . . . the State was using its ownership interest in or control of a corporation specifically in order to achieve a particular result, the conduct in question has been attributed to the State'.[36]

Therefore, attribution to the state of conduct under the 'direction or control' of the state requires not only that the entity is generally controlled by the state but that the individual operation in question was effectively controlled and that the act was a genuine part of that operation.

Key terms of the Articles were drafted with a broad brush in general terms, leaving their application to tribunals addressing specific factual settings. Thus, simple reference to the text of the Articles cannot replace an appropriate analysis and explanation of the manner in which the specific setting of the case has to be understood in light of the Articles. In specific cases, the text of the Articles may have to serve as the starting point rather then the end of the reasoning.

It has been pointed out that the levels of control required for attribution under Article 8 in the context of an investment dispute may differ from the standard applied in other areas of international law, such as in the laws on armed intervention or international criminal responsibility.[37]

(c) Judicial practice on attribution

In practice, tribunals have often used a combination of the criteria of structure, function, and control.[38]

---

[35] J Crawford, *The International Law Commission's Articles on State Responsibility* (2002).
[36] Crawford, n 35, pp 112–13.
[37] See *Bayindir v Pakistan*, Award, 27 August 2009, para 130.
[38] For a detailed overview of tribunal practice, see J Crawford, 'Investment Arbitration and the ILC Articles on State Responsibility (with Appendix)' (2010) 25 *ICSID Review* 127.

This was particularly so where entities exercised diverse functions. In *Maffezini v Spain*,[39] the Tribunal made some general remarks about the different principles to be applied in deciding on attribution. It considered structure, function, and control:

The question whether or not SODIGA is a State entity must be examined first from a formal or structural point of view. Here a finding that the entity is owned by the State, directly or indirectly, gives rise to a rebuttable presumption that it is a State entity. The same result will obtain if an entity is controlled by the State, directly or indirectly. A similar presumption arises if an entity's purpose or objectives is the carrying out of functions which are governmental in nature or which are otherwise normally reserved to the State, or which by their nature are not usually carried out by private businesses or individuals.[40]

The *Maffezini* Tribunal examined various activities of a state entity, including giving advice to the investor and transfer of funds from the personal account of the investor by the entity. The Tribunal considered the advisory part as commercial and the transfer of funds as an exercise of public functions.[41] The Tribunal said:

In dealing with these questions, the Tribunal must again rely on the functional test, that is, it must establish whether specific acts or omissions are essentially commercial rather than governmental in nature or, conversely, whether their nature is essentially governmental rather than commercial. Commercial acts cannot be attributed to the Spanish State, while governmental acts should be so attributed.[42]

In *Salini v Morocco*,[43] the Tribunal ruled on the status of a Moroccan company (ADM) entrusted with the construction, maintenance, and operation of highways and major communication routes. The Tribunal considered, on the structural side, that ADM was a commercial company, incorporated as a limited liability company with its own legal personality. The state held 89 per cent of the stock of the company. The Board of Directors included, as President of ADM, the Minister of Infrastructure and a number of officials who depended upon the Minister of Economy and Finance. Thus, de facto, the state controlled and managed ADM. On the functional side, the Tribunal noted that the tasks of ADM, that is, the building of highways and communication routes, were matters of the state.[44] The Tribunal said:

---

[39] *Maffezini v Spain*, Decision on Jurisdiction, 25 January 2000. For a detailed analysis, see A Cohen Smutny, 'State Responsibility and Attribution. When Is a State Responsible for the Acts of State Enterprises? *Emilio Agustín Maffezini v The Kingdom of Spain*' in T Weiler (ed), *International Investment Law and Arbitration* (2005) 17.

[40] At para 77.

[41] Giving advice to a foreign investor regarding the cost of a project was deemed commercial, given that other commercial entities provide the same service. Advice on environmental legislation also did not give rise to state responsibility. However, the state entity was seen to carry out a governmental function when it transferred funds from the investor's account by way of granting a loan, not authorized by the investor, to a Spanish entity.

[42] At para 52.

[43] *Salini v Morocco*, Decision on Jurisdiction, 23 July 2001, paras 31 et seq.

[44] At para 33. See also *LESI/Dipenta v Algeria*, Award, 10 January 2005.

ADM being, both from a structural and functional point of view, a body distinguishable from the State only by virtue of its legal status, the Tribunal . . . concludes that the Italian companies have shown that ADM is a State company, acting in the name of the Kingdom of Morocco.[45]

The Tribunal in *Noble Ventures v Romania*,[46] had to consider the status of two Romanian entities, possessing legal personality, that were entrusted with the task of implementing a privatization programme under the control of the government. The two agencies exercised the state's rights in shareholder meetings, undertook measures to prepare for privatization, and sold shares held by the government. The Board of the agencies was appointed and dismissed by the Prime Minister and it included ex officio the President of the Romanian Development Agency.

In the Tribunal's view, the agencies could not be considered state organs within the meaning of Article 4 of the ILC Articles, since they were separate legal entities. However, the decision concludes that the two agencies 'acted as the empowered public institution under the Privatization Law'.[47] Therefore:

the Tribunal concludes that SOF and APAPS were entitled by law to represent the Respondent and did so in all of their actions as well as omissions. The acts allegedly in violation of the BIT are therefore attributable to the Respondent for the purposes of assessment under the BIT.[48]

In contrast to *Maffezini*, *Noble Ventures* rejected the position that governmental and commercial conduct is to be distinguished for purposes of attribution. The Tribunal stated:

in the context of responsibility, it is difficult to see why commercial acts, so called *acta iure gestionis*, should by definition not be attributable while governmental acts, so called *acta iure imperii*, should be attributable. The ILC-Draft does not maintain or support such a distinction. Apart from the fact that there is no reason why one should not regard commercial acts as being in principle also attributable, it is difficult to define whether a particular act is governmental. There is a widespread consensus in international law, as in particular expressed in the discussions in the ILC regarding attribution, that there is no common understanding in international law of what constitutes a governmental or public act.[49]

However, this position differs from the ILC Articles. They assume that attribution, regardless of the nature of the act, applies only with respect to state organs.[50] *Noble*

---

[45] At para 35.

[46] *Noble Ventures v Romania*, Award, 12 October 2005, paras 69 et seq.

[47] At para 79.

[48] At para 80. Another example of an entity exercising governmental functions is a state Board set up in Ghana, with the mission of regulating the export and marketing of cocoa, promoting production and cultivation, and undertaking research for improving the quality of cocoa. See *Hamester v Ghana*, Award, 18 June 2010, para 189.

[49] At para 82.

[50] J Crawford, *The International Law Commission's Articles on State Responsibility* (2002) 96. In this sense: *Alpha v Ukraine*, Award, 8 November 2010, para 402.

Ventures extends this position beyond state organs to separate state agencies, based on the assumption that it is difficult to define a 'governmental act'.

Impregilo v Pakistan[51] did not address an issue of state responsibility for conduct violating a rule of international law but responsibility of a state for breach of a municipal law contract. The Tribunal distinguished between governmental acts, in this case violations of the BIT, and simple breaches of contract. It said:

> a clear distinction exists between the responsibility of a State for the conduct of an entity that violates international law (e.g. a breach of Treaty), and the responsibility of a State for the conduct of an entity that breaches a municipal law contract (i.e. Impregilo's Contract Claims).[52]

On this basis, the Tribunal found that its jurisdiction did not extend to mere breach of a contract to which an entity other than the state was a named party.[53]

In *Toto v Lebanon*,[54] the Tribunal had to rule on the attribution of the acts of a Lebanese entity (CEPG) which undertook public works projects entrusted to it by the Ministry of Public Works and Projects. The funding of CEPG came from the state and the top management of CEPG was appointed by the Council of Ministers. A second entity (CDR), the successor of CEPG, acted as an agent of the state, as a consultant to the Ministry and the legislative branch, and all its plans and projects were subject to approval by the Council of Ministers. The Tribunal found that both CEPG and CDR exercised governmental authority in the sense of Article 5 of the ILC Articles.

Other decisions similarly look at a combination of structure, function, and control in order to determine the attribution of actions of state entities to the state.[55] In strict theory, the presence of any one of the possible criteria (status as state organ, governmental function, control) would suffice to establish attribution. In practice, tribunals have not followed the strict separation of these categories but have typically looked at them in conjunction.

Generally, the practice of tribunals is consistent with the position that delegating the state's activities to separate entities will not permit avoidance of responsibility for breach of a treaty.

---

[51] *Impregilo v Pakistan*, Decision on Jurisdiction, 22 April 2005.

[52] At para 210.

[53] In support of its decision, the Tribunal cited *RFCC v Morocco*, Decision on Jurisdiction, 16 July 2001, para 68 and *Cable Television of Nevis v Federation of St Kitts and Nevis*, Award, 13 January 1997, para 2.22.

[54] *Toto v Lebanon*, Decision on Jurisdiction, 11 September 2009, paras 51 et seq.

[55] *Wintershall v Qatar*, Partial Award, 5 February 1988, 28 ILM 795, 811 et seq; *Nycomb v Latvia*, Award, 16 December 2003, sec 4.2; *Waste Management v Mexico*, Award, 30 April 2004, para 75; *LESI-Dipenta v Algeria*, Award, 10 January 2005, para 19; *EnCana Corp v Ecuador*, Award, 3 February 2006, para 154; *Jan de Nul v Egypt*, Decision on Jurisdiction, 16 June 2006, paras 83–9; *Helnan v Egypt*, Decision on Jurisdiction, 17 October 2006, paras 91–3; *AMTO v Ukraine*, Award, 26 March 2008, paras 31, 101–2; *LESI v Algeria*, Award, 12 November 2008, paras 102–16; *Bayindir v Pakistan*, Award, 27 August 2009, paras 111–30; *EDF v Romania*, Award, 8 October 2009, paras 185–214.

(d) State responsibility for failure to protect

In addition to these forms of attribution, a state may be liable as a consequence of acts of entities if it was under an obligation to protect the investor from adverse action but failed to do so. In this situation, state responsibility does not arise from attribution but as a consequence of an independent obligation to protect the investor. This obligation may arise either as part of the international minimum standard under customary international law or on the basis of an obligation contained in a BIT or other treaty. Under customary international law, as well as under investment treaties, host states are under an obligation to protect investors against illegal interference. In BITs this standard is either described as full protection and security[56] or is seen as part of the fair and equitable treatment standard.[57] The duty to protect is not directed specifically at state entities; it also includes protection against the acts of private persons within the limits of due diligence. But in view of the supervision and control exercised by the state over state entities, as well as of the knowledge of their planned and actual activities, there is a heightened duty to protect the investor against adverse actions of such entities.

In *Amco v Indonesia*,[58] PT Wisma took over the hotel that was the investment by force, with the assistance of members of the Indonesian armed forces. In the Tribunal's view, the fact that PT Wisma had a close relationship with the army did not make its acts attributable to Indonesia. But the assistance and lack of protection by the army/police in connection with the act of illegal self-help committed by PT Wisma was an international wrong for which the Republic bore responsibility. In that respect:

The Tribunal finds that although it is proven that a close relationship exists between PT Wisma and Inkopad, and between the latter and the armed forces . . . this fact in itself does not attribute the acts of PT Wisma or its leadership to the Government of Indonesia. . . .

It is a generally accepted rule of international law, clearly stated in international awards and judgments and generally accepted in the literature, that a State has a duty to protect aliens and their investment against unlawful acts committed by some of its citizens. . . .

. . . [T]he acts of PT Wisma . . . were illegal self-help and the assistance to these acts given to PT Wisma and lack of protection afforded to PT Amco, a foreign investor in Indonesia by the army/police was an international wrong attributable to the Republic.[59]

In *Wena Hotels v Egypt*,[60] agents of EHC had taken over the investment by force. EHC had the status of a public sector company and its sole shareholder was Egypt. The shareholder assembly was chaired by the Minister of Tourism who appointed one half of the Directors of the company, nominated its Chairman, and had the power to dismiss members of the Board. Moreover, ECH operated within broad policy guidelines issued by the government and EHC's money was treated as 'public money' by the government. Despite these findings relating to structure,

---

[56] See pp 160 et seq.   [57] See pp 130 et seq.
[58] *Amco v Indonesia*, Award, 20 November 1984.
[59] At paras 162, 172, and 178.
[60] *Wena Hotels v Egypt*, Award, 8 December 2000.

function, and control,[61] the Tribunal preferred to base its decision on Egypt's failure to protect the investment:

The Tribunal agrees with Wena that Egypt violated its obligation under Article 2(2) of the IPPA [the BIT] to accord Wena's investment 'fair and equitable treatment' and 'full protection and security.' Although it is not clear that Egyptian officials other than officials of EHC directly participated in the April 1, 1991 seizures, there is substantial evidence that Egypt was aware of EHC's intentions to seize the hotels and took no actions to prevent EHC from doing so.[62]

3. Party status for constituent subdivisions or agencies under the ICSID Convention

The Convention on the Settlement of Investment Disputes between States and Nationals of Other States (ICSID Convention) in Article 25(1) and (3) foresees the possibility that a constituent subdivision or agency of a state may become a party to arbitration proceedings provided it has been designated to ICSID and if the consent of that entity has been approved by the state.[63] Little use has been made of this provision.[64] Its procedural aspects are described in Chapter X on dispute settlement.[65]

The possibility of designating territorial subdivisions and entities and making them parties to proceedings does not affect the attribution of their actions to the central government.[66] The jurisdictional nature of Article 25 makes it clear that the rule addresses the determination of jurisdiction *ratione personae*.[67] Article 25(1) does not set forth any principle of attribution to the state, but merely opens the possibility for the host state to delegate party status to its territorial subdivision or entity for jurisdictional and procedural purposes.

The question whether a particular constituent subdivision or entity is eligible for this purpose is left to the relevant domestic law. The consequence of a designation is that the entity itself may become a party to ICSID proceedings if a dispute arises out of a relationship between the investor and the legal entity, provided that the entity has consented to ICSID jurisdiction and the state has approved the consent by the entity.[68]

---

[61] At paras 65–9.   [62] At para 84.

[63] Article 25(1) of the ICSID Convention, after the reference to the contracting state party to the proceedings, adds in parentheses, '(or any constituent subdivision or agency of a Contracting State designated to the Centre by that State)'. Article 25(3) provides: 'Consent by a constituent subdivision or agency of a Contracting State shall require the approval of that State unless that State notifies the Centre that no such approval is required.'

[64] A number of states have made designations that are listed on ICSID's website at <http://icsid.worldbank.org/ICSID/Index.jsp>. See also *Tanzania Electric v Independent Power Tanzania*, Award, 12 July 2001, para 13.

[65] See pp 249–50.

[66] *Vivendi v Argentina*, Award, 21 November 2000, paras 46–9.

[67] C Schreuer et al, *The ICSID Convention: A Commentary* (2009), Art 25, paras 230 et seq.

[68] For details, see Schreuer, n 67, paras 230 et seq and 903 et seq.

IX

Political Risk Insurance

The risk for the investor inherent in major investment projects has led to the evolution of a market for investment insurance schemes.[1] The first phase of insurance programmes commenced in the 1950s and was entirely dominated by insurers run by national governments, which sought to promote the outgoing investments of their nationals. In the United States, the Agency for International Development carried out the task until the Overseas Private Investment Corporation (OPIC) took over in 1971. In the early 1970s, private insurers entered the market, beginning with Lloyd's in London and the American International Group (AIG) in New York. In 1985 the member states of the World Bank decided to establish an international organization, the Multilateral Investment Guarantee Agency (MIGA), for the same purpose. The Inter Arab Development Bank is charged primarily with underwriting investment insurance on the regional level.[2]

The purpose of national programmes is tied to the promotion of the national economy. Often, protection is granted only to national companies and their projects in countries friendly to the investor's home country. Covered risks are usually expropriation, non-convertibility of currency, and political violence. OPIC, for instance, covers matters of expropriation, non-convertibility, and losses due to war, revolution, insurrection, and civil strife.[3]

Some of the national programmes are subsidized, such as the German one, while others such as OPIC in the United States purport to act without a burden to the taxpayer. The creation of the MIGA was prompted, according to its Preamble, by the recognition 'that the flow of foreign investment to developing countries would be facilitated and further encouraged by alleviating concerns related to non-commercial risks.'

Private companies entered the investment insurance market on the assumption of higher efficiency and an acceptable margin of profit. In its original context and design, the private programmes emerged as extensions of traditional forms of marine insurance.

Private insurers seek to diversify their own risk by schemes of mutual cooperation with other companies and also by leveraging their operations by reliance on reinsurers. They have the advantage, vis-à-vis the public sector, of being able to

---

[1] According to a report published in 2009, only 14 per cent of the total global flow of foreign direct investment is covered by insurance, see MIGA Report, *World Investment and Political Risk* (2009) 34.

[2] See I Shihata, 'Regional Investment Insurance Project' (1972) 6 *J World Trade Law* 185.

[3] See USC § 2194.

tailor their products to the needs of the individual company insured. They can price and accept or reject risk based on commercial considerations and are able to act speedily and flexibly. According to an agreement among private insurers (Waterborne Agreement), they exclude nuclear risks, but will otherwise underwrite war risk on a controlled basis as part of a political risk account and now routinely insure against terrorism, although this risk is often supported by government-backed reinsurance. Private insurers do not in practice cover the risk of currency devaluation or depreciation.

The strongest difference between private and public insurers concerns the time horizon of the insurance offered: whereas the public sector has been prepared to offer coverage for up to 20 years, private companies typically limit their risk by offering protection for much shorter periods. While some private market political risk insurers offer coverage for up to 15 years, others limit themselves to much shorter periods, sometimes only for three years, subject to renewal.

The existence, side by side, of these actors presents a unique panorama of competitive and complementary services by the private sector, national governmental agencies, and international actors. Expectations held previously that the activities of the private sector might obviate or crowd out the need for the service of public institutions turned out to be unrealistic, at least over the past decades. Some government agencies, notably OPIC, seek to cooperate with the private sector and not just to compete with it. The result is often coinsurance and reinsurance.

To some extent, governmental insurance programmes reflect foreign policy goals of the government especially as regards eligibility of projects. Also, major types of investment risks have remained so difficult to assess in mathematical terms or so risk prone that private insurers have decided not to cover them. Thus, national insurance agencies work in a hybrid manner, reflecting principles of prudent private risk management but also governmental characteristics.

As for competition between domestic insurers, private and public, and MIGA, they differ in their willingness to accept various types of risk and offer different rates for different packages of insurance. Altogether, overlapping elements exist among the policies and activities of the different insurers, and the divergences are explained by the different goals and institutional settings. The various existing regimes diverge in part in regard to the types of investment covered. Exports are covered by MIGA if they contribute significantly to a specific investment.[4] Activities of the host state when acting as a purchaser, supplier, manager, and creditor are excluded from coverage by OPIC.[5] MIGA is only prepared to insure an investment that satisfies its understanding of economic soundness and has received host country approval.[6] The rules of MIGA do not, however, require specific standards of protection of foreign investment in the host country. This is because MIGA only insures

---

[4] 'Commentary on the Convention Establishing the Multilateral Investment Guarantee Agency' (1986) 1 *ICSID Review-FILJ* 193, 201.

[5] See Art 4.03(b) of the OPIC Contract of Insurance Against Inconvertibility, Expropriation, Political Violence (Form 234 KGT 12–85, 2nd rev), reprinted in R D Bishop, J Crawford, and W M Reisman, *Foreign Investment Disputes* (2005) 517, 519.

[6] See Convention Establishing the Multilateral Investment Guarantee Agency, Arts 12(d) and 15.

risk in 'MIGA member' countries where there is a bilateral agreement between MIGA and the host government.

It has been the general practice of government insurers to conclude agreements with host countries that provide for subrogation. This means that the investor's rights against the host country are assigned to the insurer upon payment under the insurance contract. Some countries, such as Germany, include clauses to this effect in bilateral investment treaties (BITs), whereas others, such as the United States, conclude specific agreements for this purpose. In Germany, governmental insurance will only be granted for investments in countries that have concluded a BIT with Germany or in which a similar degree of legal security exists.

With regard to the types of risk covered, these are similar to those addressed in BITs. Beyond the protection of assets, most programmes offer protection against non-compliance with contracts. Also, the risks of currency inconvertibility and restrictions on currency transfer are covered. Of course, all schemes provide for protection against direct and indirect expropriation, and some government insurers, for example OPIC, and most private insurers also cover cases of business interruption. Remarkably, the MIGA Convention in Chapter III, Article 11(a)(ii) specifically provides that no loss is covered arising from 'non-discriminatory measures of general application which governments normally take for the purpose of regulating economic activity in their territories'. Risks of war and civil disturbance are generally covered. OPIC (and most other government insurers and the larger private sector underwriters) will not cover projects that violate international environmental standards, create unreasonable health risks, or fail to respect human rights, in particular workers' rights.[7]

Concerning protection of non-compliance with contracts, repudiation or breach is covered by MIGA if the holder of the guarantee does not have access to a judicial and arbitral forum or the decision of such a forum is not rendered within a reasonable period as defined by MIGA, or such a decision is not enforced.[8] Non-payment of an obligation under an arbitral award may constitute an expropriation as understood in international law and as covered by an insurance contract, even if the host country considers that it is not able to pay the amount due under the arbitral award.[9]

Disputes have arisen between insured investors and the insurer when the two sides have disagreed on the interpretation or application of the insurance contract. Typically, such disputes are resolved through arbitration provided for in the insurance contracts. Often, the resulting decisions deal with legal issues that appear

---

[7] See generally M Perry, 'A Model for Efficient Aid: The Case for Political Risk Insurance Activities of the Overseas Private Investment Corporation' (1996) 36 *Virginia J Int'l L* 511; see USC 22, §§ 2199 et seq.

[8] See MIGA Convention, Ch III, Art 11(a)(ii).

[9] See eg *MidAmerican Energy Holdings Company v OPIC*, citing the *Restatement (Third) of Foreign Relations Law* (1999), § 712, cmt h and the Harvard Draft Convention on the International Responsibility of States for Injuries to Aliens; an excerpt of the case is reprinted in D Bishop, J Crawford, and M Reisman, *Foreign Investment Disputes* (2005) 563 et seq. But see also the position that non-payment of debts will not amount to an expropriation (*Waste Management*), p 129.

similar to those that arise in the relationship between the host state and the investor in the context of a BIT. For instance, the investor may claim that its treatment by the host state amounts to an indirect expropriation as covered by an insurance contract.

In a number of disputes, tribunals set up under insurance contracts have addressed legal issues of expropriation, currency inconvertibility, breaches of contract, the consequences of political violence, and attribution. Some decisions of these tribunals set up under insurance contracts have been relied upon in disputes between investors and states.[10] The authority of arbitral awards rendered under insurance contracts to disputes between states and foreign investors will depend, not least, on whether the provisions in insurance contracts and the standards of protection in treaties and customary international law are the same.

---

[10] The Award in *Revere Copper v OPIC*, Award, 24 August 1978, 56 ILR (1980) 258, is often cited in the context of defining an indirect expropriation.

X

Settling Investment Disputes

1. State v state disputes

(a) Diplomatic protection

Under traditional international law investors did not have direct access to international remedies to pursue claims against foreign states for violation of their rights. They depended on diplomatic protection by their home states. A state exercising diplomatic protection espouses the claim of its national against another state and pursues it in its own name.[1] The Permanent Court of International Justice (PCIJ) explained in the *Mavrommatis Palestine Concessions* case:

> It is an elementary principle of international law that a State is entitled to protect its subjects, when injured by acts contrary to international law committed by another State, from whom they have been unable to obtain satisfaction through the ordinary channels. By taking up the case of one of its subjects and by resorting to diplomatic action or international judicial proceedings on his behalf, a State is in reality asserting its own rights—its right to ensure, in the person of its subjects, respect for the rules of international law.[2]

Diplomatic protection is subject to several conditions. The investor, whether it is an individual or a corporation, must be a national of the protecting state. This bond of nationality must have existed continuously from the time of the injury until the claim is presented or, according to some, until the claim is settled. In addition, the investor must have exhausted the local remedies in the state that has allegedly committed the violation.

The usefulness of diplomatic protection is limited. The investor has no right to diplomatic protection but depends on the political discretion of its government. The government may refuse to take up the claim, it may discontinue diplomatic protection at any time, and it may even waive the national's claim or agree to a reduced settlement. In other words, the investor is never in control of the process. As the International Court of Justice (ICJ) said in the *Barcelona Traction* case:[3]

---

[1] The International Law Commission adopted Draft Articles on Diplomatic Protection in 2006. See Official Records of the General Assembly, 61st Session, Supplement No 10 (A/61/10). The General Assembly took note of the draft articles in Res 61/35.

[2] *Mavrommatis Palestine Concessions Case*, PCIJ, Series A, No 2, 12.

[3] *Barcelona Traction, Light and Power Co, Ltd (Belgium v Spain)*, Judgment, 5 February 1970, ICJ Reports (1970) 44.

79. The State must be viewed as the sole judge to decide whether its protection will be granted, to what extent it is granted, and when it will cease. It retains in this respect a discretionary power the exercise of which may be determined by considerations of a political or other nature, unrelated to the particular case. Since the claim of the State is not identical with that of the individual or corporate person whose cause is espoused, the State enjoys complete freedom of action.

Diplomatic protection on behalf of investors also carries important disadvantages for the states concerned.[4] It can seriously disrupt their international relations, leading to protracted disputes. Developing countries resent pressure from capital-exporting countries whether it is exercised bilaterally or in multilateral fora such as international lending institutions. Diplomatic protection in investment disputes by capital-exporting countries against developing countries has been a frequent source of irritation for the latter.

Some countries have gone as far as challenging the permissibility of diplomatic protection. Under the so-called Calvo Doctrine, Latin American countries have sought to exclude any special rights for foreigners.[5] This has led them to reject diplomatic protection as an undesirable or even impermissible interference in their internal affairs or to limit it to cases of denial of justice.

Where the investor's state of nationality decides to exercise diplomatic protection, the primary method of dispute settlement is negotiation. If negotiations prove fruitless, the protecting state may resort to international adjudication, including the ICJ. Examples of cases involving the protection of investors brought to the ICJ are the *Barcelona Traction* case and the *ELSI* case.[6] Diplomatic protection may also lead to arbitration between the two states.[7] Nearly all bilateral investment treaties (BITs) contain arbitration clauses for the settlement of disputes arising from their application between the contracting states. The arbitration clauses are often supplemented by provisions that require consultations and negotiations.

Alternatively, states may resort to unfriendly measures or countermeasures (reprisals). This right is limited by the prohibition of the use of force. Therefore, armed force against a host state is not a permissible means of protecting the rights of foreign investors.

As will be described below, in many cases investors have been granted direct access to effective means of international dispute settlement. As a consequence, investment disputes between states have become rare. In many situations investors no longer depend on the diplomatic protection by their home states.

The right to exercise diplomatic protection may be curtailed by treaty provisions. The Convention on the Settlement of Investment Disputes between States and Nationals of Other States (ICSID Convention) provides in Article 27(1) that,

---

[4] I Shihata, 'Towards a Greater Depoliticization of Investment Disputes: the Roles of ICSID and MIGA' in I Shihata, *The World Bank in a Changing World* (1991) 309.
[5] See D Shea, *The Calvo Clause* (1955).
[6] *Case Concerning the Elettronica Sicula SpA (ELSI) (US v Italy)*, Judgment, 20 July 1989, ICJ Reports (1989) 15.
[7] See eg the *Martini Case*, Award, 3 May 1930, 2 RIAA 974; *Canevaro Case*, Award, 3 May 1912, 11 RIAA 397; *Italy v Cuba*, Award, 15 January 2008.

where consent to investor-state arbitration under the Convention exists, a contracting state may not give diplomatic protection or bring an international claim. However, under Article 27(2) this does not exclude informal diplomatic exchanges for the sole purpose of facilitating settlement of the dispute. In the course of the Convention's drafting, the exclusion of diplomatic protection was explained, inter alia, in terms of the removal of the dispute from the realm of politics and diplomacy into the realm of law.[8] The guarantee against diplomatic protection may constitute a strong incentive for host states to consent to investor-state arbitration. Any violation of the prohibition to exercise diplomatic protection under Article 27(1) of the ICSID Convention would not affect the jurisdiction of the ICSID tribunal.[9]

Even under the ICSID Convention, the right to diplomatic protection continues to exist in favour of an investor who has prevailed in investor-state arbitration if the host state fails to comply with the award. Until recently, diplomatic protection to secure compliance with awards appears to have played little, if any, practical role.

Article 64 of the ICSID Convention provides that a dispute between parties to the Convention concerning its interpretation or application is to be referred to the ICJ unless it can be settled by negotiation or the states concerned agree on another method of settlement. The context of this provision and its drafting history make it clear that this procedure is not to be used to interfere in investor-state dispute settlement proceedings.[10]

(b) Direct disputes between states

Apart from the espousal of a particular investor's claim, a dispute may arise between states simply as a consequence of a general violation of international law, in particular of a treaty protecting investments.

BITs typically contain two clauses on dispute settlement: one offers arbitration between the host state and an investor; another provides for arbitration between the contracting parties to the treaty. During the ICSID Convention's drafting there seemed to be consensus that inter-state arbitration should neither interfere in investor-state cases nor affect the finality of ICSID awards.[11]

In *Lucchetti v Peru*, the investor had initiated arbitration against the host state under a BIT. Thereupon the respondent state initiated inter-state proceedings under the BIT against Chile, the investor's home state, and sought a suspension of the investor-state proceedings. Peru argued that interpretative priority should be given to the state-state proceedings. The Tribunal in the investor-state proceedings declined the request for the suspension of proceedings[12] and Peru did not subsequently pursue the inter-state proceedings.

---

[8] *History of the Convention*, vol II, Part 1, pp 242, 273, 303, 372, 464.
[9] *Banro American v Congo*, Award, 1 September 2000, paras 18, 19; *Autopista v Venezuela*, Decision on Jurisdiction, 27 September 2001, paras 75, 140.
[10] See especially the Report of the Executive Directors to the Convention, para 45.
[11] *History of the Convention*, vol II, pp 65–6, 273, 274, 349, 350, 433, 435, 527–8, 576–7.
[12] *Lucchetti v Peru*, Award on Jurisdiction, 7 February 2005, paras 7, 9.

In a case brought under the BIT between Italy and Cuba,[13] Italy relied on the clause for the settlement of disputes between the two contracting states. Italy presented two types of claim: one category was based on the diplomatic protection of its nationals; the other concerned Italy's own rights under the BIT. The Tribunal held that the exhaustion of local remedies was required for the claims based on diplomatic protection but not for Italy's pursuit of its own rights. The several claims failed for a variety of jurisdictional and merits-related reasons.

2. Investor v state disputes

(a) The limited usefulness of domestic courts

In the absence of an agreement to the contrary, an investment dispute between a state and a foreign investor would normally have to be settled by the host state's courts. Conflict of laws rules will normally point to these courts since the dispute is likely to have the closest connection to the state in which the investment is made.

From the investor's perspective, this is not an attractive solution. Rightly or wrongly, the investor will fear a lack of impartiality from the courts of the state against which it wishes to pursue its claim. In many countries, an independent judiciary cannot be taken for granted and executive interventions in court proceedings or a sense of judicial loyalty to the forum state are likely to influence the outcome. This is particularly so where large amounts of money are involved.

Not infrequently, legislation is the cause of complaints by investors. Domestic courts will often be bound to apply the local law even if it is at odds with international legal rules protecting the rights of investors. In fact, in some countries the relevant treaties may not even be part of the domestic legal order. At times, domestic courts may be the perpetrators of the alleged violation of investor rights.[14] Even where courts decide in the investor's favour, the executive may ignore their decisions.[15] In all these situations domestic courts cannot offer an effective remedy to foreign investors.

The courts of the investor's home country and of third states are usually not a viable alternative. In most cases they lack territorial jurisdiction over investments taking place in another state. An agreement on forum selection for investment disputes in a state other than the host state is unlikely to be accepted by the latter. The only exception is loan contracts which are often subject to the jurisdiction and the law of a major financial centre.

An additional obstacle to using domestic courts outside the host state would be rules of state immunity. Host states dealing with foreign investors will frequently act in the exercise of sovereign powers (*jure imperii*) rather than in a commercial capacity (*jure gestionis*). Therefore, even in countries which follow a doctrine of

---

[13] *Italy v Cuba*, Award, 15 January 2008.
[14] *Saipem v Bangladesh*, Award, 30 June 2009.
[15] *Siag v Egypt*, Award, 1 June 2009, paras 436, 448, 453–6.

restrictive immunity, lawsuits against foreign states arising from investment disputes are likely to fail.[16] An explicit waiver of immunity is possible but will be difficult to obtain.

In addition to sovereign immunity, other judicial doctrines are likely to stand in the way of lawsuits in domestic courts. The act-of-state doctrine enjoins courts from examining the legality of official acts of foreign states in their own territory. For instance, the US Supreme Court has stated that it would not examine the validity of a taking of property by a foreign government in its territory even if its illegality under international law is alleged.[17] Further obstacles to lawsuits against host states in domestic courts of other states would be related doctrines of non-justiciability, political questions, and lack of a close connection to the local legal system.[18]

It is mainly for these reasons that alternative methods have been created for the settlement of disputes between states and foreign investors. They consist primarily of granting the foreign investor direct access to arbitration with the host state.

(b) Arbitration and conciliation

The gaps left by the traditional methods of dispute settlement (diplomatic protection and action in domestic courts) has led to the idea of offering investors direct access to effective international procedures, especially arbitration. This carries advantages for both the investor and the host state. The advantage for the investor is obvious: it gains access to an effective international remedy. The advantage to the host state is twofold: by offering an international procedure for dispute settlement it improves its investment climate and is likely to attract more foreign investment. Also, by consenting to international arbitration the host state shields itself against other processes, notably diplomatic protection.

In addition, arbitration is usually more efficient than litigation through regular courts. It offers the parties the opportunity to select arbitrators who enjoy their confidence and who have the necessary expertise in the field. Moreover, the private nature of arbitration, assuring the confidentiality of proceedings, is often valued by parties to major economic development projects. But confidentiality has also come under attack, leading to calls for more transparency.[19]

In the vast majority of cases the method chosen for the international settlement of investor-state disputes is arbitration. A second method is conciliation. Conciliation is flexible and relatively informal. It is designed to assist the parties in reaching an agreed settlement. It takes place before a conciliation commission that examines the facts and prepares a report that suggests a solution but is not binding on the parties. The ICSID Convention treats conciliation and arbitration as equivalent

---

[16] See *SGS v Pakistan*, Decision on Jurisdiction, 6 August 2003, paras 20–5 for a description of proceedings before the courts of Switzerland.

[17] *Banco Nacional de Cuba v Sabbatino*, 376 US 398, 3 ILM 381 (1964).

[18] *Chilean Copper Case*, Landgericht Hamburg, 22 January 1973, 13 March 1974.

[19] See below pp 286–8.

alternatives.[20] But conciliation is rarely used, whereas there is frequent resort to arbitration. The reason is evidently that conciliation leaves the final word with the disputing parties. Occasionally, a conciliation procedure is a necessary prerequisite for arbitration.

Some dispute settlement clauses offer both arbitration and conciliation by either mentioning both or by referring to the ICSID Convention without further specification. In a situation of this kind, the choice between the two methods is with the party initiating proceedings. In *SPP v Egypt*,[21] jurisdiction was based on domestic legislation which provided for the settlement of disputes 'within the framework of the [ICSID] Convention'. Egypt argued that this phrase was insufficient to express consent to arbitration since it did not refer expressly to arbitration. The Tribunal rejected this argument:

Nowhere...does the [ICSID] Convention say that consent to the Centre's jurisdiction must specify whether the consent is for purposes of arbitration or conciliation. Once consent has been given 'to the jurisdiction of the Centre', the Convention and its implementing regulations afford the means for making the choice between the two methods of dispute settlement. The Convention leaves that choice to the party instituting the proceedings.[22]

In contrast to conciliation, arbitration is more formal and adversarial. Most importantly, it leads to a binding decision based on law. This is the reason why claimants prefer arbitration over conciliation. In most cases it seems wiser to direct the necessary effort and expense to proceedings that lead to a binding decision.

The existence of an effective system of dispute settlement is likely to have an effect even without its actual use. The mere availability of an effective remedy will influence the behaviour of parties to potential disputes. It is likely to have a restraining influence on investors as well as on host states. Both sides will try to avoid actions that might involve them in arbitration that they are likely to lose. In addition, the parties' willingness to settle a dispute amicably will be strengthened by the existence of an arbitration clause.

Investment arbitration uses a mechanism originally developed for the settlement of commercial disputes between private parties. The main characteristics of commercial disputes are often also present in investor-state arbitrations. But the application of international law rules governing the conduct of the state means that investor-state arbitration has its own distinctive features. In some respects investment arbitration performs the function of judicial review of administrative acts. This situation finds expression in the fact that states have negotiated the ICSID Convention as a distinct set of rules for investment disputes. At the same time, mechanisms that have been devised primarily for classical commercial disputes between two private entities are also used for the settlement of investment disputes.

---

[20] The ICSID Convention deals with conciliation in Arts 28–35.
[21] *SPP v Egypt*, Decision on Jurisdiction II, 14 April 1988.
[22] At para 102.

(c) Arbitration institutions and regimes

Arbitration between a host state and a foreign investor may take place in the framework of a variety of institutions or rules. If arbitration is not supported by a particular arbitration institution, it is referred to as ad hoc arbitration. Ad hoc arbitration requires an arbitration agreement that regulates a number of issues. These include selection of arbitrators, applicable law, and a large number of procedural questions. A number of institutions, such as UNCITRAL, have developed standard rules that may be incorporated into the parties' agreement.

aa. ICSID

The majority of cases are brought under the Convention on the Settlement of Investment Disputes between States and Nationals of Other States.[23] The Convention was drafted in the framework of the World Bank, was adopted on 18 March 1965 in Washington DC, and entered into force on 14 October 1966. It created the International Centre for Settlement of Investment Disputes which is why the Convention is commonly referred to as the ICSID Convention. Sometimes it is also referred to as the Washington Convention. By summer 2012, 148 states were parties to the Convention.[24]

The aim of the ICSID Convention, as expressed in its Preamble, is to promote economic development through the creation of a favourable investment climate. ICSID provides a system of dispute settlement that is designed exclusively for investor-state disputes. It offers standard clauses for use by the parties, detailed rules of procedure, and institutional support.[25] The institutional support extends not only to the selection of arbitrators but also to the conduct of arbitration proceedings: for instance, each tribunal is assisted by a legal secretary who is a staff member of ICSID; venues for hearings are arranged by ICSID; and all financial arrangements surrounding the arbitration are administered by ICSID. The Secretary-General of ICSID exercises a screening power over requests for arbitration and will refuse to register a request that is manifestly outside ICSID's jurisdiction.

The jurisdiction of ICSID requires an investment dispute of a legal nature between a state party to the Convention and a national of another state that is also a party to the Convention. In addition, the two parties to the dispute (the host state and the investor) must have consented to ICSID's jurisdiction.[26] Participation

---

[23] 575 UNTS 159; 4 ILM 524 (1965).

[24] Three states have terminated their participation by denouncing the ICSID Convention in accordance with its Art 71: Bolivia on 2 May 2007; Ecuador on 6 July 2009; and Venezuela on 24 January 2012.

[25] For a concise overview, see L Reed, J Paulsson, and N Blackaby, *Guide to ICSID Arbitration* (2004). For a more detailed exposition, see C Schreuer, L Malintoppi, A Reinisch, and A Sinclair, *The ICSID Convention: A Commentary*, 2nd edn (2009).

[26] ICSID Convention, Art 25(1) provides in relevant part:

The jurisdiction of the Centre shall extend to any legal dispute arising directly out of an investment, between a Contracting State (or any constituent subdivision or agency of a

in the ICSID Convention is not sufficient to establish jurisdiction since it does not amount to consent to jurisdiction.[27]

Proceedings under the ICSID Convention are self-contained. This means that they are independent of the intervention of any outside bodies. In particular, domestic courts have no power to stay, to compel, or to otherwise influence ICSID proceedings. Nor do domestic courts have the power to set aside or otherwise review ICSID awards.

ICSID proceedings are not threatened by the non-cooperation of a party. If one of the parties fails to act, the proceedings will not be stalled. The Convention provides a watertight system against the frustration of proceedings by a recalcitrant party: arbitrators not appointed by the parties will be appointed by the Centre;[28] the decision on whether there is jurisdiction in a particular case is with the tribunal;[29] non-submission of memorials or non-appearance at hearings by a party will not stall the proceedings;[30] and non-cooperation by a party will not affect the award's binding force and enforceability.

ICSID Awards are binding and final and not subject to review except under the narrow conditions provided by the Convention itself (Arts 49–52). Non-compliance with an Award by a state would be a breach of the Convention and would lead to a revival of the right to diplomatic protection by the investor's state of nationality (Arts 53 and 27). The Convention provides its own system of enforcement: awards are recognized as final in all states parties to the Convention. Pecuniary obligations arising from Awards are to be enforced in the same way as final judgments of the local courts in all states parties to the Convention (Art 54).

ICSID had a slow start—the Convention entered into force in 1966 but the first case was not registered until 1972. The 1970s and 1980s saw steady but only intermittent action; one or two cases per year were typical for that period. Since the mid-1990s there has been a dramatic increase in activity. In 1995 there were four ICSID arbitrations pending and in summer 2012 about 150 cases were pending.[31] During 2011 the Secretary-General registered 33 new cases.

Contracting State designated to the Centre by that State) and a national of another Contracting State, which the parties to the dispute consent in writing to submit to the Centre.

[27] ICSID Convention, Preamble, para 7:

Declaring that no Contracting State shall by the mere fact of its ratification, acceptance or approval of this Convention and without its consent be deemed to be under any obligation to submit any particular dispute to conciliation or arbitration . . .

[28] Article 38.
[29] Article 41.
[30] Article 45.
[31] For detailed information on pending cases, see <http://www.worldbank.org/icsid/cases/pending.htm>.

bb. ICSID Additional Facility

In 1978 the Administrative Council of ICSID created the Additional Facility.[32] It is open to parties that submit to its jurisdiction in certain cases that are outside ICSID's jurisdiction. The most important situation involves cases in which only one side is either a party the ICSID Convention or a national of a party to the ICSID Convention. Additional categories include cases which do not directly arise from an investment and fact-finding.[33]

The practical relevance of the Additional Facility lies in cases where either the host state or the investor's home state is not a party to the ICSID Convention. This has become especially important in the context of the North American Free Trade Agreement (NAFTA) since only the United States has ratified the ICSID Convention but Canada and Mexico have not.[34] Article 1120 of the NAFTA offers consent to arbitration alternatively under the ICSID Convention, the Additional Facility, and the UNCITRAL Arbitration Rules. Many cases under the NAFTA are conducted under the Additional Facility. Additional Facility proceedings receive institutional support from ICSID in a similar way to proceedings under the ICSID Convention.

Arbitration under the Additional Facility is not governed by the ICSID Convention but by separate Additional Facility Rules. This means, in particular, that the ICSID Convention's provisions on the recognition and enforcement of awards are not applicable to awards rendered under the Additional Facility. Rather, the

---

[32] The Additional Facility Rules are available from ICSID's homepage at <http://www.worldbank. org/icsid/facility/facility.htm>. The Additional Facility, Rules together with four schedules are also reproduced in 1 ICSID Reports 213–80. Generally on the Additional Facility, see A Broches, 'The "Additional Facility" of the International Centre for Settlement of Investment Disputes (ICSID)' (1979) 4 *Yearbook Commercial Arbitration* 373; P Toriello, 'The Additional Facility of the International Centre for Settlement of Investment Disputes' (1978–79) 4 *Italian Yearbook of Int'l L* 59; C Schreuer et al, *The ICSID Convention: A Commentary*, 2nd edn (2009), Art 6, para 25; Art 11, para 15; Art 25, paras 9–13, 30–4, 87, 202–10, 300–1, 409, 443–6, 457–63, 623; Art 26, paras 22, 113, 179, 180; Art 36, paras 7, 47, 61; Art 42, paras 142, 275; Art 43, para 3; Art 47, para 7; Art 52, para 5; Art 53, paras 5–9; Art 54, paras 12–22; Art 62, paras 7–10.

[33] The Additional Facility Rules, Art 2 provides:

The Secretariat of the Centre is hereby authorized to administer, subject to and in accordance with these Rules, proceedings between a State (or a constituent subdivision or agency of a State) and a national of another State, falling within the following categories:

(a) conciliation and arbitration proceedings for the settlement of legal disputes arising directly out of an investment which are not within the jurisdiction of the Centre because either the State party to the dispute or the State whose national is a party to the dispute is not a Contracting State;

(b) conciliation and arbitration proceedings for the settlement of legal disputes which are not within the jurisdiction of the Centre because they do not arise directly out of an investment, provided that either the State party to the dispute or the State whose national is a party to the dispute is a Contracting State; and

(c) fact-finding proceedings.

[34] The North American Free Trade Agreement (NAFTA), 32 ILM 605 (1993), was ratified by Canada, Mexico, and the United States. See pp 15–17.

Convention on the Recognition and Enforcement of Foreign Arbitral Award of 1958 (the New York Convention) applies. Also, awards rendered under the Additional Facility, unlike ICSID awards, are not exempt from the scrutiny of and setting aside by competent national courts.[35]

cc. Non-ICSID investment arbitration

ICSID has become the main forum for the settlement of disputes between a foreign investor and the host state. However, ICSID is not the only institution for foreign investment arbitration. Not all states have become parties to the ICSID Convention. Moreover, it is not unusual for BITs to leave the investor with a choice between ICSID and other types of arbitration. Despite clear differences between classical commercial arbitration and investment arbitration, institutions dealing primarily with commercial arbitration such as the International Chamber of Commerce (ICC) or the London Court of International Arbitration (LCIA), do not exclude investor-state arbitration. This includes also the Regional Arbitration Centres in Frankfurt, Vienna, Cairo, Kuala Lumpur, and Hong Kong, or the China International Economic and Trade Arbitration Commission (CIETAC). In current practice, such arbitrations are most commonly conducted under the UNCITRAL Arbitration Rules of 1976 (revised in 2010) and under the ICC Arbitration Rules of 1998 (revised in 2011).

As to the procedural law applicable in fora other than ICSID, the clear tendency is to reduce or eliminate the role of the domestic arbitration law at the place of arbitration and instead to develop and apply rules designed specifically for international proceedings.[36]

All procedures have in common that the parties can control the composition of the tribunal and the law applicable in the proceedings. Other common elements include the power of tribunals to decide on their own competence,[37] the tribunal's power to determine the rules of procedure in the absence of a choice by the parties,[38] and the principle of confidentiality.[39] Basic procedural requirements are set forth in broad terms. For instance, the ICC Rules state that a tribunal 'shall act fairly and impartially and ensure that each party has a reasonable opportunity to present its case'.[40] Some variations exist in regard to document production, the taking of evidence, ethical standards for arbitrators and counsel, and the cost

---

[35] See *United Mexican States v Metalclad Corp*, Supreme Court of British Columbia, 2 May 2001, 5 ICSID Reports 236.

[36] Compare G Sauser-Hall's Reports for the Institut de Droit International, *Annuaire de l'Institut de Droit International*, vol 44 I, 469–592 (1952), vol 48 II, 264–361 (1958), with the contributions in 'Pervasive Problems in International Arbitration', LA Mistelis and JDM Lew eds, 2006, especially H Alvarez, 'Autonomy of International Arbitration Process', pp 119 et seq.

[37] See eg UNCITRAL Rules, Art 23 sec 1; ICC Rules, Art 6 secs 3 and 5.

[38] UNCITRAL Rules, Art 17; ICC Rules, Art 19.

[39] UNCITRAL Rules, Art 28 sec 3; ICC Rules, Art 22(3).

[40] ICC Arbitration Rules, Art 22 sec 4; see also UNCITRAL Rules, Art 17 sec 1 ('parties are treated with equality and that at an appropriate stage of the proceedings each party is given a reasonable opportunity of presenting its case').

structure.[41] Of course, the laws of the seat of arbitration will also differ. Given the freedom of arbitrators to determine the procedure, a major difference often lies less with the written rules than with the personal background and experience of the arbitrator, especially in regard to their familiarity with the principles of common law and civil law.

i. The International Chamber of Commerce

The most established international arbitral institution is the ICC,[42] which has its seat in Paris and has been in existence since 1923. Its current rules date from 2012. Its most distinctive feature is the administrative assistance and guidance provided by the so-called 'International Court of Arbitration'. Despite its name, this is an administrative body made up of representatives from different countries. Similar to the 'Permanent Court of Arbitration',[43] the ICC Court only provides technical assistance and a list of arbitrators, but will not itself render a judgment or award. The Court will appoint the arbitrator(s) unless the parties agree otherwise.

A special feature in ICC proceedings are the 'Terms of Reference' which the arbitrators will usually draw up once they receive the files of the case from the ICC Secretariat.[44] Generally speaking, these terms provide for a short character-ization of the case, including a summary of the claims and, especially, a list of the issues to be decided. While these Terms are helpful for the parties and the tribunal in their focus on the relevant issues, the Terms reflect the impression of the Tribunal at an early stage, and the issues may evolve substantially during the proceedings.

Another peculiar feature concerns the manner in which an ICC tribunal reaches its final award. Once the tribunal has agreed on a draft, this document is forwarded to the ICC Court of Arbitration, and the Court will check the formalities, ensuring that all relevant matters are covered and that there are no obvious mathematical errors or misprints in the draft.[45] However, responsibility for the final substance of the award remains with the tribunal and not with the Court.

ii. The London Court of International Arbitration

The London Court of International Arbitration (LCIA)[46] has existed since 1986, as a successor to the London Chamber of Arbitration established in 1892. Regardless of the nationalities of the parties, the LCIA is designed to deal with disputes arising out of commercial transactions, including investor-state disputes. The 'Arbitration Court' includes practitioners from all the major trading countries. The current Rules were adopted in 1998. If requested, the Court will also apply the UNCI-TRAL Rules or act as an appointing authority.

---

[41] See Alvarez, n 36, pp 124 et seq.
[42] <http://www.iccwbo.org/court/arbitration/id4199/index.html>.
[43] See p 244.
[44] ICC Rules, Art 23.
[45] ICC Rules, Art 33.
[46] For detailed information, see <http://www.lcia.org/>.

iii. The UNCITRAL Rules

The UNCITRAL Rules of Arbitration, revised in 2010,[47] differ fundamentally from the previously described settings. They are rules only and do not establish a machinery to administer proceedings in a particular case. It is up to the parties to provide an administrative framework for a case, and they may create an ad hoc tribunal anywhere in the world. Alternatively, the UNCITRAL Rules may be applied by an existing institution such as ICSID or the LCIA.[48]

The UNCITRAL Rules are considered to reflect a modern, universally established set of international arbitration rules. The 43 Articles essentially address all matters that may arise in international proceedings, from the notice of arbitration to the appointment of arbitrators, interim measures, the rules governing the proceedings, and the form and effect of an award including the decision on costs.

UNCITRAL has also influenced the development of international arbitration by way of a proposal for national legislation called the UNCITRAL Model Law on International Commercial Arbitration (1985) and a corresponding proposal on international conciliation (2002). The useful UNCITRAL Notes on Organizing Arbitral Proceedings (1996)[49] list and describe issues which will come up in international arbitrations. The 19 points cover matters such as decision-making, agreement on rules, language, place of arbitration, form of communications, confidentiality, evidence, and rules on hearings and on the award.

iv. The Iran–United States Claims Tribunal

Starting with the Jay Treaty* in 1794[50] between Great Britain and the United States, states have often set up arbitral tribunals and mixed commissions[51] in order to resolve claims arising out of specific wars, revolutions, civil strife, or other major events affecting foreign nationals. The Iran–United States Claims Tribunal was established in 1981 by the Algiers Declaration for the resolution of claims of both US and Iranian nationals and companies arising out of events during the Iranian

---

[47] For the text of the revised UNCITRAL Arbitration Rules adopted by GA Res 65/22, see <http://www.uncitral.org/pdf/english/texts/arbitration/arb-rules-revised/arb-rules-revised-2010-e.pdf>.

[48] See *OEPC v Ecuador*, Award, 1 July 2004, arbitrated at the LCIA; *CME v Czech Republic*, Award, 14 March 2003, arbitrated at Stockholm; *Saluka v Czech Republic*, Partial Award, 17 March 2006, arbitrated in Geneva; *Lauder v Czech Republic*, Award, 3 September 2001, arbitrated in London; see on the Czech cases G Sacerdoti, 'Investment Arbitration Under ICSID and UNCITRAL Rules: Prerequisites, Applicable Law, Review of Awards' (2004) 19 *ICSID Review-FILJ* 1. In some cases proceedings under the UNCITRAL Rules are administered by the PCA. See *Chevron and Texaco v Ecuador*, Final Award, 31 August 2011. The UNCITRAL Rules are also used in proceedings under the NAFTA. See *Chemtura v Canada*, Award, 2 August 2010. The UN Compensation Commission set up to deal with damages caused by Iraq was also guided by the UNCITRAL Rules. The Iran–US Claims Tribunal operates under modified UNCITRAL Rules.

[49] For the text of the Notes, see <http://www.uncitral.org/pdf/english/texts/arbitration/arb-notes/arb-notes-e.pdf>.

[50] See K S Ziegler, 'Jay Treaty (1794)' in R Wolfrum (ed), *Max Planck Encyclopedia of Public International Law*, vol VI (1997) 449.

[51] See R Dolzer, 'Mixed Claims Commissions' in R Wolfrum (ed), *Max Planck Encyclopedia of Public International Law*, vol VII (2012) 295.

Revolution. The Algiers Declaration described the law applicable as: 'such choice of law rules and principles of commercial and international law as the Tribunal determines to be applicable, taking into account relevant usages of trade, contract provisions and changed circumstances.'

Since its inception, the Tribunal, which is seated in The Hague, has addressed general issues of international law relating to foreign investment, such as matters of expropriation, state responsibility, nationality, and international arbitral procedure.

The jurisprudence of the Tribunal has made valuable contributions to the clarification and evolution of international law in general and investment law in particular, with its decisions often cited by other tribunals and commentators. It is a remarkable achievement by a machinery set up to deal effectively with sensitive legal matters arising between two states with radically different political and legal values.

The Tribunal has still not concluded its work after more than 30 years and has not yet ruled on all key claims of the Iranian Government. But the Tribunal has decided the vast majority of the 3,800 claims filed, often involving complex factual and legal matters.

v. The Permanent Court of Arbitration

The Permanent Court of Arbitration (PCA) has its seat in The Hague. It was initially established in 1899 by the Hague Peace Conference which adopted the Convention on Pacific Settlement of International Disputes. In 1907 the Second Peace Conference decided to retain the Court.[52]

The PCA is not, strictly speaking, a court. It only administers or facilitates arbitration, conciliation, and fact-finding. The parties to proceedings may be states, private parties, and international organizations. It may address disputes both under public international law and private international law. Cases pertaining to foreign investment also fall within its wide range of activities. The PCA's Secretariat—the International Bureau—may register a case, provide legal support to tribunals, process documents, and conduct communications between parties, as well as provide legal research and organize meetings and hearings. The Bureau also maintains a list of arbitrators who may be chosen by the parties to a dispute. The current procedural rules of the PCA are based on the 1976 UNCITRAL Rules. The Secretary-General of the Bureau may serve as appointing authority in UNCITRAL arbitrations or may be requested to designate an appointing authority, and may rule on the challenge of an arbitrator.[53]

---

[52] For details, see N Ando, 'Permanent Court of Arbitration' in R Wolfrum (ed), *Max Planck Encyclopedia of Public International Law*, vol VIII (2012) 251.

[53] In the past, arbitrations before the Court have included famous cases such as *Russian Indemnity Arbitration* (1912) and the *Norwegian Shipowners Claims Arbitration* (1922). After decades with a low profile, the services of the PCA have more recently been in increasing demand. From a political point of view, the arbitration Commissions for disputes between Ethiopia and Eritrea have recently been most visible. Cases such as *Saluka v Czech Republic*, Partial Award, 17 March 2006, or *Frontier Petroleum v Czech Republic*, Final Award, 12 November 2010, are more important in the present context.

(d) The subject matter of the dispute (jurisdiction *ratione materiae*)

The existence of a legal dispute concerning an investment is a jurisdictional requirement in investment arbitration. If proceedings are to be conducted under the ICSID Convention, the test is that there is a 'legal dispute arising directly out of an investment' (Art 25(1)). Each of these elements, the existence of a dispute, the legal nature of the dispute, the directness of the dispute, and the existence of an investment, may raise jurisdictional questions.

aa. The dispute

The ICJ has defined a dispute as 'a disagreement on a point of law or fact, a conflict of legal views or interests between parties'.[54] In another case, the ICJ referred to 'a situation in which the two sides held clearly opposite views concerning the question of the performance or non-performance of certain treaty obligations'.[55] The Tribunal in *Texaco v Libya* referred to a 'present divergence of interests and opposition of legal views'.[56] ICSID tribunals have adopted similar definitions of 'disputes'.[57]

In *RDC v Guatemala*,[58] jurisdiction depended, inter alia, on whether the dispute had broken out before or after the entry into force of the Dominican Republic–Central America–United States Free Trade Agreement (CAFTA). The Tribunal defined the concept of a dispute 'as a conflict of views on points of law or fact which requires sufficient communication between the parties for each to know the other's views and oppose them'.[59] On that basis it found that the dispute had crystallized after CAFTA had entered into force and hence affirmed its jurisdiction.

bb. The legal nature of the dispute

Disputes are legal if they 'concern the existence or scope of a legal right or obligation, or the nature or extent of the reparation to be made for breach of a

---

[54] See *Case Concerning East Timor*, ICJ Reports (1995) 89, 99 and the references to earlier cases cited therein.

[55] *Interpretation of the Peace Treaties with Bulgaria, Hungary and Romania* (first phase), ICJ Reports (1950) 65, 74; *Case Concerning Certain Property (Liechtenstein v Germany)*, ICJ Reports (2005), paras 20–7.

[56] *Texaco Overseas Petroleum Company and California Asiatic Oil Company v Libyan Arab Republic*, Preliminary Award, 27 November 1975, 53 ILR 389, 416.

[57] *AGIP v Congo*, Award, 30 November 1979, 1 ICSID Reports 306, paras 38–42; *Maffezini v Spain*, Decision on Jurisdiction, 25 January 2000, 40 ILM 1129 (2001), paras 93–8; *Tokios Tokelės v Ukraine*, Decision on Jurisdiction, 29 April 2004, paras 106, 107; *Lucchetti v Peru*, Award, 7 February 2005, para 48; *Impregilo v Pakistan*, Decision on Jurisdiction, 22 April 2005, paras 302, 303; *El Paso Energy Intl Co v Argentina*, Decision on Jurisdiction, 27 April 2006, para 61; *Suez, Sociedad General de Aguas de Barcelona SA, and InterAguas Servicios Integrales del Agua SA v Argentina*, Decision on Jurisdiction, 16 May 2006, para 29; *Helnan v Egypt*, Decision on Jurisdiction, 17 October 2006, para 52; *AMTO v Ukraine*, Award, 26 March 2008; *Victor Pey Casado v Chile*, Award, 8 May 2008, paras 440–7; *ATA v Jordan*, Award, 18 May 2010, paras 98–109, 115–20; *Burlington Resources v Ecuador*, Decision on Jurisdiction, 2 June 2010, paras 254–340.

[58] *Railroad Development Corp (RDC) v Guatemala*, Second Decision on Jurisdiction, 18 May 2010.

[59] At paras 129, 126–38.

legal obligation'.[60] Respondents have sometimes argued that a tribunal lacked jurisdiction because the dispute before it was not legal but rather of a political or economic nature. Tribunals have invariably rejected these arguments since the claims had been presented in legal terms. In *Suez v Argentina* the Tribunal found that the claimant had made legal claims:

A legal dispute, in the ordinary meaning of the term, is a disagreement about legal rights or obligations. . . . In the present case, the Claimants clearly base their case on legal rights which they allege have been granted to them under the bilateral investment treaties that Argentina has concluded with France and Spain. In their written pleadings and oral arguments, the Claimants have consistently presented their case in legal terms. . . . the dispute as presented by the Claimants is legal in nature.[61]

Other tribunals have adopted similar descriptions of legal disputes and have rejected attempts to contest their jurisdiction on the ground that the disputes before them were political or economic.[62]

cc. The directness of the dispute in relation to the investment

The element of directness applies to the dispute in relation to the investment.[63] It does not relate to the investment as such. In *Fedax v Venezuela*, the respondent argued that the disputed transaction—debt instruments issued by the Republic of Venezuela—was not a 'direct foreign investment' and therefore could not qualify as an investment under the ICSID Convention. The Tribunal rejected this argument. It pointed out that:

jurisdiction can exist even in respect of investments that are not direct, so long as the dispute arises directly from such transaction.[64]

An investment operation typically involves a number of ancillary transactions and legal contacts. They include financing, the lease of property, purchase of various

---

[60] Report of the Executive Directors to the ICSID Convention, para 26, 1 ICSID Reports 28.

[61] *Suez, Sociedad General de Aguas de Barcelona SA, and InterAguas Servicios Integrales del Agua SA v Argentina*, Decision on Jurisdiction, 16 May 2006, paras 34–7 at 37.

[62] See *CSOB v Slovakia*, Decision on Jurisdiction, 24 May 1999, para 61; *Maffezini v Spain*, Decision on Jurisdiction, 25 January 2000, paras 94–8; *Gas Natural SDG, SA v Argentina*, Decision on Jurisdiction, 17 June 2005, paras 20–3; *Camuzzi v Argentina*, Decision on Jurisdiction, 11 May 2005, para 55; *AES Corp v Argentina*, Decision on Jurisdiction, 26 April 2005, paras 40–7; *Sempra Energy Intl v Argentina*, Decision on Jurisdiction, 11 May 2005, paras 67, 68; *Continental Casualty Company v Argentina*, Decision on Jurisdiction, 22 February 2006, para 67; *El Paso Energy Intl Co v Argentina*, Decision on Jurisdiction, 27 April 2006, paras 47–62; *Jan de Nul et al v Egypt*, Decision on Jurisdiction, 16 June 2006, para 74; *National Grid plc v Argentina*, Decision on Jurisdiction, 20 June 2006, paras 142, 143, 160; *Pan American v Argentina*, Decision on Preliminary Objections, 27 July 2006, paras 71–91; *Saipem v Bangladesh*, Decision on Jurisdiction, 21 March 2007, paras 93–7; *Noble Energy v Ecuador*, Decision on Jurisdiction, 5 March 2008, paras 121–3; *Perenco v Ecuador*, Decision on Jurisdiction, 30 June 2011, paras 132–47.

[63] The NAFTA, Art 1101(1) refers to measures 'relating to' investors or investments. On the interpretation of this term, see *Methanex v United States*, Decision on Jurisdiction, 7 August 2002, paras 127–47.

[64] *Fedax v Venezuela*, Decision on Jurisdiction, 11 June 1997, para 24. See also *Siemens v Argentina*, Decision on Jurisdiction, 3 August 2004, para 150.

goods, marketing of produced goods, and tax liabilities. In economic terms, these transactions and contacts are all more or less linked to the investment. But whether these peripheral activities arise directly out of an investment for purposes of ICSID's jurisdiction may be subject to doubt and has to be decided on a case-by-case basis.[65]

In *CSOB v Slovakia* the claimant had granted a loan to a Slovak collection company that was secured by a guarantee of the Slovak Ministry of Finance. When the Slovak collection company defaulted in its payment, CSOB instituted ICSID proceedings against Slovakia. Slovakia argued that the claims against it did not arise directly out of the loan and were, therefore, outside the Tribunal's jurisdiction. The Tribunal rejected this argument:

An investment is frequently a rather complex operation, composed of various interrelated transactions, each element of which, standing alone, might not in all cases qualify as an investment. Hence, a dispute that is brought before the Centre must be deemed to arise directly out of an investment even when it is based on a transaction which, standing alone, would not qualify as an investment under the Convention, provided that the particular transaction forms an integral part of an overall operation that qualifies as an investment.[66]

The Tribunal added that the Slovak Republic's obligation was closely related to the loan made by CSOB. The loan, in turn, was part of the overall operation of consolidating CSOB and developing its banking activity in the Slovak Republic. Therefore, the dispute arose directly out of the investment. Other tribunals have endorsed the idea of the general unity of the investment operation.[67]

In a number of cases Argentina argued that the measures it had taken were of a general nature, were designed to serve the national welfare, and were not specifically directed to the particular investor's operation. Therefore, in Argentina's view, the dispute concerning these measures did not arise directly out of the investment. The Tribunal in *CMS v Argentina* did not accept this argument. It stated:

the Tribunal concludes on this point that it does not have jurisdiction over measures of general economic policy adopted by the Republic of Argentina and cannot pass judgment on whether they are right or wrong. The Tribunal also concludes, however, that it has jurisdiction to examine whether specific measures affecting the Claimant's investment or

---

[65] For examples, see *Holiday Inns v Morocco*, as summarized in C Schreuer et al, *The ICSID Convention: A Commentary*, 2nd edn (2009), Art 25, para 95; *SOABI v Senegal*, Award, 25 February 1988, paras 8.01–8.23; *Amco v Indonesia*, Resubmitted Case: Decision on Jurisdiction, 10 May 1988, 1 ICSID Reports 543, 562–5; *Tokios Tokelés v Ukraine*, Decision on Jurisdiction, 29 April 2004, paras 87–93; *Lemire v Ukraine*, Decision on Jurisdiction and Liability, 14 January 2010, paras 92–8; *Alpha v Ukraine*, Award, 8 November 2010, paras 250–3.

[66] *CSOB v Slovakia*, Decision on Jurisdiction, 24 May 1999, para 72.

[67] *Enron v Argentina*, Decision on Jurisdiction, 14 January 2004, paras 58–60, 70; *PSEG v Turkey*, Decision on Jurisdiction, 4 June 2004, paras 106–24; *Joy Mining v Egypt*, Award on Jurisdiction, 6 August 2004, para 54; *Duke Energy v Peru*, Decision on Jurisdiction, 1 February 2006, paras 92, 100 et seq; *Saipem v Bangladesh*, Decision on Jurisdiction, 21 March 2007, paras 110, 114; *OKO Pankki v Estonia*, Award, 19 November 2007, paras 204, 208; *RSM Production v Grenada*, Award, 13 March 2009, paras 255 et seq; *ATA Construction v Jordan*, Award, 18 May 2010, paras 96, 97; *Alpha Projektholding v Ukraine*, Award, 8 November 2010, para 272; *Fraport v Philippines*, Decision on Annulment, 23 December 2010, para 113. See further pp 61–2.

measures of general economic policy having a direct bearing on such investment have been adopted in violation of legally binding commitments made to the investor in treaties, legislation or contracts.[68]

Other tribunals have followed this line of argument.[69] It follows that a host state cannot rely on the general policy nature of measures taken by it if these measures had a concrete effect on the investment and violated specific commitments and obligations. These commitments may arise from legislation, a contract, or a treaty.[70]

dd. The investment

The existence of an investment is a cornerstone of ICSID's jurisdiction. Yet, the ICSID Convention offers no definition of the term 'investment'. Nevertheless, some tribunals have assumed that an 'investment' will be defined in objective terms which cannot be substituted by agreement of the parties. The relevant issues have been discussed in the chapter on investments.[71] For the purposes of Article 25, as discussed above,[72] many tribunals have adopted a list of descriptors that they regard as typical for investments.[73] These include:

- a substantial commitment;
- a certain duration;
- an element of risk; and
- significance for the host state's development.

---

[68] *CMS v Argentina*, Decision on Jurisdiction, 17 July 2003, para 33.

[69] *LG&E v Argentina*, Decision on Jurisdiction, 30 April 2004, para 67; *AES Corporation v Argentina*, Decision on Jurisdiction, 26 April 2005, paras 56, 57; *Sempra Energy International v Argentina*, Decision on Jurisdiction, 11 May 2005, para 71; *Camuzzi Intl SA v Argentina*, Decision on Jurisdiction, 11 May 2005, paras 56 et seq; *Gas Natural SDG, SA v Argentina*, Decision on Jurisdiction, 17 June 2005, paras 37–40; *Continental Casualty Company v Argentina*, Decision on Jurisdiction, 22 February 2006, para 74; *Suez, Sociedad General de Aguas de Barcelona SA, and InterAguas Servicios Integrales del Agua SA v Argentina*, Decision on Jurisdiction, 16 May 2006, paras 27–30; *El Paso Energy Intl Co v Argentina*, Decision on Jurisdiction, 27 April 2006, paras 89–100; *National Grid plc v Argentina*, Decision on Jurisdiction, 20 June 2006, paras 123–41; *Pan American v Argentina*, Decision on Preliminary Objections, 27 July 2006, paras 55–70.

[70] See further pp 115, 120 et seq (expropriation).

[71] See Chapter III.2.

[72] See pp 65–74.

[73] *Salini Costruttori SpA et Italstrade SpA v Morocco*, Decision on Jurisdiction, 23 July 2001, para 53; *SGS v Pakistan*, Decision on Jurisdiction, 6 August 2003, para 133 footnote 113; *Joy Mining Machinery Ltd v Egypt*, Award on Jurisdiction, 6 August 2004, paras 53, 57, 62; *AES Corporation v Argentina*, Decision on Jurisdiction, 26 April 2005, para 88; *Bayindir Insaat Turizm Ticaret Ve Sanayi AS v Pakistan*, Decision on Jurisdiction, 14 November 2005, paras 130–8; *Jan de Nul et al v Egypt*, Decision on Jurisdiction, 16 June 2006, paras 90–6; *Helnan v Egypt*, Decision on Jurisdiction, 17 October 2006, para 77; *Mitchell v DR Congo*, Decision on Annulment, 1 November 2006, paras 23–48; *Saipem v Bangladesh*, Decision on Jurisdiction, 21 March 2007, paras 99–102, 109–11; *Malaysian Historical Salvors v Malaysia*, Award, 17 May 2007, paras 44, 48–148, Decision on Annulment, 16 April 2009, paras 57–81.

(e) The parties to the dispute (jurisdiction *ratione personae*)

Investment arbitration is mixed in the sense that it involves a sovereign state (the host state), on one side, and a private foreign investor, on the other.

aa. The host state

ICSID's jurisdiction extends to contracting states, that is, parties to the ICSID Convention. Whether a particular state has ratified the Convention is evident from the List of Contracting States and Other Signatories of the Convention maintained by the Centre. It is available on the Centre's website.[74]

The critical time for the status of a state as a contracting state is the date of the registration of the request for arbitration by the Secretary-General of ICSID. A state may give its consent to submit to the Centre's jurisdiction before becoming a contracting state; but this consent becomes effective only once the state satisfies the requirements of a contracting state. A state that is not a contracting state of the Convention, at the time of a request for arbitration, will not be subject to the Centre's jurisdiction even if it has given its consent to jurisdiction.

The host state may deal with foreign investors either through a central state organ, such as a government ministry, or through a separate entity. This may be a territorial entity such as a province or municipality;[75] it may also be a specialized government agency such as an investment board or a privatization agency. Acts in violation of international law will be attributed to the central government even if they were committed by a sub-entity of the host state. Under the international law of state responsibility, the state is responsible for all its organs including those of a territorial unit as well as for state entities exercising elements of governmental authority.[76]

The ICSID Convention contains a provision that makes it possible for a sub-entity of the host state to appear in proceedings. Article 25, after referring to the contracting state, adds in parentheses 'or any constituent subdivision or agency of a Contracting State designated to the Centre [ie ICSID] by that State'. The term 'constituent subdivisions' includes any territorial entity below the level of the state, such as a province, a state, or a municipality. The term 'agency' refers to an entity of the host state. What matters are the functions rather than the legal structure of the

---

[74] <http://www.worldbank.org/icsid/constate/c-states-en.htm>.

[75] For details, see Chapter VIII.2.

[76] See the Articles on Responsibility of States for Internationally Wrongful Acts adopted by the International Law Commission (ILC) in 2001, Art 4(1):

> The conduct of any State organ shall be considered an act of that State under international law, whether the organ exercises legislative, executive, judicial or any other functions, whatever position it holds in the organization of the State, and whatever its character as an organ of the central government or of a territorial unit of the State.

(J Crawford, *The International Law Commission's Articles on State Responsibility* (2002) 94). See further pp 216 et seq, of this title.

entity. Whether it is government-owned and whether it has separate legal personality are of secondary importance. What is relevant is that it performs public functions on behalf of the contracting state.

The Convention requires that the constituent subdivision or agency be designated to ICSID. Designation assures an investor that the particular agency or entity with which it is dealing has been properly authorized by the state. Nevertheless, Article 25(3) of the ICSID Convention requires additionally that the constituent subdivision or agency's consent to the Centre's jurisdiction be approved by the state to which it belongs. ICSID maintains a public register of designated subdivisions and agencies of states[77] but relatively few countries have made designations under this provision. Constituent subdivisions or agencies have played a limited role in ICSID practice.[78]

In *Cable Television v St Kitts and Nevis*,[79] the claimant had entered into a contract with the Nevis Island Administration (NIA) containing consent to ICSID arbitration. The Tribunal found that the NIA was a constituent subdivision of the Federation of St Kitts and Nevis, a sovereign state, and a party to the ICSID Convention. But NIA had not been designated to ICSID as a constituent subdivision or agency in accordance with Article 25(1) of the ICSID Convention. Nor had its consent been approved by the Federation in accordance with Article 25(3). In turn, the Federation was not a party to the contract containing consent to ICSID's jurisdiction. The Tribunal found that it had no jurisdiction.[80]

bb. The investor

In most instances investors are juridical persons, that is, corporations. At times, individuals also appear as claimants in investment arbitration.[81]

Investment arbitration is designed for the protection of private investors. The ICSID Convention's Preamble speaks specifically of the role of private international investment. This would indicate that the investor must be a private individual or corporation. But state-owned corporations and state entities may be accepted as investors if they act in a private commercial capacity.

In *CSOB v Slovakia*, the respondent contested the Tribunal's competence arguing that the claimant, a bank, was a state agency of the Czech Republic rather than an independent commercial entity and that it was discharging essentially governmental activities. The Tribunal rejected this contention. It held that access

---

[77] Designations by Contracting States Regarding Constituent Subdivisions or Agencies (Art 25(1) and (3) of the Convention): see <http://www.worldbank.org/icsid/pubs/icsid-8/icsid-8-c.htm>.

[78] But see *Tanzania Electric v Independent Power Tanzania*, Award, 12 July 2001, para 13; *Repsol v Petroecuador*, Decision on Annulment, 8 January 2007; *Noble Energy v Ecuador*, Decision on Jurisdiction, 5 March 2008, para 6.

[79] *Cable Television v St Kitts and Nevis*, Award, 13 January 1997.

[80] See also *Hamester v Ghana*, Award, 18 June 2010, paras 27, 62, where the Secretary-General of ICSID refused to register a Request for Arbitration against an undesignated state agency.

[81] See eg *Robert Azinian and others v Mexico; Feldman v Mexico; Antoine Goetz and others v Burundi; Gruslin v Malaysia; Emilio Augustín Maffezini v Spain; Olguín v Paraguay; Hussein Nuaman Soufraki v United Arab Emirates*.

to arbitration did not depend upon whether the company was partially or wholly owned by the government. The decisive test was whether the company was discharging essentially governmental functions. CSOB's banking activities had to be judged by their nature and not by their purpose and, hence, were commercial.[82]

It has always been beyond doubt that arbitral proceedings are open to more than one claimant in one and the same case. The practice under the ICSID Convention shows numerous proceedings with more than one party on the claimants' side.[83] One and the same case may even involve several BITs and may be conducted under more than one set of procedural rules.[84]

In *Abaclat et al v Argentina*[85] a group of more than 180,000 Italian bondholders, later reduced to about 60,000, instituted arbitration proceedings against Argentina for failing to honour government bonds. The Tribunal noted that this was not a class action since each investor had individually consented to the arbitration. Argentina's offer of consent, given through its BIT with Italy, included claims presented by multiple claimants in a single proceeding. The Tribunal, alluding to the fact that the BIT's definition of investment covered bonds, said:

where the BIT covers investments which are susceptible of involving a high number of investors, and where such investments require a collective relief in order to provide effective protection to such investment, it would be contrary to the purpose of the BIT, and to the spirit of ICSID, to require in addition to the consent to ICSID arbitration in general, a supplementary express consent to the form of such arbitration.[86]

The Tribunal also rejected Argentina's objections to the admissibility of the proceeding. Any adaptations of the standard procedure under the ICSID Convention that may become necessary were within the Tribunal's powers. The claims were sufficiently homogeneous for the claimants to be treated as a group and to justify a simplification of the procedure.

Sometimes claimants start separate proceedings that are closely related because they arise from the same set of facts. Some arbitration systems, such as Article 1126

---

[82] *CSOB v Slovakia*, Decision on Jurisdiction, 24 May 1999, paras 15–27. See also *Telenor v Hungary*, Award, 13 September 2006, para 16: the fact that Telenor was 75 per cent owned by the state of Norway did not give rise to jurisdictional difficulties. See also *Rumeli Telekom v Kazakhstan*, Award, 29 July 2008, paras 325–8: the Tribunal found that the extent of any control over the claimants by the Turkish Government and the possibility that the proceeds of any award might be remitted to the Turkish Treasury did not deprive the claimants of their status as commercial entities.

[83] See eg *Antoine Goetz and others v Republic of Burundi*, Award, 2 September 1998, paras 84–9; *Champion Trading Company, Ameritrade International, Inc, James T Wahba, John B Wahba, Timothy T Wahba v Egypt*, Decision on Jurisdiction, 21 October 2003, para 1; *Foresti et al v South Africa*, Award, 4 August 2010, para 1.

[84] See *Suez, Sociedad General de Aguas de Barcelona SA, and Vivendi Universal SA v Argentina* (ICSID) and *AWG Group Ltd v Argentina* (UNCITRAL), Decision on Jurisdiction, 3 August 2006, paras 1–4, 7.

[85] *Abaclat et al v Argentina*, Decision on Jurisdiction, 4 August 2011, paras 216, 294–8, 480–92, 506–51. The case had previously been known by the name *a Beccara v Argentina*.

[86] At para 518.

of the NAFTA, foresee the consolidation of closely related proceedings.[87] Consolidation of separate proceedings may also simply be based on an agreement of the parties.[88] Exceptionally, claims arising from the same overall transaction between the same parties but subject to several jurisdictional instruments may call for consolidation.[89] Another possible method to coordinate separate claims that are closely related because they arise from the same set of facts consists in the creation of tribunals that are formally separate but are identically composed.[90]

cc. The investor's nationality

The investor's nationality is relevant for several purposes. In order to gain access to dispute settlement under the ICSID Convention, there is a positive as well as a negative nationality requirement: an investor is required to be a 'national of another Contracting State', that is, of a state that is a party to the ICSID Convention. Also, the investor must not be a national of the host state (Art 25).

If the investor relies on a jurisdictional clause in a treaty he or she must also have the nationality of one of the states parties to the treaty. In the case of arbitration based on a BIT, the host state must be one of the parties to the BIT and the investor must demonstrate that it is a national of the other party.

In the case of natural persons (individuals) the nationality of the contracting state to the ICSID Convention must exist at two separate dates: an individual investor has to be a national of a contracting state at the time the parties consent to submit to the Centre's jurisdiction and also on the date the request for arbitration or conciliation is registered by the Centre. In addition, the individual investor must not be a national of the host state on these two dates.

An individual's nationality[91] is determined primarily by the domestic legislation of the state whose nationality is claimed. A certificate of nationality is strong evidence but not conclusive proof of nationality.

An investor's nationality has to be objectively determined irrespective of an agreement between the host state and the investor. An agreement between a host state and an investor may specifically state the investor's nationality. Such an agreement creates a presumption but may not be conclusive. In particular, it cannot create a nationality that does not objectively exist.

Investors who hold the nationality of the host state are barred from bringing claims before the Centre. The purpose of ICSID is to encourage the settlement of disputes that involve states and private foreign investors. This also applies to

---

[87] See *Canfor v United States, Tembec et al v United States, Terminal Forest Products v United States*, Order of the Consolidation Tribunal, 7 September 2005; *Corn Products v Mexico, Archer Daniels Midland and Tate & Lyle v Mexico*, Order of the Consolidation Tribunal, 20 May 2005.

[88] *Pan American v Argentina*, Decision on Preliminary Objections, 27 July 2006, paras 1–4, 7.

[89] *Noble Energy v Ecuador*, Decision on Jurisdiction, 5 March 2008, paras 186–207.

[90] See *Alcoa Minerals v Jamaica, Kaiser Bauxite v Jamaica, Reynolds v Jamaica. Camuzzi v Argentina*, Decision on Jurisdiction, 11 May 2005, para 4; *Sempra Energy Intl v Argentina*, Decision on Jurisdiction, 11 May 2005, para 5.

[91] For more detailed treatment of the nationality of individual investors, see Chapter III.1(b).

investors with dual nationality if one of the two nationalities is that of the host state even if it is not the effective one.

A juridical person (company) must have the nationality of a state party to the ICSID Convention only on the day the parties consented to submit to ICSID's jurisdiction. Juridical persons will qualify as nationals of contracting states through their place of incorporation or seat of business.[92]

An agreement on the nationality of the investor between the host state and a corporate investor constitutes strong evidence that the nationality requirement has been fulfilled. Such an agreement will carry great weight, but it cannot create a nationality that does not exist.

A juridical person may, however, possess the host state's nationality and still qualify as a national of another contracting state under an exception contained in Article 25(2)(b).[93]

The prevalence of investment arbitration based on treaties has led to a decline in the importance of this possibility for locally incorporated companies that are under foreign control to institute ICSID arbitration. Many of these treaties include shareholding or participation in companies in their definitions of investment. This allows the foreign shareholders in the locally incorporated company to pursue the claim internationally.[94]

dd. The significance of the Additional Facility

As set out above, under Article 25(1) of the ICSID Convention the host state and the investor's state of nationality must be contracting states. If one or the other of these states is not a party to the Convention, the requirements *ratione personae* are not fulfilled and there is no jurisdiction.

If only one of the two states is a party to the ICSID Convention, the Additional Facility[95] offers a method of dispute settlement. The Additional Facility enables a non-contracting state or a national of a non-contracting state to the ICSID Convention to participate in dispute settlement proceedings administered by ICSID. Under the Additional Facility either the host state or the state of the investor's nationality must be a contracting party to the Convention. If neither state is a party to the ICSID Convention not even the Additional Facility is available. If both states are parties to the Convention, the parties must use the procedure under the Convention and may not use the Additional Facility. Also, there must be a separate submission to dispute settlement under the Additional Facility.

---

[92] For more detailed treatment of the nationality of corporate investors, including the element of control, see Chapter III.1(c).

[93] For more detailed treatment of the application of Article 25(2)(b) of the ICSID Convention, see Chapter III.1(d).

[94] For more detailed treatment, see Chapter III.1(g).

[95] For a description of the Additional Facility, see Section 2(c).

(f) Consent to arbitration

Like any form of arbitration, investment arbitration is always based on an agreement. Consent to arbitration by the host state and by the investor is an indispensable requirement for a tribunal's jurisdiction. Participation in treaties plays an important role for the jurisdiction of tribunals but cannot, by itself, establish jurisdiction. Both parties must have expressed their consent.

In practice, consent is given in one of three ways: first, a consent clause may be included in a direct agreement between the parties. Dispute settlement clauses providing for investor-state arbitration are common in contracts between states and foreign investors.

A second technique to give consent to arbitration is a provision in the national legislation of the host state. Such a provision offers arbitration to foreign investors in general terms. Many capital-importing countries have adopted such provisions. Since consent to arbitration is always based on an agreement between the parties, the mere existence of such a provision in national legislation will not suffice. But the investor may accept the offer in writing at any time while the legislation is in effect, and the acceptance may also be made simply by instituting proceedings.

The third method to give consent to arbitration is through a treaty between the host state and the investor's state of nationality. Most BITs contain clauses offering arbitration to the nationals of one state party to the treaty against the other state party to the treaty. The same method is employed by a number of regional multilateral treaties such as the NAFTA and the Energy Charter Treaty (ECT). Offers of consent contained in treaties must also be perfected by an acceptance on the part of the investor.

In some cases claimants relied on several instruments to establish consent. Jurisdiction was said to exist on the basis of a contract as well as on a treaty[96] or on the basis of legislation and a treaty.[97]

aa. Consent by direct agreement

An agreement between the parties recording consent to arbitration may be achieved through a compromissory clause in an investment agreement between the host state and the investor submitting future disputes arising from the investment operation to arbitration.[98] It is equally possible to submit a dispute that has already arisen

---

[96] *Noble Energy v Ecuador*, Decision on Jurisdiction, 5 March 2008, paras 22, 23, 150, 178; *Duke Energy v Ecuador*, Award, 18 August 2008, paras 99, 102, 111–89; *Lemire v Ukraine*, Decision on Jurisdiction and Liability, 14 January 2010, para 60; *Millicom v Senegal*, Decision on Jurisdiction, 16 July 2010, para 26.

[97] *Rumeli v Kazakhstan*, Award, 29 July 2008, paras 162, 165, 220–2; *Mobil v Venezuela*, Decision on Jurisdiction, 10 June 2010, para 24; *Pac Rim v El Salvador*, Decision on Preliminary Objections, 2 August 2010, paras 21–3, 242, 253; *CEMEX v Venezuela*, Decision on Jurisdiction, 30 December 2010, para 59.

[98] ICSID has developed a set of Model Clauses to facilitate the drafting of consent clauses in investment contracts. See ICSID Model Clauses, Doc ICSID/5/Rev 2 of 1993. Reproduced in

between the parties through consent expressed in a *compromis*. Therefore, consent may be given with respect to existing or future disputes.[99]

The agreement on consent between the parties need not be recorded in a single instrument. An investment application made by the investor may provide for arbitration. If the application is approved by the competent authority of the host state there is consent to arbitration by both parties.[100]

The parties are free to delimit their consent to arbitration by defining it in general terms, by excluding certain types of disputes, or by listing the questions they are submitting to arbitration. In practice, broad inclusive consent clauses are the norm. Consent clauses contained in investment agreements typically refer to 'any dispute' or to 'all disputes' under the respective agreements.[101]

Investment operations sometimes involve complex arrangements expressed in a number of successive agreements. Arbitration clauses may be contained in some of these agreements but not in others. The question arises whether the consent to arbitration extends to the entire operation or is confined to the specific agreements containing the arbitration clauses.

Tribunals have generally taken a broad view of expressions of consent of this kind. The arbitration clauses were not applied narrowly to the specific document containing them but were read in the context of the parties' overall relationship. The interrelated contracts were seen as representing the legal framework for one investment operation. Therefore, arbitration clauses contained in some, though not all, of the different contracts were interpreted as applying to the entire operation.[102]

In *Duke Energy v Peru* the investor had concluded several successive contracts with Peru in relation to the same investment. Only one of the contracts contained a clause whereby the parties consented to ICSID arbitration. The Tribunal applied the principle of the 'unity of the investment'[103] as developed, in particular, in *CSOB v Slovakia*.[104] At the same time it held that the claimant would have to substantiate its claims by reference to the contract containing the arbitration clause. The other contracts would be taken into consideration for the purpose of interpreting and applying that contract.[105]

---

4 ICSID Reports 357. Available at <http://icsid.worldbank.org/ICSID/StaticFiles/model-clauses-en/main-eng.htm>.

[99] Agreements to submit existing disputes to arbitration are rare. But see *MINE v Guinea*, Award, 6 January 1988, 4 ICSID Reports 61, 67; *Compania del Desarrollo de Santa Elena SA v Costa Rica*, Award, 17 February 2000, para 26.

[100] *Amco v Indonesia*, Decision on Jurisdiction, 25 September 1983, paras 10, 25.

[101] See eg *World Duty Free v Kenya*, Award, 4 October 2006, para 6.

[102] See *Holiday Inns v Morocco*, Decision on Jurisdiction, 12 May 1974; P Lalive, 'The First "World Bank" Arbitration (*Holiday Inns v Morocco*)—Some Legal Problems' (1980) 51 *BYIL* 123, 156–9; *Klöckner v Cameroon*, Award, 21 October 1983, 2 ICSID Reports 9, 13, 65–9; *SOABI v Senegal*, Decision on Jurisdiction, 1 August 1984, paras 47–58; Award, 25 February 1988, paras 4.01–4.52.

[103] See Chapter III.2(b).

[104] *CSOB v Slovakia*, Decision on Jurisdiction, 24 May 1999, paras 72, 74–5, 80, 82. See also in the same case, Decision on Further and Partial Objection to Jurisdiction, 1 December 2000, para 28.

[105] *Duke Energy v Peru*, Decision on Jurisdiction, 1 February 2006, paras 119–34; Decision on Annulment, 1 March 2011, paras 145–60.

bb. Consent through host state legislation

The host state may offer consent to arbitration to foreign investors in general terms. However, not every reference to investment arbitration in national legislation amounts to consent to jurisdiction. Therefore, the respective provisions in national laws must be studied carefully.

Some national investment laws provide unequivocally for dispute settlement by international arbitration. For instance, Article 8(2) of the Albanian Law on Foreign Investment of 1993 states in part:

the foreign investor may submit the dispute for resolution and the Republic of Albania hereby consents to the submission thereof, to the International Centre for Settlement of Investment Disputes.[106]

Other provisions are less explicit but still indicate that they express the state's consent to international arbitration. National laws may state that 'the investors may submit' the dispute to, or that the dispute 'shall be settled' by, international arbitration.

Other references in national legislation to investment arbitration may not amount to consent. Some provisions make it clear that further action by the host state is required to establish consent. This would be the case where the law in question provides that the parties 'may agree' to settle investment disputes through arbitration.[107]

Some provisions may be unclear and lead to a dispute as to whether the host state has given its consent.[108] The Venezuelan Investment Law of 1999 contains an Article 22 which, translated, reads:

Disputes arising between an international investor whose country of origin has in effect with Venezuela a treaty or agreement on the promotion and protection of investments, or disputes to which are applicable the provision of the Convention Establishing the Multilateral Investment Guarantee Agency (OMGI–MIGA) or the Convention on the Settlement of Investment Disputes between States and National of other States (ICSID), shall be submitted to international arbitration according to the terms of the respective treaty or agreement, if it so provides, without prejudice to the possibility of making use, when appropriate, of the dispute resolution means provided for under the Venezuelan legislation in effect.

In *Mobil v Venezuela*, the claimants sought to rely on this clause to establish ICSID's jurisdiction. The Tribunal undertook a detailed analysis of this text. It noted that the provision contrasted with clear expressions of consent in some of Venezuela's BITs. The Tribunal reached the conclusion that an intention of Venezuela to offer consent to ICSID's jurisdiction on the basis of this ambiguous

---

[106] See *Tradex v Albania*, Decision on Jurisdiction, 24 December 1996, 5 ICSID Reports 47, 54.
[107] *Biwater Gauff v Tanzania*, Award, 24 July 2008, paras 326–37.
[108] See *SPP v Egypt*, Decision on Jurisdiction I, 27 November 1985, paras 70–8; Decision on Jurisdiction II, 14 April 1988, paras 53–117.

clause could not be established.[109] Other tribunals interpreting Article 22 of the Venezuelan Investment Law reached the same result.[110]

A legislative provision containing consent to arbitration is merely an offer by the state to investors. In order to perfect an arbitration agreement, that offer must be accepted by the investor. The investor may accept the offer simply by instituting arbitration.[111] The host state may repeal its offer at any time unilaterally as long as it has not been accepted. Therefore, an investor would be well advised to accept the offer of consent to arbitration through a written communication as early as possible.[112]

The investor's acceptance of consent can be given only to the extent of the offer made in the legislation. But it is entirely possible for the investor's acceptance to be narrower than the offer and to extend only to certain matters or only to a particular investment operation.

Some offers of consent to arbitration in national laws are quite broad and refer to disputes concerning foreign investment in general terms.[113] Others delimit the questions covered by consent clauses. This may include the requirement that the dispute must be in respect of an approved enterprise. Other references to international arbitration relate only to the application and interpretation of the piece of legislation in question.[114]

The host state's offer of consent contained in its legislation may be subject to certain conditions, time limits, or formalities. In a number of investment laws, the investor's consent is linked to the process of obtaining an investment authorization.[115] Other investment laws require that the investor must accept the offer of consent to arbitration within certain time limits.

cc. Consent through bilateral investment treaties

Most investment arbitration cases in recent years have been based on jurisdiction established through BITs. The basic mechanism is the same as in the case of national legislation: the states parties to the BIT offer consent to arbitration to investors who are nationals of the other contracting party. The arbitration agreement is perfected through the acceptance of that offer by an eligible investor.

[109] *Mobil v Venezuela*, Decision on Jurisdiction, 10 June 2010, paras 67–140. The Tribunal found that it had jurisdiction on the basis of the BIT between the Netherlands and Venezuela, at paras 142–206.
[110] *CEMEX v Venezuela*, Decision on Jurisdiction, 30 December 2010, paras 63–139; *Brandes v Venezuela*, Award, 2 August 2011, paras 79–118.
[111] *Tradex v Albania*, Decision on Jurisdiction, 24 December 1996, 5 ICSID Reports 47, 63; *Zhinvali v Georgia*, Award, 24 January 2003, para 342.
[112] *SPP v Egypt*, Decision on Jurisdiction I, 27 November 1985, para 40.
[113] *Inceysa v El Salvador*, Award, 2 August 2006, para 331.
[114] See the consent clause in *SPP v Egypt*, Decision on Jurisdiction I, 27 November 1985, para 70.
[115] In *Inceysa v El Salvador*, Award, 2 August 2006, at paras 331–4, the Tribunal found that the investor was unable to avail itself of an ICSID consent clause in the host state's Investment Law because the investment did not meet the requirement of legality. See pp 95–6.

The vast majority of BITs contain clauses referring to investment arbitration.[116] Most investor-state dispute settlement clauses in BITs offer unequivocal consent to arbitration. This will be the case where the treaty states that each contracting party 'hereby consents' or where the dispute 'shall be submitted' to arbitration.[117]

Not all references to investor-state arbitration in BITs necessarily constitute binding offers of consent by the host state. Some clauses in BITs referring to arbitration are phrased in terms of an undertaking by the host state to give consent in the future. For instance, states may promise to accede to a demand by an investor to submit to arbitration by stating that the host state 'shall consent' to arbitration in the event of a dispute.[118] In *Millicom v Senegal*, the BIT provided that the state concerned '*devra consentir*' ('shall assent') to a dispute's submission to ICSID arbitration. Senegal objected on the ground that this did not amount to consent but that under this formula the state retained discretionary power to give or withhold consent. The Tribunal rejected this objection and found that the treaty provision amounted to 'a unilateral offer and a commitment by Senegal to submit itself to ICSID jurisdiction'.[119]

Some references to arbitration in BITs merely provide that the host state will give sympathetic consideration to a request for dispute settlement through arbitration. A clause of this kind does not amount to consent by the host state. Also, some BITs merely envisage a future agreement between the host state and the investor containing consent to arbitration.

Many dispute settlement clauses in BITs offer several alternatives. These may include the domestic courts of the host state, procedures agreed to by the parties to the dispute, ICSID arbitration, ICC arbitration, and ad hoc arbitration often under the UNCITRAL Rules. The precise legal effect of such clauses depends upon their wording. Some of these composite settlement clauses require subsequent agreement by the disputing parties to select one of these procedures. Others contain the state's advance consent to all of them, thereby giving the party that initiates arbitration a choice. Some BITs offering several methods of settlement specifically state that the choice between them lies with the investor.

A provision on consent to arbitration in a BIT is merely an offer by the respective states that requires acceptance by the other party. That offer may be accepted by a national of the other state party to the BIT.

It is established practice that an investor may accept an offer of consent contained in a BIT by instituting ICSID proceedings.[120] The Tribunal in *Generation Ukraine v Ukraine* said:

it is firmly established that an investor can accept a State's offer of ICSID arbitration contained in a bilateral investment treaty by instituting ICSID proceedings. There is

---

[116] See R Dolzer and M Stevens, *Bilateral Investment Treaties* (1995) 129 et seq; K J Vandevelde, *Bilateral Investment Treaties* (2010) 433 et seq.

[117] *RosInvest v Russia*, Award on Jurisdiction, 1 October 2007, paras 56–75.

[118] See Japan-Pakistan BIT of 1998, Art 10(2).

[119] *Millicom v Senegal*, Decision on Jurisdiction, 16 July 2010, paras 56, 61–6.

[120] See eg *Toto v Lebanon*, Decision on Jurisdiction, 11 September 2009, para 94.

nothing in the BIT to suggest that the investor must communicate its consent in a different form directly to the State;... It follows that the Claimant validly consented to ICSID arbitration by filing its Notice of Arbitration at the ICSID Centre.[121]

In the case of arbitration clauses contained in treaties, a withdrawal of an offer of consent before its acceptance would be more difficult than in the case of national legislation. An offer of arbitration in a treaty remains valid notwithstanding an attempt to terminate it, unless there is a basis for the termination under the law of treaties. Nevertheless, early acceptance is advisable. Once the arbitration agreement is perfected through the acceptance of the offer contained in the treaty, it remains in existence even if the states parties to the BIT agree to amend or terminate the treaty. In a number of cases investors had, in fact, accepted offers of consent contained in BITs prior to the institution of proceedings.[122]

Some BITs contain inducements to investors to give their consent. Submission to arbitration may be made a condition for admission of investments in the host state and may form part of the licensing process. BITs may provide specifically that their benefits will extend only to investors that have consented to arbitration.

dd. Consent through multilateral treaties

A number of multilateral treaties also offer consent to arbitration. The ICSID Convention is not one of these treaties. The Convention offers a detailed framework for the settlement of investment disputes but requires separate consent by the host state and by the foreign investor. The last paragraph of the Preamble to the Convention makes this quite clear by stating:

no Contracting State shall by the mere fact of its ratification, acceptance or approval of this Convention and without its consent be deemed to be under any obligation to submit any particular dispute to conciliation or arbitration;

In contrast, a number of regional treaties do offer consent to arbitration. Article 1122 of the NAFTA[123] provides in relevant part:

1. Each Party consents to the submission of a claim to arbitration in accordance with the procedures set out in this Agreement.

Article 1120 of the NAFTA specifies that an investor may submit a claim to arbitration under the ICSID Convention, the ICSID Additional Facility Rules, or the UNCITRAL Arbitration Rules.

The ECT[124] also provides consent to investment arbitration. Article 26(3)(a) provides in relevant part:

---

[121] *Generation Ukraine v Ukraine*, Award, 16 September 2003, paras 12.2, 12.3.
[122] See eg *ADC v Hungary*, Award, 2 October 2006, para 363.
[123] North American Free Trade Agreement, December 1992, 32 ILM 605 (1993). The CAFTA, Art 10.17 contains a similar clause.
[124] 34 ILM 360, 399 (1995).

each Contracting Party hereby gives its unconditional consent to the submission of a dispute to international arbitration or conciliation in accordance with this Article.

Under the ECT, the investor may submit the dispute to arbitration under the ICSID Convention, the ICSID Additional Facility Rules, the UNCITRAL Arbitration Rules, or the Arbitration Institute of the Stockholm Chamber of Commerce.[125] Here, too, the institution of proceedings constitutes the investor's acceptance of the offer of consent.[126]

ee. The scope of consent

The scope of consent to arbitration offered in treaties varies. Many BITs in their consent clauses contain phrases such as 'all disputes concerning investments' or 'any legal dispute concerning an investment'. These provisions do not restrict a tribunal's jurisdiction to claims arising from the BIT's substantive standards. By their own terms, these consent clauses encompass disputes that go beyond the interpretation and application of the BIT itself and would include disputes that arise from a contract in connection with the investment.

In *Salini v Morocco*, Article 8 of the applicable BIT defined ICSID's jurisdiction in terms of '[t]ous les différends ou divergences...concernant un investissement'.[127] The Tribunal noted that the terms of this provision were very general and included not only a claim for violation of the BIT but also a claim based on contract: 'Article 8 obliges the State to respect the jurisdictional choice arising by reason of breaches of the bilateral Agreement and of any breach of a contract which binds it directly.'[128]

In *Compañía de Aguas del Aconquija, SA & Vivendi Universal*[129] Article 8 of the BIT between France and Argentina, applicable in that case, offered consent for '[a]ny dispute relating to investments'. In its discussion of the BIT's fork-in-the-road clause, the ad hoc Committee said:

Article 8 deals generally with disputes 'relating to investments made under this Agreement between one Contracting Party and an investor of the other Contracting Party'. It is those disputes which may be submitted, at the investor's option, either to national or international adjudication. Article 8 does not use a narrower formulation, requiring that the investor's claim allege a breach of the BIT itself. Read literally, the requirements for arbitral jurisdiction in Article 8 do not necessitate that the Claimant allege a breach of the BIT itself: it is sufficient that the dispute relate to an investment made under the BIT. This may be contrasted, for example, with Article 11 of the BIT [dealing with state-state dispute settlement], which refers to disputes 'concerning the interpretation or application of this Agreement', or with Article 1116 of the NAFTA, which provides that an investor may

[125] ECT, Art 26(4).
[126] *AMTO v Ukraine*, Award, 26 March 2008, paras 44–7.
[127] Italy-Morocco BIT, Art 8.
[128] *Salini v Morocco*, Decision on Jurisdiction, 23 July 2001, *Journal de Droit International* 196 (2002), 6 ICSID Reports 400, para 61.
[129] *Compañía de Aguas del Aconquija, SA & Vivendi Universal v Argentina*, Decision on Annulment, 3 July 2002.

submit to arbitration under Chapter 11 'a claim that another Party has breached an obligation under' specified provisions of that Chapter.[130]

The Tribunal in *SGS v Pakistan* reached a different conclusion. Article 9 of the applicable BIT between Switzerland and Pakistan referred to 'disputes with respect to investments'. The Tribunal found that the phrase was merely descriptive of the factual subject matter of the disputes and did not relate to the legal basis of the claims or cause of action asserted in the claims. The Tribunal said: 'from that description alone, without more, we believe that no implication necessarily arises that both BIT and purely contract claims are intended to be covered by the Contracting Parties in Article 9.'[131]

Therefore, the Tribunal held that it had no jurisdiction with respect to contract claims which did not also constitute breaches of the substantive standards of the BIT.[132]

That decision has attracted some criticism.[133] In *SGS v Philippines*,[134] Article VIII(2) of the Switzerland-Philippines BIT offered consent to arbitration for 'disputes with respect to investments'. The Tribunal found that the clause in question was entirely general allowing for the submission of all investment disputes. Therefore, the Tribunal found that the term included a dispute arising from an investment contract.[135]

Other BIT clauses offering consent to arbitration do not refer to investment disputes in general terms but circumscribe the types of dispute that are submitted to arbitration. A provision that is typical for US BITs is contained in Article VII of the Argentina-US BIT of 1991. It offers consent for investment disputes, which are defined as follows:

a dispute between a Party and a national or company of the other Party arising out of or relating to (a) an investment agreement between that Party and such national or company; (b) an investment authorization granted by that Party's foreign investment authority (if any such authorization exists) to such national or company; or (c) an alleged breach of any right conferred or created by this Treaty with respect to an investment.

A narrower offer of consent to arbitration in BITs covers only violations of the BIT's substantive standards. For instance, the BIT between El Salvador and the Netherlands contains a submission to arbitration in Article 9 only for 'disputes which arise within the scope of this agreement between one Contracting Party and an investor of the other Contracting Party concerning an investment'.

Similarly, under Article 1116 of the NAFTA the scope of the consent to arbitration is limited to claims arising from alleged breaches of the NAFTA itself.

---

[130] At para 55.

[131] *SGS v Pakistan*, Decision on Jurisdiction, 6 August 2003, para 161.

[132] *SGS v Pakistan*, Decision on Jurisdiction, 6 August 2003, para 161.

[133] See also *Tokios Tokelès v Ukraine*, Decision on Jurisdiction, 29 April 2004, para 52.

[134] *SGS v Philippines*, Decision on Jurisdiction, 29 January 2004.

[135] At paras 131–5. In the same sense: *Chevron & Texaco v Ecuador*, Interim Award, 1 December 2008, paras 203, 209–11; *SGS v Paraguay*, Decision on Jurisdiction, 12 February 2010, paras 129, 183; *Alpha v Ukraine*, Award, 8 November 2010, para 243.

Also, under Article 26(1) of the ECT the scope of the consent is limited to claims arising from alleged breaches of the ECT itself.[136]

An umbrella clause in the BIT should extend the jurisdiction of tribunals to violations of contracts even if the consent to arbitration is restricted to claims arising from breaches of the treaty.[137] If it is true that under the operation of an umbrella clause, violations of a contract relating to the investment become treaty violations, it would follow that even a provision in a BIT merely offering consent to arbitration for violations of the BIT extends to contract violations covered by the umbrella clause.

The subject matter of some expressions of consent to arbitration is narrowly confined. Typical examples of narrow clauses of this kind are expressions of consent that are limited to disputes relating to expropriations[138] or to the amount of compensation for expropriations.[139] For instance, the China-Hungary BIT of 1991 provides in Article 10(1):

Any dispute between either Contracting State and the investor of the other Contracting State concerning the amount of compensation for expropriation may be submitted to an arbitral tribunal.

Some national laws also offer consent only in respect of narrowly circumscribed issues. In *Tradex v Albania* the consent expressed in the Albanian Law on Foreign Investment was limited in the following terms:

if the dispute arises out of or relates to expropriation, compensation for expropriation, or discrimination and also for the transfers in accordance with Article 7 ...[140]

After a detailed examination of the facts, the Tribunal found that the claimant had not been able to prove that an expropriation had occurred.[141]

ff. The interpretation of consent

Where consent is based on a treaty it would seem obvious to apply principles of treaty interpretation.[142] Reliance on domestic law principles of interpretation appears attractive where consent is based on a clause in domestic legislation. But it must be kept in mind that the perfected consent is neither a treaty nor simply a provision of domestic law, but an agreement between the host state and the foreign investor.

---

[136] *Kardassopoulos v Georgia*, Decision on Jurisdiction, 6 July 2007, paras 249–51.

[137] On umbrella clauses, see Chapter VII.3.

[138] *Saipem v Bangladesh*, Decision on Jurisdiction, 21 March 2007, paras 116, 129–33; Award, 30 June 2009, paras 120–32.

[139] *Telenor v Hungary*, Award, 13 September 2006, paras 18(2), 25, 57, 81–3; *ADC v Hungary*, Award, 2 October 2006, paras 12, 445; *Tza Yap Shum v Peru*, Decision on Jurisdiction, 19 June 2009, paras 129–88.

[140] *Tradex v Albania*, Decision on Jurisdiction, 24 December 1996, 5 ICSID Reports 47, 54–5.

[141] *Tradex v Albania*, Award, 29 April 1999, paras 132–205.

[142] For a general discussion of treaty interpretation in the context of investment law, see Chapter II.1.

In *CSOB v Slovakia* consent to arbitration was based on a contract between the parties that referred to a BIT. Although the BIT had never entered into force, the Tribunal concluded that the parties, by referring to the BIT, had intended to incorporate the arbitration clause in the BIT into their contract. With respect to the interpretation of the consent agreement, the Tribunal had no doubt that it was governed by international law:

> The question of whether the parties have effectively expressed their consent to ICSID jurisdiction is not to be answered by reference to national law. It is governed by international law as set out in Article 25(1) of the ICSID Convention.[143]

Tribunals have also held more generally that questions of jurisdiction are not subject to the law applicable to the merits of the case. Rather, questions of jurisdiction are governed by their own system which is defined by the instruments determining jurisdiction.[144] In the words of the Tribunal in *CMS v Argentina*:

> Article 42 [of the ICSID Convention][145] is mainly designed for the resolution of disputes on the merits and, as such, it is in principle independent from the decision on jurisdiction, governed solely by Article 25 of the [ICSID] Convention and those other provisions of the consent instrument which might be applicable, in the instant case the Treaty provisions.[146]

The host state's domestic law is relevant to jurisdiction if the consent to arbitration is based on a provision in its legislation.[147] In *Mobil v Venezuela*, the claimant relied on an ambiguous clause in Venezuela's Investment Law that referred to the ICSID Convention.[148] The Tribunal said:

> Legislation and more generally unilateral acts by which a State consents to ICSID jurisdiction must be considered as standing offers to foreign investors under the ICSID Convention. Those unilateral acts must accordingly be interpreted according to the ICSID Convention itself and to the rules of international law governing unilateral declarations of States.[149]

In a number of cases the respondents argued that an expression of consent to arbitration should be construed restrictively. Most tribunals have rejected this argument. Some tribunals seemed to lean more towards an extensive interpretation

---

[143] *CSOB v Slovakia*, Decision on Jurisdiction, 24 May 1999, para 35.

[144] *Azurix v Argentina*, Decision on Jurisdiction, 8 December 2003, paras 48–50; *Enron v Argentina*, Decision on Jurisdiction, 14 January 2004, para 38; *Siemens v Argentina*, Decision on Jurisdiction, 3 August 2004, paras 29–31; *Camuzzi v Argentina*, Decision on Jurisdiction, 11 May 2005, paras 15–17, 57; *AES Corp v Argentina*, Decision on Jurisdiction, 26 April 2005, paras 34–9; *Jan de Nul NV, Dredging Intl NV v Egypt*, Decision on Jurisdiction, 16 June 2006, paras 65–8.

[145] Article 42 of the ICSID Convention deals with the law applicable to the dispute.

[146] *CMS v Argentina*, Decision on Jurisdiction, 17 July 2003, para 88.

[147] *SPP v Egypt*, Decision on Jurisdiction II, 14 April 1988, paras 55–61; *Inceysa v El Salvador*, Award, 2 August 2006, paras 131, 222–64; *Zhinvali v Georgia*, Award, 24 January 2003, paras 229, 339, 340.

[148] See p 256.

[149] *Mobil v Venezuela*, Decision on Jurisdiction, 10 June 2010, para 85. See also *CEMEX v Venezuela*, Decision on Jurisdiction, 30 December 2010, para 79; *Brandes v Venezuela*, Award, 2 August 2011, para 36.

of consent clauses[150] but the majority of tribunals have subscribed to a balanced approach that accepts neither a restrictive nor an expansive approach to the interpretation of consent clauses.[151]

In *SPP v Egypt*, the argument of the restrictive interpretation of jurisdictional instruments was raised in relation to an arbitration clause in national legislation. The Tribunal found that there was no presumption of jurisdiction and that jurisdiction only existed insofar as consent thereto had been given by the parties. Equally, there was no presumption against the conferment of jurisdiction with respect to a sovereign state. After referring to a number of international judgments and awards, the Tribunal said:

> Thus, jurisdictional instruments are to be interpreted neither restrictively nor expansively, but rather objectively and in good faith, and jurisdiction will be found to exist if—but only if—the force of the arguments militating in favor of it is preponderant.[152]

(g) Conditions for the institution of proceedings

aa. The requirement to resort to domestic courts

Under traditional international law, before an international claim on behalf of an investor may be put forward in international proceedings, the investor must have exhausted the domestic remedies offered by the host state's legal system. But it is well established that, where consent has been given to investor-state arbitration, there is generally no need to exhaust local remedies. One of the purposes of investor-state arbitration is to avoid the vagaries of proceedings in the host state's courts. Article 26 of the ICSID Convention specifically excludes the requirement to exhaust remedies 'unless otherwise stated'.[153]

---

[150] *SGS v Philippines*, Decision on Jurisdiction, 29 January 2004, para 116; *Eureko v Poland*, Partial Award, 19 August 2005, para 248; *Tradex v Albania*, Decision on Jurisdiction, 24 December 1996, para 68; *Millicom v Senegal*, Decision on Jurisdiction, 16 July 2010, para 98.

[151] *Amco v Indonesia*, Decision on Jurisdiction, 25 September 1983, paras 12–24; *SOABI v Senegal*, Award, 25 February 1988, paras 4.08–4.10; *Cable TV v St Kitts and Nevis*, Award, 13 January 1997, para 6.27; *CSOB v Slovakia*, Decision on Jurisdiction, 24 May 1999, para 34; *Ethyl Corp v Canada*, Decision on Jurisdiction, 24 June 1998, para. 55; *Loewen v United States*, Decision on Competence and Jurisdiction, 9 January 2001, para 51; *Methanex v United States*, Preliminary Award on Jurisdiction, 7 August 2002, paras 103–5; *Mondev Intl Ltd v United States*, Award, 11 October 2002, paras 42, 43; *Aguas del Tunari, SA v Bolivia*, Decision on Jurisdiction, 21 October 2005, para 91; *El Paso Energy Intl Co v Argentina*, Decision on Jurisdiction, 27 April 2006, paras 68–70; *Suez, Sociedad General de Aguas de Barcelona SA, and InterAguas Servicios Integrales del Agua SA v Argentina*, Decision on Jurisdiction, 16 May 2006, paras 59, 64; *Pan American v Argentina*, Decision on Preliminary Objections, 27 July 2006, paras 97–9; *Duke Energy v Ecuador*, Award, 18 August 2008, paras 129–30; *Austrian Airlines v Slovakia*, Final Award, 9 October 2009, paras 119–21; *Mobil v Venezuela*, Decision on Jurisdiction, 10 June 2010, paras 112–19; *CEMEX v Venezuela*, Decision on Jurisdiction, 30 December 2010, paras 104 et seq.

[152] *SPP v Egypt*, Decision on Jurisdiction, 14 April 1988, para 63.

[153] Article 26 of the ICSID Convention provides:

> Consent of the parties to arbitration under this Convention shall, unless otherwise stated, be deemed consent to such arbitration to the exclusion of any other remedy. A Contracting State may require the exhaustion of local administrative or judicial remedies as a condition of its consent to arbitration under this Convention.

ICSID[154] and non-ICSID tribunals[155] have confirmed that the claimants were entitled to institute international arbitration directly without first exhausting the remedies offered by local courts.

It is open to a host state to make the exhaustion of local remedies a condition of its consent to arbitration. In fact, some BITs offering consent require the exhaustion of local remedies. But clauses of this kind are rare and are found mostly in older BITs. In the absence of such a proviso, the investor does not need to exhaust local remedies before starting an international arbitration. The Tribunal in *Generation Ukraine v Ukraine* stated:

13.4 The first sentence of Article 26 secures the exclusivity of a reference to ICSID arbitration vis-à-vis any other remedy. A logical consequence of this exclusivity is the waiver by Contracting States to the ICSID Convention of the remedies rule, so that the investor is not compelled to pursue remedies in the respondent State's domestic courts or tribunals before the institution of ICSID proceedings. This waiver is implicit in the second sentence of Article 26, which nevertheless allows Contracting States to reserve its right to insist upon the prior exhaustion of local remedies as a condition of its consent.[156]

In some cases tribunals have required an attempt to obtain redress in domestic courts, not as a matter of jurisdiction or admissibility, but as part of the evidence that the relevant standard of international law had indeed been violated. The Tribunal in *Waste Management* described this phenomenon in the following terms: 'in this context the notion of exhaustion of local remedies is incorporated into the substantive standard and is not only a procedural prerequisite to an international claim.'[157]

In a similar vein, the Tribunal in *Generation Ukraine v Ukraine* said:

the failure to seek redress from national authorities disqualifies the international claim, not because there is a requirement of *exhaustion* of local remedies but because the very reality of conduct tantamount to expropriation is doubtful in the absence of a reasonable—not necessarily exhaustive—effort by the investor to obtain correction.[158]

Therefore, under this theory an attempt to seek redress in the domestic courts would be required to demonstrate that a substantive standard, such as protection against uncompensated expropriation or fair and equitable treatment, has indeed been violated.

This theory has been severely criticized. In *Helnan v Egypt*, the Tribunal relied on the above passage from *Generation Ukraine*. It found that the claimant's failure

---

[154] *Amco v Indonesia*, Decision on Annulment, 16 May 1986, para 63; *Lanco v Argentina*, Decision on Jurisdiction, 8 December 1998, para 39; *IBM v Ecuador*, Decision on Jurisdiction, 22 December 2003, paras 77–84; *AES v Argentina*, Decision on Jurisdiction, 26 April 2005, paras 69, 70; *Saipem v Bangladesh*, Award, 30 June 2009, paras 174–84.

[155] *CME v Czech Republic*, Final Award, 14 March 2003, para 412; *Yaung Chi Oo v Myanmar*, Award, 31 March 2003, para 40; *Nycomb v Latvia*, Award, 16 December 2003, sec 2.4. But see *Loewen v United States*, Award, 26 June 2003, paras 142–217.

[156] *Generation Ukraine, Inc v Ukraine*, Award, 16 September 2003, para 13.4.

[157] *Waste Management v Mexico*, Award, 30 April 2004, para 97. Footnote omitted.

[158] *Generation Ukraine, Inc v Ukraine*, Award, 16 September 2003, para 20.30. See also *EnCana v Ecuador*, Award, 3 February 2006, para 194.

to challenge a key ministerial decision in the Egyptian administrative courts meant that there was no violation of the BIT's standards of protection.[159] This particular finding was subsequently annulled. The ad hoc Committee noted:

A requirement to pursue local court remedies would have the effect of disentitling a claimant from pursuing its direct treaty claim for failure by the executive to afford fair and equitable treatment, even where the decision was taken at the highest level of government within the host State.... Such a consequence would be contrary to the express provisions of Article 26...[160]

Some BITs provide that before an investor can bring a dispute before an international tribunal he or she must seek resolution before the host state's domestic courts for a certain period, often 18 months. The investor may proceed to international arbitration if the domestic proceedings do not result in the dispute's settlement during that period or if the dispute persists after the domestic decision. For instance, the Argentina-Germany BIT provides in Article 10(2) that any investment dispute shall first be submitted to the host state's competent tribunals. The provision continues:

(3) The dispute may be submitted to an international arbitration tribunal in any of the following circumstances:

(a) at the request of one of the parties to the dispute if no decision on the merits of the claim has been rendered after the expiration of a period of eighteen months from the date in which the court proceedings referred to in para. 2 of this Article have been initiated, or if such decision has been rendered, but the dispute between the parties persist;

Tribunals have held that this was not an application of the exhaustion of local remedies rule.[161] The usefulness of such a requirement is questionable: it creates a considerable burden to the party seeking arbitration with little chance of advancing the settlement of the dispute. A substantive decision by the domestic courts in a complex investment dispute is unlikely within 18 months, certainly if one includes the possibility of appeals. Even if such a decision is rendered, the dispute is likely to persist if the investor is dissatisfied with the decision's outcome. Therefore, arbitration remains an option after the expiry of the 18-month period. It follows that the most likely effect of a clause of this kind is delay and additional cost, since it is unlikely that the dispute will be resolved before the domestic courts within that time frame. One tribunal called a provision of this kind 'nonsensical from a practical point of view'.[162]

In actual practice, investors were often able to avoid the application of such a rule by invoking most-favoured-nation (MFN) clauses in the same BITs which allowed

---

[159] *Helnan v Egypt*, Award, 3 July 2008, para 148.

[160] *Helnan v Egypt*, Decision on Annulment, 14 June 2010, paras 43–57 at para 53.

[161] *Maffezini v Spain*, Decision on Jurisdiction, 25 January 2000, para 28; *Siemens v Argentina*, Decision on Jurisdiction, 3 August 2004, para 104; *Gas Natural SDG, SA v Argentina*, Decision on Jurisdiction, 17 June 2005, para 30.

[162] *Plama v Bulgaria*, Decision on Jurisdiction, 8 February 2005, para 224.

them to rely on other BITs of the host state that did not contain that requirement.[163]

bb. The fork in the road

Another way in which BITs sometimes refer to domestic courts is a so-called fork-in-the-road provision. Such a clause provides that the investor must choose between the litigation of its claims in the host state's domestic courts or through international arbitration and that the choice, once made, is final.[164] For instance, Article 8(2) of the Argentina-France BIT provides:

Once an investor has submitted the dispute either to the jurisdictions of the Contracting Party involved or to international arbitration, the choice of one or the other of these procedures shall be final.

Similarly, under the ECT consent of the states parties listed in Annex ID does not apply where the investor has previously submitted the dispute to the host state's courts.[165]

Investors are often drawn into local legal disputes of one sort or another in the course of investment activities. However, not every appearance before a court or tribunal of the host state will constitute a choice under a fork-in-the-road provision. While such disputes may relate in some way to the investment, they are not necessarily identical to the dispute before the international tribunal. Therefore, the appearance before a domestic court does not necessarily reflect a choice that would preclude international arbitration. Tribunals have held that the loss of access to international arbitration under a fork-in-the-road clause applies only if the same dispute involving the same cause of action between the same parties has been submitted to the domestic courts of the host state.[166] Only rarely did tribunals find

---

[163] *Maffezini v Spain*, Decision on Jurisdiction, 25 January 2000, paras 54–64; *Siemens v Argentina*, Decision on Jurisdiction, 3 August 2004, paras 32–110; *Gas Natural SDG, SA v Argentina*, Decision on Jurisdiction, 17 June 2005, paras 24–49; *Suez, Sociedad General de Aguas de Barcelona SA, and InterAguas Servicios Integrales del Agua SA v Argentina*, Decision on Jurisdiction, 16 May 2006, paras 52–66; *National Grid plc v Argentina*, Decision on Jurisdiction, 20 June 2006, paras 80–93; *Suez, Sociedad General de Aguas de Barcelona SA, and Vivendi Universal SA v Argentina and AWG Group Ltd v Argentina*, Decision on Jurisdiction, 3 August 2006, paras 52–68. But see *Wintershall v Argentina*, Award, 8 December 2008, paras 158–97; *ICS Inspection v Argentina*, Award, 10 February 2012, paras 243–327.

[164] The NAFTA, in Art 1121, does not, strictly speaking, contain a fork-in-the-road provision. However, it requires, as a condition of consent to arbitration, that the claimant submits a waiver of the right to initiate or continue before domestic judiciaries any proceedings with respect to the measures taken by the respondent that are alleged to be in breach of the NAFTA. See *Waste Management v Mexico*, Award, 2 June 2000; *Thunderbird v Mexico*, Award, 26 January 2006, paras 111–18. The CAFTA contains a similar provision in Art 10.18. See *Railroad Development v Guatemala*, Decision on Jurisdiction, 17 November 2008; *Commerce Group v El Salvador*, Award, 14 March 2011.

[165] See ECT, Art 26(3)(b)(i).

[166] *Olguín v Paraguay*, Decision on Jurisdiction, 8 August 2000, para 30; *Vivendi v Argentina*, Award, 21 November 2000, paras 53–5; Decision on Annulment, 3 July 2002, paras 36–43, 53–5; *Genin v Estonia*, Award, 25 June 2001, paras 321, 330–3; *Lauder v Czech Republic*, Final Award, 3 September 2001, paras 156–66; *Middle East Cement v Egypt*, Award, 12 April 2002, paras 70–3; *Azurix v Argentina*, Decision on Jurisdiction, 8 December 2003, paras 37–41, 86–92; *Enron v*

that the fundamental basis of the claim before them was the same as before the domestic courts[167]

CMS v Argentina[168] addressed the fork-in-the-road provision in the Argentina-US BIT. Argentina argued that the investor had taken the fork in the road since the local company, TGN, in which the investor held shares, had appealed a judicial decision to the Federal Supreme Court and had sought other administrative remedies.[169]

The Tribunal rejected Argentina's contention. It pointed out that the appeal had been taken by the local company TGN rather than by the foreign investor. Also, the steps taken consisted only of defensive and reactive actions. Most importantly, the subject matter in the domestic proceedings was not the same as the one in the ICSID arbitration. TGN's claims concerned the contractual arrangements under a licence while those of CMS concerned treaty rights.[170] The Tribunal said:

80. Decisions of several ICSID tribunals have held that as contractual claims are different from treaty claims, even if there had been or there currently was a recourse to the local courts for breach of contract, this would not have prevented submission of the treaty claims to arbitration. This Tribunal is persuaded that with even more reason this view applies to the instant dispute, since no submission has been made by CMS to local courts and since, even if TGN had done so—which is not the case—, this would not result in triggering the 'fork in the road' provision against CMS. Both the parties and the causes of action under separate instruments are different.

cc. An attempt at amicable settlement

A common condition in treaties providing for investor-state arbitration is that an amicable settlement must first be attempted through consultations or negotiations. This requirement is subject to certain time limits ranging from 3 to 12 months. If no settlement is reached within that period the claimant may proceed to arbitration. A typical waiting period under BITs would be six months. The NAFTA (Arts 1118–20) also prescribes a waiting period of six months after the events giving rise to the claim.[171] Article 26(2) of the ECT offers consent to arbitration if the dispute cannot be settled within three months from the date on which either party requested amicable settlement.[172] National legislation offering consent to arbitration may similarly provide for waiting periods.[173]

Argentina, Decision on Jurisdiction, 14 January 2004, paras 95–8; *Occidental v Ecuador*, Award, 1 July 2004, paras 37–63; *LG&E v Argentina*, Decision on Jurisdiction, 30 April 2004, paras 75, 76; *Champion Trading v Egypt*, Decision on Jurisdiction, 21 October 2003, sec 3.4.3; *Pan American v Argentina*, Decision on Preliminary Objections, 27 July 2006, paras 155–7; *Toto v Lebanon*, Decision on Jurisdiction, 11 September 2009, paras 203–17; *Victor Pey Casado v Chile*, Award, 8 May 2008, paras 467–98; *Total v Argentina*, Decision on Liability, 27 December 2010, paras 442–3.

[167] *Pantechniki v Albania*, Award, 30 July 2009, paras 53–67.
[168] *CMS v Argentina*, Decision on Jurisdiction, 17 July 2003, paras 77–82.
[169] At para 77.
[170] At paras 78–82.
[171] *Metalclad v Mexico*, Award, 30 August 2000, paras 64–9.
[172] *Petrobart v Kyrgyz Republic*, Award, 29 March 2005, sec VIII.7.
[173] *Tradex v Albania*, Decision on Jurisdiction, 24 December 1996, 5 ICSID Reports 47, 60–1.

The reaction of tribunals to these provisions requiring an attempt at amicable settlement before the institution of arbitration has not been uniform.[174] In the majority of cases the tribunals found that the claimants had complied with these waiting periods before proceeding to arbitration.[175] In other cases the tribunals found that non-compliance with the waiting periods did not affect their jurisdiction.[176]

In *Biwater Gauff v Tanzania*, the UK-Tanzania BIT provided for a six-month period for settlement. There had been attempts to resolve the dispute but the six-month period had not yet elapsed when the Request for Arbitration was filed. The Tribunal held that this did not preclude it from proceeding. It said:

this six-month period is procedural and directory in nature, rather than jurisdictional and mandatory. Its underlying purpose is to facilitate opportunities for amicable settlement. Its purpose is not to impede or obstruct arbitration proceedings, where such settlement is not possible. Non-compliance with the six month period, therefore, does not preclude this Arbitral Tribunal from proceeding. If it did so, the provision would have curious effects, including:

- preventing the prosecution of a claim, and forcing the claimant to do nothing until six months have elapsed, even where further negotiations are obviously futile, or settlement obviously impossible for any reason;

- forcing the claimant to recommence an arbitration started too soon, even if the six-month period has elapsed by the time the Arbitral Tribunal considers the matter.[177]

---

[174] For the practice of the ICJ see *Military and Paramilitary Activities in and against Nicaragua* (*Nicaragua v United States*), Judgment (Jurisdiction and Admissibility), 26 November 1984, ICJ Reports (1984) 427–9 and *Case Concerning Application of the International Convention on the Elimination of all forms of Racial Discrimination* (*Georgia v Russia*), Judgment, 1 April 2011, paras 115–84.

[175] *Salini v Morocco*, Decision on Jurisdiction, 23 July 2001, paras 15–23; *CMS v Argentina*, Decision on Jurisdiction, 17 July 2003, paras 121–3; *Generation Ukraine v Ukraine*, Award, 16 September 2003, paras 14.1–14.6; *Azurix v Argentina*, Decision on Jurisdiction, 8 December 2003, para 55; *Tokios Tokelės v Ukraine*, Decision on Jurisdiction, 29 April 2004, paras 101–7; *LG&E v Argentina*, Decision on Jurisdiction, 30 April 2004, para 80; *MTD v Chile*, Award, 25 May 2004, para 96; *Occidental v Ecuador*, Award, 1 July 2004, para 7; *Siemens v Argentina*, Decision on Jurisdiction, 3 August 2004, paras 163–73; *LESI—DIPENTA v Algérie*, Award, 10 January 2005, paras 32, 33; *AES Corp v Argentina*, Decision on Jurisdiction, 26 April 2005, paras 62–71; *Continental Casualty v Argentina*, Decision on Jurisdiction, 22 February 2006, para 6; *Berschader v Russia*, Award, 21 April 2006, paras 98–104; *El Paso v Argentina*, Decision on Jurisdiction, 27 April 2006, para 38; *Pan American v Argentina*, Decision on Preliminary Objections, 27 July 2006, paras 39, 41; *AMTO v Ukraine*, Award, 26 March 2008, paras 50, 53, 57–8; *Occidental v Ecuador*, Decision on Jurisdiction, 9 September 2008, paras 90–5; *AFT v Slovakia*, Award, 5 March 2011, paras 200–12.

[176] In *Ethyl Corp v Canada*, Decision on Jurisdiction, 24 June 1998, paras 76–88, the Tribunal dismissed the objection based on the six-month provision since further negotiations would have been pointless. In *Lauder v Czech Republic*, Final Award, 3 September 2001, para 187, the Tribunal found that the waiting period of six months was not a jurisdictional provision. In *SGS v Pakistan*, Decision on Jurisdiction, 6 August 2003, para 184, the Tribunal found that the waiting period was procedural rather than jurisdictional and that negotiations would have been futile. Similarly in *Bayindir v Pakistan*, Decision on Jurisdiction, 14 November 2005, paras 88–103, the Tribunal found that a requirement to give notice of the dispute for the purpose of reaching a negotiated settlement was not a precondition for jurisdiction.

[177] *Biwater Gauff v Tanzania*, Award, 24 July 2008, paras 338–50 at 343.

Other tribunals have reached the opposite conclusion.[178] In *Burlington Resources v Ecuador*, the BIT between Ecuador and the United States provided for consultation and negotiation in the event of a dispute. ICSID arbitration would become available six months after the dispute had arisen. The Tribunal found that the claimant had only informed the respondent of the dispute with its submission of the dispute to ICSID arbitration. It followed that the claim was inadmissible:

by imposing upon investors an obligation to voice their disagreement at least six months prior to the submission of an investment dispute to arbitration, the Treaty effectively accords host States the right to be informed about the dispute at least six months before it is submitted to arbitration. The purpose of this right is to grant the host State an *opportunity* to redress the problem before the investor submits the dispute to arbitration. In this case, Claimant has deprived the host State of that opportunity. That suffices to defeat jurisdiction.[179]

It would seem that the decisive question is whether there was a promising opportunity for a settlement. There is little point in declining jurisdiction and sending the parties back to the negotiating table if negotiations are obviously futile. Even if the institution of arbitration was premature, the waiting period will often have expired by the time the tribunal is ready to make a decision on jurisdiction. Under these circumstances, declining jurisdiction and compelling the claimant to start the proceedings anew would be uneconomical. An alternative way to deal with non-compliance with a waiting period is a suspension of proceedings to allow additional time for negotiations if these appear promising.

(h) The applicability of MFN clauses to dispute settlement

An MFN clause contained in a treaty will extend the better treatment granted to a third state or its nationals to a beneficiary of the treaty.[180] Most BITs and some other treaties for the protection of investments[181] contain MFN clauses. Some of these MFN clauses will specify to which parts of the treaty they apply. For instance, the MFN clause may specify that it includes, or that it excludes, dispute settlement.[182] But most MFN clauses are worded in a general way and typically refer only to the treatment of investments.[183]

This has led to the question of whether the effect of MFN clauses extends to the provisions on dispute settlement in these treaties. Put differently, is it possible to

---

[178] *Goetz v Burundi*, Award, 10 February 1999, paras 90–3; *Enron v Argentina*, Decision on Jurisdiction, 14 January 2004, para 88; *Wintershall v Argentina*, Award, 8 December 2008, paras 133–57; *Murphy v Ecuador*, Award, 15 December 2010, paras 90–157.

[179] *Burlington Resources v Ecuador*, Decision on Jurisdiction, 2 June 2010, paras 312–18, 332–40 at para 315. Emphasis in original.

[180] See also R Dolzer and T Myers, 'After *Tecmed*: Most-Favored-Nation Clauses in Investment Protection Agreements' (2004) 19 *ICSID Review-FILJ* 49.

[181] See NAFTA, Art 1103; ECT, Art 10(7).

[182] The UK Model BIT confirms 'for the avoidance of doubt' that MFN treatment applies to a list of Articles that include the settlement of investor-state disputes. The BIT between Austria and Kazakhstan specifically includes dispute settlement in its MFN clause.

[183] Generally on MFN clauses, see Chapter VII.9.

avoid the conditions and limitations attached to consent to arbitration in a treaty by relying on an MFN clause in the treaty provided the respondent state has entered into a treaty with a third state that contains a consent clause without these conditions and limitations? Or even more radically, if the treaty containing the MFN clause does not offer consent to arbitration, is it possible to rely on consent to arbitration in a treaty of the respondent state with a third party?

In *Maffezini v Spain*[184] the consent clause in the Argentina-Spain BIT required resort to the host state's domestic courts for 18 months before the institution of arbitration. That BIT contained the following MFN clause: 'In all matters subject to this Agreement, this treatment shall not be less favorable than that extended by each Party to the investments made in its territory by investors of a third country.'

On the basis of that clause, the Argentinian claimant relied on the Chile-Spain BIT which does not contain the requirement to seek redress in the host state's courts for 18 months. The Tribunal undertook a detailed analysis of the applicability of MFN clauses to dispute settlement arrangements[185] and concluded:

the most favored nation clause included in the Argentine-Spain BIT embraces the dispute settlement provisions of this treaty.... the Tribunal concludes that Claimant had the right to submit the instant dispute to arbitration without first accessing the Spanish courts.[186]

At the same time, the *Maffezini* Tribunal warned against exaggerated expectations attached to the operation of MFN clauses and distinguished between the legitimate extension of rights and benefits and disruptive treaty-shopping.[187] In particular, the MFN clause should not override public policy considerations that the contracting parties had in mind as fundamental conditions for their acceptance of the agreement.[188]

Subsequent decisions dealing with the application of MFN clauses to the requirement to seek a settlement in domestic courts for 18 months have mostly adopted the same solution.[189] The tribunals confirmed that the claimants were entitled to rely on the MFN clause in the applicable treaty to invoke the more favourable dispute settlement clause of another treaty that did not contain the 18-month rule.[190] At the same time these tribunals expressed their conviction that arbitration was an important part of the protection of foreign investors and that MFN clauses

---

[184] *Maffezini v Spain*, Decision on Jurisdiction, 25 January 2000.

[185] At paras 38–64.

[186] At para 64.

[187] At para 63.

[188] At para 62.

[189] For notable exceptions, see *Wintershall v Argentina*, Award, 8 December 2008, paras 158–97; *ICS Inspection v Argentina*, Award, 10 February 2012, paras 243–327.

[190] *Siemens v Argentina*, Decision on Jurisdiction, 3 August 2004, paras 94–110; *Gas Natural SDG, SA v Argentina*, Decision on Jurisdiction, 17 June 2005, paras 24–31, 41–9; *Suez, Sociedad General de Aguas de Barcelona SA, and InterAguas Servicios Integrales del Agua SA v Argentina*, Decision on Jurisdiction, 16 May 2006, paras 52–66; *National Grid plc v Argentina*, Decision on Jurisdiction, 20 June 2006, paras 53–94; *Suez, Sociedad General de Aguas de Barcelona SA, and Vivendi Universal SA v Argentina and AWG Group Ltd v Argentina*, Decision on Jurisdiction, 3 August 2006, paras 52–68; *Impregilo v Argentina*, Award, 21 June 2011, paras 51–109; *Hochtief v Argentina*, Decision on Jurisdiction, 24 October 2011.

should apply to dispute settlement. For instance the Tribunal in *Gas Natural v Argentina* said:

assurance of independent international arbitration is an important—perhaps the most important—element in investor protection. Unless it appears clearly that the state parties to a BIT or the parties to a particular investment agreement settled on a different method for resolution of disputes that may arise, most-favored-nation provisions in BITs should be understood to be applicable to dispute settlement.[191]

Another group of cases demonstrates a more sceptical attitude towards the applicability of MFN clauses to dispute settlement. Most of these cases did not concern procedural obstacles to the institution of arbitration proceedings but the scope of the consent clauses in question.[192]

In *Salini v Jordan*[193] the dispute was whether the consent to arbitration contained in the Italy-Jordan BIT extended to contract claims as well as to treaty claims. The MFN clause in that treaty provides:

Both Contracting Parties, within the bounds of their own territory, shall grant investments effected by, and the income accruing to, investors of the other Contracting Party, no less favourable treatment than that accorded to investments effected by, and income accruing to, its own nationals or investors of Third States.

The Tribunal refused to apply the MFN clause to the question of whether it had jurisdiction over contract claims. It seemed to proceed from a presumption against the application of a generally worded MFN clause to dispute settlement and concluded that the MFN clause 'does not apply insofar as dispute settlement clauses are concerned'.[194]

In *Plama v Bulgaria*[195] the Tribunal had found that it had jurisdiction on the basis of Article 26 of the ECT.[196] The claimant had additionally attempted to base the Tribunal's jurisdiction on the BIT between Bulgaria and Cyprus. That BIT does not provide for investor-state arbitration. But it contains the following MFN clause in its Article 3(1): 'Each Contracting Party shall apply to the investments in its territory by investors of the other Contracting Party a treatment which is not less favourable than that accorded to investments by investors of third states.'

The claimant had sought to use this MFN clause to avail itself of the Bulgaria-Finland BIT in order to establish ICSID's jurisdiction. Therefore, reliance on the MFN clause was not merely directed at overcoming a procedural obstacle but was an attempt to create a jurisdiction that would not have otherwise existed.

The Tribunal concluded that the MFN clause could not be interpreted as providing consent to submit a dispute to ICSID arbitration.[197] It said:

---

[191] *Gas Natural SDG, SA v Argentina*, Decision on Jurisdiction, 17 June 2005, para 49.

[192] In addition to the cases discussed below, see *Berschader v Russia*, Award, 21 April 2006, paras 159–208; *Tza Yap Shum v Peru*, Decision on Jurisdiction, 19 June 2009, paras 189–220; *Austrian Airlines v Slovakia*, Final Award, 9 October 2009, paras 109–40.

[193] *Salini v Jordan*, Decision on Jurisdiction, 29 November 2004.

[194] At para 119.

[195] *Plama v Bulgaria*, Decision on Jurisdiction, 8 February 2005.

[196] At para 179.　　　　[197] At paras 183, 184, 227.

an MFN provision in a basic treaty does not incorporate by reference dispute settlement provisions in whole or in part set forth in another treaty, unless the MFN provision in the basic treaty leaves no doubt that the Contracting Parties intended to incorporate them.[198]

In *Telenor v Hungary*[199] the clause in the BIT between Hungary and Norway, offering consent to investor-state arbitration, was limited to compensation or other consequences of expropriation. Here, the claimant sought to rely on the MFN clause in the BIT to benefit from wider dispute resolution provisions in BITs between Hungary and other countries. The MFN clause in Article IV(1) of the BIT provided:

Investments made by Investors of one Contracting Party in the territory of the other Contracting Party, as also the returns therefrom, shall be accorded treatment no less favourable than that accorded to investments made by Investors of any third State.

The Tribunal endorsed the solution adopted in *Plama*. It found that the term 'treatment' contained in the MFN clause referred to substantive but not to procedural rights. Deciding otherwise would lead to undesirable treaty-shopping creating uncertainty and instability. Also, the jurisdiction of an arbitral tribunal as determined by a BIT was not to be inferentially extended by an MFN clause since Hungary and Norway had made a deliberate choice to limit arbitration.[200] It said:

The Tribunal therefore concludes that in the present case the MFN clause cannot be used to extend the Tribunal's jurisdiction to categories of claim other than expropriation, for this would subvert the common intention of Hungary and Norway in entering into the BIT in question.[201]

A possible exception to this pattern is *RosInvest v Russia*.[202] In that case the UK-Russia BIT offered consent to jurisdiction over the amount of compensation in the event of an expropriation. On the basis of an MFN clause in that treaty, the Tribunal applied a dispute settlement provision in the Denmark-Russia BIT which covered any dispute in connection with an investment. The Tribunal noted that the very character of an MFN clause is that protection not accepted in one treaty is widened by transferring the protection accorded in another treaty.[203] But the Tribunal's conclusion was limited to finding that the MFN clause enabled it to decide whether there had, in fact, been a valid expropriation.

The two sets of cases may be distinguishable on factual grounds. Most of the cases in which the tribunals accepted the applicability of the MFN clauses to dispute settlement concerned procedural obstacles. Most of the cases in which the effect of the MFN clauses was denied concerned attempts to extend the scope of jurisdiction substantively to issues not covered by the arbitration clauses in the basic treaties. Nevertheless, there is substantial contradiction in the reasoning of

---

[198] At para 223.
[199] *Telenor v Hungary*, Award, 13 September 2006.
[200] At paras 90–7.
[201] At para 100.
[202] *RosInvest v Russia*, Award on Jurisdiction, October 2007, paras 124–39.
[203] At para 131.

the tribunals. In particular, both groups of tribunals made broad statements as to the applicability, or otherwise, of MFN clauses to dispute settlement in general. These broad statements are impossible to reconcile.

The widespread disagreement on this point is further illustrated by the fact that decisions dealing with the effect of MFN clauses are not infrequently accompanied by carefully drafted dissenting opinions. This applies both to decisions permitting the use of MFN clauses in connection with dispute settlement[204] and to decisions disallowing their use.[205]

The acceptance of MFN clauses for the purposes of attracting substantive standards from other treaties[206] but their rejection when it comes to dispute settlement, leads to a paradoxical situation. The importation of additional substantive standards of protection by way of an MFN clause inevitably has effects on the jurisdiction of tribunals. This is particularly evident where the jurisdiction of a tribunal is limited to violations of the treaty. If the basic treaty does not contain an umbrella clause or a guarantee of fair and equitable treatment, the applicability of these standards by way of an MFN clause will also widen the jurisdiction of a tribunal. The effect is that certain jurisdictional limitations in clauses dealing with dispute settlement can be overcome with the help of an MFN clause while others cannot.

A further open question is the effect of a successful invocation of an MFN clause. Does the MFN clause attract only those provisions of the third party treaty that are beneficial to the party invoking it? Or does it lead to the substitution of the basic treaty by the third party treaty including those provisions that are less beneficial? For instance, if the MFN clause is used to avoid a requirement to resort to domestic courts for a certain period of time, would a fork-in-the-road clause in the third party treaty, that is not contained in the basic treaty, become applicable?

The Tribunal in *Siemens v Argentina* took the view that the party invoking the MFN clause could pick and choose. It noted that:

a benefit by the operation of an MFN clause does not carry with it the acceptance of all the terms of the treaty which provides for such benefit whether or not they are considered beneficial to the party making the claim;[207]
... its application will be related only to the benefits that the treaty of reference may grant and to the extent that benefits are perceived to be such.[208]

The Tribunal in *Hochtief v Argentina* reached a different result. It found that the claimant could not use an MFN clause to avoid the requirement to litigate in domestic courts for 18 months without at the same time being subject to a fork-in-the-road

---

[204] *Impregilo v Argentina*, Award, 21 June 2011, paras 51–109 (Diss Op B Stern); *Hochtief v Argentina*, Decision on Jurisdiction, 24 October 2011 (Diss Op C Thomas).

[205] *Renta4 v Russia*, Award on Preliminary Objections, 20 March 2009, paras 68–120 (Sep Op C Brower); *Austrian Airlines v Slovakia*, Final Award, 9 October 2009, paras 109–40 (Sep Op C Brower).

[206] See pp 209 et seq.

[207] *Siemens v Argentina*, Decision on Jurisdiction, 3 August 2004, para 109.

[208] At para 120. See also *RosInvest v Russia*, Final Award, 12 September 2010, paras 269–71.

provision in the third party treaty. The Tribunal said: 'The MFN provision does not permit the selective picking of components from each set of conditions, so as to manufacture a synthetic set of conditions to which *no* State's nationals would be entitled.'[209]

(i) The selection of domestic courts in contracts

Contracts between host states and foreign investors frequently contain forum selection clauses that refer disputes arising from the application of these contracts to the host states' domestic courts. When disputes in connection with the investments arose, investors would invoke the provisions of treaties, usually BITs, granting them access to international arbitration. In turn, the host states would rely on the forum selection clauses in the contracts arguing that the investors had waived their right to international arbitration.

The arbitral tribunals confronted with these arguments have taken a differentiated attitude.[210] *Compañía de Aguas del Aconquija, SA & Compagnie Générale des Eaux v Argentine Republic* (the *Vivendi I* case)[211] involved a concession contract between the French investor and a province of Argentina. The contract contained a forum selection that referred disputes arising from the contract to the jurisdiction of the province's courts. The investor, seeking to bring its claim before an international tribunal rather than before a domestic court, relied on the BIT between Argentina and France to establish the jurisdiction of ICSID. Argentina challenged the ICSID Tribunal's jurisdiction by relying on the forum selection clause in the concession contract.

The ICSID Tribunal distinguished between claims based on the BIT and claims based on the concession contract. The forum selection clause in the concession contract did not affect the claimant's right to go to international arbitration to pursue violations of the BIT.[212] Nevertheless, the Tribunal found that all of the claims were closely linked to the performance of the concession contract and that it was impossible to separate the two types of claim. Therefore, resort to ICSID arbitration should be open to the claimants only after they had failed in their pursuit of the claims before the domestic courts. The Tribunal added that the need to resort to domestic courts was not based on a requirement to exhaust local remedies but was based on the concession contract's forum selection clause.[213]

---

[209] *Hochtief v Argentina*, Decision on Jurisdiction, 24 October 2011, para 98.

[210] In some cases tribunals denied the existence of forum selection, on the basis that domestic courts had jurisdiction in any event under domestic law and that this jurisdiction was not subject to agreement or waiver: *LANCO v Argentina*, Decision on Jurisdiction, 8 December 1998, para 26; *Salini v Morocco*, Decision on Jurisdiction, 23 July 2001, paras 25–7.

[211] *Compañía de Aguas del Aconquija, SA & Compagnie Générale des Eaux v Argentina*, Award, 21 November 2000.

[212] At paras 53, 54.

[213] Award, paras 77–81.

The Award was partly annulled.[214] The ad hoc Committee, which had to decide on the request for annulment of the Award, found that the Tribunal had manifestly exceeded its powers by not examining the merits of some of the claims before it. The Committee ruled that a particular investment dispute may at the same time involve issues of the interpretation and application of a treaty and of a contract.[215] On the relation between breach of treaty and breach of contract, the ad hoc Committee pointed out that these related to independent standards:

A state may breach a treaty without breaching a contract, and *vice versa* . . . whether there has been a breach of the BIT and whether there has been a breach of contract are different questions. . . . [T]he existence of an exclusive jurisdiction clause in a contract between the claimant and the respondent state or one of its subdivisions cannot operate as a bar to the application of the treaty standard. . . . A state cannot rely on an exclusive jurisdiction clause in a contract to avoid the characterisation of its conduct as internationally unlawful under a treaty.[216]

The tribunals have since followed the distinction between contract claims, which are subject to contractual forum selection clauses, and treaty claims, which are unaffected by such clauses. Under this consistent practice the treaty-based jurisdiction of international arbitral tribunals to decide on violations of these treaties is not affected by domestic forum selection clauses in contracts. The contractual selection of domestic courts is restricted to violations of the respective contracts.[217]

For instance, in *AES v Argentina*,[218] the jurisdiction of the international tribunal was based on an offer of consent, accepted by the investor, in the BIT between Argentina and the United States. Argentina relied on forum selection clauses

---

[214] *Compañía de Aguas del Aconquija, SA & Vivendi Universal v Argentina*, Decision on Annulment, 3 July 2002.

[215] Decision on Annulment, paras 60, 72, 76.

[216] Decision on Annulment, paras 95, 96, 101, 103.

[217] *CMS v Argentina*, Decision on Jurisdiction, 17 July 2003, paras 70–6; *SGS v Pakistan*, Decision on Jurisdiction, 6 August 2003, paras 43–74, 147–73; *Azurix v Argentina*, Decision on Jurisdiction, 8 December 2003, paras 26–36, 75–9; *Enron v Argentina*, Decision on Jurisdiction, 14 January 2004, paras 89–94; *SGS v Philippines*, Decision on Jurisdiction, 29 January 2004, paras 136–55, 160–3; *LG&E v Argentina*, Decision on Jurisdiction, 30 April 2004, paras 58–62; *Siemens v Argentina*, Decision on Jurisdiction, 3 August 2004, paras 174–83; *Salini v Jordan*, Decision on Jurisdiction, 29 November 2004, paras 92–6; *Impregilo v Pakistan*, Decision on Jurisdiction, 22 April 2005, paras 286–9; *Camuzzi Intl SA v Argentina*, Decision on Jurisdiction, 11 May 2005, paras 105–19; *Sempra Energy International v Argentina*, Decision on Jurisdiction, 11 May 2005, paras 116–28; *Eureko v Poland*, Partial Award, 19 August 2005, paras 81, 89, 92–114; *Aguas del Tunari, SA v Bolivia*, Decision on Jurisdiction, 21 October 2005, paras 94–123; *Bayindir v Pakistan*, Decision on Jurisdiction, 14 November 2005, paras 139–67; *Suez, Sociedad General de Aguas de Barcelona SA, and InterAguas Servicios Integrales del Agua SA v Bolivia*, Decision on Jurisdiction, 16 May 2006, paras 41–5; *National Grid plc v Argentina*, Decision on Jurisdiction, 20 June 2006, paras 167–70; *Inceysa v El Salvador*, Award, 2 August 2006, paras 43, 212–17; *Total v Argentina*, Decision on Jurisdiction, 25 August 2006, paras 82–5; *Fraport v Philippines*, Award, 16 August 2007, paras 388–91; *Vivendi v Argentina*, Resubmitted Case: Award, 20 August 2007, paras 7.3.1–7.3.11; *Helnan v Egypt*, Award, 3 July 2008, paras 102–3; *TSA Spectrum v Argentina*, Award, 19 December 2008, paras 42–66; *Enron v Argentina*, Decision on Annulment, 30 July 2010, paras 128–50; *Impregilo v Argentina*, Award, 21 June 2011, paras 141–89; *SGS v Paraguay*, Decision on Jurisdiction, 12 February 2010, paras 173–85; Award, 10 February 2012, paras 75, 96–109.

[218] *AES Corp v Argentina*, Decision on Jurisdiction, 26 April 2005.

contained in concession contracts and objected to ICSID's jurisdiction. The Tribunal rejected Argentina's argument. It said:

the Entities concerned have consented to a forum selection clause electing Administrative Argentine law and exclusive jurisdiction of Argentine administrative tribunals in the concession contracts and related documents. But this exclusivity only plays within the Argentinean legal order, for matters in relation with the execution of these concession contracts. They do not preclude AES from exercising its rights as resulting, within the international legal order from two international treaties, namely the US-Argentina BIT and the ICSID Convention.

In other terms, the present Tribunal has jurisdiction over any alleged breach by Argentina of its obligations under the US-Argentina BIT.[219]

The distinction between contract claims and treaty claims has appeared in many investment arbitrations.[220] The respondent's objection that the case only involves contract claims and the claimant's insistence that treaty rights are involved, have become routine features of many cases. As it turns out, the distinction between treaty claims and contract claims is not always easy. A particular course of action by the host state may well constitute a breach of contract and a violation of international law. The two categories are not mutually exclusive. Rather, two different standards have to be applied to determine whether one or the other or both have been violated.

The situation is made even more complex by the fact that some treaties offer jurisdiction for any investment dispute, which would include contract claims, while other treaties restrict jurisdiction to alleged violations of the treaty. The jurisdiction of a treaty-based tribunal is not necessarily restricted to violations of the treaty's substantive provisions. A tribunal's jurisdiction is not determined by its establishment through a treaty but by the wording of the clause governing its jurisdiction. In addition, umbrella clauses will convert contract breaches into treaty breaches, although this point is not undisputed.[221]

The separate treatment of contract claims and treaty claims leads to situations where the claimant may be compelled to pursue part of its claim through national procedures and another part through international procedures. This has undesirable consequences. The need to dissect cases into contract claims and treaty claims to be dealt with by separate fora requires claim splitting and has the potential of

---

[219] At paras 93, 94.

[220] See eg *El Paso v Argentina*, Decision on Jurisdiction, 27 April 2006, paras 63–5; *Jan de Nul v Egypt*, Decision on Jurisdiction, 16 June 2006, paras 79–82; *LESI & Astaldi v Algeria*, Decision on Jurisdiction, 12 July 2006, para 84; *Telenor v Hungary*, Award, 13 September 2006, paras 32, 50, 47(1), 50; *Saipem v Bangladesh*, Decision on Jurisdiction, 21 March 2007, paras 139–42; *Parkerings v Lithuania*, Award, 11 September 2007, paras 257, 260–6, 289, 317, 345; *BG Group v Argentina*, Final Award, 24 December 2007, paras 177–85; *Helnan v Egypt*, Award, 3 July 2008, paras 102, 107; *Biwater Gauff v Tanzania*, Award, 24 July 2008, paras 468–75; *Rumeli v Kazakhstan*, Award, 29 July 2008, para 330; *Bayindir v Pakistan*, Award, 27 August 2009, paras 133–9, 197, 367–75; *Toto v Lebanon*, Decision on Jurisdiction, 11 September 2009, paras 95–130; *Burlington Resources v Ecuador*, Decision on Jurisdiction, 2 June 2010, paras 76–81; *Helnan v Egypt*, Decision on Annulment, 14 June 2010, paras 58–66; *Hamester v Ghana*, Award, 18 June 2010, paras 325–31.

[221] See Chapter VII.3.

leading to parallel proceedings. This is uneconomical and contrary to the goal of reaching final and comprehensive resolutions of disputes.

Even worse, the separation of types of claim arising from the same set of facts can lead to retaliatory proceedings. A host state, threatened by a treaty claim before an international tribunal, may start domestic proceedings in order to counteract and frustrate the international proceedings. In this way, the host state can exert pressure on the investor to settle or withdraw the treaty claim. Alternatively, the host state can use the domestic proceedings to recoup the money awarded in the international award through an action for breach of contract against the investor. Put differently, allowing the host state to pursue contract claims arising from the same dispute in its own domestic forum can undermine the procedural protection granted to the foreign investor in the BIT.

(j) Procedure

aa. Arbitration Rules

Arbitration requires a comprehensive body of procedural rules. In investment arbitration the most commonly applied set of rules are those provided in the ICSID Convention and in the ICSID Arbitration Rules. In addition, ICSID offers a set of Institution Rules as well as Administrative and Financial Regulations. The Regulations and Rules are adopted by ICSID's Administrative Council. The latest amendment to the ICSID Regulations and Rules came into effect on 10 April 2006.[222]

Article 44 of the ICSID Convention provides that arbitration proceeding are to be conducted in accordance with the Convention and, except as the parties otherwise agree, in accordance with the Arbitration Rules in effect on the date on which the parties consented to arbitration. Any question of procedure not covered in this manner is to be decided by the tribunal. Therefore, ICSID proceedings are self-contained and denationalized—that is, they are independent of any national law including the law of the tribunal's seat. Domestic courts do not have the power to intervene.

Non-ICSID arbitration is governed by other sets of rules. Proceedings under the Additional Facility are subject to the Arbitration (Additional Facility) Rules.[223] Proceedings under the auspices of other arbitration institutions are subject to the respective rules provided by these institutions. For ad hoc arbitration, the parties frequently select the UNCITRAL Arbitration Rules.[224] Non-ICSID proceedings are not insulated from national law. For the sake of convenience, this chapter focuses on ICSID procedure.

---

[222] See <http://icsid.worldbank.org/ICSID/ICSID/RulesMain.jsp>.
[223] See <http://icsid.worldbank.org/ICSID/ICSID/AdditionalFacilityRules.jsp>.
[224] The original UNCITRAL Arbitration Rules were adopted in 1976, 15 ILM 701 (1976). A revised version was adopted by UN GA Res 65/22 in 2010.

bb. Institution of proceedings

ICSID proceedings are initiated by a request for arbitration directed to the Secretary-General of ICSID.[225] The request may be submitted by either the investor or the host state. In practice, the investor is nearly always the claimant. The request must be drafted in one of ICSID's official languages (English, French, and Spanish) and a non-refundable lodging fee of US$25,000 is payable at the time of the request. After the constitution of the tribunal, an administrative fee of US$32,000 is payable per year.

The request for arbitration must contain information concerning the dispute, the parties, and the jurisdictional requirements, including the basis of consent.[226] The Secretary-General will register the request unless he finds that the dispute is manifestly outside the Centre's jurisdiction.[227] Registration is often preceded by correspondence with both parties and a call by ICSID for further clarifications. Once the request is registered, the Secretary-General will notify the parties in writing.

cc. The tribunal and its composition

Tribunals are nearly always composed of three arbitrators. Sole arbitrators are relatively rare. Under the standard procedure for the appointment of arbitrators at ICSID, each party appoints one arbitrator and the third, who is the tribunal's president, is appointed by agreement of the parties.[228] A different mode of appointment may be agreed by the parties.[229] Sometimes the two party-appointed arbitrators are charged with appointment of the tribunal's president.

If the tribunal is not constituted after 90 days, either party may request the Chairman of the Administrative Council[230] to make any outstanding appointments.[231] In doing so, the Chairman will consult with the parties as far as possible. The purpose of this provision is to avoid a stalemate if one party is uncooperative. The Chairman is bound to make this appointment from the Panel of Arbitrators kept by ICSID.[232] Arbitrators thus appointed must not be nationals of the state party to the dispute or co-nationals of the investor party to the dispute.

In the case of party-appointed arbitrators, national arbitrators are also excluded.[233] But this prohibition would not apply if each individual member of the tribunal is appointed by agreement of the parties. The idea behind this rule is to guarantee maximum objectivity of the arbitrators.

---

[225] Article 36(1).   [226] Article 36(2); Institution Rule 2.
[227] Article 36(3).   [228] Article 37(2)(b).   [229] Arbitration Rule 2.
[230] Under Art 5 of the Convention, the President of the International Bank for Reconstruction and Development is *ex officio* Chairman of ICSID's Administrative Council.
[231] Article 38.
[232] Article 40(1). Articles 12–16 of the Convention establish a Panel of Arbitrators to be maintained by the Centre.
[233] This effect is achieved through Art 39 and Arbitration Rule 1(3).

Arbitrators must be of high moral character, have recognized competence in the fields of law, commerce, industry, or finance, and may be relied upon to exercise independent judgement.[234] In addition, arbitrators must be independent of the parties. Each arbitrator must sign a declaration providing details of any relationships with the parties.[235] A conflict of interest is a bar to appointment and may lead to the arbitrator's disqualification.

In the case of death, incapacity, or resignation of an arbitrator, the resulting vacancy will be filled by the same method that was applied for the original appointment.[236]

A party may propose disqualification of an arbitrator on the ground that the arbitrator manifestly lacks the qualities required for his or her appointment.[237] Proposals for disqualification typically involve allegations of a conflict of interest or other lack of independent judgement,[238] although non-compliance with the nationality requirements under the Convention is another possible ground.[239] The decision on a proposal to disqualify is made by the unchallenged members of the tribunal. If the unchallenged members do not agree, the decision is made by the Chairman of the Administrative Council who also decides if a sole arbitrator or a majority of the arbitrators is challenged.[240]

In *Compañía de Aguas del Aconquija, SA & Vivendi Universal v Argentina*[241] the President of the ad hoc Committee[242] had disclosed that a partner of his law firm was giving legal advice to the claimant. The respondent's proposal to disqualify him was unsuccessful. The members of the Committee found particularly relevant that: (a) the relationship was immediately and fully disclosed; (b) there had never been a personal lawyer–client relationship; (c) the work in question had nothing to do with the case before the Committee and (d) only concerned a specific transaction; and (e) the relationship was about to come to an end.[243] The ad hoc Committee stated:

the mere existence of some professional relationship with a party is not an automatic basis for disqualification of an arbitrator or Committee member. All the circumstances need to be

---

[234] Articles 14(1) and 40(2).   [235] Arbitration Rule 6(2).

[236] Article 56(1); Arbitration Rule 8. Exceptionally under Art 56(3) in the case of a resignation by a party-appointed arbitrator without the consent of the tribunal, the resulting vacancy is to be filled by the Chairman.

[237] Article 57.

[238] See *Amco v Indonesia*, Decision on Jurisdiction, 25 September 1983: the challenge is reported by W M Tupman, 'Challenge and Disqualification of Arbitrators in International Commercial Arbitration' (1989) 38 *ICLQ* 26, 44–5; *Generation Ukraine, Inc v Ukraine*, Award, 16 September 2003, paras 4.8–4.18; *Salini v Jordan*, Award, 31 January 2006, paras 5, 9.

[239] *Olguín v Paraguay*, Decision on Jurisdiction, 8 August 2000, paras 12–13; Award, 26 July 2001, paras 15–16.

[240] Article 58; Arbitration Rule 9. See *Abaclat et al v Argentina*, Decision on Challenge, 21 December 2011.

[241] *Compañía de Aguas del Aconquija, SA & Vivendi Universal v Argentina*, Decision on the Challenge to the President of the Committee, 3 October 2001.

[242] Under Art 52 of the Convention an award may be annulled under certain circumstances by an ad hoc committee. See pp 301 et seq.

[243] At para 26.

considered in order to determine whether the relationship is significant enough to justify entertaining reasonable doubts as to the capacity of the arbitrator or member to render a decision freely and independently.[244]

dd. Provisional measures

Under the ICSID Convention the tribunal has the possibility of taking provisional measures.[245] The purpose of provisional measures is to induce behaviour by the parties that is conducive to a successful conduct of the proceedings. The measures have to be taken at a time when the outcome of a dispute is still uncertain. In fact, provisional measures are often requested before the tribunal has made a decision on jurisdiction. Therefore, the tribunal has to strike a careful balance between the urgency of a request for provisional measures and the need not to prejudge the case. Tribunals have held that they have the power to take provisional measures on the basis of their prima facie evaluation of jurisdiction and that this is without prejudice to a subsequent determination of jurisdiction.[246]

The guiding principles for the indication of provisional measures are urgency and necessity. For instance, it may be necessary to induce the parties to cooperate in the proceedings and to furnish all relevant evidence; it may be necessary to take early measures to secure compliance with an eventual award; it may be necessary to stop the parties from resorting to self-help or seeking relief through other remedies; and it may be necessary to prevent a general aggravation of the situation through unilateral action.

Parties to proceedings have requested provisional measures in a number of situations. In some cases, tribunals have used provisional measures to secure access to evidence essential to the proceedings;[247] in other cases, parties have unsuccessfully requested provisional measures directed at the posting of financial guarantees to secure recovery of the cost of the proceedings.[248] Yet another situation involved allegations of 'hostile propaganda' or adverse publications.[249]

---

[244] At para 27.

[245] Article 47; Arbitration Rule 39. Under Arbitration Rule 39(6) provisional measures by domestic courts are possible in ICSID proceedings only in the unlikely event that the parties have so agreed in their consent agreement.

[246] *Casado v Chile*, Decision on Provisional Measures, 25 September 2001, paras 5–14; *SGS v Pakistan*, Procedural Order No 2, 16 October 2002, 8 ICSID Reports 388, 391–2; *Azurix v Argentina*, Decision on Provisional Measures, 6 August 2003, paras 29–31; *Biwater Gauff v Tanzania*, Procedural Order No 1, 31 March 2006, paras 32, 47, 70; *Occidental v Ecuador*, Decision on Provisional Measures, 17 August 2007, para 55.

[247] *AGIP v Congo*, Award, 30 November 1979, paras 7–9; *Vacuum Salt v Ghana*, Decision on Provisional Measures, 14 June 1993; Award, 16 February 1994, paras 13–22; *Biwater Gauff v Tanzania*, Procedural Order No 1, 31 March 2006, paras 16, 20, 45–6, 56, 77–81, 84–8; *Railroad Development Corp v Guatemala*, Decision on Provisional Measures, 15 October 2008; *Fakes v Turkey*, Award, 14 July 2010, para 13.

[248] *Maffezini v Spain*, Procedural Order No 2, 28 October 1999; *Casado v Chile*, Decision on Provisional Measures, 25 September 2001, paras 78–89; *Bayindir v Pakistan*, Award, 27 August 2009, para 55; *Cementownia v Turkey*, Award, 17 September 2009, paras 34, 36; *Anderson v Costa Rica*, Award, 19 May 2010, para 9; *Hamester v Ghana*, Award, 18 June 2010, paras 15, 17.

[249] *Amco v Indonesia*, Decision on Provisional Measures, 9 December 1983; *World Duty Free v Kenya*, Award, 4 October 2006, para 16; *EDF v Romania*, Procedural Order No 2, 30 May 2008.

The most important category of provisional measures involves requests to order the termination or suspension of related domestic proceedings.[250] In *SGS v Pakistan*[251] the Supreme Court of Pakistan had granted a motion by the respondent that the claimant be permanently enjoined from taking any steps to participate in the ICSID proceedings. The claimant requested provisional measures from the ICSID tribunal. One request was to the effect that the respondent should immediately withdraw from all proceedings in the courts of Pakistan relating in any way to the ICSID arbitration and cause these proceedings to be discontinued.[252]

The Tribunal noted that under Article 41 of the ICSID Convention the tribunal is the judge of its own competence. It pointed out that the Supreme Court judgment, although final under the law of Pakistan, did not bind the Tribunal as a matter of international law. The Tribunal said:

> The right to seek access to international adjudication must be respected and cannot be constrained by an order of a national court. Nor can a State plead its internal law in defence of an act that is inconsistent with its international obligations. Otherwise, a Contracting State could impede access to ICSID arbitration by operation of its own law.[253]

On that basis the Tribunal issued the following provisional measure:

> the Tribunal recommends that the Government of Pakistan not take any step to initiate a complaint for contempt [of court]. It recommends further that, in the event that any other party, including the Supreme Court of Pakistan *sua sponte*, were to initiate a complaint, the Government of Pakistan take all necessary steps to inform the Court of the current standing of this proceeding and of the fact that this Tribunal must discharge its duty to determine whether it has the jurisdiction to consider the international claim on the merits. The Government of Pakistan should ensure that if contempt proceedings are initiated by any party, such proceedings not be acted upon.[254]

The wording and drafting history of the ICSID Convention would suggest that a decision for provisional measures under Article 47 is not binding but merely a

---

[250] *MINE v Guinea*, Award, 6 January 1988, 4 ICSID Reports 61, at 69, 77; *Vacuum Salt v Ghana*, Decision on Provisional Measures, 14 June 1993; Award, 16 February 1994, paras 13–22; *CSOB v Slovakia*, Procedural Order No 2, 9 September 1998, Procedural Order No 3, 5 November 1998, Procedural Order No 4, 11 January 1999, Procedural Order No 5, 1 March 2000; *Tanzania Electric v Independent Power Tanzania*, Award, 12 July 2001, paras 26, 29; *Casado v Chile*, Decision on Provisional Measures, 25 September 2001, paras 28–66; *Azurix v Argentina*, Decision on Provisional Measures, 6 August 2003; *Tokios Tokelės v Ukraine*, Decision on Jurisdiction, 29 April 2004, paras 11, 12; *Bayindir v Pakistan*, Decision on Jurisdiction, 14 November 2005, para 46; Award, 27 August 2009, paras 52–66, 487, 488; *Duke Energy v Peru*, Decision on Jurisdiction, 1 February 2006, paras 15–18; *Saipem v Bangladesh*, Decision on Jurisdiction, 21 March 2007, paras 162–85; *Plama v Bulgaria*, Award, 27 August 2008, paras 23–6; *Burlington v Ecuador*, Decision on Jurisdiction, 2 June 2010, paras 65–75; *Millicom v Senegal*, Decision on Jurisdiction, 16 July 2010, paras 29–31, 33–5, 37; *ATA v Jordan*, Decision on Interpretation, 7 March 2011, paras 10–12, 46.

[251] *SGS v Pakistan*, Procedural Order No 2, 16 October 2002.

[252] At p 392.

[253] At p 393. Footnote omitted.

[254] At p 397.

recommendation.[255] Nevertheless, tribunals have come to the conclusion that decisions on provisional measures are binding upon the parties.[256] In *Maffezini v Spain*, the Tribunal compared the word 'recommend' used in connection with provisional measures, to the word 'order' used elsewhere in the Arbitration Rules. It said:

The Tribunal does not believe that the parties to the Convention meant to create a substantial difference in the effect of these two words. The Tribunal's authority to rule on provisional measures is no less binding than that of a final award. Accordingly, for the purposes of this Order, the Tribunal deems the word 'recommend' to be of equivalent value as the word 'order.'[257]

Apart from the question of binding force, non-compliance with provisional measures will be taken into account by the tribunal when making the award.[258]

ee. Summary procedure

Under ICSID Arbitration Rule 41(5), introduced in 2006, a party may within 30 days of the tribunal's constitution object on the ground that the claim is manifestly without merit. This gives the tribunal the possibility of dismissing an evidently unmeritorious case expeditiously and at an early stage.

For an objection under Rule 41(5) to be successful, the lack of merit must be manifest. The Tribunal in *Trans-Global Petroleum v Jordan* found that the ordinary meaning of the word 'manifestly' required the respondent to 'establish its objection clearly and obviously, with relative ease and despatch'.[259]

The Secretary-General's screening power before registering a request for arbitration under Article 36(3) is restricted to jurisdiction and does not extend to the merits. The summary procedure under Rule 41(5) fills this gap but is not limited to challenges on the merits. It can also be used to dispute jurisdiction.[260] The Tribunal in *Brandes v Venezuela* said:

There exist no objective reasons why the intent not to burden the parties with a possibly long and costly proceeding when dealing with such unmeritorious claims should be limited to an evaluation of the merits of the case and should not also englobe an examination of the jurisdictional basis on which the tribunal's powers to decide the case rest.[261]

---

[255] Article 47: 'the Tribunal may . . . recommend any provisional measures'. By contrast, under Art 41 of its Statute, the ICJ may 'indicate' provisional measures. Under Art 290 of the United Nations Convention on the Law of the Sea the court or tribunal may 'prescribe' provisional measures.

[256] *Casado v Chile*, Decision on Provisional Measures, 25 September 2001, paras 17–23; *Tokios Tokelés v Ukraine*, Procedural Order No 1, 1 July 2003, para 4; *Biwater Gauff v Tanzania*, Procedural Order No 2, 31 March 2006, paras 87–8, 97–8, 104–6; *Occidental v Ecuador*, Decision on Provisional Measures, 17 August 2007, para 58.

[257] *Maffezini v Spain*, Procedural Order No 2, 28 October 1999, para 9.

[258] See *AGIP v Congo*, Award, 30 November 1979, para 42.

[259] *Trans-Global Petroleum v Jordan*, Decision under Arbitration Rule 41(5), 12 May 2008, para 88.

[260] *Global Trading v Ukraine*, Award, 1 December 2010, paras 30–1; *RSM v Grenada*, Award, 10 December 2010, para 6.1.1.

[261] *Brandes v Venezuela*, Decision under Arbitration Rule 41(5), 2 February 2009, para 52.

At the same time there appears to be agreement that the objection must be based on a question of law and not of fact.[262]

In *Global Trading v Ukraine* the Tribunal found that the activities underlying the dispute 'are pure commercial transactions that cannot on any interpretation be considered to constitute "investments" within the meaning of Article 25 of the ICSID Convention'.[263] It therefore held that the claims put forward were manifestly without legal merit under Rule 41(5) and rendered an award to that effect.

Despite its summary nature, this expedited procedure requires that both parties be properly heard both in writing and orally. A decision upholding an objection results in an award which, under Article 48(3) of the ICSID Convention, must deal with every question submitted to the tribunal and must contain a full statement of reasons.

ff. Written and oral procedure

Procedural questions are typically addressed at the tribunal's first session with the parties. The questions include representation of the parties, the place and language of proceedings, the number and sequence of the pleadings, a calendar with time limits for the submission of pleadings, and the date of hearings, records of hearings, and production of evidence.

Typically proceedings involve a written phase followed by an oral one. The written phase is opened by a memorial of the claimant followed by a counter-memorial of the respondent. In most cases there is another round of written exchanges termed reply and rejoinder. A memorial must contain a statement of the facts, a statement of the law, and the party's submissions. A counter-memorial also must address the facts and legal arguments and make submissions.[264] In addition, the parties often submit voluminous supporting documentation.

If the respondent raises objections to the tribunal's jurisdiction, the proceedings on the merits are suspended. Such an objection is to be submitted not later than at the time the counter-memorial is due. Typically, the proceedings are then bifurcated, that is, the jurisdictional question is heard first, followed, if the tribunal finds that it has jurisdiction, by a resumption of the proceedings on the merits. Alternatively, the tribunal may decide to join the jurisdictional question to the merits. In most cases the procedure dealing with jurisdiction also consists of a written and an oral phase.[265]

If the tribunal decides that the dispute is not within the jurisdiction of the Centre or outside its competence, or that all claims are manifestly without legal merit, it will render an award to that effect[266] and the proceedings are closed. Otherwise, the tribunal will resume the proceedings on the merits.

---

[262] *Brades v Venezuela*, n 261 paras 56–61; *Global Trading v Ukraine*, Award, 1 December 2010, para 31; *RSM v Grenada*, Award, 10 December 2010, para 6.1.1.

[263] *Global Trading v Ukraine*, Award, 1 December 2010, para 57.

[264] Arbitration Rule 31.

[265] Article 41; Arbitration Rule 41.

[266] Arbitration Rule 41(6).

The oral phase consists of a hearing in the presence of the tribunal, its officers, and the parties and their representatives. In addition to the parties, the tribunal may hear witnesses and experts. Most hearings are closed to the public.[267]

The evidence presented by the parties to the tribunal consists of documents, witness testimony, and expert opinions.[268] The tribunal has discretion in deciding on the relevance,[269] credibility,[270] and admissibility[271] of evidence. The tribunal may call upon the parties to produce further evidence.[272] In a number of cases tribunals have issued orders for the production of documents and have developed criteria for their materiality, relevance, and specificity.[273]

Default—that is, non-participation of an uncooperative party—will not stall the proceedings. If one party fails to present its case, the other party may request the tribunal to proceed and render an award. Before doing so, the tribunal will give the non-appearing party another chance to cooperate. The appearing party's assertions will not be accepted simply because the other party does not cooperate and hence does not contest them. Rather, the tribunal has to examine all questions and decide whether the appearing party's submissions are well founded in fact and in law.[274]

Default by a party puts an extra burden on the tribunal and also on the cooperating party. The tribunal must examine the cooperating party's submissions on its own motion. The cooperating party may be called upon to prove assertions which might otherwise be accepted as uncontested. Default has occurred in only relatively few cases.[275] In some cases, the respondent states did not cooperate initially but appeared at a later stage in the proceedings.[276]

The parties may at any time agree to settle or otherwise discontinue the case. A settlement may be incorporated into an award if the parties so request and submit their settlement in writing.[277] Alternatively, a party may unilaterally request

---

[267] On transparency, see pp 286–8.

[268] Arbitration Rules 33–5.

[269] See *Aguas del Tunari, SA v Bolivia*, Decision on Jurisdiction, 21 October 2005, para 25.

[270] See *ADC v Hungary*, Award, 2 October 2006, para 257; *Rumeli Telekom v Kazakhstan*, Award, 29 July 2008, paras 442–8.

[271] *Methanex v United States*, Award, 3 August 2005, Part II, Ch I, paras 1–60.

[272] Article 43(a).

[273] *Pope & Talbot v Canada*, Ruling on Claim of Crown Privilege, 6 September 2000, 7 ICSID Reports 99; *UPS v Canada*, Tribunal Decision Relating to Canada's Claim of Cabinet Privilege, 8 October 2004; *CSOB v Slovakia*, Award, 29 December 2004, para 9; *Noble Ventures v Romania*, Award, 12 October 2005, paras 19, 20; *Aguas del Tunari v Bolivia*, Decision on Jurisdiction, 21 October 2005, paras 24–8, 324–7; *Duke Energy v Peru*, Decision on Jurisdiction, 1 February 2006, para 19; *Biwater Gauff (Tanzania) Ltd v Tanzania*, Procedural Order No 2, 24 May 2006; *Azurix v Argentina*, Award, 14 July 2006, paras 22–7, 29, 31; *ADC v Hungary*, Award, 2 October 2006, paras 30, 33–7; *Champion Trading v Egypt*, Decision on Jurisdiction, 21 October 2003, paras 15, 17–23; *Bayindir v Pakistan*, Procedural Order No 4, Document Production, 27 November 2006.

[274] Article 45; Arbitration Rules 34(3), 42.

[275] *Kaiser Bauxite v Jamaica*, Decision on Jurisdiction, 6 July 1975, 1 ICSID Reports 299, paras 5–10; *LETCO v Liberia*, Award, 31 March 1986, 2 ICSID Reports 346, pp 354–7; *Goetz v Burundi*, Decision, 2 September 1998, 6 ICSID Reports 5, paras 33–57.

[276] *Benvenuti & Bonfant v Congo*, Award, 15 August 1980, paras 1.7–1.12, 1.17–1.34; *AMT v Zaire*, Award, 21 February 1997, paras 2.01–3.01.

[277] Arbitration Rule 43.

discontinuance of the proceedings, which the tribunal will grant if the other party does not object.[278] In addition, the proceedings will be discontinued if both parties fail to take any steps for six consecutive months.[279]

gg. The award

After the pleadings of the parties are completed, the tribunal deliberates on the award. Only the members of the tribunal take part in the deliberations and their substance remains secret.[280]

Awards are rendered in writing and are signed by the members of the tribunal. Most awards are rendered unanimously, but majority decisions are possible.[281] A member of the tribunal may attach a dissenting opinion or a declaration.

Awards must deal with all questions submitted to the tribunal and contain a full statement of reasons. Under the ICSID Convention, an award finally disposes of all questions before the tribunal. A failure to deal with all questions, or serious shortcomings in the reasoning, may lead to a charge of excess of powers or failure to state the reasons, both of which are grounds for annulment.[282]

The award is dispatched promptly to the parties. The date of the award is not the date of signature by the arbitrators but the date of dispatch to the parties.[283] This is important for the exact determination of the time limits for any post-award remedies.[284]

Awards are final and binding; they are subject to review only under limited circumstances.[285] The binding force of awards is limited to the parties. It does not extend to other cases before different tribunals and does not create binding precedents. Tribunals have emphasized on many occasions that they are not bound by previous decisions. At the same time they have also stated that they will take due account of previous cases when making their decisions.[286] In fact, parties routinely rely on earlier decisions of other international tribunals and of international courts, and tribunals frequently refer to and rely on earlier decisions.

hh. Transparency

Confidentiality is traditionally considered one of the major advantages of international commercial arbitration between private parties. But in investment arbitration the presence of issues of public interest have increasingly led to demands for more openness and transparency. Two issues are typically discussed under the heading of transparency: access to information and third party participation.

---

[278] Arbitration Rule 44.   [279] Arbitration Rule 45.   [280] Arbitration Rule 15.
[281] Arbitration Rule 16(1) provides that all decisions of the tribunal may be rendered by majority vote.
[282] See pp 304, 307.   [283] Article 49(1).   [284] See pp 301, 309.
[285] See pp 300 et seq.   [286] See pp 33–4.

The Secretary-General of ICSID is under an obligation to publish information about the existence and progress of pending cases.[287] This is achieved primarily through the Centre's website at <http://icsid.worldbank.org/ICSID/Index.jsp>.

Awards are not published automatically. ICSID will publish awards only with the consent of both parties,[288] but under an amendment to the Arbitration Rules introduced in 2006 the Centre is now under an obligation to publish excerpts of the legal reasoning of each award.[289] The parties are free to release awards and other decisions for publication unless otherwise agreed. Most ICSID awards have been published in one way or another but there are some awards and other decisions that have remained unpublished. Non-ICSID awards are published sporadically. It is impossible to discover how many non-ICSID arbitrations have taken place since there is no central register of these proceedings.

The situation with respect to documents relating to pending arbitration proceedings is complex.[290] The parties are not prohibited from publishing their pleadings, but they may come to an understanding to refrain from doing so. The parties are free to agree on total or partial publication of documents relating to a proceeding.[291]

Most hearings are closed to the public. In principle, only the members of the tribunal, officers of the tribunal, the parties and their representatives, and witnesses while giving testimony may attend. But under a rule introduced in 2006, the tribunal may, unless a party objects and after consultation with the Secretary-General of ICSID, allow other persons to attend all or part of the hearings.[292] Some investment treaties provide that investor-state arbitration hearings shall be open to the public.

In some cases ICSID tribunals have permitted the submission of *amicus curiae* briefs by non-disputing parties.[293] Under a procedure introduced in 2006 the tribunal may, after consulting the parties, allow an entity that is not a party to file a written submission regarding a matter within the scope of the dispute.[294]

Non-ICSID tribunals operating in the framework of the NAFTA under the UNCITRAL Rules, have allowed third parties to make written submissions.[295] In

---

[287] Administrative and Financial Regulations 22 and 23.

[288] Article 48(5).

[289] Arbitration Rule 48(4).

[290] For detailed discussion, see *Biwater Gauff v Tanzania*, Procedural Order No 3, 29 September 2006 and Procedural Order No 5, 2 February 2007. See also *World Duty Free v Kenya*, Award, 4 October 2006, para 16.

[291] See *Malaysian Historical Salvors v Malaysia*, Award, 17 May 2007, para 32.

[292] Arbitration Rule 32.

[293] See *Aguas Argentinas et al v Argentina*, Order in Response to a Petition for Transparency and Participation as *Amicus Curiae*, 19 May 2005; *Methanex v United States*, Award, 3 August 2005, Part II, Ch C, paras 26–30; *Aguas del Tunari, SA v Bolivia*, Decision on Jurisdiction, 21 October 2005, paras 15–18, Appendix III; *Aguas Provinciales de Santa Fe et al v Argentina*, Order in Response to a Petition for Participation as *Amicus Curiae*, 17 March 2006.

[294] Arbitration Rule 37(2). For an application of this procedure, see eg *Biwater Gauff v Tanzania*, Award, 24 July 2008, paras 356–92.

[295] *Methanex v United States* (UNCITRAL), Decision on *Amici Curiae*, 15 January 2001; *United Parcel Services v Canada* (UNCITRAL), Decision of the Tribunal on Petitions for Intervention and Participation as *Amici Curiae*, 17 October 2001.

October 2003 the NAFTA Free Trade Commission issued a statement regarding the participation of non-disputing parties.[296]

(k) Applicable law

Foreign investments are regulated by international as well as national rules. There is a considerable body of substantive international law protecting foreign investors. It consists of treaty law, contained mostly in BITs, but also multilateral treaties such as the NAFTA and the ECT. But there is also a good deal of customary international law that remains relevant. This customary international law includes various aspects of state responsibility and such issues as denial of justice, the law on expropriation, and rules relating to the nationality of individuals and corporations.

Investments are typically complex operations involving numerous transactions of different kinds. Many of these transactions will take place under the local law and will have their closest connection to the host state's legal system. The relevant legislation relates to commercial law, company law, administrative law, labour law, tax law, foreign exchange regulations, real estate law, and many other areas of the host state's legal system. At the same time, the application of international law gives the investor assurance that the international minimum standard will be observed.

The parties to the dispute, that is the host state and the investor, may agree on the governing law. Some contracts governing investments simply refer to the host state's domestic law.[297] The choice of the law of the investor's home country or of the law of a third state is rare but not unheard of.[298] In the majority of cases, agreements between the parties on applicable law include international law as well as host state law.[299]

Some treaties and other international documents providing for arbitration refer to the parties' agreement on choice of law.[300] Some of the relevant treaties contain their own choice of law clauses in case there is no agreement on applicable law between the parties. For instance, Article 42 of the ICSID Convention refers primarily to any agreement on choice of law that the parties may have reached.

---

[296] NAFTA Free Trade Commission Statement on Non-Disputing Party Participation, 7 October 2003, 44 ILM 796 (2005).

[297] See eg *Attorney-General v Mobil Oil NZ Ltd*, New Zealand, High Court, 1 July 1987, 4 ICSID Reports 117, 123; *MINE v Guinea*, Decision on Annulment, 22 December 1989, para 6.31.

[298] See eg *SPP v Egypt*, Award, 20 May 1992, para 225. The choice of English law to the exclusion of Egyptian law turned out to be decisive for the computation of interest. *Azpetrol v Azerbaijan*, Award, 8 September 2009, paras 49–65.

[299] See the Deeds of Concession concluded between Libya and two US companies between 1955 and 1968 in *Texaco v Libya*, Award, 19 January 1977, 53 ILR 389, at 404. See also *LIAMCO v Libya*, Award, 12 April 1977, 62 ILR 141, at 172; *British Petroleum v Libya*, 10 October 1973, 53 ILR 297, at 303; *AGIP v Congo*, Award, 30 November 1979, para 18; *Kaiser Bauxite v Jamaica*, Decision on Jurisdiction, 6 July 1975, para 12; *CSOB v Slovakia*, Award, 29 December 2004, paras 58–63; *Duke Energy v Ecuador*, Award, 18 August 2008, paras 190–7.

[300] ICSID Convention, Art 42; ICSID Additional Facility Rules, Art 54. See also UNCITRAL Arbitration Rules, Art 35.

In the absence of such an agreement, it provides for the application of the host state's law and international law:

Article 42

(1) The Tribunal shall decide a dispute in accordance with such rules of law as may be agreed by the parties. In the absence of such agreement, the Tribunal shall apply the law of the Contracting State party to the dispute (including its rules on the conflict of laws) and such rules of international law as may be applicable.

Both the UNCITRAL Rules (Art 35(1)) and the ICC Rules (Art 21(1)) state that a tribunal will apply the law designated by the parties. If there is no choice of law clause, the UNCITRAL Rules refer to 'the law which it determines to be appropriate' and to 'any usage of trade applicable to the transaction' which the tribunal shall take into account (Art 35(3)). For ICC proceedings, its Rules provide in such a case that the Tribunal 'shall apply the rules of law which it determines to be appropriate' (Art 21(1)) and that the Tribunal 'shall take account of the provisions of the contract, if any, between the parties and of any relevant trade usages' (Art 21(2)). Many of the treaty provisions that offer investor-state arbitration, such as the NAFTA, the ECT, and some BITs, also contain provisions on applicable law. By taking up the offer of arbitration, the investor also accepts the choice of law clause contained in the treaty's dispute settlement provision. In this way, the treaty's provision on applicable law becomes part of the arbitration agreement. In other words, the clause on applicable law in the treaty becomes a choice of law agreed by the parties to the arbitration.[301]

Some clauses in treaties governing the applicable law in investment disputes refer exclusively to international law. For instance, Chapter 11, Section B of the NAFTA, dealing with the settlement of investor-state disputes, refers only to international law including the NAFTA itself:

Article 1131: Governing law

1. A Tribunal established under this Section shall decide the issues in dispute in accordance with this Agreement and applicable rules of international law.[302]

Similarly, the ECT's provision on investor-state dispute settlement provides:

Article 26 Settlement of disputes between an investor and a contracting party

. . .

(6) A tribunal established under paragraph (4) shall decide the issues in dispute in accordance with this Treaty and applicable rules and principles of international law.[303]

---

[301] A R Parra, 'Provisions on the Settlement of Investment Disputes in Modern Investment Laws, Bilateral Investment Treaties and Multilateral Instruments on Investment' (1997) 12 *ICSID Review-FILJ* 287, 332; P Peters, 'Dispute Settlement Arrangements in Investment Treaties' (1991) 22 *Netherlands Yearbook of Int'l L* 91, 147–8 (1991); I F I Shihata and A R Parra, 'The Experience of the International Centre for Settlement of Investment Disputes' (1999) 14 *ICSID Review-FILJ* 299, 336. See also the analysis in *Antoine Goetz v Burundi*, Award, 10 February 1999, para 94 and in *Siemens v Argentina*, Award, 6 February 2007, para 76.
[302] 32 ILM 605, 645 (1993).
[303] 34 ILM 360, 400 (1995).

A number of BITs also merely refer to international law including the substantive rules of the BIT itself.[304]

Other BITs, in provisions dealing with applicable law, combine the host state's domestic law with international law. A frequently used formula lists: (a) the host state's law; (b) the BIT itself as well as other treaties; (c) any contract relating to the investment; and (d) general international law. In *Antoine Goetz v Burundi*[305] the relevant Belgium-Burundi BIT contained a provision on applicable law of this type. The Tribunal found that it had to apply a combination of domestic law and international law.[306] The Tribunal made the following general statement:

a complementary relationship must be allowed to prevail. That the Tribunal must apply Burundian law is beyond doubt, since this last is also cited in the first place by the relevant provision of the Belgium-Burundi investment treaty. As regards international law, its application is obligatory for two reasons. First, because, according to the indications furnished to the Tribunal by the claimants, Burundian law seems to incorporate international law and thus to render it directly applicable; . . . Furthermore, because the Republic of Burundi is bound by the international law obligations which it freely assumed under the Treaty for the protection of investments . . .[307]

The Tribunal then stated that an application of international law and of domestic law might lead to different results. The Tribunal first undertook an analysis of the dispute from the perspective of the law of Burundi. This analysis led to the conclusion that under the law of Burundi the actions in question were legal.[308] The Tribunal then examined the same issue from the perspective of international law, in particular in light of the BIT. This examination led to the result that the legality of the measures taken by Burundi depended on the payment of adequate and effective compensation which was still outstanding.[309]

A slightly different provision on applicable law that combines host state law and international law may be found in the BIT between Argentina and Spain:

The Arbitral Tribunal shall decide the dispute in accordance with the provisions of this Agreement, the terms of other Agreements concluded between the parties, the law of the Contracting Party in whose territory the investment was made, including its rules on conflict of laws, and general principles of international law.[310]

That treaty provision was applicable in *Maffezini v Spain*[311] where the subject of the dispute was the construction of a chemical plant. The Tribunal did not enter into a theoretical discussion on the law applicable to the case before it; it applied

---

[304] For a detailed list of examples, see E Gaillard and Y Banifatemi, 'The Meaning of "and" in Article 42(1), Second Sentence, of the Washington Convention: The Role of International Law in the ICSID Choice of Law Process' (2003) 18 *ICSID Review-FILJ* 375, 377.

[305] *Antoine Goetz v Burundi*, Award, 10 February 1999.

[306] At para 95.

[307] At para 98.

[308] At paras 100–19.

[309] At paras 120–33.

[310] Argentina-Spain BIT, Art 10(5).

[311] *Maffezini v Spain*, Award, 13 November 2000.

international law to some questions and host state law to other questions. For instance, on the issue of whether Spain was responsible for the actions of a state entity the Tribunal relied on the international law of state responsibility for the question of attribution[312] and on the Spanish Law on Public Administration and Common Administrative Procedure to elucidate the structure and functions of the entity.[313] Having reached an affirmative reply on attribution, it then applied the BIT.[314] On the issue of an environmental impact assessment, the Tribunal applied international law,[315] Spanish legislation,[316] a European Community directive,[317] and the BIT.[318] To the question of whether a contract had been perfected between the investor and the state entity, the Tribunal applied the Spanish Civil Code and the Spanish Commercial Code together with authoritative commentaries.[319] On the issue of a statute of limitation under Spanish legislation, the Tribunal found that it did not apply to claims filed under the ICSID Convention.[320]

Not all BITs contain provisions on applicable law. Where jurisdiction is based on a BIT that does not contain a provision on governing law, tribunals have sometimes construed such a choice from the BIT's invocation.

In *AAPL v Sri Lanka*,[321] jurisdiction was based on the BIT between Sri Lanka and the United Kingdom. This BIT did not contain a provision on applicable law. The Tribunal found that by arguing their case on the basis of the BIT, the parties had expressed their choice of the BIT as the applicable law as 'both Parties acted in a manner that demonstrates their mutual agreement to consider the provisions of the Sri Lanka/UK Bilateral Investment Treaty as being the primary source of the applicable legal rules'.[322]

The Tribunal in *AAPL v Sri Lanka* went on to state that the BIT was not a closed legal system but had to be seen in a wider juridical context. This wider juridical context, as well as the parties' submissions, led it to apply customary international law as well as domestic law.[323] Other tribunals have similarly found that in cases involving disputes under BITs the primary source of law had to be the BIT itself and other rules of international law.[324]

In the absence of an agreement on the governing law, Article 42 of the ICSID Convention provides that the tribunal apply host state law and applicable rules of international law. Most tribunals applying this provision examined the issues before

---

[312] At paras 50, 52, 57, 77, 83.   [313] At paras 47–9.   [314] At para 83.
[315] At para 67.   [316] At paras 68, 69.   [317] At para 69.
[318] At para 71.   [319] At paras 89, 90.
[320] At paras 92, 93. For a similar methodology on applicable law, see also *BG Group v Argentina*, Final Award, 24 December 2007, paras 89–103; *National Grid v Argentina*, Award, 3 November 2008, paras 81–90.
[321] *AAPL v Sri Lanka*, Award, 27 June 1990.
[322] At para 20.
[323] At paras 18–24.
[324] *Wena Hotels v Egypt*, Award, 8 December 2000, paras 78, 79; *ADC v Hungary*, Award, 2 October 2006, paras 288–91; *LG&E v Argentina*, Decision on Liability, 3 October 2006, paras 85, 97–8; *Saipem v Bangladesh*, Award, 30 June 2009, para 99; *Bayindir v Pakistan*, Award, 27 August 2009, paras 109, 110.

them under both systems of law.[325] In some cases the tribunals were simply content to find that both systems of law reached the same result.[326]

A widely held theory on the relationship of international law to host state law under the second sentence of Article 42(1) is the doctrine of the supplemental and corrective function of international law vis-à-vis domestic law.[327] The ad hoc Committee in *Amco v Indonesia* described this doctrine as follows:

Article 42(1) of the Convention authorizes an ICSID tribunal to apply rules of international law only to fill up lacunae in the applicable domestic law and to ensure precedence to international law norms where the rules of the applicable domestic law are in collision with such norms.[328]

It is questionable whether this doctrine accurately reflects reality. Tribunals have given international law more than a mere ancillary or subsidiary role. The Tribunal in the resubmitted case of *Amco v Indonesia* called this a distinction without a difference:

40. This Tribunal notes that Article 42(1) refers to the application of host-state law and international law. If there are no relevant host-state laws on a particular matter, a search must be made for the relevant international laws. And, where there are applicable host-state laws, they must be checked against international laws, which will prevail in case of conflict. Thus international law is fully applicable and to classify its role as 'only' 'supplemental and corrective' seems a distinction without a difference.[329]

Under the residual rule of Article 42(1) of the ICSID Convention both legal systems, that is international law and host state law, have a role to play.[330] In *CMS v Argentina* the Tribunal said:

there is here a close interaction between the legislation and the regulations governing the gas privatization, the License and international law, as embodied both in the Treaty and in

---

[325] But see *SOABI v Senegal*, Award, 25 February 1988, paras 5.02 et seq where the Tribunal restricted itself to the application of Senegalese law.

[326] *Adriano Gardella v Côte d'Ivoire*, Award, 29 August 1977, para 4.3; *Benvenuti & Bonfant v Congo*, Award, 15 August 1980, para 4.64; *Klöckner v Cameroon*, Award, 21 October 1983, 2 ICSID Reports 9, at p 63; *Amco v Indonesia*, Award, 20 November 1984, paras 147–8, 188, 201, 245–50, 265–8, 281; *Duke Energy v Peru*, Award, 18 August 2008, paras 144–61; *Aguaytia v Peru*, Award, 11 December 2008, paras 71–4.

[327] *Klöckner v Cameroon*, Decision on Annulment, 3 May 1985, para 69; *LETCO v Liberia*, Award, 31 March 1986, 2 ICSID Reports 343, at 358–9; *Amco v Indonesia*, Resubmitted Case: Award, 5 June 1990, para 38; *SPP v Egypt*, Award, 20 May 1992, para 84; *Autopista v Venezuela*, Award, 23 September 2003, paras 101–5.

[328] *Amco v Indonesia*, Decision on Annulment, 16 May 1986, para 20.

[329] *Amco v Indonesia*, Resubmitted Case: Award, 5 June 1990, para 40.

[330] See E Gaillard and Y Banifatemi, 'The Meaning of "and" in Article 42(1), Second Sentence, of the Washington Convention: The Role of International Law in the ICSID Choice of Law Process' (2003) 18 *ICSID Review-FILJ* 375, 403–11; R Dolzer, 'Contemporary Law of Foreign Investment: Revisiting the Status of International Law' in C Binder, U Kriebaum, A Reinisch, and S Wittich (eds), *International Investment Law for the 21st Century* (2009) 818; Z Douglas, *The International Law of Investment Claims* (2009) 39–133.

customary international law. All of these rules are inseparable and will, to the extent justified, be applied by the Tribunal.[331]

It is only where there is a conflict between the host state's law and international law that a tribunal has to make a decision on precedence. The Tribunal in *LG&E v Argentina* emphasized that ultimately international law is controlling: 'International law overrides domestic law when there is a contradiction since a State cannot justify non-compliance of its international obligations by asserting the provisions of its domestic law.'[332]

In non-ICSID arbitration between investors and host states, tribunals also apply a combination of international law and host state law. The UNCITRAL Arbitration Rules refer the tribunal to the law designated by the parties. In the absence of a choice of law, the tribunal is to apply the law which it determines to be appropriate.[333]

In *Occidental v Ecuador* the arbitration was conducted under the UNCITRAL Rules of 1976. The Tribunal listed a mix of sources of law under host state law and under international law:

> The dispute in the present case is related to various sources of applicable law. It is first related to the Contract ... ; it is next related to Ecuadorian tax legislation; this is followed by specific Decisions adopted by the Andean Community and issues that arise under the law of the WTO. In particular the dispute is related to the rights and obligations of the parties under the Treaty [ie the US-Ecuador BIT] and international law.[334]

Therefore, in most cases the applicable substantive law in investment arbitration combines international law and host state law. This is so whether or not the parties have made a choice of law that combines international law with host state law. In the majority of cases tribunals have, in fact, applied both systems of law. Where there was a contradiction between the two, international law had to prevail. It is left to the tribunals to identify the various issues before them to which international law or host state law is to apply.

(I) Remedies

aa. Restitution and satisfaction

Under the international law of state responsibility, reparation for a wrongful act takes the form of restitution, compensation, or satisfaction.[335] In investment

---

[331] *CMS v Argentina*, Award, 12 May 2005, para 117. See also *Wena v Egypt*, Decision on Annulment, 5 February 2002, paras 37–40; *Azurix v Argentina*, Award, 14 July 2006, para 67; *LG&E v Argentina*, Decision on Liability, 3 October 2006, paras 82–99; *Enron v Argentina*, Award, 22 May 2007, paras 203–9; *Tokios Tokelės v Ukraine*, Award, 26 July 2007, paras 138–45; *Sempra v Argentina*, Award, 28 September 2007, paras 231–40.

[332] *LG&E v Argentina*, Decision on Liability, 3 October 2006, para 94. See also *CDSE v Costa Rica*, Award, 17 February 2000, paras 64, 65; *Duke Energy v Peru*, Decision on Jurisdiction, 1 February 2006, para 162.

[333] UNCITRAL Arbitration Rules 2010, Art 35(1).

[334] *Occidental v Ecuador*, Final Award, 1 July 2004, para 93. See also *Eastern Sugar v Czech Republic*, Partial Award, 27 March 2007, paras 191–7.

[335] Articles on Responsibility of States for Internationally Wrongful Acts adopted by the ILC in 2001, Art 34. J Crawford, *The International Law Commission's Articles on State Responsibility* (2002) 211.

arbitration, the remedy nearly always consists of monetary compensation. Satisfaction plays a subordinate role in investment law.[336] Restitution in kind or specific performance is ordered infrequently.[337] This is not due to any inherent limitation on tribunals but the consequence of the situations in which most disputes arise and the way in which the claims are put forward. In a number of cases, tribunals did in fact order restitution[338] or affirmed their power to do so.[339]

In *Enron v Argentina* the claimants requested that the Tribunal declare certain taxes unlawful and issue a permanent injunction against their collection.[340] Argentina argued that the Tribunal did not have the power to order injunctive relief. In Argentina's view, the Tribunal could only establish whether there had been an illegal expropriation and determine the corresponding compensation.[341] The Tribunal found that it had the power to order specific performance:

An examination of the powers of international courts and tribunals to order measures concerning performance or injunction and of the ample practice that is available in this respect, leaves this Tribunal in no doubt about the fact that these powers are indeed available.[342]

bb. Damages for an illegal act

The calculation of monetary reparation can be a complex undertaking, often requiring the involvement of valuation experts.[343] If an illegal act has been committed, the guiding principle is that reparation must, as far as possible, restore the situation that would have existed had the illegal act not been committed.[344] In the *Chorzów Factory Case*, the PCIJ expressed this principle in the following words:

The essential principle contained in the actual notion of an illegal act—a principle which seems to be established by international practice and in particular by the decisions of arbitral

---

[336] *Biwater Gauff v Tanzania*, Award, 24 July 2008, paras 465–7, 807; *Europe Cement v Turkey*, Award, 13 August 2009, paras 146–8, 176, 181.

[337] See C Schreuer, 'Non-Pecuniary Remedies in ICSID Arbitration' (2004) 20 *Arbitration International* 325.

[338] *Martini Case (Italy v Venezuela)*, Award, 3 May 1930, 25 *AJIL* 554 (1931), at 585; *Texaco Overseas Petroleum Company and California Asiatic Oil Company v Government of the Libyan Arab Republic*, Award on the Merits, 19 January 1977, 53 ILR 389, at 497–511; *Antoine Goetz and others v Republic of Burundi*, Award, 2 September 1998 and 10 February 1999, paras 132–3; *Semos v Mali*, Award, 25 February 2003, 10 ICSID Reports 116, 129; *ADC v Hungary*, Award, 2 October 2006, para 523; *Siemens v Argentina*, Award, 6 February 2007, para 403(5); *ATA v Jordan*, Award, 18 May 2010, paras 129–32.

[339] *Nycomb v Latvia*, Award, 16 December 2003, sec 5.1; *Micula v Romania*, Decision on Jurisdiction and Admissibility, 24 September 2008, paras 158–68. But see *LG&E v Argentina*, Award, 25 July 2007, paras 84–7; *Occidental v Ecuador*, Decision on Provisional Measures, 17 August 2007, paras 66–86.

[340] *Enron v Argentina*, Decision on Jurisdiction, 14 January 2004, para 77.

[341] At para 76.

[342] At para 79.

[343] For a concise overview, see I Marboe, 'Compensation and Damages in International Law, The Limits of "Fair Market Value"' (2006) 7 *J World Investment & Trade* 723.

[344] Articles on Responsibility of States for Internationally Wrongful Acts adopted by the ILC in 2001, Arts 31, 36.

tribunals—is that reparation must, as far as possible, wipe out all the consequences of the illegal act and re-establish the situation which would, in all probability, have existed if that act had not been committed.[345]

Under this principle, damages for a violation of international law have to reflect the damage actually suffered by the victim. In other words, the victim's actual situation has to be compared with the one that would have prevailed had the act not been committed. Therefore, punitive or moral damages will not usually be granted.[346] This subjective method includes any consequential damage but also incidental benefits arising as a consequence of the illegal act. According to the Tribunal in *Petrobart v Kyrgyz Republic*:

in so far as it appears that Petrobart has suffered damage as a result of the Republic's breaches of the Treaty, Petrobart shall so far as possible be placed financially in the position in which it would have found itself, had the breaches not occurred.[347]

One method for calculating damages would be to look at the replacement value of property that has been taken or destroyed. This presupposes that the equipment in question is actually replaceable. Another method is to look at the actual losses, that is, the amount invested as well as costs and expenses incurred by the investor.[348]

If the illegal act results in deprivation of income, damages may have to include lost profits.[349] Lost profits will be awarded only if they are not speculative, that is, in cases where the investment has a record of profitability or there are other clear indicators of future profits.[350] Also a risk element has to be factored into any calculation of future profits. In addition, care must be taken to avoid double counting. This may occur if actual expenses are combined with expected future profits.

Tribunals have also taken negligent behaviour by the investors into account when calculating damages due to them. In *MTD v Chile* the Tribunal found that the investors had made decisions that unnecessarily increased their risks and for which they bore responsibility. It followed that the damages due were to be appropriately reduced:

---

[345] *Case Concerning the Factory at Chorzów*, Merits, 1928, PCIJ, Series A, No 17, p 47.

[346] *Siag v Egypt*, Award, 1 June 2009, paras 544–8; *Europe Cement v Turkey*, Award, 13 August 2009, paras 177–81; *Cementownia v Turkey*, Award, 17 September 2009, paras 164–72; *Lemire v Ukraine*, Decision on Jurisdiction and Liability, 14 January 2010, paras 426–86. But see *Desert Line v Yemen*, Award, 6 February 2008, paras 284–91.

[347] *Petrobart v Kyrgyz Republic*, Award, 29 March 2005, VIII.7, in Stockholm Int'l Arb Rev 2005:3, 45 at 84. See also *MTD v Chile*, Award, 25 May 2004, para 238.

[348] *Metalclad v Mexico*, Award, 30 August 2000, para 122; *Azurix v Argentina*, Award, 14 July 2006, para 425.

[349] See eg *Amco v Indonesia*, Resubmitted Case: Award, 5 June 1990, paras 163–284; *LETCO v Liberia*, Award, 31 March 1986, 2 ICSID Reports 346, at 373–7.

[350] *AAPL v Sri Lanka*, Award, 27 June 1990, paras 105–8; *SPP v Egypt*, Award, 20 May 1992, paras 186–9; *Metalclad Corp v United Mexican States*, Award, 30 August 2000, paras 120–2; *Wena Hotels Ltd v Arab Republic of Egypt*, Award, 8 December 2000, paras 123–4; *SD Myers v Canada*, Award on Damages, 21 October 2002, paras 173 et seq; *Tecmed v United Mexican States*, Award, 29 May 2003, para 186; *Autopista v Venezuela*, Award, 23 September 2003, paras 351–65; *PSEG v Turkey*, Award, 19 January 2007, paras 310–15; *LG&E v Argentina*, Award, 25 July 2007, paras 88–91.

The Tribunal considers therefore that the Claimants should bear part of the damages suffered and the Tribunal estimates that share to be 50% after deduction of the residual value of their investment . . .[351]

Events subsequent to the illegal act may affect the damage caused and must be taken into account.[352] All information available at the time of the award should be reflected in the calculation; this may include consequential damage or a diminution of damage. A subsequent increase in the value of the investment will also be relevant. In *ADC v Hungary* the Tribunal, after noting that the value of the investment had risen very considerably after the date of the illegal expropriation, said:

the application of the *Chorzów Factory* standard requires that the date of valuation should be the date of the Award and not the date of expropriation, since this is what is necessary to put the Claimants in the same position as if the expropriation had not been committed.[353]

cc. Compensation for expropriation

The calculation of compensation for a lawful expropriation follows different standards.[354] Compensation is one of the requirements for a legal expropriation together with a public purpose, non-discrimination, and fair procedure.[355] Most BITs and other treaties for the protection of investments contain this requirement.[356] These treaties often refer to 'adequate' or 'appropriate' compensation. The World Bank Guidelines on the Treatment of Foreign Direct Investment state that:

Compensation will be deemed 'adequate' if it is based on the fair market value of the taken asset as such value is determined immediately before the time at which the taking occurred or the decision to take the asset became publicly known.[357]

Many of the treaties dealing with compensation for expropriation also refer to the expropriated investment's fair market value.[358] For instance, the Argentina-US BIT provides:

Compensation shall be equivalent to the fair market value of the expropriated investment immediately before the expropriatory action was taken or became known, whichever is earlier;[359]

---

[351] *MTD v Chile*, Award, 25 May 2004, para 243; *Azurix v Argentina*, Award, 14 July 2006, paras 425 et seq.

[352] *Siemens v Argentina*, Award, 6 February 2007, paras 352, 353, 360.

[353] *ADC v Hungary*, Award, 2 October 2006, para 497.

[354] For decisions clearly distinguishing between compensation for expropriation and damages for an illegal act, see *Nycomb v Latvia*, Award, 16 December 2003, sec 5.1; *MTD v Chile*, Award, 25 May 2004, para 238; *ADC v Hungary*, Award, 2 October 2006, paras 481, 483; *Siemens v Argentina*, Award, 6 February 2007, paras 349–52; *LG&E v Argentina*, Award, 25 July 2007, paras 29–58.

[355] See pp 99–101.

[356] NAFTA, Art 1110; ECT, Art 13.

[357] Guideline IV (3), 31 ILM 1379, at 1382.

[358] NAFTA, Art 1110(2); ECT, Art 13(1).

[359] Argentina-US BIT, Art IV(1).

Tribunals have frequently relied on the fair market value as the appropriate standard for compensation.[360]

Whereas damages for an illegal act look at the victim's subjective position, compensation for expropriation, as expressed in the investment's fair market value, is an objective standard that looks at the amount that a willing buyer would normally pay to a willing seller in a free transaction, at arm's length. On the other hand, a market value will often be a fiction, especially where a market for large and complex investments does not exist. Therefore, market value is often determined on the basis of the future prospects or earning capacity of the investment.

The most frequently used method for determining market value is the discounted cash flow (DCF) method which looks at the projected likely income created by the investment in the future. The underlying assumption is that this is the standard for the price that a hypothetical buyer would be willing to pay. Under this method, an estimate is made of cash flows that may be expected in the future. In order to calculate the present value of future cash flows, a discount factor has to be applied in order to take account of the time value of money and of risk. Past data are relevant but not necessarily decisive for the determination of future prospects. Other 'value drivers' may also be indicative of future cash flows. Risk may be influenced by macroeconomic factors or political crises but also by the specific risk borne by the investment.

If the investment has not yet produced income or is unlikely to produce further income in the future, the appropriate method for valuation may be the liquidation value. This is the price at which the remaining assets could be sold under conditions of liquidation. This method usually yields a much lower value than valuation on the basis of a going concern.

The valuation date in the case of expropriations should be the date immediately before the fact of the expropriation became publicly known. This is designed to avoid any influence of the impending expropriation on the investment's market value.

dd. Interest

An award of damages or compensation normally includes interest.[361] Interest is a sum paid or payable as compensation for the temporary withholding of money. If the investor had to take out a loan as a consequence of the deprivation, interest is designed to cover the cost of the loan. If no loan was taken, interest may reflect the lost earning capacity of the money in question.

Interest is due from the date at which the principal amount was due. In the case of damages, this is normally the date of the wrongful act.[362] In *AAPL v Sri Lanka* the Tribunal stated that:

---

[360] See eg *Biloune v Ghana*, Award on Jurisdiction and Liability, 27 October 1989, 95 ILR 184, at 211; *SPP v Egypt*, Award, 20 May 1992, para 197; *Compania del Desarrollo de Santa Elena SA v Costa Rica*, Award, 17 February 2000, para 70.

[361] Generally, see J Y Gotanda, 'Awarding Interest in International Arbitration' (1996) 90 *AJIL* 40.

[362] In some cases this date may be difficult to determine. See *PSEG v Turkey*, Award, 19 January 2007, paras 349–51.

the case-law elaborated by international arbitral tribunals strongly suggests that in assessing the liability due for losses incurred the interest becomes an integral part of the compensation itself, and should run consequently from the date when the State's international responsibility became engaged[363]

In the case of compensation, interest is normally due from the date of the expropriation, although that date may be difficult to determine with indirect or creeping expropriations. The appropriate date will be the day when the investor definitely lost control over the investment.

The rate of interest may be calculated on the basis of the legal interest rate in an applicable legal system or on an inter-bank rate such as the London Interbank Offered Rate (LIBOR).[364]

The practice of tribunals shows a trend towards compounding interest, that is, interest is capitalized at certain intervals and will then itself bear interest. While some tribunals have rejected compound interest,[365] it has been accepted in the majority of recent decisions.[366]

(m) Costs

The costs of major investment arbitrations can be considerable and may run into millions of dollars for complex cases.[367] The costs consist of three elements: the charges for the use of the facilities and expenses of ICSID[368] or other arbitration institution, the fees and expenses of the arbitrators, and the expenses incurred by

---

[363] *AAPL v Sri Lanka*, Award, 27 June 1990, para 114. See also *SPP v Egypt*, Award, 20 May 1992, para 234; *Metalclad Corp v United Mexican States*, Award, 30 August 2000, para 128.

[364] *PSEG v Turkey*, Award, 19 January 2007, para 348; *Sempra v Argentina*, Award, 28 September 2007, paras 483–6; *Rumeli Telekom v Kazakhstan*, Award, 29 July 2008, para 818; *National Grid v Argentina*, Award, 3 November 2008, para 291; *Siag v Egypt*, Award, 1 June 2009, paras 594–8.

[365] *CME v Czech Republic*, Final Award, 14 March 2003, paras 642–7; *Autopista v Venezuela*, Award, 23 September 2003, paras 393–7; *Eastern Sugar v Czech Republic*, Partial Award, 27 March 2007, para 374; *Duke Energy v Ecuador*, Award, 18 August 2008, para 473.

[366] *Atlantic Triton v Guinea*, Award, 21 April 1986, 3 ICSID Reports 13, at 33, 43; *Compania del Desarrollo de Santa Elena SA v Costa Rica*, Award, 17 February 2000, paras 104, 105; *Metalclad v Mexico*, Award, 30 August 2000, para 128; *Maffezini v Spain*, Award, 13 November 2000, para 96; *Wena Hotels v Egypt*, Award, 8 December 2000, para 129; *Middle East Cement v Egypt*, Award, 12 April 2002, para 174; *Pope & Talbot v Canada*, Award in Respect of Damages, 31 May 2002, para 90; *Tecmed v United Mexican States*, Award, 29 May 2003, para 196; *MTD v Chile*, Award, 25 May 2004, para 253(4); *Azurix v Argentina*, Award, 14 July 2006, paras 439–40; *ADC v Hungary*, Award, 2 October 2006, para 522; *PSEG v Turkey*, Award, 19 January 2007, para 348; *Enron v Argentina*, Award, 22 May, 2007, paras 451–2; *Compañía de Aguas del Aconquija, SA & Vivendi Universal v Argentina*, Award, 20 August 2007, paras 9.1.1–9.2.8; *BG Group v Argentina*, Final Award, 24 December 2007, paras 456–7; *Sempra v Argentina*, Award, 28 September 2007, paras 483–6; *OKO Pankki v Estonia*, Award, 19 November 2007, paras 343–56; *Continental Casualty v Argentina*, Award, 5 September 2008, paras 306–16; *Funnekotter v Zimbabwe*, Award, 22 April 2009, paras 141–6; *Siag v Egypt*, Award, 1 June 2009, paras 594–8; *Impregilo v Argentina*, Award, 21 June 2011, paras 382–4.

[367] Eg in *PSEG v Turkey*, the total amount of costs claimed was US$20,851,636.62. See Award, 19 January 2007, para 352. The Award in *Libananco v Turkey*, 2 September 2011, paras 558–9, seems to have set a record with combined costs for both parties at US$60 million.

[368] The details are set out in ICSID's Administrative and Financial Regulations at <http://www.worldbank.org/icsid/basicdoc/partC.htm> as well as in a Schedule of Fees at <http://www.worldbank.org/icsid/schedule/fees.pdfsee>.

the parties in connection with the proceedings. Of these three categories, the third, consisting mainly of the costs for legal representation, is typically by far the largest.

The ICSID Convention in Article 61(2) leaves it to the tribunal's discretion by whom these costs are to be paid, unless the parties agree otherwise. Other arbitration rules may provide differently. For instance, the UNCITRAL Arbitration Rules state that the costs of arbitration shall in principle be borne by the unsuccessful party.[369] But in a particular case, both parties may be partly successful.

The practice of tribunals on the attribution of costs is far from uniform. In many cases the tribunals found that the fees and expenses of the Centre and of the arbitrators were to be shared equally and that each party had to bear its own expenses.[370] In some cases the tribunals awarded costs as a sanction for the improper conduct of one of the parties. This has been the case where the tribunal found that the claim had been frivolous or fraudulent or that there had been dilatory or otherwise improper conduct.[371] In *LETCO v Liberia* the Tribunal awarded the full costs of the arbitration to the claimants including their own expenses. The Tribunal said:

This decision is based largely on Liberia's procedural bad faith. Not only did Liberia fail to partake in these arbitral proceedings, contrary to its contractual agreement, but it has also undertaken judicial proceedings in Liberia in order to nullify the results of this arbitration.[372]

More recently tribunals have shown a growing inclination to adopt the principle that costs follow the event. An award of costs against the losing party may be total

[369] Article 42 (1).

[370] See eg *Adriano Gardella v Ivory Coast*, Award, 29 August 1977, para 4.12; *Klöckner v Cameroon*, Award, 21 October 1983, 2 ICSID Reports 9 at 77; *Atlantic Triton v Guinea*, Award, 21 April 1986, 3 ICSID Reports 17 at 42, 44; *SOABI v Senegal*, Award, 25 February 1988, para 12.05; *Amco v Indonesia*, Resubmitted Case: Award, 5 June 1990, paras 285–91; *Vacuum Salt v Ghana*, Award, 16 February 1994, paras 56–60; *Cable TV v St Kitts and Nevis*, Award, 13 January 1997, paras 8.04–8.06; *Tradex v Albania*, Award, 29 April 1999, paras 206–7; *Robert Azinian and others v Mexico*, Award, 1 November 1999, paras 125–7; *CDSE v Costa Rica*, Award, 17 February 2000, para 109; *Maffezini v Spain*, Award, 13 November 2000, paras 98–9; *Middle East Cement v Egypt*, Award, 12 April 2002, para 176; *Compañía de Aguas del Aconquija, SA & Vivendi Universal v Argentina*, Decision on Annulment, 3 July 2002, paras 117–18; *Autopista v Venezuela*, Award, 23 September 2003, para 425; *MTD v Chile*, Award, 25 May 2004, para 252; *Salini v Jordan*, Award, 31 January 2006, paras 101–4; *World Duty Free v Kenya*, Award, 4 October 2006, paras 189–91; *Mitchell v Congo*, Decision on Annulment, 1 November 2006, para 67; *Enron v Argentina*, Award, 22 May 2007, para 453; *Duke Energy v Peru*, Award, 18 August 2008, paras 494–500; *RSM Production v Grenada*, Award, 13 March 2009, paras 487–99; *RosInvest v Russia*, Final Award, 12 September 2010, para 701; *AES Summit v Hungary*, Award, 23 September 2010, para 15.3.3; *Grand River Enterprises v United States*, Award, 12 January 2011, paras 239–47; *Brandes v Venezuela*, Award, 2 August 2011, para 120.

[371] *Benvenuti & Bonfant v Congo*, Award, 15 August 1980, paras 4.127–4.129; *MINE v Guinea*, Award, 6 January 1988, 4 ICSID Reports 61, at 77; *Generation Ukraine, Inc v Ukraine*, Award, 16 September 2003, para 24.2; *Azurix v Argentina*, Award, 14 July 2006, para 441; *Compañía de Aguas del Aconquija, SA & Vivendi Universal v Argentina*, Award, 20 August 2007, paras 10.2.2–10.2.6; *Plama v Bulgaria*, Award, 27 August 2008, paras 321–2; *Phoenix v Czech Republic*, Award, 15 April 2009, paras 151–2; *Europe Cement v Turkey*, Award, 13 August 2009, paras 185–6; *Cementownia v Turkey*, Award, 17 September 2009, paras 177–8; *Fakes v Turkey*, Award, 14 July 2010, paras 153–4.

[372] *LETCO v Liberia*, Award, 31 March 1986, 2 ICSID Reports 370, at 378.

or, more frequently, may cover a certain proportion of the overall costs.[373] In *ADC v Hungary* the claimant prevailed with its claim for illegal expropriation and other BIT violations. On the issue of costs, the Tribunal said:

it can be seen from previous awards that ICSID arbitrators do in practice award costs in favour of the successful party and sometimes in large sums . . . In the present case, the Tribunal can find no reason to depart from the starting point that the successful party should receive reimbursement from the unsuccessful party. . . . Were the Claimants not to be reimbursed their costs . . . it could not be said that they were being made whole.[374]

(n) Challenge and review of decisions

Awards are final and not subject to any appeals procedures.[375] It is only under very limited circumstances that a review of awards is possible. Two potentially conflicting principles are at work in the process of review of a judicial decision: the principle of finality and the principle of correctness. Finality serves the purpose of efficiency in terms of an expeditious and economical settlement of disputes. Correctness is an elusive goal that takes time and effort and may involve several layers of control, a phenomenon that is well known from appeals in domestic court procedure. In arbitration, the principle of finality is typically given more weight than the principle of correctness.

aa. Review in non-ICSID arbitration

In non-ICSID arbitration, including arbitration under the Additional Facility, the normal way to challenge an award is through national courts. This is done in the courts of the country in which the tribunal has its seat or by the courts charged with the task of enforcing the award.

---

[373] *AGIP v Congo*, Award, 30 November 1979, 1 ICSID Reports 309, at 329; *AAPL v Sri Lanka*, Award, 27 June 1990, para 116; *SPP v Egypt*, Award, 20 May 1992, paras 205–11; *Scimitar v Bangladesh*, Award, 5 April 1994, paras 30–2; *Wena Hotels v Egypt*, Award, 8 December 2000, para 130; *Compañía de Aguas del Aconquija, SA & Vivendi Universal v Argentina*, Decision on Supplementation and Rectification of Annulment Decision, 28 May 2003, paras 43–4; *Generation Ukraine, Inc v Ukraine*, Award, 16 September 2003, para 24.1; *CDC v Seychelles*, Award, 17 December 2003, para 63; *Soufraki v United Arab Emirates*, Award, 7 July 2004, para 85; *CDC v Seychelles*, Decision on Annulment, 29 June 2005, paras 88–90; *Eureko v Poland*, Partial Award, 19 August 2005, para 261; *Thunderbird v Mexico*, Award, 26 January 2006, paras 210–21; *Inceysa v El Salvador*, Award, 2 August 2006, para 338; *Telenor v Hungary*, Award, 13 September 2006, paras 104–8; *ADC v Hungary*, Award, 2 October 2006, paras 525–42; *Champion Trading v Egypt*, Award, 27 October 2006, paras 165–78; *PSEG v Turkey*, Award, 19 January 2007, paras 352–3; *OKO Pankki v Estonia*, Award, 19 November 2007, paras 368–75; *BG Group v Argentina*, Final Award, 24 December 2007, paras 458–66; *Rumeli Telekom v Kazakhstan*, Award, 29 July 2008, para 819; *National Grid v Argentina*, Award, 3 November 2008, para 295; *Funnekotter v Zimbabwe*, Award, 22 April 2009, para 147; *Siag v Egypt*, Award, 1 June 2009, paras 599–630; *EDF v Romania*, Award, 8 October 2009, paras 321–9; *Chemtura v Canada*, Award, 2 August 2010, paras 272–3; *Alpha v Ukraine*, Award, 8 November 2010, para 516; *RSM Production v Grenada*, Award, 10 December 2010, paras 8.3.4–8.3.6; *AFT v Slovakia*, Award, 5 March 2011, paras 260–70.

[374] *ADC v Hungary*, Award, 2 October 2006, paras 531, 533.

[375] See ICSID Convention, Art 53.

The New York Convention on the Recognition and Enforcement of Foreign Arbitral Awards of 1958[376] in its Article V lists a number of grounds on the basis of which recognition and enforcement of a non-national arbitral award may be refused at the request of a party. The UNCITRAL Model Law on International Commercial Arbitration of 1985 foresees a limited number of grounds for the setting aside or non-recognition of an international commercial award by a domestic court, which are based on Article V of the New York Convention.[377] In many countries, national arbitration laws, including the rules on setting aside arbitral awards, are modelled on the UNCITRAL Model Law.

The most important grounds for the setting aside of awards under these laws are the invalidity of the arbitration agreement, lack of proper notice of the arbitration proceedings, a decision in the award beyond the scope of the submission to arbitration, improper composition of the tribunal, a subject matter not capable of settlement by arbitration under the law of the state in question, and an award that is in conflict with the public policy of that state. Proceedings for setting aside awards in non-ICSID investment arbitration have taken place in a number of cases.[378]

bb. Annulment under the ICSID Convention

ICSID awards are not subject to annulment or any other form of scrutiny by domestic courts. Rather, the ICSID Convention offers its own self-contained system for review. Under this procedure, an ad hoc committee may annul an award upon the request of a party. An ad hoc committee consists of three persons, appointed by the Chairman of ICSID's Administrative Council.[379] The request for annulment must come from one of the parties to the arbitration and has to be submitted within 120 days of the award's dispatch to the parties.[380] There is no *ex officio* annulment. Typically, a party requesting annulment hopes for a decision that is more favourable to it after annulment.

Only awards are subject to annulment; there is no annulment in respect of other decisions, such as decisions upholding jurisdiction or decisions on provisional measures, except if they are subsequently incorporated into the award. A decision by a tribunal declining jurisdiction is an award and therefore subject to annulment. Requests for partial annulment and annulment of parts of awards are possible.

Under Article 52(5) of the ICSID Convention, an ad hoc committee may stay the enforcement of the award while annulment proceedings are pending.[381] Before the constitution of an ad hoc committee the stay will be automatic if it is requested in the application for annulment. Some ad hoc committees have required a bank

[376] 330 UNTS 38 (1959).
[377] UNCITRAL Model Law, Arts 34 and 36, 24 ILM 1302, 1311–13 (1985).
[378] For a list of decisions on challenges of investment awards in national courts, see <http://italaw.com/annulment_judicialreview.htm>.
[379] The President of the World Bank holds this office *ex officio*.
[380] Articles 52(2) and 49(1).
[381] Arbitration Rule 54.

guarantee or similar security from the award debtor for the eventual payment of the award as a condition for the stay of enforcement. The guarantee will be operative if annulment is rejected and the award becomes enforceable.[382] Other ad hoc committees have declined to order such a security.[383]

Annulment is different from an appeal.[384] Annulment is concerned only with the legitimacy of the process of the decision but not with its substantive correctness. Appeal is concerned with both. Appeal may result in the replacement of the decision by a new decision, whereas annulment merely removes the original decision without replacing it. Therefore, an ad hoc committee acting under the ICSID Convention does not have the power to render its own decision on the merits. After annulment, the dispute can be resubmitted to a new tribunal. ICSID ad hoc committees dealing with requests for annulment in previous cases have stressed the distinction between annulment and appeal.[385]

The ad hoc Committee in *CDC v Seychelles* described the function of annulment in the following terms:

This mechanism protecting against errors that threaten the fundamental fairness of the arbitral process (but not against incorrect decisions) arises from the ICSID Convention's drafters' desire that Awards be final and binding, which is an expression of 'customary law based on the concepts *of pacta sunt servanda* and *res judicata*,' and is in keeping with the object and purpose of the Convention. Parties use ICSID arbitration (at least in part)

[382] *Amco v Indonesia*, Decision on Annulment, 16 May 1986, paras 8–9; *Amco v Indonesia*, Resubmitted Case, Interim Order No 1, 2 March 1991, para 19; *Wena v Egypt*, Decision on Annulment, 5 February 2002, paras 5–6; *CDC v Seychelles*, Decision on Continued Stay, 14 July 2004, Decision on Annulment, 29 June 2005, para 16; *Repsol v Ecuador*, Decision on Annulment, 8 January 2007, paras 8, 12; *Compañía de Aguas del Aconquija, SA & Vivendi Universal v Argentina*, Decision on Stay of Enforcement, 4 November 2008; *Sempra v Argentina*, Decision on Continued Stay of Enforcement, 5 March 2009; Decision on Termination of Stay of Enforcement, 7 August 2009.

[383] *MINE v Guinea*, Interim Order No 1 on Guinea's Application for Stay of Enforcement of the Award, 12 August 1988, 4 ICSID Reports 111; *Mitchell v Congo*, Decision on the Stay of Enforcement, 30 November 2004; *MTD v Chile*, Decision on Continued Stay of Enforcement, 1 June 2005; *CMS v Argentina*, Decision on Continued Stay of Enforcement, 1 September 2006; *Azurix v Argentina*, Decision on Continued Stay of Enforcement, 28 December 2007; *Enron v Argentina*, Decision on Second Request to Lift Stay of Enforcement, 20 May 2009; *Rumeli v Kazakhstan*, Decision on Annulment, 25 March 2010, paras 10–24; *Victor Pey Casado v Chile*, Decision on Stay of Enforcement, 5 May 2010.

[384] See especially D D Caron, 'Reputation and Reality in the ICSID Annulment Process: Understanding the Distinction Between Annulment and Appeal' (1992) 7 *ICSID Review-FILJ* 21.

[385] *Klöckner v Cameroon*, Decision on Annulment, 3 May 1985, paras 83, 118, 120, 178; *Amco v Indonesia*, Decision on Annulment, 16 May 1986, paras 43, 110; *MINE v Guinea*, Decision on Annulment, 22 December 1989, paras 4.04, 5.08, 6.55; *Wena v Egypt*, Decision on Annulment, 5 February 2002, para 18; *Compañía de Aguas del Aconquija, SA & Vivendi Universal v Argentina*, Decision on Annulment, 3 July 2002, para 62; *CDC v Seychelles*, Decision on Annulment, 29 June 2005, paras 35, 36; *Mitchell v Congo*, Decision on Annulment, 1 November 2006, para 19; *Soufraki v UAE*, Decision on Annulment, 5 June 2007, paras 20, 24; *Repsol v Petroecuador*, Decision on Annulment, 8 January 2007, para 38; *MTD v Chile*, Decision on Annulment, 21 March 2007, para 31; *CMS v Argentina*, Decision on Annulment, 25 September 2007, paras 43, 44, 135, 136, 158; *Rumeli v Kazakhstan*, Decision on Annulment, 25 March 2010, para 70; *Sempra v Argentina*, Decision on Annulment, 29 June 2010, paras 73, 74; *Enron v Argentina*, Decision on Annulment, 30 July 2010, paras 63–5; *Vivendi II v Argentina*, Decision on Annulment, 10 August 2010, para 247; *Fraport v Philippines*, Decision on Annulment, 23 December 2010, para 76.

because they wish a more efficient way of resolving disputes than is possible in a national court system with its various levels of trial and appeal, or even in non-ICSID Convention arbitrations (which may be subject to national courts' review under local laws and whose enforcement may also be subject to defenses available under, for example, the New York Convention).[386]

The grounds for annulment under the ICSID Convention are listed exhaustively in Article 52(1):

(a) that the Tribunal was not properly constituted;

(b) that the Tribunal has manifestly exceeded its powers;

(c) that there was corruption on the part of a member of the Tribunal;

(d) that there has been a serious departure from a fundamental rule of procedure; or

(e) that the award has failed to state the reasons on which it is based.

Annulment is restricted to these five grounds. Any request for annulment must be brought under one or several of these grounds and an ad hoc committee may not annul on other grounds. Also, a party may not present new arguments on fact or law that it failed to put forward in the original arbitral proceeding. Therefore, Article 52 of the ICSID Convention offers a review process limited to a few fundamental standards of a mostly procedural nature.

Under Article 52(3) of the ICSID Convention an ad hoc committee has the authority to annul the award. Therefore, an ad hoc committee has discretion and is not under an obligation to annul if it finds that there is a ground for annulment listed in Article 52(1). An ad hoc committee has to decide whether the fault is sufficiently grave to warrant annulment, especially whether it has made a material difference to the position of one of the parties.[387] The ad hoc Committee in *Vivendi* said:

it appears to be established that an *ad hoc* committee has a certain measure of discretion as to whether to annul an award, even if an annullable error is found. Article 52(3) provides that a committee 'shall have the authority to annul the award or any part thereof', and this has been interpreted as giving committees some flexibility in determining whether annulment is appropriate in the circumstances. Among other things, it is necessary for an *ad hoc* committee to consider the significance of the error relative to the legal rights of the parties.[388]

Only three of the grounds for annulment listed above have played a role in practice: excess of powers, serious departure from a fundamental rule of procedure, and

---

[386] *CDC v Seychelles*, Decision on Annulment, 29 June 2005, para 36. Footnotes omitted.

[387] *MINE v Guinea*, Decision on Annulment, 22 December 1989, paras 4.09–4.10; *CDC v Seychelles*, Decision on Annulment, 29 June 2005, paras 37, 65. But see the earlier decision to the contrary in *Klöckner v Cameroon*, Decision on Annulment, 3 May 1985, paras 80, 116, 151, 179.

[388] *Compañía de Aguas del Aconquija, SA & Vivendi Universal v Argentina*, Decision on Annulment, 3 July 2002, para 66. Footnote omitted. See also at paras 63, 86.

failure to state reasons. Parties requesting annulment have almost invariably claimed the presence of more than one of these defects justifying annulment.[389]

i. Excess of powers

An excess of powers occurs where the tribunal deviates from the parties' agreement to arbitrate. This would be the case if a tribunal makes a decision on the merits although it does not have jurisdiction or if it exceeds its jurisdiction. Jurisdiction is determined by Article 25 of the Convention. The requirements listed there must be met; otherwise there is no jurisdiction. This would be the case if there is no legal dispute arising directly out of an investment. Similarly, if the nationality requirements under the ICSID Convention are not met, there is no jurisdiction and a decision on the merits would be an excess of powers. Absence of valid consent to arbitration would also mean that there is no jurisdiction and an award on the merits would be an excess of powers.

An excess of powers must be manifest in order to constitute a ground for annulment. Manifest means that the excess of powers must be obvious.[390]

In *Mitchell v Congo* the request for annulment argued that the Tribunal had committed a manifest excess of powers by assuming jurisdiction although the dispute had not arisen from an investment. The ad hoc Committee held that a contribution to the host state's economic development was an indispensable element of the concept of an investment under the ICSID Convention. The ad hoc Committee found that there was no indication that the claimant's business—a legal counselling firm—had made such a contribution. It followed for the ad hoc Committee that there was no investment in the sense of Article 25 of the ICSID Convention and that the Tribunal had consequently committed a manifest excess of powers by assuming jurisdiction.[391]

Failure to exercise an existing jurisdiction also constitutes an excess of powers. In *Vivendi*[392] the ad hoc Committee said:

---

[389] *Klöckner v Cameroon*, Decision on Annulment, 3 May 1985, para 166; *Amco v Indonesia*, Decision on Annulment, 16 May 1986, paras 4, 84; *MINE v Guinea*, Decision on Annulment, 22 December 1989, para 6.97; *CDC v Seychelles*, Decision on Annulment, 29 June 2005, para 38; *Rumeli v Kazakhstan*, Decision on Annulment, 25 March 2010, para 3; *Helnan v Egypt*, Decision on Annulment, 14 June 2010, para 8; *Sempra v Argentina*, Decision on Annulment, 29 June 2010, para 43; *Compañía de Aguas del Aconquija, SA & Vivendi Universal v Argentina*, Decision on Annulment, 10 August 2010, paras 2, 17.

[390] *Klöckner v Cameroon*, Decision on Annulment, 3 May 1985, 2 ICSID Reports 95, at paras 17, 52(e); *Wena v Egypt*, Decision on Annulment, 5 February 2002, 6 ICSID Reports 129, at para 25; *CDC v Seychelles*, Decision on Annulment, 29 June 2005, paras 41, 42; *Mitchell v Congo*, Decision on Annulment, 1 November 2006, para 20; *Repsol v Petroecuador*, Decision on Annulment, 8 January 2007, para 36; *Soufraki v UAE*, Decision on Annulment, 5 June 2007, para 40; *Azurix v Argentina*, Decision on Annulment, 1 September 2009, paras 63–70; *Sempra v Argentina*, Decision on Annulment, 29 June 2010, paras 211–19; *Fraport v Philippines*, Decision on Annulment, 23 December 2010, paras 39–45, 112.

[391] *Mitchell v Congo*, Decision on Annulment, 1 November 2006, paras 23–48.

[392] *Compañía de Aguas del Aconquija, SA & Vivendi Universal v Argentina*, Decision on Annulment, 3 July 2002.

It is settled, and neither party disputes, that an ICSID tribunal commits an excess of powers not only if it exercises a jurisdiction which it does not have . . . but also if it fails to exercise a jurisdiction which it possesses . . .[393]

The Tribunal had not decided certain claims that were before it but had referred the claimants to the domestic courts. The ad hoc Committee found that the Tribunal had thereby committed an excess of powers:

In the Committee's view, it is not open to an ICSID tribunal having jurisdiction under a BIT in respect of a claim based upon a substantive provision of that BIT, to dismiss the claim on the ground that it could or should have been dealt with by a national court. . . . [T]he Committee concludes that the Tribunal exceeded its powers in the sense of Article 52(1)(b), in that the Tribunal, having jurisdiction over the Tucumán claims, failed to decide those claims.[394]

Article 52(1) of the ICSID Convention does not, in express terms, provide for annulment for failure to apply the proper law. But the provisions on applicable law are an essential element of the parties' agreement to arbitrate. Therefore, the application of a law other than that agreed to by the parties may constitute an excess of powers and can be a valid ground for annulment. On the other hand, an error in the application of the proper law, even if it leads to an incorrect decision, is not a ground for annulment. Ad hoc committees, although recognizing this distinction in principle, have grappled with the dividing line between non-application and erroneous application of the proper law.[395]

In *Wena v Egypt*, the proper law was host state law and applicable rules of international law. In the annulment proceedings Egypt argued that the Tribunal, by awarding interest at the rate of nine per cent, compounded quarterly, had failed to apply the proper law since such a calculation of interest was contrary to Egyptian law. The ad hoc Committee rejected this argument. It found that under the BIT compensation had to amount to the market value of the investment expropriated. This had to be read as including a determination of appropriate interest. The ad hoc Committee said:

53. The option the Tribunal took was in the view of this Committee within the Tribunal's power. International law and ICSID practice, unlike the Egyptian Civil Code, offer a variety

---

[393] At para 86.

[394] At paras 102, 115.

[395] *Klöckner v Cameroon*, Decision on Annulment, 3 May 1985, paras 59–61; *Amco v Indonesia*, Decision on Annulment, 16 May 1986, paras 21–8; *MINE v Guinea*, Decision on Annulment, 22 December 1989, paras 5.02–5.04; *Wena v Egypt*, Decision on Annulment, 5 February 2002, paras 26–53; *CDC v Seychelles*, Decision on Annulment, 29 June 2005, para 46; *Mitchell v Congo*, Decision on Annulment, 1 November 2006, paras 55–7; *MTD v Chile*, Decision on Annulment, 21 March 2007, paras 44–8, 58–77; *Soufraki v UAE*, Decision on Annulment, 5 June 2007, paras 85–102; *CMS v Argentina*, Decision on Annulment, 25 September 2007, paras 128–36; *Azurix v Argentina*, Decision on Annulment, 1 September 2009, paras 46–8, 131–77, 314–29; *Sempra v Argentina*, Decision on Annulment, 29 June 2010, paras 186–210; *Enron v Argentina*, Decision on Annulment, 30 July 2010, paras 218–20, 377–405; *Duke Energy Intl v Peru*, Decision on Annulment, 1 March 2011, para 212.

of alternatives that are compatible with those objectives. These alternatives include the compounding of interest in some cases.[396]

ii. Serious departure from a fundamental rule of procedure

Under the ICSID Convention, a violation of a rule of procedure is a ground for annulment only if the departure from the rule was serious and the rule concerned is fundamental. The seriousness of the departure requires that it is more than minimal and that it must have had a material effect on a party. A minor and inconsequential breach of a rule of procedure is no ground for annulment. A rule is fundamental only if it affects the fairness of the proceedings.[397]

An example for a fundamental rule of procedure is the right to be heard.[398] In several cases involving the charge of a violation of the right to be heard, a party complained that the award was based on a theory that had not been discussed by the parties before the tribunal. Ad hoc committees have rejected the idea that tribunals, in drafting their awards, are restricted to the arguments presented to them by the parties.[399] In *Klöckner v Cameroon* the ad hoc Committee said:

> arbitrators must be free to rely on arguments which strike them as the best ones, even if those arguments were not developed by the parties (although they could have been). Even if it is generally desirable for arbitrators to avoid basing their decision on an argument that has not been discussed by the parties, it obviously does not follow that they therefore commit a 'serious departure from a fundamental rule of procedure.'[400]

Other instances of invocations of fundamental rules of procedure concerned impartiality and equal treatment of the parties[401] and issues of evidence.[402]

A party that is aware of a violation of a rule of procedure by the tribunal must react immediately by stating its objection and by demanding compliance. Under Arbitration Rule 27 failure to do so will be interpreted as a waiver to object at a later stage. If a party has failed to protest against a perceived procedural irregularity before the tribunal, it cannot subsequently claim in annulment proceedings

---

[396] *Wena v Egypt*, Decision on Annulment, 5 February 2002, para 53. Footnote omitted.

[397] *Klöckner v Cameroon*, Decision on Annulment, 3 May 1985, paras 82bis–113; *MINE v Guinea*, Decision on Annulment, 22 December 1989, paras 5.05–5.06; *Wena v Egypt*, Decision on Annulment, 5 February 2002, paras 56–8; *CDC v Seychelles*, Decision on Annulment, 29 June 2005, paras 48, 49; *Azurix v Argentina*, Decision on Annulment, 1 September 2009, paras 49–52, 234; *Enron v Argentina*, Decision on Annulment, 30 July 2010, paras 70, 71.

[398] *MINE v Guinea*, Decision on Annulment, 22 December 1989, para 5.06; *Amco v Indonesia*, Resubmitted Case: Decision on Annulment, 3 December 1992, paras 9.05–9.10; *Wena v Egypt*, Decision on Annulment, 5 February 2002, para 57; *Lucchetti v Peru (sub nom Industria Nacional de Alimentos)*, Decision on Annulment, 5 September 2007, para 122; *Helnan v Egypt*, Decision on Annulment, 14 June 2010, para 38; *Fraport v Philippines*, Decision on Annulment, 23 December 2010, paras 127–33, 144–247.

[399] *Wena v Egypt*, Decision on Annulment, 5 February 2002, paras 66–70; *Compañía de Aguas del Aconquija, SA & Vivendi Universal v Argentina*, Decision on Annulment, 3 July 2002, paras 82–5.

[400] *Klöckner v Cameroon*, Decision on Annulment, 3 May 1985, para 91.

[401] *Klöckner*, n 400, paras 93–113; *Amco v Indonesia*, Decision on Annulment, 16 May 1986, paras 30, 32, 36, 88, 122–3; *CDC v Seychelles*, Decision on Annulment, 29 June 2005, paras 51–5.

[402] *Azurix v Argentina*, Decision on Annulment, 1 September 2009, paras 207–39.

that this irregularity constituted a serious departure from a fundamental rule of procedure.[403]

iii. Failure to state reasons

The purpose of a statement of reasons is to explain to the reader of the award, especially to the parties, how and why the tribunal reached its decision. Article 48(3) of the ICSID Convention contains a clear obligation to state reasons for the award. Therefore, a total absence of reasons is extremely unlikely, but requests for annulment have repeatedly alleged the absence of reasons on particular points. In addition, complaints have been directed at insufficient and inadequate reasons, contradictory reasons, or a failure to deal with every question before the tribunal.

If reasons on a particular point are missing, an ad hoc committee may reconstruct the omitted reasons. Therefore, an award will not be annulled if the reasons for a decision, though not stated explicitly, are readily apparent to the ad hoc committee. Implicit reasoning is sufficient as long as it can be inferred reasonably from the terms and conclusions of the award.[404]

Insufficiency and inadequacy of reasons have been invoked repeatedly. This is a particularly subjective criterion and ad hoc committees have stated that reasons had to be 'sufficiently relevant', 'appropriate', and 'to allow the parties to understand the Tribunal's decision'.[405] The ad hoc Committee in *Vivendi* said in this respect:

> annulment under Article 52(1)(e) should only occur in a clear case. This entails two conditions: first, the failure to state reasons must leave the decision on a particular point essentially lacking in any expressed rationale; and second, that point must itself be necessary to the tribunal's decision.[406]

---

[403] *Klöckner v Cameroon*, Decision on Annulment, 3 May 1985, para 88; *CDC v Seychelles*, Decision on Annulment, 29 June 2005, paras 51–3; *Fraport v Philippines*, Decision on Annulment, 23 December 2010, paras 204–8, 233–4.

[404] *Amco v Indonesia*, Decision on Annulment, 16 May 1986, para 58; *MINE v Guinea*, Decision on Annulment, 22 December 1989, paras 6.103–6.104; *Wena v Egypt*, Decision on Annulment, 5 February 2002, paras 81–3, 93, 98, 106; *Compañía de Aguas del Aconquija, SA & Vivendi Universal v Argentina*, Decision on Annulment, 3 July 2002, paras 87–91; *CDC v Seychelles*, Decision on Annulment, 29 June 2005, paras 81, 87; *Soufraki v UAE*, Decision on Annulment, 5 June 2007, para 24; *CMS v Argentina*, Decision on Annulment, 25 September 2007, paras 125–7; *Rumeli v Kazakhstan*, Decision on Annulment, 25 March 2010, paras 83, 138; *Compañía de Aguas del Aconquija, SA & Vivendi Universal v Argentina*, Decision on Annulment, 10 August 2010, para 248; *Fraport v Philippines*, Decision on Annulment, 23 December 2010, paras 264–6. But see an earlier decision to the contrary: *Klöckner v Cameroon*, Decision on Annulment, 3 May 1985, para 144.

[405] *Klöckner v Cameroon*, Decision on Annulment, 3 May 1985, paras 117–20; *Amco v Indonesia*, Decision on Annulment, 16 May 1986, paras 38–43; *MINE v Guinea*, Decision on Annulment, 22 December 1989, paras 5.08–5.09; *Wena v Egypt*, Decision on Annulment, 5 February 2002, paras 75–83; *CDC v Seychelles*, Decision on Annulment, 29 June 2005, paras 66–71, 75; *Mitchell v Congo*, Decision on Annulment, 1 November 2006, paras 21, 39–41, 46, 65; *Soufraki v UAE*, Decision on Annulment, 5 June 2007, paras 121–34; *Lucchetti v Peru (sub nom Industria Nacional de Alimentos)*, Decision on Annulment, 5 September 2007, paras 126–30; *CMS v Argentina*, Decision on Annulment, 25 September 2007, paras 86–98, 125–7; *Fraport v Philippines*, Decision on Annulment, 23 December 2010, paras 248–80.

[406] *Compañía de Aguas del Aconquija, SA & Vivendi Universal v Argentina*, Decision on Annulment, 3 July 2002, para 65.

It is also accepted that contradictory reasons may amount to a failure to state reasons since they will not enable the reader to understand the tribunal's motives. Genuinely contradictory reasons would cancel each other out.[407]

The tribunal's obligation to deal with every question submitted to it is contained in Article 48(3) of the ICSID Convention. Failure to deal with every question is not listed as a separate ground for annulment but ad hoc committees have found that it is covered by failure to state reasons.[408] But this obligation does not mean that the tribunal has to address every single argument put forward by a party; only a crucial or decisive argument would be a 'question' in this context. An argument is decisive if its acceptance would have affected the tribunal's decision.

A decision by an ad hoc committee upholding a request for annulment for any of the grounds listed in Article 52(1) invalidates the original award, but it does not replace it with a new decision on the merits. Under Article 52(6) of the ICSID Convention, if the award is annulled, the dispute is to be submitted to a new tribunal at the request of either party. If the award is partially annulled, only the annulled portion of the award falls to be re-litigated while the unannulled part remains *res judicata*.[409]

Any determinations of fact and law made by the ad hoc committee are not binding on the tribunal hearing the resubmitted case. Only the annulment of the award but not the reasoning accompanying it is binding.[410] In addition, in the resubmitted case the parties may not introduce new claims that they did not present to the first tribunal.[411]

cc. Supplementation and rectification under the ICSID Convention

Under Article 49(2) of the ICSID Convention, the tribunal may upon the request of a party decide any question it had omitted to decide in the award and shall rectify technical errors in the award.[412] This gives the tribunal the possibility of correcting

---

[407] *Klöckner v Cameroon*, Decision on Annulment, 3 May 1985, para 116; *Amco v Indonesia*, Decision on Annulment, 16 May 1986, para 97; *MINE v Guinea*, Decision on Annulment, 22 December 1989, para 6.105; *Compañía de Aguas del Aconquija, SA & Vivendi Universal v Argentina*, Decision on Annulment, 3 July 2002, paras 64, 65, 72; *CDC v Seychelles*, Decision on Annulment, 29 June 2005, paras 77–86; *Azurix v Argentina*, Decision on Annulment, 1 September 2009, paras 364–6; *Duke Energy Intl v Peru*, Decision on Annulment, 1 March 2011, para 166.

[408] *Klöckner v Cameroon*, Decision on Annulment, 3 May 1985, para 115; *Amco v Indonesia*, Decision on Annulment, 16 May 1986, para 32; *MINE v Guinea*, Decision on Annulment, 22 December 1989, para 5.13; *Wena v Egypt*, Decision on Annulment, 5 February 2002, paras 102–10; *Azurix v Argentina*, Decision on Annulment, 1 September 2009, paras 240–6; *MCI v Ecuador*, Decision on Annulment, 19 October 2009, paras 66–9; *Rumeli v Kazakhstan*, Decision on Annulment, 25 March 2010, para 84.

[409] Arbitration Rule 55(3). *Amco v Indonesia*, Resubmitted Case: Decision on Jurisdiction, 10 May 1988, 1 ICSID Reports 543, at 545–61; *Compañía de Aguas del Aconquija, SA & Vivendi Universal SA v Argentina*, Resubmitted Case: Decision on Jurisdiction, 14 November 2005, paras 30–1.

[410] *Amco v Indonesia*, Resubmitted Case: Decision on Jurisdiction, 10 May 1988, 1 ICSID Reports 543, at 552.

[411] *Amco*, n 410, at 560–1, 566–7.

[412] Arbitration Rule 49.

inadvertent omissions and minor technical errors. This remedy is not designed for substantive amendments of the award. The request has to be made within 45 days.

dd. Interpretation under the ICSID Convention

In the case of a dispute between the parties concerning the meaning or scope of an award, either party may request an interpretation under Article 50 of the ICSID Convention.[413] There is no time limit for such a request. If possible, the original tribunal is to decide upon the request and, if this is not possible, a new tribunal will be constituted for the purpose. Once the interpretation has been given, the award will be binding as interpreted.

The purpose of an interpretation is to clarify points that were decided in the award and not to decide new points.[414] In addition, the dispute on the award's interpretation must have some practical relevance to the award's implementation.[415] The Tribunal in *ATA v Jordan* summarized the function of a decision on interpretation as follows:

(1) there must be a dispute between the parties over 'the meaning or scope' of the award;

(2) the purpose of the application must be to obtain a true interpretation of the award, rather than to reopen the matter; and

(3) the requested interpretation 'must have some practical relevance to the Award's implementation'.[416]

ee. Revision under the ICSID Convention

If decisive new facts come to light after the award has been rendered, a party may, in accordance with Article 51 of the ICSID Convention, request the award's revision.[417] The new facts must have been unknown to the applicant at the time the award was rendered.[418] A request for revision must be made within 90 days of discovery of the new facts and within three years of the award being rendered. If possible, the original tribunal is to decide upon the request. If this is not possible, a new tribunal will be constituted for this purpose.

The new facts must be capable of affecting the award decisively, that is, they would have led to a different decision had they been known to the tribunal. The request for revision must come from one of the parties. The tribunal may not revise the award on its own initiative. The award will be binding as revised.

---

[413] Arbitration Rules 50 and 51.
[414] *Wena v Egypt*, Decision on Interpretation, 31 October 2005, paras 103–7, 127–31, 133, 138.
[415] *Wena v Egypt*, n 414, paras 81, 87.
[416] *ATA v Jordan*, Decision on Interpretation, 7 March 2011, para 35.
[417] Arbitration Rules 50 and 51.
[418] *RSM v Grenada*, Award, 10 December 2010, paras 7.1.15–7.1.30.

(o) Enforcement of awards

Arbitral awards are binding upon the parties and create an obligation to comply with them. Except for the limited possibilities for review described in the preceding chapter, they are final. Article 53 of the ICSID Convention specifically provides for the finality of awards. The issues decided in awards are also *res judicata*. This means that the parties may not seek another remedy before another tribunal or in a domestic court.

The enforcement of non-ICSID awards, including Additional Facility awards, is subject to the national law of the place of enforcement and to the New York Convention on the Recognition and Enforcement of Foreign Arbitral Awards.[419] Article V of that Convention lists a number of grounds on which recognition and enforcement may be refused. The most important of these grounds are the invalidity of the arbitration agreement, lack of proper notice of the arbitration proceedings, a decision in the award outside the submission to arbitration, improper composition of the tribunal, an award that is not yet binding or has been set aside, a subject matter not capable of settlement by arbitration under the law of the state in which enforcement is sought, and an award that is in conflict with the public policy of that state.

The regime for the enforcement of ICSID awards is different. Under Article 54 of the ICSID Convention awards are to be recognized as binding and their pecuniary obligations are to be enforced in the same way as final domestic judgments in all states parties to the Convention. The obligation to recognize an award extends to any type of obligation under it. By contrast, the obligation to enforce is limited to pecuniary obligations under the award.

Recognition and enforcement may be sought not only in the host state or in the investor's state of nationality, but in any state that is a party to the ICSID Convention. The prevailing party may select a state where enforcement seems most promising. This choice is likely to be determined by the availability of suitable assets.

The procedure for the enforcement of ICSID awards is governed by the law on the execution of judgments in each country. Contracting states are to designate a competent court or authority for this purpose.[420]

The party seeking recognition and enforcement must furnish a copy of the award certified by the Secretary-General of ICSID. If a stay of enforcement is in force, the duty to enforce is suspended. A stay of enforcement may be granted while proceedings for the interpretation, revision, or annulment are in progress.

There is no review of ICSID awards by domestic courts in the course of proceedings for recognition and enforcement. Therefore, the domestic court or authority may not examine whether the ICSID tribunal had jurisdiction, whether it

---

[419] 330 UNTS 38; 7 ILM 1046 (1968).

[420] See Designations of Courts or Other Authorities Competent for the Recognition and Enforcement of Awards Rendered Pursuant to the Convention at <http://www.worldbank.org/icsid/pubs/icsid-8/icsid-8-e.htm>.

adhered to the proper procedure, or whether the award is substantively correct. It may not even examine whether the award is in conformity with the forum state's *ordre public* (public policy). The domestic court or authority is limited to verifying that the award is authentic.

Proceedings for the recognition and enforcement of ICSID awards may be initiated in several states simultaneously. This may be necessary to secure their *res judicata* effect. If enforcement is sought in more than one state, appropriate steps must be taken to prevent double or multiple recovery.

Under Article 55 of the ICSID Convention, the obligation to enforce pecuniary obligations arising from ICSID awards does not affect any immunity from execution that states enjoy. State immunity is regulated by customary international law. A number of states have passed legislation in this field.[421] A United Nations Convention dealing with state immunity is not yet in force.[422]

For purposes of state immunity from execution, a distinction is usually made between commercial and non-commercial property. Execution is permitted against commercial property but not against property serving official or governmental functions. The exact dividing line between the two types of property is not always easy to draw.[423] In particular, there is some uncertainty as to whether a public purpose of the property is the only decisive criterion for immunity from execution. Diplomatic property, including embassy accounts[424] as well as accounts held by national central banks,[425] enjoys special protection from execution. A waiver of immunity from execution may be possible but will be difficult to obtain from a host state. Occasionally, domestic rules on state immunity from execution actually place limits on the possibility of agreeing on waivers.

Some national rules on immunity from execution display special features. The US Foreign Sovereign Immunities Act of 1976 (FSIA) provides for an exception to state immunity from execution in respect of a foreign state's property in the United States used for commercial activity in the United States only if that property is or was used for the commercial activity upon which the claim is based.[426] Another exception to immunity from execution under the same Act concerns commercial property which was taken in violation of international law or which was exchanged

---

[421] United States: Foreign Sovereign Immunities Act (FSIA) 1976, 28 USC §§ 1330, 1602–11, 15 ILM 1388 (1976), as amended in 1988, 28 ILM 396 (1989) and in 1996/7, 36 ILM 759 (1997); United Kingdom: State Immunity Act (SIA) 1978, 17 ILM 1123 (1978); Australia: Foreign States Immunities Act 1985, 25 ILM 715 (1986).

[422] United Nations Convention on Jurisdictional Immunities of States and their Property, 2004, Adopted by the General Assembly of the United Nations on 2 December 2004. See GA Res 59/38, annex, Official Records of the General Assembly, 59th Session, Supplement No 49 (A/59/49).

[423] *LETCO v Liberia*, District Court, SDNY, 5 September and 12 December 1986; *Benvenuti & Bonfant v Congo*, Tribunal de grande instance, Paris, 13 January 1981, Cour d'appel, Paris, 26 June 1981; *SOABI v Senegal*, Cour d'appel, Paris, 5 December 1989, Cour de cassation, 11 June 1991.

[424] *LETCO v Liberia*, US District Court for the District of Columbia, 16 April 1987.

[425] *AIG Capital Partners Inc and another v Republic of Kazakhstan (National Bank of Kazakhstan Intervening)*, High Court, Queen's Bench Division (Commercial Court), 20 October 2005 [2005] EWHC 2239 (Comm), 11 ICSID Reports 118.

[426] FSIA, 28 USC § 1610(a)(2).

for such property.[427] Also under the FSIA, there is a special exception to state immunity from execution for the purposes of executing arbitral awards.[428]

State immunity from execution is merely a procedural bar to the award's enforcement but does not affect the obligation of the state to comply with it. Therefore, successful reliance on state immunity does not alter the fact that non-compliance with an award is a breach of the ICSID Convention. The ad hoc Committee in *MINE v Guinea* noted in this respect that:

It should be clearly understood ... that State immunity may well afford a legal defense to forcible execution, but it provides neither argument nor excuse for failing to comply with an award. In fact, the issue of State immunity from forcible execution of an award will typically arise if the State party refuses to comply with its treaty obligations. Non-compliance by a State constitutes a violation by that State of its international obligations and will attract its own sanctions.[429]

Under Article 27 of the ICSID Convention the right of diplomatic protection will revive in the event of non-compliance with the award. Therefore, diplomatic protection is an alternative and supplement to the judicial enforcement of awards under Article 54. In particular, diplomatic protection will be available if enforcement is unsuccessful because of the award debtor state's immunity from execution. But diplomatic protection may be exercised only by the aggrieved investor's state of nationality.

---

[427] FSIA, 28 USC § 1610(a)(3).

[428] FSIA, 28 USC § 1610(a)(6).

[429] *MINE v Guinea*, Interim Order No 1 on Guinea's Application for Stay of Enforcement of the Award, 12 August 1988, para 25.

ANNEXES

Convention on the Settlement of Investment Disputes Between States and Nationals of Other States (ICSID Convention)

Preamble

The Contracting States

Considering the need for international cooperation for economic development, and the role of private international investment therein;

Bearing in mind the possibility that from time to time disputes may arise in connection with such investment between Contracting States and nationals of other Contracting States;

Recognizing that while such disputes would usually be subject to national legal processes, international methods of settlement may be appropriate in certain cases;

Attaching particular importance to the availability of facilities for international conciliation or arbitration to which Contracting States and nationals of other Contracting States may submit such disputes if they so desire;

Desiring to establish such facilities under the auspices of the International Bank for Reconstruction and Development;

Recognizing that mutual consent by the parties to submit such disputes to conciliation or to arbitration through such facilities constitutes a binding agreement which requires in particular that due consideration be given to any recommendation of conciliators, and that any arbitral award be complied with; and

Declaring that no Contracting State shall by the mere fact of its ratification, acceptance or approval of this Convention and without its consent be deemed to be under any obligation to submit any particular dispute to conciliation or arbitration,

Have agreed as follows:

Chapter I International Centre for Settlement of Investment Disputes

Section 1
Establishment and Organization
Article 1

(1) There is hereby established the International Centre for Settlement of Investment Disputes (hereinafter called the Centre).

(2) The purpose of the Centre shall be to provide facilities for conciliation and arbitration of investment disputes between Contracting States and nationals of other Contracting States in accordance with the provisions of this Convention.

Article 2

The seat of the Centre shall be at the principal office of the International Bank for Reconstruction and Development (hereinafter called the Bank). The seat may be moved to another place by decision of the Administrative Council adopted by a majority of two-thirds of its members.

Article 3

The Centre shall have an Administrative Council and a Secretariat and shall maintain a Panel of Conciliators and a Panel of Arbitrators.

Section 2
The Administrative Council

Article 4

(1) The Administrative Council shall be composed of one representative of each Contracting State. An alternate may act as representative in case of his principal's absence from a meeting or inability to act.
(2) In the absence of a contrary designation, each governor and alternate governor of the Bank appointed by a Contracting State shall be *ex officio* its representative and its alternate respectively.

Article 5

The President of the Bank shall be *ex officio* Chairman of the Administrative Council (hereinafter called the Chairman) but shall have no vote. During his absence or inability to act and during any vacancy in the office of President of the Bank, the person for the time being acting as President shall act as Chairman of the Administrative Council.

Article 6

(1) Without prejudice to the powers and functions vested in it by other provisions of this Convention, the Administrative Council shall:
  (a) adopt the administrative and financial regulations of the Centre;
  (b) adopt the rules of procedure for the institution of conciliation and arbitration proceedings;
  (c) adopt the rules of procedure for conciliation and arbitration proceedings (hereinafter called the Conciliation Rules and the Arbitration Rules);
  (d) approve arrangements with the Bank for the use of the Bank's administrative facilities and services;
  (e) determine the conditions of service of the Secretary-General and of any Deputy Secretary-General;
  (f) adopt the annual budget of revenues and expenditures of the Centre;
  (g) approve the annual report on the operation of the Centre.
The decisions referred to in sub-paragraphs (a), (b), (c) and (f) above shall be adopted by a majority of two-thirds of the members of the Administrative Council.
(2) The Administrative Council may appoint such committees as it considers necessary.
(3) The Administrative Council shall also exercise such other powers and perform such other functions as it shall determine to be necessary for the implementation of the provisions of this Convention.

Article 7

(1) The Administrative Council shall hold an annual meeting and such other meetings as may be determined by the Council, or convened by the Chairman, or convened by the Secretary-General at the request of not less than five members of the Council.

(2) Each member of the Administrative Council shall have one vote and, except as otherwise herein provided, all matters before the Council shall be decided by a majority of the votes cast.

(3) A quorum for any meeting of the Administrative Council shall be a majority of its members.

(4) The Administrative Council may establish, by a majority of two-thirds of its members, a procedure whereby the Chairman may seek a vote of the Council without convening a meeting of the Council. The vote shall be considered valid only if the majority of the members of the Council cast their votes within the time limit fixed by the said procedure.

Article 8

Members of the Administrative Council and the Chairman shall serve without remuneration from the Centre.

Section 3
The Secretariat

Article 9

The Secretariat shall consist of a Secretary-General, one or more Deputy Secretaries-General and staff.

Article 10

(1) The Secretary-General and any Deputy Secretary-General shall be elected by the Administrative Council by a majority of two-thirds of its members upon the nomination of the Chairman for a term of service not exceeding six years and shall be eligible for re-election. After consulting the members of the Administrative Council, the Chairman shall propose one or more candidates for each such office.

(2) The offices of Secretary-General and Deputy Secretary-General shall be incompatible with the exercise of any political function. Neither the Secretary-General nor any Deputy Secretary-General may hold any other employment or engage in any other occupation except with the approval of the Administrative Council.

(3) During the Secretary-General's absence or inability to act, and during any vacancy of the office of Secretary-General, the Deputy Secretary-General shall act as Secretary-General. If there shall be more than one Deputy Secretary-General, the Administrative Council shall determine in advance the order in which they shall act as Secretary-General.

Article 11

The Secretary-General shall be the legal representative and the principal officer of the Centre and shall be responsible for its administration, including the appointment of staff, in accordance with the provisions of this Convention and the rules adopted by the Administrative Council. He shall perform the function of registrar and shall have the power to authenticate arbitral awards rendered pursuant to this Convention, and to certify copies thereof.

Section 4
The Panels
Article 12

The Panel of Conciliators and the Panel of Arbitrators shall each consist of qualified persons, designated as hereinafter provided, who are willing to serve thereon.

Article 13

(1) Each Contracting State may designate to each Panel four persons who may but need not be its nationals.
(2) The Chairman may designate ten persons to each Panel. The persons so designated to a Panel shall each have a different nationality.

Article 14

(1) Persons designated to serve on the Panels shall be persons of high moral character and recognized competence in the fields of law, commerce, industry or finance, who may be relied upon to exercise independent judgment. Competence in the field of law shall be of particular importance in the case of persons on the Panel of Arbitrators.
(2) The Chairman, in designating persons to serve on the Panels, shall in addition pay due regard to the importance of assuring representation on the Panels of the principal legal systems of the world and of the main forms of economic activity.

Article 15

(1) Panel members shall serve for renewable periods of six years.
(2) In case of death or resignation of a member of a Panel, the authority which designated the member shall have the right to designate another person to serve for the remainder of that member's term.
(3) Panel members shall continue in office until their successors have been designated.

Article 16

(1) A person may serve on both Panels.
(2) If a person shall have been designated to serve on the same Panel by more than one Contracting State, or by one or more Contracting States and the Chairman, he shall be deemed to have been designated by the authority which first designated him or, if one such authority is the State of which he is a national, by that State.
(3) All designations shall be notified to the Secretary-General and shall take effect from the date on which the notification is received.

Section 5
Financing the Centre
Article 17

If the expenditure of the Centre cannot be met out of charges for the use of its facilities, or out of other receipts, the excess shall be borne by Contracting States which are members of the Bank in proportion to their respective subscriptions to the capital stock of the Bank, and by Contracting States which are not members of the Bank in accordance with rules adopted by the Administrative Council.

Section 6
Status, Immunities and Privileges
Article 18

The Centre shall have full international legal personality. The legal capacity of the Centre shall include the capacity:

(a) to contract;
(b) to acquire and dispose of movable and immovable property;
(c) to institute legal proceedings.

Article 19

To enable the Centre to fulfil its functions, it shall enjoy in the territories of each Contracting State the immunities and privileges set forth in this Section.

Article 20

The Centre, its property and assets shall enjoy immunity from all legal process, except when the Centre waives this immunity.

Article 21

The Chairman, the members of the Administrative Council, persons acting as conciliators or arbitrators or members of a Committee appointed pursuant to paragraph (3) of Article 52, and the officers and employees of the Secretariat

(a) shall enjoy immunity from legal process with respect to acts performed by them in the exercise of their functions, except when the Centre waives this immunity;
(b) not being local nationals, shall enjoy the same immunities from immigration restrictions, alien registration requirements and national service obligations, the same facilities as regards exchange restrictions and the same treatment in respect of travelling facilities as are accorded by Contracting States to the representatives, officials and employees of comparable rank of other Contracting States.

Article 22

The provisions of Article 21 shall apply to persons appearing in proceedings under this Convention as parties, agents, counsel, advocates, witnesses or experts; provided, however, that sub-paragraph (b) thereof shall apply only in connection with their travel to and from, and their stay at, the place where the proceedings are held.

Article 23

(1) The archives of the Centre shall be inviolable, wherever they may be.
(2) With regard to its official communications, the Centre shall be accorded by each Contracting State treatment not less favourable than that accorded to other international organizations.

Article 24

(1) The Centre, its assets, property and income, and its operations and transactions authorized by this Convention shall be exempt from all taxation and customs duties. The Centre shall also be exempt from liability for the collection or payment of any taxes or customs duties.
(2) Except in the case of local nationals, no tax shall be levied on or in respect of expense allowances paid by the Centre to the Chairman or members of the Administrative Council, or on or in respect of salaries, expense allowances or other emoluments paid by the Centre to officials or employees of the Secretariat.

(3) No tax shall be levied on or in respect of fees or expense allowances received by persons acting as conciliators, or arbitrators, or members of a Committee appointed pursuant to paragraph (3) of Article 52, in proceedings under this Convention, if the sole jurisdictional basis for such tax is the location of the Centre or the place where such proceedings are conducted or the place where such fees or allowances are paid.

Chapter II Jurisdiction of the Centre

Article 25

(1) The jurisdiction of the Centre shall extend to any legal dispute arising directly out of an investment, between a Contracting State (or any constituent subdivision or agency of a Contracting State designated to the Centre by that State) and a national of another Contracting State, which the parties to the dispute consent in writing to submit to the Centre. When the parties have given their consent, no party may withdraw its consent unilaterally.

(2) "National of another Contracting State" means:

    (a) any natural person who had the nationality of a Contracting State other than the State party to the dispute on the date on which the parties consented to submit such dispute to conciliation or arbitration as well as on the date on which the request was registered pursuant to paragraph (3) of Article 28 or paragraph (3) of Article 36, but does not include any person who on either date also had the nationality of the Contracting State party to the dispute; and

    (b) any juridical person which had the nationality of a Contracting State other than the State party to the dispute on the date on which the parties consented to submit such dispute to conciliation or arbitration and any juridical person which had the nationality of the Contracting State party to the dispute on that date and which, because of foreign control, the parties have agreed should be treated as a national of another Contracting State for the purposes of this Convention.

(3) Consent by a constituent subdivision or agency of a Contracting State shall require the approval of that State unless that State notifies the Centre that no such approval is required.

(4) Any Contracting State may, at the time of ratification, acceptance or approval of this Convention or at any time thereafter, notify the Centre of the class or classes of disputes which it would or would not consider submitting to the jurisdiction of the Centre. The Secretary-General shall forthwith transmit such notification to all Contracting States. Such notification shall not constitute the consent required by paragraph (1).

Article 26

Consent of the parties to arbitration under this Convention shall, unless otherwise stated, be deemed consent to such arbitration to the exclusion of any other remedy. A Contracting State may require the exhaustion of local administrative or judicial remedies as a condition of its consent to arbitration under this Convention.

Article 27

(1) No Contracting State shall give diplomatic protection, or bring an international claim, in respect of a dispute which one of its nationals and another Contracting State shall have consented to submit or shall have submitted to arbitration under this Convention,

unless such other Contracting State shall have failed to abide by and comply with the award rendered in such dispute.

(2) Diplomatic protection, for the purposes of paragraph (1), shall not include informal diplomatic exchanges for the sole purpose of facilitating a settlement of the dispute.

Chapter III Conciliation

Section 1
Request for Conciliation
Article 28

(1) Any Contracting State or any national of a Contracting State wishing to institute conciliation proceedings shall address a request to that effect in writing to the Secretary-General who shall send a copy of the request to the other party.

(2) The request shall contain information concerning the issues in dispute, the identity of the parties and their consent to conciliation in accordance with the rules of procedure for the institution of conciliation and arbitration proceedings.

(3) The Secretary-General shall register the request unless he finds, on the basis of the information contained in the request, that the dispute is manifestly outside the jurisdiction of the Centre. He shall forthwith notify the parties of registration or refusal to register.

Section 2
Constitution of the Conciliation Commission
Article 29

(1) The Conciliation Commission (hereinafter called the Commission) shall be constituted as soon as possible after registration of a request pursuant to Article 28.

(2) (a) The Commission shall consist of a sole conciliator or any uneven number of conciliators appointed as the parties shall agree.

　(b) Where the parties do not agree upon the number of conciliators and the method of their appointment, the Commission shall consist of three conciliators, one conciliator appointed by each party and the third, who shall be the president of the Commission, appointed by agreement of the parties.

Article 30

If the Commission shall not have been constituted within 90 days after notice of registration of the request has been dispatched by the Secretary-General in accordance with paragraph (3) of Article 28, or such other period as the parties may agree, the Chairman shall, at the request of either party and after consult-ing both parties as far as possible, appoint the conciliator or conciliators not yet appointed.

Article 31

(1) Conciliators may be appointed from outside the Panel of Conciliators, except in the case of appointments by the Chairman pursuant to Article 30.

(2) Conciliators appointed from outside the Panel of Conciliators shall possess the qualities stated in paragraph (1) of Article 14.

Section 3
Conciliation Proceedings
Article 32

(1) The Commission shall be the judge of its own competence.

(2) Any objection by a party to the dispute that that dispute is not within the jurisdiction of the Centre, or for other reasons is not within the competence of the Commission, shall be considered by the Commission which shall determine whether to deal with it as a preliminary question or to join it to the merits of the dispute.

Article 33

Any conciliation proceeding shall be conducted in accordance with the provisions of this Section and, except as the parties otherwise agree, in accordance with the Conciliation Rules in effect on the date on which the parties consented to conciliation. If any question of procedure arises which is not covered by this Section or the Conciliation Rules or any rules agreed by the parties, the Commission shall decide the question.

Article 34

(1) It shall be the duty of the Commission to clarify the issues in dispute between the parties and to endeavour to bring about agreement between them upon mutually acceptable terms. To that end, the Commission may at any stage of the proceedings and from time to time recommend terms of settlement to the parties. The parties shall cooperate in good faith with the Commission in order to enable the Commission to carry out its functions, and shall give their most serious consideration to its recommendations.

(2) If the parties reach agreement, the Commission shall draw up a report noting the issues in dispute and recording that the parties have reached agreement. If, at any stage of the proceedings, it appears to the Commission that there is no likelihood of agreement between the parties, it shall close the proceedings and shall draw up a report noting the submission of the dispute and recording the failure of the parties to reach agreement. If one party fails to appear or participate in the proceedings, the Commission shall close the proceedings and shall draw up a report noting that party's failure to appear or participate.

Article 35

Except as the parties to the dispute shall otherwise agree, neither party to a conciliation proceeding shall be entitled in any other proceeding, whether before arbitrators or in a court of law or otherwise, to invoke or rely on any views expressed or statements or admissions or offers of settlement made by the other party in the conciliation proceedings, or the report or any recommendations made by the Commission.

Chapter IV Arbitration

Section 1
Request for Arbitration
Article 36

(1) Any Contracting State or any national of a Contracting State wishing to institute arbitration proceedings shall address a request to that effect in writing to the Secretary-General who shall send a copy of the request to the other party.

(2) The request shall contain information concerning the issues in dispute, the identity of the parties and their consent to arbitration in accordance with the rules of procedure for the institution of conciliation and arbitration proceedings.

(3) The Secretary-General shall register the request unless he finds, on the basis of the information contained in the request, that the dispute is manifestly outside the jurisdiction of the Centre. He shall forthwith notify the parties of registration or refusal to register.

Section 2
Constitution of the Tribunal
Article 37

(1) The Arbitral Tribunal (hereinafter called the Tribunal) shall be constituted as soon as possible after registration of a request pursuant to Article 36.

(2) (a) The Tribunal shall consist of a sole arbitrator or any uneven number of arbitrators appointed as the parties shall agree.

    (b) Where the parties do not agree upon the number of arbitrators and the method of their appointment, the Tribunal shall consist of three arbitrators, one arbitrator appointed by each party and the third, who shall be the president of the Tribunal, appointed by agreement of the parties.

Article 38

If the Tribunal shall not have been constituted within 90 days after notice of registration of the request has been dispatched by the Secretary-General in accordance with paragraph (3) of Article 36, or such other period as the parties may agree, the Chairman shall, at the request of either party and after consulting both parties as far as possible, appoint the arbitrator or arbitrators not yet appointed. Arbitrators appointed by the Chairman pursuant to this Article shall not be nationals of the Contracting State party to the dispute or of the Contracting State whose national is a party to the dispute.

Article 39

The majority of the arbitrators shall be nationals of States other than the Contracting State party to the dispute and the Contracting State whose national is a party to the dispute; provided, however, that the foregoing provisions of this Article shall not apply if the sole arbitrator or each individual member of the Tribunal has been appointed by agreement of the parties.

Article 40

(1) Arbitrators may be appointed from outside the Panel of Arbitrators, except in the case of appointments by the Chairman pursuant to Article 38.

(2) Arbitrators appointed from outside the Panel of Arbitrators shall possess the qualities stated in paragraph (1) of Article 14.

Section 3
Powers and Functions of the Tribunal
Article 41

(1) The Tribunal shall be the judge of its own competence.

(2) Any objection by a party to the dispute that that dispute is not within the jurisdiction of the Centre, or for other reasons is not within the competence of the Tribunal, shall be considered by the Tribunal which shall determine whether to deal with it as a preliminary question or to join it to the merits of the dispute.

Article 42

(1) The Tribunal shall decide a dispute in accordance with such rules of law as may be agreed by the parties. In the absence of such agreement, the Tribunal shall apply the law of the Contracting State party to the dispute (including its rules on the conflict of laws) and such rules of international law as may be applicable.

(2) The Tribunal may not bring in a finding of *non liquet* on the ground of silence or obscurity of the law.

(3) The provisions of paragraphs (1) and (2) shall not prejudice the power of the Tribunal to decide a dispute *ex aequo et bono* if the parties so agree.

Article 43

Except as the parties otherwise agree, the Tribunal may, if it deems it necessary at any stage of the proceedings,

(a) call upon the parties to produce documents or other evidence, and

(b) visit the scene connected with the dispute, and conduct such inquiries there as it may deem appropriate.

Article 44

Any arbitration proceeding shall be conducted in accordance with the provisions of this Section and, except as the parties otherwise agree, in accordance with the Arbitration Rules in effect on the date on which the parties consented to arbitration. If any question of procedure arises which is not covered by this Section or the Arbitration Rules or any rules agreed by the parties, the Tribunal shall decide the question.

Article 45

(1) Failure of a party to appear or to present his case shall not be deemed an admission of the other party's assertions.

(2) If a party fails to appear or to present his case at any stage of the proceedings the other party may request the Tribunal to deal with the questions submitted to it and to render an award. Before rendering an award, the Tribunal shall notify, and grant a period of grace to, the party failing to appear or to present its case, unless it is satisfied that that party does not intend to do so.

Article 46

Except as the parties otherwise agree, the Tribunal shall, if requested by a party, determine any incidental or additional claims or counterclaims arising directly out of the subject-matter of the dispute provided that they are within the scope of the consent of the parties and are otherwise within the jurisdiction of the Centre.

Article 47

Except as the parties otherwise agree, the Tribunal may, if it considers that the circumstances so require, recommend any provisional measures which should be taken to preserve the respective rights of either party.

Section 4
The Award
Article 48

(1) The Tribunal shall decide questions by a majority of the votes of all its members.

(2) The award of the Tribunal shall be in writing and shall be signed by the members of the Tribunal who voted for it.

(3) The award shall deal with every question submitted to the Tribunal, and shall state the reasons upon which it is based.

(4) Any member of the Tribunal may attach his individual opinion to the award, whether he dissents from the majority or not, or a statement of his dissent.

(5) The Centre shall not publish the award without the consent of the parties.

Article 49

(1) The Secretary-General shall promptly dispatch certified copies of the award to the parties. The award shall be deemed to have been rendered on the date on which the certified copies were dispatched.

(2) The Tribunal upon the request of a party made within 45 days after the date on which the award was rendered may after notice to the other party decide any question which it had omitted to decide in the award, and shall rectify any clerical, arithmetical or similar error in the award. Its decision shall become part of the award and shall be notified to the parties in the same manner as the award. The periods of time provided for under paragraph (2) of Article 51 and paragraph (2) of Article 52 shall run from the date on which the decision was rendered.

Section 5
Interpretation, Revision and Annulment of the Award
Article 50

(1) If any dispute shall arise between the parties as to the meaning or scope of an award, either party may request interpretation of the award by an application in writing addressed to the Secretary-General.

(2) The request shall, if possible, be submitted to the Tribunal which rendered the award. If this shall not be possible, a new Tribunal shall be constituted in accordance with Section 2 of this Chapter. The Tribunal may, if it considers that the circumstances so require, stay enforcement of the award pending its decision.

Article 51

(1) Either party may request revision of the award by an application in writing addressed to the Secretary-General on the ground of discovery of some fact of such a nature as decisively to affect the award, provided that when the award was rendered that fact was unknown to the Tribunal and to the applicant and that the applicant's ignorance of that fact was not due to negligence.

(2) The application shall be made within 90 days after the discovery of such fact and in any event within three years after the date on which the award was rendered.

(3) The request shall, if possible, be submitted to the Tribunal which rendered the award. If this shall not be possible, a new Tribunal shall be constituted in accordance with Section 2 of this Chapter.

(4) The Tribunal may, if it considers that the circumstances so require, stay enforcement of the award pending its decision. If the applicant requests a stay of enforcement of the award in his application, enforcement shall be stayed provisionally until the Tribunal rules on such request.

Article 52

(1) Either party may request annulment of the award by an application in writing addressed to the Secretary-General on one or more of the following grounds:
   (a) that the Tribunal was not properly constituted;
   (b) that the Tribunal has manifestly exceeded its powers;
   (c) that there was corruption on the part of a member of the Tribunal;
   (d) that there has been a serious departure from a fundamental rule of procedure; or
   (e) that the award has failed to state the reasons on which it is based.

(2) The application shall be made within 120 days after the date on which the award was rendered except that when annulment is requested on the ground of corruption such application shall be made within 120 days after discovery of the corruption and in any event within three years after the date on which the award was rendered.

(3) On receipt of the request the Chairman shall forthwith appoint from the Panel of Arbitrators an ad hoc Committee of three persons. None of the members of the Committee shall have been a member of the Tribunal which rendered the award, shall be of the same nationality as any such member, shall be a national of the State party to the dispute or of the State whose national is a party to the dispute, shall have been designated to the Panel of Arbitrators by either of those States, or shall have acted as a conciliator in the same dispute. The Committee shall have the authority to annul the award or any part thereof on any of the grounds set forth in paragraph (1).

(4) The provisions of Articles 41–45, 48, 49, 53 and 54, and of Chapters VI and VII shall apply *mutatis mutandis* to proceedings before the Committee.

(5) The Committee may, if it considers that the circumstances so require, stay enforcement of the award pending its decision. If the applicant requests a stay of enforcement of the award in his application, enforcement shall be stayed provisionally until the Committee rules on such request.

(6) If the award is annulled the dispute shall, at the request of either party, be submitted to a new Tribunal constituted in accordance with Section 2 of this Chapter.

Section 6
Recognition and Enforcement of the Award

Article 53

(1) The award shall be binding on the parties and shall not be subject to any appeal or to any other remedy except those provided for in this Convention. Each party shall abide by and comply with the terms of the award except to the extent that enforcement shall have been stayed pursuant to the relevant provisions of this Convention.

(2) For the purposes of this Section, "award" shall include any decision interpreting, revising or annulling such award pursuant to Articles 50, 51 or 52.

Article 54

(1) Each Contracting State shall recognize an award rendered pursuant to this Convention as binding and enforce the pecuniary obligations imposed by that award within its territories as if it were a final judgment of a court in that State. A Contracting State with

a federal constitution may enforce such an award in or through its federal courts and may provide that such courts shall treat the award as if it were a final judgment of the courts of a constituent state.

(2) A party seeking recognition or enforcement in the territories of a Contracting State shall furnish to a competent court or other authority which such State shall have designated for this purpose a copy of the award certified by the Secretary-General. Each Contracting State shall notify the Secretary-General of the designation of the competent court or other authority for this purpose and of any subsequent change in such designation.

(3) Execution of the award shall be governed by the laws concerning the execution of judgments in force in the State in whose territories such execution is sought.

Article 55

Nothing in Article 54 shall be construed as derogating from the law in force in any Contracting State relating to immunity of that State or of any foreign State from execution.

Chapter V Replacement and Disqualification of Conciliators and Arbitrators

Article 56

(1) After a Commission or a Tribunal has been constituted and proceedings have begun, its composition shall remain unchanged; provided, however, that if a conciliator or an arbitrator should die, become incapacitated, or resign, the resulting vacancy shall be filled in accordance with the provisions of Section 2 of Chapter III or Section 2 of Chapter IV.

(2) A member of a Commission or Tribunal shall continue to serve in that capacity notwithstanding that he shall have ceased to be a member of the Panel.

(3) If a conciliator or arbitrator appointed by a party shall have resigned without the consent of the Commission or Tribunal of which he was a member, the Chairman shall appoint a person from the appropriate Panel to fill the resulting vacancy.

Article 57

A party may propose to a Commission or Tribunal the disqualification of any of its members on account of any fact indicating a manifest lack of the qualities required by paragraph (1) of Article 14. A party to arbitration proceedings may, in addition, propose the disqualification of an arbitrator on the ground that he was ineligible for appointment to the Tribunal under Section 2 of Chapter IV.

Article 58

The decision on any proposal to disqualify a conciliator or arbitrator shall be taken by the other members of the Commission or Tribunal as the case may be, provided that where those members are equally divided, or in the case of a proposal to disqualify a sole conciliator or arbitrator, or a majority of the conciliators or arbitrators, the Chairman shall take that decision. If it is decided that the proposal is well-founded the conciliator or arbitrator to whom the decision relates shall be replaced in accordance with the provisions of Section 2 of Chapter III or Section 2 of Chapter IV.

Chapter VI Cost of Proceedings

Article 59

The charges payable by the parties for the use of the facilities of the Centre shall be determined by the Secretary-General in accordance with the regulations adopted by the Administrative Council.

Article 60

(1) Each Commission and each Tribunal shall determine the fees and expenses of its members within limits established from time to time by the Administrative Council and after consultation with the Secretary-General.

(2) Nothing in paragraph (1) of this Article shall preclude the parties from agreeing in advance with the Commission or Tribunal concerned upon the fees and expenses of its members.

Article 61

(1) In the case of conciliation proceedings the fees and expenses of members of the Commission as well as the charges for the use of the facilities of the Centre, shall be borne equally by the parties. Each party shall bear any other expenses it incurs in connection with the proceedings.

(2) In the case of arbitration proceedings the Tribunal shall, except as the parties otherwise agree, assess the expenses incurred by the parties in connection with the proceedings, and shall decide how and by whom those expenses, the fees and expenses of the members of the Tribunal and the charges for the use of the facilities of the Centre shall be paid. Such decision shall form part of the award.

Chapter VII Place of Proceedings

Article 62

Conciliation and arbitration proceedings shall be held at the seat of the Centre except as hereinafter provided.

Article 63

Conciliation and arbitration proceedings may be held, if the parties so agree,

(a) at the seat of the Permanent Court of Arbitration or of any other appropriate institution, whether private or public, with which the Centre may make arrangements for that purpose; or

(b) at any other place approved by the Commission or Tribunal after consultation with the Secretary-General.

Chapter VIII Disputes between Contracting States

Article 64

Any dispute arising between Contracting States concerning the interpretation or application of this Convention which is not settled by negotiation shall be referred to the International Court of Justice by the application of any party to such dispute, unless the States concerned agree to another method of settlement.

Chapter IX Amendment

Article 65

Any Contracting State may propose amendment of this Convention. The text of a proposed amendment shall be communicated to the Secretary-General not less than 90 days prior to the meeting of the Administrative Council at which such amendment is to be considered and shall forthwith be transmitted by him to all the members of the Administrative Council.

Article 66

(1) If the Administrative Council shall so decide by a majority of two-thirds of its members, the proposed amendment shall be circulated to all Contracting States for ratification, acceptance or approval. Each amendment shall enter into force 30 days after dispatch by the depositary of this Convention of a notification to Contracting States that all Contracting States have ratified, accepted or approved the amendment.

(2) No amendment shall affect the rights and obligations under this Convention of any Contracting State or of any of its constituent subdivisions or agencies, or of any national of such State arising out of consent to the jurisdiction of the Centre given before the date of entry into force of the amendment.

Chapter X Final Provisions

Article 67

This Convention shall be open for signature on behalf of States members of the Bank. It shall also be open for signature on behalf of any other State which is a party to the Statute of the International Court of Justice and which the Administrative Council, by a vote of two-thirds of its members, shall have invited to sign the Convention.

Article 68

(1) This Convention shall be subject to ratification, acceptance or approval by the signatory States in accordance with their respective constitutional procedures.

(2) This Convention shall enter into force 30 days after the date of deposit of the twentieth instrument of ratification, acceptance or approval. It shall enter into force for each State which subsequently deposits its instrument of ratification, acceptance or approval 30 days after the date of such deposit.

Article 69

Each Contracting State shall take such legislative or other measures as may be necessary for making the provisions of this Convention effective in its territories.

Article 70

This Convention shall apply to all territories for whose international relations a Contracting State is responsible, except those which are excluded by such State by written notice to the depositary of this Convention either at the time of ratification, acceptance or approval or subsequently.

Article 71

Any Contracting State may denounce this Convention by written notice to the depositary of this Convention. The denunciation shall take effect six months after receipt of such notice.

Article 72

Notice by a Contracting State pursuant to Articles 70 or 71 shall not affect the rights or obligations under this Convention of that State or of any of its constituent subdivisions or agencies or of any national of that State arising out of consent to the jurisdiction of the Centre given by one of them before such notice was received by the depositary.

Article 73

Instruments of ratification, acceptance or approval of this Convention and of amendments thereto shall be deposited with the Bank which shall act as the depositary of this Convention. The depositary shall transmit certified copies of this Convention to States members of the Bank and to any other State invited to sign the Convention.

Article 74

The depositary shall register this Convention with the Secretariat of the United Nations in accordance with Article 102 of the Charter of the United Nations and the Regulations thereunder adopted by the General Assembly.

Article 75

The depositary shall notify all signatory States of the following:
- (a) signatures in accordance with Article 67;
- (b) deposits of instruments of ratification, acceptance and approval in accordance with Article 73;
- (c) the date on which this Convention enters into force in accordance with Article 68;
- (d) exclusions from territorial application pursuant to Article 70;
- (e) the date on which any amendment of this Convention enters into force in accordance with Article 66; and
- (f) denunciations in accordance with Article 71.

DONE at Washington, in the English, French and Spanish languages, all three texts being equally authentic, in a single copy which shall remain deposited in the archives of the International Bank for Reconstruction and Development, which has indicated by its signature below its agreement to fulfil the functions with which it is charged under this Convention.

The Energy Charter Treaty (excerpts)

PART I
Definitions and Purpose
Article 1
Definitions

As used in this Treaty:

(1) "Charter" means the European Energy Charter adopted in the Concluding Document of the Hague Conference on the European Energy Charter signed at The Hague on 17 December 1991; signature of the Concluding Document is considered to be signature of the Charter.

(2) "Contracting Party" means a state or Regional Economic Integration Organization which has consented to be bound by this Treaty and for which the Treaty is in force.

(3) "Regional Economic Integration Organization" means an organization constituted by states to which they have transferred competence over certain matters a number of which are governed by this Treaty, including the authority to take decisions binding on them in respect of those matters.

(4) "Energy Materials and Products", based on the Harmonized System of the Customs Co-operation Council and the Combined Nomenclature of the European Communities, means the items included in Annex EM.

(5) "Economic Activity in the Energy Sector" means an economic activity concerning the exploration, extraction, refining, production, storage, land transport, transmission, distribution, trade, marketing, or sale of Energy Materials and Products except those included in Annex NI, or concerning the distribution of heat to multiple premises.[1]

(6) "Investment" means every kind of asset, owned or controlled directly or indirectly by an Investor and includes:[2]

    (a) tangible and intangible, and movable and immovable, property, and any property rights such as leases, mortgages, liens, and pledges;

    (b) a company or business enterprise, or shares, stock, or other forms of equity participation in a company or business enterprise, and bonds and other debt of a company or business enterprise;

    (c) claims to money and claims to performance pursuant to contract having an economic value and associated with an Investment;

    (d) Intellectual Property;

    (e) Returns;

    (f) any right conferred by law or contract or by virtue of any licences and permits granted pursuant to law to undertake any Economic Activity in the Energy Sector.

A change in the form in which assets are invested does not affect their character as investments and the term "Investment" includes all investments, whether existing at or made after the later of the date of entry into force of this Treaty for the Contracting Party

---

[1] See Final Act of the European Energy Charter Conference, Understandings, n. 2. with respect to Article 1 (5), p. 25.

[2] See Final Act of the European Energy Charter Conference, Understandings, n. 3. with respect to Article 1(6), p. 26; Final Act of the European Energy Charter Conference, Declarations, n. 1. with respect to Article 1(6), p. 30; and note 22, p. 54.

of the Investor making the investment and that for the Contracting Party in the Area of which the investment is made (hereinafter referred to as the "Effective Date") provided that the Treaty shall only apply to matters affecting such investments after the Effective Date.

"Investment" refers to any investment associated with an Economic Activity in the Energy Sector and to investments or classes of investments designated by a Contracting Party in its Area as "Charter efficiency projects" and so notified to the Secretariat.

(7) "Investor" means:
   (a) with respect to a Contracting Party:
       (i) a natural person having the citizenship or nationality of or who is permanently residing in that Contracting Party in accordance with its applicable law;
       (ii) a company or other organization organized in accordance with the law applicable in that Contracting Party;[3]
   (b) with respect to a "third state", a natural person, company or other organization which fulfils, mutatis mutandis, the conditions specified in subparagraph (a) for a Contracting Party.

(8) "Make Investments" or "Making of Investments" means establishing new Investments, acquiring all or part of existing Investments or moving into different fields of Investment activity.[4]

(9) "Returns" means the amounts derived from or associated with an Investment, irrespective of the form in which they are paid, including profits, dividends, interest, capital gains, royalty payments, management, technical assistance or other fees and payments in kind.

(10) "Area" means with respect to a state that is a Contracting Party:
   (a) the territory under its sovereignty, it being understood that territory includes land, internal waters and the territorial sea; and
   (b) subject to and in accordance with the international law of the sea: the sea, sea-bed and its subsoil with regard to which that Contracting Party exercises sovereign rights and jurisdiction.

With respect to a Regional Economic Integration Organization which is a Contracting Party, Area means the Areas of the member states of such Organization, under the provisions contained in the agreement establishing that Organization.

(11) (a) "GATT" means "GATT 1947" or "GATT 1994", or both of them where both are applicable.
   (b) "GATT 1947" means the General Agreement on Tariffs and Trade, dated 30 October 1947, annexed to the Final Act Adopted at the Conclusion of the Second Session of the Preparatory Committee of the United Nations Conference on Trade and Employment, as subsequently rectified, amended or modified.
   (c) "GATT 1994" means the General Agreement on Tariffs and Trade as specified in Annex 1A of the Agreement Establishing the World Trade Organization, as subsequently rectified, amended or modified. A party to the Agreement Establishing the World Trade Organization is considered to be a party to GATT 1994.
   (d) "Related Instruments" means, as appropriate:

---

[3] See Decisions with respect to the Energy Charter Treaty (Annex 2 to the Final Act of the European Energy Charter Conference), n. 5. with Respect to Articles 24(4)(a) and 25, p. 137; note 38, p. 70; and note 39, p. 71.

[4] See Final Act of the European Energy Charter Conference, Understandings, n. 4. with respect to Article 1(8), p. 26.

(i) agreements, arrangements or other legal instruments, including decisions, declarations and understandings, concluded under the auspices of GATT 1947 as subsequently rectified, amended or modified; or

(ii) the Agreement Establishing the World Trade Organization including its Annex 1 (except GATT 1994), its Annexes 2, 3 and 4, and the decisions, declarations and understandings related thereto, as subsequently rectified, amended or modified.

(12) "Intellectual Property" includes copyrights and related rights, trademarks, geographical indications, industrial designs, patents, layout designs of integrated circuits and the protection of undisclosed information.[5]

(13) (a) "Energy Charter Protocol" or "Protocol" means a treaty, the negotiation of which is authorized and the text of which is adopted by the Charter Conference, which is entered into by two or more Contracting Parties in order to complement, supplement, extend or amplify the provisions of this Treaty with respect to any specific sector or category of activity within the scope of this Treaty, or to areas of co-operation pursuant to Title III of the Charter.

(b) "Energy Charter Declaration" or "Declaration" means a non-binding instrument, the negotiation of which is authorized and the text of which is approved by the Charter Conference, which is entered into by two or more Contracting Parties to complement or supplement the provisions of this Treaty.

(14) "Freely Convertible Currency" means a currency which is widely traded in international foreign exchange markets and widely used in international transactions.

Article 2
Purpose Of The Treaty

This Treaty establishes a legal framework in order to promote long-term cooperation in the energy field, based on complementarities and mutual benefits, in accordance with the objectives and principles of the Charter.

Part III
Investment Promotion and Protection
Article 10
Promotion, Protection and Treatment of Investments[6]

(1) Each Contracting Party shall, in accordance with the provisions of this Treaty, encourage and create stable, equitable, favourable and transparent conditions for Investors of other Contracting Parties to make Investments in its Area. Such conditions shall include a commitment to accord at all times to Investments of Investors of other Contracting Parties fair and equitable treatment. Such Investments shall also enjoy the most constant protection and security and no Contracting Party shall in any way impair by unreasonable or discriminatory measures their management, maintenance, use, enjoyment or disposal. In no case shall such Investments be accorded treatment less

---

[5] See Final Act of the European Energy Charter Conference, Understandings, n. 5. with respect to Article 1(12), p. 27.

[6] See Final Act of the European Energy Charter Conference, Understandings, n. 9. with respect to Articles 9, 10 and Part V, p. 27 and Declarations, n. 4. with respect to Article 10, p. 31.

favourable than that required by international law, including treaty obligations.[7] Each Contracting Party shall observe any obligations it has entered into with an Investor or an Investment of an Investor of any other Contracting Party.[8]

(2) Each Contracting Party shall endeavour to accord to Investors of other Contracting Parties, as regards the Making of Investments in its Area, the Treatment described in paragraph (3).

(3) For the purposes of this Article, "Treatment" means treatment accorded by a Contracting Party which is no less favourable than that which it accords to its own Investors or to Investors of any other Contracting Party or any third state, whichever is the most favourable.

(4) A supplementary treaty shall, subject to conditions to be laid down therein, oblige each party thereto to accord to Investors of other parties, as regards the Making of Investments in its Area, the Treatment described in paragraph (3). That treaty shall be open for signature by the states and Regional Economic Integration Organizations which have signed or acceded to this Treaty. Negotiations towards the supplementary treaty shall commence not later than 1 January 1995, with a view to concluding it by 1 January 1998.[9]

(5) Each Contracting Party shall, as regards the Making of Investments in its Area, endeavour to:
(a) limit to the minimum the exceptions to the Treatment described in paragraph (3);
(b) progressively remove existing restrictions affecting Investors of other Contracting Parties.

(6) (a) A Contracting Party may, as regards the Making of Investments in its Area, at any time declare voluntarily to the Charter Conference, through the Secretariat, its intention not to introduce new exceptions to the Treatment described in paragraph (3).
(b) A Contracting Party may, furthermore, at any time make a voluntary commitment to accord to Investors of other Contracting Parties, as regards the Making of Investments in some or all Economic Activities in the Energy Sector in its Area, the Treatment described in paragraph(3). Such commitments shall be notified to the Secretariat and listed in Annex VC and shall be binding under this Treaty.

(7) Each Contracting Party shall accord to Investments in its Area of Investors of other Contracting Parties, and their related activities including management, maintenance, use, enjoyment or disposal, treatment no less favourable than that which it accords to Investments of its own Investors or of the Investors of any other Contracting Party or any third state and their related activities including management, maintenance, use, enjoyment or disposal, whichever is the most favourable.[10]

(8) The modalities of application of paragraph (7) in relation to programmes under which a Contracting Party provides grants or other financial assistance, or enters into contracts, for energy technology research and development, shall be reserved for the supplemen-

---

[7] See Final Act of the European Energy Charter Conference, Understandings, n. 17. with respect to Articles 26 and 27, p. 28 and Chairman's Statement at Adoption Session on 17 December 1994, p. 157.

[8] See Article 26(3)(c), p. 73; Article 27(2), p. 75 and Annex 1A, p. 98.

[9] See Final Act of the European Energy Charter Conference, Understandings, n. 10. with respect to Article 10(4), p. 27; n. 11 with respect to Articles 10(4) and 29(6), p. 28; Final Act of the European Energy Charter Conference, Declarations, n. 1. with respect to Article 1(6), p. 30 and Chairman's Statement at Adoption Session on 17 December 1994, p. 157.

[10] See Decisions with respect to the Energy Charter Treaty (Annex 2 to the Final Act of the European Energy Charter Conference), n. 2. with respect to Article 10(7), p. 135; Article 32(1), p. 79 and Annex T pp. 113 and 126.

tary treaty described in paragraph (4). Each Contracting Party shall through the Secretariat keep the Charter Conference informed of the modalities it applies to the programmes described in this paragraph.

(9) Each state or Regional Economic Integration Organization which signs or accedes to this Treaty shall, on the date it signs the Treaty or deposits its instrument of accession, submit to the Secretariat a report summarizing all laws, regulations or other measures relevant to:

(a) exceptions to paragraph (2); or

(b) the programmes referred to in paragraph (8).

A Contracting Party shall keep its report up to date by promptly submitting amendments to the Secretariat. The Charter Conference shall review these reports periodically.

In respect of subparagraph (a) the report may designate parts of the energy sector in which a Contracting Party accords to Investors of other Contracting Parties the Treatment described in paragraph (3).

In respect of subparagraph (b) the review by the Charter Conference may consider the effects of such programmes on competition and Investments.

(10) Notwithstanding any other provision of this Article, the treatment described in paragraphs (3) and (7) shall not apply to the protection of Intellectual Property; instead, the treatment shall be as specified in the corresponding provisions of the applicable international agreements for the protection of Intellectual Property rights to which the respective Contracting Parties are parties.

(11) For the purposes of Article 26, the application by a Contracting Party of a trade-related investment measure as described in Article 5(1) and (2) to an Investment of an Investor of another Contracting Party existing at the time of such application shall, subject to Article 5(3) and (4), be considered a breach of an obligation of the former Contracting Party under this Part.[11]

(12) Each Contracting Party shall ensure that its domestic law provides effective means for the assertion of claims and the enforcement of rights with respect to Investments, investment agreements, and investment authorizations.

Article 11
Key Personnel

(1) A Contracting Party shall, subject to its laws and regulations relating to the entry, stay and work of natural persons, examine in good faith requests by Investors of another Contracting Party, and key personnel who are employed by such Investors or by Investments of such Investors, to enter and remain temporarily in its Area to engage in activities connected with the making or the development, management, maintenance, use, enjoyment or disposal of relevant Investments, including the provision of advice or key technical services.

(2) A Contracting Party shall permit Investors of another Contracting Party which have Investments in its Area, and Investments of such Investors, to employ any key person of the Investor's or the Investment's choice regardless of nationality and citizenship provided that such key person has been permitted to enter, stay and work in the Area of the former Contracting Party and that the employment concerned conforms to the terms, conditions and time limits of the permission granted to such key person.

---

[11] See Final Act of the European Energy Charter Conference, Declarations, n. 2. with respect to Articles 5 and 10(11), p. 30.

Article 12
Compensation for Losses

(1) Except where Article 13 applies, an Investor of any Contracting Party which suffers a loss with respect to any Investment in the Area of another Contracting Party owing to war or other armed conflict, state of national emergency, civil disturbance, or other similar event in that Area, shall be accorded by the latter Contracting Party, as regards restitution, indemnification, compensation or other settlement, treatment which is the most favourable of that which that Contracting Party accords to any other Investor, whether its own Investor, the Investor of any other Contracting Party, or the Investor of any third state.

(2) Without prejudice to paragraph (1), an Investor of a Contracting Party which, in any of the situations referred to in that paragraph, suffers a loss in the Area of another Contracting Party resulting from

    (a) requisitioning of its Investment or part thereof by the latter's forces or authorities; or

    (b) destruction of its Investment or part thereof by the latter's forces or authorities, which was not required by the necessity of the situation, shall be accorded restitution or compensation which in either case shall be prompt, adequate and effective.

Article 13
Expropriation

(1) Investments of Investors of a Contracting Party in the Area of any other Contracting Party shall not be nationalized, expropriated or subjected to a measure or measures having effect equivalent to nationalization or expropriation (hereinafter referred to as "Expropriation") except where such Expropriation is:

    (a) for a purpose which is in the public interest;

    (b) not discriminatory;

    (c) carried out under due process of law; and

    (d) accompanied by the payment of prompt, adequate and effective compensation.

Such compensation shall amount to the fair market value of the Investment expropriated at the time immediately before the Expropriation or impending Expropriation became known in such a way as to affect the value of the Investment (hereinafter referred to as the "Valuation Date").

Such fair market value shall at the request of the Investor be expressed in a Freely Convertible Currency on the basis of the market rate of exchange existing for that currency on the Valuation Date. Compensation shall also include interest at a commercial rate established on a market basis from the date of Expropriation until the date of payment.

(2) The Investor affected shall have a right to prompt review, under the law of the Contracting Party making the Expropriation, by a judicial or other competent and independent authority of that Contracting Party, of its case, of the valuation of its Investment, and of the payment of compensation, in accordance with the principles set out in paragraph (1).

(3) For the avoidance of doubt, Expropriation shall include situations where a Contracting Party expropriates the assets of a company or enterprise in its Area in which an Investor of any other Contracting Party has an Investment, including through the ownership of shares.

Article 14
Transfers Related to Investments[12]

(1) Each Contracting Party shall with respect to Investments in its Area of Investors of any other Contracting Party guarantee the freedom of transfer into and out of its Area, including the transfer of:

    (a) the initial capital plus any additional capital for the maintenance and development of an Investment;

    (b) Returns;

    (c) payments under a contract, including amortization of principal and accrued interest payments pursuant to a loan agreement;

    (d) unspent earningsi[13] and other remuneration of personnel engaged from abroad in connection with that Investment;

    (e) proceeds from the sale or liquidation of all or any part of an Investment;

    (f) payments arising out of the settlement of a dispute;

    (g) payments of compensation pursuant to Articles 12 and 13.

(2) Transfers under paragraph (1) shall be effected without delay and (except in case of a Return in kind) in a Freely Convertible Currency.[14]

(3) Transfers shall be made at the market rate of exchange existing on the date of transfer with respect to spot transactions in the currency to be transferred. In the absence of a market for foreign exchange, the rate to be used will be the most recent rate applied to inward investments or the most recent exchange rate for conversion of currencies into Special Drawing Rights, whichever is more favourable to the Investor.

(4) Notwithstanding paragraphs (1) to (3), a Contracting Party may protect the rights of creditors, or ensure compliance with laws on the issuing, trading and dealing in securities and the satisfaction of judgements in civil, administrative and criminal adjudicatory proceedings, through the equitable, non- discriminatory, and good faith application of its laws and regulations.

(5) Notwithstanding paragraph (2), Contracting Parties which are states that were constituent parts of the former Union of Soviet Socialist Republics may provide in agreements concluded between them that transfers of payments shall be made in the currencies of such Contracting Parties, provided that such agreements do not treat Investments in their Areas of Investors of other Contracting Parties less favourably than either Investments of Investors of the Contracting Parties which have entered into such agreements or Investments of Investors of any third state.[15]

(6) Notwithstanding subparagraph (1)(b), a Contracting Party may restrict the transfer of a Return in kind in circumstances where the Contracting Party is permitted under Article 29(2)(a) or the GATT and Related Instruments to restrict or prohibit the exportation or the sale for export of the product constituting the Return in kind; provided that a Contracting Party shall permit transfers of Returns in kind to be effected as authorized or specified in an investment agreement, investment authorization, or other written

---

[12] See Decisions with respect to the Energy Charter Treaty (Annex 2 to the Final Act of the European Energy Charter Conference), n. 3. with respect to Article 14, p. 135.

[13] See Article 32(1), p. 79 and Annex T, pp. 113 and 127.

[14] See Decisions with respect to the Energy Charter Treaty (Annex 2 to the Final Act of theEuropean Energy Charter Conference), n. 4. with respect to Article 14 (2), p. 136.

[15] See Final Act of the European Energy Charter Conference, Understandings, n. 12. withrespect to Article 14(5), p. 28.

agreement between the Contracting Party and either an Investor of another Contracting Party or its Investment.

Article 15
Subrogation

(1) If a Contracting Party or its designated agency (hereinafter referred to as the "Indemnifying Party") makes a payment under an indemnity or guarantee given in respect of an Investment of an Investor (hereinafter referred to as the "Party Indemnified") in the Area of another Contracting Party (hereinafter referred to as the "Host Party"), the Host Party shall recognize:

  (a) the assignment to the Indemnifying Party of all the rights and claims in respect of such Investment; and

  (b) the right of the Indemnifying Party to exercise all such rights and enforce such claims by virtue of subrogation.

(2) The Indemnifying Party shall be entitled in all circumstances to:

  (a) the same treatment in respect of the rights and claims acquired by it by virtue of the assignment referred to in paragraph (1); and

  (b) the same payments due pursuant to those rights and claims, as the Party Indemnified was entitled to receive by virtue of this Treaty in respect of the Investment concerned.

(3) In any proceeding under Article 26, a Contracting Party shall not assert as a defence, counterclaim, right of set-off or for any other reason, that indemnification or other compensation for all or part of the alleged damages has been received or will be received pursuant to an insurance or guarantee contract.

Article 16
Relation to other Agreements[16]

Where two or more Contracting Parties have entered into a prior international agreement, or enter into a subsequent international agreement, whose terms in either case concern the subject matter of Part III or V of this Treaty,

(1) nothing in Part III or V of this Treaty shall be construed to derogate from any provision of such terms of the other agreement or from any right to dispute resolution with respect thereto under that agreement; and

(2) nothing in such terms of the other agreement shall be construed to derogate from any provision of Part III or V of this Treaty or from any right to dispute resolution with respect thereto under this Treaty,

where any such provision is more favourable to the Investor or Investment.

Article 17
Non-Application of Part III in Certain Circumstances

Each Contracting Party reserves the right to deny the advantages of this Part to:

(1) a legal entity if citizens or nationals of a third state own or control such entity and if that entity has no substantial business activities in the Area of the Contracting Party in which it is organized; or

---

[16] See Decisions with respect to the Energy Charter Treaty (Annex 2 to the Final Act of theEuropean Energy Charter Conference), n. 1. with respect to the Treaty as a whole, p. 135 and n. 3. with respect to Article 14, p. 135.

(2) an Investment, if the denying Contracting Party establishes that such Investment is an Investment of an Investor of a third state with or as to which the denying Contracting Party:
    (a) does not maintain a diplomatic relationship; or
    (b) adopts or maintains measures that:
        (i) prohibit transactions with Investors of that state; or
        (ii) would be violated or circumvented if the benefits of this Part were accorded to Investors of that state or to their Investments.

PART V
Dispute Settlement[17]

Article 26
Settlement of Disputes between an Investor and a Contracting Party[18]

(1) Disputes between a Contracting Party and an Investor of another Contracting Party relating to an Investment of the latter in the Area of the former, which concern an alleged breach of an obligation of the former under Part III shall, if possible, be settled amicably.
(2) If such disputes can not be settled according to the provisions of paragraph (1) within a period of three months from the date on which either party to the dispute requested amicable settlement, the Investor party to the dispute may choose to submit it for resolution:
    (a) to the courts or administrative tribunals of the Contracting Party party to the dispute[19]
    (b) in accordance with any applicable, previously agreed dispute settlement procedure; or
    (c) in accordance with the following paragraphs of this Article.
(3) (a) Subject only to subparagraphs (b) and (c), each Contracting Party hereby gives its unconditional consent to the submission of a dispute to international arbitration or conciliation in accordance with the provisions of this Article.
    (b) (i) The Contracting Parties listed in Annex ID do not give such unconditional consent where the Investor has previously submitted the dispute under subparagraph (2)(a) or (b).
        (ii) For the sake of transparency, each Contracting Party that is listed in Annex ID shall provide a written statement of its policies, practices and conditions in this regard to the Secretariat no later than the date of the deposit of its instrument of ratification, acceptance or approval in accordance with Article 39 or the deposit of its instrument of accession in accordance with Article 41.
    (c) A Contracting Party listed in Annex IA does not give such unconditional consent with respect to a dispute arising under the last sentence of Article 10(1).
(4) In the event that an Investor chooses to submit the dispute for resolution under subparagraph (2)(c), the Investor shall further provide its consent in writing for the dispute to be submitted to:

---

[17] See Decisions with respect to the Energy Charter Treaty (Annex 2 to the Final Act of the European Energy Charter Conference), n. 1. with respect to the Treaty as a whole, p. 135 and Final Act of the European Energy Charter Conference, Understandings, n. 9. with respect to Articles 9,10 and Part V, p. 27.
[18] See Final Act of the European Energy Charter Conference, Understandings, n. 17. with respect to Articles 26 and 27, p. 28.
[19] See Final Act of the European Energy Charter Conference, Understandings, n. 16. with respect to Article 26(2)(a), p. 28.

(a) (i) The International Centre for Settlement of Investment Disputes, established pursuant to the Convention on the Settlement of Investment Disputes between States and Nationals of other States opened for signature at Washington, 18 March 1965 (hereinafter referred to as the "ICSID Convention"), if the Contracting Party of the Investor and the Contracting Party party to the dispute are both parties to the ICSID Convention; or

    (ii) The International Centre for Settlement of Investment Disputes, established pursuant to the Convention referred to in subparagraph (a) (i), under the rules governing the Additional Facility for the Administration of Proceedings by the Secretariat of the Centre (hereinafter referred to as the "Additional Facility Rules"), if the Contracting Party of the Investor or the Contracting Party party to the dispute, but not both, is a party to the ICSID Convention;

(b) a sole arbitrator or ad hoc arbitration tribunal established under the Arbitration Rules of the United Nations Commission on International Trade Law (hereinafter referred to as "UNCITRAL"); or

(c) an arbitral proceeding under the Arbitration Institute of the Stockholm Chamber of Commerce.

(5) (a) The consent given in paragraph (3) together with the written consent of the Investor given pursuant to paragraph (4) shall be considered to satisfy the requirement for:

    (i) written consent of the parties to a dispute for purposes of Chapter II of the ICSID Convention and for purposes of the Additional Facility Rules;

    (ii) an "agreement in writing" for purposes of article II of the United Nations Convention on the Recognition and Enforcement of Foreign Arbitral Awards, done at New York, 10 June 1958 (hereinafter referred to as the "New York Convention"); and

    (iii) "the parties to a contract [to] have agreed in writing" for the purposes of article 1 of the UNCITRAL Arbitration Rules.

(b) Any arbitration under this Article shall at the request of any party to the dispute be held in a state that is a party to the New York Convention. Claims submitted to arbitration hereunder shall be considered to arise out of a commercial relationship or transaction for the purposes of article I of that Convention.

(6) A tribunal established under paragraph (4) shall decide the issues in dispute in accordance with this Treaty and applicable rules and principles of international law.

(7) An Investor other than a natural person which has the nationality of a Contracting Party party to the dispute on the date of the consent in writing referred to in paragraph (4) and which, before a dispute between it and that Contracting Party arises, is controlled by Investors of another Contracting Party, shall for the purpose of article 25(2)(b) of the ICSID Convention be treated as a "national of another Contracting State" and shall for the purpose of article 1(6) of the Additional Facility Rules be treated as a "national of another State".

(8) The awards of arbitration, which may include an award of interest, shall be final and binding upon the parties to the dispute. An award of arbitration concerning a measure of a sub-national government or authority of the disputing Contracting Party shall provide that the Contracting Party may pay monetary damages in lieu of any other remedy granted. Each Contracting Party shall carry out without delay any such award and shall make provision for the effective enforcement in its Area of such awards.

Article 27
Settlement of Disputes between Contracting Parties[20]

(1) Contracting Parties shall endeavour to settle disputes concerning the application or interpretation of this Treaty through diplomatic channels.

(2) If a dispute has not been settled in accordance with paragraph (1) within a reasonable period of time, either party thereto may, except as otherwise provided in this Treaty or agreed in writing by the Contracting Parties, and except as concerns the application or interpretation of Article 6 or Article 19 or, for Contracting Parties listed in Annex IA, the last sentence of Article 10(1), upon written notice to the other party to the dispute submit the matter to an ad hoc tribunal under this Article.

(3) Such an ad hoc arbitral tribunal shall be constituted as follows:

  (a) The Contracting Party instituting the proceedings shall appoint one member of the tribunal and inform the other Contracting Party to the dispute of its appointment within 30 days of receipt of the notice referred to in paragraph (2) by the other Contracting Party;

  (b) Within 60 days of the receipt of the written notice referred to in paragraph (2), the other Contracting Party party to the dispute shall appoint one member. If the appointment is not made within the time limit prescribed, the Contracting Party having instituted the proceedings may, within 90 days of the receipt of the written notice referred to in paragraph (2), request that the appointment be made in accordance with subparagraph (d);

  (c) A third member, who may not be a national or citizen of a Contracting Party party to the dispute, shall be appointed by the Contracting Parties parties to the dispute. That member shall be the President of the tribunal. If, within 150 days of the receipt of the notice referred to in paragraph (2), the Contracting Parties are unable to agree on the appointment of a third member, that appointment shall be made, in accordance with subparagraph (d), at the request of either Contracting Party submitted within 180 days of the receipt of that notice;

  (d) Appointments requested to be made in accordance with this paragraph shall be made by the Secretary-General of the Permanent Court of International Arbitration within 30 days of the receipt of a request to do so. If the Secretary-General is prevented from discharging this task, the appointments shall be made by the First Secretary of the Bureau. If the latter, in turn, is prevented from discharging this task, the appointments shall be made by the most senior Deputy;

  (e) Appointments made in accordance with subparagraphs (a) to (d) shall be made with regard to the qualifications and experience, particularly in matters covered by this Treaty, of the members to be appointed;

  (f) In the absence of an agreement to the contrary between the Contracting Parties, the Arbitration Rules of UNCITRAL shall govern, except to the extent modified by the Contracting Parties parties to the dispute or by the arbitrators. The tribunal shall take its decisions by a majority vote of its members;

  (g) The tribunal shall decide the dispute in accordance with this Treaty and applicable rules and principles of international law;

  (h) The arbitral award shall be final and binding upon the Contracting Parties parties to the dispute;

---

[20] See Final Act of the European Energy Charter Conference, Understandings, n. 17. withrespect to Articles 26 and 27, p. 28 and Article 28, p. 76.

(i) Where, in making an award, a tribunal finds that a measure of a regional or local government or authority within the Area of a Contracting Party listed in Part I of Annex P is not in conformity with this Treaty, either party to the dispute may invoke the provisions of Part II of Annex P;

(j) The expenses of the tribunal, including the remuneration of its members, shall be borne in equal shares by the Contracting Parties parties to the dispute. The tribunal may, however, at its discretion direct that a higher proportion of the costs be paid by one of the Contracting Parties parties to the dispute;

(k) Unless the Contracting Parties parties to the dispute agree otherwise, the tribunal shall sit in The Hague, and use the premises and facilities of the Permanent Court of Arbitration;

(l) A copy of the award shall be deposited with the Secretariat which shall make it generally available.

Article 28
Non-Application of Article 27 to Certain Disputes

A dispute between Contracting Parties with respect to the application or interpretation of Article 5 or 29 shall not be settled under Article 27 unless the Contracting Parties parties to the dispute so agree.

North American Free Trade Agreement (Chapter Eleven)

Section A – Investment
Article 1101
Scope and Coverage

1. This Chapter applies to measures adopted or maintained by a Party relating to:
   (a) investors of another Party;
   (b) investments of investors of another Party in the territory of the Party; and
   (c) with respect to Articles 1106 and 1114, all investments in the territory of the Party.
2. A Party has the right to perform exclusively the economic activities set out in Annex III and to refuse to permit the establishment of investment in such activities.
3. This Chapter does not apply to measures adopted or maintained by a Party to the extent that they are covered by Chapter Fourteen (Financial Services).
4. Nothing in this Chapter shall be construed to prevent a Party from providing a service or performing a function such as law enforcement, correctional services, income security or insurance, social security or insurance, social welfare, public education, public training, health, and child care, in a manner that is not inconsistent with this Chapter.

Article 1102
National Treatment

1. Each Party shall accord to investors of another Party treatment no less favorable than that it accords, in like circumstances, to its own investors with respect to the establishment, acquisition, expansion, management, conduct, operation, and sale or other disposition of investments.
2. Each Party shall accord to investments of investors of another Party treatment no less favorable than that it accords, in like circumstances, to investments of its own investors with respect to the establishment, acquisition, expansion, management, conduct, operation, and sale or other disposition of investments.
3. The treatment accorded by a Party under paragraphs 1 and 2 means, with respect to a state or province, treatment no less favorable than the most favorable treatment accorded, in like circumstances, by that state or province to investors, and to investments of investors, of the Party of which it forms a part.
4. For greater certainty, no Party may:
   (a) impose on an investor of another Party a requirement that a minimum level of equity in an enterprise in the territory of the Party be held by its nationals, other than nominal qualifying shares for directors or incorporators of corporations; or
   (b) require an investor of another Party, by reason of its nationality, to sell or otherwise dispose of an investment in the territory of the Party.

Article 1103
Most-Favored-Nation Treatment

1. Each Party shall accord to investors of another Party treatment no less favorable than that it accords, in like circumstances, to investors of any other Party or of a non-Party with respect to the establishment, acquisition, expansion, management, conduct, operation, and sale or other disposition of investments.

2. Each Party shall accord to investments of investors of another Party treatment no less favorable than that it accords, in like circumstances, to investments of investors of any other Party or of a non-Party with respect to the establishment, acquisition, expansion, management, conduct, operation, and sale or other disposition of investments.

Article 1104
Standard of Treatment

Each Party shall accord to investors of another Party and to investments of investors of another Party the better of the treatment required by Articles 1102 and 1103.

Article 1105
Minimum Standard of Treatment

1. Each Party shall accord to investments of investors of another Party treatment in accordance with international law, including fair and equitable treatment and full protection and security.
2. Without prejudice to paragraph 1 and notwithstanding Article 1108(7)(b), each Party shall accord to investors of another Party, and to investments of investors of another Party, non-discriminatory treatment with respect to measures it adopts or maintains relating to losses suffered by investments in its territory owing to armed conflict or civil strife.
3. Paragraph 2 does not apply to existing measures relating to subsidies or grants that would be inconsistent with Article 1102 but for Article 1108(7)(b).

Article 1106
Performance Requirements

1. No Party may impose or enforce any of the following requirements, or enforce any commitment or undertaking, in connection with the establishment, acquisition, expansion, management, conduct or operation of an investment of an investor of a Party or of a non-Party in its territory:
   (a) to export a given level or percentage of goods or services;
   (b) to achieve a given level or percentage of domestic content;
   (c) to purchase, use or accord a preference to goods produced or services provided in its territory, or to purchase goods or services from persons in its territory;
   (d) to relate in any way the volume or value of imports to the volume or value of exports or to the amount of foreign exchange inflows associated with such investment;
   (e) to restrict sales of goods or services in its territory that such investment produces or provides by relating such sales in any way to the volume or value of its exports or foreign exchange earnings;
   (f) to transfer technology, a production process or other proprietary knowledge to a person in its territory, except when the requirement is imposed or the commitment or undertaking is enforced by a court, administrative tribunal or competition authority to remedy an alleged violation of competition laws or to act in a manner not inconsistent with other provisions of this Agreement; or
   (g) to act as the exclusive supplier of the goods it produces or services it provides to a specific region or world market.
2. A measure that requires an investment to use a technology to meet generally applicable health, safety or environmental requirements shall not be construed to be inconsistent with paragraph 1(f). For greater certainty, Articles 1102 and 1103 apply to the measure.

3. No Party may condition the receipt or continued receipt of an advantage, in connection with an investment in its territory of an investor of a Party or of a non-Party, on compliance with any of the following requirements:
   (a) to achieve a given level or percentage of domestic content;
   (b) to purchase, use or accord a preference to goods produced in its territory, or to purchase goods from producers in its territory;
   (c) to relate in any way the volume or value of imports to the volume or value of exports or to the amount of foreign exchange inflows associated with such investment; or
   (d) to restrict sales of goods or services in its territory that such investment produces or provides by relating such sales in any way to the volume or value of its exports or foreign exchange earnings.

4. Nothing in paragraph 3 shall be construed to prevent a Party from conditioning the receipt or continued receipt of an advantage, in connection with an investment in its territory of an investor of a Party or of a non-Party, on compliance with a requirement to locate production, provide a service, train or employ workers, construct or expand particular facilities, or carry out research and development, in its territory.

5. Paragraphs 1 and 3 do not apply to any requirement other than the requirements set out in those paragraphs.

6. Provided that such measures are not applied in an arbitrary or unjustifiable manner, or do not constitute a disguised restriction on international trade or investment, nothing in paragraph 1(b) or (c) or 3(a) or (b) shall be construed to prevent any Party from adopting or maintaining measures, including environmental measures:
   (a) necessary to secure compliance with laws and regulations that are not inconsistent with the provisions of this Agreement;
   (b) necessary to protect human, animal or plant life or health; or
   (c) necessary for the conservation of living or non-living exhaustible natural resources.

Article 1107
Senior Management and Boards of Directors

1. No Party may require that an enterprise of that Party that is an investment of an investor of another Party appoint to senior management positions individuals of any particular nationality.

2. A Party may require that a majority of the board of directors, or any committee thereof, of an enterprise of that Party that is an investment of an investor of another Party, be of a particular nationality, or resident in the territory of the Party, provided that the requirement does not materially impair the ability of the investor to exercise control over its investment.

Article 1108
Reservations and Exceptions

1. Articles 1102, 1103, 1106 and 1107 do not apply to:
   (a) any existing non-conforming measure that is maintained by
       (i) a Party at the federal level, as set out in its Schedule to Annex I or III,
       (ii) a state or province, for two years after the date of entry into force of this Agreement, and thereafter as set out by a Party in its Schedule to Annex I in accordance with paragraph 2, or
       (iii) a local government;
   (b) the continuation or prompt renewal of any non-conforming measure referred to in subparagraph (a); or

(c) an amendment to any non-conforming measure referred to in subparagraph (a) to the extent that the amendment does not decrease the conformity of the measure, as it existed immediately before the amendment, with Articles 1102, 1103, 1106 and 1107.

2. Each Party may set out in its Schedule to Annex I, within two years of the date of entry into force of this Agreement, any existing nonconforming measure maintained by a state or province, not including a local government.

3. Articles 1102, 1103, 1106 and 1107 do not apply to any measure that a Party adopts or maintains with respect to sectors, subsectors or activities, as set out in its Schedule to Annex II.

4. No Party may, under any measure adopted after the date of entry into force of this Agreement and covered by its Schedule to Annex II, require an investor of another Party, by reason of its nationality, to sell or otherwise dispose of an investment existing at the time the measure becomes effective.

5. Articles 1102 and 1103 do not apply to any measure that is an exception to, or derogation from, the obligations under Article 1703 (Intellectual Property National Treatment) as specifically provided for in that Article.

6. Article 1103 does not apply to treatment accorded by a Party pursuant to agreements, or with respect to sectors, set out in its Schedule to Annex IV.

7. Articles 1102, 1103 and 1107 do not apply to:
   (a) procurement by a Party or a state enterprise; or
   (b) subsidies or grants provided by a Party or a state enterprise, including government supported loans, guarantees and insurance.

8. The provisions of:
   (a) Article 1106(1)(a), (b) and (c), and (3)(a) and (b) do not apply to qualification requirements for goods or services with respect to export promotion and foreign aid programs;
   (b) Article 1106(1)(b), (c), (f) and (g), and (3)(a) and (b) do not apply to procurement by a Party or a state enterprise; and
   (c) Article 1106(3)(a) and (b) do not apply to requirements imposed by an importing Party relating to the content of goods necessary to qualify for preferential tariffs or preferential quotas.

Article 1109
Transfers

1. Each Party shall permit all transfers relating to an investment of an investor of another Party in the territory of the Party to be made freely and without delay. Such transfers include:
   (a) profits, dividends, interest, capital gains, royalty payments, management fees, technical assistance and other fees, returns in kind and other amounts derived from the investment;
   (b) proceeds from the sale of all or any part of the investment or from the partial or complete liquidation of the investment;
   (c) payments made under a contract entered into by the investor, or its investment, including payments made pursuant to a loan agreement;
   (d) payments made pursuant to Article 1110; and
   (e) payments arising under Section B.

2. Each Party shall permit transfers to be made in a freely usable currency at the market rate of exchange prevailing on the date of transfer with respect to spot transactions in the currency to be transferred.

3. No Party may require its investors to transfer, or penalize its investors that fail to transfer, the income, earnings, profits or other amounts derived from, or attributable to, investments in the territory of another Party.

4. Notwithstanding paragraphs 1 and 2, a Party may prevent a transfer through the equitable, non-discriminatory and good faith application of its laws relating to:
   (a) bankruptcy, insolvency or the protection of the rights of creditors;
   (b) issuing, trading or dealing in securities;
   (c) criminal or penal offenses;
   (d) reports of transfers of currency or other monetary instruments; or
   (e) ensuring the satisfaction of judgments in adjudicatory proceedings.

5. Paragraph 3 shall not be construed to prevent a Party from imposing any measure through the equitable, non-discriminatory and good faith application of its laws relating to the matters set out in subparagraphs (a) through (e) of paragraph 4.

6. Notwithstanding paragraph 1, a Party may restrict transfers of returns in kind in circumstances where it could otherwise restrict such transfers under this Agreement, including as set out in paragraph 4.

Article 1110
Expropriation and Compensation

1. No Party may directly or indirectly nationalize or expropriate an investment of an investor of another Party in its territory or take a measure tantamount to nationalization or expropriation of such an investment ("expropriation"), except:
   (a) for a public purpose;
   (b) on a non-discriminatory basis;
   (c) in accordance with due process of law and Article 1105(1); and
   (d) on payment of compensation in accordance with paragraphs 2 through 6.

2. Compensation shall be equivalent to the fair market value of the expropriated investment immediately before the expropriation took place ("date of expropriation"), and shall not reflect any change in value occurring because the intended expropriation had become known earlier. Valuation criteria shall include going concern value, asset value including declared tax value of tangible property, and other criteria, as appropriate, to determine fair market value.

3. Compensation shall be paid without delay and be fully realizable.

4. If payment is made in a G7 currency, compensation shall include interest at a commercially reasonable rate for that currency from the date of expropriation until the date of actual payment.

5. If a Party elects to pay in a currency other than a G7 currency, the amount paid on the date of payment, if converted into a G7 currency at the market rate of exchange prevailing on that date, shall be no less than if the amount of compensation owed on the date of expropriation had been converted into that G7 currency at the market rate of exchange prevailing on that date, and interest had accrued at a commercially reasonable rate for that G7 currency from the date of expropriation until the date of payment.

6. On payment, compensation shall be freely transferable as provided in Article 1109.

7. This Article does not apply to the issuance of compulsory licenses granted in relation to intellectual property rights, or to the revocation, limitation or creation of intellectual property rights, to the extent that such issuance, revocation, limitation or creation is consistent with Chapter Seventeen (Intellectual Property).

8. For purposes of this Article and for greater certainty, a non-discriminatory measure of general application shall not be considered a measure tantamount to an expropriation of

a debt security or loan covered by this Chapter solely on the ground that the measure imposes costs on the debtor that cause it to default on the debt.

Article 1111
Special Formalities and Information Requirements

1. Nothing in Article 1102 shall be construed to prevent a Party from adopting or maintaining a measure that prescribes special formalities in connection with the establishment of investments by investors of another Party, such as a requirement that investors be residents of the Party or that investments be legally constituted under the laws or regulations of the Party, provided that such formalities do not materially impair the protections afforded by a Party to investors of another Party and investments of investors of another Party pursuant to this Chapter.
2. Notwithstanding Articles 1102 or 1103, a Party may require an investor of another Party, or its investment in its territory, to provide routine information concerning that investment solely for informational or statistical purposes. The Party shall protect such business information that is confidential from any disclosure that would prejudice the competitive position of the investor or the investment. Nothing in this paragraph shall be construed to prevent a Party from otherwise obtaining or disclosing information in connection with the equitable and good faith application of its law.

Article 1112
Relation to Other Chapters

1. In the event of any inconsistency between this Chapter and another Chapter, the other Chapter shall prevail to the extent of the inconsistency.
2. A requirement by a Party that a service provider of another Party post a bond or other form of financial security as a condition of providing a service into its territory does not of itself make this Chapter applicable to the provision of that crossborder service. This Chapter applies to that Party's treatment of the posted bond or financial security.

Article 1113
Denial of Benefits

1. A Party may deny the benefits of this Chapter to an investor of another Party that is an enterprise of such Party and to investments of such investor if investors of a non-Party own or control the enterprise and the denying Party:
   (a) does not maintain diplomatic relations with the non-Party; or
   (b) adopts or maintains measures with respect to the non-Party that prohibit transactions with the enterprise or that would be violated or circumvented if the benefits of this Chapter were accorded to the enterprise or to its investments.
2. Subject to prior notification and consultation in accordance with Articles 1803 (Notification and Provision of Information) and 2006 (Consultations), a Party may deny the benefits of this Chapter to an investor of another Party that is an enterprise of such Party and to investments of such investors if investors of a non-Party own or control the enterprise and the enterprise has no substantial business activities in the territory of the Party under whose law it is constituted or organized.

Article 1114
Environmental Measures

1. Nothing in this Chapter shall be construed to prevent a Party from adopting, maintaining or enforcing any measure otherwise consistent with this Chapter that it considers

appropriate to ensure that investment activity in its territory is undertaken in a manner sensitive to environmental concerns.

2. The Parties recognize that it is inappropriate to encourage investment by relaxing domestic health, safety or environmental measures. Accordingly, a Party should not waive or otherwise derogate from, or offer to waive or otherwise derogate from, such measures as an encouragement for the establishment, acquisition, expansion or retention in its territory of an investment of an investor. If a Party considers that another Party has offered such an encouragement, it may request consultations with the other Party and the two Parties shall consult with a view to avoiding any such encouragement.

Section B
Settlement of Disputes between a Party and an Investor of Another Party
Article 1115
Purpose

Without prejudice to the rights and obligations of the Parties under Chapter Twenty (Institutional Arrangements and Dispute Settlement Procedures), this Section establishes a mechanism for the settlement of investment disputes that assures both equal treatment among investors of the Parties in accordance with the principle of international reciprocity and due process before an impartial tribunal.

Article 1116
Claim by an Investor of a Party on Its Own Behalf

1. An investor of a Party may submit to arbitration under this Section a claim that another Party has breached an obligation under:
   (a) Section A or Article 1503(2) (State Enterprises), or
   (b) Article 1502(3)(a) (Monopolies and State Enterprises) where the monopoly has acted in a manner inconsistent with the Party's obligations under Section A,
   and that the investor has incurred loss or damage by reason of, or arising out of, that breach.

2. An investor may not make a claim if more than three years have elapsed from the date on which the investor first acquired, or should have first acquired, knowledge of the alleged breach and knowledge that the investor has incurred loss or damage.

Article 1117
Claim by an Investor of a Party on Behalf of an Enterprise

1. An investor of a Party, on behalf of an enterprise of another Party that is a juridical person that the investor owns or controls directly or indirectly, may submit to arbitration under this Section a claim that the other Party has breached an obligation under:
   (a) Section A or Article 1503(2) (State Enterprises), or
   (b) Article 1502(3)(a) (Monopolies and State Enterprises) where the monopoly has acted in a manner inconsistent with the Party's obligations under Section A, and that the enterprise has incurred loss or damage by reason of, or arising out of, that breach.

2. An investor may not make a claim on behalf of an enterprise described in paragraph 1 if more than three years have elapsed from the date on which the enterprise first acquired, or should have first acquired, knowledge of the alleged breach and knowledge that the enterprise has incurred loss or damage.

3. Where an investor makes a claim under this Article and the investor or a noncontrolling investor in the enterprise makes a claim under Article 1116 arising out of the same events that gave rise to the claim under this Article, and two or more of the claims are submitted to arbitration under Article 1120, the claims should be heard together by a Tribunal established under Article 1126, unless the Tribunal finds that the interests of a disputing party would be prejudiced thereby.

4. An investment may not make a claim under this Section.

Article 1118
Settlement of a Claim through Consultation and Negotiation

The disputing parties should first attempt to settle a claim through consultation or negotiation.

Article 1119
Notice of Intent to Submit a Claim to Arbitration

The disputing investor shall deliver to the disputing Party written notice of its intention to submit a claim to arbitration at least 90 days before the claim is submitted, which notice shall specify:

   (a) the name and address of the disputing investor and, where a claim is made under Article 1117, the name and address of the enterprise;

   (b) the provisions of this Agreement alleged to have been breached and any other relevant provisions;

   (c) the issues and the factual basis for the claim; and

   (d) the relief sought and the approximate amount of damages claimed.

Article 1120
Submission of a Claim to Arbitration

1. Except as provided in Annex 1120.1, and provided that six months have elapsed since the events giving rise to a claim, a disputing investor may submit the claim to arbitration under:

   (a) the ICSID Convention, provided that both the disputing Party and the Party of the investor are parties to the Convention;

   (b) the Additional Facility Rules of ICSID, provided that either the disputing Party or the Party of the investor, but not both, is a party to the ICSID Convention; or

   (c) the UNCITRAL Arbitration Rules.

2. The applicable arbitration rules shall govern the arbitration except to the extent modified by this Section.

Article 1121
Conditions Precedent to Submission of a Claim to Arbitration

1. A disputing investor may submit a claim under Article 1116 to arbitration only if:

   (a) the investor consents to arbitration in accordance with the procedures set out in this Agreement; and

   (b) the investor and, where the claim is for loss or damage to an interest in an enterprise of another Party that is a juridical person that the investor owns or controls directly or indirectly, the enterprise, waive their right to initiate or continue before any administrative tribunal or court under the law of any Party, or other dispute settlement procedures, any proceedings with respect to the measure of the disputing Party that is alleged to be a breach referred to in Article 1116, except for proceedings for injunctive, declaratory or other extraordinary relief, not involving the payment of damages, before an administrative tribunal or court under the law of the disputing Party.

2. A disputing investor may submit a claim under Article 1117 to arbitration only if both the investor and the enterprise:
   (a) consent to arbitration in accordance with the procedures set out in this Agreement; and
   (b) waive their right to initiate or continue before any administrative tribunal or court under the law of any Party, or other dispute settlement procedures, any proceedings with respect to the measure of the disputing Party that is alleged to be a breach referred to in Article 1117, except for proceedings for injunctive, declaratory or other extraordinary relief, not involving the payment of damages, before an administrative tribunal or court under the law of the disputing Party.

3. A consent and waiver required by this Article shall be in writing, shall be delivered to the disputing Party and shall be included in the submission of a claim to arbitration.

4. Only where a disputing Party has deprived a disputing investor of control of an enterprise:
   (a) a waiver from the enterprise under paragraph 1(b) or 2(b) shall not be required; and
   (b) Annex 1120.1(b) shall not apply.

Article 1122
Consent to Arbitration

1. Each Party consents to the submission of a claim to arbitration in accordance with the procedures set out in this Agreement.

2. The consent given by paragraph 1 and the submission by a disputing investor of a claim to arbitration shall satisfy the requirement of:
   (a) Chapter II of the ICSID Convention (Jurisdiction of the Centre) and the Additional Facility Rules for written consent of the parties;
   (b) Article II of the New York Convention for an agreement in writing; and
   (c) Article I of the InterAmerican Convention for an agreement.

Article 1123
Number of Arbitrators and Method of Appointment

Except in respect of a Tribunal established under Article 1126, and unless the disputing parties otherwise agree, the Tribunal shall comprise three arbitrators, one arbitrator appointed by each of the disputing parties and the third, who shall be the presiding arbitrator, appointed by agreement of the disputing parties.

Article 1124
Constitution of a Tribunal When a Party Fails to Appoint an Arbitrator or the Disputing Parties are Unable to Agree on a Presiding Arbitrator

1. The Secretary-General shall serve as appointing authority for an arbitration under this Section.

2. If a Tribunal, other than a Tribunal established under Article 1126, has not been constituted within 90 days from the date that a claim is submitted to arbitration, the Secretary-General, on the request of either disputing party, shall appoint, in his discretion, the arbitrator or arbitrators not yet appointed, except that the presiding arbitrator shall be appointed in accordance with paragraph 3.

3. The Secretary-General shall appoint the presiding arbitrator from the roster of presiding arbitrators referred to in paragraph 4, provided that the presiding arbitrator shall not be a national of the disputing Party or a national of the Party of the disputing investor. In the event that no such presiding arbitrator is available to serve, the Secretary-General shall appoint, from the ICSID Panel of Arbitrators, a presiding arbitrator who is not a national of any of the Parties.

4. On the date of entry into force of this Agreement, the Parties shall establish, and thereafter maintain, a roster of 45 presiding arbitrators meeting the qualifications of the Convention and rules referred to in Article 1120 and experienced in international law and investment matters. The roster members shall be appointed by consensus and without regard to nationality.

Article 1125
Agreement to Appointment of Arbitrators

For purposes of Article 39 of the ICSID Convention and Article 7 of Schedule C to the ICSID Additional Facility Rules, and without prejudice to an objection to an arbitrator based on Article 1124(3) or on a ground other than nationality:

(a) the disputing Party agrees to the appointment of each individual member of a Tribunal established under the ICSID Convention or the ICSID Additional Facility Rules;

(b) a disputing investor referred to in Article 1116 may submit a claim to arbitration, or continue a claim, under the ICSID Convention or the ICSID Additional Facility Rules, only on condition that the disputing investor agrees in writing to the appointment of each individual member of the Tribunal; and

(c) a disputing investor referred to in Article 1117(1) may submit a claim to arbitration, or continue a claim, under the ICSID Convention or the ICSID Additional Facility Rules, only on condition that the disputing investor and the enterprise agree in writing to the appointment of each individual member of the Tribunal.

Article 1126
Consolidation

1. A Tribunal established under this Article shall be established under the UNCITRAL Arbitration Rules and shall conduct its proceedings in accordance with those Rules, except as modified by this Section.

2. Where a Tribunal established under this Article is satisfied that claims have been submitted to arbitration under Article 1120 that have a question of law or fact in common, the Tribunal may, in the interests of fair and efficient resolution of the claims, and after hearing the disputing parties, by order:

(a) assume jurisdiction over, and hear and determine together, all or part of the claims; or

(b) assume jurisdiction over, and hear and determine one or more of the claims, the determination of which it believes would assist in the resolution of the others.

3. A disputing party that seeks an order under paragraph 2 shall request the Secretary-General to establish a Tribunal and shall specify in the request:

(a) the name of the disputing Party or disputing investors against which the order is sought;

(b) the nature of the order sought; and

(c) the grounds on which the order is sought.

4. The disputing party shall deliver to the disputing Party or disputing investors against which the order is sought a copy of the request.

5. Within 60 days of receipt of the request, the Secretary-General shall establish a Tribunal comprising three arbitrators. The Secretary-General shall appoint the presiding arbitrator from the roster referred to in Article 1124(4). In the event that no such presiding arbitrator is available to serve, the Secretary-General shall appoint, from the ICSID Panel of Arbitrators, a presiding arbitrator who is not a national of any of the Parties. The Secretary-General shall appoint the two other members from the roster referred to in Article 1124(4), and to the extent not available from that roster, from the ICSID Panel of Arbitrators, and to the extent not available from that Panel, in the discretion of the Secretary- General. One member shall be a national of the disputing Party and one member shall be a national of a Party of the disputing investors.

6. Where a Tribunal has been established under this Article, a disputing investor that has submitted a claim to arbitration under Article 1116 or 1117 and that has not been named in a request made under paragraph 3 may make a written request to the Tribunal that it be included in an order made under paragraph 2, and shall specify in the request:
   (a) the name and address of the disputing investor;
   (b) the nature of the order sought; and
   (c) the grounds on which the order is sought.

7. A disputing investor referred to in paragraph 6 shall deliver a copy of its request to the disputing parties named in a request made under paragraph 3.

8. A Tribunal established under Article 1120 shall not have jurisdiction to decide a claim, or a part of a claim, over which a Tribunal established under this Article has assumed jurisdiction.

9. On application of a disputing party, a Tribunal established under this Article, pending its decision under paragraph 2, may order that the proceedings of a Tribunal established under Article 1120 be stayed, unless the latter Tribunal has already adjourned its proceedings.

10. A disputing Party shall deliver to the Secretariat, within 15 days of receipt by the disputing Party, a copy of:
    (a) a request for arbitration made under paragraph (1) of Article 36 of the ICSID Convention;
    (b) a notice of arbitration made under Article 2 of Schedule C of the ICSID Additional Facility Rules; or
    (c) a notice of arbitration given under the UNCITRAL Arbitration Rules.

11. A disputing Party shall deliver to the Secretariat a copy of a request made under paragraph 3:
    (a) within 15 days of receipt of the request, in the case of a request made by a disputing investor;
    (b) within 15 days of making the request, in the case of a request made by the disputing Party.

12. A disputing Party shall deliver to the Secretariat a copy of a request made under paragraph 6 within 15 days of receipt of the request.

13. The Secretariat shall maintain a public register of the documents referred to in paragraphs 10, 11 and 12.

Article 1127
Notice

A disputing Party shall deliver to the other Parties:

(a) written notice of a claim that has been submitted to arbitration no later than 30 days after the date that the claim is submitted; and

(b) copies of all pleadings filed in the arbitration.

Article 1128
Participation by a Party

On written notice to the disputing parties, a Party may make submissions to a Tribunal on a question of interpretation of this Agreement.

Article 1129
Documents

1. A Party shall be entitled to receive from the disputing Party, at the cost of the requesting Party a copy of:
   (a) the evidence that has been tendered to the Tribunal; and
   (b) the written argument of the disputing parties.
2. A Party receiving information pursuant to paragraph 1 shall treat the information as if it were a disputing Party.

Article 1130
Place of Arbitration

Unless the disputing parties agree otherwise, a Tribunal shall hold an arbitration in the territory of a Party that is a party to the New York Convention, selected in accordance with:
   (a) the ICSID Additional Facility Rules if the arbitration is under those Rules or the ICSID Convention; or
   (b) the UNCITRAL Arbitration Rules if the arbitration is under those Rules.

Article 1131
Governing Law

1. A Tribunal established under this Section shall decide the issues in dispute in accordance with this Agreement and applicable rules of international law.
2. An interpretation by the Commission of a provision of this Agreement shall be binding on a Tribunal established under this Section.

Article 1132
Interpretation of Annexes

1. Where a disputing Party asserts as a defense that the measure alleged to be a breach is within the scope of a reservation or exception set out in Annex I, Annex II, Annex III or Annex IV, on request of the disputing Party, the Tribunal shall request the interpretation of the Commission on the issue. The Commission, within 60 days of delivery of the request, shall submit in writing its interpretation to the Tribunal.
2. Further to Article 1131(2), a Commission interpretation submitted under paragraph 1 shall be binding on the Tribunal. If the Commission fails to submit an interpretation within 60 days, the Tribunal shall decide the issue.

Article 1133
Expert Reports

Without prejudice to the appointment of other kinds of experts where authorized by the applicable arbitration rules, a Tribunal, at the request of a disputing party or, unless the disputing parties disapprove, on its own initiative, may appoint one or more experts to report to it in writing on any factual issue concerning environmental, health, safety or other scientific matters raised by a disputing party in a proceeding, subject to such terms and conditions as the disputing parties may agree.

Article 1134
Interim Measures of Protection

A Tribunal may order an interim measure of protection to preserve the rights of a disputing party, or to ensure that the Tribunal's jurisdiction is made fully effective, including an order to preserve evidence in the possession or control of a disputing party or to protect the Tribunal's jurisdiction. A Tribunal may not order attachment or enjoin the application of the measure alleged to constitute a breach referred to in Article 1116 or 1117. For purposes of this paragraph, an order includes a recommendation.

Article 1135
Final Award

1. Where a Tribunal makes a final award against a Party, the Tribunal may award, separately or in combination, only:
    (a) monetary damages and any applicable interest;
    (b) restitution of property, in which case the award shall provide that the disputing Party may pay monetary damages and any applicable interest in lieu of restitution.
    A tribunal may also award costs in accordance with the applicable arbitration rules.
2. Subject to paragraph 1, where a claim is made under Article 1117(1):
    (a) an award of restitution of property shall provide that restitution be made to the enterprise;
    (b) an award of monetary damages and any applicable interest shall provide that the sum be paid to the enterprise; and
    (c) the award shall provide that it is made without prejudice to any right that any person may have in the relief under applicable domestic law.
3. A Tribunal may not order a Party to pay punitive damages.

Article 1136
Finality and Enforcement of an Award

1. An award made by a Tribunal shall have no binding force except between the disputing parties and in respect of the particular case.
2. Subject to paragraph 3 and the applicable review procedure for an interim award, a disputing party shall abide by and comply with an award without delay.
3. A disputing party may not seek enforcement of a final award until:
    (a) in the case of a final award made under the ICSID Convention
        (i) 120 days have elapsed from the date the award was rendered and no disputing party has requested revision or annulment of the award, or
        (ii) revision or annulment proceedings have been completed; and
    (b) in the case of a final award under the ICSID Additional Facility Rules or the UNCITRAL Arbitration Rules
        (i) three months have elapsed from the date the award was rendered and no disputing party has commenced a proceeding to revise, set aside or annul the award, or
        (ii) a court has dismissed or allowed an application to revise, set aside or annul the award and there is no further appeal.
4. Each Party shall provide for the enforcement of an award in its territory.

5. If a disputing Party fails to abide by or comply with a final award, the Commission, on delivery of a request by a Party whose investor was a party to the arbitration, shall establish a panel under Article 2008 (Request for an Arbitral Panel). The requesting Party may seek in such proceedings:
   (a) a determination that the failure to abide by or comply with the final award is inconsistent with the obligations of this Agreement; and
   (b) a recommendation that the Party abide by or comply with the final award.
6. A disputing investor may seek enforcement of an arbitration award under the ICSID Convention, the New York Convention or the InterAmerican Convention regardless of whether proceedings have been taken under paragraph 5.
7. A claim that is submitted to arbitration under this Section shall be considered to arise out of a commercial relationship or transaction for purposes of Article I of the New York Convention and Article I of the InterAmerican Convention.

Article 1137
General

Time when a Claim is Submitted to Arbitration
1. A claim is submitted to arbitration under this Section when:
   (a) the request for arbitration under paragraph (1) of Article 36 of the ICSID Convention has been received by the Secretary-General;
   (b) the notice of arbitration under Article 2 of Schedule C of the ICSID Additional Facility Rules has been received by the Secretary- General; or
   (c) the notice of arbitration given under the UNCITRAL Arbitration Rules is received by the disputing Party.

Service of Documents
2. Delivery of notice and other documents on a Party shall be made to the place named for that Party in Annex 1137.2.

Receipts under Insurance or Guarantee Contracts
3. In an arbitration under this Section, a Party shall not assert, as a defense, counterclaim, right of setoff or otherwise, that the disputing investor has received or will receive, pursuant to an insurance or guarantee contract, indemnification or other compensation for all or part of its alleged damages.

Publication of an Award
4. Annex 1137.4 applies to the Parties specified in that Annex with respect to publication of an award.

Article 1138
Exclusions

1. Without prejudice to the applicability or non-applicability of the dispute settlement provisions of this Section or of Chapter Twenty (Institutional Arrangements and Dispute Settlement Procedures) to other actions taken by a Party pursuant to Article 2102 (National Security), a decision by a Party to prohibit or restrict the acquisition of an investment in its territory by an investor of another Party, or its investment, pursuant to that Article shall not be subject to such provisions.
2. The dispute settlement provisions of this Section and of Chapter Twenty shall not apply to the matters referred to in Annex 1138.2.

Section C - Definitions
Article 1139
Definitions

For purposes of this Chapter:

disputing investor means an investor that makes a claim under Section B;

disputing parties means the disputing investor and the disputing Party;

disputing party means the disputing investor or the disputing Party;

disputing Party means a Party against which a claim is made under Section B;

enterprise means an "enterprise" as defined in Article 201 (Definitions of General Application), and a branch of an enterprise;

enterprise of a Party means an enterprise constituted or organized under the law of a Party, and a branch located in the territory of a Party and carrying out business activities there.

equity or debt securities includes voting and non-voting shares, bonds, convertible debentures, stock options and warrants;

G7 Currency means the currency of Canada, France, Germany, Italy, Japan, the United Kingdom of Great Britain and Northern Ireland or the United States;

ICSID means the International Centre for Settlement of Investment Disputes;

ICSID Convention means the *Convention on the Settlement of Investment Disputes between States and Nationals of other States*, done at Washington, March 18, 1965;

InterAmerican Convention means the InterAmerican Convention on International Commercial Arbitration, done at Panama, January 30, 1975;

investment means:

(a) an enterprise;

(b) an equity security of an enterprise;

(c) a debt security of an enterprise
   (i) where the enterprise is an affiliate of the investor, or
   (ii) where the original maturity of the debt security is at least three years, but does not include a debt security, regardless of original maturity, of a state enterprise;

(d) a loan to an enterprise
   (i) where the enterprise is an affiliate of the investor, or
   (ii) where the original maturity of the loan is at least three years,
   but does not include a loan, regardless of original maturity, to a state enterprise;

(e) an interest in an enterprise that entitles the owner to share in income or profits of the enterprise;

(f) an interest in an enterprise that entitles the owner to share in the assets of that enterprise on dissolution, other than a debt security or a loan excluded from subparagraph (c) or (d);

(g) real estate or other property, tangible or intangible, acquired in the expectation or used for the purpose of economic benefit or other business purposes; and

(h) interests arising from the commitment of capital or other resources in the territory of a Party to economic activity in such territory, such as under
   (i) contracts involving the presence of an investor's property in the territory of the Party, including turnkey or construction contracts, or concessions, or
   (ii) contracts where remuneration depends substantially on the production, revenues or profits of an enterprise;

but investment does not mean,

(i) claims to money that arise solely from

      (i)   commercial contracts for the sale of goods or services by a national or enterprise in the territory of a Party to an enterprise in the territory of another Party, or

     (ii) the extension of credit in connection with a commercial transaction, such as trade financing, other than a loan covered by subparagraph (d); or

(j) any other claims to money,

that do not involve the kinds of interests set out in subparagraphs (a) through (h);

investment of an investor of a Party means an investment owned or controlled directly or indirectly by an investor of such Party;

investor of a Party means a Party or state enterprise thereof, or a national or an enterprise of such Party, that seeks to make, is making or has made an investment;

investor of a non-Party means an investor other than an investor of a Party, that seeks to make, is making or has made an investment;

New York Convention means the *United Nations Convention on the Recognition and Enforcement of Foreign Arbitral Awards*, done at New York, June 10, 1958;

Secretary-General means the Secretary-General of ICSID;

transfers means transfers and international payments;

Tribunal means an arbitration tribunal established under Article 1120 or 1126; and

UNCITRAL Arbitration Rules means the arbitration rules of the United Nations Commission on International Trade Law, approved by the United Nations General Assembly on December 15, 1976.

Annex 1120.1
Submission of a Claim to Arbitration Mexico

With respect to the submission of a claim to arbitration:

  (a) an investor of another Party may not allege that Mexico has breached an obligation under:

      (i)   Section A or Article 1503(2) (State Enterprises), or

     (ii) Article 1502(3)(a) (Monopolies and State Enterprises) where the monopoly has acted in a manner inconsistent with the Party's obligations under Section A, both in an arbitration under this Section and in proceedings before a Mexican court or administrative tribunal; and

  (b) where an enterprise of Mexico that is a juridical person that an investor of another Party owns or controls directly or indirectly alleges in proceedings before a Mexican court or administrative tribunal that Mexico has breached an obligation under:

      (i)   Section A or Article 1503(2) (State Enterprises), or

     (ii) Article 1502(3)(a) (Monopolies and State Enterprises) where the monopoly has acted in a manner inconsistent with the Party's obligations under Section A,

the investor may not allege the breach in an arbitration under this Section.

Annex 1137.2
Service of Documents on a Party Under Section B

Each Party shall set out in this Annex and publish in its official journal by January 1, 1994, the place for delivery of notice and other documents under this Section.

Annex 1137.4
Publication of an Award Canada

Where Canada is the disputing Party, either Canada or a disputing investor that is a party to the arbitration may make an award public.

Mexico

Where Mexico is the disputing Party, the applicable arbitration rules apply to the publication of an award.

United States

Where the United States is the disputing Party, either the United States or a disputing investor that is a party to the arbitration may make an award public.

Annex 1138.2
Exclusions from Dispute Settlement Canada

A decision by Canada following a review under the Investment Canada Act, with respect to whether or not to permit an acquisition that is subject to review, shall not be subject to the dispute settlement provisions of Section B or of Chapter Twenty (Institutional Arrangements and Dispute Settlement Procedures).

Mexico

A decision by the National Commission on Foreign Investment ("Comision Nacional de Inversiones Extranjeras") following a review pursuant to Annex page IM4, with respect to whether or not to permit an acquisition that is subject to review, shall not be subject to the dispute settlement provisions of Section B or of Chapter Twenty (Institutional Arrangements and Dispute Settlement Procedures).

Agreement Between the Government of the People's Republic of China and the Government of [...] on the Promotion and Protection of Investments

The Government of the People's Republic of China and the Government of (hereinafter referred to as the Contracting Parties),

Intending to create favorable conditions for investment by investors of one Contracting Party in the territory of the other Contracting Party;

Recognizing that the reciprocal encouragement, promotion and protection of such investment will be conducive to stimulating business initiative of the investors and will increase prosperity in both States;

Desiring to intensify the cooperation of both States on the basis of equality and mutual benefits;

Have agreed as follows:

Article 1
Definitions

For the purpose of this Agreement,

1. The term "investment" means every kind of asset invested by investors of one Contracting Party in accordance with the laws and regulations of the other Contracting Party in the territory of the latter, and in particularly, though not exclusively, includes:
   (a) movable and immovable property and other property rights such as mortgages, pledges and similar rights;
   (b) shares, debentures, stock and any other kind of participation in companies;
   (c) claims to money or to any other performance having an economic value associated with an investment;
   (d) intellectual property rights, in particularly copyrights, patents, trademarks, trade-names, technical process, know-how and good-will;
   (e) business concessions conferred by law or under contract permitted by law, including concessions to search for, cultivate, extract or exploit natural resources.
   Any change in the form in which assets are invested does not affect their character as investments provided that such change is in accordance with the laws and regulations of the Contracting Party in whose territory the investment has been made.

2. The term "investor" means,
   (a) natural persons who have nationality of either Contracting Party in accordance with the laws of that Contracting Party;
   (b) legal entities, including companies, associations, partnerships and other organizations, incorporated or constituted under the laws and regulations of either Contracting Party and have their seats in that Contracting Party.

3. The term "return" means the amounts yielded from investments, including profits, dividends, interests, capital gains, royalties, fees and other legitimate income.

Article 2
Promotion and Protection of Investment

1. Each Contracting Party shall encourage investors of the other Contracting Party to make investments in its territory and admit such investments in accordance with its laws and regulations.

2. Investments of the investors of either Contracting Party shall enjoy the constant protection and security in the territory of the other Contracting Party.
3. Without prejudice to its laws and regulations, neither Contracting Party shall take any unreasonable or discriminatory measures against the management, maintenance, use, enjoyment and disposal of the investments by the investors of the other Contracting Party.
4. Subject to its laws and regulations, one Contracting Party shall provide assistance in and facilities for obtaining visas and working permit to nationals of the other Contracting Party engaging in activities associated with investments made in the territory of that Contracting Party.

Article 3
Treatment of Investment

1. Investments of investors of each Contracting Party shall all the time be accorded fair and equitable treatment in the territory of the other Contracting Party.
2. Without prejudice to its laws and regulations, each Contracting Party shall accord to investments and activities associated with such investments by the investors of the other Contracting Party treatment not less favorable than that accorded to the investments and associated activities by its own investors.
3. Neither Contracting Party shall subject investments and activities associated with such investments by the investors of the other Contracting Party to treatment less favorable than that accorded to the investments and associated activities by the investors of any third State.
4. The provisions of Paragraphs 3 of this Article shall not be construed so as to oblige one Contracting Party to extend to the investors of the other Contracting Party the benefit of any treatment, preference or privilege by virtue of:
   (a) any customs union, free trade zone, economic union and any international agreement resulting in such unions, or similar institutions;
   (b) any international agreement or arrangement relating wholly or mainly to taxation;
   (c) any arrangements for facilitating small scale frontier trade in border areas.

Article 4
Expropriation

1. Neither Contracting Party shall expropriate, nationalize or take other similar measures (hereinafter referred to as "expropriation") against the investments of the investors of the other Contracting Party in its territory, unless the following conditions are met:
   (a) for the public interests;
   (b) under domestic legal procedure;
   (c) without discrimination;
   (d) against compensation.
2. The compensation mentioned in Paragraph 1 of this Article shall be equivalent to the value of the expropriated investments immediately before the expropriation is taken or the impending expropriation becomes public knowledge, whichever is earlier. The value shall be determined in accordance with generally recognized principles of valuation. The compensation shall include interest at a normal commercial rate from the date of expropriation until the date of payment. The compensation shall also be made without delay, be effectively realizable and freely transferable.

Article 5
Compensation for Damages and Losses

Investors of one Contracting Party whose investments in the territory of the other Contracting Party suffer losses owing to war, a state of national emergency,insurrection, riot or other similar events in the territory of the latter Contracting Party, shall be accorded by the latter Contracting Party treatment, as regards restitution, indemnification, compensation and other settlements no less favorable than that accorded to the investors of its own or any third State, whichever is more favorable to the investor concerned.

Article 6
Transfers

1. Each Contracting Party shall, subject to its laws and regulations, guarantee to the investors of the other Contracting Party the transfer of their investments and returns held in its territory, including:
   (a) profits, dividends, interests and other legitimate income;
   (b) proceeds obtained from the total or partial sale or liquidation of investments;
   (c) payments made pursuant to a loan agreement in connection with investments;
   (d) royalties in relation to the matters in Paragraph 1 (d) of Article 1;
   (e) payments of technical assistance or technical service fee, management fee;
   (f) payments in connection with contracting projects;
   (g) earnings of nationals of the other Contracting Party who work in connection with an investment in its territory.
2. Nothing in Paragraph 1 of this Article shall affect the free transfer of compensation paid under Article 4 and 5 of this Agreement.
3. The transfer mentioned above shall be made in a freely convertible currency and at the prevailing market rate of exchange applicable within the Contracting Party accepting the investments and on the date of transfer.

Article 7
Subrogation

If one Contracting Party or its designated agency makes a payment to its investors under a guarantee or a contract of insurance against non-commercial risks it has accorded in respect of an investment made in the territory of the other Contracting Party, the latter Contracting Party shall recognize:
   (a) the assignment, whether under the law or pursuant to a legal transaction in the former Contracting Party, of any rights or claims by the investors to the former Contracting Party or to its designated agency, as well as,
   (b) that the former Contracting Party or its designated agency is entitled by virtue of subrogation to exercise the rights and enforce the claims of that investor and assume the obligations related to the investment to the same extent as the investor.

Article 8
Settlement of Disputes between Contracting Parties

1. Any dispute between the Contracting Parties concerning the interpretation or application of this Agreement shall, as far as possible, be settled with consultation through diplomatic channel.
2. If a dispute cannot thus be settled within six months, it shall, upon the request of either Contracting Party, be submitted to an ad hoc arbitral tribunal.
3. Such tribunal comprises of three arbitrators. Within two months of the receipt of the written notice requesting arbitration, each Contracting Party shall appoint one arbitra-

tor. Those two arbitrators shall, within further two months, together select a national of a third State having diplomatic relations with both Contracting Parties as Chairman of the arbitral tribunal.

4. If the arbitral tribunal has not been constituted within four months from the receipt of the written notice requesting arbitration, either Contracting Party may, in the absence of any other agreement, invite the President of the International Court of Justice to make any necessary appointments. If the President is a national of either Contracting Party or is otherwise prevented from discharging the said functions, the Member of the International Court of Justice next in seniority who is not a national of either Contracting Party or is not otherwise prevented from discharging the said functions shall be invited to make such necessary appointments.

5. The arbitral tribunal shall determine its own procedure. The arbitral tribunal shall reach its award in accordance with the provisions of this Agreement and the principles of international law recognized by both Contracting Parties.

6. The arbitral tribunal shall reach its award by a majority of votes. Such award shall be final and binding upon both Contracting Parties. The arbitral tribunal shall, upon the request of either Contracting Party, explain the reasons of its award.

7. Each Contracting Party shall bear the costs of its appointed arbitrator and of its representation in arbitral proceedings. The relevant costs of the Chairman and tribunal shall be borne in equal parts by the Contracting Parties.

Article 9
Settlement of Disputes between Investors and One Contracting Party

1. Any legal dispute between an investor of one Contracting Party and the other Contracting Party in connection with an investment in the territory of the other Contracting Party shall, as far as possible, be settled amicably through negotiations between the parties to the dispute.

2. If the dispute cannot be settled through negotiations within six months from the date it has been raised by either party to the dispute, it shall be submitted by the choice of the investor:
   (a) to the competent court of the Contracting Party that is a party to the dispute;
   (b) to International Center for Settlement of Investment Disputes (ICSID) under the Convention on the Settlement of Disputes between States and Nationals of Other States, done at Washington on March 18,1965, provided that the Contracting Party involved in the dispute may require the investor concerned to go through the domestic administrative review procedures specified by the laws and regulations of that Contracting Party before the submission to the ICSID.
   Once the investor has submitted the dispute to the competent court of the Contracting Party concerned or to the ICSID, the choice of one of the two procedures shall be final.

3. The arbitration award shall be based on the law of the Contracting Party to the dispute including its rules on the conflict of laws, the provisions of this Agreement as well as the universally accepted principles of international law.

4. The arbitration award shall be final and binding upon both parties to the dispute. Both Contracting Parties shall commit themselves to the enforcement of the award.

Article 10
Other Obligations

1. If the legislation of either Contracting Party or international obligations existing at present or established hereafter between the Contracting Parties result in a position entitling invest-

ments by investors of the other Contracting Party to a treatment more favorable than is provided for by the Agreement, such position shall not be affected by this Agreement.

2. Each Contracting Party shall observe any commitments it may have entered into with the investors of the other Contracting Party as regards to their investments.

Article 11
Application

This Agreement shall apply to investment made prior to or after its entry into force by investors of one Contracting Party in the territory of the other Contracting Party in accordance with the laws and regulations of the Contracting Party concerned, but not apply to the dispute arose before its entry into force.

Article 12
Consultations

1. The representatives of the Contracting Parties shall hold meetings from time to time for the purpose of:
   (a) reviewing the implementation of this Agreement;
   (b) exchanging legal information and investment opportunities;
   (c) resolving disputes arising out of investments;
   (d) forwarding proposals on promotion of investment;
   (e) studying other issues in connection with investment.
2. Where either Contracting Party requests consultation on any matter of Paragraph 1 of this Article, the other Contracting Party shall give prompt response and the consultation be held alternatively in Beijing and

Article 13
Entry into Force, Duration and Termination

1. This Agreement shall enter into force on the first day of the following month after the date on which both Contracting Parties have notified each other in writing that their respective internal legal procedures necessary therefor have been fulfilled and remain in force for a period of ten years.
2. This Agreement shall continue to be in force unless either Contracting Party has given a written notice to the other Contracting Party to terminate this Agreement one year before the expiration of the initial ten year period or at any time thereafter.
3. With respect to investments made prior to the date of termination of this Agreement, the provisions of Article 1 to 12 shall continue to be effective for a further period of ten years from such date of termination.
4. This Agreement may be amended by written agreement between the Contracting Parties. Any amendment shall enter into force under the same procedures required for entry into force of the present Agreement.

IN WITNESS WHEREOF the undersigned, duly authorized thereto by respective Governments, have signed this Agreement.

Done in duplicate aton, in the Chinese, and English languages, all texts being equally authentic. In case of divergent interpretation, the English text shall prevail.

. . . .,

For the Government of   For the Government of
The People's Republic of China

Treaty between the Federal Republic of Germany and [...] concerning the Encouragement and Reciprocal Protection of Investments

The Federal Republic of Germany
and

....,

desiring to intensify economic co-operation between the two States,

intending to create favourable conditions for investments by investors of either State in the territory of the other State,

recognizing that the encouragement and contractual protection of such investments are apt to stimulate private business initiative and to increase the prosperity of both nations,

have agreed as follows:

Article 1
Definitions

Within the meaning of this Treaty,

1. the term "investments" comprises every kind of asset which is directly or indirectly invested by investors of one Contracting State in the territory of the other Contracting State. The investments include in particular:
   (a) movable and immovable property as well as any other rights in rem, such as mortgages, liens and pledges;
   (b) shares of companies and other kinds of interest in companies;
   (c) claims to money which has been used to create an economic value or claims to any performance having an economic value;
   (d) intellectual property rights, in particular copyrights and related rights, patents, utility-model patents, industrial designs, trademarks, plant variety rights;
   (e) trade-names, trade and business secrets, technical processes, know-how, and good-will;
   (f) business concessions under public law, including concessions to search for, extract or exploit natural resources;
   any alteration of the form in which assets are invested shall not affect their classification as investment. In the case of indirect investments, in principle only those indirect investments shall be covered which the investor realizes via a company situated in the other Contracting State;

2. the term "returns" means the amounts yielded by an investment for a definite period, such as profit, dividends, interest, royalties or fees;
3. the term "investor" means
   (a) in respect of the Federal Republic of Germany:
       – any natural person who is a German within the meaning of the Basic Law of the Federal Republic of Germany or a national of a Member State of the European Union or of the European Economic Area who, within the context of freedom of establishment pursuant to Article 43 of the EC Treaty, is established in the Federal Republic of Germany;

    – any juridical person and any commercial or other company or association with or without legal personality which is founded pursuant to the law of the Federal Republic of Germany or the law of a Member State of the European Union or the European Economic Area and is organized pursuant to the law of the Federal Republic of Germany, registered in a public register in the Federal Republic of Germany or enjoys freedom of establishment as an agency or permanent establishment in Germany pursuant to Articles 43 and 48 of the EC Treaty;
    which in the context of entrepreneurial activity is the owner, possessor or shareholder of an investment in the territory of the other Contracting State, irrespective of whether or not the activity is directed at profit;

  (b) in respect of . . . .:
. . . .
. . . .
. . . .
. . . .
. . . .
. . . .

4. the term "territory" refers to the area of each Contracting State including the exclusive economic zone and the continental shelf insofar as international law allows the Contracting State concerned to exercise sovereign rights or jurisdiction in these areas.

Article 2
Admission and protection of investments

(1) Each Contracting State shall in its territory promote as far as possible investments by investors of the other Contracting State and admit such investments in accordance with its legislation.

(2) Each Contracting State shall in its territory in every case accord investments by investors of the other Contracting State fair and equitable treatment as well as full protection under this Treaty.

(3) Neither Contracting State shall in its territory impair by arbitrary or discriminatory measures the activity of investors of the other Contracting State with regard to investments, such as in particular the management, maintenance, use, enjoyment or disposal of such investments. This provision shall be without prejudice to Article 7 (3).

(4) Returns from an investment, as well as returns from reinvested returns, shall enjoy the same protection as the original investment.

Article 3
National and most-favoured-nation treatment

(1) Neither Contracting State shall in its territory subject investments owned or controlled by investors of the other Contracting State to treatment less favourable than it accords to investments of its own investors or to investments of investors of any third State.

(2) Neither Contracting State shall in its territory subject investors of the other Contracting State, as regards their activity in connection with investments, to treatment less favourable than it accords to its own investors or to investors of any third State. The following shall, in particular, be deemed treatment less favourable within the meaning of this Article:
  1. different treatment in the event of restrictions on the procurement of raw or auxiliary materials, of energy and fuels, and of all types of means of production and operation;

2. different treatment in the event of impediments to the sale of products at home and abroad; and

3. other measures of similar effect.

Measures that have to be taken for reasons of public security and order shall not be deemed treatment less favourable within the meaning of this Article.

(3) Such treatment shall not relate to privileges which either Contracting State accords to investors of third States on account of its membership of, or association with, a customs or economic union, a common market or a free trade area.

(4) The treatment granted under this Article shall not relate to advantages which either Contracting State accords to investors of third States by virtue of an agreement for the avoidance of double taxation in the field of taxes on income and assets or other agreements regarding matters of taxation.

(5) This Article shall not oblige a Contracting State to extend to investors resident in the territory of the other Contracting State tax privileges, tax exemptions and tax reductions which according to its tax laws are granted only to investors resident in its territory.

(6) The Contracting States shall within the framework of their national legislation give sympathetic consideration to applications for the entry and sojourn of persons of either Contracting State who wish to enter the territory of the other Contracting State in connection with an investment; the same shall apply to employed persons of either Contracting State who in connection with an investment wish to enter the territory of the other Contracting State and sojourn there to take up employment. Where necessary, applications for work permits shall also be given sympathetic consideration.

(7) Notwithstanding any bilateral or multilateral agreements which are binding on both Contracting States, the investors of the Contracting States are free to select the means of transport for the international transportation of persons and of capital goods directly related to an investment within the meaning of this Treaty. Transport companies of the Contracting States shall not be discriminated against thereby.

Article 4
Compensation in case of expropriation

(1) Investments by investors of either Contracting State shall enjoy full protection and security in the territory of the other Contracting State.

(2) Investments by investors of either Contracting State may not directly or indirectly be expropriated, nationalized or subjected to any other measure the effects of which would be tantamount to expropriation or nationalization in the territory of the other Contracting State except for the public benefit and against compensation. Such compensation must be equivalent to the value of the expropriated investment immediately before the date on which the actual or threatened expropriation, nationalization or other measure became publicly known. The compensation must be paid without delay and shall carry the usual bank interest until the time of payment; it must be effectively realizable and freely transferable. Provision must have been made in an appropriate manner at or prior to the time of expropriation, nationalization or other measure for the determination and payment of such compensation. The legality of any such expropriation, nationalization or other measure and the amount of compensation must be subject to review by due process of law.

(3) Investors of either Contracting State whose investments suffer losses in the territory of the other Contracting State owing to war or other armed conflict, revolution, a state of national emergency, or revolt, shall be accorded treatment no less favourable by such other Contracting State than that State accords to its own investors as regards restitution,

indemnification, compensation or other valuable consideration. Such payments must be freely transferable.

(4) Investors of either Contracting State shall enjoy most-favoured-nation treatment in the territory of the other Contracting State in respect of the matters provided for in the present Article.

Article 5
Free transfer

(1) Each Contracting State shall guarantee to investors of the other Contracting State the free transfer of payments in connection with an investment, in particular
  1. the principal and additional amounts to maintain or increase the investment;
  2. the returns;
  3. the repayment of loans;
  4. the proceeds from the liquidation or the sale of the whole or any part of the investment;
  5. the compensation provided for in Article 4.
(2) Transfers under Article 4 (2) or (3), under the present Article or Article 6, shall be made without delay at the market rate of exchange applicable on the day of the transfer. A transfer shall be deemed to have been made without delay if made within such period as is normally required for the completion of transfer formalities. The period shall commence with the submission of the corresponding application, where such an application is necessary, or the notification of the intended transfer, and must in no circumstances exceed two months.
(3) Should it not be possible to ascertain a market rate pursuant to paragraph (2), the cross rate obtained from those rates which would be applied by the International Monetary Fund on the date of payment for conversions of the currencies concerned into Special Drawing Rights shall apply.

Article 6
Subrogation

If either Contracting State makes payment to any of its investors under a guarantee it has assumed in respect of an investment in the territory of the other Contracting State, the latter Contracting State shall, without prejudice to the rights of the former Contracting State under Article 9, recognize the assignment, whether under a law or pursuant to a legal transaction, of any right or claim from such investors to the former Contracting State. Furthermore, the latter Contracting State shall recognize the subrogation of that Contracting State to any such right or claim (assigned claim), which that Contracting State shall be entitled to assert to the same extent as its predecessor in title. As regards the transfer of payments on the basis of such assignment, Article 4 (1) and (2) and Article 5 shall apply mutatis mutandis.

Article 7
Other provisions

(1) If the legislation of either Contracting State or international obligations existing at present or established hereafter between the Contracting States in addition to this Treaty contain any provisions, whether general or specific, entitling investments by investors of the other Contracting State to a treatment more favourable than is provided for by this Treaty, such provisions shall prevail over this Treaty to the extent that they are more favourable.
(2) Each Contracting State shall fulfil any other obligations it may have entered into with regard to investments in its territory by investors of the other Contracting State.

(3) With regard to the treatment of income and assets for the purpose of taxation, precedence shall be given to the application of the agreements in force at the time between the Federal Republic of Germany and . . . for the avoidance of double taxation in the field of taxes on income and assets.

Article 8
Scope of application

This Treaty shall also apply to investments made prior to its entry into force by investors of either Contracting State in the territory of the other Contracting State consistent with the latter's legislation.

Article 9
Settlement of disputes between the Contracting States

(1) Disputes between the Contracting States concerning the interpretation or application of this Treaty should as far as possible be settled by the Governments of the two Contracting States.

(2) If a dispute cannot thus be settled, it shall upon the request of either Contracting State be submitted to an arbitral tribunal.

(3) The arbitral tribunal shall be constituted for each case as follows: each Contracting State shall appoint one member, and these two members shall agree upon a national of a third State as their chairman to be appointed by the Governments of the two Contracting States. The members shall be appointed within two months, and the chairman within three months, from the date on which either Contracting State has informed the other Contracting State that it wants to submit the dispute to an arbitral tribunal.

(4) If the periods specified in paragraph (3) have not been observed, either Contracting State may, in the absence of any other relevant agreement, invite the President of the International Court of Justice to make the necessary appointments. If the President is a national of either Contracting State or if he is otherwise prevented from discharging the said function, the Vice-President should make the necessary appointments. If the Vice-President is a national of either Contracting State or if he, too, is prevented from discharging the said function, the Member of the Court next in seniority who is not a national of either Contracting State should make the necessary appointments.

(5) The arbitral tribunal shall reach its decisions by a majority of votes. Its decisions shall be binding. Each Contracting State shall bear the cost of its own member and of its representatives in the arbitration proceedings; the cost of the chairman and the remaining costs shall be borne in equal parts by the Contracting States. The arbitral tribunal may make a different regulation concerning costs. In all other respects, the arbitral tribunal shall determine its own procedure.

Article 10
Settlement of disputes between a Contracting
State and an investor of the other Contracting State

(1) Disputes concerning investments between a Contracting State and an investor of the other Contracting State should as far as possible be settled amicably between the parties to the dispute. To help them reach an amicable settlement, the parties to the dispute also have the option of agreeing to institute conciliation proceedings under the Convention on the Settlement of Investment Disputes between States and Nationals of Other States of 18 March 1965 (ICSID).

(2) If the dispute cannot be settled within six months of the date on which it was raised by one of the parties to the dispute, it shall, at the request of the investor of the other

Contracting State, be submitted to arbitration. The two Contracting States hereby declare that they unreservedly and bindingly consent to the dispute being submitted to one of the following dispute settlement mechanisms of the investor's choosing:

1. arbitration under the auspices of the International Centre for Settlement of Investment Disputes pursuant to the Convention on the Settlement of Investment Disputes between States and Nationals of Other States of 18 March 1965 (ICSID), provided both Contracting States are members of this Convention, or
2. arbitration under the auspices of the International Centre for Settlement of Investment Disputes pursuant to the Convention on the Settlement of Investment Disputes between States and Nationals of Other States of 18 March 1965 (ICSID) in accordance with the Rules on the Additional Facility for the Administration of Proceedings by the Secretariat of the Centre, where the personal or factual preconditions for proceedings pursuant to figure 1 do not apply, but at least one Contracting State is a member of the Convention referred to therein, or
3. an individual arbitrator or an ad-hoc arbitral tribunal which is established in accordance with the rules of the United Nations Commission on International Trade Law (UNCITRAL) as in force at the commencement of the proceedings, or
4. an arbitral tribunal which is established pursuant to the Dispute Resolution Rules of the International Chamber of Commerce (ICC), the London Court of International Arbitration (LCIA) or the Arbitration Institute of the Stockholm Chamber of Commerce, or
5. any other form of dispute settlement agreed by the parties to the dispute.

(3) The award shall be binding and shall not be subject to any appeal or remedy other than those provided for in the Convention or arbitral rules on which the arbitral proceedings chosen by the investor are based. The award shall be enforced by the Contracting States as a final and absolute ruling under domestic law.

(4) Arbitration proceedings pursuant to this Article shall take place at the request of one of the parties to the dispute in a State which is a Contracting Party to the United Nations Convention on the Recognition and Enforcement of Foreign Arbitral Awards of 10 June 1958.

(5) During arbitration proceedings or the enforcement of an award, the Contracting State involved in the dispute shall not raise the objection that the investor of the other Contracting State has received compensation under an insurance contract in respect of all or part of the damage.

Article 11
Relations between the Contracting States

This Treaty shall be in force irrespective of whether or not diplomatic or consular relations exist between the Contracting States.

Article 12
Registration clause

Registration of this Treaty with the Secretariat of the United Nations, in accordance with Article 102 of the United Nations Charter, shall be initiated immediately following its entry into force by the Contracting State in which the signing took place. The other Contracting State shall be informed of registration, and of the UN registration number, as soon as this has been confirmed by the Secretariat of the United Nations.

Article 13
Entry into force, duration and notice of termination

(1) This Treaty shall be subject to ratification; the instruments of ratification shall be exchanged as soon as possible.

(2) This Treaty shall enter into force on the first day of the second month following the exchange of the instruments of ratification. It shall remain in force for a period of ten years and shall continue in force thereafter for an unlimited period unless denounced in writing through diplomatic channels by either Contracting State twelve months before its expiration. After the expiry of the period of ten years this Treaty may be denounced at any time by either Contracting State giving twelve months' notice.

(3) In respect of investments made prior to the date of termination of this Treaty, the provisions of the above Articles shall continue to be effective for a further period of twenty years from the date of termination of this Treaty.

Done in on in duplicate in the German and ....
languages, both texts being equally authentic.

For the For

Federal Republic of Germany...

Draft Agreement Between the Government of the United Kingdom of Great Britain and Northern Ireland and the Government of [...] for the Promotion and Protection of Investments

The Government of the United Kingdom of Great Britain and Northern Ireland and the Government of_____;

Desiring to create favourable conditions for greater investment by nationals and companies of one State in the territory of the other State;

Recognising that the encouragement and reciprocal protection under international agreement of such investments will be conducive to the stimulation of individual business initiative and will increase prosperity in both States;

Have agreed as follows:

Article 1
Definitions

For the purposes of this Agreement:

(a) "investment" means every kind of asset and in particular, though not exclusively, includes:
  (i) movable and immovable property and any other property rights such as mortgages, liens or pledges;
  (ii) shares in and stock and debentures of a company and any other form of participation in a company;
  (iii) claims to money or to any performance under contract having a financial value;
  (iv) intellectual property rights, goodwill, technical processes and knowhow;
  (v) business concessions conferred by law or under contract, including concessions to search for, cultivate, extract or exploit natural resources.

  A change in the form in which assets are invested does not affect their character as investments and the term "investment" includes all investments, whether made before or after the date of entry into force of this Agreement;

(b) "returns" means the amounts yielded by an investment and in particular, though not exclusively, includes profit, interest, capital gains, dividends, royalties and fees;

(c) "nationals" means:
  (i) in respect of the United Kingdom: physical persons deriving their status as United Kingdom nationals from the law in force in the United Kingdom;
  (ii) in respect of_____:_____;

(d) "companies" means:
  (i) in respect of the United Kingdom: corporations, firms and associations incorporated or constituted under the law in force in any part of the United Kingdom or in any territory to which this Agreement is extended in accordance with the provisions of Article 12;
  (ii) in respect of_____:_____;

(e) "territory" means:
  (i) in respect of the United Kingdom: Great Britain and Northern Ireland, including the territorial sea and maritime area situated beyond the territorial sea of the United Kingdom which has been or might in the future be designated under the national law of the United Kingdom in accordance with international law as an area within which the United Kingdom may exercise rights with regard to the sea-bed and subsoil and the natural resources and any territory to which this Agreement is extended in accordance with the provisions of Article 12;
  (ii) in respect of_____:_____.

Article 2
Promotion and Protection of Investment

(1) Each Contracting Party shall encourage and create favourable conditions for nationals or companies of the other Contracting Party to invest capital in its territory, and, subject to its right to exercise powers conferred by its laws, shall admit such capital.
(2) Investments of nationals or companies of each Contracting Party shall at all times be accorded fair and equitable treatment and shall enjoy full protection and security in the territory of the other Contracting Party. Neither Contracting Party shall in any way impair by unreasonable or discriminatory measures the management, maintenance, use, enjoyment or disposal of investments in its territory of nationals or companies of the other Contracting Party. Each Contracting Party shall observe any obligation it may have entered into with regard to investments of nationals or companies of the other Contracting Party.

Article 3
National Treatment and Most-favoured-nation Provisions

(1) Neither Contracting Party shall in its territory subject investments or returns of nationals or companies of the other Contracting Party to treatment less favourable than that which it accords to investments or returns of its own nationals or companies or to investments or returns of nationals or companies of any third State.
(2) Neither Contracting Party shall in its territory subject nationals or companies of the other Contracting Party, as regards their management, maintenance, use, enjoyment or disposal of their investments, to treatment less favourable that that which it accords to its own nationals or companies or to nationals or companies of any third State.
(3) For the avoidance of doubt it is confirmed that the treatment provided for in paragraphs (1) and (2) above shall apply to the provisions of Articles 1 to 11 of this Agreement.

Article 4
Compensation for Losses

(1) Nationals or companies of one Contracting Party whose investments in the territory of the other Contracting Party suffer losses owing to war or other armed conflict, revolution, a state of national emergency, revolt, insurrection or riot in the territory of the latter Contracting Party shall be accorded by the latter Contracting Party treatment, as regards restitution, indemnification, compensation or other settlement, no less favourable that that which the latter Contracting Party accords to its own nationals or companies or to nationals or companies of any third State. Resulting payments shall be freely transferable.
(2) Without prejudice to paragraph (1) of this Article, nationals or companies of one Contracting Party who in any of the situations referred to in that paragraph suffer losses in the territory of the other Contracting Party resulting from:

(a) requisitioning of their property by its forces or authorities, or

(b) destruction of their property by its forces or authorities, which was not caused in combat action or was not required by the necessity of the situation, shall be accorded restitution or adequate compensation. Resulting payments shall be freely transferable.

Article 5
Expropriation

(1) Investments of nationals or companies of either Contracting Party shall not be nationalised, expropriated or subjected to measures having effect equivalent to nationalisation or expropriation (hereinafter referred to as "expropriation") in the territory of the other Contracting Party except for a public purpose related to the internal needs of that Party on a non-discrimina- tory basis and against prompt, adequate and effective compensation. Such compensation shall amount to the genuine value of the investment expropriated immediately before the expropriation or before the impending expropriation became public knowledge, whichever is the earlier, shall include interest at a normal commercial rate until the date of payment, shall be made without delay, be effectively realizable and be freely transferable. The national or company affected shall have a right, under the law of the Contracting Party making the expropriation, to prompt review, by a judicial or other independent authority of that Party, of his or its case and of the valuation of his or its investment in accordance with the principles set out in this paragraph.

(2) Where a Contracting Party expropriates the assets of a company which is incorporated or constituted under the law in force in any part of its own territory, and in which nationals or companies of the other Contracting Party own shares, it shall ensure that the provisions of paragraph (1) of this Article are applied to the extent necessary to guarantee prompt, adequate and effective compensation in respect of their investment to such nationals or companies of the other Contracting Party who are owners of those shares.

Article 6
Repatriation of Investment and Returns

Each Contracting Party shall in respect of investments guarantee to nationals or companies of the other Contracting Party the unrestricted transfer of their investments and returns. Transfers shall be effected without delay in the convertible currency in which the capital was originally invested or in any other convertible currency agreed by the investor and the Contracting Party concerned. Unless otherwise agreed by the investor transfers shall be made at the rate of exchange applicable on the date of transfer pursuant to the exchange regulations in force.

Article 7
Exceptions

The provisions of this Agreement relative to the grant of treatment not less favourable than that accorded to the nationals or companies of either Contracting Party or of any third State shall not be construed so as to oblige one Contracting Party to extend to the nationals or companies of the other the benefit of any treatment, preference or privilege resulting from:

(a) any existing or future customs union or similar international agreement to which either of the Contracting Parties is or may become a party; or

(b) any international agreement or arrangement relating wholly or mainly to taxation or any domestic legislation relating wholly or mainly to taxation.

(c) any requirements of European Community law resulting from the United Kingdom's membership of the European Union prohibiting, restricting or limiting the movement of capital to or from any third country.

Article 8 [Preferred]
Reference to International Centre for Settlement of Investment Disputes

(1) Each Contracting Party hereby consents to submit to the International Centre for the Settlement of Investment Disputes (hereinafter referred to as "the Centre") for settlement by conciliation or arbitration under the Convention on the Settlement of Investment Disputes between States and Nationals of Other States opened for signature at Washington DC on 18 March 1965 any legal dispute arising between that Contracting Party and a national or company of the other Contracting Party concerning an investment of the latter in the territory of the former.

(2) A company which is incorporated or constituted under the law in force in the territory of one Contracting Party and in which before such a dispute arises the majority of shares are owned by nationals or companies of the other Contracting Party shall in accordance with Article 25 (2) (b) of the Convention be treated for the purposes of the Convention as a company of the other Contracting Party.

(3) If any such dispute should arise and agreement cannot be reached within three months between the parties to this dispute through pursuit of local remedies or otherwise, then, if the national or company affected also consents in writing to submit the dispute to the Centre for settlement by conciliation or arbitration under the Convention, either party may institute proceedings by addressing a request to that effect to the Secretary-General of the Centre as provided in Articles 28 and 36 of the Convention. In the event of disagreement as to whether conciliation or arbitration is the more appropriate procedure the national or company affected shall have the right to choose. The Contracting Party which is a party to the dispute shall not raise as an objection at any stage of the proceedings or enforcement of an award the fact that the national or company which is the other party to the dispute has received in pursuance of an insurance contract an indemnity in respect of some or all of his or its losses.

(4) Neither Contracting Party shall pursue through the diplomatic channel any dispute referred to the Centre unless:
  (a) the Secretary-General of the Centre, or a conciliation commission or an arbitral tribunal constituted by it, decides that the dispute is not within the jurisdiction of the Centre; or
  (b) the other Contracting Party shall fail to abide by or to comply with any award rendered by an arbitral tribunal.

Article 8 [Alternative]
Settlement of Disputes between an Investor and a Host State

(1) Disputes between a national or company of one Contracting Party and the other Contracting Party concerning an obligation of the latter under this Agreement in relation to an investment of the former which have not been amicably settled shall, after a period of three months from written notification of a claim, be submitted to international arbitration if the national or company concerned so wishes.

(2) Where the dispute is referred to international arbitration, the national or company and the Contracting Party concerned in the dispute may agree to refer the dispute either to:
  (a) the International Centre for the Settlement of Investment Disputes (having regard to the provisions, where applicable, of the Convention on the Settlement of

Investment Disputes between States and Nationals of other States, opened for signature at Washington DC on 18 March 1965 and the Additional Facility for the Administration of Conciliation, Arbitration and Fact-Finding Proceedings); or

(b) the Court of Arbitration of the International Chamber of Commerce; or

(c) an international arbitrator or ad hoc arbitration tribunal to be appointed by a special agreement or established under the Arbitration Rules of the United Nations Commission on International Trade Law.

If after a period of three months from written notification of the claim there is no agreement to one of the above alternative procedures, the dispute shall at the request in writing of the national or company concerned be submitted to arbitration under the Arbitration Rules of the United Nations Commission on International Trade Law as then in force. The parties to the dispute may agree in writing to modify these Rules.

Article 9
Disputes between the Contracting Parties

(1) Disputes between the Contracting Parties concerning the interpretation or application of this Agreement should, if possible, be settled through the diplomatic channel.

(2) If a dispute between the Contracting Parties cannot thus be settled, it shall upon the request of either Contracting Party be submitted to an arbitral tribunal.

(3) Such an arbitral tribunal shall be constituted for each individual case in the following way. Within two months of the receipt of the request for arbitration, each Contracting Party shall appoint one member of the tribunal. Those two members shall then select a national of a third State who on approval by the two Contracting Parties shall be appointed Chairman of the tribunal. The Chairman shall be appointed within two months from the date of appointment of the other two members.

(4) If within the periods specified in paragraph (3) of this Article the necessary appointments have not been made, either Contracting Party may, in the absence of any other agreement, invite the President of the International Court of Justice to make any necessary appointments. If the President is a national of either Contracting Party or if he is otherwise prevented from discharging the said function, the Vice-President shall be invited to make the necessary appointments. If the Vice-President is a national of either Contracting Party or if he too is prevented from discharging the said function, the Member of the International Court of Justice next in seniority who is not a national of either Contracting Party shall be invited to make the necessary appointments.

(5) The arbitral tribunal shall reach its decision by a majority of votes. Such decision shall be binding on both Contracting Parties. Each Contracting Party shall bear the cost of its own member of the tribunal and of its representation in the arbitral proceedings; the cost of the Chairman and the remaining costs shall be borne in equal parts by the Contracting Parties. The tribunal may, however, in its decision direct that a higher proportion of costs shall be borne by one of the two Contracting Parties, and this award shall be binding on both Contracting Parties. The tribunal shall determine its own procedure.

Article 10
Subrogation

(1) If one Contracting Party or its designated Agency ("the first Contracting Party") makes a payment under an indemnity given in respect of an investment in the territory of the other Contracting Party ("the second Contracting Party"), the second Contracting Party shall recognise:

(a) the assignment to the first Contracting Party by law or by legal transaction of all the rights and claims of the party indemnified; and

(b) that the first Contracting Party is entitled to exercise such rights and enforce such claims by virtue of subrogation, to the same extent as the party indemnified.

(2) The first Contracting Party shall be entitled in all circumstances to the same treatment in respect of:

(a) the rights and claims acquired by it by virtue of the assignment, and

(b) any payments received in pursuance of those rights and claims, as the party indemnified was entitled to receive by virtue of this Agreement in respect of the investment concerned and its related returns.

(3) Any payments received in non-convertible currency by the first Contracting Party in pursuance of the rights and claims acquired shall be freely available to the first Contracting Party for the purpose of meeting any expenditure incurred in the territory of the second Contracting Party.

Article 11
Application of other Rules

If the provisions of law of either Contracting Party or obligations under international law existing at present or established hereafter between the Contracting Parties in addition to the present Agreement contain rules, whether general or specific, entitling investments by nationals or companies of the other Contracting Party to a treatment more favourable than is provided for by the present Agreement, such rules shall to the extent that they are more favourable prevail over the present Agreement.

Article 12
Territorial Extension

At the time of [signature] [entry into force] [ratification] of this Agreement, or at any time thereafter, the provisions of this Agreement may be extended to such territories for whose international relations the Government of the United Kingdom are responsible as may be agreed between the Contracting Parties in an Exchange of Notes.

Article 13
Entry into Force

[This Agreement shall enter into force on the day of_____signature.]

or

[Each Contracting Party shall notify the other in writing of the completion of the constitutional formalities required in its territory for the entry into force of this Agreement. This Agreement shall enter into force on the date of the latter of the two notifications.]

or

[The Agreement shall be ratified and shall enter into force on the exchange of Instruments of Ratification.]

Article 14
Duration and Termination

This Agreement shall remain in force for a period of ten years. Thereafter it shall continue in force until the expiration of twelve months from the date on which either Contracting Party shall have given written notice of termination to the other. Provided that in respect of investments made whilst the Agreement is in force, its provisions shall continue in effect with respect to such investments for a period of twenty years after the date of termination and without prejudice to the application thereafter of the rules of general international law.

In witness whereof the undersigned, duly authorised thereto by their respective Governments, have signed this Agreement.

Done in duplicate at_____this_____day of_____200_ [in the English and . . . languages, both texts being equally authoritative].

For the Government of   For the Government of
the United Kingdom of Great Britain and   :
Northern Ireland:

Treaty Between the Government of the United States of America and the Government of [Country] Concerning the Encouragement and Reciprocal Protection of Investment

The Government of the United States of America and the Government of [Country] (hereinafter the "Parties");

Desiring to promote greater economic cooperation between them with respect to investment by nationals and enterprises of one Party in the territory of the other Party;

Recognizing that agreement on the treatment to be accorded such investment will stimulate the flow of private capital and the economic development of the Parties;

Agreeing that a stable framework for investment will maximize effective utilization of economic resources and improve living standards;

Recognizing the importance of providing effective means of asserting claims and enforcing rights with respect to investment under national law as well as through international arbitration;

Desiring to achieve these objectives in a manner consistent with the protection of health, safety, and the environment, and the promotion of internationally recognized labor rights;

Having resolved to conclude a Treaty concerning the encouragement and reciprocal protection of investment;

Have agreed as follows:

Section A

Article 1
Definitions

For purposes of this Treaty:

"**central level of government**" means:

    (a) for the United States, the federal level of government; and

    (b) for [Country], [_____].

"**Centre**" means the International Centre for Settlement of Investment Disputes ("ICSID") established by the ICSID Convention.

"**claimant**" means an investor of a Party that is a party to an investment dispute with the other Party.

"**covered investment**" means, with respect to a Party, an investment in its territory of an investor of the other Party in existence as of the date of entry into force of this Treaty or established, acquired, or expanded thereafter.

"**disputing parties**" means the claimant and the respondent.

"**disputing party**" means either the claimant or the respondent.

"**enterprise**" means any entity constituted or organized under applicable law, whether or not for profit, and whether privately or governmentally owned or controlled, including a corporation, trust, partnership, sole proprietorship, joint venture, association, or similar organization; and a branch of an enterprise.

"**enterprise of a Party**" means an enterprise constituted or organized under the law of a Party, and a branch located in the territory of a Party and carrying out business activities there.

"**existing**" means in effect on the date of entry into force of this Treaty.

"**freely usable currency**" means "freely usable currency" as determined by the International Monetary Fund under its *Articles of Agreement.*

"**GATS**" means the *General Agreement on Trade in Services*, contained in Annex 1B to the WTO Agreement.

"**government procurement**" means the process by which a government obtains the use of or acquires goods or services, or any combination thereof, for governmental purposes and not with a view to commercial sale or resale, or use in the production or supply of goods or services for commercial sale or resale.

"**ICSID Additional Facility Rules**" means the *Rules Governing the Additional Facility for the Administration of Proceedings by the Secretariat of the International Centre for Settlement of Investment Disputes.*

"**ICSID Convention**" means the *Convention on the Settlement of Investment Disputes between States and Nationals of Other States,* done at Washington, March 18, 1965.

["**Inter-American Convention**" means the *Inter-American Convention on International Commercial Arbitration,* done at Panama, January 30, 1975.]

"**investment**" means every asset that an investor owns or controls, directly or indirectly, that has the characteristics of an investment, including such characteristics as the commitment of capital or other resources, the expectation of gain or profit, or the assumption of risk. Forms that an investment may take include:

(a) an enterprise;

(b) shares, stock, and other forms of equity participation in an enterprise;

(c) bonds, debentures, other debt instruments, and loans;[1]

(d) futures, options, and other derivatives;

(e) turnkey, construction, management, production, concession, revenue-sharing, and other similar contracts;

(f) intellectual property rights;

(g) licenses, authorizations, permits, and similar rights conferred pursuant to domestic law;[2, 3] and

(h) other tangible or intangible, movable or immovable property, and related property rights, such as leases, mortgages, liens, and pledges.

---

[1] Some forms of debt, such as bonds, debentures, and long-term notes, are more likely to have the characteristics of an investment, while other forms of debt, such as claims to payment that are immediately due and result from the sale of goods or services, are less likely to have such characteristics.

[2] Whether a particular type of license, authorization, permit, or similar instrument (including a concession, to the extent that it has the nature of such an instrument) has the characteristics of an investment depends on such factors as the nature and extent of the rights that the holder has under the law of the Party. Among the licenses, authorizations, permits, and similar instruments that do not have the characteristics of an investment are those that do not create any rights protected under domestic law. For greater certainty, the foregoing is without prejudice to whether any asset associated with the license, authorization, permit, or similar instrument has the characteristics of an investment.

[3] The term "investment" does not include an order or judgment entered in a judicial or administrative action.

"**investment agreement**" means a written agreement[4] between a national authority[5] of a Party and a covered investment or an investor of the other Party, on which the covered investment or the investor relies in establishing or acquiring a covered investment other than the written agreement itself, that grants rights to the covered investment or investor:

    (a) with respect to natural resources that a national authority controls, such as for their exploration, extraction, refining, transportation, distribution, or sale;

    (b) to supply services to the public on behalf of the Party, such as power generation or distribution, water treatment or distribution, or telecommunications; or

    (c) to undertake infrastructure projects, such as the construction of roads, bridges, canals, dams, or pipelines, that are not for the exclusive or predominant use and benefit of the government.

"**investment authorization**"[6] means an authorization that the foreign investment authority of a Party grants to a covered investment or an investor of the other Party.

"**investor of a non-Party**" means, with respect to a Party, an investor that attempts to make, is making, or has made an investment in the territory of that Party, that is not an investor of either Party.

"**investor of a Party**" means a Party or state enterprise thereof, or a national or an enterprise of a Party, that attempts to make, is making, or has made an investment in the territory of the other Party; provided, however, that a natural person who is a dual national shall be deemed to be exclusively a national of the State of his or her dominant and effective nationality.

"**measure**" includes any law, regulation, procedure, requirement, or practice.

"**national**" means:

    (a) for the United States, a natural person who is a national of the United States as defined in Title III of the Immigration and Nationality Act; and

    (b) for [Country], [____].

"**New York Convention**" means the *United Nations Convention on the Recognition and Enforcement of Foreign Arbitral Awards,* done at New York, June 10, 1958.

"**non-disputing Party**" means the Party that is not a party to an investment dispute.

"**person**" means a natural person or an enterprise.

"**person of a Party**" means a national or an enterprise of a Party.

"**protected information**" means confidential business information or information that is privileged or otherwise protected from disclosure under a Party's law.

"**regional level of government**" means:

    (a) for the United States, a state of the United States, the District of Columbia, or Puerto Rico; and

    (b) for [Country], [____].

---

[4] "Written agreement" refers to an agreement in writing, executed by both parties, whether in a single instrument or in multiple instruments, that creates an exchange of rights and obligations, binding on both parties under the law applicable under Article 30[Governing Law](2). For greater certainty, (a) a unilateral act of an administrative or judicial authority, such as a permit, license, or authorization issued by a Party solely in its regulatory capacity, or a decree, order, or judgment, standing alone; and (b) an administrative or judicial consent decree or order, shall not be considered a written agreement.

[5] For purposes of this definition, "national authority" means (a) for the United States, an authority at the central level of government; and (b) for [Country], [ ].

[6] For greater certainty, actions taken by a Party to enforce laws of general application, such as competition laws, are not encompassed within this definition.

"**respondent**" means the Party that is a party to an investment dispute.

"**Secretary-General**" means the Secretary-General of ICSID.

"**state enterprise**" means an enterprise owned, or controlled through ownership interests, by a Party.

"**territory**" means:
- (a) with respect to the United States,
    - (i) the customs territory of the United States, which includes the 50 states, the District of Columbia, and Puerto Rico;
    - (ii) the foreign trade zones located in the United States and Puerto Rico.
- (b) with respect to [Country,] [_____].
- (c) with respect to each Party, the territorial sea and any area beyond the territorial sea of the Party within which, in accordance with customary international law as reflected in the United Nations Convention on the Law of the Sea, the Party may exercise sovereign rights or jurisdiction.

"**TRIPS Agreement**" means the *Agreement on Trade-Related Aspects of Intellectual Property Rights*, contained in Annex 1C to the WTO Agreement.[7]

"**UNCITRAL Arbitration Rules**" means the arbitration rules of the United Nations Commission on International Trade Law.

"**WTO Agreement**" means the *Marrakesh Agreement Establishing the World Trade Organization*, done on April 15, 1994.

Article 2
Scope and Coverage

1. This Treaty applies to measures adopted or maintained by a Party relating to:
   - (a) investors of the other Party;
   - (b) covered investments; and
   - (c) with respect to Articles 8 [Performance Requirements], 12 [Investment and Environment], and 13 [Investment and Labor], all investments in the territory of the Party.
2. A Party's obligations under Section A shall apply:
   - (a) to a state enterprise or other person when it exercises any regulatory, administrative, or other governmental authority delegated to it by that Party;[8] and
   - (b) to the political subdivisions of that Party.
3. For greater certainty, this Treaty does not bind either Party in relation to any act or fact that took place or any situation that ceased to exist before the date of entry into force of this Treaty.

Article 3
National Treatment

1. Each Party shall accord to investors of the other Party treatment no less favorable than that it accords, in like circumstances, to its own investors with respect to the establishment, acquisition, expansion, management, conduct, operation, and sale or other disposition of investments in its territory.

---

[7] For greater certainty, "TRIPS Agreement" includes any waiver in force between the Parties of any provision of the TRIPS Agreement granted by WTO Members in accordance with the WTO Agreement.

[8] For greater certainty, government authority that has been delegated includes a legislative grant, and a government order, directive or other action transferring to the state enterprise or other person, or authorizing the exercise by the state enterprise or other person of, governmental authority.

2. Each Party shall accord to covered investments treatment no less favorable than that it accords, in like circumstances, to investments in its territory of its own investors with respect to the establishment, acquisition, expansion, management, conduct, operation, and sale or other disposition of investments.

3. The treatment to be accorded by a Party under paragraphs 1 and 2 means, with respect to a regional level of government, treatment no less favorable than the treatment accorded, in like circumstances, by that regional level of government to natural persons resident in and enterprises constituted under the laws of other regional levels of government of the Party of which it forms a part, and to their respective investments.

Article 4
Most-Favored-Nation Treatment

1. Each Party shall accord to investors of the other Party treatment no less favorable than that it accords, in like circumstances, to investors of any non-Party with respect to the establishment, acquisition, expansion, management, conduct, operation, and sale or other disposition of investments in its territory.

2. Each Party shall accord to covered investments treatment no less favorable than that it accords, in like circumstances, to investments in its territory of investors of any non-Party with respect to the establishment, acquisition, expansion, management, conduct, operation, and sale or other disposition of investments.

Article 5
Minimum Standard of Treatment[9]

1. Each Party shall accord to covered investments treatment in accordance with customary international law, including fair and equitable treatment and full protection and security.

2. For greater certainty, paragraph 1 prescribes the customary international law minimum standard of treatment of aliens as the minimum standard of treatment to be afforded to covered investments. The concepts of "fair and equitable treatment" and "full protection and security" do not require treatment in addition to or beyond that which is required by that standard, and do not create additional substantive rights. The obligation in paragraph 1 to provide:
   (a) "fair and equitable treatment" includes the obligation not to deny justice in criminal, civil, or administrative adjudicatory proceedings in accordance with the principle of due process embodied in the principal legal systems of the world; and
   (b) "full protection and security" requires each Party to provide the level of police protection required under customary international law.

3. A determination that there has been a breach of another provision of this Treaty, or of a separate international agreement, does not establish that there has been a breach of this Article.

4. Notwithstanding Article 14 [Non-Conforming Measures](5)(b) [subsidies and grants], each Party shall accord to investors of the other Party, and to covered investments, non-discriminatory treatment with respect to measures it adopts or maintains relating to losses suffered by investments in its territory owing to armed conflict or civil strife.

5. Notwithstanding paragraph 4, if an investor of a Party, in the situations referred to in paragraph 4, suffers a loss in the territory of the other Party resulting from:
   (a) requisitioning of its covered investment or part thereof by the latter's forces or authorities; or

---

[9] Article 5 [Minimum Standard of Treatment] shall be interpreted in accordance with Annex A.

(b) destruction of its covered investment or part thereof by the latter's forces or authorities, which was not required by the necessity of the situation,

the latter Party shall provide the investor restitution, compensation, or both, as appropriate, for such loss. Any compensation shall be prompt, adequate, and effective in accordance with Article 6[Expropriation and Compensation](2) through (4), *mutatis mutandis.*

6. Paragraph 4 does not apply to existing measures relating to subsidies or grants that would be inconsistent with Article 3 [National Treatment] but for Article 14 [Non-Conforming Measures](5)(b) [subsidies and grants].

Article 6
Expropriation and Compensation[10]

1. Neither Party may expropriate or nationalize a covered investment either directly or indirectly through measures equivalent to expropriation or nationalization ("expropriation"), except:
   (a) for a public purpose;
   (b) in a non-discriminatory manner;
   (c) on payment of prompt, adequate, and effective compensation; and
   (d) in accordance with due process of law and Article 5 [Minimum Standard of Treatment](1) through (3).

2. The compensation referred to in paragraph 1(c) shall:
   (a) be paid without delay;
   (b) be equivalent to the fair market value of the expropriated investment immediately before the expropriation took place ("the date of expropriation");
   (c) not reflect any change in value occurring because the intended expropriation had become known earlier; and
   (d) be fully realizable and freely transferable.

3. If the fair market value is denominated in a freely usable currency, the compensation referred to in paragraph 1(c) shall be no less than the fair market value on the date of expropriation, plus interest at a commercially reasonable rate for that currency, accrued from the date of expropriation until the date of payment.

4. If the fair market value is denominated in a currency that is not freely usable, the compensation referred to in paragraph 1(c) - converted into the currency of payment at the market rate of exchange prevailing on the date of payment - shall be no less than:
   (a) the fair market value on the date of expropriation, converted into a freely usable currency at the market rate of exchange prevailing on that date, plus
   (b) interest, at a commercially reasonable rate for that freely usable currency, accrued from the date of expropriation until the date of payment.

5. This Article does not apply to the issuance of compulsory licenses granted in relation to intellectual property rights in accordance with the TRIPS Agreement, or to the revocation, limitation, or creation of intellectual property rights, to the extent that such issuance, revocation, limitation, or creation is consistent with the TRIPS Agreement.

Article 7
Transfers

1. Each Party shall permit all transfers relating to a covered investment to be made freely and without delay into and out of its territory. Such transfers include:

---

[10] Article 6 [Expropriation] shall be interpreted in accordance with Annexes A and B.

(a) contributions to capital;

(b) profits, dividends, capital gains, and proceeds from the sale of all or any part of the covered investment or from the partial or complete liquidation of the covered investment;

(c) interest, royalty payments, management fees, and technical assistance and other fees;

(d) payments made under a contract, including a loan agreement;

(e) payments made pursuant to Article 5 [Minimum Standard of Treatment](4) and (5) and Article 6 [Expropriation and Compensation]; and

(f) payments arising out of a dispute.

2. Each Party shall permit transfers relating to a covered investment to be made in a freely usable currency at the market rate of exchange prevailing at the time of transfer.

3. Each Party shall permit returns in kind relating to a covered investment to be made as authorized or specified in a written agreement between the Party and a covered investment or an investor of the other Party.

4. Notwithstanding paragraphs 1 through 3, a Party may prevent a transfer through the equitable, non-discriminatory, and good faith application of its laws relating to:

(a) bankruptcy, insolvency, or the protection of the rights of creditors;

(b) issuing, trading, or dealing in securities, futures, options, or derivatives;

(c) criminal or penal offenses;

(d) financial reporting or record keeping of transfers when necessary to assist law enforcement or financial regulatory authorities; or

(e) ensuring compliance with orders or judgments in judicial or administrative proceedings.

Article 8
Performance Requirements

1. Neither Party may, in connection with the establishment, acquisition, expansion, management, conduct, operation, or sale or other disposition of an investment of an investor of a Party or of a non-Party in its territory, impose or enforce any requirement or enforce any commitment or undertaking:[11]

(a) to export a given level or percentage of goods or services;

(b) to achieve a given level or percentage of domestic content;

(c) to purchase, use, or accord a preference to goods produced in its territory, or to purchase goods from persons in its territory;

(d) to relate in any way the volume or value of imports to the volume or value of exports or to the amount of foreign exchange inflows associated with such investment;

(e) to restrict sales of goods or services in its territory that such investment produces or supplies by relating such sales in any way to the volume or value of its exports or foreign exchange earnings;

(f) to transfer a particular technology, a production process, or other proprietary knowledge to a person in its territory;

(g) to supply exclusively from the territory of the Party the goods that such investment produces or the services that it supplies to a specific regional market or to the world market; or

---

[11] For greater certainty, a condition for the receipt or continued receipt of an advantage referred to in paragraph 2 does not constitute a "commitment or undertaking" for the purposes of paragraph 1.

(h) (i) to purchase, use, or accord a preference to, in its territory, technology of the Party or of persons of the Party[12]; or

   (ii) that prevents the purchase or use of, or the according of a preference to, in its territory, particular technology,

so as to afford protection on the basis of nationality to its own investors or investments or to technology of the Party or of persons of the Party.

2. Neither Party may condition the receipt or continued receipt of an advantage, in connection with the establishment, acquisition, expansion, management, conduct, operation, or sale or other disposition of an investment in its territory of an investor of a Party or of a non-Party, on compliance with any requirement:

   (a) to achieve a given level or percentage of domestic content;

   (b) to purchase, use, or accord a preference to goods produced in its territory, or to purchase goods from persons in its territory;

   (c) to relate in any way the volume or value of imports to the volume or value of exports or to the amount of foreign exchange inflows associated with such investment; or

   (d) to restrict sales of goods or services in its territory that such investment produces or supplies by relating such sales in any way to the volume or value of its exports or foreign exchange earnings.

3. (a) Nothing in paragraph 2 shall be construed to prevent a Party from conditioning the receipt or continued receipt of an advantage, in connection with an investment in its territory of an investor of a Party or of a non-Party, on compliance with a requirement to locate production, supply a service, train or employ workers, construct or expand particular facilities, or carry out research and development, in its territory.

   (b) Paragraphs 1(f) and (h) do not apply:

      (i) when a Party authorizes use of an intellectual property right in accordance with Article 31 of the TRIPS Agreement, or to measures requiring the disclosure of proprietary information that fall within the scope of, and are consistent with, Article 39 of the TRIPS Agreement; or

      (ii) when the requirement is imposed or the commitment or undertaking is enforced by a court, administrative tribunal, or competition authority to remedy a practice determined after judicial or administrative process to be anticompetitive under the Party's competition laws.[13]

   (c) Provided that such measures are not applied in an arbitrary or unjustifiable manner, and provided that such measures do not constitute a disguised restriction on international trade or investment, paragraphs 1(b), (c), (f), and (h), and 2(a) and (b), shall not be construed to prevent a Party from adopting or maintaining measures, including environmental measures:

      (i) necessary to secure compliance with laws and regulations that are not inconsistent with this Treaty;

      (ii) necessary to protect human, animal, or plant life or health; or

      (iii) related to the conservation of living or non-living exhaustible natural resources.

---

[12] For purposes of this Article, the term "technology of the Party or of persons of the Party" includes technology that is owned by the Party or persons of the Party, and technology for which the Party holds, or persons of the Party hold, an exclusive license.

[13] The Parties recognize that a patent does not necessarily confer market power.

(d) Paragraphs 1(a), (b), and (c), and 2(a) and (b), do not apply to qualification requirements for goods or services with respect to export promotion and foreign aid programs.

(e) Paragraphs 1(b), (c), (f), (g), and (h), and 2(a) and (b), do not apply to government procurement.

(f) Paragraphs 2(a) and (b) do not apply to requirements imposed by an importing Party relating to the content of goods necessary to qualify for preferential tariffs or preferential quotas.

4. For greater certainty, paragraphs 1 and 2 do not apply to any commitment, undertaking, or requirement other than those set out in those paragraphs.

5. This Article does not preclude enforcement of any commitment, undertaking, or requirement between private parties, where a Party did not impose or require the commitment, undertaking, or requirement.

Article 9
Senior Management and Boards of Directors

1. Neither Party may require that an enterprise of that Party that is a covered investment appoint to senior management positions natural persons of any particular nationality.

2. A Party may require that a majority of the board of directors, or any committee thereof, of an enterprise of that Party that is a covered investment, be of a particular nationality, or resident in the territory of the Party, provided that the requirement does not materially impair the ability of the investor to exercise control over its investment.

Article 10
Publication of Laws and Decisions Respecting Investment

1. Each Party shall ensure that its:
   (a) laws, regulations, procedures, and administrative rulings of general application; and
   (b) adjudicatory decisions
   respecting any matter covered by this Treaty are promptly published or otherwise made publicly available.

2. For purposes of this Article, "administrative ruling of general application" means an administrative ruling or interpretation that applies to all persons and fact situations that fall generally within its ambit and that establishes a norm of conduct but does not include:
   (a) a determination or ruling made in an administrative or quasi-judicial proceeding that applies to a particular covered investment or investor of the other Party in a specific case; or
   (b) a ruling that adjudicates with respect to a particular act or practice.

Article 11
Transparency

1. The Parties agree to consult periodically on ways to improve the transparency practices set out in this Article, Article 10 and Article 29.

2. Publication
   To the extent possible, each Party shall:
   (a) publish in advance any measure referred to in Article 10(1)(a) that it proposes to adopt; and

    (b) provide interested persons and the other Party a reasonable opportunity to comment on such proposed measures.

3. With respect to proposed regulations of general application of its central level of government respecting any matter covered by this Treaty that are published in accordance with paragraph 2(a), each Party:

    (a) shall publish the proposed regulations in a single official journal of national circulation and shall encourage their distribution through additional outlets;

    (b) should in most cases publish the proposed regulations not less than 60 days before the date public comments are due;

    (c) shall include in the publication an explanation of the purpose of and rationale for the proposed regulations; and

    (d) shall, at the time it adopts final regulations, address significant, substantive comments received during the comment period and explain substantive revisions that it made to the proposed regulations in its official journal or in a prominent location on a government Internet site.

4. With respect to regulations of general application that are adopted by its central level of government respecting any matter covered by this Treaty, each Party:

    (a) shall publish the regulations in a single official journal of national circulation and shall encourage their distribution through additional outlets; and

    (b) shall include in the publication an explanation of the purpose of and rationale for the regulations.

5. Provision of Information

    (a) On request of the other Party, a Party shall promptly provide information and respond to questions pertaining to any actual or proposed measure that the requesting Party considers might materially affect the operation of this Treaty or otherwise substantially affect its interests under this Treaty.

    (b) Any request or information under this paragraph shall be provided to the other Party through the relevant contact points.

    (c) Any information provided under this paragraph shall be without prejudice as to whether the measure is consistent with this Treaty.

6. Administrative Proceedings

With a view to administering in a consistent, impartial, and reasonable manner all measures referred to in Article 10(1)(a), each Party shall ensure that in its administrative proceedings applying such measures to particular covered investments or investors of the other Party in specific cases:

    (a) wherever possible, covered investments or investors of the other Party that are directly affected by a proceeding are provided reasonable notice, in accordance with domestic procedures, when a proceeding is initiated, including a description of the nature of the proceeding, a statement of the legal authority under which the proceeding is initiated, and a general description of any issues in controversy;

    (b) such persons are afforded a reasonable opportunity to present facts and arguments in support of their positions prior to any final administrative action, when time, the nature of the proceeding, and the public interest permit; and

    (c) its procedures are in accordance with domestic law.

7. Review and Appeal

    (a) Each Party shall establish or maintain judicial, quasi-judicial, or administrative tribunals or procedures for the purpose of the prompt review and, where warranted, correction of final administrative actions regarding matters covered by this Treaty.

Such tribunals shall be impartial and independent of the office or authority entrusted with administrative enforcement and shall not have any substantial interest in the outcome of the matter.

(b) Each Party shall ensure that, in any such tribunals or procedures, the parties to the proceeding are provided with the right to:
    (i) a reasonable opportunity to support or defend their respective positions; and
    (ii) a decision based on the evidence and submissions of record or, where required by domestic law, the record compiled by the administrative authority.

(c) Each Party shall ensure, subject to appeal or further review as provided in its domestic law, that such decisions shall be implemented by, and shall govern the practice of, the offices or authorities with respect to the administrative action at issue.

8. Standards-Setting
(a) Each Party shall allow persons of the other Party to participate in the development of standards and technical regulations by its central government bodies.[14] Each Party shall allow persons of the other Party to participate in the development of these measures, and the development of conformity assessment procedures by its central government bodies, on terms no less favorable than those it accords to its own persons.

(b) Each Party shall recommend that non-governmental standardizing bodies in its territory allow persons of the other Party to participate in the development of standards by those bodies. Each Party shall recommend that non-governmental standardizing bodies in its territory allow persons of the other Party to participate in the development of these standards, and the development of conformity assessment procedures by those bodies, on terms no less favorable than those they accord to persons of the Party.

(c) Subparagraphs 8(a) and 8(b) do not apply to:
    (i) sanitary and phytosanitary measures as defined in Annex A of the World Trade Organization (WTO) Agreement on the Application of Sanitary and Phytosanitary Measures; or
    (ii) purchasing specifications prepared by a governmental body for its production or consumption requirements.

(d) For purposes of subparagraphs 8(a) and 8(b), "central government body", "standards", "technical regulations" and "conformity assessment procedures" have the meanings assigned to those terms in Annex 1 of the WTO Agreement on Technical Barriers to Trade. Consistent with Annex 1, the three latter terms do not include standards, technical regulations or conformity assessment procedures 'for the supply of a service.

Article 12
Investment and Environment

1. The Parties recognize that their respective environmental laws and policies, and multilateral environmental agreements to which they are both party, play an important role in protecting the environment.

2. The Parties recognize that it is inappropriate to encourage investment by weakening or reducing the protections afforded in domestic environmental laws. Accordingly, each

---

[14] A Party may satisfy this obligation by, for example, providing interested persons a reasonable opportunity to provide comments on the measure it proposes to develop and taking those comments into account in the development of the measure.

Party shall ensure that it does not waive or otherwise derogate from or offer to waive or otherwise derogate from its environmental laws[15] in a manner that weakens or reduces the protections afforded in those laws, or fail to effectively enforce those laws through a sustained or recurring course of action or inaction, as an encouragement for the establishment, acquisition, expansion, or retention of an investment in its territory.

3. The Parties recognize that each Party retains the right to exercise discretion with respect to regulatory, compliance, investigatory, and prosecutorial matters, and to make decisions regarding the allocation of resources to enforcement with respect to other environmental matters determined to have higher priorities. Accordingly, the Parties understand that a Party is in compliance with paragraph 2 where a course of action or inaction reflects a reasonable exercise of such discretion, or results from a *bona fide* decision regarding the allocation of resources.

4. For purposes of this Article, "environmental law" means each Party's statutes or regulations,[16] or provisions thereof, the primary purpose of which is the protection of the environment, or the prevention of a danger to human, animal, or plant life or health, through the:

   (a) prevention, abatement, or control of the release, discharge, or emission of pollutants or environmental contaminants;

   (b) control of environmentally hazardous or toxic chemicals, substances, materials, and wastes, and the dissemination of information related thereto; or

   (c) protection or conservation of wild flora or fauna, including endangered species, their habitat, and specially protected natural areas,

   in the Party's territory, but does not include any statute or regulation, or provision thereof, directly related to worker safety or health.

5. Nothing in this Treaty shall be construed to prevent a Party from adopting, maintaining, or enforcing any measure otherwise consistent with this Treaty that it considers appropriate to ensure that investment activity in its territory is undertaken in a manner sensitive to environmental concerns.

6. A Party may make a written request for consultations with the other Party regarding any matter arising under this Article. The other Party shall respond to a request for consultations within thirty days of receipt of such request. Thereafter, the Parties shall consult and endeavor to reach a mutually satisfactory resolution.

7. The Parties confirm that each Party may, as appropriate, provide opportunities for public participation regarding any matter arising under this Article.

Article 13
Investment and Labor

1. The Parties reaffirm their respective obligations as members of the International Labor Organization ("ILO") and their commitments under the *ILO Declaration on Fundamental Principles and Rights at Work and its Follow-Up*.

---

[15] Paragraph 2 shall not apply where a Party waives or derogates from an environmental law pursuant to a provision in law providing for waivers or derogations.

[16] For the United States, "statutes or regulations" for the purposes of this Article means an act of the United States Congress or regulations promulgated pursuant to an act of the United States Congress that is enforceable by action of the central level of government.

2. The Parties recognize that it is inappropriate to encourage investment by weakening or reducing the protections afforded in domestic labor laws. Accordingly, each Party shall ensure that it does not waive or otherwise derogate from or offer to waive or otherwise derogate from its labor laws where the waiver or derogation would be inconsistent with the labor rights referred to in subparagraphs (a) through (e) of paragraph 3, or fail to effectively enforce its labor laws through a sustained or recurring course of action or inaction, as an encouragement for the establishment, acquisition, expansion, or retention of an investment in its territory.

3. For purposes of this Article, "labor laws" means each Party's statutes or regulations,[17] or provisions thereof, that are directly related to the following:
   (a) freedom of association;
   (b) the effective recognition of the right to collective bargaining;
   (c) the elimination of all forms of forced or compulsory labor;
   (d) the effective abolition of child labor and a prohibition on the worst forms of child labor;
   (e) the elimination of discrimination in respect of employment and occupation; and
   (f) acceptable conditions of work with respect to minimum wages, hours of work, and occupational safety and health.

4. A Party may make a written request for consultations with the other Party regarding any matter arising under this Article. The other Party shall respond to a request for consultations within thirty days of receipt of such request. Thereafter, the Parties shall consult and endeavor to reach a mutually satisfactory resolution.

5. The Parties confirm that each Party may, as appropriate, provide opportunities for public participation regarding any matter arising under this Article.

Article 14
Non-Conforming Measures

1. Articles 3 [National Treatment], 4 [Most-Favored-Nation Treatment], 8 [Performance Requirements], and 9 [Senior Management and Boards of Directors] do not apply to:
   (a) any existing non-conforming measure that is maintained by a Party at:
      (i) the central level of government, as set out by that Party in its Schedule to Annex I or Annex III,
      (ii) a regional level of government, as set out by that Party in its Schedule to Annex I or Annex III, or
      (iii) a local level of government;
   (b) the continuation or prompt renewal of any non-conforming measure referred to in subparagraph (a); or
   (c) an amendment to any non-conforming measure referred to in subparagraph (a) to the extent that the amendment does not decrease the conformity of the measure, as it existed immediately before the amendment, with Article 3 [National Treatment], 4 [Most-Favored-Nation Treatment], 8 [Performance Requirements], or 9 [Senior Management and Boards of Directors].

2. Articles 3 [National Treatment], 4 [Most-Favored-Nation Treatment], 8 [Performance Requirements], and 9 [Senior Management and Boards of Directors] do not apply to any

---

[17] For the United States, "statutes or regulations" for purposes of this Article means an act of the United States Congress or regulations promulgated pursuant to an act of the United States Congress that is enforceable by action of the central level of government.

measure that a Party adopts or maintains with respect to sectors, subsectors, or activities, as set out in its Schedule to Annex II.

3. Neither Party may, under any measure adopted after the date of entry into force of this Treaty and covered by its Schedule to Annex II, require an investor of the other Party, by reason of its nationality, to sell or otherwise dispose of an investment existing at the time the measure becomes effective.

4. Articles 3 [National Treatment] and 4 [Most-Favored-Nation Treatment] do not apply to any measure covered by an exception to, or derogation from, the obligations under Article 3 or 4 of the TRIPS Agreement, as specifically provided in those Articles and in Article 5 of the TRIPS Agreement.

5. Articles 3 [National Treatment], 4 [Most-Favored-Nation Treatment], and 9 [Senior Management and Boards of Directors] do not apply to:
   (a) government procurement; or
   (b) subsidies or grants provided by a Party, including government-supported loans, guarantees, and insurance.

Article 15
Special Formalities and Information Requirements

1. Nothing in Article 3 [National Treatment] shall be construed to prevent a Party from adopting or maintaining a measure that prescribes special formalities in connection with covered investments, such as a requirement that investors be residents of the Party or that covered investments be legally constituted under the laws or regulations of the Party, provided that such formalities do not materially impair the protections afforded by a Party to investors of the other Party and covered investments pursuant to this Treaty.

2. Notwithstanding Articles 3 [National Treatment] and 4 [Most-Favored-Nation Treatment], a Party may require an investor of the other Party or its covered investment to provide information concerning that investment solely for informational or statistical purposes. The Party shall protect any confidential business information from any disclosure that would prejudice the competitive position of the investor or the covered investment. Nothing in this paragraph shall be construed to prevent a Party from otherwise obtaining or disclosing information in connection with the equitable and good faith application of its law.

Article 16
Non-Derogation

This Treaty shall not derogate from any of the following that entitle an investor of a Party or a covered investment to treatment more favorable than that accorded by this Treaty:
1. laws or regulations, administrative practices or procedures, or administrative or adjudicatory decisions of a Party;
2. international legal obligations of a Party; or
3. obligations assumed by a Party, including those contained in an investment authorization or an investment agreement.

Article 17
Denial of Benefits

1. A Party may deny the benefits of this Treaty to an investor of the other Party that is an enterprise of such other Party and to investments of that investor if persons of a non-Party own or control the enterprise and the denying Party:
   (a) does not maintain diplomatic relations with the non-Party; or

(b) adopts or maintains measures with respect to the non-Party or a person of the nonParty that prohibit transactions with the enterprise or that would be violated or circumvented if the benefits of this Treaty were accorded to the enterprise or to its investments.

2. A Party may deny the benefits of this Treaty to an investor of the other Party that is an enterprise of such other Party and to investments of that investor if the enterprise has no substantial business activities in the territory of the other Party and persons of a non-Party, or of the denying Party, own or control the enterprise.

Article 18
Essential Security

Nothing in this Treaty shall be construed:

1. to require a Party to furnish or allow access to any information the disclosure of which it determines to be contrary to its essential security interests; or

2. to preclude a Party from applying measures that it considers necessary for the fulfillment of its obligations with respect to the maintenance or restoration of international peace or security, or the protection of its own essential security interests.

Article 19
Disclosure of Information

Nothing in this Treaty shall be construed to require a Party to furnish or allow access to confidential information the disclosure of which would impede law enforcement or otherwise be contrary to the public interest, or which would prejudice the legitimate commercial interests of particular enterprises, public or private.

Article 20
Financial Services

1. Notwithstanding any other provision of this Treaty, a Party shall not be prevented from adopting or maintaining measures relating to financial services for prudential reasons, including for the protection of investors, depositors, policy holders, or persons to whom a fiduciary duty is owed by a financial services supplier, or to ensure the integrity and stability of the financial system.[18] Where such measures do not conform with the provisions of this Treaty, they shall not be used as a means of avoiding the Party's commitments or obligations under this Treaty.

2. (a) Nothing in this Treaty applies to non-discriminatory measures of general application taken by any public entity in pursuit of monetary and related credit policies or exchange rate policies. This paragraph shall not affect a Party's obligations under Article 7 [Transfers] or Article 8 [Performance Requirements].[19]

    (b) For purposes of this paragraph, "public entity" means a central bank or monetary authority of a Party.

3. Where a claimant submits a claim to arbitration under Section B [Investor-State Dispute Settlement], and the respondent invokes paragraph 1 or 2 as a defense, the following provisions shall apply:

---

[18] It is understood that the term "prudential reasons" includes the maintenance of the safety, soundness, integrity, or financial responsibility of individual financial institutions, as well as the maintenance of the safety and financial and operational integrity of payment and clearing systems.

[19] For greater certainty, measures of general application taken in pursuit of monetary and related credit policies or exchange rate policies do not include measures that expressly nullify or amend contractual provisions that specify the currency of denomination or the rate of exchange of currencies.

(a) The respondent shall, within 120 days of the date the claim is submitted to arbitration under Section B, submit in writing to the competent financial authorities[20] of both Parties a request for a joint determination on the issue of whether and to what extent paragraph 1 or 2 is a valid defense to the claim. The respondent shall promptly provide the tribunal, if constituted, a copy of such request. The arbitration may proceed with respect to the claim only as provided in subparagraph (d).

(b) The competent financial authorities of both Parties shall make themselves available for consultations with each other and shall attempt in good faith to make a determination as described in subparagraph (a). Any such determination shall be transmitted promptly to the disputing parties and, if constituted, to the tribunal. The determination shall be binding on the tribunal.

(c) If the competent financial authorities of both Parties, within 120 days of the date by which they have both received the respondent's written request for a joint determination under subparagraph (a), have not made a determination as described in that subparagraph, the tribunal shall decide the issue or issues left unresolved by the competent financial authorities. The provisions of Section B shall apply, except as modified by this subparagraph.

    (i) In the appointment of all arbitrators not yet appointed to the tribunal, each disputing party shall take appropriate steps to ensure that the tribunal has expertise or experience in financial services law or practice. The expertise of particular candidates with respect to the particular sector of financial services in which the dispute arises shall be taken into account in the appointment of the presiding arbitrator.

    (ii) If, before the respondent submits the request for a joint determination in conformance with subparagraph (a), the presiding arbitrator has been appointed pursuant to Article 27(3), such arbitrator shall be replaced on the request of either disputing party and the tribunal shall be reconstituted consistent with subparagraph (c)(i). If, within 30 days of the date the arbitration proceedings are resumed under subparagraph (d), the disputing parties have not agreed on the appointment of a new presiding arbitrator, the Secretary-General, on the request of a disputing party, shall appoint the presiding arbitrator consistent with subparagraph (c)(i).

    (iii) The tribunal shall draw no inference regarding the application of paragraph 1 or 2 from the fact that the competent financial authorities have not made a determination as described in subparagraph (a).

    (iv) The non-disputing Party may make oral and written submissions to the tribunal regarding the issue of whether and to what extent paragraph 1 or 2 is a valid defense to the claim. Unless it makes such a submission, the non-disputing Party shall be presumed, for purposes of the arbitration, to take a position on paragraph 1 or 2 not inconsistent with that of the respondent.

(d) The arbitration referred to in subparagraph (a) may proceed with respect to the claim:

    (i) 10 days after the date the competent financial authorities' joint determination has been received by both the disputing parties and, if constituted, the tribunal; or

---

[20] For purposes of this Article, "competent financial authorities" means, for the United States, the Department of the Treasury for banking and other financial services, and the Office of the United States Trade Representative, in coordination with the Department of Commerce and other agencies, for insurance; and for [Country], [ ].

(ii) 10 days after the expiration of the 120-day period provided to the competent financial authorities in subparagraph (c).

(e) On the request of the respondent made within 30 days after the expiration of the 120-day period for a joint determination referred to in subparagraph (c), or, if the tribunal has not been constituted as of the expiration of the 120-day period, within 30 days after the tribunal is constituted, the tribunal shall address and decide the issue or issues left unresolved by the competent financial authorities as referred to in subparagraph (c) prior to deciding the merits of the claim for which paragraph 1or 2 has been invoked by the respondent as a defense. Failure of the respondent to make such a request is without prejudice to the right of the respondent to invoke paragraph 1 or 2 as a defense at any appropriate phase of the arbitration.

4. Where a dispute arises under Section C and the competent financial authorities of one Party provide written notice to the competent financial authorities of the other Party that the dispute involves financial services, Section C shall apply except as modified by this paragraph and paragraph 5.

(a) The competent financial authorities of both Parties shall make themselves available for consultations with each other regarding the dispute, and shall have 180 days from the date such notice is received to transmit a report on their consultations to the Parties. A Party may submit the dispute to arbitration under Section C only after the expiration of that 180-day period.

(b) Either Party may make any such report available to a tribunal constituted under Section C to decide the dispute referred to in this paragraph or a similar dispute, or to a tribunal constituted under Section B to decide a claim arising out of the same events or circumstances that gave rise to the dispute under Section C.

5. Where a Party submits a dispute involving financial services to arbitration under Section C in conformance with paragraph 4, and on the request of either Party within 30 days of the date the dispute is submitted to arbitration, each Party shall, in the appointment of all arbitrators not yet appointed, take appropriate steps to ensure that the tribunal has expertise or experience in financial services law or practice. The expertise of particular candidates with respect to financial services shall be taken into account in the appointment of the presiding arbitrator.

6. Notwithstanding Article 11(2)-(4) [Transparency - Publication], each Party, to the extent practicable,

(a) shall publish in advance any regulations of general application relating to financial services that it proposes to adopt and the purpose of the regulation;

(b) shall provide interested persons and the other Party a reasonable opportunity to comment on such proposed regulations; and

(c) should at the time it adopts final regulations, address in writing significant substantive comments received from interested persons with respect to the proposed regulations.

7. The terms "financial service" or "financial services" shall have the same meaning as in subparagraph 5(a) of the Annex on Financial Services of the GATS.

8. For greater certainty, nothing in this Treaty shall be construed to prevent the adoption or enforcement by a party of measures relating to investors of the other Party, or covered investments, in financial institutions that are necessary to secure compliance with laws or regulations that are not inconsistent with this Treaty, including those related to the prevention of deceptive and fraudulent practices or that deal with the effects of a default on financial services contracts, subject to the requirement that such measures are not applied in a manner which would constitute a means of arbitrary or unjustifiable

discrimination between countries where like conditions prevail, or a disguised restriction on investment in financial institutions.

Article 21
Taxation

1. Except as provided in this Article, nothing in Section A shall impose obligations with respect to taxation measures.
2. Article 6 [Expropriation] shall apply to all taxation measures, except that a claimant that asserts that a taxation measure involves an expropriation may submit a claim to arbitration under Section B only if:
   (a) the claimant has first referred to the competent tax authorities[21] of both Parties in writing the issue of whether that taxation measure involves an expropriation; and
   (b) within 180 days after the date of such referral, the competent tax authorities of both Parties fail to agree that the taxation measure is not an expropriation.
3. Subject to paragraph 4, Article 8 [Performance Requirements] (2) through (4) shall apply to all taxation measures.
4. Nothing in this Treaty shall affect the rights and obligations of either Party under any tax convention. In the event of any inconsistency between this Treaty and any such convention, that convention shall prevail to the extent of the inconsistency. In the case of a tax convention between the Parties, the competent authorities under that convention shall have sole responsibility for determining whether any inconsistency exists between this Treaty and that convention.

Article 22
Entry into Force, Duration, and Termination

1. This Treaty shall enter into force thirty days after the date the Parties exchange instruments of ratification. It shall remain in force for a period of ten years and shall continue in force thereafter unless terminated in accordance with paragraph 2.
2. A Party may terminate this Treaty at the end of the initial ten-year period or at any time thereafter by giving one year's written notice to the other Party.
3. For ten years from the date of termination, all other Articles shall continue to apply to covered investments established or acquired prior to the date of termination, except insofar as those Articles extend to the establishment or acquisition of covered investments.

Section B
Article 23
Consultation and Negotiation

In the event of an investment dispute, the claimant and the respondent should initially seek to resolve the dispute through consultation and negotiation, which may include the use of nonbinding, third-party procedures.

---

[21] For the purposes of this Article, the "competent tax authorities" means:
   (a) for the United States, the Assistant Secretary of the Treasury (Tax Policy), Department of the Treasury; and
   (b) for [Country], [ ].

Article 24
Submission of a Claim to Arbitration

1. In the event that a disputing party considers that an investment dispute cannot be settled by consultation and negotiation:
   (a) the claimant, on its own behalf, may submit to arbitration under this Section a claim
      (i) that the respondent has breached
         (A) an obligation under Articles 3 through 10,
         (B) an investment authorization, or
         (C) an investment agreement;
      and
      (ii) that the claimant has incurred loss or damage by reason of, or arising out of, that breach; and
   (b) the claimant, on behalf of an enterprise of the respondent that is a juridical person that the claimant owns or controls directly or indirectly, may submit to arbitration under this Section a claim
      (i) that the respondent has breached
         (A) an obligation under Articles 3 through 10,
         (B) an investment authorization, or
         (C) an investment agreement;
      and
      (ii) that the enterprise has incurred loss or damage by reason of, or arising out of, that breach,
   provided that a claimant may submit pursuant to subparagraph (a)(i)(C) or (b)(i)(C) a claim for breach of an investment agreement only if the subject matter of the claim and the claimed damages directly relate to the covered investment that was established or acquired, or sought to be established or acquired, in reliance on the relevant investment agreement.
2. At least 90 days before submitting any claim to arbitration under this Section, a claimant shall deliver to the respondent a written notice of its intention to submit the claim to arbitration ("notice of intent"). The notice shall specify:
   (a) the name and address of the claimant and, where a claim is submitted on behalf of an enterprise, the name, address, and place of incorporation of the enterprise;
   (b) for each claim, the provision of this Treaty, investment authorization, or investment agreement alleged to have been breached and any other relevant provisions;
   (c) the legal and factual basis for each claim; and
   (d) the relief sought and the approximate amount of damages claimed.
3. Provided that six months have elapsed since the events giving rise to the claim, a claimant may submit a claim referred to in paragraph 1:
   (a) under the ICSID Convention and the ICSID Rules of Procedure for Arbitration Proceedings, provided that both the respondent and the non-disputing Party are parties to the ICSID Convention;
   (b) under the ICSID Additional Facility Rules, provided that either the respondent or the non-disputing Party is a party to the ICSID Convention;
   (c) under the UNCITRAL Arbitration Rules; or
   (d) if the claimant and respondent agree, to any other arbitration institution or under any other arbitration rules.
4. A claim shall be deemed submitted to arbitration under this Section when the claimant's notice of or request for arbitration ("notice of arbitration"):

(a) referred to in paragraph 1 of Article 36 of the ICSID Convention is received by the Secretary-General;

(b) referred to in Article 2 of Schedule C of the ICSID Additional Facility Rules is received by the Secretary-General;

(c) referred to in Article 3 of the UNCITRAL Arbitration Rules, together with the statement of claim referred to in Article 20 of the UNCITRAL Arbitration Rules, are received by the respondent; or

(d) referred to under any arbitral institution or arbitral rules selected under paragraph 3 (d) is received by the respondent.

A claim asserted by the claimant for the first time after such notice of arbitration is submitted shall be deemed submitted to arbitration under this Section on the date of its receipt under the applicable arbitral rules.

5. The arbitration rules applicable under paragraph 3, and in effect on the date the claim or claims were submitted to arbitration under this Section, shall govern the arbitration except to the extent modified by this Treaty.

6. The claimant shall provide with the notice of arbitration:

(a) the name of the arbitrator that the claimant appoints; or

(b) the claimant's written consent for the Secretary-General to appoint that arbitrator.

Article 25
Consent of Each Party to Arbitration

1. Each Party consents to the submission of a claim to arbitration under this Section in accordance with this Treaty.

2. The consent under paragraph 1 and the submission of a claim to arbitration under this Section shall satisfy the requirements of:

(a) Chapter II of the ICSID Convention (Jurisdiction of the Centre) and the ICSID Additional Facility Rules for written consent of the parties to the dispute; [and]

(b) Article II of the New York Convention for an "agreement in writing[."] [;" and

(c) Article I of the Inter-American Convention for an "agreement."]

Article 26
Conditions and Limitations on Consent of Each Party

1. No claim may be submitted to arbitration under this Section if more than three years have elapsed from the date on which the claimant first acquired, or should have first acquired, knowledge of the breach alleged under Article 24(1) and knowledge that the claimant (for claims brought under Article 24(1)(a)) or the enterprise (for claims brought under Article 24(1)(b)) has incurred loss or damage.

2. No claim may be submitted to arbitration under this Section unless:

(a) the claimant consents in writing to arbitration in accordance with the procedures set out in this Treaty; and

(b) the notice of arbitration is accompanied,

(i) for claims submitted to arbitration under Article 24(1)(a), by the claimant's written waiver, and

(ii) for claims submitted to arbitration under Article 24(1)(b), by the claimant's and the enterprise's written waivers

of any right to initiate or continue before any administrative tribunal or court under the law of either Party, or other dispute settlement procedures, any proceeding with respect to any measure alleged to constitute a breach referred to in Article 24.

3. Notwithstanding paragraph 2(b), the claimant (for claims brought under Article 24(1)(a)) and the claimant or the enterprise (for claims brought under Article 24(1)(b)) may initiate or continue an action that seeks interim injunctive relief and does not involve the payment of monetary damages before a judicial or administrative tribunal of the respondent, provided that the action is brought for the sole purpose of preserving the claimant's or the enterprise's rights and interests during the pendency of the arbitration.

Article 27
Selection of Arbitrators

1. Unless the disputing parties otherwise agree, the tribunal shall comprise three arbitrators, one arbitrator appointed by each of the disputing parties and the third, who shall be the presiding arbitrator, appointed by agreement of the disputing parties.
2. The Secretary-General shall serve as appointing authority for an arbitration under this Section.
3. Subject to Article 20(3), if a tribunal has not been constituted within 75 days from the date that a claim is submitted to arbitration under this Section, the Secretary-General, on the request of a disputing party, shall appoint, in his or her discretion, the arbitrator or arbitrators not yet appointed.
4. For purposes of Article 39 of the ICSID Convention and Article 7 of Schedule C to the ICSID Additional Facility Rules, and without prejudice to an objection to an arbitrator on a ground other than nationality:
    (a) the respondent agrees to the appointment of each individual member of a tribunal established under the ICSID Convention or the ICSID Additional Facility Rules;
    (b) a claimant referred to in Article 24(1)(a) may submit a claim to arbitration under this Section, or continue a claim, under the ICSID Convention or the ICSID Additional Facility Rules, only on condition that the claimant agrees in writing to the appointment of each individual member of the tribunal; and
    (c) a claimant referred to in Article 24(1)(b) may submit a claim to arbitration under this Section, or continue a claim, under the ICSID Convention or the ICSID Additional Facility Rules, only on condition that the claimant and the enterprise agree in writing to the appointment of each individual member of the tribunal.

Article 28
Conduct of the Arbitration

1. The disputing parties may agree on the legal place of any arbitration under the arbitral rules applicable under Article 24(3). If the disputing parties fail to reach agreement, the tribunal shall determine the place in accordance with the applicable arbitral rules, provided that the place shall be in the territory of a State that is a party to the New York Convention.
2. The non-disputing Party may make oral and written submissions to the tribunal regarding the interpretation of this Treaty.
3. The tribunal shall have the authority to accept and consider *amicus curiae* submissions from a person or entity that is not a disputing party.
4. Without prejudice to a tribunal's authority to address other objections as a preliminary question, a tribunal shall address and decide as a preliminary question any objection by the respondent that, as a matter of law, a claim submitted is not a claim for which an award in favor of the claimant may be made under Article 34.
    (a) Such objection shall be submitted to the tribunal as soon as possible after the tribunal is constituted, and in no event later than the date the tribunal fixes for

the respondent to submit its counter-memorial (or, in the case of an amendment to the notice of arbitration, the date the tribunal fixes for the respondent to submit its response to the amendment).

(b) On receipt of an objection under this paragraph, the tribunal shall suspend any proceedings on the merits, establish a schedule for considering the objection consistent with any schedule it has established for considering any other preliminary question, and issue a decision or award on the objection, stating the grounds therefor.

(c) In deciding an objection under this paragraph, the tribunal shall assume to be true claimant's factual allegations in support of any claim in the notice of arbitration (or any amendment thereof) and, in disputes brought under the UNCITRAL Arbitration Rules, the statement of claim referred to in Article 20 of the UNCITRAL Arbitration Rules. The tribunal may also consider any relevant facts not in dispute.

(d) The respondent does not waive any objection as to competence or any argument on the merits merely because the respondent did or did not raise an objection under this paragraph or make use of the expedited procedure set out in paragraph 5.

5. In the event that the respondent so requests within 45 days after the tribunal is constituted, the tribunal shall decide on an expedited basis an objection under paragraph 4 and any objection that the dispute is not within the tribunal's competence. The tribunal shall suspend any proceedings on the merits and issue a decision or award on the objection(s), stating the grounds therefor, no later than 150 days after the date of the request. However, if a disputing party requests a hearing, the tribunal may take an additional 30 days to issue the decision or award. Regardless of whether a hearing is requested, a tribunal may, on a showing of extraordinary cause, delay issuing its decision or award by an additional brief period, which may not exceed 30 days.

6. When it decides a respondent's objection under paragraph 4 or 5, the tribunal may, if warranted, award to the prevailing disputing party reasonable costs and attorney's fees incurred in submitting or opposing the objection. In determining whether such an award is warranted, the tribunal shall consider whether either the claimant's claim or the respondent's objection was frivolous, and shall provide the disputing parties a reasonable opportunity to comment.

7. A respondent may not assert as a defense, counterclaim, right of set-off, or for any other reason that the claimant has received or will receive indemnification or other compensation for all or part of the alleged damages pursuant to an insurance or guarantee contract.

8. A tribunal may order an interim measure of protection to preserve the rights of a disputing party, or to ensure that the tribunal's jurisdiction is made fully effective, including an order to preserve evidence in the possession or control of a disputing party or to protect the tribunal's jurisdiction. A tribunal may not order attachment or enjoin the application of a measure alleged to constitute a breach referred to in Article 24. For purposes of this paragraph, an order includes a recommendation.

9. (a) In any arbitration conducted under this Section, at the request of a disputing party, a tribunal shall, before issuing a decision or award on liability, transmit its proposed decision or award to the disputing parties and to the non-disputing Party. Within 60 days after the tribunal transmits its proposed decision or award, the disputing parties may submit written comments to the tribunal concerning any aspect of its proposed decision or award. The tribunal shall consider any such comments and issue its decision or award not later than 45 days after the expiration of the 60-day comment period.

(b) Subparagraph (a) shall not apply in any arbitration conducted pursuant to this Section for which an appeal has been made available pursuant to paragraph 10.

10. In the event that an appellate mechanism for reviewing awards rendered by investor-State dispute settlement tribunals is developed in the future under other institutional arrangements, the Parties shall consider whether awards rendered under Article 34 should be subject to that appellate mechanism. The Parties shall strive to ensure that any such appellate mechanism they consider adopting provides for transparency of proceedings similar to the transparency provisions established in Article 29.

Article 29
Transparency of Arbitral Proceedings

1. Subject to paragraphs 2 and 4, the respondent shall, after receiving the following documents, promptly transmit them to the non-disputing Party and make them available to the public:
   (a) the notice of intent;
   (b) the notice of arbitration;
   (c) pleadings, memorials, and briefs submitted to the tribunal by a disputing party and any written submissions submitted pursuant to Article 28(2) [Non-Disputing Party submissions] and (3) [*Amicus* Submissions] and Article 33 [Consolidation];
   (d) minutes or transcripts of hearings of the tribunal, where available; and
   (e) orders, awards, and decisions of the tribunal.
2. The tribunal shall conduct hearings open to the public and shall determine, in consultation with the disputing parties, the appropriate logistical arrangements. However, any disputing party that intends to use information designated as protected information in a hearing shall so advise the tribunal. The tribunal shall make appropriate arrangements to protect the information from disclosure.
3. Nothing in this Section requires a respondent to disclose protected information or to furnish or allow access to information that it may withhold in accordance with Article 18 [Essential Security Article] or Article 19 [Disclosure of Information Article].
4. Any protected information that is submitted to the tribunal shall be protected from disclosure in accordance with the following procedures:
   (a) Subject to subparagraph (d), neither the disputing parties nor the tribunal shall disclose to the non-disputing Party or to the public any protected information where the disputing party that provided the information clearly designates it in accordance with subparagraph (b);
   (b) Any disputing party claiming that certain information constitutes protected information shall clearly designate the information at the time it is submitted to the tribunal;
   (c) A disputing party shall, at the time it submits a document containing information claimed to be protected information, submit a redacted version of the document that does not contain the information. Only the redacted version shall be provided to the non-disputing Party and made public in accordance with paragraph 1; and
   (d) The tribunal shall decide any objection regarding the designation of information claimed to be protected information. If the tribunal determines that such information was not properly designated, the disputing party that submitted the information may (i) withdraw all or part of its submission containing such information, or (ii) agree to resubmit complete and redacted documents with corrected designations in accordance with the tribunal's determination and subparagraph (c). In either case, the other disputing party shall, whenever necessary, resubmit complete and redacted documents which either remove the information withdrawn under (i) by the disputing party that first submitted the information or redesignate the

information consistent with the designation under (ii) of the disputing party that first submitted the information.

5. Nothing in this Section requires a respondent to withhold from the public information required to be disclosed by its laws.

Article 30
Governing Law

1. Subject to paragraph 3, when a claim is submitted under Article 24(1)(a)(i)(A) or Article 24(1)(b)(i)(A), the tribunal shall decide the issues in dispute in accordance with this Treaty and applicable rules of international law.

2. Subject to paragraph 3 and the other terms of this Section, when a claim is submitted under Article 24(1)(a)(i)(B) or (C), or Article 24(1)(b)(i)(B) or (C), the tribunal shall apply:
   (a) the rules of law specified in the pertinent investment authorization or investment agreement, or as the disputing parties may otherwise agree; or
   (b) if the rules of law have not been specified or otherwise agreed:
       (i) the law of the respondent, including its rules on the conflict of laws;[22] and
       (ii) such rules of international law as may be applicable.

3. A joint decision of the Parties, each acting through its representative designated for purposes of this Article, declaring their interpretation of a provision of this Treaty shall be binding on a tribunal, and any decision or award issued by a tribunal must be consistent with that joint decision.

Article 31
Interpretation of Annexes

1. Where a respondent asserts as a defense that the measure alleged to be a breach is within the scope of an entry set out in Annex I, II, or III, the tribunal shall, on request of the respondent, request the interpretation of the Parties on the issue. The Parties shall submit in writing any joint decision declaring their interpretation to the tribunal within 90 days of delivery of the request.

2. A joint decision issued under paragraph 1 by the Parties, each acting through its representative designated for purposes of this Article, shall be binding on the tribunal, and any decision or award issued by the tribunal must be consistent with that joint decision. If the Parties fail to issue such a decision within 90 days, the tribunal shall decide the issue.

Article 32
Expert Reports

Without prejudice to the appointment of other kinds of experts where authorized by the applicable arbitration rules, a tribunal, at the request of a disputing party or, unless the disputing parties disapprove, on its own initiative, may appoint one or more experts to report to it in writing on any factual issue concerning environmental, health, safety, or other scientific matters raised by a disputing party in a proceeding, subject to such terms and conditions as the disputing parties may agree.

---

[22] The "law of the respondent" means the law that a domestic court or tribunal of proper jurisdiction would apply in the same case.

Article 33
Consolidation

1. Where two or more claims have been submitted separately to arbitration under Article 24(1) and the claims have a question of law or fact in common and arise out of the same events or circumstances, any disputing party may seek a consolidation order in accordance with the agreement of all the disputing parties sought to be covered by the order or the terms of paragraphs 2 through 10.

2. A disputing party that seeks a consolidation order under this Article shall deliver, in writing, a request to the Secretary-General and to all the disputing parties sought to be covered by the order and shall specify in the request:

   (a) the names and addresses of all the disputing parties sought to be covered by the order;

   (b) the nature of the order sought; and

   (c) the grounds on which the order is sought.

3. Unless the Secretary-General finds within 30 days after receiving a request under paragraph 2 that the request is manifestly unfounded, a tribunal shall be established under this Article.

4. Unless all the disputing parties sought to be covered by the order otherwise agree, a tribunal established under this Article shall comprise three arbitrators:

   (a) one arbitrator appointed by agreement of the claimants;

   (b) one arbitrator appointed by the respondent; and

   (c) the presiding arbitrator appointed by the Secretary-General, provided, however, that the presiding arbitrator shall not be a national of either Party.

5. If, within 60 days after the Secretary-General receives a request made under paragraph 2, the respondent fails or the claimants fail to appoint an arbitrator in accordance with paragraph 4, the Secretary-General, on the request of any disputing party sought to be covered by the order, shall appoint the arbitrator or arbitrators not yet appointed. If the respondent fails to appoint an arbitrator, the Secretary-General shall appoint a national of the disputing Party, and if the claimants fail to appoint an arbitrator, the Secretary-General shall appoint a national of the nondisputing Party.

6. Where a tribunal established under this Article is satisfied that two or more claims that have been submitted to arbitration under Article 24(1) have a question of law or fact in common, and arise out of the same events or circumstances, the tribunal may, in the interest of fair and efficient resolution of the claims, and after hearing the disputing parties, by order:

   (a) assume jurisdiction over, and hear and determine together, all or part of the claims;

   (b) assume jurisdiction over, and hear and determine one or more of the claims, the determination of which it believes would assist in the resolution of the others; or

   (c) instruct a tribunal previously established under Article 27 [Selection of Arbitrators] to assume jurisdiction over, and hear and determine together, all or part of the claims, provided that

      (i) that tribunal, at the request of any claimant not previously a disputing party before that tribunal, shall be reconstituted with its original members, except that the arbitrator for the claimants shall be appointed pursuant to paragraphs 4 (a) and 5; and

      (ii) that tribunal shall decide whether any prior hearing shall be repeated.

7. Where a tribunal has been established under this Article, a claimant that has submitted a claim to arbitration under Article 24(1) and that has not been named in a request made

under paragraph 2 may make a written request to the tribunal that it be included in any order made under paragraph 6, and shall specify in the request:

(a) the name and address of the claimant;

(b) the nature of the order sought; and

(c) the grounds on which the order is sought.

The claimant shall deliver a copy of its request to the Secretary-General.

8. A tribunal established under this Article shall conduct its proceedings in accordance with the UNCITRAL Arbitration Rules, except as modified by this Section.

9. A tribunal established under Article 27 [Selection of Arbitrators] shall not have jurisdiction to decide a claim, or a part of a claim, over which a tribunal established or instructed under this Article has assumed jurisdiction.

10. On application of a disputing party, a tribunal established under this Article, pending its decision under paragraph 6, may order that the proceedings of a tribunal established under Article 27 [Selection of Arbitrators] be stayed, unless the latter tribunal has already adjourned its proceedings.

Article 34
Awards

1. Where a tribunal makes a final award against a respondent, the tribunal may award, separately or in combination, only:

(a) monetary damages and any applicable interest; and

(b) restitution of property, in which case the award shall provide that the respondent may pay monetary damages and any applicable interest in lieu of restitution.

A tribunal may also award costs and attorney's fees in accordance with this Treaty and the applicable arbitration rules.

2. Subject to paragraph 1, where a claim is submitted to arbitration under Article 24(1)(b):

(a) an award of restitution of property shall provide that restitution be made to the enterprise;

(b) an award of monetary damages and any applicable interest shall provide that the sum be paid to the enterprise; and

(c) the award shall provide that it is made without prejudice to any right that any person may have in the relief under applicable domestic law.

3. A tribunal may not award punitive damages.

4. An award made by a tribunal shall have no binding force except between the disputing parties and in respect of the particular case.

5. Subject to paragraph 6 and the applicable review procedure for an interim award, a disputing party shall abide by and comply with an award without delay.

6. A disputing party may not seek enforcement of a final award until:

(a) in the case of a final award made under the ICSID Convention,

(i) 120 days have elapsed from the date the award was rendered and no disputing party has requested revision or annulment of the award; or

(ii) revision or annulment proceedings have been completed; and

(b) in the case of a final award under the ICSID Additional Facility Rules, the UNCITRAL Arbitration Rules, or the rules selected pursuant to Article 24(3)(d),

(i) 90 days have elapsed from the date the award was rendered and no disputing party has commenced a proceeding to revise, set aside, or annul the award; or

(ii) a court has dismissed or allowed an application to revise, set aside, or annul the award and there is no further appeal.

7. Each Party shall provide for the enforcement of an award in its territory.
8. If the respondent fails to abide by or comply with a final award, on delivery of a request by the non-disputing Party, a tribunal shall be established under Article 37 [State-State Dispute Settlement]. Without prejudice to other remedies available under applicable rules of international law, the requesting Party may seek in such proceedings:
   (a) a determination that the failure to abide by or comply with the final award is inconsistent with the obligations of this Treaty; and
   (b) a recommendation that the respondent abide by or comply with the final award.
9. A disputing party may seek enforcement of an arbitration award under the ICSID Convention or the New York Convention [or the Inter-American Convention] regardless of whether proceedings have been taken under paragraph 8.
10. A claim that is submitted to arbitration under this Section shall be considered to arise out of a commercial relationship or transaction for purposes of Article I of the New York Convention [and Article I of the Inter-American Convention].

Article 35
Annexes and Footnotes

The Annexes and footnotes shall form an integral part of this Treaty.

Article 36
Service of Documents

Delivery of notice and other documents on a Party shall be made to the place named for that Party in Annex C.

Section C
Article 37
State-State Dispute Settlement

1. Subject to paragraph 5, any dispute between the Parties concerning the interpretation or application of this Treaty, that is not resolved through consultations or other diplomatic channels, shall be submitted on the request of either Party to arbitration for a binding decision or award by a tribunal in accordance with applicable rules of international law. In the absence of an agreement by the Parties to the contrary, the UNCITRAL Arbitration Rules shall govern, except as modified by the Parties or this Treaty.
2. Unless the Parties otherwise agree, the tribunal shall comprise three arbitrators, one arbitrator appointed by each Party and the third, who shall be the presiding arbitrator, appointed by agreement of the Parties. If a tribunal has not been constituted within 75 days from the date that a claim is submitted to arbitration under this Section, the Secretary-General, on the request of either Party, shall appoint, in his or her discretion, the arbitrator or arbitrators not yet appointed.
3. Expenses incurred by the arbitrators, and other costs of the proceedings, shall be paid for equally by the Parties. However, the tribunal may, in its discretion, direct that a higher proportion of the costs be paid by one of the Parties.
4. Articles 28(3) [*Amicus Curiae* Submissions], 29 [Investor-State Transparency], 30(1) and (3) [Governing Law], and 31 [Interpretation of Annexes] shall apply *mutatis mutandis* to arbitrations under this Article.
5. Paragraphs 1 through 4 shall not apply to a matter arising under Article 12 or Article 13.

IN WITNESS WHEREOF, the respective plenipotentiaries have signed this Treaty.

DONE in duplicate at [city] this [number] day of [month, year], in the English and [foreign] languages, each text being equally authentic.

FOR THE GOVERNMENT OF   FOR THE GOVERNMENT OF
THE UNITED STATES OF AMERICA: [Country]:

Annex A
Customary International Law

The Parties confirm their shared understanding that "customary international law" generally and as specifically referenced in Article 5 [Minimum Standard of Treatment] and Annex B [Expropriation] results from a general and consistent practice of States that they follow from a sense of legal obligation. With regard to Article 5 [Minimum Standard of Treatment], the customary international law minimum standard of treatment of aliens refers to all customary international law principles that protect the economic rights and interests of aliens.

Annex B
Expropriation

The Parties confirm their shared understanding that:

1. Article 6 [Expropriation and Compensation](1) is intended to reflect customary international law concerning the obligation of States with respect to expropriation.
2. An action or a series of actions by a Party cannot constitute an expropriation unless it interferes with a tangible or intangible property right or property interest in an investment.
3. Article 6 [Expropriation and Compensation](1) addresses two situations. The first is direct expropriation, where an investment is nationalized or otherwise directly expropriated through formal transfer of title or outright seizure.
4. The second situation addressed by Article 6 [Expropriation and Compensation](1) is indirect expropriation, where an action or series of actions by a Party has an effect equivalent to direct expropriation without formal transfer of title or outright seizure.
   (a) The determination of whether an action or series of actions by a Party, in a specific fact situation, constitutes an indirect expropriation, requires a case-by- case, fact-based inquiry that considers, among other factors:
      (i) the economic impact of the government action, although the fact that an action or series of actions by a Party has an adverse effect on the economic value of an investment, standing alone, does not establish that an indirect expropriation has occurred;
      (ii) the extent to which the government action interferes with distinct, reasonable investment-backed expectations; and
      (iii) the character of the government action.
   (b) Except in rare circumstances, non-discriminatory regulatory actions by a Party that are designed and applied to protect legitimate public welfare objectives, such as public health, safety, and the environment, do not constitute indirect expropriations.

Annex C
Service of Documents on a Party

United States

Notices and other documents shall be served on the United States by delivery to:
Executive Director (L/EX)
Office of the Legal Adviser
Department of State
Washington, D.C. 20520
United States of America

[Country]

Notices and other documents shall be served on [Country] by delivery to:
[insert place of delivery of notices and other documents for [Country]]

Index